mgov.

UNITED NATIONS
STATISTICAL
COMMISSION

UNITED NATIONS
ECONOMIC COMMISSION
FOR EUROPE

STATISTICAL DATA EDITING

Volume No. 3

IMPACT ON DATA QUALITY

UNITED NATIONS
New York and Geneva, 2006

NOTE

Symbols of United Nations documents are composed of capital letters combined with figures. Mention of such symbol indicates a reference to a United Nations document.

The designations employed and the presentation of the material in this publication do not imply the expression of any opinion whatsoever on the part of the Secretariat of the United Nations concerning the legal status of any country, territory, city or area, or of its authorities, or concerning the delimitation of its frontier or boundaries.

UNITED NATIONS PUBLICATION

Sales No. E.06.II.E.16

ISBN 13: 978-92-116952-2
ISSN 0069-8458

PREFACE

Statistical Data Editing: Impact on Data Quality, is the third in the series of Statistical Data Editing publications produced by the participants of the United Nations Economic Commission for Europe (UN/ECE) Work Sessions on Statistical Data Editing (SDE). While the first two volumes dealt with the topics of what is data editing and how is it performed, the principal focus of this volume is its impact on the quality of the outgoing estimates.

The aim of this publication is to assist National Statistical Offices in assessing the impact of the data editing process on data quality, that is, in assessing how well the process is working. We hope that this publication will help the statistical community of the ECE region to improve the quality of official statistics.

Marek Belka
Executive Secretary and Under Secretary General
United Nations Economic Commission for Europe

INTRODUCTION – John Kovar, Statistics Canada

Data editing is an integral and expensive part of the survey process; its impact is far reaching. In this volume we examine how editing affects data quality. We use the broadly accepted meaning of data quality, that is, its fitness for use, or fitness for purpose. We thus address issues of accuracy, relevance, coherence and interpretability. We also take into account the various stakeholders in the survey process, such as the users, respondents or data producers themselves.

Firstly, in Chapter 1, we provide examples of evaluation frameworks of the editing process: what to plan for; what to measure; what to retain, so we can learn from the process. This Chapter also illustrates the practical implementation with an example from the Italian National Statistical Institute.

Chapter 2 addresses specific issues of what to measure. Various quality indicators are proposed, both from a theoretical and practical point of view. We examine how editing affects data quality in a quantitative way. The impact of imputation on the total survey error is taken into account. The chapter concludes by suggesting what quality information should be provided to the data users and in what way.

Chapter 3 addresses the problem of improving data quality. What can we learn from the editing process in order to be able to continuously improve the product? Detailed examples of how the data editing process should fit into the statistical infrastructure are presented. More globally, we also address the problem of where and how editing should fit into the various modes of data collection, as it relates to electronic data reporting and the use of alternate data sources.

Finally, in Chapter 4 we consider quality in its full breadth. We review what has been done, and what was planned but not done, in evaluating quality. We argue that editing should be considered in a wider perspective by providing information to other survey processes in a systematic way. Some future directions are outlined.

The material was prepared within the framework of the project on Statistical Data Editing, which is in the programme of work of the Conference of European Statisticians. It comprises selected papers presented at the Statistical Data Editing Work Sessions held in Prague (October 1997), Rome (June 1999), Cardiff (October 2000), Helsinki (June 2002), and Madrid (October 2003). The publication comprises updated versions of these papers as well as new papers that were tabled at the Ottawa meeting (May 2005). The volume was compiled and edited by the UN/ECE Statistical Division. It represents an extensive voluntary effort on the part of the authors. The readers are also encouraged to visit the group's data editing knowledge base at http://amrads.jrc.cec.eu.int/k-base/ for a complete documentation of the SDE efforts.

Acknowledgement

The editors express their thanks to all authors who contributed to the publication. Special thanks also go to the members of the steering group for coordinating and introducing the individual chapters, and for helping to compile and edit the material, namely: Leopold Granquist (Statistics Sweden), John Kovar (Statistics Canada), Carsten Kuchler (Statistisches Bundesamt, Germany), Pedro Revilla (Instituto Nacional de Estadística, Spain), Natalie Shlomo (Central Bureau of Statistics, Israel and Southampton Social Statistics Research Institute, University of Southampton, United Kingdom), Heather Wagstaff (Office for National Statistics, United Kingdom), and Paula Weir (Energy Information Administration, United States). Their joint efforts have contributed significantly to the preparation of the publication as a whole.

CONTENTS

Chapter 1

FRAMEWORK OF EVALUATION

Foreword – John Kovar, Statistics Canada

Three papers were selected for this introductory chapter that examines how to plan and implement evaluation studies. First, Svein Nordbotten explores how one should approach the problem of evaluating the efficiency of every data editing problem by providing a general framework. He investigates the issues of what to measure and how to measure it. He considers opportunities for systematic exploration and evaluation of relationships among statistical product quality and the editing process variables with the aim of developing a causal model of the editing process in order to design a more efficient editing process.

The paper by Ray Chambers concentrates on the evaluation criteria of approaches with the goal of establishing a "best practice". The proposed criteria should assess the performance of the methods when the "true" values are known. They may therefore not be appropriate for assessing the performance of methods with a specific real data set where the true values are not known. However, the described approaches provide guidance in finding effective edit and imputation methods. This emphasizes the need for good benchmark data sets that could be shared between researchers.

The Italian paper examines the evaluation phase to assess whether the edit and imputation process is capable of achieving the dual objective of editing. This dual objective aims at continually improving data quality and providing information on the survey process - including the editing and imputation (E&I) process itself. The paper explores evaluation objectives, presents an extensive bibliography and provides a discussion of their experiences.

The evaluation of overall statistical processes, and particularly the edit and imputation process, is a new domain in need of continuous study. The first paper identifies some tasks for future research in this area.

EVALUATING EFFICIENCY OF STATISTICAL DATA EDITING: GENERAL FRAMEWORK

By Svein Nordbotten, Statistics Sweden

PREFACE

The methodological material, "Evaluating Efficiency of Statistical Data Editing: General Framework", was prepared based on the request of countries participating in the activities on statistical data editing organised by the UNECE Statistical Division within the framework of the programme of work of the Conference of European Statisticians.

The document was reviewed at the Work Session on Statistical Data Editing in June 1999. National Statistical Offices of the UNECE member countries and the Food and Agriculture Organisation (FAO) participated in this meeting. The material reflects the outcome of the discussion on the document.

At its 1999 plenary session, the Conference of European Statisticians agreed to reproduce this document and to distribute it to the interested statistical offices as a methodological material.

1. WHY IS DATA EDITING A FOCAL POINT

Data editing is a step in the preparation of statistics, the goal of which is to improve the quality of the statistical information. International research indicates that in a typical statistical survey, the editing may consume up to 40% of all costs. The following questions have been raised:

- Is the use of these resources spent on editing justified?
- Can more effective editing strategies be applied? or
- Can the quality perhaps be improved by allocating some of the editing resources to other statistical production processes to prevent errors [Granquist 1996 and 1997]?

Large statistical organisations and national statistical offices regard their activities as processes producing many statistical *products* in parallel. Each production can be considered as a thread through a sequence of special processes. The overall task for a statistical organisation is to specify, tune and run each thread of processes to deliver a product with as high a quality as possible taking the available resources into account.

We assume that quality can be conceived as a measure of how well the statistical producer succeeds in serving his users. The success will depend on the market demand for statistical products and how the producer allocates his resources to the production of each product and to each process in the production. The better knowledge the statistical producer can acquire about the market for statistical products and the production processes, the better his chances will be for a successful and efficient statistical production. Editing has a particular role in statistical production because its only aim is to improve the quality of the statistical products.

The purpose of this paper is to present a general framework for evaluating the efficiency of statistical data editing in improving the quality of statistical products. The paper includes discussion of:

- The market for statistical products,
- The statistical quality in a market perspective,
- How the quality depends on editing process variables,
- How to measure quality and editing process performance data,
- Model tools to support the design of editing processes.

Further work is needed, and the presentation is concluded by suggestions for some important tasks for future research.

2. STATISTICAL QUALITY IN A MARKET PERSPECTIVE

The different needs for statistical information are likely to be so numerous that it would be prohibitive for a statistical producer to serve them all. Different users will therefore frequently have to use the same statistical product as a substitute for their varying user needs.

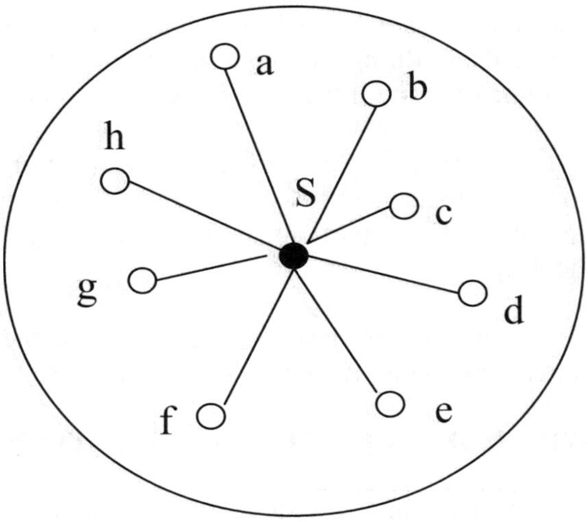

Figure 1: Individual target needs served by one statistical target

Consider a conceptual definition *S* of a statistical product as the centre of a circle symbolising all conceptual definitions for which the definition of *S* can be considered to be a feasible substitute. *Figure 1* illustrates a situation in which the applications *a-h* have different conceptual needs symbolised by a different spatial location in a circle. As long as the conceptual distances from the centre are within an acceptable length represented by the radius of the circle, the users can be served by the statistical concept *S*. For example, users needing a certain population estimate for different points of time, may all use statistics from a census as long as the census was taken within an acceptable time distance.

As a simplification, we ignore the multiplicity of user conceptual needs for statistical products and assume that all needs in the circle can be served by the statistical concept symbolised in the figure by the black circle in the centre. When measured by a perfect process, the statistical concept will be referred to as the *target* product and the attribute value of the product will be referred to as the target *size*[1]. Needs outside the circle cannot be served satisfactorily by this product.

The quality related to a statistical product, is determined by a number of factors including product *relevance* (correspondence between the concept measured and the concept required by the application), *timeliness* (the period between the time of the observations and the time to which the application refers), and *accuracy* (the deviation between the target size determined by a perfect process and the product size determined by the imperfect process) [Depoutot 1998]. Wider quality concepts, as used for example by Statistics Canada, include also accessibility, interpretability and coherence [Statistics Canada 1998].

Figure 2 symbolises by arrows how the 3 factors may pull the statistical product size (the black circle) away from target size (the white circle). The deviation between the actual product size and the ideal target size, is an inverse indicator of quality and frequently referred to as the error of the statistical product.

---

[1] We use product *size* as a general term for the measurement to avoid confusion with the utility value of the product for a user. A measured population total, an average income, a percentage, etc. are examples of different product sizes.

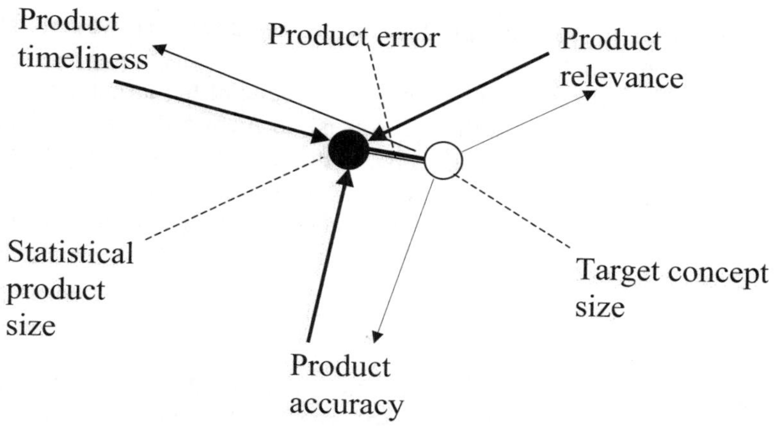

To justify the preparation of statistics, the users must benefit from the products. We can imagine a market place in which the statistical producers and users trade. We assume that any statistical product has a certain economic value for each user determined by the product quality.

The market value for a statistical product can be described by a sum of all user values. This sum may be considered as a function of the product quality. The cost of production can also be conceived as a function of the product quality.

The market value for a statistical product can be described by a sum of all user values. This sum may be considered as a function of the product quality. The cost of production can also be conceived as a function of the product quality.

Figure 3 presents a simple graphical model of such a market. According to elementary theory of production, the statistical producer should aim at a quality level, which justifies the costs, i.e. at a quality level for which the product value curve is above the cost curve. The market would theoretically be in optimal economic balance when the marginal value and cost are equal.

The *users* want data about quality to decide if the supplied statistics are suitable for their needs, while the *producers* need data on quality to analyse alternative production strategies and to

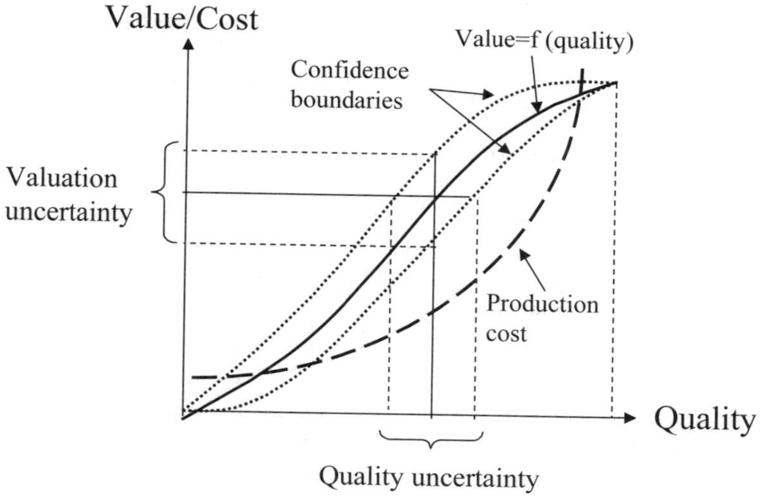

Figure 3: A statistical market mechanism

allocate resources for improving overall production performance. However, quality can never be precise. One obvious reason is that
the precise quality of a statistical product presumes knowledge of the target size, and then there would be no need for measuring the fact. Another reason is, as mentioned above, that the desired target concept may vary among the users. While a quality statement expresses uncertainty about a statistical product, uncertainty will also be a part of the quality measurement itself. This is illustrated by the stippled curves in *Figure 3* indicating a confidence interval for the value-quality curve.

3. STATISTICAL EDITING

The preparation of statistics can be presented as a number of threads, each representing a separate product passing through a sequence of processes. In this paper, we shall limit the discussion to a single product and thread even though we are aware of the interdependence among the threads competing for available resources. *Figure 4* illustrates how each statistical product can be considered as being described by two main variables, the *size* representing the product demanded by the users and the *quality* expressing how reliable the product is. Both variables will depend on how the different processes are designed and how the resources including the available professional competence, are allocated to each process.

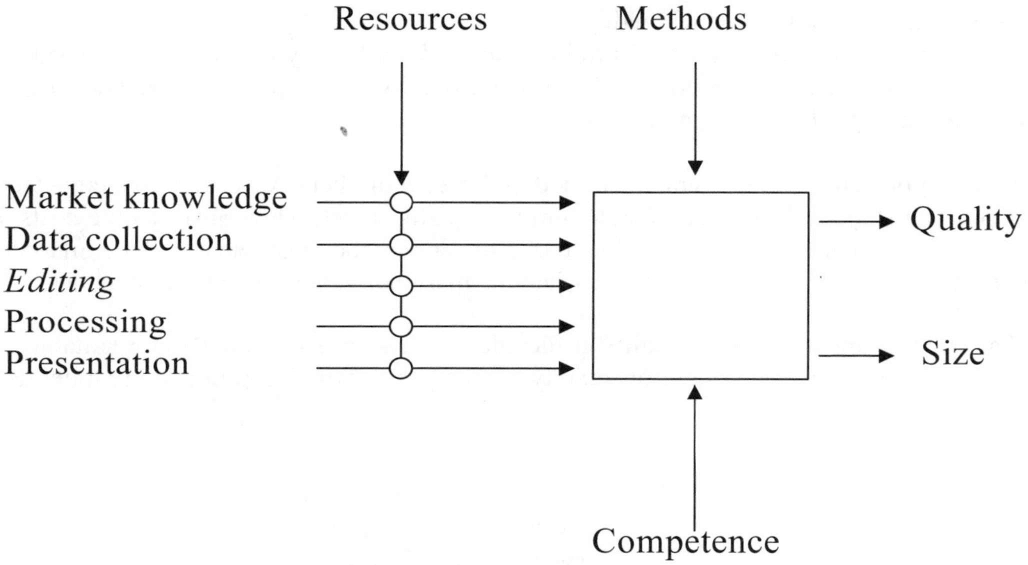

Figure 4: Allocations to statistical processes

Each of the processes can be described by several variables. We would like to identify how the quality of a product is determined by these variables. If we succeed, we shall be able to discuss if the resources are efficiently allocated and if the editing process for the product considered should have 10%, 20% or 40% of the resources allocated to the product considered.

The target size can only be measured correctly by means of a statistical process carried out according to an ideal procedure without any resource restrictions. But because an ideal production usually will be prohibitive for the producer, errors appear in connection with the observation and processing of data for the individual units. In designing a statistical product, resources should first be allocated to statistical processes, which can effectively prevent errors to be generated. The aim of the editing process is to catch individual errors, which are too expensive to prevent efficiently by other processes.

While the result of the editing process is described by data on *quality*, the execution of the process is the source for *performance* data. Description of an editing process requires four types of data:

- Data about the editing *architecture* describing how the process is set up using different methods. For example, this may be a control algorithm for detecting errors, an algorithm for imputing one category of errors and instructions for manual actions of another category of rejected data. The architecture data inform us how the designer wanted the process to be constructed and are obtained during the design of the process.

- Data about the *implementation* of the editing process with numerical characteristics, such as specific bounds for edit ratios, imputation functions, etc. These data describe how the process was implemented with all its detailed specifications.

- *Performance* data, which document the operational characteristics of the process applied on a specific set of data. They include data on the quality of the editing process.

- *Cost* data on which kind of resources were used and how they were spent on different activities.

The first two types of data are obtained during the preparation of the process while the last two types are collected during the execution of the process.

A description of the editing process by means of these four types of data will, in addition to being useful information for evaluating and trimming the process, also provide indications about alternative ways to improve the quality of statistical products, and about opportunities for studying the relationship between the editing process and the statistical product quality.

4. MEASURING STATISTICAL QUALITY AND EDITING PERFORMANCE

In the two previous sections, the statistical product quality and the editing process were discussed from a rather abstract perspective. To be useful, these theoretical notions must be replaced by operational variables, which can be measured and processed. In this section we associate the abstract variables from the previous sections with operational variables that can be observed.

4.1 Measuring quality

Quality cannot usually be observed by an exact measurement, but can, subject to a specified risk, be predicted as an upper bound for the product error, i.e. for the deviation of the product size from the target size.

Consider the expression:

$$Pr\,(|Y'-Y|>D)=1-p \qquad 4.1$$

which implies that the probability or risk is $(1-p)$ that the product size Y' deviates from its target size Y by more than an amount D. We shall denote D as a *quality predictor* even though it decreases by increasing quality and in fact is an error indicator. Because D is unknown, we shall substitute it with the prediction D' [Nordbotten 1998]. It can be demonstrated that $D' = \alpha\,(p)*var\ Y'$ where the value of α is determined by the probability distribution of Y' and the assumed value of p. Assuming that Y' has a normal distribution, α is easily available in statistical tables. The variance of the product size Y' can be derived from a small sample as described below.

To compute a prediction D', we need a small sample of individual records with edited as well as raw data. If the raw records for these units can be re-edited in as ideal a manner as possible to obtain a third set of records containing individual target data, we can compute Y as well as D' for different confidence levels p. It can be shown that as expected, a smaller risk $(1-p)$ is related to a larger D' for the same product and sample.

Because D' is itself subject to errors, the prediction may or may not provide satisfactory credibility. It is therefore important to test the prediction empirically. In experiments with individual data for which both edited and target data versions exist, we can perform statistical tests comparing predicted quality D' and actual quality D of the edited data [Nordbotten 1998 and Weir 1997].

		Actual		**Total**
		D<=5	**D>5**	
Predicted deviation D'	**D'<=5**	363	67	430
	D'>5	51	23	74
	Total	414	90	504

Table 1: Testing 504 product estimates requiring $|Y'-Y| <= 5$ *assuming* $p=0.75$.

Table 1 illustrates how *504* products or estimates were classified in an experiment to evaluate accuracy predictions [Nordbotten 1999]. The figures, which are based on 1990 Norwegian Population Census data, refer to imputed population totals compared with the corresponding target totals. Only estimates with a deviation from the target with *5* or less people were assumed acceptable. The quality prediction algorithm classified *430* product estimates (first row sum) as satisfactory while *414* (first column sum) were within the pre-set requirement. *51* estimates were predicted as outside the boundary while they in fact were acceptable, a typical Type 1 classification error. On the other hand, *67* values were predicted acceptable while their deviations were greater than *5*, misclassifications of Type 2.

With a normal distribution and a $p=0.75$, we should expect that *25* percent of the values (i.e. 126 product estimates) would be subjected to a Type 1 misclassification. As the table shows, the number of Type 1 errors (51) is well within the expected limit. The explanation of this unexpected result is that the distribution of D' does not approximate closely the normal distribution.

Manzari and Della Rocca distinguish *between output-oriented approaches and input-oriented approaches* to evaluation of editing and imputation procedures [Manzari and Della Rocca 1999]. In an output- oriented approach they focus on the effect of the editing on resulting products, while in an input-oriented approach they concentrate on the effect of the editing on the individual data items. Because they evaluate editing processes by means of data with synthetic errors introduced, they are able to follow an input-oriented approach. The quality indicator D' presented in this section is a typical example of an output-oriented approach. In the next section, we will also discuss an input-oriented approach.

4.2 Measuring process and cost data

In section 3, we stressed the need for identifying the variables of the editing process, which determined the quality of a statistical product. Two logical steps constitute the editing process:

- *Classification* of an observation as acceptable or suspicious, and

- *Correction* of components believed to be wrong.

Before the advent of automation in statistical production, subject matter experts carried out editing, frequently with few formal editing guidelines. Later, computers were introduced and provided new possibilities for more efficient editing, but required also a formalisation of the process [Nordbotten 1963]. Editing principles were developed and implemented in a number of tools for practical application. Today, a wide spectrum of different methods and tools exists. An editing architecture adjusted to a particular survey can be designed by a combination of available tools [UNECE 1997].

While the quality evaluation focused on the *final effects* of the editing process on the statistical products, the objective of the process evaluation is to describe what is happening with data *during* the editing process [Engström 1996 and 1997]. But because of the close relationship between the performance of the process and the quality of the results, properties of the editing process can also be useful quality indicators.

The measurement of the quality effects of editing is based on comparisons between edited data and target data. The process measurement on the other hand, is based on comparison between raw (unedited) and edited data. Process data are generated during the process itself and can therefore be frequently used for continuous monitoring of the process. Continuous monitoring of the process permits changes during the editing process execution based on the operational variables observed.

N:	Total number of observations
N_C:	Number of observations rejected as suspicious
N_I:	Number of imputed observations
X:	Raw value sum for all observations
X_C:	Raw value sum for rejected observations
Y_I:	Imputed value sum of rejected observations
Y:	Edited value sum of all observations
K_C:	Cost of editing controls
K_I:	Cost of imputations

List 1: Typical operational and cost variables

Some typical variables, which can be recorded during the process, are shown in *List 1.* These basic variables give us important facts about the editing process. They are descriptive facts, and can be useful if we learn how to combine and interpret them correctly. Since we have no theoretical system guiding us with respect to selecting which variables to observe, the approach of this section is explorative.

If the number of observations rejected as suspicious in a periodic survey increased from one period to another, it can for example be interpreted as an indication that the raw data have decreasing quality. On the other hand, it can also be regarded as indication of increased quality of the final results, because more units are rejected for careful inspection. A correct conclusion may require that several of the variables be studied simultaneously. As a first step toward a better understanding of the editing process, the basic variables can be combined in different ways. *List 2* gives examples of a few composite variables frequently being used for monitoring and evaluating the editing process.

Frequencies:	
$F_C = N_C/N$	(Reject frequency)
$F_I = N_I/N$	(Impute frequency)
Ratios:	
$R_C = X_C/X$	(Reject ratio)
$R_I = Y_I/X$	(Impute ratio)
Per unit values:	
$\underline{K}_C = K_C/N$	(Cost per rejected unit)
$\underline{K}_I = K_I/N$	(Cost per imputed unit)

List 2: Some typical operational and cost ratios

The *reject frequency, F_C*, indicates the relative extent of the control work performed. This variable gives a measure of the workload that a certain control method implies, and is used to tune the control criteria according to available resources. In an experimental design stage, the reject frequency is used to compare and choose between alternative methods.

The imputation effects on the rejected set of N_C observations are the second group of variables. The *impute frequency*, F_I, indicates the relative number of observations which have their values changed during the process. F_I should obviously not be larger than F_C. If the difference F_c - F_I is significant, it may be an indication that the rejection criteria are too narrow, or perhaps that more resources should be allocated to make the inspection and imputation of rejected observations more effective.

The *rejected value ratio*, R_C, measures the impact of the rejected values relative to the raw value sum for all observations. A small rejected value ratio may indicate that the suspicious values are an insignificant part of the total of values. If combined with a high F_C, a review of the process may conclude that the resources spent on inspection of rejected values cannot be justified and are in fact better used for some other process. R_C may show that even though the F_C is large, the R_C may be small which may be another indication that the current editing procedure is not well balanced.

The *impute ratio*, R_I, indicates the overall effect of the editing and imputation on the raw observations. If R_I is small, we may suspect that resources may be wasted on editing.

Costs per rejected unit, K_C, and *cost per imputed unit*, K_I, add up to the total editing cost per unit. The costs per product (item) have to be computed based on a cost distribution scheme since only totals will be available from the accounting system.

The process data are computed from both raw and edited micro data. The importance of preserving also the original raw data has now become obvious and it should become usual practice that the files of raw and edited micro data are carefully stored.

As already pointed out, we have yet no theory for the operational aspects of the editing process. The process variables computed are often used independently of each other. The editing process can easily be evaluated differently depending on which variables are used. The purpose of the next section is to investigate how the process can be described by a set of interrelated variables, which may provide further knowledge about the nature of the editing process and a basis for improved future designs.

5. ANALYSIS

Metadata of the type outlined in section 4 offer opportunities for systematic exploration and evaluation of relationships among the statistical product quality and the editing process variables considered. The research objective is to develop a model of the editing process, which describes the *causal* relationships among the variables discussed and can serve as a tool for designing efficient editing processes.

The set of editing architectures, the users' demands and the available resources including mental and stored knowledge and experience, are the environmental conditions within which the implementation for a specific statistical product can be selected. The selected implementation is assumed to determine the operational performance and finally the quality and cost of the editing associated with the product.

Figure 5 outlines the general structure of a model in mind. On the left are the 3 classes of input variables available for the implementation design. Each class may comprise several variables, which in turn can take a set of values representing different alternatives. There may be, for example, variables identifying alternative control and correction methods, variables representing different edit criteria and imputation parameters, etc. For these variables, values must be selected, designed or estimated. The selection of an implementation design is usually done based on knowledge, which may be mental or represented in a metadata system maintained systematically. When executed, the implementation design is assumed to determine the product quality, cost and performance levels.

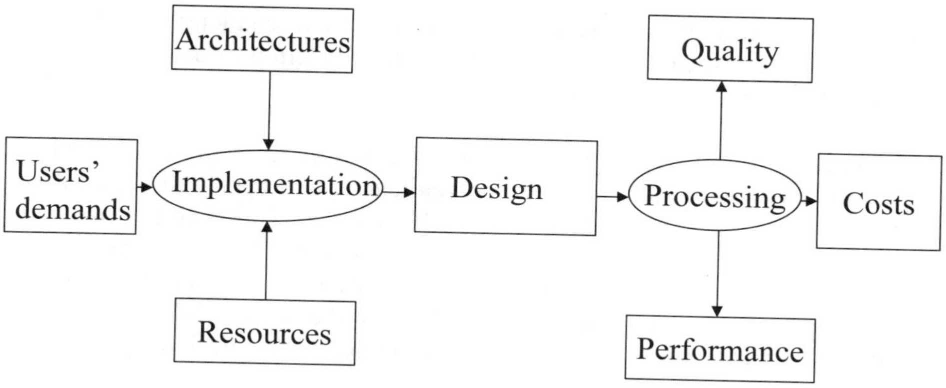

Figure 5: Causal model

The causal relations among the different sets of variables are symbolised by arrows in the figure. Using the notation already introduced, we can write down the model in symbolic form by:

$I=f(A,D, R)$, 5.1

where *A, D* and *R* are variables representing architectures, users' demands and levels of available resources, respectively, from the available sets **A**, **D**, **R**. The design variables are represented by the implementation variable *I* from the set **I**. The mapping *f* represents the mappings from the elements in **A**, **D** and **R** to the elements in **I** and corresponds to the implementation design activity. The selected implementation design I determines the editing process represented by the mappings *q, p* and *k*, the quality *Q*, the performance variables *P* and the costs variables *K* from the available sets **Q**, **P** and **K**:

$Q= q (I)$, 5.2

$P= p(I)$ 5.3

and

$K= k (I)$. *5.4*

The expressions *5.2* and *5.3* illustrate that the performance variables may be considered as indicators of quality. If the relations *5.2* and *5.3* exist, combination of the two relations may give a new relation:

$Q= q'(P)$ 5.5

where the new mapping *q'* symbolising the mapping from P to *Q*. This expression indicates that *P* can be used as an indicator of *Q* if the *q'* can be determined.

When the quality *Q* and costs *K* both are determined, *Q* needs to be compared with *K*. A model corresponding to the market *Figure 3* is needed, i.e. an equation reflecting the relationship between the quality *Q* and the market value *V*:

$V= v (Q)$. 5.6

The market value *V* can be compared and evaluated with the associated costs *K*. Alternative designs, i.e. different implementations, could also be evaluated, compared and ranked.

Exploring these relations empirically will be an important challenge and long-term objective for research in editing of statistical data. It will require the collection of data from several surveys as well as observations from the statistical market.

The aim stated above was the development of a model to support the producer in finding answers to the questions about which is the 'best' architecture and design of an editing process for a given market situation and available architectures and resources. To create a tool for improving the editing strategy, we 'turn around' the causal model discussed in the last paragraphs to a decision support model. This transformed model is outlined in Figure 6. The variables on the left side are available architectures and resource alternatives, while at the upper right side we have required quality. On the lower right side, the output of the model is the design specifications and cost estimates.

When a statistical market demands a statistical product, the decision support model should assist the statistical producer to investigate:

- If a feasible architecture exists given the repository of editing methods/techniques and the financial and human resources he commands;
- Which editing process design can be implemented within the input constraints;

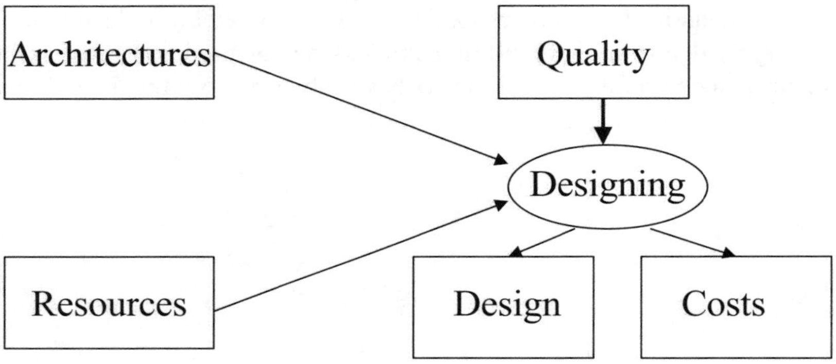

Figure 6: Strategy model

- What the cost will be of the designed process.

There may be several editing designs, which satisfy the input conditions. Based on the discussion in section 2 and the causal model, we search the implementation design I that gives the highest non-negative solution to the expression:

$$H=V(q(I))-K(I) \qquad 5.7$$

In the long run, research must be extended to study also the impact of other statistical processes, e.g. data acquisition, estimation and presentation of statistical products, on statistical quality and how other statistical processes interact with editing [Jong 1996, Nordbotten 1957]. Only such research may give the necessary tools for tuning resource allocations across all processes in order to obtain the best quality statistics in a general sense.

6. NEEDS FOR FURTHER RESEARCH

There exists no overall theory from which the producers of official statistics can obtain support for their design and management decisions. So far, producers have relied on theories from several disciplines for separate statistical processes. For some processes and tasks, well-developed theory is available. The theory of sample survey design and estimation is an example of a theory that is an important foundation for design decisions. It illustrates how errors due to random sampling can be taken into account in designing effective samples and evaluating the quality in results due to the sample design. In the last couple of decades, the theory of databases is another example of a theory that has become an important basis for the producers.

Control and correction of non-random errors, on the other hand, have a less strong theoretical basis. Up to now, a large set of editing methods has been developed [Winkler 1999]. Little progress has been seen so far, however, in integrating the different theories into a general theory of statistical quality.

We can characterise much of the research and methodological development in official statistics as fragmented and explorative associated with different processes. One explanation may be that the purpose of producing statistical information has not been clearly stated and widely understood and that different types of specialists have been involved in different statistical production processes.

There is therefore a need for a general theory of statistical systems and their environments permitting systematic, empirical research and co-operation among the different groups of specialists. *Figure 7* illustrates how the research in editing can be envisaged as a part in a wider scheme for research i statistical production.

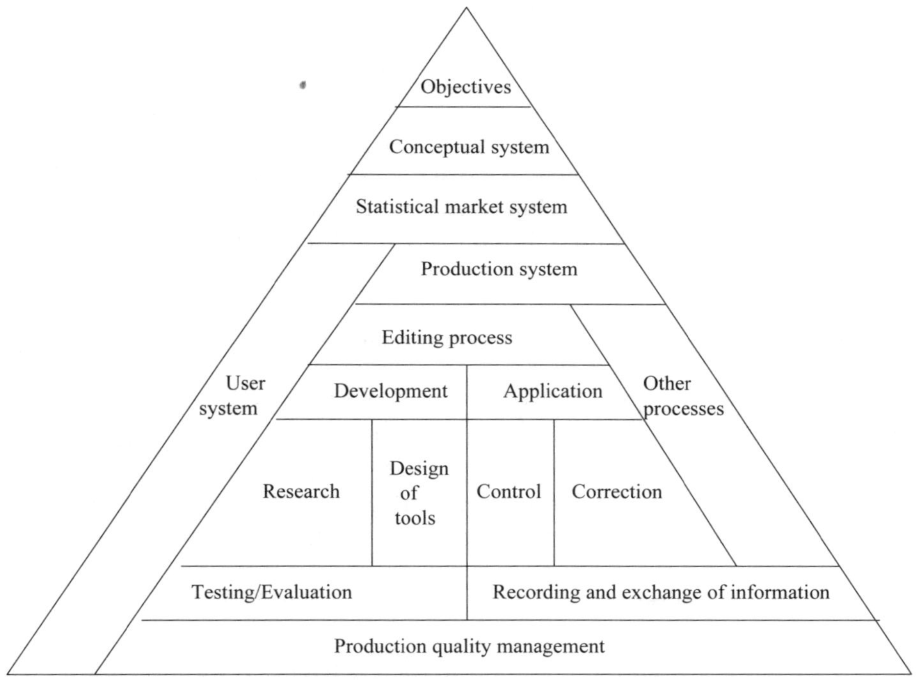

Figure 7: A framework for research in statistical editing

This paper focuses on the editing process, but also takes into account other statistical production processes and their environment as outlined in section 2. It emphasises the interactions between the editing process, the other statistical processes and the statistical production environment.

The proposed framework does not intend to be the missing theory for official production of statistics. Its purpose is limited to proposing some relevant research activities connected to editing and aimed at improving the statistical product qualities, and suggesting some research topics and an infrastructure to work within.

Some tasks for future research in statistical data editing may be:

- Development of a conceptual framework for description of editing processes.

A common language for communication is needed. The UNECE Draft Glossary of Terms Used in Data Editing has recently been updated [Winkler 1999a]. There are terms still missing and the glossary should be continuously updated with terms used, for example, in papers contributed in the UNECE Work Sessions on Statistical Data Editing.

- Collecting empirical data sets suitable for experimentation.

From statements given at the Work Session in Rome, available data sets suitable for testing new editing methods and architectures are missing and would be appreciated by many researchers. Such sets should be stored in a standard form in a repository and made accessible to researchers working with statistical editing method development and evaluation. Both raw and edited microdata should be stored. When existing, a sample of re-edited ('target') data will be very useful for quality evaluations. Mainly because of confidentiality rules, it is very difficult today to obtain access to data sets used by colleagues in their research. If real data sets cannot be made available, an alternative is data sets with synthetic data as discussed by Manzari and Della Rocca [Manzari and Della Rocca 1999].

- Comparison and evaluation of relative merits of available editing tools.

Useful information can be made available by systematic comparison of the functionality of editing methods based on their description [Poirier 1999]. However, the essential condition for comparison and evaluation of editing architectures is access to empirical microdata. So far, few examples of data sets exchanged and used for comparison of methods have been reported [Kovar and Winkler 1996].

- Research on causal model description of the editing process.

Research on causal models will require detailed data from the editing process of the type pointed out above. Data from simulations can in many situations be a substitute for real data. In some situations, synthetic data can even be superior for studying in detail how different editing methods handle special error types. How to construct useful generators for synthetic data and errors, is therefore also a relevant research task in connection with evaluation of editing methods.

- Exchange of information on research.

UNECE made an important contribution to the exchange of information on editing research work by compiling the statistical editing bibliography [UNECE 1996]. In a field like statistical data editing it is important that this bibliography be kept up-to-date. Internet can be exploited more effectively for dissemination of research ideas, experience, references, general problems with answers, etc. Internet can also be used as a highway for researchers to data sets released for comparative research, to stored editing methods, programs and systems made available by authors and developers who wish to share their products with colleagues for comments and applications.

References

[1] Depoutot, R. (1998): *Quality Of International Statistics: Comparability and Coherence.* Conference on Methodological Issues in Official Statistics. Stockholm.

[2] Engström, P. (1996): *Monitoring the Editing Process.* Working Paper No. 9, UNECE Work Session on Statistical Data Editing. Voorburg.

[3] Engström, P. (1997): A *Small Study on Using Editing Process Data for Evaluation of the European Structure of Earnings Survey.* Working Paper No. 19, UNECE Work Session on Statistical Data Editing, Prague.

[4] Engström, P. and Granquist, L. (1999): *Improving Quality by Modern Editing.* Working Paper No. 23, UNECE Work Session on Statistical Data Editing, Rome.

[5] Granquist, L. (1996): *The New View on Editing.* UNECE Work Session on Statistical Data Editing, Voorburg. Also published in the International Statistical Review, Vol. 65, No. 3, pp.381-387.

[6] Granquist, L (1997): *An Overview Of Methods Of Evaluating Data Editing Procedures.* Statistical Data Editing. Methods and Techniques, Vol. 2. Statistical Standards and Studies No 48. UNECE. pp. 112 122.

[7] Jong, W.A.M. de (1996): *Designing a Complete Edit Strategy - Combining Techniques.* Working Paper No. 29, UNECE Work Session on Statistical Data Editing, Voorburg.

[8] Kovar. J. and Winkler, E.W. (1996): *Editing Economic Data.* Working Paper No. 12, UNECE Work Session on Statistical Data Editing. Voorburg.

[9] Manzari, A. and Della Rocca, G. (1999): *A Generalized System Based on Simulation Approach to Test the Quality of Editing and Imputation Procedures.* Working Paper No. 13, UNECE Work Session on Statistical Data Editing, Rome.

[10] Nordbotten, S. (1957): *On Errors and Optimal Allocation in a Census.* Skandinavisk Aktuarietidskrift. pp. 1-10.

[11] Nordbotten, S. (1963): *Automatic Editing of Individual Statistical Observations.* Statistical Standards and Studies. Handbook No. 2. United Nations, N.Y.

[12] Nordbotten, S. (1995): *Editing Statistical Records by Neural Networks.* Journal of Official Statistics, Vol.11, No. 4, pp. 391-411.

[13] Nordbotten, S. (1998): *Estimating Population Proportions from Imputed Data.* Computational Statistics & Data Analysis, Vol. 27, pp. 291-309.

[14] Nordbotten, S. (1999): *Small Area Statistics from Survey and Imputed Data.* To be published.

[15] Poirier, C. (1999): *A Functional Evaluation of Edit and Imputation Tools.* Working Paper No. 12, UNECE Work Session on Statistical Data Editing. Rome.

[16] Statistics Canada (1998): *Quality Guidelines.* Third Edition, Ottawa.

[17] UNECE (1996): *Bibliography On Statistical Data Editing.* Working Paper No. 5, UNECE Work Session on Statistical Data Editing. Voorburg.

[18] UNECE (1997): *Statistical Data Editing Methods and Techniques.* Vol. 2. Statistical Standards and Studies No. 48. UNECE, N.Y. and Geneva.

[19] Weir, P. (1997): *Data Editing and Performance Measures*. Working Paper No. 38, UNECE Work Session on Statistical Data Editing, Prague.

[20] Winkler, W.E. (1999a): *Draft Glossary of Terms Used in Data Editing*. Working Paper No. 2, UNECE Work Session on Statistical Data Editing. Rome.

[21] Winkler, W.E. (1999b): *State of Statistical Data Editing and Current Research Problems.* Working Paper No. 29, UNECE Work Session on Statistical Data Editing, Rome.

EVALUATION CRITERIA FOR EDITING AND IMPUTATION IN EUREDIT

By Ray Chambers, Department of Social Statistics, University of Southampton, United Kingdom

1. THE EUREDIT PROJECT

Euredit, or to give it its full title "The Development and Evaluation of New Methods for Editing and Imputation" is a large research project funded under the FP5 Information Societies Technology Programme of the European Commission. The objectives of Euredit are quite ambitious, and include the development of new methods for editing and imputation, the comparative evaluation of these methods together with "standard" methods and the dissemination of these results via a software product as well as publications.

The main focus of Euredit is editing and imputation for the types of data collected by national statistical agencies. Reflecting this, the participants in Euredit include the UK Office for National Statistics, the Netherlands Central Bureau of Statistics, the Italian National Statistical Institute, Statistics Denmark, Statistic Finland and the Swiss Federal Statistics Office. From a methodological point of view, the main "new" methods that will be investigated within Euredit will be those based on the application of neural net and related computationally intensive methods, as well as the application of modern outlier robust statistical methods. The neural net and computationally intensive methods will be developed by the University of York, the University of Jyvaeskylae and Royal Holloway University, with Statistics Denmark, while the outlier robust methods will be largely developed by the University of Southampton and Insiders GmbH, with the Swiss Federal Statistics Office and the Netherlands Central Bureau of Statistics. Numerical Algorithms Group (NAG) will be responsible for creating the software product that will form the key dissemination vehicle for the research output of the project.

Since Euredit will involve a large number of different institutions all developing methods for editing and imputation, it was recognized right from the project's inception that there would need to be a common core of evaluation procedures that all Euredit developers would have to apply to a common core of data sets to ensure comparability of performance. The core of "test" data sets has been put together by the ONS from contributions by different members of the Euredit consortium. The purpose of this paper is to describe the core of evaluation criteria that will be applied to edit and imputation outcomes for these data that will be generated by the different methodologies being investigated within Euredit. At this stage it is envisaged that a substantial number of these criteria will be incorporated into the Euredit software product.

In what follows we first discuss the assessment of editing performance within Euredit, followed by imputation performance. Ancillary issues related to special types of data structures commonly found in official statistics data sets are then discussed, as well as the very important issue of practical implementation of an edit and imputation method. A more extensive document setting out the detail of the evaluation formulae to be used in Euredit is available from its website (http://www.cs.york.ac.uk/Euredit).

2. WHAT IS EDITING?

Editing is the process of detecting errors in statistical data. An error is the difference between a *measured* value for a datum and the corresponding *true* value of this datum. The true value is defined as the value that would have been recorded if an ideal (and expensive) measurement procedure had been used in the data collection process.

Editing can be of two different types. *Logical* editing is where the data values of interest have to obey certain pre-defined rules, and editing is the process of checking to see whether this is the case. A data value that fails a logical edit must be wrong. *Statistical* editing on the other hand is about the identification of data values that might be wrong. Ideally, it should be highly likely that a data value that fails a statistical edit is wrong, but there is always the chance that in fact it is correct. Since the context in which the edit is applied (e.g. the presence or absence of external information, and its associated quality) modifies the way an edit is classified, Euredit will not attempt to distinguish between evaluation of logical editing performance and evaluation of statistical editing performance. It will only be concerned with evaluation of overall editing performance (i.e. detection of data fields with errors).

One can also distinguish editing from *error localization.* The latter corresponds to the process of deciding which of the fields in a particular record that "fail" the edit process should be modified (e.g. parent/child age above). The key aspect of performance here is finding the "smallest" set of fields in a record such that at least one of these fields is in error. This type of evaluation depends on application of the Felligi-Holt principle of minimum change and requires access to the full set of edit rules for the data set of interest. Since it is infeasible to include every possible edit rule with the evaluation data sets being developed in Euredit, the evaluation procedures used by Euredit will not be concerned with the localization aspects of editing.

2.1 Performance Requirements for Statistical Editing

Two basic requirements for a good statistical editing procedure have been identified in Euredit.

(i) Efficient Error Detection: Subject to constraints on the cost of editing, the editing process should be able to detect virtually all errors in the data set of interest.

(ii) Influential Error Detection: The editing process should be able to detect those errors in the data set that would lead to significant errors in analysis if they were ignored.

2.2 Efficient Error Detection

Typically, the concern is detection of the maximum number of true errors (measured value $\neq$ true value) in the data set for a specified detection cost. This detection cost rises as the number of incorrect detections (measured value = true value) made increases, while the number of true errors detected obviously decreases as the number of undetected true errors increases. Consequently, Euredit will evaluate the error detection performance of an editing procedure in terms of the both the number of incorrect detections it makes as well as the number of correct detections that it fails to make for each variable in the data set of interest.

In many situations, a data record that has at least one variable value flagged as "suspicious" will have all its data values flagged in the same way. This is equivalent to defining a *case-level* editing process. Euredit will also apply evaluation measures to correct/incorrect case level detections.

The above measures are essentially "averages", and so will vary across subgroups of the data set of interest. An important part of the evaluation of an editing procedure in Euredit will therefore be to show how these measures vary across identifiable subgroups of this data set. For example, in a business survey application, the performance of an editing procedure may well vary across different industry groups.

2.3 Influential Error Reduction

In this case the aim in editing is not so much to find as many errors as possible, but to find the errors that matter (i.e. the influential errors) and then to correct them. From this point of view the size of the error in the measured data (measured value - true value) is the important characteristic, and the aim of the editing process is to detect measured data values that have a high probability of being "far" from their associated true values.

In order to evaluate the error reduction brought about by editing, Euredit will assume that all values flagged as suspicious by the editing process are checked, and their actual true values determined. Suppose the variable Y is scalar. Then the editing procedure leads to a set of post-edit values defined by $\hat{Y}_i = E_i Y_i + (1 - E_i) Y_i^*$ where Y_i is the measured value for this variable for the ith case and Y_i^* is the corresponding "true" value. The key performance criterion in this situation is the "distance" between the distribution of the true values Y_i^* and the distribution of the post-edited values $\hat{Y}_i$. The aim is to have an editing procedure where these two distributions are as close as possible, or equivalently where the difference between the two distributions is as close to zero as possible.

When Y is scalar, the errors in the post-edited data are $D_i = \hat{Y}_i - Y_i^* = E_i(Y_i - Y_i^*)$. For intrinsically positive variables, the evaluation measures that will be used in Euredit will be the average of both the D_i and the square of the D_i. For strictly positive variables these averages will be expressed as a proportion of the average of the true values (suitably sample weighted if required). In addition, other, more "distributional" measures related to the spread of the D_i will be computed, for example the ratio of the range of the D_i to the interquartile distance of the corresponding true values.

With a categorical variable one cannot define an error by simple differencing. Instead Euredit will tabulate the joint distribution of the post-edit and true values, and a "good" editing procedure is then one such that the weighted frequency of "mismatches" in this joint distribution is small. When the variable of interest is ordinal, this weighted frequency measures will be modified by the "distance" between the categories that contribute to a mismatch.

A slightly different approach to evaluating whether an editing procedure has found the "errors that matter" is to check whether any remaining errors in the post-edited survey data do not lead to estimates that are significantly different from what would be obtained if editing was "perfect". Euredit will check this by comparing estimates based on the post-edited data with those based on the true data, e.g. via calculation of appropriately standardized differences. In the case of linear estimates for scalar variables this is equivalent to calculating a t-statistic for testing the hypothesis that the weighted mean of the D_i is not significantly different from zero.

When the variable of interest is categorical, with A categories, the D_i values above will be computed as

$$D_i = \sum_a \sum_{b \neq a} I(\hat{Y}_i = a) I(Y_i^* = b).$$

Here I(Yi = a) is the indicator function for when case i takes category a. If Y is ordinal rather than nominal then

$$D_i = \sum_a \sum_{b \neq a} d(a,b) I(\hat{Y}_i = a) I(Y_i^* = b)$$

where d(a,b) is a measure of the distance between category a and category b. Evaluation then proceeds as outlined above.

2.4 Evaluating the Outlier Detection Performance of an Editing Procedure

Statistical outlier detection can be considered a form of editing. As with "standard" editing, the aim is to identify data values that are inconsistent with what is expected, or what the majority of the data values indicate should be the case. However, in this case there are no true values that can be ascertained. Instead, the aim is to remove these values from the data being analysed, in the hope that the outputs from this analysis will then be closer to the truth than an analysis that includes these values (i.e. with the detected outliers included).

In order to evaluate how well an editing procedure detects outliers, the moments and distribution of the outlier-free data values will be compared with the corresponding moments and distribution of the true values. Similarly, the distribution of the "outlier-free" values will be compared with that of the true values over a range of values that covers the distribution of the true values, e.g. the deciles of the distribution of the true values.

3. WHAT IS IMPUTATION?

Imputation is the process by which values in a data set that are missing or suspicious (e.g. edit failures) are replaced by known acceptable values. Euredit will not distinguish between imputation due to missingness or imputation as a method for correcting for edit failure, since imputation is carried out for any variable for which true values are missing. Reasons for imputation vary, but typically it is because the data processing system has been designed to work with a complete dataset, i.e. one where all values are acceptable (satisfy edits) and there are no "holes".

Methods of imputation for missing data vary considerably depending on the type of data set, its extent and the characteristics of the missingness in the data. However, there are two broad classes of missingness for which different imputation methods are typically applied. These are *unit missingness,* where all the data for a case are missing, and *item missingness,* where part of the data for a case are missing. The extent of item missingness may well (and often does) vary between different records.

An important characteristic of missingness is *identifiability.* Missingness is identifiable if we know which records in the dataset are missing, even though we do not know the values contained in these records. Missingness due to edit failure is always identifiable. Missingness brought about through underenumeration (as in a population census) or undercoverage (as in a sample survey) is typically not identifiable. The importance of identifiability is that it allows one at least in theory to cross-classify the missing records according to their true and imputed values, and hence evaluate the efficacy of the imputation process. Euredit will only be concerned with imputation of identifiable missingness.

3.1 Performance Requirements for Imputation

Ideally, an imputation procedure should be capable of effectively reproducing the key outputs from a "complete data" statistical analysis of the data set of interest. However, this is usually impossible, soalternative measures of performance are of interest. The basis for these measures is set out in the following list of desirable properties for an imputation procedure. The list itself is ranked from properties that are hardest to achieve to those that are easiest. **This does NOT mean that the ordering reflects desirability**. In fact, in most uses of imputation within national statistical agencies the aim is to produce aggregated estimates from a data set and criteria (i) and (ii) below will be irrelevant. On the other hand, if the data set is to be publicly released or used for development of prediction models, then (i) and (ii) become rather more relevant.

(i) **Predictive Accuracy:** The imputation procedure should maximize preservation of true values. That is, it should result in imputed values that are "close" as possible to the true values.

(ii) **Ranking Accuracy:** The imputation procedure should maximize preservation of order in the imputed values. That is, it should result in ordering relationships between imputed values that are the same (or very similar) to those that hold in the true values.

(iii) **Distributional Accuracy:** The imputation procedure should preserve the distribution of the true data values. That is, marginal and higher order distributions of the imputed data values should be essentially the same as the corresponding distributions of the true values.

(iv) **Estimation Accuracy:** The imputation procedure should reproduce the lower order moments of the distributions of the true values. In particular, it should lead to unbiased and efficient inferences for parameters of the distribution of the true values (given that these true values are unavailable).

(v) **Imputation Plausibility:** The imputation procedure should lead to imputed values that are plausible. In particular, they should be acceptable values as far as the editing procedure is concerned.

It should be noted that not all the above properties are meant to apply to every variable that is imputed. In particular, property (ii) requires that the variable be at least ordinal, while property (iv) is only distinguishable from property (iii) when the variable being imputed is scalar. Consequently the imputation evaluation measures used in Euredit will depend on the scale of measurement of the variable being imputed.

An additional point to note about property (iv) above is that it represents a compromise. Ideally, this property should correspond to "preservation of analysis", in the sense that the results of any statistical analysis of the imputed data should lead to the same conclusions as the same analysis of the complete data. However, since it is impossible to a priori identify all possible analyses that could be carried out on a data set containing imputed data, this criterion has been modified to focus on preservation of estimated moments of the variables making up the data set of interest.

Furthermore in all cases performance relative to property (v) above ("plausibility") can be checked by treating the imputed values as measured values and assessing how well they perform relative to the statistical editing criteria described earlier in this paper.

Finally, unless specifically stated to the contrary below, all imputation evaluation measures used in Euredit will be defined with respect to the set of n imputed values within a data set, rather than the set of all values making up this set.

3.2 Imputation Performance Measures for a Nominal Categorical Variable

The extent to which an imputation procedure preserves the marginal distribution of a categorical variable with c+1 categories can be assessed by calculating the value of a Wald-type statistic that compares the imputed and true distributions of the variable across these categories. This statistic is the extension (Stuart, 1955) of McNemar's statistic (without a continuity correction) for marginal homogeneity in a 2 x 2 table. It is given by

$$W = (\mathbf{R} - \mathbf{S})^t \left[\mathrm{diag}(\mathbf{R} + \mathbf{S}) - \mathbf{T} - \mathbf{T}^t\right]^{-1} (\mathbf{R} - \mathbf{S}).$$

Here **R** is the c-vector of imputed counts for the first c categories of the variable, **S** is the c-vector of actual counts for these categories and **T** is the square matrix of order c corresponding to the crossclassification of actual vs. imputed counts for these categories. Assuming some form of stochastic imputation is used, the large sample distribution of W is chi-square with c degrees of freedom, and so a statistical test of whether the imputation method preserves the distribution of the categorical variable of interest can be carried out.

Note that adding any number of "correct" imputations to the set of imputed values being tested does not alter the value of W. That is, it is only the extent of the "incorrect" imputations in the data set that determines whether the hypothesis of preservation of marginal distributions is supported or rejected.

The extension of W to the case where more than one categorical variable is being imputed is straightforward. One just defines Y as the single categorical variable corresponding to all possible outcomes from the joint distribution of these categorical variables and then computes W as above.

It is also important in Euredit to assess how well an imputation process preserves true values for a categorical variable Y with c+1 categories. An obvious measure of how closely the imputed values "track" the true values for this variable is given by the proportion of off-diagonal entries for the square

table T^+ of order c+1 obtained by cross-classifying these imputed and actual values. This is

$$D = 1 - n^{-1}\sum_{i=1}^{n} I(\hat{Y}_i = Y_i^*)$$

where $\hat{Y}_i$ denotes the imputed version of Y and Y_i^* is its true value.

Provided the hypothesis that the imputation method preserves the marginal distribution of Y cannot be rejected, the variance of D can be estimated by

$$\hat{V}(D) = n^{-1} - n^{-2}\mathbf{1}^t\{\text{diag}(\mathbf{R}+\mathbf{S}) - \mathbf{T} - \text{diag}(\mathbf{T})\}\mathbf{1} = n^{-1}(1 - D)$$

where 1 denotes a c-vector of ones. If the imputation method preserves individual values, D should be identically zero. To allow for the fact that the imputation method may "almost" preserve true values, one can test whether the expected value of D is significantly greater than a small positive constant ε. That is, one is willing to allow up to a maximum expected proportion ε of incorrect imputations and still declare that the imputation method preserves true values. Consequently, if

$$D > \varepsilon + 2\sqrt{\hat{V}(D)}$$

one can say that the imputation method has an expected incorrect imputation rate that is significantly larger than ε and hence does not preserve true values. The choice of ε will depend on the application. In Euredit this constant is set to

$$\varepsilon^* = \max\left(0, D - 2\sqrt{\hat{V}(D)}\right).$$

The smaller this value, the better the imputation process is at preserving true values. An imputation method that generates a value of zero for ε^* for a particular data set will be said to have preserved true values in that data set.

3.3 Imputation Performance Measures for an Ordinal Categorical Variable

When Y is ordinal, preservation of order becomes an issue. To illustrate, consider the following 4 imputed by actual cross-classifications for an ordinal variable Y taking values 1, 2 and 3. In all cases the value of W is zero, so the issue is one of preserving values, not distributions. The D statistic value for each table is also shown. Using a subscript to denote a particular table it can be seen that $D_a < D_b < D_c < D_d$ so the imputation method underlying table (a) appears "best".

However, one could question whether this actually means method (a) IS better than methods (b), (c) and (d). Thus method (a) twice imputes a value of 1 when the actual value is 3, and similarly twice imputes a value of 3 when the actual value is 1, a total of 4 "major" errors. In comparison, method (b) only makes 2 corresponding major errors, but also makes an additional 4 "minor" errors. The total error count (6) for (b) is clearly larger than that of (a), but its "major error count" (2) is smaller. The corresponding count for (c) is smaller still (0). It may well be that method (c) is in fact the best of all the four methods!

(a)

	$Y^*=1$	$Y^*=2$	$Y^*=3$	
$\hat{Y}=1$	3	0	2	5
$\hat{Y}=2$	0	5	0	5
$\hat{Y}=3$	2	0	3	5
	5	5	5	D = 4/15

(b)

	$Y^*=1$	$Y^*=2$	$Y^*=3$	
$\hat{Y}=1$	3	1	1	5
$\hat{Y}=2$	1	3	1	5
$\hat{Y}=3$	1	1	3	5
	5	5	5	D = 6/15

(c)

	$Y^*=1$	$Y^*=2$	$Y^*=3$	
$\hat{Y}=1$	3	2	0	5
$\hat{Y}=2$	2	1	2	5
$\hat{Y}=3$	0	2	3	5
	5	5	5	D = 8/15

(d)

	$Y^*=1$	$Y^*=2$	$Y^*=3$	
$\hat{Y}=1$	0	0	5	5
$\hat{Y}=2$	0	5	0	5
$\hat{Y}=3$	5	0	0	5
	5	5	5	D = 10/15

A way of allowing not only the absolute number of imputation errors, but also their "size" to influence assessment, is to compute a generalized version of D, where the "distance" between imputed and true values is taken into account. That is, we compute

$$D = n^{-1}\sum_{i=1}^{n} d(\hat{Y}_i, Y_i^*)$$

where d(a, b) is the "distance" from category a to category b. Thus, if we put d(a, b) equal to the "block metric" distance function, then $d(\hat{Y}_i, Y_i^*) = 1$ if $\hat{Y} = a$ and $Y^* = a-1$ or $a+1$ and $d(\hat{Y}_i, Y_i^*) = 2$ if $\hat{Y} = a$ and $Y^* = a-2$ or $a+2$. With this definition we see that $D_a = D_b = D_c = 8/15$ and $D_d = 20/15$. That is, there is in fact nothing to choose between (a), (b) and (c). On the other hand, suppose that $d(\hat{Y}_i, Y_i^*)$ = 1 if $\hat{Y} = a$ and $Y^* = a-1$ or $j+1$ and $d(\hat{Y}_i, Y_i^*) = 4$ if $\hat{Y} = a$ and $Y^* = a-2$ or $a+2$. That is, major errors are four times as bad as minor errors (a squared error rule). Then $D_a = 16/15$, $D_b = 12/15$, $D_c = 8/15$ and $D_d = 40/15$. Here we see that method (c) is the best of the four.

Assuming the categories are numbered from 1 to A, the following compromise definition will be used by Euredit:

$$d(a,b) = \frac{1}{2}\left[\frac{|a-b|}{A-1} + I(a \neq b)\right].$$

3.4 Imputation Performance Measures for a Scalar Variable

The statistics W and D can be easily extended to evaluating imputation for a continuous scalar variable by first categorizing that variable. If the variable is integer-valued the categorization is obvious, though "rare" tail values may need to be grouped. For truly continuous variables (e.g. income) a more appropriate categorization would be on the basis of the actual distribution of the variable in the population (e.g. decile groups). Here again, "rare" groups may need special attention. However, Euredit will avoid the arbitrariness of categorizing a continuous variable by using imputation performance measures that are directly applicable to scalar variables.

To start, consider preservation of true values. If this property holds, then $\hat{Y}$ should be close to Y^* for cases where imputation has been carried out. One way this "closeness" can be assessed

therefore is by calculating the weighted Pearson moment correlation between $\hat{Y}$ and Y^* for imputed cases. For data that are reasonably "normal" looking this should give a good measure of imputation performance. For data
that are highly skewed however, the non-robustness of the correlation coefficient means that it is preferable to focus on estimates of the regression of Y^* on $\hat{Y}$, particular those that are robust to outliers and influential values.

The regression approach evaluates the performance of the imputation procedure by fitting a linear model of the form $Y^* = \beta \hat{Y} + \varepsilon$ to the imputed data values using a (preferably sample weighted) robust estimation method. Let b denote the fitted value of β that results. Evaluation then proceeds by testing whether β = 1. If this test does not indicate a significant difference, then a measure of the regression mean square error

$$\hat{\sigma}^2 = \frac{1}{n-1}\sum_{i=1}^{n} w_i (Y_i^* - b\hat{Y}_i)^2$$

can be computed. A good imputation method will have a non-significant p-value for the test of $\beta = 1$ as well as a low value of $\hat{\sigma}^2$.

Underlying the above regression-based approach to evaluation is the idea of measuring the performance of an imputation method by the distance $d(\hat{Y}_i, Y_i^*)$ between the n-vector $\hat{Y}$ of imputed values and the corresponding n-vector Y^* of true values. An important class of such measures is defined by the weighted Lp distance between $\hat{Y}$ and Y^*. Euredit will calculate these measures for p =1 and p = 2.

Preservation of ordering for a scalar variable will be evaluated by replacing Y and Y above by their ranks in the full data set (not just in the set of imputed cases).

The distance between the weighted empirical distribution functions $F_{Y^*_n}(t)$ and $F_{\hat{Y}_n}(t)$ defined by the true and imputed values respectively provides a measure of how well the imputation procedure "preserves distributions". Such a distance is

$$d_\alpha(F_{Y^*_n}, F_{\hat{Y}_n}) = \frac{1}{t_{2n} - t_0}\sum_{j=1}^{2n} (t_j - t_{j-1}) \left| F_{Y^*_n}(t_j) - F_{\hat{Y}_n}(t_j) \right|^\alpha$$

where the $\{t_j\}$ values are the 2n jointly ordered true and imputed values of Y with t_0 equal to the largest integer smaller than or equal to t_1.and α is a "suitable" positive constant. Larger values of α attach more importance to larger differences between $F_{Y^*_n}(t)$ and $F_{\hat{Y}_n}(t)$. Euredit will use α = 1 and α = 2.

Finally, one can consider preservation of aggregates when imputing values of a scalar variable. The most important case here is preservation of the raw moments of the empirical distribution of the true values. For k = 1, 2, ..., Euredit will measure how well these are preserved by computing

$$m_k = \left| \sum_{i=1}^{n} w_i (Y_i^{*k} - \hat{Y}_i^k) / \sum_{i=1}^{n} w_i \right| = \left| m(Y^{*k}) - m(\hat{Y}^k) \right|.$$

Preservation of derived moments, particularly moments around the mean, is also of interest in Euredit. In this case the data values (true and imputed) will be replaced by the corresponding differences. For example, preservation of moments around the mean will be assessed by calculating mk above with

Y_i^* replaced by $Y_i^* - m(Y^*)$ and $\hat{Y}_i$ replaced by $\hat{Y}_i - m(\hat{Y})$. Similarly, preservation of joint second order moments for two variables Y_1 and Y_2 will be measured by calculating m_k, but now replacing Y_i^* by $(Y_{1i}^* - m(\mathbf{Y}_1^*))(Y_{2i}^* - m(\mathbf{Y}_2^*))$, and $\hat{Y}_i$ by $(\hat{Y}_{1i} - m(\hat{\mathbf{Y}}_1))(\hat{Y}_{2i} - m(\hat{\mathbf{Y}}_2))$.

3.5 Evaluating Outlier Robust Imputation

The outlier robustness of an imputation procedure can be assessed by the "robustness" of the analyses based on the imputed values, compared to the analyses based on the true data (which can contain outliers). This is a rather different type of performance criterion from that investigated so far, in that the aim here is not to get "close" to the unknown true values but to enable analyses that are more "efficient" than would be the case if they were based on the true data values.

For the Euredit project the emphasis will be on assessing efficiency in terms of mean squared error for estimating the corresponding population mean using a weighted mean based on the imputed data values. Note that this measure uses all N data values in the data set rather than just the n imputed values, and is given by

$$MSE = \left(\sum_{i=1}^{N} w_i\right)^{-1}\left(\sum_{i=1}^{N} w_i I(\hat{Y}_i = Y_i^*)\right)^{-1}\sum_{i=1}^{N} w_i^2(\hat{Y}_i - m_N(\hat{Y}))^2 + \left[m_N(\hat{Y}) - m_N(Y^*)\right].$$

Here $m_N(Y)$ refers to the weighted mean of the variable Y defined over all N values in the data set of interest. Observe that the variance term in (30) includes a penalty for excessive imputation.

4. EVALUATING IMPUTATION PERFORMANCE FOR MIXTURE TYPE VARIABLES

Mixture type variables occur regularly in most official statistics collections. These are scalar variables that can take exact values with non-zero probability and are continuously distributed otherwise. An example is a non-negative variable that takes the value zero with positive probability π, and is distributed over the positive real line with probability $1 - \pi$. The most straightforward way to evaluate imputation performance for such variables is to evaluate this performance separately for the "mixing" variable and for the actual values at each level of the mixing variable.

5. EVALUATING IMPUTATION PERFORMANCE IN PANEL AND TIME SERIES DATA

A panel data structure exists when there are repeated observations made on the same set of cases. Typically these are at regularly spaced intervals, but they do not have to be. The vector of repeated observations on a variable Y in this type of data set can therefore be considered as a realisation of a multivariate random variable. Euredit will therefore calculate multivariate versions of the measures described earlier in order to evaluate imputation performance for this type of data.

For time series data the situation is a little different. Here i = 1, ..., n indexes the different time series of interest, with each series corresponding to a multivariate observation indexed by time. For such data most methods of analysis are based on the estimated autocorrelation structure of the different series. Hence an important evaluation measure where imputed values are present is preservation of these estimated autocorrelations. Let r_{ik}^* denote the true value of the estimated autocorrelation at lag k for the series defined by variable Y_i with $\hat{r}_{jk}$ the corresponding estimated lag k autocorrelation based on the imputed data. The Euredit measure of the relative discrepancy between the estimated lag k autocorrelations for the true and imputed versions of these series is then

$$R_k = \left| \sum_{i=1}^{n} (r_{ik}^* - \hat{r}_{ik}) / \sum_{i=1}^{n} r_{ik}^* \right|.$$

6. COMPARING TWO (OR MORE) IMPUTATION METHODS

A key analysis in the Euredit project will be the comparison of a number of imputation methods. Simple tabular and graphical analyses will often be sufficient in this regard. For example, Madsen and Larson (2000) compare MLP neural networks with logistic regression at different levels of "error probabilities" and display their results in tabular and graphical format showing how various performance measures for error detection for these methods vary with these probability levels.

A more sophisticated statistical analysis would involve the independent application of the different methods to distinct subsets of the data set (e.g. industry or regional groups) and then computing the performance measure of interest for each of the different methods within each of these groups. A repeated measures ANCOVA analysis of these values (maybe after suitable transformation) with imputation method as a factor will then be carried out.

Alternatively, pairwise "global" comparisons of imputation methods will be carried out in Euredit using a measure of the form

$$r_{L\alpha}(\hat{Y}, \tilde{Y}) = \frac{d_{L\alpha}(\hat{Y}, Y^*)}{d_{L\alpha}(\tilde{Y}, Y^*)} = \left\{ \sum_{i=1}^{n} w_i \left| \hat{Y}_i - Y_i^* \right|^{\alpha} / \sum_{i=1}^{n} w_i \left| \tilde{Y}_i - Y_i^* \right|^{\alpha} \right\}^{1/\alpha}.$$

Here $\hat{Y}$ and $\tilde{Y}$ are two imputed versions of Y, and $\alpha = 1$ or 2.

7. OPERATIONAL EFFICIENCY

Editing and imputation methods have to be operationally efficient in order for them to be attractive to most "large scale" users. This means that an important aspect of assessment for an editing and imputation method is the ease with which it can be implemented, maintained and applied to large scale data sets. The following criteria will be used in Euredit to determine the operational efficiency of an editing and imputation (E&I) method:

(a) What resources are needed to implement the E&I method in the production process?
(b) What resources are needed to maintain the E&I method?
(b) What is the required expertise needed to apply the E&I method in practice?
(d) What are the hardware and software requirements?
(e) Are there any data limitations (e.g. size/complexity of data set to be imputed)?
(f) What feedback does the E&I method produce? Can this feedback be used to "tune" the process in order to improve its efficiency?
(g) What resources are required to modify the operation of the E&I method? Is it possible to quickly change its operating characteristics and rerun it?
(h) A key aspect of maintaining an E&I system is its *transparency*. Is the underlying methodology intuitive? Are the algorithms and code accessible and well documented?

8. PLAUSIBILITY

The plausibility of the imputed values is *a binding requirement* for an imputation procedure, in the sense that an imputation procedure is unacceptable if it generates implausible values. This is particularly important for applications within NSIs. Within Euredit plausibility will be assessed by the imputed data passing all "fatal" edits, where these are defined. The *degree* of plausibility will be measured by calculating the edit performance measures described earlier, treating the imputed data values as the pre-edit "raw" values.

9. QUALITY MEASUREMENT

In the experimental situations that will be explored in Euredit, it is possible to use simulation methods to assess the quality of the E&I method, by varying the experimental conditions and observing the change in E&I performance. However, in real life applications the true values for the missing/incorrect data are unknown, and so this approach is not feasible. In particular, information on the quality of the editing and imputation outcomes in such cases can only be based on the data available for imputation.

In this context editing quality can be assessed by treating the imputed values as the true values and computing the different edit performance measures described earlier. Of course, the quality of these quality measures is rather suspect if the imputed values are themselves unreliable. Consequently an important property of an imputation method should be that it produces measures of the quality its imputations. One important measure (assuming that the imputation method preserves distributions) is the so-called imputation variance. This is the *additional* variability, over and above the "complete data variability", associated with inference based on the imputed data. It is caused by the extra uncertainty associated with randomness in the imputation method. This additional variability can be measured by repeating the imputation process and applying multiple imputation theory. Repeatability of the imputation process is therefore an important quality measure.

References

[1] Madsen, B. and Bjoern Steen Larsen, B. S. (2000). The uses of neural networks in data editing. Invited paper, International Conference on Establishment Surveys (ICES II), June 2000, Buffalo, N.Y.

[2] Stuart, A. (1955). A test for homogeneity of the marginal distributions in a two-way classification. *Biometrika 42,* pg. 412.

EVALUATING EDITING AND IMPUTATION PROCESSES: THE ITALIAN EXPERIENCE

By Marco Di Zio, Orietta Luzi, Antonia Manzari, ISTAT, Italy

1. INTRODUCTION

Statisticians working in the context of data editing and imputation (E&I in the following) in National Statistical Offices agree that the two main goals of performing E&I on statistical survey data are reducing the effects of non-sampling errors on survey results (*quality of the data*), and providing information on the overall survey process, including E&I (*quality of the process*). E&I processes are to be designed and applied in order to meet these requirements as much as possible. The capability of E&I processes of reaching these objectives can be verified on the basis of appropriate evaluation studies. Within the last few years, evaluation has been recognized as a central aspect in the area of E&I, particularly because of the increasing demand for information about the characteristics of this survey phase and its impact on data quality, and the need of keeping under control the variability of results due to E&I.

In this paper we limit the discussion to the evaluation of E&I performed at the data editing stage, excluding all the data verification activities performed at the previous survey stages (data capturing, data entry).

On the basis of some tests performed or still in progress at ISTAT, some general problems in the context of the evaluation of E&I procedures are identified in the paper, and the solutions adopted at ISTAT for dealing with different evaluation objectives are illustrated.

The paper is structured as follows. In section 2 a general framework for evaluation problem is defined, taking into account the complexity of the E&I phase and some different evaluation objectives. Sections 3, 4 and 5 deal more in depth with specific evaluation objectives, with a discussion based on the Italian experience.

2. EVALUATING E&I: GENERAL PROBLEMS

In recent years the problem of how to evaluate the quality of E&I has been widely discussed in literature from both a theoretical and an operational point of view. The concept of *quality* of E&I has to be firstly defined.

Nordbotten (1999) defines the quality of statistical data editing as "a measure of how well the statistical process succeeds in satisfying users and producers needs": users expect information about the data reliability, producers want information on the reliability of the E&I process for improving the resources allocation and the overall production performance.

A unique definition of the quality of an E&I process cannot be provided since it depends on the particular E&I aspect we are interested in. Hence the evaluation of E&I quality depends on the definition of the specific process characteristic we want to highlight. Granquist (1997) performs a broad analysis of evaluation objectives through the description of several applications and studies presented in literature.

In this paper, we report the Italian experience in the following areas:

1. verifying the statistical properties of a specific E&I approach for a specific data problem;
2. choosing the *best* technique for a given data problem;

3. monitoring and optimising the performance of a given E&I method/process;
4. obtaining information on errors and error sources;
5. measuring the E&I impact on original (*raw*) data.

Objectives 1 through 4 are related to the producer's needs of information about the process reliability, while objective 5 aims at providing users with information about the data reliability.

In practice, each objective corresponds to one of the steps that normally are to be carried out when designing, implementing and applying an E&I procedure. Depending on the step, different quality and/or documentation needs are to be satisfied.

Typically, in the *planning* phase, objectives 1 and 2 aim at analysing and measuring the potential performance, the possible benefits and the operational characteristics relating to the use of a new or a traditional methodology when applied to a given E&I problem or to a particular survey context. For example, objective 1 is pursued when the statistical properties of a new E&I method are to be tested on real or simulated data reproducing the theoretical situation the method is designed to deal with. Objective 2 is typical of studies in which the evaluation aim is assessing the quality of competitive E&I methods in terms of their capability of correctly deal with a real data problem.

Relating to this point, it is worthwhile emphasizing that the evaluation problem is generally a complex task because of the typical complex structure of E&I procedures. In fact, an E&I process generally consists of many sub-phases, performing each a particular step of the whole E&I process (Jong, 1996; Di Zio *et al.*, 2002b; Manzari, 2004). The simplest distinction refers to error localisation and error imputation, but many other sub-processes can be identified, depending on the variables nature (ordinal, nominal, continuous), the error typologies (systematic or stochastic, influential or not influential, etc.), the survey characteristics (censuses, sampling surveys, panels), and so on. Therefore, an E&I process can be viewed as a completely integrated set of different techniques dealing each with a different E&I sub-problem but having the common aim of improving the overall quality of final results. Correspondingly, the problem of evaluating an E&I process can be split in the evaluation of simpler sub-problems, focusing each on a specific E&I sub-phase. It is obvious that different evaluation criteria will be used depending on the particular E&I sub-phase, on the features of the specific E&I method, on the survey objectives. For example, if our goal is to evaluate the performance of a technique in dealing with influential data, a relevant quality criteria is the method capability of preserving aggregates reducing costs and respondent burden resulting from interactive editing activities. If our aim is to verify the quality of an imputation method for data to be used to develop forecasting models, the most important quality criteria could be the preservation of micro data.

Once a given set of techniques have been selected as elements of an E&I strategy, the strategy itself has to be *designed, implemented* and *tested*. Generally these activities are supported by an iterative evaluation process, which aims at tuning and improving the performance of the E&I process (objective 3). Appropriate evaluation criteria and the corresponding measurements are to be defined in order to facilitate the continuous monitoring of each E&I sub-process.

An important objective in the context of evaluating E&I processes is obtaining information on non-sampling errors (objective 4). Once the final E&I procedure has been defined and tuned, the analysis of errors and error structure represent a valid support for identifying the most likely sources of errors contaminating data. A typical product of objective 4 is the so-called *error profile*, i.e. a description of the characteristics of all identified errors and their internal structure (Cirianni *et al.*, 2000). This information is generally used for improving the survey organization in future survey repetitions, and when specific studies on particular error types or mechanisms are to be carried out (objectives 1 and 2).

Measuring the impact of E&I on original data (objective 5) is the minimal requirement to be met by each statistical survey. In fact, the objective of this type of evaluation is obtaining basic products like:

- documentation of the E&I processing flow;
- assessment of the E&I statistical effects on data;
- assessment of the quality of collected data.

In each evaluation study, a critical aspect is represented by the identification of *standard indicators* quantifying the corresponding quality criteria. A good research has been carried on in this area (Chambers, 2000; Stefanowicz, 1997; Madsen *et al.*, 2000; Fortini *et al.*, 1999; Nordbotten, 1997; Nordbotten, 2000). The need of defining generalised measures is increasing due to many reasons:

- the increasing need of internal and external comparability of E&I processes;
- the increasing need of international comparability of E&I processes;
- the development of new or improved E&I techniques;
- the increasing demand of information on data processing coming from end users.

The assessment of the quality of both data and data processing, as well as quality reporting, are central problems not only at National Statistical Offices level, where the effort is concentrated in the definition and dissemination of *statistical guidelines* and *quality reports* (National Centre for Education Statistics, 1992; Statistics Canada, 1998), but also in an international perspective: as an example, growing attention is devoted to these aspects at Eurostat, where increasing importance is given to the problem of non-sampling error documentation and measurement (LEG, 2001).

Once an evaluation objective and the corresponding quality criteria have been stated, the design of the evaluation study implies to define *how* the evaluation has to be carried out, i.e. which particular evaluation approach has to be adopted. A general distinction can be made between *observational* and *experimental* studies (Biemer *et al.*, 1995). In the first context, the investigators study the phenomenon as they find it. For the purpose of this paper, we mean that the assessment of the quality of an E&I process is based only on observed data, eventually enriched with all available information on surveyed units and variables (e.g. coming from historical or administrative sources of information, or collected through re-interviews or complete data revision processes) (Granquist, 1995; Granquist, 1997; Biemer *et al.*, 1995; Poulsen, 1997). In the experimental approach, we generally investigate the phenomenon having a certain control on the mechanism ruling some key aspects of the phenomenon itself. In our context, it means that we simulate the situations we would investigate, and make inference from the simulation results obtained for assessing the quality of a procedure (an E&I procedure, or a single technique) (Kovar *et al.*, 1996).

Given the evaluation objective, the choice is sometimes obvious. For instance, if the objective is to choose the *best* technique for dealing with a specific E&I problem, an experimental approach is more appropriate than an observational one. On the contrary, measuring the effects on data of an E&I process is a typical observational study. In other cases, however, there are other elements influencing the choice of the approach; the most important are the available resources (budget, human, tools, other costs), the timeliness requirements, and the available external information.

3. EVALUATING THE QUALITY OF E&I: THE SIMULATION APPROACH

In this section, objectives 1 and 2 mentioned in the previous section are synthetically discussed, and a general description of the most recent experiences performed at ISTAT in these areas is provided. As already mentioned in section 2, both objectives aim at providing data producers with information on E&I process at the planning phase: this information is generally used for improving the efficacy (in terms of quality of results) and the efficiency (in terms of costs) of E&I activities performed at each sub-phase, hence the performance of the overall E&I process.

The experiences performed at ISTAT until now are both observational and experimental. In the observational context, the evaluation of E&I methods has been performed essentially in the following area: for a given E&I problem, starting from raw data, verifying the usefulness of a new methodology by comparing its results with those obtained by using the current approach (Di Zio *et al.*, 2002a), or identifying the most appropriate technique among different alternative approaches (Cirianni *et al.*, 2001).

As already mentioned, the experimental approach is the natural framework where the evaluation of the quality of E&I methods can be embedded. At ISTAT the simulation approach (Barcaroli *et al.*, 1997; Luzi *et al.*, 1998; Della Rocca *et. al.*, 2000;) is at present adopted in many evaluation studies. This approach consists of the following main steps:

(i) corrupt original true values with errors and/or missing values;
(ii) apply the E&I strategy under study in order to obtain the edited and imputed data;
(iii) compare some quantities computed on the true values with the same quantities computed on the edited and imputed data.

The simulation approach is effective for both the evaluation objectives 1 and 2 (see section 2). In fact, the first objective consists of verifying the behaviour of a technique in some theoretical situations; for example, if we want to evaluate the capability of two techniques to deal with random errors, we can simulate random errors in our data and draw conclusions from the comparison of the results produced by the techniques under study.

Concerning objective 2 (choosing the *best* set of techniques for a given survey application), we first simulate errors trying to reproduce real situations; then we evaluate the set of integrated methods with respect to these error situations. In this context, it is important to analyse the *error profile* of the survey data we are going to investigate, in order to reproduce, at least for the main aspects, the error mechanisms affecting data.

The main advantages of the simulation approach with respect to other ones are low costs and the possibility of controlling some critical aspects of the applications. Drawbacks mainly relate to the effort required for modelling errors and error patterns.

Some interesting experiences in this area have been carried out at ISTAT in different contexts: comparing the performance of different approaches for a given E&I problem (Manzari *et al.*, 2001), assessing the capability of a new approach of dealing with some specific kinds of errors (Manzari, 1999; Coppola *et al.*, 2002) and, in the context of the European EUREDIT project (www.cs.york.ac.uk/euredit/), evaluating the *best* method in an overall survey context. In the latter case, the evaluation criteria and the corresponding performance indicators are those described in Chambers (2000).

In the following, we will stress some theoretical aspects relating to the use of the simulation approach. Let us suppose we have observed k variables on n units. Let $X=(X_1, ..., X_k)$ be the vector of original true values, let $Y=(Y_1, ..., Y_k)$ be the vector of corrupted values and let $X'=(X'_1, ..., X'_k)$ be the vector of final edited data. As so far introduced, for evaluating the E&I procedure, we generally compare the generic quantities $Q(X)$ and $Q(X')$ through a suitable generic loss function $D(Q(X), Q(X'))$[1]. The X' values can be thought as a realisation of a random vector from a multivariate probability distribution depending on different random mechanisms: the corruption of the original values with probability law f (error mechanism), the error localisation method (with probability law g when it is not deterministic), the imputation method (with probability law h when it is not deterministic). This process is represented in Figure 1.

[1] One of the possible choice is for instance $Q(X)=X$ and $D(Q(X),Q(X'))=(Q(X-Q(X'))^2$ the square of the difference between original and edited values.

Figure 1: E&I in a simulation context

(*Error Mechanism*)		(*Error Localization Mechanism*)		(*Imputation Mechanism*)	
	$\varepsilon \sim f$		$L \sim g$		$I \sim h$
Original data	⟶ Contaminated data		⟶ Localized errors		⟶ Final data
$(X_1, \ldots, X_k)$	$(Y_1, \ldots, Y_k)$		$(Y_1, \ldots, Y_k)$		$(X'_1, \ldots, X'_k)$

In this context, to evaluate statistically the quality of the E&I process we have to consider all the stochastic mechanisms affecting the results. Thus if we want to evaluate fairly the performance of the E&I process through a suitable generic function $D(Q(X),Q(X'))$, we should need to compute it with respect to the distributions of the stochastic mechanisms present in the process. One natural way is to compute the expected value of D :

$$E_{\varepsilon,\, L,\, I}[D(Q(X)\, ,\, Q(X')\,)] = E(D)$$

where (ε, L, I) represent the random mechanism influencing the final results. Choosing $D(Q(X),Q(X')) = (Q(X) - Q(X'))^2$, we obtain the well known Mean Square Error. Generally the expected value $E(D)$ cannot be computed analytically because of the difficulty of modelling the joint distribution of the random variables X'. On the other hand, we are often able to draw observations from the joint distribution of the random variable $X'(\varepsilon,L,I)$. In this context we can use a Monte Carlo integration method to approximate the expected value $E(D)$ (Rubinstein, 1981). If we repeat m times the E&I process, we obtain $(X'^{(1)}, \ldots, X'^{(m)})$ that can be thought as a m sample drawn from the distribution of X', hence for m sufficiently large:

$$\frac{1}{m}\sum_{i=1}^{m} D(Q(X), Q(X'^{(i)})) \cong E_{\varepsilon,L,I}(D(Q(X), Q(X')))$$

As illustrated in Figure 1, since the process is hierarchical, it could be interesting to assess the impact on the final data of each single stochastic mechanism. This can be achieved through the usual formulae with respect to the natural conditioning arising from the stream depicted in Figure 1. For example if we suppose that the imputation mechanism is not stochastic, we can decompose the total variance in a part induced by the error localisation mechanism and by the corruption method used, i.e.

$$Var_{\varepsilon,L}\, (\, D(Q(X),Q(X')\,)\,) = E_{\varepsilon}\, [\, Var_{L|\varepsilon}\, (D(Q(X),\, Q(X')\,)\,)] + Var_{\varepsilon}\, [\, E_{L|\varepsilon}\, (D(Q(X),\, Q(X')\,))\,]$$

where $E_{\varepsilon}\, [Var_{L|\varepsilon}\, (D(Q(X),Q(X')\,))\,]$ gives the part of total variance expressed by the variability of the error localisation random mechanism, and $Var_{\varepsilon}\, [E_{L|\varepsilon}\, (D(Q(X),Q(X')\,))]$ quantify the part of total variance expressed by the variability of the error introduction random mechanism. All these quantities can be computed through simulations by Monte Carlo methods.

4. TUNING E&I PROCESSES

The importance of optimising the performance of E&I processes in terms of quality and resources allocation has been continuously underlined in literature. Possible ways of pursuing this objective have been discussed by many authors (among others, Granquist, 1995; Lepp *et al.*, 1993). General problems relating to the optimal design and application of E&I processes have been examined in Granquist (1995), together with possible solutions: in particular, the Author identifies three types of costs connected with editing (producer costs, respondent cost and losses in timeliness), and he suggests some possible ways of improving the cost-benefit trade-off of editing processes (e.g. performing specific evaluations, improving edits, improving questionnaire design, limiting manual follow-up to those flagged records with the heaviest potential impact on estimates).

Since each E&I procedure is a complex process consisting of several integrated methods, there is not a unique way of applying it to data: the actual strategy depends on the specification of a number of elements as the hierarchy among units/errors/variables, the editing approaches and the type of edits, the stratification variables, the imputation algorithms, and so on. Therefore, once the components of an E&I procedure have been defined (in terms of approaches/methods/algorithms chosen to deal with the different data problems), its actual operational characteristics are to be *designed* and *implemented,* and the overall strategy has to be *tested* and *tuned* on the observed data. These tasks are generally performed through an iterative evaluation process in which the subject matter expert deals with the E&I elements to improve the performance of data processing.

The problem of tuning an E&I process corresponds to analysing what is happening to data *during* its execution (Nordbotten, 2000; Thomas, 1997). In this case, the evaluation objectives correspond to:

- verifying the effectiveness of the adopted editing methods in terms of results reliability;
- verifying that the E&I process results in terms of costs and timeliness correspond to those expected in the planning phase;
- verifying that resources are allocated in the appropriate way through the different (sub-)phases of the E&I process.

A great help in specifying and setting an E&I process is represented by possible knowledge on the methods under study coming from previous *quality evaluation studies* or *past experiences*, maybe performed on other survey processes. The existing documentation can assist the statistician in choosing some solutions and in discarding some others. However, the subject matter expert has to deal with new collected data, so, although the hints provided by the existing documentation, he needs information suitable to analyse alternative settings and to choose the one which provides the *best* E&I process in his production context.

It is good practice to supply each E&I process with E&I diagnostics in order to continuously monitor its execution and be able of identifying possible problems as soon as they appear. Diagnostics are helpful tools whatever the survey features and the E&I system used. These diagnostics represent performance indicators to be used for monitoring the reliability and suitability of the applied techniques. Performance criteria that can be used in this evaluation context, in which generally only raw and edited data are available, are, for example, data processing costs, timeliness, amount of creative editing and over-editing, respondent burden, preservation of micro and macro data, consistency and usefulness of edits, data coherence with other sources of information. Some of these criteria are common to many E&I sub-phases, like costs and timeliness, while other ones are more appropriate for specific data processing activities: for example, in automatic data processing, the preservation of both micro data and data distributions are relevant quality requirements, while respondent burden and preservation of aggregates mainly relates to selective editing and interactive editing (De Pol, 1997; Engstrom, 1995; Latouche *et al.*, 1995).

In recent years ISTAT researchers essentially worked in two main directions: improving the trade off between timeliness and data quality in automatic editing (in both households and business surveys) and reducing costs and time related to the manual/interactive editing (particularly in business surveys).

In the latter area, the problem of improving the identification of relevant units (in terms of their impact on estimates) has been faced through the approaches of *macro editing* (Barcaroli et al, 1995) and *selective editing* (Luzi *et al.*, 1999; Di Zio *et al.*, 2002b; Cirianni *et al.*, 2000). Encouraging results have been obtained in all the performed studies and applications. Further research is needed in this area.

In the field of automatic data processing, lot of experience has been gathered at ISTAT in the use of performance measures produced by generalised software dealing with random not influential errors.

As known, generalised software facilitates the standardisation of E&I processes through the use of approaches and methods specifically designed to deal with particular data problems. The use of this software gives guarantees about quality requirements since they implement theoretically consolidated algorithms. Furthermore, they allow saving resources and time by eliminating the need of developing ad hoc code.

A further advantage of using generalized systems relates to the possibility of verifying edit rules in terms of redundancy and consistency. Redundancy between edits does not affect the correctness of their definition but can affect the efficiency of the E&I process. On the contrary, inconsistency between edits can be originated by errors in the definition of some edits, and this generally affects the efficacy of the E&I process. An overall description of possible problems and drawbacks related to the incorrect use of edits is done in Granquist (1995). Here we refer to the use of validity checks and consistency edits used in automatic data E&I.

Another important advantage related to the use of generalised software is generally the standardisation of evaluation and documentation measures through the production of sets of indicators and reports useful for monitoring and calibrating the effects of the data processing actions performed on data. Examples of these reports are those produced by systems like SCIA (Riccini *et al.*, 1995) and GEIS (Kovar *et al.*, 1996), currently used at ISTAT for dealing with random errors in categorical and continuous variables respectively. Both software are based on the Fellegi and Holt approach (Fellegi *et al.*, 1976), hence they give some guarantees to the user about the quality of results in terms of minimum change of original data, final data plausibility with respect to the user-defined edits, preservation of original distributions under specific conditions. A new software, called DIESIS (Bruni *et al.*, 2001; Bruni *et al.*, 2002), has been developed for dealing with categorical and continuous data, implementing the *data driven* and the *minimum change* approaches.

Examples of operational tools usually provided by generalized software for supporting the monitoring E&I activities are:

1. the *number* of *passing* and *failing* records;
2. the *rates of edit failures*;
3. the *imputation frequency* and the *edits* mostly involved in the imputation process;
4. the *frequency distributions* before and after imputation and the *transition matrices* containing the frequencies of occurrence between values before and after imputation (for qualitative variables);

These tools support the subject-matter expert in the analysis of the automatic data processing through the observation of its effects on data: for example, a too high difference between the number of *failing* and *passing* records provides a first insight that something is going wrong in data or in the E&I process; the *failure rates of edits* can reveal errors in the definition of edits, they can also help in checking the nature of the errors in data (random or systematic) and in reducing possible over-editing of data; the analysis of the *transition matrices* is useful to evaluate some aspects of the performed corrections: if concentration of frequencies are noted in cells outside the main diagonal and the marginal distribution does not show the same pattern, this can be due to errors in the definition of edits and/or to the presence of residual systematic errors.

5. ANALYSING THE IMPACT OF E&I PROCESSES

In the area of E&I, National Statistical Offices and Eurostat are paying increasing attention to the problem of defining standard quality indicators and producing standard quality reports for process documentation. Many studies can be found in recent literature dealing with the problem of assessing and documenting the impact of E&I on survey data (among others, Madsen, 2000; Nordbotten 2000; Lindell, 1997; Whitridge *et al.*, 1999; Cirianni *et al.* 2000), and several indicators have been proposed for evaluating the E&I effects on raw data. In this context, the term *quality* relates more strictly to the transparency, reliability and suitability of an E&I procedure with respect to the planned objectives.

Regardless of the adopted procedure, the production of standard quality indicators for documenting the data processing activities performed at the E&I stage and assessing the E&I impact on collected data is always recommended. Generally, standard indicators are to be produced for satisfying both users and producers needs. In particular, they are selected in order to met some main purposes:

i. providing users with information about the characteristics of the E&I process, the quality of collected data and the data modifications due to the E&I process;
ii. providing subject-matter experts with information about the characteristics of errors in order to facilitate the identification of their possible sources;
iii. providing subject-matter experts with documentation on the E&I impact on data in each survey repetition in order to allow data and process monitoring over the time;
iv. providing National Statistical Offices with information about both data and process quality for each survey in order to allow comparisons among *similar* survey processes.

According to Granquist and Kovar (1997), all these objectives aim at "gathering intelligence related to significant difference in the data for analytical purposes" and "providing feedback that can lead to improvements in data collection and processing".

In particular, researchers and subject matter experts agree on the importance of editing activities as source of information on error sources: the analysis of error patterns and error characteristics generally give precious information about possible lacks and inefficiencies in some survey phases (including E&I) originating them. This information can be used to plan the appropriate modifications of the survey organisation in the next survey repetitions.

On the other hand, the analysis of the E&I impact in terms of time, costs, and modifications produced on the statistical properties of data, allows statisticians to verify the reliability and the usefulness of the adopted methodologies and to plan revised or new approaches for improving the performance of the E&I process.

Similarly, the analysis over time of appropriate quality indicators for a given survey can highlight structural modifications in the surveyed phenomena or occasional problems needing adjustments in future survey repetitions.

The comparison of standard measures among similar surveys is a powerful tool that survey managers and National Statistical Offices can use for identifying structural of methodological lacks in surveys or data processing strategies, thus stimulating their revision and improvement.

Objectives i.÷iv. are characterized by some common problems:
- identifying appropriate standard indicators;
- supporting data producers providing them with tools for computing such indicators in a standard way;
- convincing data producers about the need of the evaluation task and the advantages that can be obtained from the availability of standard quality indicators.

In recent years ISTAT researchers have been working mainly in the following directions:
1. providing survey managers with an information system especially dedicated to documenting and analysing the quality of the survey production process, including the E&I phase;

2. providing subject-matter experts with a generalised tool for analysing the impact of their own E&I processes on the statistical properties of collected data;
3. encouraging the production and the use of standard indicators and measures for documenting the E&I strategies and their impact on observed data, and monitoring the effects of E&I procedures over the time.

Concerning the first area, the centralised information system SIDI (Brancato *et. al.*, 1998) has been designed and developed at ISTAT to support the quality control activity through the monitoring of the survey production process, the documentation of data production activities and the dissemination of suitable information on data quality to the final users. The adopted approach focuses on the production process according to the concept that the quality of final data benefits of improvements in the process. To this purposes, SIDI manages not only quantitative information (quality indicators) but also qualitative information (metadata on the survey production process characteristics). Relating to the E&I phase, the standard quality indicators and the metadata on the E&I phase included at present in SIDI (Fortini *et al.*, 1999) are as much general as possible for allowing the comparative evaluations of surveys. All indicators are based on the comparison of *raw* and *clean* data and allow the survey managers to analyse the impact of the E&I activities on both units and variables.

Relating to point 2, in order to facilitate and standardise the production of evaluation indicators measuring the statistical effects on data of E&I, a generalized software implementing both the SIDI indicators and other statistical measures has been designed and implemented (Della Rocca *et al.*, 2003). The available indices correspond to quality criteria like impact on elementary data, impact on aggregates and distributions, impact on data relations, partly exploiting the results obtained in the context of the EUREDIT project.

Concerning the third area, as mentioned in section II detailed reports on the effect of automatic E&I procedures are directly provided by generalised software used at ISTAT. These reports can be used for documenting the impact of automatic E&I on observed data. They also provide some information on the type of errors affecting data. For these reasons, the production and use of similar descriptive measures and reports is recommended also in case of both automatic editing performed by using *ad hoc* software, and manual/interactive editing.

References

[1] Barcaroli G., Ceccarelli C., Luzi O. (1995). An edit and imputation system for quantitative variables based on macroediting techniques. *Proceedings of the International Conference on Survey Measurement and Process Quality*, Bristol (UK), 1-4 Aprile, pp.12-17.

[2] Barcaroli G. and D'Aurizio L. (1997). Evaluating Editing Procedures: the Simulation Approach. *UN/ECE Work Session on Statistical Data Editing*, Prague, October 1997.

[3] Biemer, P., Fecso, R.S. (1995). Evaluating and Controlling Measurement Error in Business. In *Business Survey Methods*, eds. B.G. Cox, D.A. Binder, B.N. Chinappa, A. Christianson, M.J. Colledge, and P.S. Kott, New York: Wiley, pp.267-275.

[4] Brancato G., D'Angiolini G., Signore M. (1998). Building up the quality profile of ISTAT surveys. *Proceedings of the conference Statistics for Economics and Social Development*, Aguascalientes (Mexico), September 1-4.

[5] Bruni R., Reale A., Torelli R. (2001). Optimisation Techniques for Edit Validation and Data Imputation. *Proceedings of the XVIIIth Statistics Canada International Symposium on Methodological Issues "Achieving Data Quality in a Statistical Agency: a Methodological Perspective*".

[6] Bruni R., Reale A., Torelli R. (2002). DIESIS: a New Software System for Editing and Imputation. *Proceedings of the Conference of the Italian Statistical Society*, Milano, 2002.

[7] Chambers R. (2000). *Evaluation Criteria for Statistical Editing and Imputation.* T001.05, EUREDIT report.

[8] Cirianni A., Di Zio M., Luzi O., Seeber A.C. (2000). The new integrated data editing procedure for the Italian Labour Cost survey: measuring the effects on data of combined techniques. *Proceedings of the International Conference on Establishment Surveys II*, Buffalo, June 17-21.

[9] Cirianni A., Di Zio M., Luzi O., Palmieri A., Seeber A.C. (2001). Comparing the effect of different adjustment methods for units with large amounts of item non-response: a case study. *Proceedings of the International Conference on Quality in Official Statistics* (First version), Stockholm, Sweden, May 14-15.

[10] Coppola L., Di Zio M., Luzi O., Ponti A., Scanu M. (2002). On the use of Bayesian Networks in Official Statistics. *Proceedings of the DataClean Conference*, Finland, May 2002.

[11] Della Rocca G., Di Zio M., Manzari A., Luzi O. (2000). E.S.S.E. Editing System Standard Evaluation. *Proceedings of the SEUGI 18*, Dublin, June 20-23.

[12] Della Rocca G., Di Zio M., Luzi O., Signore M., Scavalli E., Simeoni G. (2003). Documenting and monitoring Editing and Imputation Processes in the Italian Institute of Statistics, *UN/ECE Work Session on Statistical Data Editing*, Madrid, October 20-22.

[13] Di Zio M., Luzi O. (2002a). Comparing a purely deterministic and a semi-probabilistic approach for editing and imputation of Agricultural Census data. *Scritti di Statistica Economica*, Vol. 9, September 2002.

[14] Di Zio M., Luzi O., (2002b). Combining methodologies in a data editing procedure: an experiment on the survey of Balance Sheets of Agricultural Firms. *Italian Journal of Applied Statistics*, Vol. 14, No 1, pp. 59-80.

[15] De Pol F. (1997). Selective Editing in the Netherlands Annual Construction Survey. *Statistical Data Editing Methods and Techniques Vol. II*, Conference of European Statisticians, United Nations, 1997.

[16] Engstrom, P. (1995). A Study on Using Selective Editing in the Swedish Survey on Wages and Employment in Industry. *UN/ECE Work Session on Statistical Data Editing*, 1995.

[17] Fellegi I. P. and Holt D. (1976). A systematic approach to edit e imputation, *Journal of the American Statistical Association,* Vol.71, pp. 17-35.

[18] Fortini M., Scanu M. and Signore M. (1999). Measuring and Analysing the Data Editing Activity in ISTAT Information System for Survey Documentation. *UN/ECE Work Session on Statistical Data Editing*, Rome, June 2-4.

[19] Granquist, L. (1995). Improving the Traditional Editing Process. In *Business Survey Methods*, eds. B.G. Cox, D.A. Binder, B.N. Chinappa, A. Christianson, M.J. Colledge, and P.S. Kott, New York: Wiley, pp. 385-401.

[20] Granquist, L. (1997). An overview of Methods of Evaluating Data Editing Procedures. *Statistical Data Editing Methods and Techniques Vol. II,* Conference of European Statisticians, United Nations, 1997.

[21] Granquist L. and Kovar J. (1997). Editing of Survey Data: How Much is Enough? In *Survey Measurement and Process Quality,* eds. L. Lyberg, P. Biemer, M. Collins, E. de Leeuw, C. Dippo, N. Schwarz, and D. Trewin, New York: Wiley, pp. 415-435.

[22] Kovar J. and Winkler E.W. (1996). Editing Economic Data. *UN/ECE Work Session on Statistical Data Editing*, 1996.

[23] Latouche M., Bureau M., Croal J. (1995). Development of cost-effective edit and follow-up process: the Canadian survey of employment experience. *UN/ECE Work Session on Statistical Data Editing*, 1995.

[24] LEG (2001) *Proceedings of the International Conference on Quality in Official Statistics* (First version), Stockholm, Sweden, May 14-15.

[25] Lepp H. and Linacre S.J. (1993),. Improving the efficency and Effectiveness of Editing in a Statistical Agency, *Bulletin of the International Statistical Institute*, *Proceedingsof the 48th Session,* Florence, 11-112.

[26] Lindell K. (1997). Impact of Editing on the Salary Statistics for Employees in County Council. *Statistical Data Editing Methods and Techniques Vol. II*, Conference of European Statisticians, United Nations, 1997.

[27] Luzi O. and Della Rocca G. (1998). A Generalised Error Simulation System to Test the Performance of Editing Procedures, *Proceedings of the SEUGI 16*, Prague, June 9-12.

[28] Luzi O. and Pallara A. (1999). Combining Macroediting and Selective Editing to Detect Influential Observations in Cross-Sectional Survey Data. *UN/ECE Work Session on Statistical Data Editing*, Rome, June 2-4.

[29] Madsen B. and Solheim L. (2000). How to measure the effect of data editing. *UN/ECE Work Session on Statistical Data Editing*, Cardiff, October 18-20.

[30] Manzari A. (1999). A New Imputation Methodology: an Experimental Application to Italian Population Census Data. *Proceedings of the Conference of the Italian Statistical Society*, Udine, 1999 (in italian).

[31] Manzari A. and Reale A. (2001). Towards a new system for edit and imputation of the 2001 Italian Population Census data: A comparison with the Canadian Nearest-neighbour Imputation Methodology. *Proceedings Actes of the International Association of Survey Statisticians, Invited Papers, August 2001, Seoul, pp. 634-655.*

[32] Manzari A. (2004). Combining Editing and Imputation methods: an Experimental Application on Population Census Data. *Journal of the Royal Statistical Society Series A,* Vol. 167 (2), pp. 295-307.

[33] National Center for Education Statistics (1992). *NCES Statistical Standards.*

[34] Nordbotten S. (1997). *Metrics for the Quality of Editing, Imputation and Prediction.* Statistics Sweden Technical Report, SN, 3-Oct-97.

[35] Nordbotten S. (2000). *Evaluating Efficiency of Statistical Data Editing: A General Framework.* United Nations, 2000.

[36] Poulsen M.E. (1997). Evaluating Data Editing Process Using Survey Data and Register Data. *Statistical Data Editing Methods and Techniques Vol. 2,* Conference of European Statisticians, United Nations, 1997.

[37] Riccini E., Silvestri F., Barcaroli G., Ceccarelli C., Luzi O., Manzari A. (1995). *The Methodology of Editing and Imputation by Qualitative Variables Implemented in SCIA.* Technical Report. Italian National Institute of Statistics.

[38] Rubinstein, R. Y. (1981). *Simulation and the Monte Carlo method.* New York: Wiley.

[39] Stefanowicz, B. (1997). Selected issues of Data Editing. *Statistical Data Editing Methods and Techniques Vol. II*, Conference of European Statisticians, United Nations, 1997.

[40] Statistics Canada (1998). *Statistics Canada Quality Guidelines.*

[41] Thomas, J. (1997). Statistical measurement and monitoring of data editing and imputation in the 2001 United Kingdom Census of Population. *Statistical Data Editing Methods and Techniques Vol. II*, Conference of European Statisticians, United Nations, 1997.

[42] Whitridge P. and Benier J. (1999). The impact of Editing on Data Quality. *UN/ECE Work Session on Statistical Data Editing*, Rome, June 2-4.

Chapter 2

QUALITY MEASURES

Foreword – Paula Weir, U.S. Energy Information Administration

Chapter 2 contains four sections that focus on the actual measurement and communication of quality with respect to edit and imputation.

The first section proposes a variety of performance indicators categorized by purpose and data type. It suggests how to perform the measurement to evaluate effectively the quality of the E&I process and its relationship to overall survey quality. The papers in this section address not only bias due to the process, but also the effect on variance.

The second section explores the evaluation of methods and procedures from both the functional and empirical points of view, to determine the impact of the process on the final data and the estimates produced. One paper introduces plausibility indicators to determine the most effective edit process path. Another compares the performance of software packages and algorithms. The results from the Euredit project are also provided.

The third section addresses the precision of estimates by examining the impact of the E&I process on the variance from the theoretical and empirical points of view.

The fourth section concludes the chapter by examining what knowledge and metadata on E&I should be shared and disseminated to the data users and data producers to understand the attributes of the product (the statistics). It also examines how the sharing of information with internal users can help the continuous improvement of the E&I process.

Section 2.1

INDICATORS

Foreword – Carsten Kuchler, Statistisches Bundesamt, Germany

When considering indicators of data quality, two main questions arise - what to measure and how to measure it . What are the concepts of quality to be measured by the indicators, and how and to what extent can they be applied to a particular survey. The contributions in this section address both questions on the impact of data editing and imputation on overall data quality.

The first three contributions discuss the "what-to-measure" question. Di Zio et al. (2005) derive some basic indicators on comparisons between true, raw and processed data, and then discuss problems of measuring these indicators in a simulation approach. Thus, their focus is more on evaluating methods using synthetic data to provide a priori criteria for the selection of methods. Della Rocca et al. (2005) on the other hand, focus on characterizing a particular survey. They begin with a brief discussion of some fundamental criteria applied to the editing and imputation process, such as preserving individual data, marginal and joint distributions, aggregates, etc.. They prepare the ground for measures to be applied to a specific data set at the editing and imputation stage.

Unlike the first two papers that mainly address the bias due to editing and imputation, Rancourt (2002) deals with the impact of editing interventions in terms of variance measures. Editing needs to be considered as a statistical process that causes missing data. Under this assumption, Rancourt adopts well-established approaches for estimating the variance due to imputation to derive a general measure for estimating the increase of variance due to editing.

Beyond these abstract quality indicators, the contributions point to the crucial role of software tools in deciding what to measure and how to measure it. To do this, software tools must focus on two problems: (a) how to evaluate editing and imputation methods using these indicators in controlled circumstances, and (b) how to integrate this evaluation into a survey process.

Rancourt and Di Zio et al. address the first question by presenting simulation environments that can be used to test editing and imputation methods on a given data set. This allows for the selection of the most suitable method. In addition, they discuss the generation of synthetic data that bring the conditions of data production under the methodologists' control. Such synthetic data sets are required for the comparison of the true and processed data as proposed by Di Zio et al. for estimating the bias component due to specific editing and imputation procedures.

Della Rocca et al. address the second problem concerning the costly evaluation of indicators. They present the IDEA system that generates the proposed indicators at the same time as performing the edit and imputation steps. Instead of reducing costs by generating indicators automatically in the application flow, Smith and Weir (2000) argue that the number of indicators to be evaluated may be reduced to the most meaningful ones. These indicators are identified by means of Principal Component Analysis for a reference survey. Indicators of low explanatory value can be left out in subsequent surveys. Smith and Weir show the effect of this approach in two examples. After having derived a variety of data quality indicators for the past years, this new approach provides a reasonable criterion in assessing indicators for a particular survey.

EVALUATING THE QUALITY OF EDITING AND IMPUTATION: THE SIMULATION APPROACH

By Marco Di Zio, Ugo Guarnera, Orietta Luzi, and Antonia Manzari, Italian National Statistical Institute (ISTAT)

1. INTRODUCTION

In statistical surveys, non-sampling errors correspond to deviations of the collected data of the surveyed variables from the corresponding actual (*true*) values. These errors may derive from different sources, like response, measurement, data processing. It is well known that non-sampling errors may account for the greater proportion of the total error. For this reason, non-sampling errors are to be detected and eliminated from data. *Editing and imputation* (E&I) generally indicate the set of activities done at the post-data capturing stage for the identification and treatment of errors.

In order to evaluate the quality of an E&I process we need to define which component we are interested in and the indicators to quantify it. In this paper we focus on the capability of an E&I process to correctly detect errors and eliminate them by restoring the corresponding true values without introducing new errors in data (*accuracy*).

The evaluation of the accuracy of an E&I method can be performed only when, for a given set of raw data, the corresponding *true* values are known. In this situation the accuracy of E&I can be assessed by comparing the *final* (edited and imputed) data with the corresponding *true* ones.

The first problem is how to obtain true and raw data. One of the possible approaches consists in artificially generating them. In this paper we discuss some aspects relating to the use of the simulation approach for obtaining artificial data to be used for evaluation purposes.

The second main problem is identifying appropriate statistical measures, based on the comparison of final data with the corresponding true ones, for the assessment of the E&I capability to deal with the specific types of non-sampling errors contaminating data. Different measures can be defined depending on the evaluation aim: indicators measuring the capability of E&I of correctly identifying and correcting errors (*micro* level indicators), and other measures for assessing the statistical impact of E&I on target estimates (*macro* level indicators). In this paper a set of micro level indicators are proposed and discussed.

A software for evaluating E&I procedures based on the simulation approach has been developed at ISTAT. This software, called ESSE, allows simulating sets of raw data by the controlled contamination of given sets of true values based on predefined error models/mechanisms. Micro level indicators are directly provided based on the adopted simulation strategy and the E&I results.

The paper is structured as follows. The experimental framework based on the use of simulation, as well as its statistical implications are illustrated in section 2. The artificial generation of synthetic data is discussed in section 3. Some aspects relating to obtaining *true* and/or *raw* data are discussed respectively in sections 4 and 5. A set of quality indicators measuring the E&I accuracy at micro level are discussed in section 6. In section 7 the error models available in the software ESSE for obtaining artificial raw data are illustrated.

2. EVALUATING EDITING AND IMPUTATION METHODS: THE SIMULATION APPROACH

In specialized literature, E&I is viewed not only as the set of methods, activities, and tools aiming at identifying and eliminating errors from a set of statistical survey data, but also as a possible source of non-sampling errors that may cause an estimate not to be in perfect agreement with the parameter it is supposed to estimate (Rancourt, 2002), and, if it contains stochastic elements, as an additional source of data variability. Therefore, the problem of measuring the *quality* of E&I is twofold: 1) assessing its capability of correctly dealing with non-sampling errors affecting data, i.e. its accuracy, and 2) measuring its impact on target estimates.

When dealing with the problem of designing and implementing an optimal E&I procedure, the natural question to be answered is how is it possible to evaluate the quality of E&I. Let $X_1, \ldots, X_p$ be the p variables of interest, i.e. the set of phenomena to be investigated by a specific survey process. The quality of an E&I method can be evaluated when it is possible to compare the final data with the corresponding true ones, i.e. when the following three sets of data are available:

1) the *true* data, i.e. the n x p matrix X of the actual values of the p variables on the n units;
2) the *raw* data, i.e. the n x p matrix Y corresponding to contaminated data;
3) the *edited* data, i.e. the n x p matrix X' of final (edited and imputed) values resulting from the application to Y of the E&I method under evaluation.

In this framework, given the target phenomenon, under predefined assumptions on the error typologies possibly contaminating them, designing an evaluation study for a specific E&I method implies the definition of the following main elements:

1) how to obtain true data;
2) how to obtain raw data;
3) how to measure the E&I accuracy.

Concerning the first two aspects, different approaches have been proposed in literature. The choice among them mainly depends on the available resources and evaluation objectives (Granquist, 1997; Norbotten, 2000).

For true data, a number of alternative solutions can be adopted. As errors arise mainly at the data collection and data entry phases, one possible way to obtain more accurate data could be to repeat these activities under better conditions (e.g. using professional interviewers, computer assisted interviewing, reconciliation of current answers with previous ones, etc.) (Lesseler *et al.*, 1995). The main disadvantage of this approach is that it is rather expensive in terms of both resources spent and respondent's burden. Furthermore, in spite of whatever action is taken, a given amount of errors will continue contaminating data. For these reasons this approach can seldom be adopted.

A set of *true* data might be obtained by linking information coming from appropriate alternative sources of information (statistical or administrative) (Poulsen, 1997). The problem here is the difficulty of obtaining data from the same sampling units, on the same phenomena of interest and for the same period of time.

An alternative solution is to define as *true* an artificially generated set of data. In this case, the quality of the performed analyses strongly depends on the models chosen to generate data, in particular on how well these models represent data.

Concerning raw data, these can correspond to either observed survey data, or to artificially generated data. In the latter case, starting from a set of true data, pre-defined rates of pre-specified types of errors are introduced based on specific error mechanisms (Barcaroli et al., 1997).

For both true and raw data, when using the simulation approach the goal is investigating the phenomenon of interest having a certain control on the mechanism ruling some key aspects of the phenomenon itself. It means that we simulate the situation we want to investigate, and use the obtained results for assessing the quality of either a single technique or an overall E&I procedure in the specific simulated situation. The main advantages of the simulation approach with respect to other ones are low costs and the possibility of controlling some critical aspects of the applications. Drawbacks concern mainly the effort required for modelling the data and/or errors. The simulation approach is also useful for the comparative evaluation of different E&I methods or procedures. This is the case of the research activities carried out in the context of the EUREDIT project (http://www.cs.york.uk/euredit/) where, starting from predefined sets of data assumed as true, raw data sets have been artificially generated in order to perform comparative evaluations of different E&I techniques.

Concerning the problem of how to measure the E&I accuracy, the comparison of the final data with the corresponding true ones allows computing indicators that summarize the performance of the E&I process at the *micro* or reported level, as well as the *macro* or aggregate level (Garcia *et al.*, 1994; Stefanowicz, 1997; Chambers, 2001). In the first case the measures are based on the changes occurring in the individual data items while in the second case the focus is on the changes occurring in the estimates and/or distributions. Both types of measures can be computed and a hierarchy (in terms of relevance) generally depends on the level at which the data are released.

In order to understand better the evaluation problem in a simulation context, as well as its statistical implications, it is useful to graphically represent the overall data and process flow characterizing the simulation-based evaluation framework. In Figure 1 (Di Zio et al., 2002) all the stochastic elements influencing the final results are depicted.

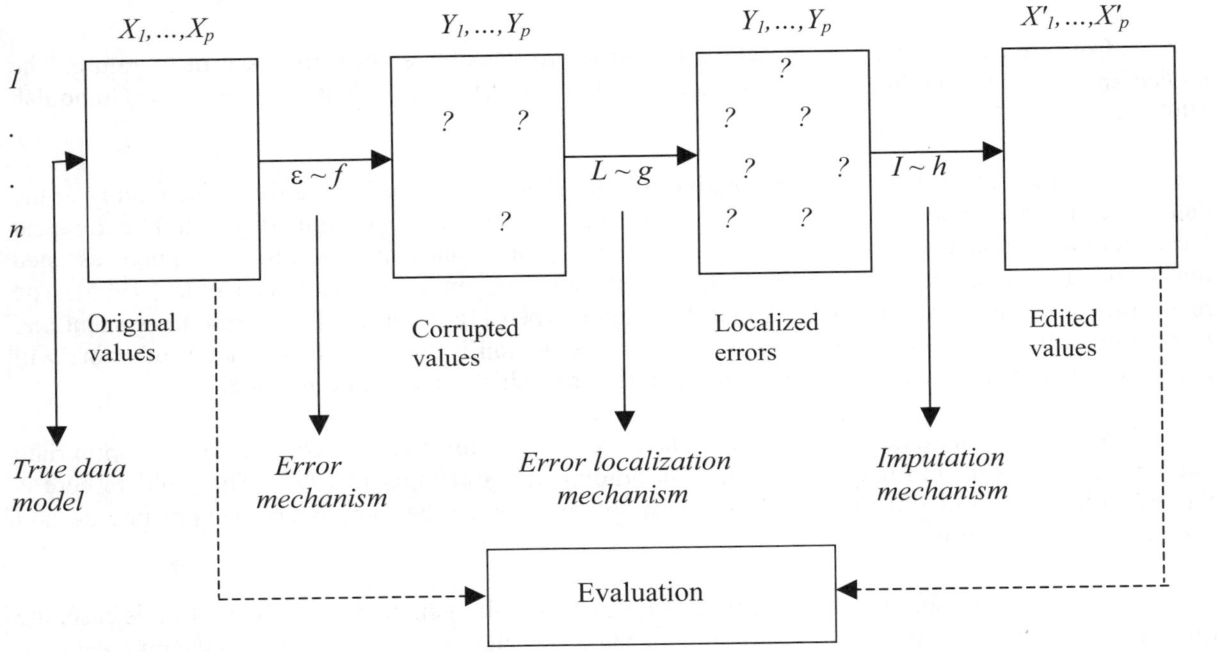

Figure 1: Evaluating editing and imputation processes in a simulation context

Suppose for the sake of simplicity that the initial data are fixed. In our simulation context, the X' values can be thought of as a realization of a random vector from a multivariate probability distribution depending on different random mechanisms: the corruption of the original values with probability law f (*error and missing data mechanism*), the error localization method (with probability law g when it is not deterministic) and the imputation method (with probability law h when it is not deterministic).

To statistically evaluate the quality of the E&I process we generally compare two quantities $Q(X)$ and $Q(X')$, where $Q(\cdot)$ is a generic function of the data (possibly vector valued), through a suitable generic loss function $d(Q(X),Q(X'))$ taking into account all the different stochastic mechanisms affecting the results. One natural way of doing that is to compute the expected value:

$$E_{\varepsilon, L, I}[\, d(Q(X), Q(X'))] \qquad [1]$$

where (ε, L, I) represents the random mechanisms as in Figure 1. For instance, for X univariate, if we define $Q(X)=X$ and, for each pair of n-dimensional vectors $\mathbf{u},\mathbf{v}$, $d(\mathbf{u},\mathbf{v})= \sum_{i=1}^{n}\delta(u_i, v_i)$, where $\delta(s,t) = \begin{cases} 1 & if\ s \neq t \\ 0 & otherwise \end{cases}$, we obtain the basic elements of the class of micro indicators described in section 6. An analytical computation of the expected value [1] is generally not feasible because of the difficulty of modelling the joint distribution of the random variables X'. On the other hand, we are often able to draw observations from the joint distribution of the random variable $X'(\varepsilon,L,I)$. In this context we can use a Monte Carlo integration method to approximate the expected value [1] (Rubinstein, 1981).

Given the hierarchical process represented in Figure 1, if we are interested in assessing the impact on final results of each single stochastic mechanism, we can decompose the expected value [1] in parts corresponding each to the effect induced by each mechanism present in the process. Most of the methods proposed in literature deal with the problem of estimating the components due to missing data and to imputation (see for example Lee *et al.*, 2002; Rubin, 1987). Concerning editing, Rancourt (2002) and Ghosh-Dastidar *et al.* (2003) discuss the problem of evaluating the component due to error localization.

One way of estimating the effects of each random mechanism affecting final results (including E&I) is based on the use of a Monte Carlo approach, consisting in iterating the editing and/or the imputation methods under evaluation conditionally to the other stochastic mechanisms that hierarchically precede them. For example, if we aim at measuring the components due to a specific missing mechanisms and to a given imputation model, we have to iterate k times the contamination process under the assumed missing model (thus generating k *raw* data sets) and, conditionally to each contaminated data set, we have to apply j times the imputation method under evaluation. Analyzing the resulting distributions of the predefined quality indicators, the different contributions (e.g. in terms of bias and variance) of the various mechanisms taken into account in the experimental study can be measured.

3. SIMULATION OF SYNTHETIC DATA

In this section we discuss issues related to data simulation. Let $(X_1, \ldots, X_p)$ be a random variable following the probability function $F(x_1, \ldots, x_p ; \theta)$.
If we know $F(x_1, \ldots, x_p ; \theta)$, by simply generating random sample from it, it is possible to use Monte Carlo techniques as discussed in section 2 (Devroye, 1986).
Of course, more real and interesting is the case when $F(x_1, \ldots, x_p ;\theta)$ is unknown. In this case we can replace $F(x_1, \ldots, x_p ;\theta)$ with its estimate $\hat{F}(x_1, \ldots, x_p ;\theta)$ (having a random sample $\mathbf{x}^{(1)},\ldots, \mathbf{x}^{(n)}$, where $\mathbf{x}^{(i)}=(x^{(i)}_1, \ldots, x^{(i)}_p)$, available) and draw samples using this estimated p.d.f.. Different techniques can be used to estimate F, and we mainly divide them in parametric and non-parametric.

In the parametric approach, obviously it is necessary to first specify a parametric form for the distribution $F(x_1, \ldots, x_p ;\theta)$, e.g. the Gaussian distribution. Then the parameters θ can be estimated, for instance using the maximum likelihood estimators, thus obtaining $\hat{F}(x_1,\ldots, x_p;\hat{\theta})$. Finally B random samples from $\hat{F}(x_1, \ldots, x_p ;\hat{\theta})$ can be drawn in order to compute the quantity of interest.

In the non-parametric approach, we can obtain a random sample from the empirical distribution $\hat{F}_n(x_1, \ldots, x_p ; \theta)$ by drawing B random samples with replacement $\mathbf{x}^{(1)},\ldots, \mathbf{x}^{(B)}$ from the initial sample $\mathbf{x}^{(1)},\ldots, \mathbf{x}^{(n)}$.

The connection of the above data generation methods with the re-sampling method techniques is evident. In particular they are related to the bootstrap techniques, where theory is established to compute estimates and variance of estimates of target quantities (Efron *et al.*, 1993; Efron, 1994).

Following the scheme in Figure 1, $F(x_1, \ldots, x_p ; \theta)$ is the result of different random mechanisms that interact in a very complex way. It results that building step-by-step $F(x_1, \ldots, x_p ; \theta)$ is in turn a very complex task. The re-sampling methods allow starting from the end of the process (the sample observed from $F(x_1, \ldots, x_p ; \theta)$. For instance if we want to evaluate a method by varying the processes of generating data and non-responses, instead of specifying the two random mechanisms and the interaction between them, we can resample the initial sample (comprehensive of missingness) in order to reproduce the "real" mechanisms generating them.

4. OBTAINING TRUE DATA

Following the previous section, the data generation can be made either through a non-parametric or a parametric approach. While the non-parametric data generation is clear, more words are needed in the case of parametric generation, especially when data has to mime "true" data. Apart from the classical Gaussian and multinomial distributions, we want to focus on the situation when data distribution is asymmetric. This happens in most of the surveys dealing with continuous variables, for instance incomes, expenditures. A first way of handling this issue is through the use of the log-normal distribution. The log-normal distribution refers to data that after the logarithmic transformation can be considered normal. From a practical point of view simulating this type of data consists in generating data from the normal distribution and transforming them through the exponential function. In multivariate context exponential transformations are generally component-wise and it is difficult to obtain data having the desired distributional characteristics in terms of joint relations between variables. However other asymmetric multivariate distributions have been introduced (see Johnson *et al.*, 1972), and it is worth mentioning them. For their tractability, a special mention is due to hyperbolic distribution Barndorff-Nielsen *et al.* (1983) and the multivariate skew-normal and skew-t distribution (Azzalini *et al.*, 1999; Azzalini *et al.*, 2003). In a practical context we remark that for the hyperbolic distribution, for skew-normal and for skew-t distributions specialized libraries have been implemented in the open source code R (http://cran.r-project.org/). In particular, packages are available for parameters estimates of these distributions. This is particularly useful when, in a simulation context, the parameters of the distributions to be generated have to be estimated from some set of available data and the log-normality cannot be assumed.

5. OBTAINING RAW DATA

One of the most critical issues in evaluating E&I procedures based on the simulation approach, is generating raw data. Since, as already noticed, a "best" E&I method in all practical situations does not exist, in the experimental context we have the problem of setting up "typical" situations in order to evaluate different methods for specific error typologies. To this aim we need modelling error as well as non-response, or, in other words, we have to model the distribution of the raw data conditional on the true ones.

As far as non-response is concerned, a first issue to deal with is the nature of the mechanism that generates missing data. In fact it is well known that most of the imputation procedures assume, more or less explicitly, at least MAR mechanism for non-response (Little *et al.*, 2003). One of the most common ways for simulating a MAR mechanism on a data-set with n observations and p variables consists of drawing from a suitably specified probability distribution $P(\boldsymbol{R}|\,\boldsymbol{Z};\vartheta)$ where $\boldsymbol{R}$ is a random matrix whose entries represent the response indicators (i.e. $R_{ij}=1$ if the j-th variable on the i-th observation is observed and 0 otherwise), $\boldsymbol{Z}$ is a set of covariates without missing values and ϑ is a set of parameters. Simulating a non-MAR mechanism could be also useful in order to check the robustness of E&I strategy with respect to departure from the ignorability assumption. Furthermore, in some special cases (Tang *et al.*, 2003), consistent data analyses can be performed even in the presence of a non-ignorable non-response mechanism.

Artificial perturbation of data through introduction of errors is an even more difficult task. In fact, unlike missing values, measurement errors are characterized not only by their occurrence pattern (i.e. the set of items in error), but also by their "intensity", that is the extent (generally expressed in terms of ratio or difference) to which erroneous data deviate from true ones. Hence, modelling measurement errors generally requires more care than modelling non-response. One approach, that could be defined non-parametric (Barcaroli *et al.,* 1997), consists of introducing errors according to some known mechanism such as *unity measure errors* in the compilation phase or *digits permutation* at the data entry stage. Specialized software have been used in ISTAT to simulate easily some of the most common non-sampling errors in the different survey phases (Luzi *et al.,* 1998; Manzari *et al.,* 2000; Della Rocca *et al.*, 2000). This approach has the advantage of being independent of explicit parametric model assumptions for the error mechanism. Another commonly adopted approach consists of drawing samples from a probability distribution $P(Y|X;\ \xi)$ of the corrupted values conditional on the true ones (ξ denotes a set of parameters). In this context error typology reflects on the distributional characteristics of $P(\cdot)$. For instance, in case of quantitative data, "random errors" are represented by probability distributions $P(Y|X;\ \xi)$ such that $E(Y|X;\ \xi) = 0$, and *independent errors* are associated with distributions that can be factorized into as many univariate distributions as the number of involved variables. In many cases (Hansen, 1953) measurement errors are modelled through an additive mechanism $Y_i=X_i+\varepsilon_i$ where typically it is assumed that the errors have zero mean and are independent of each other. Often independence between ε_i and X_i is also assumed. This mechanism can be easily simulated by generating errors from a normal distribution with zero mean and diagonal variance-covariance matrix. Straightforward extensions are obtained by considering non-diagonal variance-covariance matrices and non-zero mean vectors.

Another important issue in modelling and simulating non-sampling errors is the assumption of the "intermittent" nature of errors. In the additive model, this means that the ε_i's are generated by semi-continuous distributions or, in other words, the distribution of the corrupted data is a mixture whose components are associated with the different error patterns. In this context, the objective of an editing procedure can be viewed as that of assigning each observation to one pattern, that is, to "localize" items in error. In many editing procedures, localization of items in error is performed with the aid of a set of logical or arithmetical rules (*edits*). For each record failing one or more edits, the procedure tries to identify the items responsible for edit violation. Typically this is accomplished with the aid of some further ad hoc assumptions such as the *minimum change principle* (MCP) according to which the minimum number of items has to be changed in order the record pass all the edits. Based on the MCP, a lot of methods and software have been developed and are being widely used in the context of Official Statistics (Fellegi *et al.*, 1976; Kovar *et al.*, 1988). They all assume that errors in data are comparatively rare, so that better accuracy is obtained by changing data as little as possible. Thus, the MCP implies particular assumptions on the error mechanism. For instance, in presence of three numerical variables (X_1, X_2, X_3) related by the equality $X_1+X_2 = X_3$, the MCP implies that not more than one variable can be affected by error. Note that in this model errors are not independent of each other. In the simulative approach to the evaluation of an editing procedure, it is interesting to assess the performance of the procedure when the MCP is met by the error mechanism (that is when errors in data are rare) and, on the other hand, to test the robustness of the method in different situations where the assumptions underlying the MCP are no longer valid. In the just mentioned example, the two experimental situations can be simulated as follows:

a) *no more than one error per record*

a1) for each record i an error indicator z_i is drawn from a bernoullian distribution $P(z_i)$ with parameter π $[P(z_i)= \pi^{z_i}(1- \pi)^{1-z_i}]$. If $z_i = 1$, then the observation i is to be perturbed, otherwise it is left unchanged;

a2) for each unit to be perturbed, a value j^* is selected from the set of indices $\{1,2,3\}$ according to the probabilities $\{p_1, p_2, p_3\}$ previously defined;

a3) the variable X_{j^*} is perturbed by adding to the true value a random error ε_j drawn, for example, from a normal density $N(0, \sigma_j^2)$;

b) *independent errors*

for every unit i an error ε_{ij} is added to each variable X_j (j=1,..,3) with semi-continuous distribution, i.e. ε_{ij} is zero with probability $(1- \pi_j)$ and $N(0, \sigma_j^2)$ with probability π_j.

In the above example, the probability for a variable of being in error as well as the "error intensity" are independent of the variables to be analysed. In analogy to non-response, we could refer to such a situation as a *Error Completely at Random* (ECAR): in other words, when the error mechanism is ECAR, the subset of units in error are a simple random sample of the whole set of data and the error distribution is independent of the true values. However, as for non-response, it is plausible that units with different characteristics have different probabilities of being in error and that the error magnitude depends on the value of some attribute. For instance, in business surveys, small enterprises are more likely to provide data with lower precision, and in social surveys the income variables tend to have negative bias in units with larger income. In these cases errors are not completely at random, and analogously to the non-response case, we could attempt to introduce the concept of *Error at Random* (EAR) mechanism for referring to situation of independence between errors and true values conditional on some set of not corrupted variables correlated with the contaminated variables.

Simulating simple EAR mechanisms is easy. For instance, considering case a) of the previous example, one could generate the z_i's through a logistic or probit model using a set of k reliable covariates $\mathbf{v} = (v_1,..,v_k)$ and, conditional on $z_i =1$, draw errors from a Gaussian density $N(\mu_{\mathbf{v}}, \sigma_{\mathbf{v}}^2)$ with parameters $(\mu_{\mathbf{v}}, \sigma_{\mathbf{v}})$ depending on the covariates $\mathbf{v}$.

A last concern is the extent to which perturbed data are coherent with respect to a prefixed set of logical or arithmetical rules that, plausibly, will be used as edits in most editing strategies. Calibrating the parameters of the error model allows setting the relative frequency of errors determining "out of domain" units with respect to errors that do not affect the eligibility of data.

6. QUALITY INDICATORS

In this section we focus on the evaluation of the accuracy of E&I using some micro indicators based on the *number* of detected, undetected, introduced and corrected errors (Stefanowicz, 1997; Manzari *et al.*, 2000). In particular, the ability of the editing process in detecting the maximum number of errors without introducing new ones (editing as *error detection*) and the ability of the imputation process in restoring the individual true values are evaluated using some "*hit rate*" measures: the higher the proportion of corrected errors on the total, and the less the quantity of new errors introduced, the more accurate is the E&I process. As shown in the following, this approach allows evaluating the accuracy of the editing and the imputation processes separately considered, as well as of the E&I process as a whole.

Other sets of indicators based on the *differences* between values, distributions or aggregates have been proposed (Granquist, 1997; Chambers, 2000), and could be used to evaluate the accuracy of E&I. In this case, different types of *distance* measures are used to evaluate the ability of the editing process in reducing the total amount of error (editing as *error reduction*) and the ability of the imputation process in preserving individual values, distributions or aggregates.

In the following, accuracy indicators are first provided for the editing process and the imputation process separately, and then for the E&I process as a whole. Each indicator ranges from 0 (no accuracy) to 1 (maximum accuracy). This type of indicators has been used in studies aiming at comparing the performance of different E&I methods (Manzari *et al.* 2002; EUREDIT project http://www.cs.york.uk/euredit/).

A. Quality of Editing

Our basic choice is to consider an editing procedure like an instrument to classify each raw value into one of two states: (1) unacceptable and (2) acceptable. We put in the unacceptable class the missing values, the invalid values and the valid values considered suspicious by the editing methods. The unacceptable values will be imputed, while the acceptable values will not be imputed. Because the information about the actual erroneous/true status of the values is available, we can verify the correctness of every single choice of the editing process. We consider the editing process accurate if it classifies an erroneous value as unacceptable and a true value as acceptable. These concepts suggest evaluating the accuracy of an editing process by scoring its ability in obtain a correct classification separately for the erroneous and the true data and for the whole set of data. In other words, for each class of values, erroneous and true, and for the whole set of values, we consider the probability that the editing process correctly classifies it.

Let us consider whichever raw value of a generic variable. We regard the editing decision as the result of a screening procedure designed to detect deviations of the raw values from the original values. Accordingly to the basic concepts of diagnostic tests (Armitage *et al.*, 1971), we can define:

α : the probability of the Type-I error, that is the probability of incorrectly classifying true values as unacceptable;

β : the probability of the Type-II error, that is the probability of incorrectly classifying erroneous values as acceptable.

The analogy of editing decisions with diagnostic tests allows us to resort to familiar concepts: the probability to recognize true values as acceptable is analogous to the specificity (1-α), while the probability to recognize erroneous values as unacceptable is analogous to the sensitivity (1-β). The extent of (1-α) and (1-β) indicate the ability of the editing process in correctly classifying true and erroneous values and can be used as measures of the accuracy.

We can estimate these probabilities by applying the editing process to a set of known erroneous and true data. Each raw value can be cross-classified into one of four distinct classes: (a) erroneous and unacceptable, (b) erroneous and acceptable, (c) true and unacceptable, and (d) true and acceptable. Suppose that, for a generic variable, the application gives the following frequencies:

		Editing classification	
		unacceptable	*acceptable*
Actual status	*erroneous*	*a*	*b*
	true	*c*	*d*

Where:
a = number of erroneous data classified by the editing process as unacceptable,
b = number of erroneous data classified by the editing process as acceptable,
c = number of true data classified by the editing process as unacceptable,
d = number of true data classified by the editing process as acceptable.

Cases placed on the secondary diagonal represent the failures of the editing process, therefore, the ratio $c/(c+d)$ measures the failure of the editing process for true data and estimates α while the ratio $b/(a+b)$ measures the failure of the editing process for erroneous data and estimates β.
The specificity ($1-\alpha$) is estimated by the proportion of true data classified as acceptable:

$$\text{E\_tru} = d/(c+d)$$

Large values (close to 1) of the E_tru index indicate high ability of the editing process in preserving the true values. On the contrary, small values (close to 0) indicate that a large proportion of true values have been classified as unacceptable, in other words, the editing process introduces new errors in data.

The sensitivity ($1-\beta$) is estimated by the proportion of erroneous data classified as unacceptable:

$$\text{E\_err} = a/(a+b)$$

Large values of the E_err index indicate that the editing process is able to detect a large proportion of errors in data. On the contrary, small values indicate that only few errors have been detected by the editing process.

Note that the performance of the editing process, and therefore the values of the accuracy indices, is determined by a number of factors. For instance, in case of error localization algorithms making use of edits, a too restrictive set of edits can cause the incorrect classification of some uncommon true values, giving rise to small value of the E_tru index. Otherwise, a too loose set of edits can cause a poor ability in localizing errors, determining small values of the E_err index. What's more, even in case of well defined edits, the editing process could not detect an erroneous value in a given variable when, having defined some inconsistencies between the erroneous value and the subsets of domains of other variables, the error localization algorithm fails considering true values of other variables as suspicious. In this case there would be a double failure: with respect to the erroneous value of the current variable and with respect to the true values of other variables linked to the current one by the edits. If the failure of the error localization algorithm were systematic, we would observe a low value of the E_err index for the current variable together with low values of E_tru for at least one linked variable.

With regard to the total set of data (true and erroneous), the accuracy of the editing process (for any single variable) can be measured by the fraction of total cases that are correctly classified:

$$\text{E\_tot} = (a+d)/(a+b+c+d).$$

The reader can easily verify that the E_tot index is a linear combination of E_tru and E_err, whose weights are the fraction of the total cases that are true and the fraction of total cases that are erroneous:

$$\text{E\_tot} = \text{E\_tru}\frac{(c+d)}{(a+b+c+d)} + \text{E\_err}\frac{(a+b)}{(a+b+c+d)}.$$

Therefore, the E_tot value is strongly affected by the error proportion in data.

B. Quality of Imputation

We assume that the imputation process imputes only values previously classified by the editing process as unacceptable (missing values, invalid values and valid values considered suspicious). The new assigned value can be equal to the original one or different. In the first case the imputation process can be deemed as successful, in the latter case we say that the imputation process fails.

In the real case it is generally not necessary that the imputed value of a quantitative variable precisely equals the original value to consider the imputation as successful: it could be sufficient that the new value lies in an interval whose centre is the original value. Otherwise, in the case of qualitative variables, we consider the imputation as successful only when the imputed value equals the original one. This means that, in the case of qualitative variables, whenever the editing process classifies as unacceptable a true value we says that the imputation process fails.

We refer to the general case of both qualitative and numeric variables. The previous figures *a* and *c* can be decomposed in

$$a = as + af \qquad \text{and} \qquad c = cs + cf$$

giving rise to the following frequencies:

		Editing & Imputation classification		
		unacceptable		*acceptable*
		imputed with success	*imputed without success*	*not imputed*
Actual status	*erroneous*	a_s	a_f	b
	true	c_s	c_f	d

Where *b* and *d* are previously defined while:
a_s = number of erroneous data classified by the editing process as unacceptable and successfully imputed,
a_f= number of erroneous data classified by the editing process as unacceptable and imputed without success,
c_s= number of true data classified by the editing process as unacceptable and successfully imputed,
c_f= number of true data classified by the editing process as unacceptable and imputed without success.

The quality of the imputation process can be evaluated by the fraction of imputed data for which the imputation process is successful. For imputed erroneous values we can compute:

$$\text{I\_err} = a_s / a.$$

Large values (close to 1) of the I_err index indicate high ability of the imputation process in restoring the original values.
For imputed true values we can compute:

$$\text{I\_true} = c_s / c.$$

The fraction of imputed true values for which the imputation is successful (I_true index), is not able to evaluate the inner quality of the imputation process because the imputation consists in changing the raw values and the I_true index only measures an artificial result due to the definition of successful imputation for numeric variables (it always equals to zero for qualitative variables). In the overall E&I evaluation, we consider the I_true index as measure of the (artificial) counterbalance of the imputation process to the failure of the editing process for numeric true data.

In analogy to the editing process, the performance of the imputation process is also determined by a number of factors. For instance, if the imputation method takes into account edits and a close set of edits is defined, imposing constraints on the admissible value to impute can help in determining the original value giving rise to a large value of the I_err index (and also of the I_tru index). The same consideration holds when the range of admissible values to impute is strongly restricted by the characteristics of the domain of the variables to impute. This is true also with a loose set of edits (small value of the E_err index), because I_err measures only the imputation accuracy for the subset of erroneous values correctly classified by the editing process as unacceptable. As marginal case, when an erroneous value is recognised in a variable having only two admissible values (e.g the *sex* variable), the imputation of the true value is forced giving rise to the maximum value (1) of the I_err index.

For the total set of imputed values (erroneous and true) we can compute:

$$\text{I\_tot}=(a_s+c_s)/(a+c)$$

Note that if the imputed values ($a+c$) were only missing or invalid values, the I_tot would be suited to estimate the inner quality of the imputation process. Otherwise, as in real situation, when the imputed values ($a+c$) consist of missing values, invalid values and valid values considered suspicious by the editing process, the I_tot index under-estimates the inner quality of the imputation process because it also pays for the failure of the editing process.

C. Quality of Editing and Imputation

We can now consider the E&I process as a whole. The accuracy of the E&I process with regard to true data can be measured by estimating the probability of not introducing new errors in data. It is the total probability of two mutually exclusive events: to classify a true value as acceptable OR to impute a value close to the original one in case of incorrect editing classification of the true value. It can be estimated by:

$$\text{E\&I\_tru} = \text{E\_tru} + [(1 - \text{E\_tru})\ (\text{I\_tru})] = (c_s+d)\ /\ (c+d).$$

The accuracy of the E&I process for erroneous data can be measured by estimating the probability to correct erroneous data. It is the joint probability of a combination of two dependent events: to classify an erroneous value as unacceptable AND to restore the original value (to impute the erroneous value with success since it has been correctly classified). It can be estimated by:

$$\text{E\&I\_err} = (\text{E\_err})\ (\text{I\_err}) = a_s\ /\ (a+b).$$

For the total set of data (erroneous and true values) the accuracy of the E&I process can be measured by the fraction of total cases whose original value is correctly restored:

$$\text{E\&I\_tot} = (a_s+c_s+d)\ /\ (a+b+c+d).$$

Even in this case, it is easy to verify that the E&I_tot value is affected by the error proportion in data:

$$\text{E \& I\_tot} = (\text{E \& I\_tru})\frac{(c+d)}{(a+b+c+d)} + (\text{E \& I\_err})\frac{(a+b)}{(a+b+c+d)}.$$

7. A TOOL FOR EVALUATING EDITING AND IMPUTATION IN A SIMULATION CONTEXT: THE ESSE SOFTWARE

ESSE is an experimental software developed at ISTAT to evaluate the quality of E&I procedures in a simulation context (Luzi *et al.,* 1988; Manzari *et al.*, 2000; Della Rocca *et al.,* 2000). The software consists of two main modules: an *error simulation module* for the artificial contamination of a set of true data by a controlled generation of errors under simple error mechanisms; an *evaluation module* providing indicators measuring the accuracy of E&I processes in terms of their capability to detect as many errors as possible, to restore the true values, to avoid the introduction of new errors in data. The set of quality indicators available in ESSE have been described in section 6.

Concerning the simulation module, let X be the $n{\times}p$ data matrix containing the values of p variables observed (or simulated) on n units (*true data*). In ESSE the simulation of *raw data* consists in the modification of some of the $p{\times}n$ values based on some error models. Actually two types of mechanisms are available in ESSE: *MCAR* (Missing Completely At Random) and *MAR* (Missing At Random) models. The two approaches have been introduced in the area of *non-responses* (Rubin, 1987; Schafer, 1997), but the same stochastic mechanisms can be assumed for any type of non-sampling errors contaminating survey data.

In ESSE the user is allowed to control the *impact* of each error model on each variable, i.e. the percentage of values to be modified by using each error model. In the following, the available models under the two mechanisms are synthetically described. The aim is to reproduce as faithfully as possible the most common mechanisms generating errors in the real survey operations.

A. MCAR error models

In this context, the user can introduce several typologies of errors, which can be further grouped with respect to the nature of the variable to be treated: qualitative variables, quantitative variables or both.

a) Errors for both qualitative and quantitative variables

Item non-response: the original value of the variable X_j ($j=1,..,p$) is replaced by a missing value. The *item non-response* model generates missing values on the basis of a MCAR mechanism.

Misplacement errors: the values of two adjacent variables X_j, X_k ($j,k=1,..,p$; $j{\neq}k$) of the same type (categorical or continuous) are swapped. This model mimes a particular kind of errors due to either data capturing or data entry.

Interchange of value: if the length of a variable X_j is one digit, its value is replaced with a new one chosen in the variable domain; if the variable length is greater than one digit, a random pair of digits is chosen and swapped. Also this model mimes an error due to either data capturing or data entry.

Interchange errors: the original value of a variable X_j is replaced by a new one chosen in the variable domain. This model principally mimes response errors.

Routing errors: this model mimes the common situation in surveys where skip (or routing) instructions are used in questionnaires to indicate that the answer to a variable X_j (dependent item) is required only for some values of another variable X_k (filter item).
The condition determining the need of filling in a value for the dependent variable X_j has to be defined on the filter variable. For each unit whose condition is true the value of X_j is set to blank (categorical variables) or to zero (continuous variables). For each unit whose condition is false, the true value of X_j is replaced with a new value randomly chosen in the domain of X_j.

b) Error models for quantitative variables only

Loss or addition of zeroes: if the value of X_j ends in zero, this value is re-written adding a zero to or dropping a zero from the original value. This model principally mimes errors due to either data capturing or data entry.

Under-report error: the original value of X_j is replaced by a wrong nonnegative value lower than the true one. This model principally mimes response errors.

Outliers: the original value of X_j is replaced by a value belonging to the range $[max(X_j), 1.05 \times max(X_j)]$, where *max* is the maximum observed value of X_j.

c) Overall error

Keying error: a digit of the X_j value is replaced by a value lying in the interval [0-9]. This error model is defined as *overall* because it can affect randomly all the variables under analysis. The model mimes errors due to either data capturing or data entry.

In Figure 2 an example of how error models and the corresponding rates are defined in ESSE is shown.

B. MAR error models

A separate module in ESSE generates *item non-response* according to a MAR mechanism. This mechanism is mimed by modelling the expected probability of occurrence of a missing entry by means of a logistic model (Agresti, 1990).

Let ***X*** be the complete data set. Our goal is to introduce a given amount of missing values in one of the available variables, say X_l. Let the probability of an item of X_l to be missing, be dependent on observed data of $X_1, \dots, X_k$ ($k \neq l$) variables (independent items). According to this model, the probability to be missing for the X_l variable in the ith unit, given the observed values $x_{1i}, \dots, x_{ki}$, is:

$$P(X_{il} = missing \mid x_{1i}, \dots, x_{ki}) = \frac{e^{\beta_0 + \sum_{j=1}^{k} \beta_j x_{ij}}}{1 + e^{\beta_0 + \sum_{j=1}^{k} \beta_j x_{ij}}}$$

Once the parameters values have been properly determined, i.e. when the required expected amount $\bar{P}$ of item non responses for X_l is obtained, missing values are introduced among original data on the basis of the model so far introduced. In Figure 3 an example of how missing values can be simulated in ESSE based on a MAR mechanism is shown.

8. CONCLUDING REMARKS

In official statistics, the impact of non-sampling errors on survey results is usually not negligible, on the contrary it often accounts for the greatest part of the total error. On the other hand, the E&I activities made on entered survey data in order to deal with errors contaminating them, may to some extent affect survey results.

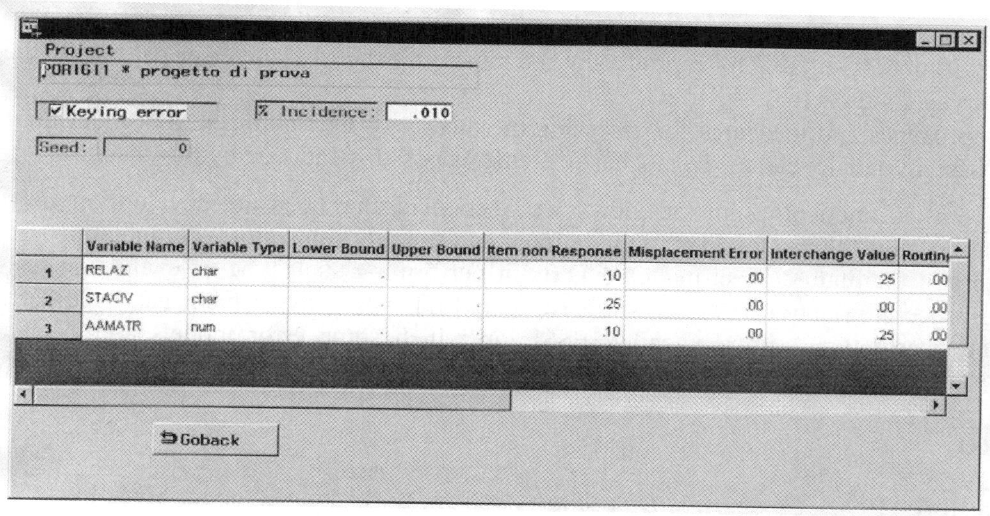

Figure 2: Generating error models in the software ESSE

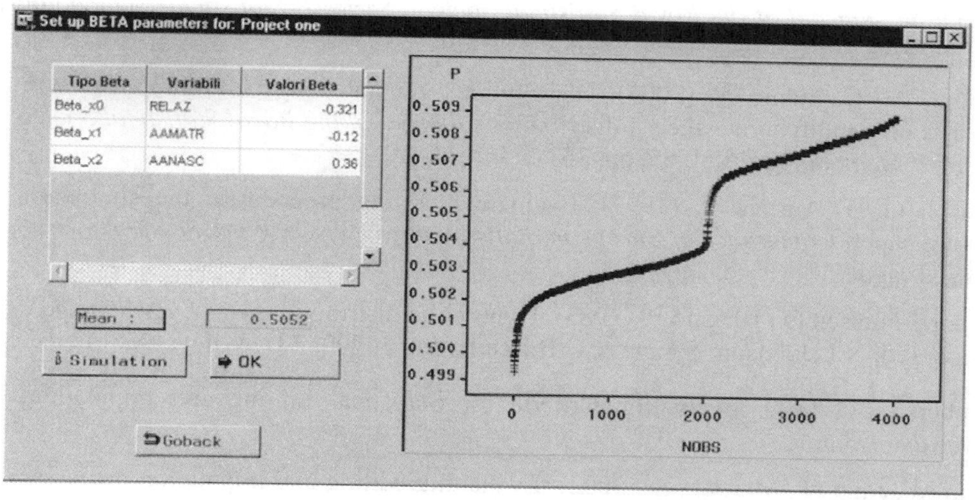

Figure 3: Generating MAR item non responses by using the software ESSE

In this paper we focused on the problem of evaluating the capability of an E&I procedure or method of correctly identifying non-sampling errors possibly affecting a given set of statistical data and recovering the true values. This evaluation can be performed only when true data are available for the phenomenon under analysis. In this situation, the evaluation can be performed by using appropriate indicators comparing the final data (obtained by using the E&I procedure under evaluation) and the corresponding true ones. In the paper the specific situation of evaluating E&I in a simulation context was analysed: some problems concerning how to artificially obtain raw and/or true sets of data were discussed, and some specific indicators suitable for assessing the capability of E&I activities of correctly identifying errors and recovering true values illustrated.

From the discussion, the need emerges for more studies and further developments from both a theoretical and a practical point of view in the specific area of official statistics. In particular, several aspects should be analysed taking into account the typical characteristics, requirements and constraints of survey processes performed at Statistical Agencies:

- data models suitable for reproducing statistical data in the different survey contexts;
- error models suitable for reproducing the most typical errors and error patterns in the different survey contexts;
- approaches and measures for assessing the quality of E&I taking into account the impact (at different data levels) of the stochastic elements possibly induced by E&I itself.

From a practical point of view, we recognize the need to develop appropriate tools implementing algorithms for data simulations and quality indicators computation in order to encourage and facilitate subject-matter experts in performing such type of evaluation tests on their own data processing activities. In this regard, at ISTAT a first experiment has been carried out in developing a prototype software, called ESSE, in which some error models and a set of quality indicators are available for evaluation purposes.

References

[1] Agresti A. (1990). *Categorical Data Analysis.* New York: John Wiley & Sons, Inc.

[2] Armitage P., Berry G. (1971) *Statistical methods in medical research.* Oxford, London, Edinburgh, Boston, Melbourne: Blackwell Scientific Publications.

[3] Azzalini, A., Capitanio A. (1999). Statistical applications of the multivariate skew-normal distribution. *Journal of the Royal Statistical Society, Series B-Statistical Methodology.* Vol. 61, pp. 579-602.

[4] Azzalini, A., Capitanio A. (2003). Distributions generated by perturbation of symmetry with emphasis on a multivariate skew-t distribution. *Journal of the Royal Statistical Society, Series B-Statistical Methodology.* Vol. 65, pp. 367-389.

[5] Barcaroli G., D'Aurizio L. (1997). Evaluating editing procedures: the simulation approach, Working paper, *Conference of European Statisticians, UN/ECE Work Session on Statistical Data Editing*, Prague.

[6] Barndorff-Nielsen O., Blæsild P. (1983). Hyperbolic distributions. In: *Encyclopedia of Statistical Sciences* (ed. N.L.Johnson, S.Kotz & C.B.Read), vol. 3, 700ñ707. Wiley, New York.

[7] Chambers, R. (2001). Evaluation Criteria for Statistical Editing and Imputation, *EUREDIT Deliverable D3.3.*

[8] Di Zio M., Luzi O., Manzari A. (2002). Evaluating editing and imputation processes: the Italian experience, *Conference of European Statisticians, UN/ECE Work Session on Statistical Data Editing*, Helsinki, May 27-29.

[9] Della Rocca G., Di Zio M., Manzari A., Luzi O. (2000). "E.S.S.E. Editing System Standard Evaluation", *Proceedings of the SEUGI 18*, Dublin, June 20-23.

[10] Devroye L. (1986). *Non-uniform Random Variate Generation.* Springer-Verlag, New York.

[11] Efron B., Tibshirani R.J. (1993). *An Introduction to the Bootstrap.* New York and London: Chapman & Hall.

[12] Efron B. (1994). Missing data, Imputation and the Bootstrap. *Journal of the American Statistical Association,* vol. 89, No. 426, pp. 463-475.

[13] Garcia E., Peirats V. (1994). Evaluation of Data Editing Procedures: Results of a Simulation Approach. In *Statistical Data Editing, Vol. 1. Methods and Techniques, Conference of European Statisticians,* Statistical Standard and Studies, No 44, pp.52-68.

[14] Genton M. G. (2004). *Skew-Elliptical Distributions and Their Applications: A Journey Beyond Normality*, Edited Volume, Chapman & Hall / CRC, Boca Raton, FL, 416 pp.

[15] Ghosh-Dastidar B., Schafer J. L. (2003). Multiple Edit/Multiple Imputation for Multivariate Continuous Data. *Journal of the American Statistical Association,* vol. 98, No. 464, pp.807-817

[16] Granquist L. (1997). An overview of methods of evaluating data editing procedures. In *Statistical Data Editing, Methods and Techniques, Vol. 2. Conference of European Statisticians,* Statistical Standard and Studies No 48, UN/ECE, pp. 112-123.

[17] Hansen M.H., Hurwitz W.N., Bershad M. (1961). Measurement Errors in Census and Surveys. *Bullettin of the International Statistical Intitute* 38(2), pp.359-374.

[18] Hosmer D. W., Lemeshow S. (1989). *Applied Logistic Regression.* John Wiley & Sons, Inc.

[19] Johnson N. L., Kotz S. (1972). *Distributions in statistics: continuous multivariate distributions.* Wiley, New York

[20] Kovar, J.G., MacMillan, J., Whitridge, P. (1988). *Overview and Strategy for the Generalized Edit and Imputation System.* Statistics Canada, Methodology Branch Working Paper No. BSMD-88-007E/F, Ottawa.

[21] Lee H., Rancourt E., Särndal C.-E. (2002). Variance Estimation from Survey Data under Single Value Imputation. In *Survey Nonresponse*, Groves R.M., Dillman D.A., Eltinge J.L., Little R.J.A. (eds), New-York:John Wiley&Sons, Inc., pp. 315-328.

[22] Lessler J.T., Kalsbeek W.D. (1995). *Non-sampling Errors in Surveys,* John Wiley.

[23] Little R.J.A., Rubin, D.B. (2003). *Statistical Analysis with Missing Data.* Wiley & Sons, New York.

[24] Luzi O., Della Rocca G. (1998). A Generalised Error Simulation System to Test the Performance of Editing Procedures, *Proceedings of the SEUGI 16*, Prague, June 9-12.

[25] Manzari A., Della Rocca G. (2000). A generalised system based on a simulation approach to test the quality of editing and imputation procedures, *ISTAT Essays* n. 6/2000, 83-103.

[26] Manzari A., Reale A. (2002). Towards a new system for edit and imputation of the 2001 Italian Population Census data: A comparison with the Canadian Nearest-neighbour Imputation Methodology, *Volume of the International Association of Survey Statisticians, Invited Papers, The 53rd Session of The International Statistical Institute, August 2001, Seoul, South Korea,*pp.634-655.

[27] Nordbotten S. (2000). Evaluating Efficiency of Statistical data Editing: General Framework. *United Nations Statistical Commission and Economic Commission for Europe, United Nations,* Geneva.

[28] Poulsen M.E. (1997). Evaluating Data Editing Process Using Survey Data and Register Data. *Statistical Data Editing Methods and Techniques Vol. II,* Conference of European Statisticians, United Nations, 1997.

[29] Rancourt E. (2002). Using Variance components to measure and evaluate the quality of editing practices, *Conference of European Statisticians, UN/ECE Work Session on Statistical Data Editing*, Helsinki, May 27-29.

[30] Rubinstein R. Y. (1981). *Simulation and the Monte Carlo method.* New York: Wiley.

[31] Schafer J. L. (1997). *Analysis of Incomplete Multivariate Data.* Chapman & Hall.

[32] Stefanowicz B. (1997). Selected issues of data editing, In *Statistical Data Editing, Methods and Techniques, Vol. 2. Conference of European Statisticians,* Statistical Standard and Studies No 48, UN/ECE, pp. 109-111.

[33] Tang G., Little R.J.A., Raghunathan T.E. (2003). Analysis of multivariate missing data with nonignorable nonresponse, *Biometrika*, 90, 4, pp. 747-764.

USING VARIANCE COMPONENTS TO MEASURE AND EVALUATE THE QUALITY OF EDITING PRACTICES

By Eric Rancourt, Household Survey Methods Division, Statistics Canada

Abstract: Sampling errors have usually attracted the attention of survey statisticians because of their direct link with the well-developed sampling theory. However, it is generally acknowledged that non-sampling errors may account for the greater proportion of the total error. This is particularly true for editing. Although there is no general methodology theory (as opposed to sampling theory) we can build on existing methods to develop tools appropriate to the editing context. One such method is the calculation of non-response and/or imputation variance, which can be extended to editing. Its use could shed light on the relative precision of approaches. In this paper, we explore ways in which the components of the total variance can be used to evaluate the quality of editing practices. We also consider how to use these variance components to help make the selection of a best editing strategy among many.

1. INTRODUCTION

Survey-taking is an exercise that comprises a large number of different activities. Since all of these activities require human intervention (or have been developed by humans), they are subject to errors. This is true regardless of whether the survey is a sample survey or a census. Therefore, there is a need not only to prevent errors, but also to measure their impact on the quality of estimates and to try to improve the situation. Even in a perfect scenario with all possible and imaginable efforts being made to avoid errors, some would still remain.

The errors are usually categorised into two types. The first type is the sampling error. It stems from the fact that only a sample of the population is investigated instead of all units. The theory and methods for this type of error have been studied at length in the past 50 years. In the context of a census, there is no sampling error, and for large surveys, it may not be the dominant source of error.

The second type is called non-sampling error. This includes all sources of errors that may cause an estimate not to be in perfect agreement with the parameter it is supposed to estimate. Non-sampling errors can be of various types and are often classified into:

(i) Coverage error, caused by a survey frame not matching exactly the target population;
(ii) Response (measurement) error, caused by respondents failing to provide "true" values to answers;
(iii) Non-response error, caused by a wide variety of reasons that lead to missing data;
(iv) Processing error, caused by any manipulation that introduces error into estimates.

The interest of this paper is in a specific cause for non-response, namely editing. Indeed, editing can be viewed as one of the causes that lead to missing data, especially when there are many inconsistencies found. With editing, it is never known to the survey manager or the survey statistician whether enough or too much is performed. Of course, it is desirable to try to find the faulty data, but beyond a certain point, good data are being erased. It is therefore important to measure the impact of editing, especially because the amount of editing can sometimes be fairly substantial or even too large.

A number of methods have been proposed to measure the impact of editing in surveys. Using estimates computed on edited and non-edited data, Madsen and Solheim (2000), defined editing bias measures. Also interested in bias, Barcaroli and D'Aurizio (1997) and Manzari and Della Rocca (1999) used simulations to produce "true" values that could then be used to compute a number of indexes they defined. In Nordbotten (1999), ratios are defined to contrast frequencies of rejected and imputed data to their associated costs.

In this paper, we are interested in using the theory of estimation of the variance under imputation (Särndal, 1992; Lee, Rancourt and Särndal, 2002) to produce an editing variance component. A similar idea was used in the metrics proposed by Nordbotten (1997) to evaluate the quality of editing and imputation by contrasting estimates based on edited and unedited values. The next section presents and defines editing as a statistical process. Section 3 follows with a description of how to measure the impact of editing using variance components. Then, some recent developments at Statistics Canada in this field are highlighted in Section 4 and the conclusion follows.

2. EDITING AS A STATISTICAL PROCESS

There are many causes for non-response. From an estimation perspective, data that are lost, deleted, misreported or corrupted may all have an impact. Therefore, editing can be seen as a process that causes missing data and needs to be followed up and monitored like any other cause whether it is manual or automated.

Conceptually, the set of non-respondents in a sample can be divided into those that have missing data as a result of editing, and those that have missing data as a result of other causes. Obviously, this breakdown is not unique and is not specific to editing. Any reason for missing data could be isolated in the same way but here the attention is on editing. In the following, the discussion is assuming total non-response, but it could also apply to partial non-response. Graphically, the situation can be pictured as follows:

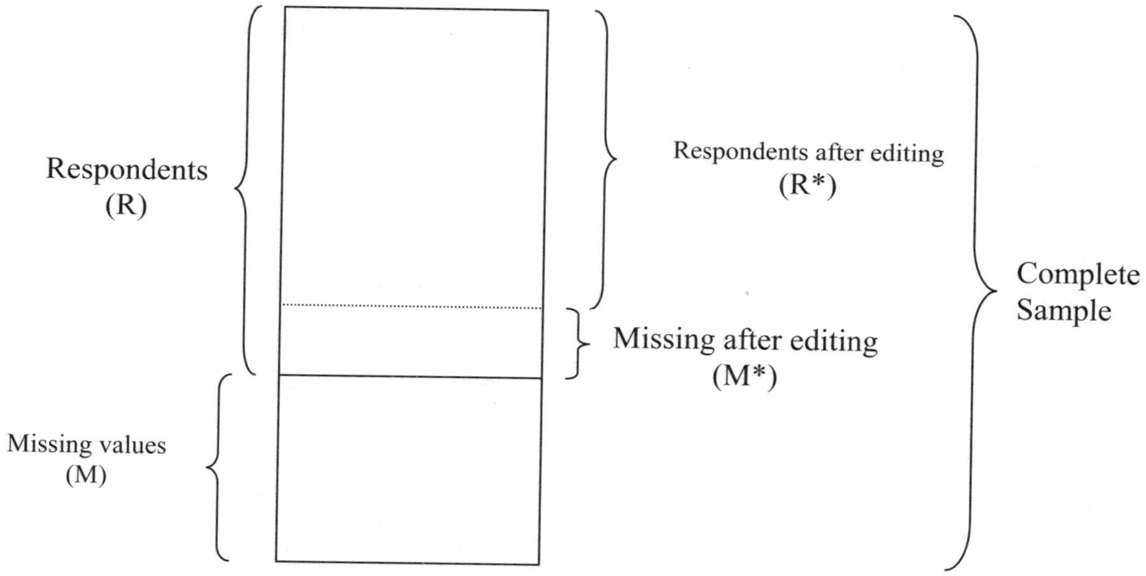

The problem with editing is to characterize it as a *statistical* process. With manual editing, the argument can be made that when reproduced, it may lead to different outcomes. In this case the errors could be assumed to behave like measurement errors and the associated theory could be used. However, with automated editing (or editing in general), the process is not necessarily stochastic but rather fixed and so, errors cannot be treated like measurement errors. In fact, it could be assumed that there are potential measurement errors and in this case, even with a fixed set of edit rules the editing process would not really be controlled. But in this paper, it is assumed that measurement errors are absent and that editing is responsible for missing data.

Editing can be considered as part of the non-response mechanism. This is often the implicit assumption when dealing with the problem of missing data. For example, the re-weighting or the imputation process is most of the time performed on all missing data without regard to the cause of missingness. However, the editing process is completely distinct from the actual response mechanism and should be studied accordingly. Then, the problem remains one of representing the editing process. Since it is fixed, it cannot really be represented by a model.

Editing does have an impact on the data. It cannot be modelled, but it affects which part of the data distribution can be observed. In surveys, the sequence of events can be represented as follows:

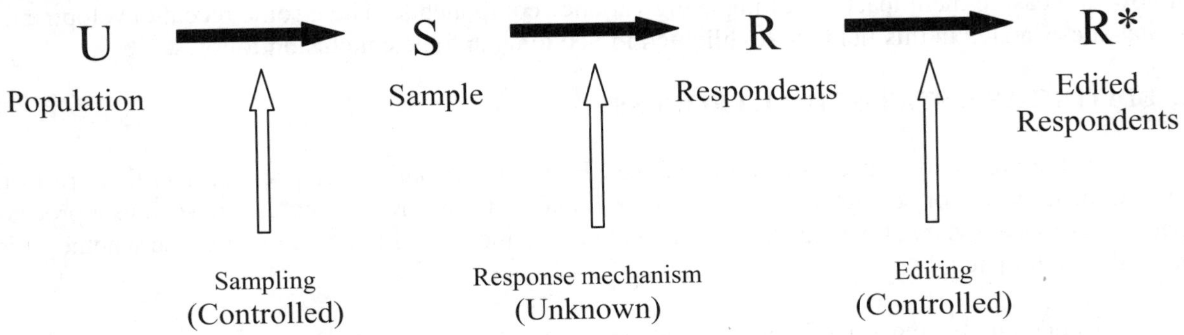

As can be seen, unlike the response mechanism, editing is a process under the survey statistician's control. For instance, with query edits, the rules are not absolute and the editor may be causing data to be missing because of edits rules that are much too tight. It is then clear that editing is not a correction tool, as the more editing is performed, the less responses are available. In the case of a census with a 100% response rate, editing becomes the only cause of missing data. One must therefore strive not to overuse editing for correction, but rather to use it to learn about the data in order to minimise other errors.

3. MEASURING THE IMPACT OF EDITING

As concluded in Granquist and Kovar (1997): "Editing will have to serve a greater function than just a data correction tool". Its goal is to improve the overall quality. The quality of individual values that have been treated for non-response is only secondary. It is with this view in mind that this section presents a tool to measure the impact of non-response.

Just like a quality control strategy in a production line, attempting to measure the quality of a process such as editing has two aspects. Firstly, the quality of the level (of estimates) must be assessed. This is why the literature has been abundant on the subject. For example, it is necessary to count how many records fail a given edit or a given set of edits. Secondly, the stability of the process must also be assessed. In this case, the literature on the subject is rather limited. There are measures of editing but not in the sense of variability of the estimates. To obtain a complete picture of the quality of editing, both types of measures (level and stability) must be used together.

Measuring the variability of processes such as non-response and editing cannot be achieved directly: A treatment must be applied. This treatment may be re-weighting and/or imputation. Therefore, the variability due to non-response (or editing) needs to be measured using the variability due to imputation or due to re-weighting. In this paper, mainly imputation will be considered.

Since an editing model cannot be used, a *data* model (ratio) such as

$$\xi : y_k = \beta x_k + \varepsilon_k, \quad \mathrm{E}_\xi(\varepsilon_k) = 0, \; \mathrm{E}_\xi(\varepsilon_k \varepsilon_{k'}) = 0, \; \mathrm{E}_\xi(\varepsilon_k^2) = \sigma^2 x_k$$

may be considered. More general models may be used, but this simplified version is sufficient for the current discussion. Under a data model, the editing process can be fixed, since the variables of interest are random. The model selected is the one that is found to best represent the data. It is important to note that the selection of a model requires the usual assessment of the fit and is not obtained as the result of a simple choice.

When imputation is used, models of the form of ξ are useful to represent the data. In Särndal (1992), a model is used to develop a framework to evaluate the precision of estimates under imputation. In this case, the variance of the estimator is represented as the sum of the sampling and the non-response (imputation) variance. In the context of editing, the variance could be further divided into components due to sampling, non-response and editing.

In the following, the imputation variance calculation approach is applied to editing. To avoid the need for evaluation of the mean squared error, estimates are assumed to be unbiased. This assumption lies on the premise that everything possible would be attempted by the survey statistician to avoid errors that may cause some bias. Of course, some bias may remain but its measure is not the focus of this paper.

Assume that the parameter of interest is the population total, $Y_U = \sum_U y_k$, where y_k is the variable of interest for unit k. The theoretical estimator that would be used under 100% response is called $\hat{Y}_{\text{FULL}}$. The estimator under no editing is $\hat{Y}_{\text{NO-EDIT}}$ and the actual one with editing is $\hat{Y}_{\text{EDIT}}$. Respectively, they are:

$$\hat{Y}_{\text{FULL}} = \sum_S w_k y_k,$$

$$\hat{Y}_{\text{NO-EDIT}} = \sum_R w_k y_k + \sum_M w_k \hat{y}_k,$$

$$\hat{Y}_{\text{EDIT}} = \sum_{R*} w_k y_k + \sum_{M*} w_k \hat{y}_k + \sum_M w_k \hat{y}_k,$$

where w_k is the final weight and $\hat{y}_k$ is a value imputed by a given method. Note that in this case, it is assumed that the same imputation model is used for values missing as a result of non-response or as a result of editing. As well, this expression does note make a distinction between records that fail an edit as a result of measurement error and those that fail strictly as a result of editing. The total error will reflect both causes.

The total error of $\hat{Y}_{\text{EDIT}}$ is

$$\hat{Y}_{\text{EDIT}} - Y_U = (\hat{Y}_{\text{EDIT}} - \hat{Y}_{\text{NO-EDIT}}) + (\hat{Y}_{\text{NO-EDIT}} - \hat{Y}_{\text{FULL}}) + (\hat{Y}_{\text{FULL}} - Y_U).$$

Turning to variance (and assuming no bias),

$$V_\xi(\hat{Y}_{\text{EDIT}}) = E_\xi(\hat{Y}_{\text{EDIT}} - Y_U)^2 = V_{\text{Editing}} + V_{\text{Nonresponse}} + V_{\text{Sampling}} + \text{ Small mix terms.}$$

For example, with ratio imputation and assuming that only units from R* are used to impute in both $M*$ and M, estimation is as follows:

$\hat{V}_{\text{Sampling}}$: As usual; or preferably computed on values imputed with residuals,

$$\hat{V}_{\text{Nonresponse}} = \left[\frac{(\sum_M w_k x_k)^2}{\sum_{R^*} x_k} + \sum_M w_k^2 x_k \right] \hat{\sigma}^2,$$

$$\hat{V}_{\text{Editing}} = \left[\frac{(\sum_{M^*} w_k x_k)^2}{\sum_{R^*} x_k} + \sum_{M^*} w_k^2 x_k \right] \hat{\sigma}^2,$$

where x_k is the auxiliary variable, $\hat{\sigma}^2 = \dfrac{\sum_{R^*} (y_k - \hat{B} x_k)^2}{\sum_{R^*} x_k}$ and $\hat{B} = \dfrac{\sum_{R^*} y_k}{\sum_{R^*} x_k}$.

These formulae are in fact the same ones that apply to estimation of the variance due to non-response when there is imputation. For example, forms for many imputation methods can be found in Lee, Rancourt and Särndal (1995) and translated into this editing framework.

With tools such as $\hat{V}_{\text{Editing}}$ and $\hat{V}_{\text{Nonresponse}}$, one can study various impacts of editing. For a given set of respondents, a number of editing strategies can be evaluated. When developing editing, it would be possible to choose among the approaches believed to be unbiased, the one with the smallest estimated variance. Another application is in repeated surveys where monitoring of the editing process could be enhanced by adding $\hat{V}_{\text{Editing}}$ to the set of edit counts and rates that are usually looked at.

There are several methods to take imputation into account. The model approach is favoured for extension to editing because it allows for production of estimates of each of the components of the total variance. Other methods such as the jackknife and the bootstrap exist for estimating the variance due to non-response and they could be used to estimate the total variance. However, the possibility of having variance components ($\hat{V}_{\text{Editing}}$, $\hat{V}_{\text{Nonresponse}}$) is not always an option for these approaches.

4. RECENT DEVELOPMENTS AT STATISTICS CANADA

Statistics Canada has produced quality guidelines (Statistics Canada, 1998) for all steps and processes of surveys. Therein, the multiple goals of editing are clearly stated. For instance, the guidelines say: "the editing process is often very complex. When editing is under the agency's control, make available detailed and up to date procedures with appropriate training to staff involved, and monitor the work itself. Consider using formal quality control procedures". The importance of measuring the impact of editing is therefore recognised. Further, it evokes the idea that editing is a process that can be submitted to quality control methods.

There has also had a Policy on informing users of data quality and methodology since the late seventies (Statistics Canada, 2001). To improve the information provided to users, large efforts have been made since 1990. A large part of it has been on estimation of the variance under imputation. As presented in Lee, Rancourt and Särndal (2000), there is now a wide array of methods to correctly account for (single) imputation variance in estimation of the total variance.

As was seen in Section 3, the methods designed to estimate the variance due to imputation can also be used to estimate the variance due to editing. Moreover, recent developments have been made in the creation of tools and software to evaluate the impact of non-response and imputation and the quality of estimates.

The first tool is a generalised simulation imputation system called GENESIS. This system allows for evaluation of imputation techniques under a simulation framework. Various imputation methods can be compared for a given population in a controlled simulation environment. Currently, a beta version can be used but it is not supported. While it is designed for imputation, GENESIS could also be used to investigate editing. Its simulation-based nature makes it a tool for investigation of the bias. At this time it is designed for evaluating the variance due to imputation, but it will eventually be extended to editing.

The second tool is a system designed to estimate the variance under non-response and imputation. The system, called SEVANI, can produce non-response and/or imputation variance components. It can produce up to three estimated variance components for processes such as re-weighting for non-response, imputation or editing. It will therefore allow for the production of variance estimates that more accurately represent the sampling and non-response variance. It should be possible to use such a system to produce measures such as $\hat{V}_{\text{Editing}}$ presented in Section 3. A beta version of the system is currently being evaluated.

Editing is an activity that is an integral part of the process in many surveys at Statistics Canada. This is acknowledged in a survey on editing practices by Gagnon, Gough and Yeo (1994). Like re-weighting and imputation, it does have an effect on estimation. Thanks to the increased awareness of this impact on final results, survey methodologists have started to consider the use of variance components to evaluate the quality of estimates. On top of the sampling variance, survey methodologists have started estimating the imputation variance and there are plans to evaluate the variance due to editing and imputation in a number of business, social and household surveys.

The Canadian Labour Force Survey is at the start of a redesign and treatment of missing and inconsistent data is at the top of the agenda. Activities that are considered in the redesign are the treatment of total non-response through re-weighting and treatment of partial non-response through imputation. As well, cross-sectional and longitudinal editing are to be re-assessed and further developed. To select the approach that will be used in production, GENESIS and SEVANI will be used to produce comparative measures of performance of the editing and imputation as well as for re-weighting for total non-response. Then, when the redesigned survey is in place, SEVANI will be used on a continuous basis to monitor the impact ($\hat{V}_{\text{Editing}}$) of editing on a monthly basis.

5. CONCLUSIONS

Editing is an important process in surveys. It can be viewed as one of the causes of non-response but unlike other response mechanisms, it is fixed. It does nonetheless have an impact on final estimates, which should be measured.

This paper has used the imputation variance estimation theory to apply it to editing. By assuming a model for the data, it is possible to use a model approach to obtain an estimate an editing variance component. As well, this information should help in better understanding the editing process. Further, adding the editing variance to the estimated variance allows for analysts to make more precise inference and for data users to be better informed of data quality.

The survey manager who has at his disposal measures of sampling, imputation and editing variance is well equipped to make decisions on how to allocate or re-direct funds in the survey. For instance, the following variance estimates may be obtained (as a percent of the total estimated variance).

Variance component	Scenario 1	Scenario 2	Scenario 3
Sampling	80 %	40 %	40 %
Non-response	10 %	50 %	20 %
Editing	10 %	10 %	40 %

Under Scenario 1, most of the variance is due to sampling. This may indicate that a larger sample could be needed. Conversely, non-response and editing appear to have a small impact on the variance. If editing and treatment of non-response require large amounts of funds and efforts, then these may be reduced. Under Scenarios 2 and 3 sampling is no longer the dominant factor contributing the overall variance. In Scenario 2, editing still has a minimal impact while it is significant in Scenario 3. In this case, the large figure (40%) may indicate that there is over-editing, that there are many errors in the data or that collection procedures need refinements. Also, since 60% of the total variance is due to editing and non-response, perhaps the sample size can be reduced to re-direct funds towards improvement of follow-up and treatment of non-response procedures.

Of course, bias is also a component of the error that cannot be neglected. The present paper does not present an approach aimed at replacing other methods to evaluate editing. It aims at providing a complementary measure in order to help in fully understanding the editing process. Since editing can be viewed as a process, its stability must be evaluated and monitored. Using the $\hat{V}_{\text{Editing}}$ component presented in Section 3 appears to be a tool of choice for this purpose.

Hopefully, the approach in this paper will help survey statisticians to develop new editing strategies or more precisely to monitor those in place.

References

[1] Barcaroli G., D'Aurizio L. – Evaluating Editing Procedures: The Simulation Approach, *Working Paper No. 17*, Conference of European Statisticians, UN\ECE Work Session on Statistical Data Editing, Prague, 1997.

[2] Gagnon F., Gough H. and Yeo D. - Survey of Editing Practices in Statistics Canada. Statistics Canada Technical Report, 1994.

[3] Granquist L. and Kovar, J. – Editing of Survey Data: How Much is Enough?. *Survey Measurement and Process Quality*, Lyberg, L et al eds., J. Wiley and Sons, New York, 1997.

[4] Lee H., Rancourt E., Särndal C.-E. – Variance Estimation in the Presence of Imputed Data for the Generalised Estimation System, *Proceedings of the Section on Survey Research Methods*, American Statistical Association, 384-389, 1995.

[5] Lee H., Rancourt E., Särndal C.-E. – Variance Estimation from Survey Data under Single Value Imputation, *Working Paper HSMD – 2000 – 006E*, Methodology Branch, Statistics Canada, 2000.

[6] Lee H., Rancourt E., Särndal C.-E. – Variance Estimation from Survey Data under Single Value Imputation, in *Survey Non-response*, Groves, R. et al eds., J. Wiley and Sons, New York, 2002.

[7] Madsen B., Solheim L. – How to Measure the Effect of Data Editing, *Working Paper No. 2*, Conference of European Statisticians, UN/ECE Work Session on Statistical Data Editing, Cardiff, 2000.

[8] Manzari A., Della Rocca G. – A Generalised System Based on a Simulation Approach to Test the Quality of Editing and Imputation Procedures, *Working Paper No. 4*, Conference of European Statisticians, UN/ECE Work Session on Statistical Data Editing, Rome, 1999.

[9] Nordbotten S. – Metrics for Predicting the Quality of Editing and Imputation, *Working Paper No. 20*, Conference of European Statisticians, UN\ECE Work Session on Statistical Data Editing, Prague, 1997.

[10] Nordbotten S. – Strategies for Improving Statistical Quality, *Working Paper No. 4*, Conference of European Statisticians, UN/ECE Work Session on Statistical Data Editing, Rome, 1999.

[11] Särndal C.-E. – Method for Estimating the Precision of Survey Estimates when Imputation Has Been Used, *Survey Methodology*, 241-252.

[12] Statistics Canada. - *Policy on Informing Users of Data Quality and Methodology*, Statistics Canada Policy Manual, 2001.

[13] Statistics Canada. - *Quality Guidelines*. Catalogue No. 12-539-XIE. Third Edition, October 1998.

QUALITY INDICATORS FOR EVALUATING AND DOCUMENTING EDITING AND IMPUTATION

By Giorgio Della Rocca, Orietta Luzi, Marina Signore, Giorgia Simeoni, ISTAT

1. INTRODUCTION

In National Statistical Offices (NSOs) the analysis of the effects on data of any processing activity has progressively assumed a central role. In this paper we concentrate on the problem of evaluating and documenting data editing and imputation processes (E&I), and in particular the E&I activities performed at the post-data collection stage.

The results provided by evaluation studies on E&I procedures are widely recognized as an important source of information on the quality of the data resulting from data capturing, on the quality of the E&I process itself and on the reliability of other aspects of the survey process. The definition of the *quality of an E&I process* depends on the particular E&I aspect that we want to investigate and evaluate (Granquist, 1997). From a general point of view, different evaluation studies are performed at different stages of the E&I *life-cycle* in order to gather different types of information on E&I (Di Zio *et al.*, 2001): information on the accuracy of an E&I method/procedure (in terms of its capability of correctly identifying and restoring "true" data) is generally collected *before* the application of the E&I method/procedure to survey data (e.g. through experimental studies); information on the effects of an E&I procedure on data for monitoring its performance and tuning it is generally obtained *during* the data processing; information needed for documentation and survey management purposes (e.g. for monitoring over time the changes of the E&I impact on data) is obtained *after* the data treatment. Furthermore, other elements are to be taken into account when assessing the quality of an E&I process, like its cost, timeliness, burden on respondents.

In the area of evaluating E&I, the most recent activities at ISTAT have been focused mainly on the following areas (Di Zio *et al.*, 2001; Brancato *et al.*, 2004): 1) evaluating the performance of E&I methods through the analysis of their statistical effects on data distributions and relations; 2) providing the subject-matter experts with detailed documentation on the process impact on data in each survey in order to permit the monitoring of process quality over time; 3) providing the NSO with information about the quality level of each survey in order to allow comparisons; 4) providing final users with information about the main characteristics of the E&I process and the data modifications due to the E&I process.

In order to meet the above-mentioned objectives, an evaluation framework has been developed at ISTAT in which both users' and producers' needs are taken into account. In this context, crucial problems like identifying appropriate indicators, standardizing their computation, supporting the survey managers in computing them have been addressed. The activities have been carried out taking into account the increasing attention paid to the identification of standard quality indicators and the production of standard quality reports at both NSO level and Eurostat level (Chambers, 2001; Linden *et al.*, 2004; Eurostat, 2000). Supporting survey managers is an important aspect because of the costs and burden due to the additional charge of producing standard quality reports for assessing and documenting the data processing activities.

In this paper we describe the recent advancements reached at ISTAT in the area of developing a comprehensive framework for evaluating E&I procedures and documenting their impact on survey data. This framework consists of a system of statistical measures corresponding to:

- performance indicators for evaluation purposes;
- standard quality indicators for documentation purposes.

It is worth mentioning that the latter are managed in the *Information System for Survey Documentation (SIDI)*, which is the centralized system for standard documentation of all ISTAT surveys. SIDI is based on the integrated management of metadata and standard quality indicators. It covers all the different stages of the data production process and includes a specific subset of standard indicators related to the E&I process.

All the proposed indicators, including those defined in the SIDI context, have been implemented in a generalized tool called IDEA (Indices for Data Editing Assessment). IDEA has then multiple goals, namely to allow survey managers to compute all the proposed indicators in a standardized and controlled way as well as to simplify and make less expensive the evaluation task thus stimulating survey managers in performing the evaluation of data processing.

A common feature of these indicators is that they can all be derived by comparing edited data and the corresponding raw data.

In addition, they can be classified as *high-level indicators* and *low-level indicators*. High-level indicators (e.g. the standard quality indicators required by SIDI) are computed taking into account all the edited variables and units. The low-level indicators are computed on subgroups of edited variables and/or subsets of units, in particular, the subset of data modified during the E&I task. Considering the subset of modified data is particularly useful when more detailed analyses are to be performed, or when the percentage of the modified values is low with respect to the overall observed values.

All the indicators can be computed on different *data domains* identified by a user-defined *stratification* item. For sample surveys, weighted indicators can also be obtained.

The paper is structured as follows: in Section 2 the indicators defined for evaluating the quality or the effects of E&I processes are described. Section 3 focuses on the standard indicators required for documenting E&I processes in the SIDI system. Issues related to the relationships between SIDI and IDEA are also illustrated. Concluding remarks are summarized in Section 4.

2. EVALUATING THE IMPACT OF EDITING AND IMPUTATION PROCEDURES

In this section we describe the approach and the indicators proposed for measuring the impact on a given set of survey data of an E&I method/procedure.

An E&I process generally consists of many sub-phases, each performing a particular step of the whole data treatment process (e.g. treatment of outliers, editing of systematic or stochastic errors on either categorical or continuous data, and so on.). As a consequence, the evaluation task can consist in the assessment of the impact on data of the overall E&I process, or it can be split in the evaluation of simpler sub-problems, each of them focused on a specific E&I sub-phase.

Furthermore, the evaluation of the impact on statistical survey data of E&I activities can be performed with different goals. One of them is monitoring and tuning the E&I process: the modifications produced on raw data are analysed in order to identify possible problems in data and data processing, and improve the efficiency of the E&I process during the data treatment itself. This type of analysis is generally performed with respect to sub-phases of the overall E&I process, in order to optimise the tuning process.

The analysis of the impact of E&I on raw data is also performed for documentation purposes, for producing information for final users, and for data analysis. For example, for a given survey, the availability of information on the statistical effects of the E&I activities over time permits a comparative analysis that could highlight structural modifications in the surveyed phenomena or occasional organisational problems requiring permanent or occasional adjustments to the survey organisation or to the E&I procedure.

Under specific conditions, the approach and the indicators illustrated in this section can also be used to measure the quality of an E&I method/procedure in terms of its capability of correctly deal with errors, e.g. the capability of an error localization process of correctly identifying not acceptable data, or the capability of an imputation technique of restoring *true* data in sampling units. This kind of evaluation implies the knowledge of *true* data for each unit[1]: in this case, the proposed indicators are to be computed by comparing the final data to the corresponding *true* ones. This type of evaluation study is typically performed at the E&I design and test phases, when the aim is assessing the suitability of a given method or approach for a specific data problem.

The performance indicators illustrated in this section have been defined starting from the results obtained during the Euredit project[2] (Charlton, 2003; Chambers, 2001), in which a general framework for evaluating the quality of E&I methods in an experimental context was developed. On the basis of the quality (or performance) criteria defined in Euredit, a set of statistical measures and graphical techniques are proposed. In particular, the impact of an E&I method/procedure is evaluated on the basis of the following performance criteria:

- impact on individual data;
- impact on marginal and joint distributions;
- impact on aggregates;
- impact on relationships between variables.

Depending on the evaluation purpose, each criterion assumes a different meaning. For example, if the aim is assessing the effects on data of an E&I method, indicators measuring the impact on individual data values provide information on the amount of changes produced on elementary data by the E&I activities, while if our goal is evaluating the quality of an E&I method, these indicators provide information on the method capability of recovering the *true* values for missing or erroneous items.

In general, the relevance and priority of the above mentioned criteria mainly depend on the investigation objectives, the investigation characteristics and the nature of the analyzed variables. For example, if our aim is to verify the quality of an imputation method and micro data have to be provided to final users, the most important quality criteria that has to be met is the preservation of both micro data and (marginal or joint) distributions. As a further example, the distributional accuracy can assume a relevant role in the case that the distributional assumptions (univariate or multivariate) on observed variables are to be analyzed or taken into account in subsequent statistical analyses.

The evaluation indicators proposed for each one of the so far introduced criteria are low-level indicators. In defining these measures, an effort was required in order to identify a common set of suitable indicators for assessing both the quality and the effects of E&I (in the following we will use the term *performance* for indicating both purposes), regardless to the fact that we are comparing either raw and clean data, or true and clean data. This task was not simple, particularly when the reference data correspond to raw datasets: in this case, the unacceptable or out of range data might affect the computation of indicators.

The proposed evaluation indicators can be applied for evaluating either the overall E&I process, or each single E&I step, depending on the evaluation purpose and the available indicators.

In the following subsections the indicators implemented in IDEA for each of the performance criteria mentioned above will be illustrated.

---

[1] A low cost consuming approach that permits this situation is based on the use of the simulation approach, also adopted in the Euredit project for the comparative evaluation of competitive E&I methods.

[2] The Euredit Project was funded under EU Fifth Framework research program (www.cs.york.ac.uk/euredit/).

2. 1 Preservation of individual data

The indicators proposed for measuring the impact of an E&I process on individual survey data depend on the nature of the investigated variable (categorical or continuous).
Let Y be the variable subject to E&I, and let Y^R_i and Y^F_i be respectively the reference and final values of Y in the ith unit (i=1,...,n), where n is the number of responding units.

a) Categorical Variables (nominal or ordinal)

a.1) If Y is a categorical variable, straightforward information on the overall amount of individual data in which the value of Y changed from one category to another category due to E&I is provided by the following *imputation rate*:

$$D_1(Y^R, Y^F) = \frac{\sum_{i=1}^{n} w_i \times I(Y_i^R, Y_i^F)}{\sum_{i=1}^{n} w_i} \times 100$$

where w_i are the possible sampling weights and $I(Y_i^R, Y_i^F)=1$ if $Y^R_i \neq Y^F_i$ and 0 otherwise. $D_1(Y^R, Y^F)$ simply measures the percentage of units in which Y has different categories in the reference and final data sets. $D_1(Y^R, Y^F)$ is 0 if all the categories are equal in the two compared data sets, while it reaches its maximum value 100 when all units assume a different category in the two data sets.

a.2) The *net imputation rate* $D_{1i}(Y^R, Y^F)$ indicates the percentage of units in which the value of Y changed from a *blank* value in the reference data set to a non *blank* value in the final data set. It is computed like $D_1(Y^R, Y^F)$ where in this case $I(Y_i^R, Y_i^F)=1$ if [$Y_i^R \neq Y_i^F$ and Y_i^R = *blank* and $Y_i^F \neq$ *blank*], and 0 otherwise.

a.3) The *modification rate* $D_{1m}(Y^R, Y^F)$ indicates the percentage of units in which the value of Y changed from a non *blank* value in the reference data set to another non *blank* value in the final data set. It is computed like $D_1(Y^R, Y^F)$ where in this case $I(Y_i^R, Y_i^F)=1$ if [$Y_i^R \neq Y_i^F$ and $Y_i^R \neq$*blank* and $Y_i^F \neq$*blank*], and 0 otherwise.

a.4) The *cancellation rate* $D_{1c}(Y^R, Y^F)$ indicates the percentage of units in which the value of Y changed from a non *blank* value in the reference data set to a *blank* value in the final data set. It is computed like $D_1(Y^R, Y^F)$ where in this case $I(Y_i^R, Y_i^F)=1$ if [$Y_i^R \neq Y_i^F$ and Y_i^R $\neq$*blank* and Y_i^F =*blank*], and 0 otherwise[3].

[3] It is obvious that, when the *blank* value is not in the domain of Y, $D_{1c}(Y^R, Y^F)$ highlights a problem in the E&I process.

a.5) Graphical representations of the frequency distributions of Y in the two compared data sets permit the visual analysis of the overall data changes. In figure 1 an example of graphical representations that can be directly performed in IDEA is shown for variable Sex.

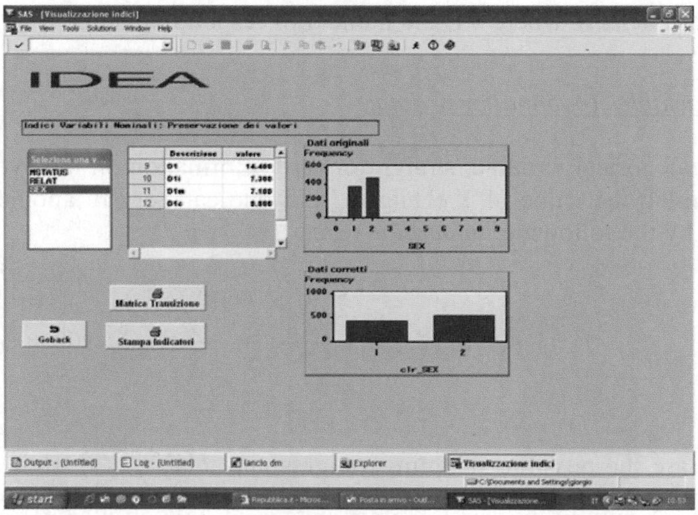

Figure 1: Frequency distribution in reference and final data for variable Sex

a.6) Useful information on changes in categories due to E&I is obtained by analysing the *transition matrix* obtained by building up a contingency table in which the categories of *Y* in the two compared data sets are crossed together. The frequencies of cells outside the main diagonal represent the number of changes due to E&I. Anomalous frequencies indicate possible biasing effects of E&I.

b) <u>*Ordinal Variables only*</u>

b.1) If *Y* is an ordinal variable, information about how much categories of *Y* have been changed due to E&I is given by the following index:

$$D_2(Y^R, Y^F) = \frac{1}{m \times \sum_{i=1}^{n} w_i} \sum_{i=1}^{n} w_i \times d(Y_i^R, Y_i^F) \times 100$$

where Y_i^R and Y_i^F are the coded categories of *Y* in the reference and in the final data sets, w_i are the possible sampling weights,

$$m = \begin{cases} (max_Y - min_Y) + 1 & \text{if the category } \textit{blank} \text{ is in the domain of } Y \\ (max_Y - min_Y) & \text{if the category } \textit{blank} \text{ is not in the domain of } Y \end{cases}$$

where max_Y, and min_Y are the higher and lower categories of *Y*, and

$$d(Y_i^R, Y_i^F) = \begin{cases} 0 & \text{if } Y_i^R = Y_i^F \\ \left|Y_i^R - Y_i^F\right| & \text{if } Y_i^R \neq Y_i^F \text{ and } Y_i^R, Y_i^F \neq blank \\ m & \\ \text{if } Y_i^R \neq Y_i^F \text{ and } (Y_i^R = blank \text{ or } Y_i^F = blank) & \end{cases}$$

$D_2(Y^R, Y^F)$ varies between 0 (all categories are equal in the two compared data sets) and 100 (maximum difference among categories).

b.2) If the value *blank* is not in the domain of variable *Y*, the index $D_2(Y^R, Y^F)$ is also computed on the subset of the $n_g \leq n$ of units in which *Y* assumes non *blank* values. In other words, once the item non-responses are discarded from the computation, the new index $D_{2n}(Y^R, Y^F)$ measures the *net* percentage of changes on *Y* values from not *blank* categories to other non *blank* categories. $D_{2n}(Y^R, Y^F)$ is useful particularly when *Y* is affected by a large amount of item non responses, in this situations in fact $d(Y_i^R, Y_i^F)$ assumes it s maximum value *m* and $D_2(Y^R, Y^F)$ results amplified by large amounts of these values.

c) Continuous Variables

c.1) If *Y* is a continuous variable, indicators $D_1(Y^R, Y^F)$, $D_{1i,}(Y^R, Y^F)$ $D_{1m}(Y^R, Y^F)$ and $D_{1c}(Y^R, Y^F)$ are still applicable, with similar meaning, and they provide information about how many data of *Y* have been changed due to E&I.

c.2) In order to evaluate both the number and the amount of changes on variable *Y*, indices belonging to the class of measures

$$D_{L\alpha}(Y^R, Y^F) = \left\{ \frac{\sum_{i=1}^{n} w_i \times \left|Y_i^R - Y_i^F\right|^{\alpha}}{\sum_{i=1}^{n} w_i} \right\}^{1/\alpha}$$

are proposed, where w_i are the possible sampling weights, and $\alpha>0$ is chosen in order to give the appropriate importance to high differences between values of *Y* in the reference and in the final data sets. The indices $D_{L1}(Y^R, Y^F)$, $D_{L2}(Y^R, Y^F)$ and $D_{L\infty}(Y^R, Y^F)$ have been implemented in IDEA, where:

$$D_{L\infty}(Y^R, Y^F) = \frac{\max_i \left|Y_i^R - Y_i^F\right|}{\sum_{i=1}^{n} w_i}$$

It is straightforward that the higher is the distance between corresponding values in the two compared data sets, the higher is the value of each one of these indices.

c.3) A set of simple statistics directly provide information on some aspects of changes in individual data, like the *number of missing and non missing observations* in the compared data sets.

c.4) A set of indices can be directly obtained by the following regression model:

$$Y_i^F = \beta \times Y_i^R$$

In particular we use the following ones:

- the *slope* β,
- the R^2 and the adjusted R^2,
- the *Root Mean Squared Error* (*RMSE*).

The graphical representation of regression results greatly helps in identifying not effective performances: in Figure 2 an example of scatter plot produced by the IDEA software for the regression analysis between raw and final data for variable *Age* is shown.

c.5) Graphical representations of the Y values in the two compared data sets permit a deepest analysis of changes in the individual data due to E&I. Box plots and histograms are useful tools in this context. In figure 3 an example of graphical representations of data through SAS Insight that can be directly performed in IDEA is shown for variable Age. Useful information on the main distributional statistics is directly provided by these representations.

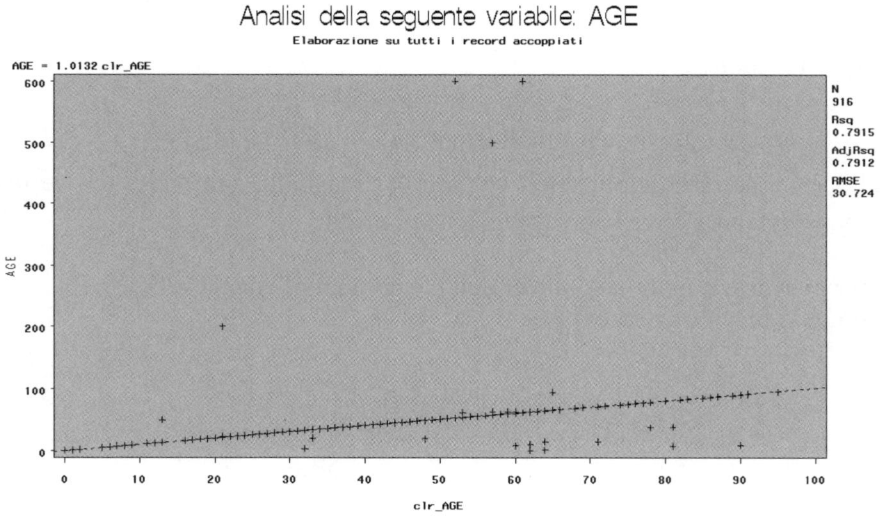

Figure 2: Results of the regression between raw and final data for variable Age

2.2 Preservation of marginal and joint distributions

The evaluation of the E&I impact on (marginal or joint) distributions can be measured by means of *descriptive* statistics (indicators, techniques of multivariate analysis) and/or *test of hypothesis* techniques. *Descriptive* indicators miss the idea of generalisation of the conclusion (inference), however they provide a simple first measurement of the distance of the distributions, and then they can give some clues to understand to what extent the compared distributions are similar.

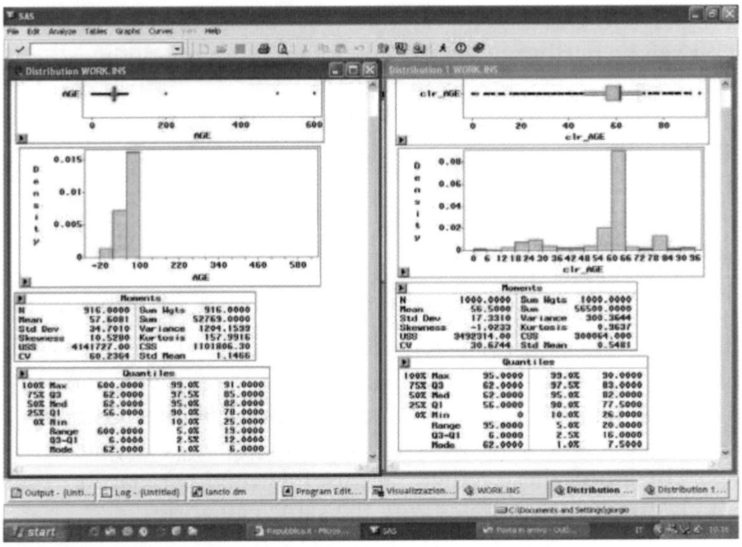

Figure 3: Box plot and histogram in reference and final data for variable Age

Relating to the use of *test of hypothesis* in the context of Official Statistics, it has to be underlined that it is always difficult to introduce a model in survey investigations, and in addition non-parametric methods require few assumptions about the underlying population from which data are obtained. Furthermore, most of the classical distribution-free tests are based on the assumptions that the random variables to be tested are independent random samples, and this property is not always satisfied in complex survey designs often adopted by NSOs. For these reasons, we propose only descriptive statistics.

d) Categorical variables (nominal or ordinal)

d.1) If Y is a categorical variable, the evaluation of the impact of E&I on its univariate distribution can be performed by using the following dissimilarity indices:

$$I_{m1} = \frac{1}{2}\sum_{k=1}^{K}\left| f_{Y_k}^{R} - f_{Y_k}^{F} \right|$$

$$I_{m2} = \left\{ \frac{1}{2}\sum_{k=1}^{K}\left| f_{Y_k}^{R} - f_{Y_k}^{F} \right|^{2} \right\}^{\frac{1}{2}}$$

where $f_{Y_k}^{R}$ and $f_{Y_k}^{F}$ are respectively the frequency of category k (possibly weighted) in the reference and in the final datasets. Both these measures assume their minimum value 0 only if the two distributions are exactly the same, while they assume the maximum value 1 when in each distribution all units have the same category of Y but that category is different in the two distributions.

It is obvious that information on changes of marginal distributions is also provided in the transition matrices so far introduced.

d.2) Graphical representations of the frequency distributions of Y in the two compared data sets permit the visual analysis of the changes of distributions due to E&I (see point a.5 in subsection 2.1).

d.3) If Y and X are two categorical variables, the evaluation of the impact of E&I on their joint distribution can be performed by using the two following indices:

$$I_{j1} = \frac{1}{2}\sum_{y}\sum_{x}\left|f_{yx} - \tilde{f}_{yx}\right|,$$

$$I_{j2} = \left\{\frac{1}{2}\sum_{y}\sum_{x}\left|f_{yx} - \tilde{f}_{yx}\right|^{2}\right\}^{\frac{1}{2}}$$

where f_{yx} and $\tilde{f}_{yx}$ are respectively the frequencies (possibly weighted) of the contingency table obtained by crossing the categories of Y and X. The indices assume values in the interval [0,1] and they can be easily extended to any set of k variables ($k \geq 2$) to make analyses on multiple distributions. Note that for variable combinations assuming few categories, I_{j1} and I_{j1} can have a value lower than the value corresponding to variable combinations having many categories. Therefore, these indices are useful when comparing results produced by different E&I methods on sets of variables with the same categories.

e) Continuous variables

e.1) If Y is a continuous variable, the Kolmogorov-Smirnov index (KS) is used to assess the difference between the marginal distributions of the variable in the compared data sets. Let Y^R_n, Y^F_n be respectively the values of Y in the reference and final data sets containing n units, and let

$$F_{Y_n^R}(t) = \frac{\sum_{i=1}^{n} w_i \times I(Y_i^R \leq t)}{\sum_{i=1}^{n} w_i}, \quad F_{Y_n^F}(t) = \frac{\sum_{i=1}^{n} w_i \times I(Y_i^F \leq t)}{\sum_{i=1}^{n} w_i}$$

be the weighted empirical distribution functions in the reference and final datasets. The KS distance is defined as:

$$KS(F_{Y_n^R}, F_{Y_n^F}) = max_t\left|F_{Y_n^R}(t) - F_{Y_n^F}(t)\right| = max_j\left|F_{Y_n^R}(t_j) - F_{Y_n^F}(t_j)\right|$$

where the $\{t_j\}$ values are the ordered values of Y. It results $KS=0$ only when $F_{Y_n^R}(t_j) = F_{Y_n^F}(t_j) \ \forall \{t_j\}$.

e.2) A set of statistics can be used in a straightforward way to obtain information on distributions changes, like the variable *mean* and *standard deviation*, the distribution *quartiles*, the *minimum* and *maximum* values of the variable Y.

e.3) A deepest analysis of changes in the marginal distribution of Y in the reference and final data sets can be performed through graphical representations of data like those mentioned in subsection 2.1 (see point c.5). Useful univariate statistics are directly provided in graphs.

2.3 Preservation of aggregates

The impact of E&I on statistical aggregates is generally evaluated in terms of: 1) non-sampling components of the variance of the aggregate estimate due to non sampling errors and E&I activities, and 2) distance between the final estimate of the aggregate and the corresponding original one.

Concerning the first aspect, it is well known that when estimating statistical parameters in presence of non-response and imputation, the variance of estimates gets inflated due to these non-sampling variability components. The most used approaches for correctly estimating variance in presence of these factors are re-sampling techniques (see, among others, Lee *et. al.*, 2001; Rao, 2001; Beaumont *et al.*, 2002) and multiple imputation (Rubin, 1987; Schafer, 1997). These aspects are not considered at this stage of research, they represent a critical area for possible future developments.

Concerning point 2), it does not take into account the different mechanisms or models underlying the generation of errors (missing and inconsistent values). In this context, the evaluation can be carried on by simply analysing the differences between point estimates of the target parameters, before and after E&I. For continuous variables, some standard aggregates (*sum of variable values, standard deviation, mean,* etc.) are directly provided by IDEA (see point c.5 in subsection 2.1, and points e.2 and e.3 in subsection 2.2).

2.4 Preservation of relations

Measuring the effects of E&I on data relations is a relevant problem to be considered when evaluating E&I. In the area of data imputation, fundamental references are the papers from Kalton *et al.* (1982), Kalton *et al.* (1986) and Little (1986). Recent research relates particularly to regression imputation (Shao *et al.*, 2002), but further research is needed with respect to other imputation techniques.
One traditional way of evaluating this aspect consists in analysing changes produced by E&I on the structure of data relations of reference data.

f) Categorical variables (nominal or ordinal)

f.1) If Y and X are categorical variables subject to E&I (either both or only one of them), the *Cramer contingency coefficient* (Kendall *et al.*, 1979) before and after the E&I process is proposed for evaluating changes in the bivariate relation between them used. For each compared data set, the *Cramer contingency coefficient* is based on the χ^2 index computed on the basis of the differences among the frequencies of the two-way contingency table crossing the r categories of Y and the c categories of X, and the corresponding theoretical frequencies. The index is equal to 0 when Y and X are not associated, while it is equal to 1 in case of complete association. Note that the index I_3 previously introduced (see subsection 2.2, point d.3) provides summary information about overall E&I effects on multivariate relationships.

g) Continuous variables

g.1) For the evaluation of the effects of E&I on bivariate relations between two continuous variables Y and X the usual measures (covariances and correlations) in the reference and in the final data sets can be used. In each data set, for each couple of items subject to E&I the following measure are then proposed:
- the *matrix of covariances*,
- the *matrix of Pearson correlations indices*.

3. DOCUMENTING EDITING AND IMPUTATION PROCESSES

The quality indicators described in section 2 refer to the evaluation of the E&I process. However, further standard quality indicators on E&I have been defined at ISTAT with documentation purposes. These indicators can also be calculated by IDEA, but they should then be imported and stored in the Information System for Survey Documentation (SIDI). As already mentioned, SIDI is the centralized information system for standard documentation of the whole data production process (from the design to the dissemination stage) for each ISTAT survey. Both a qualitative and a quantitative perspective are considered in SIDI. The documentation of E&I procedures and the standard quality indicators related to E&I are included among the more extensive information available in the SIDI system. In order to understand the framework for documentation implemented at ISTAT, the SIDI system is described in the next subsections. Besides a summary description of the whole system (subsection 3.1), particular attention is devoted to the SIDI standard quality indicators related to E&I and the interaction between SIDI and IDEA.

3.1 The SIDI system

Improving and documenting the quality of survey processes and products is a major concern for many NSOs.

The SIDI system has been designed and implemented in order to support the survey managers in such activities (Brancato *et al.*, 2004). The main purposes of the SIDI system are:

- to support the survey managers in monitoring and documenting the quality of their surveys;
- to compare the quality of different surveys;
- to provide ISTAT management with periodic reports concerning the quality of ISTAT surveys.

A very important characteristic of the SIDI system is that it manages both metadata and quality indicators in an integrated way. Indeed, besides the documentation purposes, metadata are also necessary in order to correctly interpret the quality indicators. For instance, the quality of the editing and imputation phase can be better analyzed if quantitative indicators are integrated by some information concerning the editing and imputation procedures that have been applied.

SIDI manages the following classes of metadata: i) metadata related to the information content of the survey (e.g. observed phenomena, statistical units,…); ii) metadata related to the production process, in particular the description of all the performed survey operations and of the survey quality control activities which have been carried out in order to prevent nonsampling errors, to correct them and to estimate their impact on final estimates; and iii) relevant documentation concerning specific surveys (e.g. internal documents, instructions for manual editing,…) as well as general documents (e.g. Eurostat regulations and documents on quality, …).

It is worth underlining that the quality indicators managed in SIDI are process oriented. In particular, they have been defined in order to allow the survey managers to monitor and to analyze over time the quality of the main survey phases. Indeed, the process-oriented indicators are less expensive to be calculated and are therefore a good starting point in order to create a common and standard level of quality measurement within an Institution. It can be added that sometimes process indicators might provide some insight on product quality and that improving the process quality has been largely recognized as one tool to achieve a better product quality (Lyberg et alt., 2001). To this purpose a set of quality indicators has been defined for the following survey aspects: frame; data collection, data entry, editing and imputation, timeliness, costs, and coherence. The quality indicators related to the editing and imputation phase are described in detail in subsection 3.3. Furthermore, the quality indicators are to be calculated for each survey occasion. Therefore, the system manages time series of each group of indicators and is equipped with a large set of graphical and tabular representations.

Finally, we note that in order to allow comparisons among different surveys both metadata and quality indicators have been highly standardized.

3.2 Implementing the SIDI system

The implementation of the SIDI system started in 2001. As it is well known, implementing and maintaining up-to-date information systems is a demanding task. Even if documentation is recognized as an important aspect of quality, it is a time-consuming activity and survey managers do not usually consider it as part of their current production work (Blanc *et al.*, 2001). Therefore, it is important to have a strategy for populating and keeping information systems updated.

In particular, the SIDI system has a considerable impact on current statistical activity. In fact, survey managers are required not only to provide metadata on the information content and the production process, but also to calculate groups of standard quality indicators for each survey occasion. Both aspects (documentation of survey metadata and calculation of standard indicators) require specific training and knowledge of the system definitions and functionalities. However, the calculation of quality indicators has the greatest impact from a technical and organisational point of view. With regard to survey metadata, the bigger effort is needed the first time the survey manager has to document her/his survey. Once the survey documentation has been completed, the metadata only need to be updated when a change occurs. Differently, the standard quality indicators have to be calculated for each survey occasion. Thus, their calculation implies an additional amount of work for the survey managers. Furthermore, for certain surveys it might be necessary to review some procedures in order to be able to calculate the SIDI indicators.

The awareness of such problems has brought us to define a strategy for the implementation of the SIDI system. Three main aspects of such a strategy are to be mentioned:

1. The net of quality facilitators. The quality facilitator is a new professional role for ISTAT that has been introduced for supporting the release of SIDI. More in detail, they are experts of quality issues and of the SIDI system whose task is to document and update the survey metadata, and to calculate the standard quality indicators. After attending an especially designed training course, the quality facilitators are formally appointed. It is foreseen to train a quality facilitator for each ISTAT survey, thus creating a net in the Institute. Up to now, some 65 people have already been trained.

2. The development of generalized software to support the survey managers in the computation of standard quality indicators. As already mentioned, the quality indicators managed into SIDI are process oriented. This means that they could be obtained as a by-product of the survey production process itself. Furthermore, different production processes can be considered similar with respect to the evaluation of a given set of standard quality indicators. For example; we can mention the "data entry" quality indicators for all those surveys that use external companies. For these surveys, ISTAT applies the same quality control procedure for assessing the quality of data entry. Therefore, it is planned to develop a generalized procedure for the calculation of the SIDI indicators related to this phase. The availability of generalized software for calculating quality indicators is one of the major supports that could be provided to survey managers in order to simplify and speed up their work. In fact, a main purpose is to integrate as much as possible the quality activity into statistical production processes. The software IDEA has been developed in order to satisfy also these purposes and it is now currently used to provide quality indicators for the SIDI system (see subsection 3.4).

3. The integration between SIDI and other local information systems or data bases where relevant information for the calculation of quality indicators is stored. Examples are the information system for monitoring the data collection phase for business structural statistics and the database with information on data collection related to the multipurpose surveys.

3.3 SIDI Quality indicators for Editing and Imputation

With regard to the editing and imputation phase, survey managers are asked to provide metadata on the editing technique (e.g. manual, interactive, automatic) and on the methodology for detecting and correcting the errors (e.g. deterministic or stochastic methods), as well as one or more sets of quality indicators on the impact of editing and imputation procedures on data (Fortini *et al.*, 2000). The SIDI set of standard quality indicators on E&I is described in table 1.

As a result of the process-oriented approach, all the required indicators can be obtained by comparing the raw and the final data matrices. This means that every survey that uses an E&I procedure can provide the SIDI indicators, regardless to the characteristics of the procedure (i.e. deterministic or stochastic).

While the main aim of collecting metadata in a centralized system is documentation, the presence of quality indicators could be useful also for evaluation purposes. In fact, the first group of indicators (1 to 15) concerns the overall impact of E&I procedures on the data matrix. In particular, the first three indicators provide the data matrix dimension, while the remaining ones measure specific aspects of E&I performance. For example, the imputation rate is the percentage of survey data modified in some way by the E&I procedure. It can be interpreted as "how much E&I have modified the original data". The percent composition of imputation rate suggests what the major problems are in the overall quality of collected (raw) data. A high percentage of net imputation indicates the presence of item non-response problems. Otherwise, a high percentage of modification is a sign that erroneous values are the main problem; it can then be investigated if these errors are originated by data collection or data entry. Indicators 16 to 23 concern the distributions of imputation rate by variables and by records. The indicators in this subset are voluntarily not very sensitive. They are meaningful only in the case that the impact of E&I on data is quite strong and they work as an alarm bell that indicates problems on the original data or on the E&I procedure. In fact, through the analysis of these indicators, it is possible to discover, for example, if the E&I procedure tends to work heavily on a few variables. In general terms, this subset of indicators can be useful in order to understand the behaviour of the E&I procedure: for example, if the values of these indicators are generally low, it means that the E&I procedure doesn't modify so much the data and there aren't groups of variables or records more affected than others.

As already mentioned, a survey manager can provide one or more sets of quality indicators. In fact, in a survey, different techniques and methods for E&I can be used and there can be more than one data matrix, for example related to different statistical units. Typically, household surveys have a matrix in which each record is a household and it contains only the information collected on the household itself, and another data matrix in which each record refers to an individual (household component). Furthermore, most ISTAT surveys are sampling ones, and obviously in order to evaluate the real impact of E&I on estimates it is necessary to calculate weighted standard indicators that take into account the sample weight of each statistical unit. In detail, a survey manager, for each survey occasion, has to provide two principal sets of quality indicators, one weighted and one un-weighted, related to the most important survey data matrix (e.g. statistical unit), and to the most relevant E&I methodology (if it is possible to split the different E&I steps). Then, he/she can provide other sets of quality indicators related to other statistical units and/or E&I techniques.

Table 1. Indicators on the quality of editing and imputation phase and their formulae

N	INDICATORS	FORMULAE OR DEFINITIONS
1	Total Records	
2	Total Variables	
3	Total Imputable Variables	Number of potentially imputable variables by the editing procedures[4].
4	Imputation Rate	Values modified by E&I / potentially imputable values[5]
5	Modification Rate	Changes from a value to a different imputed value / potentially imputable values
6	Net Imputation Rate	Changes from blank to a different imputed value / potentially imputable values
7	Cancellation Rate	Changes from a value to an imputed blank / potentially imputable values
8	Non Imputation Rate	Values not transformed by E&I / potentially imputable values
9	Blank Unmodified Values Rate	Blank unmodified values / potentially imputable values
10	Non Blank Unmodified Values Rate	Non blank unmodified values / potentially imputable values
Percent Components of Imputation Rate		
11	% of Modification	Changes from a value to a different imputed value / imputed values
12	% of Net Imputation	Changes from blank to a different imputed value / imputed values
13	% of Cancellation	Changes from a value to an imputed blank / imputed values
Percent Components of Non Imputation Rate		
14	% of Blank Unmodified Values	Blank unmodified values / non imputed values
15	% of Non Blank Unmodified Values	Non blank unmodified values / non imputed values
Indicators referred to Imputation Rate Distribution		
16	First Quartile of Imputation Rate Distribution by VARIABLE	Value of the imputation rate leaving the 25% of the ordered variables to the left
17	Third Quartile of Imputation Rate Distribution by VARIABLE	Value of the imputation rate leaving the 75% of the ordered variables to the left
18	Number of Variables with an imputation Rate greater than 5%	
19	Number of Variables with an Imputation Rate greater than 2%	
20	First Quartile of Imputation Rate Distribution by RECORD	*Value of the imputation rate leaving the 25% of the ordered units to the left*
21	Third Quartile of Imputation Rate Distribution by RECORD	Value of the imputation rate leaving the 75% of the ordered units to the left
22	Number of Records with an Imputation Rate greater than 5%	
23	Number of Records with an Imputation Rate greater than 2%	

For the principal sets of indicators, the system, besides the indicators' computation and tabular representation, provides various specifically designed functionalities for further analysis. Firstly, the

[4] Some variables might be excluded from the imputation process (e.g. identification codes)

[5] Potentially imputable values= Total records* Total imputable variables

indicators on the overall impact of E&I procedures on the data matrix can be analysed with regard to geographical detail. The system offers graphical representations (maps) of the indicators that permit subject matter experts to identify troubles in particular geographical areas. Through this functionality it is possible to perform a high level territorial monitoring of the quality of collected data. Secondly, through time series graphical representations, the system allows survey managers to monitor over time the values of various indicators. Using this functionality, they are able to evaluate the performance of the E&I procedure and its impact on their data through consecutive survey occasions. Finally, it is possible to make different types of comparisons for better evaluating the quality of survey data:

1. For a given survey, the system permits to compare the value of an indicator with a general mean value, obtained averaging the values of the same indicator for all surveys.
2. Furthermore, the comparison can be done with particular averages calculated within subgroup of surveys that use the same E&I methodology.
3. At last, it is possible to compare the values of the same indicator in different surveys.

3.4 The role of IDEA for SIDI quality indicators

In order to assure that SIDI quality indicators are calculated in the same standard way by each survey, quality facilitators are asked to provide in SIDI the numerators and the denominators (input values) needed for calculating the quality indicators and the system itself calculates them. After that, the indicators can be analysed (time series and/or geographical analyses) and compared (among different surveys and with general and specific mean values). With regard to E&I, the input values to be inserted in SIDI are reported in table 1. To this purpose, quality facilitators need to compare raw and clean data sets for the same survey occasion. This would have required the quality facilitators to prepare some ad hoc programmes in order to calculate the input values for SIDI, implying possible errors in computations and loss in timeliness. As mentioned before, such a work was needed for every survey using an E&I procedure, regardless to the procedure used (i.e. deterministic or stochastic imputation). Therefore, the best way to support quality facilitators in this specific task was to develop generalized software that could automatically produce the input values for SIDI by comparing raw and clean data sets. The software IDEA easily provides such values in a standard way for all ISTAT surveys.

A quality facilitator who wants to use IDEA to calculate SIDI indicators has only to provide the raw and clean SAS datasets with the following requirements: i) corresponding variables in the two datasets should have the same names; ii) both datasets should contain variable representing the records' id; iii) a variable that identifies the geographical area should be present in at least one of the two datasets. In addition, if the weighted set of indicators is calculated, a variable containing the weights should be present in the clean dataset. Such organized datasets are generally already available or easily obtainable for each survey. Starting from this input, IDEA provides an output file containing the SIDI input values, in a specific format that can be directly imported in SIDI. Furthermore, IDEA displays the SIDI indicators, and therefore the quality facilitator can control the values before importing them in SIDI (Figure 4).

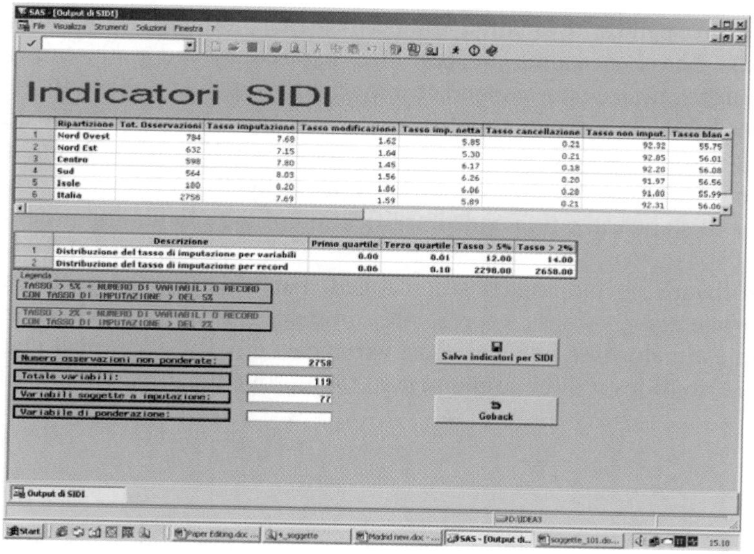

Figure 4: Output of IDEA for SIDI

Other relevant typologies of quality indicators can be calculated considering the SIDI indicators computable with IDEA as a starting point.

In particular, the un-weighted imputation rate proposed by the Eurostat Task Force on Standard Quality Indicators (Linden and Papageorgiou, 2004) corresponds to the SIDI imputation rate obtained considering only one variable as "potentially imputable".

Furthermore, it is possible to use IDEA to compare datasets related to subgroups of units, or to specific intermediate sub-phases of the E&I procedure. The resulting indicators could then be used for more specific evaluation purposes by survey managers and could also be stored in local databases.

IDEA has gained a big success among the quality facilitators: all the ones that have provided the indicators on E&I in SIDI have used IDEA for all the survey occasions. In addition, the use of IDEA for SIDI stimulates them to perform further analysis. For example, when big changes in data were enhanced by SIDI E&I indicators, they tried to understand in which phase of the production process the errors corrected by E&I where mostly originated, and, if possible, took actions in order to avoid them in successive survey occasions.

Finally, it is worth mentioning the added value of having the possibility of performing the documentation activity required by the SIDI system for the E&I phase with the same generalized software that can be used to tune and monitor the E&I process. In fact, given the potentialities of IDEA, once it has been used to calculate SIDI indicators, the other available measures for evaluating the quality of E&I or assessing its impact on data distributions and relations are often calculated by the users, thus stimulating a quality assessment that would not have been performed without this powerful tool. Consequently, the availability of IDEA facilitates the standard documentation in SIDI and the fact that SIDI has to be populated stimulates the use of IDEA as a tool for the assessment of the production procedure.

4. CONCLUDING REMARKS AND FUTURE WORK

Information on the quality and the impact of E&I is not only a requirement at NSO level, but also a powerful tool that survey managers can use to better understand data and process characteristics. Improvements in the short and medium run can be produced on the basis of indications provided by the analysis of the performance of E&I activities on specific items, units, and errors. In this paper we proposed an evaluation framework in which different indices and statistical measures are defined, based on specific evaluation (or performance) criteria, which can be used in different evaluation contexts. These measures are partially inspired by the evaluation measures used in the Euredit project. Further indices correspond to the standard quality indicators required by the ISTAT information system SIDI. In order to simplify and make more efficient the evaluation task, as well as to support subject-matter experts, the generalized software IDEA for computing all the proposed indicators has been developed. IDEA is currently used by ISTAT survey managers because of its usefulness in terms of standardization and simplification of the calculation process.

Further software developments are planned, particularly relating to the evaluation of E&I effects on multivariate distributions. Appropriate summary measures are also needed to better evaluate the E&I impact on estimates like totals, means, variances. Finally, additional graphical representations of data and data distributions will be implemented to improve the effectiveness of the evaluation.

References

[1] Beaumont J.-F., Mitchell C. (2002). The System for Estimation of Variance due to Nonresponse and Imputation (SEVANI), *Proceedings of the Statistics Canada Symposium 2002, Modelling Survey Data for Social and Economic Research* (to appear).

[2] Blanc M., Lundholm G., Signore M. (2001). LEG chapter: Documentation, *Proceedings of the International Conference on Quality in Official Statistics*, Stockholm 14-15 May 2001, CD-ROM.

[3] Brancato G., Pellegrini C., Signore M., Simeoni G. (2004). Standardising, Evaluating and Documenting Quality: the implementation of ISTAT Information System for Survey Documentation – SIDI, *European Conference on quality and methodology in Official statistics*, Mainz, May 24-26 2004, CD-ROM.

[4] Chambers R. (2001). Evaluation Criteria for Statistical Editing and Imputation, *National Statistics Methodology Series* no 28, Office for National Statistics.

[5] Charlton J. (2003). First results from the EUREDIT project – Evaluating Methods for Data Editing and Imputation, *Proceedings of the 54th ISI Session*, Berlin, 13-20 August (to appear).

[6] Di Zio M., Manzari A., Luzi O. (2001). Evaluating Editing and Imputation Processes: the Italian Experience, *UN/ECE Work Session on Statistical Data Editing*, Helsinky, Finland, May 27-29.

[7] Eurostat (2000), *Standard Quality Report*, Eurostat Working Group on Assessment of Quality in Statistics, Eurostat/A4/Quality/00/General/Standard Report, Luxembourg, April 4-5.

[8] Fortini M., Scanu M., Signore M. (2000). Use of indicators from data editing for monitoring the quality of the survey process: the Italian information system for survey documentation (SIDI), *Statistical Journal of the United Nations ECE*, n.17, pp. 25-35.

[9] Granquist, L. (1997). An overview of Methods of Evaluating Data Editing Procedures. In *Statistical Data Editing Methods and Techniques Vol. II*, Conference of European Statisticians, United Nations, 1997.

[10] Kalton, G., Kasprzyk, D. (1986). The treatment of missing survey data, *Survey Methodology*, 12, No 1, 1-16.

[11] Kalton, G., Kasprzyk, D. (1982). Imputing for missing survey responses, *Proceedings of the section on Survey Research Methods, American Statistical Association*, pp. 22-31.

[12] Kendall M., Stuart A. (1979). *The Advanced Theory of Statistics, Vol II: Inference and Relationship*. Griffin, London.

[13] Lee H., Rancourt E., Särndal C.-E. (2001). Variance Estimation from Survey Data under Single Imputation. In Groves R.M., Dillman D.A., Eltinge J.L., Little R.J.A. (eds), *Survey Nonresponse*, New-York:John Wiley&Sons, Inc., pp. 315-328.

[14] Linden H., Papageorgiou H. (2004). Standard Quality Indicators, *European Conference on quality and methodology in Official statistics*, Mainz, May 24-26 2004, CD-ROM.

[15] Little, R.J.A. (1986). Survey nonresponse adjustments for estimates of means, *International Statistical Review*, 54, pp. 139-157.

[16] Lyberg L. et al. (2001). Summary Report from the Leadership Group (LEG) on Quality", *Proceedings of the International Conference on Quality in Official Statistics*, Stockholm 14-15 May 2001, CD-ROM.

[17] National Center for Education Statistics (1992). *NCES Statistical Standards.*

[18] Norbotten S. (2000). *Evaluating Efficiency of Statistical Data Editing: A General Framework*, United Nations, 2000.

[19] Rao, J.N.K. (2001). Variance Estimation in the Presence of Imputation for Missing Data. *Proceedings of the Second International Conference on Establishment Surveys (ICESII)*, pp. 599-608.

[20] Rubin, D. (1987). *Multiple Imputation in Surveys*. John Wiley & Sons.

[21] Schafer, J.L. (1997). *Analysis of Incomplete Multivariate Data*, Chapman & Hall.

[22] Shao, J. and Wang, H. (2002). Sample Correlation Coefficients Based on Survey Data under Regression Imputation, *Journal of the America Statistical Association*, Vol. 97, pp. 544-552.

CHARACTERISATION OF QUALITY IN SAMPLE SURVEYS USING PRINCIPAL COMPONENTS ANALYSIS

By Paul Smith, Office for National Statistics, and Paula Weir, U.S. Department of Energy

1. INTRODUCTION

There are several components of quality, and classifications to describe all of these components have been devised and applied over the last 15 years (Groves 1989, Davies & Smith 1999.) In order to get some overall measure of quality, Groves (1989) also uses the concept of *total survey error*, where the biases and variances are all evaluated and put together to give an estimate of the overall mean square error (MSE) of the estimated survey values. This measure captures overall quality, but is extremely difficult and expensive to evaluate.

Instead of taking such a minute approach, we can think of quality as a multivariate measure for any dataset. Each of the quality indicators developed by Groves (1989), Davies & Smith (1999) then becomes one dimension of the overall quality. However, these dimensions are often interrelated – a low quality response from a particular sample unit will typically affect several indicators – so the amount of additional information obtained from a new indicator may be relatively small.

In order to make the assessment of quality as straightforward (and inexpensive) as possible, it would be good to concentrate on a small number of indicators that provide most of the information about the data quality. In this paper, this is achieved from a relatively wide-ranging set of the most easily calculated indicators by using principal component analysis to find the measures which best capture the underlying variation in the data quality measures. These key measures provide direction for determining which quality indicators should be calculated and maintained for an overall view of data quality, and provide information about the role of measures on data editing failures in the overall quality view.

2. THE APPROACH

Principal component analysis is a procedure that is used to reduce the observed variables to a smaller dimension by identifying variables that may be redundant or correlated. The aim is to identify a smaller number of artificial variables or principal components that account for most of the variance of the observed variables (see for example, Mardia, Kent & Bibby, 1979.) A principal component is a linear combination of the (standardised) observed variables weighted so that the resulting component maximizes the variance accounted for in the data. The weights are obtained by solving eigenequations that satisfy the principle of least squares. The eigenvalue represents the amount of variance accounted for by the associated component. A number of components are actually extracted, but usually only the first few components account for a meaningful amount of the variance. Only these few components are retained and interpreted. The values of the resulting variables are not interpretable in an empirical sense, but represent a mapping of the observed variable space onto a space of lower dimension. Principal component analysis is similar to factor analysis, but factor analysis assumes an underlying causal model.

In principal component analysis, each of the observed variables is first standardized with a mean of zero and variance of one, so that total variance is equal to the number of observed variables. Each component accounts for the maximum remaining variance of the observed standardized variables not accounted for by the previous components and is uncorrelated with the each of the previous components. Solutions for which the components remain uncorrelated are orthogonal solutions.

A variable that is given a large weight in constructing a principal component is said to have a high loading for that component. If possible, it is best to have three or more variables loading on each retained component at completion, so more variables are specified at the onset of the analysis to allow for variables to be dropped during the analysis. Usually the analysis is conducted in a sequence of steps starting with the initial extraction of the components where the number of components extracted equals the number of variables being analyzed. Various criteria are then applied to determine how many components it is meaningful to retain. These include: the Kaiser or eigenvalue-one criterion (retain components with eigenvalues greater than 1.0); the scree test (plot of eigenvalues in descending order used to identify a break between high and low eigenvalues, and the respective components before the break); the specified proportion of variance accounted for in the data (the component eigenvalue divided by the total number of variables analyzed is greater than the specified percentage); and the interpretability criterion (a shared conceptual meaning among the variables that load on a component, the differentiation between components, and the rotated factor demonstrates simple structure with respect to the variable loadings). After the meaningful components are extracted, the unrotated factor pattern matrix is created which provides the factor loadings. The solution is normally rotated to make the solution easier to interpret. The interpretation involves identifying the variables with high loadings in a component and determining the commonality among the variables. The final solution is then evaluated to determine if it satisfies the interpretability criteria.

3. APPLICATION OF PRINCIPAL COMPONENTS ON PERFORMANCE MEASURES

Survey Data-- First Example

The survey from the UK used in this first example is the Monthly Inquiry into the Distribution and Services Sector (MIDSS), a monthly survey collecting turnover and employment information (employment from a subsample only) from a stratified sample of businesses in wholesaling and the services (but excluding retailing). Six of the survey variables are used in the analysis here:

- turnover (question code 40)
- employees (50)
- male full-time employees (51)
- male part-time employees (52)
- female full-time employees (53)
- female part-time employees (54)

The last four variables should sum to total employees. In this example, data from September 1999 are used to illustrate the approach.

Performance Indicators

Several performance measures about the survey variables are also available. The nine measures used here can be categorized into three areas of quality:

Sampling
Sampling is the most easily measured component of quality from a design-based perspective, because appropriate theory is available. The two measures available are:

1. sampling fraction
2. sampling error

Response rate

Response rate is used as an indicator of the possible size of non-response error. Several versions are used here:

3. "basic" response rate – good responses/sample size;
4. return rate – all returned questionnaires/sample size;

(the difference between the two indicators above will contain some information about the quality of the sampling frame, as it will capture the number of dead or out of scope sample members)

5. weighted response rate – response by an auxiliary variable (i.e., register turnover)
6. weighted return rate

Data editing indicators

Data editing indicators reflect both of the quality of the data contained in the responses and the quality of the data editing process. A number of different aspects are used here:

7. number of warnings (non-fatal edits) subsequently cleared without change
8. number of warnings leading to changes
9. number of errors (fatal edits) subsequently corrected

The actual set of edit rules (not optimised in this case) is given in annex 1.

These 9 indicators give 46 variables for use in this analysis – one for each of 6 survey variables, except for indicator 1 (all variables have the same sampling fraction) and indicator 9 (no fatal edit failures for the four subdivisions of employment).

Principal Components

As previously stated, the aim of principal components is to find the linear combinations of groups of related variables that have the largest variation. In order for the procedure to be used, a reasonably large number of observations is needed, so the indicators need to be calculated on a range of domains. There is undoubtedly a number of ways in which these domains could be devised, but the choice made here is to calculate them by stratum. There are 144 strata containing usable information in MIDSS.

In order to avoid the variability of measures with large units swamping the measures with small units, the columns (variables) are standardised by subtracting the mean and dividing by the standard deviation, before principal components analysis is undertaken.

Results

The 46 variables resolve into 32 distinct principal components. The remaining 14 variables are collinear (or very nearly so) with other variables in the dataset. For example, a number of the response rates for different questions show high co linearity, as there is little item non-response in this survey. The first 5 principal components explain approximately 78% of the variability in the data; the actual proportions of the variability are shown in Table 1.

Table 1. Factor Pattern

Principal component	Proportion of variation explained (%)	Cumulative proportion of variance explained (%)
1	40.49	40.49
2	19.63	60.13
3	8.23	68.35
4	6.89	75.24
5	3.13	78.37
6	2.41	80.78
7	2.30	83.08
8	2.16	85.24
9	1.85	87.09
10	1.64	88.74
11-32	11.26	100.00
33-46	0.00	100.00

The loadings (coefficients pre-multiplying the input variables to derive the principal components) give some information on what the main determinants of the principal components are (the larger coefficients show which variables are most important in each principal component). Only the first five principal components are shown in Table 2. These seem to divide naturally between the main types of indicators. The first and third principal components are derived mostly from the response rates, and are shown lightly shaded in the table. The first component picks out the information in the various response rates to give an "overall response indicator" (since all the coefficients have the same sign). The third component, in contrast, picks out the difference between the weighted and unweighted response rates (as the coefficients for the basic response rate, indicator #3, and the return rate, indicator #4, have different signs than their weighted counterparts, indicators #5 and #6).

The similarity of the coefficients between the variables, and the way in which the coefficients divide into blocks by the indicator, and not by the variables, indicates that (very) little additional information is obtained by calculating the same indicators for another question in the survey, and that more information is obtained from an additional indicator. Only a few coefficients do not agree with the blocks within which they are placed. These coefficients in components 2 and 4 are more heavily shaded in Table 2 to identify them.

The second principal component picks out sampling errors through the coefficient of variation and sampling fraction indicators, and to a smaller degree, the (non-fatal) edit warnings which are identified by the editing process, but are unchanged after follow-up. All of these contribute to the underlying variability – two through the sampling variability, and one through the estimated population variance that is increased with more variable response data. Hence, we can interpret this pc as a "sampling variability" indicator. The number of unchanged non-fatal edits does not contribute substantially to any of the other first five pcs, and hence could legitimately be left unmeasured with little loss of information on this component.

The fourth pc picks out the fatal and non-fatal errors that *are* amended during the course of survey processing, reflecting a total "proportion of errors" indicator.

The fifth pc is a less easily interpretable combination of the sampling error and the non-fatal edits which are subsequently amended, mostly with opposite signs, suggesting some further aspect of underlying sampling variability.

The amount of extra information within each variable can also be interpreted with reference to the correlation matrix for the input variables (not shown), which indicates when variables are highly correlated and where one such variable may be sufficient.

Table 2

Indicator	Question code	Loadings in				
		PC 1	PC 2	PC 3	PC 4	PC 5
3. response rate (number)	40	0.20	-0.04	-0.16	-0.05	-0.02
	50	0.21	-0.03	-0.18	-0.04	0.00
	51	0.21	-0.02	-0.19	-0.03	0.03
	52	0.21	-0.02	-0.19	-0.03	0.03
	53	0.21	-0.02	-0.19	-0.03	0.03
	54	0.21	-0.02	-0.19	-0.03	0.03
5. response rate (turnover)	40	0.17	0.07	0.06	-0.03	-0.13
	50	0:19	0.10	0.21	0.03	-0.04
	51	0.20	0.11	0.20	0.04	-0.01
	52	0.20	0.11	0.20	0.04	-0.01
	53	0.20	0.11	0.20	0.04	-0.01
	54	0.20	0.11	0.20	0.04	-0.01
4. return rate (number)	40	0.20	-0.03	-0.18	-0.03	-0.01
	50	0.21	-0.03	-0.19	-0.01	0.00
	51	0.21	-0.02	-0.20	-0.00	0.03
	52	0.21	-0.02	-0.20	-0.00	0.03
	53	0.21	-0.02	-0.20	-0.00	0.03
	54	0.21	-0.02	-0.20	-0.00	0.03
6. return rate (turnover)	40	0.16	0.08	0.06	-0.02	-0.12
	50	0.19	0.10	0.21	0.04	-0.03
	51	0.20	0.11	0.20	0.05	-0.00
	52	0.20	0.11	0.20	0.05	-0.00
	53	0.20	0.11	0.20	0.05	-0.00
	54	0.20	0.11	0.20	0.05	-0.00
7. warnings cleared w/o amendment	40	-0.03	0.14	-0.06	0.20	0.03
	50	-0.01	0.20	-0.04	0.03	-0.03
	51	0.07	-0.17	0.03	-0.04	0.09
	52	0.04	-0.12	0.10	0.02	0.15
	53	0.06	-0.20	0.11	-0.06	0.09
	54	0.04	-0.22	0.16	-0.08	-0.10
8. warnings leading to amendments	40	-0.04	0.02	-0.07	0.44	-0.06
	50	-0.04	0.03	-0.08	0.42	-0.24
	51	0.02	-0.07	0.02	0.22	0.33
	52	0.02	-0.07	0.05	0.02	-0.22
	53	0.05	-0.19	0.06	0.17	0.43
	54	0.04	-0.18	0.05	0.11	0.43
2. coefficient of variation	40	-0.03	0.23	-0.10	-0.01	-0.02
	50	-0.05	0.27	-0.00	-0.09	0.26
	51	-0.04	0.27	0.00	-0.08	0.24
	52	-0.04	0.28	-0.10	-0.07	0.17
	53	-0.07	0.27	0.00	-0.08	0.23
	54	-0.05	0.28	-0.05	-0.08	0.20
1. samp fraction	40	0.06	-0.28	0.15	-0.11	0.06
	50	0.05	-0.28	0.17	-0.10	0.03
9. no of errors	40	-0.02	0.04	-0.08	0.45	-0.15
	50	0.01	-0.10	0.00	0.44	0.21

Survey Data - Second Example

The same method was also applied to survey data from the U.S. Energy Information Administration's Annual Fuel Oil and Kerosene Sales Report. This survey collects sales volume of major petroleum products by end-use sector by state from a cross-stratified sample of retailers and resellers. Six variables were also used in this analysis which were:

- No. 2 fuel oil sales for commercial use (product-line 11)
- Low sulfur No. 2 diesel sales for commercial use (product-line 12)
- High sulfur No. 2 diesel sales for commercial use (product-line 13)
- No. 2 fuel oil sales for industrial use (product-line 16)
- Low sulfur No. 2 diesel sales for industrial use (product-line 17)
- High sulfur No. 2 diesel sales for industrial (product-line 18)

The same performance indicators for these variables were used as in the first example to the extent that the data allowed. Indicator #9, number of fatal errors subsequently corrected, was not possible for this survey because fatal failures are immediately rejected and not even written to the database. In addition, for the sampling fraction, the same sampling rate applied to all variables. The same four types of response rates were also used. However, because there is no defined partial non-response in this survey, the response rate/return rate did not vary among the variables. Partial non-response may however be reflected in the edit warning indicators. The weighted response rates did vary among the variables because of the different weights used. Consequently, the eight resulting indicators in this example contain 33 variables for the analysis performed on the sampling stratum as the observation.

Results, Second Example

In this analysis, the first five principal components explained less of the variability than the first survey, only 65 %. The 78% level was not achieved until the ninth principal component as shown in Table 3 below.

Table 3

Principal component	Proportion of variation explained (%)	Cumulative proportion of variance explained (%)
1	31.02	31.02
2	17.92	48.94
3	5.79	54.73
4	5.52	60.26
5	4.32	64.58
6	4.00	68.58
7	3.41	71.99
8	3.15	75.13
9	2.78	77.91
10	2.74	80.65
11-32	19.34	99.99
33	0.01	100.00

For this example, the principal component analysis was performed first using SAS Princomp as was done for the first example, and then using the more flexible SAS Proc Factor, rotating the first six components, as suggested by the scree plot of the eigenvalues. However, no assumptions are made regarding an underlying causal structure responsible for covariation in the data. As compared to the procedure Princomp that yields eigenvectors, Proc Factor unrotated produces the eigenvector times the square root of the eigenvalue. The six components with the factor patterns highlighted as shown in Table 4 are interpretable.

Table 4. Rotated Factor Pattern

Indicator		Factor 1	Factor 2	Factor 3	Factor 4	Factor 5	Factor 6
3. Response rate		0.31	0.18	-0.15	0.01	-0.10	0.86
5. Response rate (weighted)	11	0.51	0.11	0.18	0.68	0.09	0.22
	12	0.84	0.15	0.08	0.11	0.09	0.22
	13	0.84	0.04	0.16	0.16	0.05	0.04
	16	0.64	-0.06	0.16	0.62	0.14	-0.05
	17	0.84	0.00	0.18	0.02	0.19	0.05
	18	0.88	-0.00	0.21	0.13	0.10	0.04
4. Return rate		0.30	0.18	-0.17	0.01	-0.10	0.86
6. Return rate (weighted)	11	0.48	0.18	0.17	0.68	0.10	0.23
	12	0.82	0.22	0.06	0.15	0.09	0.23
	13	0.83	0.11	0.14	0.17	0.04	0.05
	16	0.62	0.03	0.13	0.66	0.13	-0.03
	17	0.85	0.07	0.16	0.00	0.19	0.06
	18	0.88	0.08	0.18	0.13	0.09	-0.04
7. Warnings w/o change	11	0.12	-0.08	0.61	0.14	0.48	-0.08
	12	0.19	-0.01	0.73	-0.00	0.11	-0.09
	13	0.15	-0.16	0.78	-0.01	-0.05	-0.07
	16	0.11	-0.15	0.43	0.18	0.61	-0.05
	17	0.20	-0.07	0.67	0.10	0.20	0.06
	18	0.24	-0.21	0.75	-0.02	-0.01	-0.24
8. Warnings with change	11	0.07	-0.11	0.11	0.05	0.76	-0.01
	12	0.28	-0.07	-0.08	0.04	0.52	-0.14
	13	0.10	-0.16	-0.02	0.43	0.20	-0.08
	16	0.12	-0.17	0.13	0.07	0.72	0.05
	17	0.29	0.01	0.12	-0.30	0.06	0.08
	18	0.25	-0.26	0.08	-0.01	-0.03	-0.36
2. Coefficient var.	11	-0.08	0.73	0.04	0.25	-0.08	0.23
	12	-0.01	0.81	-0.13	-0.08	-0.10	0.16
	13	0.16	0.78	-0.14	-0.04	-0.13	0.07
	16	0.08	0.73	-0.10	0.42	-0.14	0.03
	17	0.25	0.73	-0.12	-0.26	-0.04	0.09
	18	0.30	0.76	-0.09	-0.12	-0.12	0.01
1. Sampling fraction		0.46	-0.51	0.45	0.22	0.30	-0.09

The rotated factors (using varimax rotation) correspond to:

1) Weighted response and return rate (with product-lines 11 and 16 having lower loadings than the other products)
2) Coefficients of Variation
3) Edit warnings resulting in no change (with product-lines 11 and 16 having lower loadings than the other products)
4) Product-lines 11 and 16 weighted return and response rate.
5) Product-lines 11 and 16 edit warnings resulting in change or no change, and product-line 12 edit warnings resulting in change.
6) Unweighted return and response rate.

The loadings in components 1, 3, 4 and 5 with respect to product-lines 11 and 16 may indicate the variability associated with potential (edit warnings without amendment) and actual (edit warnings leading to amendments) reporting errors classified as "line switching" that occur specifically between No.2 fuel oil commercial vs. industrial. The variability accounted for in these components may therefore be interpreted as reflecting partial or item non-response as part of the editing indicators for those particular variables The sampling fraction and the warnings resulting in change for product-lines 13, 17 and 18 do not follow a simple structure.

4. CONCLUSIONS

There are several components or dimensions of quality in sample surveys. However, an overall measure of the quality for a survey, such as total survey error through mean square error, is extremely difficult and expensive to evaluate. Because of the interrelationship of these dimensions, efficiency in measuring quality can be achieved by concentrating on the subset of indicators that provide most of the information about the data quality. Using two examples of business surveys, one a monthly survey of employment and turnover from the UK, and one an annual survey of sales volumes from the US, these efficiencies were realized by using principal component analysis to determine which measures best captured the underlying variation in the data quality measures.

In this study, both examples indicated that of the set of quality indicators common to many surveys (sampling rates, sampling errors, response rates, and data editing rates), response rates explained much of the variation from among the set of quality indicators. While weighted and unweighted response rates appeared to contain different information contributing to the explained variance, little additional information was generally gained in distinguishing between the return rate (all returned questionnaires/sample size) and the "basic" response rate (good responses/sample size). Furthermore, it was found that little additional information was gained by the use of different response rates for different questions. It was also demonstrated that sampling fractions and sampling errors were second in explaining the underlying variation but contain similar information. The number of non-fatal edit failures that were not amended supplemented this "sampling error" information. In addition, the UK example showed that fatal edits failures and non-fatal edits failures that do lead to amendment also contain similar information – one of these may be sufficient as an indicator. The US example further demonstrated that specific survey response items sometimes behave differently and may need separate indicators for response rates, and edit failure rates, amended and not-amended, to account for unique respondent behaviors such as line-switching of responses, a form of partial non-response.

References

[1] Davies, P. & Smith, P. (eds.) (1999) *Model Quality Reports in Business Statistics*. ONS, UK.

[2] Groves, R. (1989) *Survey errors and survey costs*. Wiley, New York.

[3] Mardia, K.V., Kent, J.T. & Bibby, J.M. (1979) *Multivariate Analysis*. Academic Press, London. SAS Institute Inc. *Chapter 1, Principal Component Analysis*, *//support.sas.com/ publishing/pubcat/chaps55129.pdf*

Section 2.2

IMPACT OF THE EDIT AND IMPUTATION PROCESSES ON DATA QUALITY AND EXAMPLES OF EVALUATION STUDIES

Foreword – Natalie Shlomo, Central Bureau of Statistics, Israel and Southampton Social Statistics Research Institute, University of Southampton, UK

This section includes five papers covering a wide range of evaluation studies on the effects of edit and imputation procedures on the quality of statistical data. The Whitridge-Bernier paper focuses on economic business data and compares the edit and imputation carried out at both the data collection stage and the data processing stage, and its impact on the quality of the final estimates. The analysis makes use of metadata collected at various stages of the survey processes for each statistical unit and shows the importance of gathering as much information as possible for analysing the quality of statistical data.

The Hoogland paper describes experiences in evaluating several important stages of edit and imputation procedures for economic business data: the effectiveness of selective editing criteria for determining which statistical units need to be manually reviewed and which can be treated automatically; and the evaluation of automatic software for edit and imputation. It describes the methodology and implementation of plausibility indicators for channeling the statistical units to the relevant phases of data processing. In addition, it defines cut-off points for selective editing criteria and test statistics for comparing the quality of the statistical data at different stages of the edit and imputation processes for the evaluation.

A wide range of test statistics for evaluating edit and imputation procedures on the quality of statistical data can be found in the Charlton paper. The paper describes results from the Euredit Project funded under the European Union's Fifth Framework research program, which brought together twelve partners from seven European countries to collaborate on the development and evaluation of edit and imputation methods. The aim of the project was to provide a statistical framework for comparing edit and imputation methods and for determining the optimal methods according to the statistical units in the data set, the pattern of non-response and the scope and amount of erroneous and missing values.

The last two papers evaluate software packages and algorithms of the error localization problem based on subjective and objective criteria. Error localization refers to the problem of changing as few fields as possible, so that all edit checks are satisfied. The Poirier paper gives a thorough functional comparison between software packages and evaluates them with respect to their strengths and limitations, the edit and imputation methods implemented, the type of statistical data that can be treated, online help and support and other subjective criteria. The De Waal paper compares sophisticated error localization algorithms for their optimality and computational speeds. Four algorithms are evaluated and compared on real numerical data sets with different patterns and amounts of errors.

THE IMPACT OF EDITING ON DATA QUALITY

By Patricia Whitridge and Julie Bernier, Statistics Canada

1. INTRODUCTION

The Project to Improve Provincial Economic Statistics (PIPES) is one of the largest and most important initiatives at Statistics Canada (Royce, 1998). It arose out of discussions in 1996 on sales tax harmonization between the Governments of Canada and several of the provinces. In three of the ten provinces, a common sales tax with a single collection authority was adopted, reducing the administrative burden on business. A formula to allocate the pooled revenues among the participating governments was determined and Statistics Canada was asked to provide detailed provincial economic data. In order to do so, Statistics Canada would need to substantially improve the quality of its statistics on provincial and territorial economies. By the end of 2000, Statistics Canada programs will be restructured and expanded to provide detailed and reliable economic accounts for the provinces and territories (Enterprise Statistics Division, 1998).

Approximately 200 separate business surveys are conducted regularly to gather data on different industries and commodities. Most of these will be integrated into a single master survey program called the Unified Enterprise Survey (UES). The new integrated approach focuses on enterprises: it will ensure that financial data collected from the enterprise's head office will be consistent with production and sales data received from its different establishments. The UES will collect more industry and commodity detail at the provincial level and avoid overlap between different survey questionnaires.

The UES is being designed to incorporate quality improvements in four areas: (i) better consistency of the methods used across industries, (ii) better coherence of the data collected from different levels of the business, (iii) better coverage of industries and (iv) better depth of information, in the sense of more content detail and estimates for more detailed domains. All of these objectives, but especially consistency, are easier to achieve with an integrated approach.

Presently, Statistics Canada encourages the consistent use of concepts, methods and procedures among the different surveys, through a number of mechanisms. These include the standard conceptual frameworks (such as the System of National Accounts (SNA)), standard classification systems (North American Industrial Classification System (NAICS)), a common business register, common staff pools for methodology, operations and systems development, and corporate policies related to survey-taking procedures.

The objective of this paper is to present the results of a study that was conducted to examine the impact of data editing on the quality of the final survey data and estimates. This first section has provided an introduction and a context for the study. The second section will discuss editing in general and at what stages different edits are applied. The Unified Enterprise Survey (UES) is presented in the following section, with more information about how editing is performed for the survey. The fourth section discusses in detail the study that was conducted. Descriptive information is given about the sample and what happened to it as the data moved through the different processes. The results section presents and compares several different sets of estimates that can be produced under different processing scenarios. Finally, some general conclusions are drawn.

2. THE EDITING PROCESS

Non-response is an ongoing problem in surveys dealing with economic data. Such data are often highly skewed and quantitative in nature, so it may be difficult to fill in the data holes caused by non-response. In addition, some survey responses may be invalid when considered either within a questionnaire, or as part of a set of questionnaires. Such errors happen because methods of creating records in files are not consistent, because questions are not fully understood, or because of transcription or coding problems (Kovar and Winkler, 1996). Edits are used to identify fields, parts of questionnaires, or, in some cases, entire questionnaires that need to be corrected.

Typically, edits are applied at several stages during the survey process. Initially, edits are applied during data capture, as part of a CATI application, or on the keying process. These edits seek to identify missing or erroneous information within a record. The result produced by these edits may involve follow-up or confirmation questions with the respondent, turning back to a completed questionnaire form, or referring a record on to imputation.

The second major application of edits occurs during the edit and imputation stage. Here, records that are incomplete after all attempts to complete them with information provided by the respondent are further verified. Additional checks are applied that will look at the data confirmed by the respondent in different ways. Statistical edits that examine a record in terms of many records, such as within an imputation class or group may be specified. Edits that examine the relationships between different fields within a record (correlational edits) are also used for quantitative data. The result produced by the edits at this stage is to send the record either for manual review or to an automatic imputation system.

3. EDITING THE UNIFIED ENTERPRISE SURVEY

For the UES, certain integrating principles were adopted, including the harmonization of concepts, definitions and questionnaires. This logically extends to the objective of developing common methodology for all steps of the survey, of which the processing systems are a part.

In terms of data collection, all sampled businesses were sent a mail-back paper questionnaire (Communications Division, 1998). Interviewers then telephoned if they needed to clarify any aspects of the reported information, or to follow-up with businesses that had not yet returned their questionnaires. Information could be adjusted or even collected directly over the phone, using a computer assisted telephone interviewing (CATI) system. The UES also offered a basic electronic reporting option for some of its questionnaires.

The processing systems for the UES are divided into logical steps. At each step, different edits are applied, and different actions are taken. During collection, edits are applied to identify missing 'key' variables, such as totals of revenues, expenses, and employment. Arithmetic edits that verify totals within a 2% tolerance are also applied at collection. Any unit failing an edit, be it arithmetic or for a 'key' variable, or a unit where a change in the industry class is suspected, is followed-up. This is done either as confirmation during a CATI interview, or as a separate contact with the respondent for paper questionnaires. During the pre-processing step of edit and imputation, some basic edits are applied that will result in some blanks being changed to zeroes, if it is obvious that such an action should take place. After these edits have been applied and the appropriate actions taken, the file will be called the 'RAW DATA' file, and is seen to represent the collected data. Given the collection system used for the UES Pilot, it is not possible to see the original data as reported by the respondent; it is then impossible to evaluate the impact of the follow-up procedure on the estimates.

The second series of edits are applied as part of the edit and imputation system. Different types of edits are applied, with different actions. If a record fails an edit in such a way that there is only one possible value that can be used to fix the record, then the record is corrected. This is known as a deterministic edit failure. In some cases, there are default values that are assigned, depending upon the situation. For example, in some industries, if no inventory is supplied, then it is assumed that there is no inventory and the field is set to zero. Lastly, any records with remaining edit failures are passed to donor imputation for correction. This imputation system is comprised of a pre-processing program that sets the stage for the donor imputation module. During the pre-processor, the data may be transformed (for example, the distribution of components of a total may be calculated) and some flags set for use by the donor module. After donor imputation, a pro-rate program is run, which adjusts imputed values to ensure that all totals are indeed equal to the sum of their parts, as well as calculating exact dollar amounts where distributions were imputed. Once edit and imputation has been completed, all records are clean and would pass the original edits as specified. Once the data have passed through edit and imputation, they are known as the 'PROCESSED DATA'.

The third step in the process is manual review, where subject matter experts manually examine the records and try to find a solution. The following records are reviewed manually: outliers, records that fail statistical edits, cases that the edit and imputation system cannot solve, and what are called 'critical imputed units'. This last category includes records that are very large or influential within their industry and province. Once the data have passed through manual review, they are considered to be 'FINAL DATA'.

4. THE STUDY

For the first year of the UES, seven industries were chosen to form the Pilot survey – industries previously without ongoing surveys. These industries are: aquaculture, taxis, couriers, lessors of real estate, real estate agents, food services and construction. There are four data collection vehicles for the UES, defined by the type of enterprise and the type of data (enterprise-level or establishment-level) required. For this study, analysis has been limited to one industry – taxis – and one type of questionnaire – that which collects establishment-level financial data. Specifically, the impact the editing process has on the quality of the final data will be analyzed, and this for revenues and expenses.

Table 1: The Sample

Sample size	320		
Out of scope (dead, inactive, etc.)	102 (32%)		
In scope	218 (68%)	Total non response	7 (3%)
		Questionnaires to process	175 (80%)
		Fully completed questionnaires	36 (17%)

As can be seen in Table 1 above, there were 320 units selected to be sent taxi questionnaires. After the field collection, 102 units were returned with response codes out of scope, for a variety of reasons, be it wrong industry, dead, inactive, unable to contact… Of the 218 that responded, and were in scope, 7 units provided no data at all, but it was possible to discern that they are still active in the taxi industry. 175 units were identified as needing some processing to complete the record. The remaining 36 questionnaires were fully completed and required no imputation at all even though they could require some missing fields to be changed to zeroes.

The first batch of edits was developed to provide a coherent set of checks that could be used for preliminary analysis for both the data collection process and the edit and imputation process. Additional correlational and statistical edits were applied at edit and imputation. Information that could be useful for evaluation purposes was maintained throughout the edit and imputation process, as well, some basic information was retained after collection. This information can be used to evaluate the efficiency of the process, and the impact it would have on the final data quality.

For taxis, counts and basic performance measures about the collection and edit and imputation processes can be produced. In addition, a number of series of estimates can be calculated, using different hypotheses each time. The estimates can be calculated using simple domain estimation based on the raw data. A second set of estimates can be produced by eliminating records that are total non-respondents and adjusting the expansion weights for each stratum in consequence; this set is also based on the raw data. This reweighting method adjusts the weights at the stratum level. Due to the small number of units involved in the taxi survey, the strata are quite broad and heterogeneous in terms of the size of the units. A third set is based on the final data that have been fully edited, imputed and reviewed. For the data from taxis, there were not enough records changed at manual review to warrant producing separate estimates from the processed data and the final data, so we have elected not to examine the estimates calculated from the processed data. Conclusions can be drawn about the impact of editing by comparing and analyzing the different sets of estimates.

It should be noted that the estimates prepared for this paper ARE NOT those that will be published from the survey. For the official estimates, a two-phase estimator will be used, and tax data will be added to the estimate to account for the smallest businesses that were excluded from the survey. In addition, the estimates will be post-stratified to a more current version of the frame, since several months elapsed between the time when the sample was drawn and the time when the questionnaires were completed by the respondents. The estimates presented here are simply to help understand the impact of editing.

For the purpose of this paper, two sections of the questionnaire will be studied: revenues and expenses. The revenue section is composed of 14 variables (R1-R14). Respondents are asked to report R12 as the sub-total of variables R1 to R11 and to report R14 as the sub-total of R12 and R13. In addition, two sub-totals were calculated and added to the table of results: SR1 = R1 + … + R11 and SR2 = R12 + R13 in order to verify that the rules are met for estimation. There were 23 different edit rules involving these variables in the collection system. Some of the rules are validity checks or balancing rules, while other more complicated rules involve variables from other sections of the questionnaire and even some administrative information.

The expense section is composed of 40 variables (E1-E40). The variable E37 is supposed to be the sum of E1 to E36 and E40 the total of E37 to E39. In addition, two calculated sub-totals were added to the table of results: SE1 = E1 + … + E36 and SE2 = E37 + E38 + E39. There were 21 edit rules applied to the expense section during collection. Even though there were less edits on the expense section, it was a much more complicated section. Often, respondents were unable to provide the level of detailed information that was requested on the questionnaire. In the collection system, a number of temporary sub-totals were planned, to make it possible to collect as much partial information (usually at a higher level of aggregation) as could be supplied. For example, salaries and employee benefits were often specified as one value, rather than the two fields requested on the questionnaire.

Table 2: Follow-up

Revenue section

# records in scope	218		
# records without follow-up	184 (84%)		
# records through follow-up	34 (16%)	All fields confirmed	9 (27%)
		At least one field changed	25 (73%)

Expense section

# records in scope	218		
# records without follow-up	152 (70%)		
# records through follow-up	66 (30%)	All fields confirmed	30 (46%)
		At least one field changed	36 (54%)

Both sections

# records in scope	218		
# records without follow-up	143 (66%)		
# records through follow-up	75 (34%)	All fields confirmed	22 (29%)
		At least one field changed	53 (71%)

Table 2 shows the distribution of records as they moved through the collection system, in terms of the revenue section, the expense section, then both sections considered together. The follow-up strategy that was implemented for UES 1997 established a list of 'priority' units that should receive preferential follow-up, starting with the largest units and those with the greatest contribution to the estimates. In practice, since 1997 was the first year for the survey, virtually all records with an edit failure at collection were followed-up. In future years, a detailed strategy for follow-up will need to be developed.

From the table, it can be seen that 71% of the records followed-up resulted in a change being made to at least one variable on the record. It appears that there was some over-editing of the expense section, as almost half of the follow-ups of edit failures resulted in the original data being confirmed by the respondent.

It should be noted that the collection system marked records where changes had been made due to follow-up, but it did not track how many variables were changed, nor the quantity by which the values were changed. This information would be interesting for a more in-depth analysis and evaluation of the collection process.

Table 3: Edit and Imputation Flow: last change in the record

Revenue section

Collection	8 (4%)
Pre processing (0 in)	203 (93%)
Processing (imputation)	5 (2%)
Manual review	2 (1%)
Total	218

Expense section

Collection	3 (1%)
Pre processing (0 in)	184 (84%)
Processing (imputation)	28 (13%)
Manual review	3 (1%)
Total	218

Both sections

Collection	3 (1%)
Pre processing (0 in)	184 (84%)
Processing (imputation)	28 (13%)
Manual review	3 (1%)
Total	218

Table 3 presents the final status of records after all processing, including manual review, has been completed. For each field, only the final status is kept on the database. The imputation rate is derived from data coming out of processing and manual review. Records changed at manual review may or may not have been imputed previously. Unfortunately, this information is not kept by the system.

In terms of the revenue section, it can be seen that the majority of changes made to this section (93%of records) involved filling zeroes into fields where it was clear that zero was the only feasible answer. There were 7 records where this section was imputed as a result of total non-response, so there was no partial imputation for this section. The expense section required more interventions by the imputation system for partial non-response.

It should be noted that there are very few records that were 'perfect' after collection. The most common correction was to fill a blank field with zeroes – the respondents seemed reluctant to specify all zeroes that applied. The strength of the processing system was to determine when it was appropriate to fill a field with zero, depending upon the inter-relationships of the variables and the actual data supplied by the respondent.

As can be seen be seen from Table 1, there were seven records that were total non-response and required complete imputation. In addition, there were 24 records (28 changed at processing + 3 at manual review - 7 total non-response) that required at least partial imputation. In the next section, the estimates will be calculated and compared for individual fields.

5. RESULTS

Table 4 shows that, for the revenue section, the imputation rate is the same for all fields (3%) and equals the total non-response rate. This means that no partial imputation was required for this specific section. All of the records were perfectly balanced after collection, this explains why the estimates of sums are also balanced to the totals after collection (SR1=R12 and SR2=R14). As shown in the table, the reweighting provides higher estimates than the two other methods. The reweighting is not the best method here because the small sample size combined with the high out of scope rate and the out of date frame information did not leave enough units over which to re-distribute the weight. For the 218 respondents, there are 40 strata, with very small effective sample sizes. In general, it is the smallest units that tend not to respond, hence their weight is re-allocated to larger units, causing the over-estimation. For example, the fourth biggest unit (according to sampling information) had its weight re-distributed among the three biggest units in the sample.

The percentage change for a specific method has been calculated as:

$$\frac{\text{estimation with the method - estimation after collection}}{\text{estimation after collection}}$$

This percentage change after imputation appears elevated for fields R10 and R13. This is due to the fact that these items were almost always reported as zero and thus the choice of a non zero donor had a high impact on the corresponding estimate. This is aggravated when the recipient has a large weight itself. The choice of donors was approved by experts during manual review and changes were made as needed. In general, the percentage change after reweighting seems high. For the total revenue item (R14), the non-respondents represent 10% of the total revenue in the sample, according to tax revenue information. A reweighting effect of 24% seems exaggerated, but this is due to the high out of scope rate combined with the small sample size, as stated previously.

As a general comment, reweighting is based on the sample design, which relies on frame information. The frame information can be quite out of date, if there have been no previous surveys, as is the case for taxis. However, the donor imputation is based on survey data and some administrative data that are current. This accounts for some of the discrepancies between the weighted totals.

Table 4: Domain Estimation with and without Imputation

Revenue section

Variable	Imp. rate *	Weighted total after collection	Reweighted total	Weighted total after E&I	% of change when reweighted	% of change in E&I
R1	3%	157216187	202026637	163098957	29%	4%
R2	3%	28662555	31893946	28806555	11%	1%
R3	3%	26691494	30845122	31624061	16%	18%
R4	3%	3848843	4076987	3848843	6%	0%
R5	3%	3161258	4224939	3161258	34%	0%
R6	3%	629263	874003	629263	39%	0%
R7	3%	7470327	8703264	7470328	17%	0%
R8	3%	690478	770281	690478	12%	0%
R9	3%	28593	40458	28593	41%	0%
R10	3%	3512792	4586222	4844997	31%	38%
R11	3%	750131	969781	750131	29%	0%
SR1		**232661920**	**288063876**	**244953464**		
R12	3%	**232661920**	**288063876**	**244953464**	24%	5%
R13	3%	425521	504961	969086	19%	128%
SR2		**233087441**	**288568838**	**245922550**		
R14	3%	**233087441**	**288568838**	**245922550**	24%	6%

* including manual review

For the expense section, the imputation rate varies from 3% to 14%. This section does require partial imputation. Field E2 (employee benefits) is the most often imputed; this was expected. At collection, although a temporary sub-total was available to be used when salaries and employee benefits were provided together, it appears that the sub-total was not used adequately. Field E35 is the only field to show a significant decrease – this field collects "other expenses" and often imputation distributed this amount among other expense items. The imputation rate for total expenses (E40) is 6%. This is low, due to the fact that all respondents who did not supply a value in field E40 were subject to follow-up. For this section, estimates of totals based on the sum of the raw data do not balance with respondent-specified totals (SE1≠E37 and SE2≠E40); this holds true under reweighting. Fields E33 and E38 show an elevated rate of change for the same reason as R10 and R13, as explained above. Again, the 24% reweighting effect on total expenses (E40) seems exaggerated since the non-respondents represent 11% of the sample according to tax expense information. This can be explained in the same way as the revenue section – the high out of scope rate, the small sample size, and the out of date frame information all contribute to the problem.

Expense section

Variable	Imp. rate *	Weighted total after collection	Reweighted total	Weighted total after E&I	% of change when reweighted	% of change in E&I
E1	4%	96040721	121853298	103033141	27%	7%
E2	14%	5735944	7246292	5863093	26%	2%
E3	3%	7007716	9014703	7697905	29%	10%
E4	3%	4656028	5707240	4854152	23%	4%
E5	4%	852951	984756	852608	15%	0%
E6	4%	5965173	6932015	5978866	16%	0%
E7	4%	114500	115270	114500	1%	0%
E8	4%	2468151	3348184	2492200	36%	1%
E9	4%	182249	190847	182260	5%	0%
E10	4%	5611360	6976462	6037325	24%	8%
E11	4%	452490	502145	452490	11%	0%
E12	4%	8992293	11485634	9208109	28%	2%
E13	4%	3043	3043	3043	0%	0%
E14	4%	4302516	5217615	4384020	21%	2%
E15	4%	2102995	2543025	2104984	21%	0%
E16	4%	155385	217327	155405	40%	0%
E17	4%	1410369	1741278	1408617	23%	0%
E18	4%	486453	701105	482993	44%	-1%
E19	4%	864582	1006969	866850	16%	0%
E20	4%	14447910	17091199	14964906	18%	4%
E21	4%	1054388	1344969	1053882	28%	0%
E22	4%	151247	157996	151187	4%	0%
E23	4%	2717348	3331349	2814581	23%	4%
E24	4%	786890	841032	821598	7%	4%
E25	4%	1144209	1421657	1212718	24%	6%
E26	4%	11304722	13364746	11787760	18%	4%
E27	4%	7102299	9777538	7191967	38%	1%
E28	4%	482869	528567	503900	9%	4%
E29	4%	1820252	2172021	1835002	19%	1%
E30	4%	1571982	1933032	1579415	23%	0%
E31	4%	893382	1050913	893181	18%	0%
E32	4%	8177241	9978843	8329484	22%	2%
E33	4%	3956338	4667113	5949648	18%	50%
E34	4%	2764652	3581070	2764291	30%	0%
E35	4%	8049724	8642331	4874384	7%	-39%
E36	4%	2323295	2720276	2355994	17%	1%
SE1		216153670	268391860	225256458		
E37	4%	174963281	225586915	225256458	29%	29%
E38	4%	845804	902799	2339447	7%	177%
E39	3%	1815829	2274091	1898228	25%	5%
SE2		177624913	228763805	229494133		
E40	3%	215999779	268729489	229494133	24%	6%

* including manual review

6. GENERAL CONCLUSIONS

Based on this study, it has been seen that editing during collection/capture and follow-up procedures provides data of high quality, as shown by the generally low imputation rate required. By examining the weighted total based solely on the data available after collection and follow-up had taken place, it can be seen that the estimates are almost always negatively biased (underestimated) – imputation increases the estimates by approximately 5%. This is as would be expected, since imputation or reweighting are methods used to account for non-response in a manner different than simply assuming zero data. If the solution to total non-response is to re-calculate the weights, distributing the weights of the non-respondents over the respondents, then the estimated totals tend to be overestimated, often by a significant amount. On average, the estimates were increased by about 25%, although the amount ranged up to 177%. Again, this could be expected, since the sampling fraction was greater for larger units, as is often the case in business surveys, so the weight of larger units is increased, resulting in higher estimates.

The principle of minimum change as applied here tended to generate a variety of imputed records that can be expected to be similar to the natural variety of records in the population.

Reweighting does not provide final estimates of high quality when the sample size is small and there are not enough units to provide a good re-distribution of the weight. This is exacerbated by an elevated out of scope rate and out of date frame information for this particular survey. As well, this example involved broad strata that were not as homogeneous as one would hope. Here, reweighting, which is equivalent to imputing the mean does not work as well as donor imputation, which imputes small units from other small units.

When donor imputation is used in a survey with small sample sizes and hence limited choices of donor, it is important to have a manual process of review to allow experts to identify situations where an inappropriate donor might have been used, leading to unexpected estimates.

It is important to ensure that adequate performance measures or descriptive information about the collection, editing, and imputation systems are maintained for evaluation purposes. Unfortunately, the next year's survey will use a different collection system that is based on a package that does not make this information available at the end of the collection and follow-up process.

This study has helped to highlight the importance of interviewer training. This is especially important when the interviewers are being asked to use collection systems that include more sophisticated tools, such as the temporary sub-totals available for this survey.

Based on this study, it is evident that further examination of the data should take place. It would be worthwhile to repeat the study using data from the other six Pilot industries, especially since some of the other industries involve a significantly higher volume of data.

References

[1] Communications Division, STC (1998) The How and Why of Business Statistics: The Respondent's Perspective. Statistics Canada Internal Document.

[2] Enterprise Survey Division (1998) PIPES Information Package – Outline. Statistics Canada Internal Document.

[3] Kovar, J. and Winkler, W. (1996) Editing Economic Data. Proceedings of the Section on Survey Research Methods of the American Statistical Association.

[4] Royce, Don (1998). Project to Improve Provincial Economic Statistics. Proceedings of the Joint IASS/IAOS Conference in Mexico.

SELECTIVE EDITING USING PLAUSIBILITY INDICATORS AND SLICE

by Jeffrey Hoogland, Statistics Netherlands

Abstract: At Statistics Netherlands the statistical process for annual structural business statistics has been redesigned. Within the scope of IMPECT (IMPlementation EConomic Transformation process) a method for selective editing has been developed. Crucial businesses are always edited manually, because of their large impact on publication totals. However, for non-crucial records plausibility indicators decide whether a record is automatically edited or whether it is edited manually. Plausible records are edited automatically with the computer program SLICE 1. In this chapter we first discuss the construction and calibration of plausibility indicators. We then examine 12 of the 54 publication cells of the annual structural business statistics 2000 Trade and Transport that have been edited selectively. Records that were edited automatically have later been edited manually for evaluation purposes. We check for differences between raw, manually edited, and automatically edited data and see the influences of selective editing on the publication totals. The plausibility indicators do not detect all influential errors. However, differences between manually and automatically edited data are small for most variables. Sometimes there are greater differences, also for key variables. In some publication cells for Transport we found major deviations. We expect that these differences can be reduced by improving the plausibility indicators and SLICE.

1. INTRODUCTION

At Statistics Netherlands a large reorganisation has been carried out. As a result, instead of a department for each survey the Division of Business Statistics now has a department for

- **business registers**
- **observation:** adjusting, sending, receiving and editing of questionnaires
- **analysis:** imputing unit non response, weighting, macro editing, publication
- **research and support**.

An important reason for creating a new organisation is that a uniform statistical process was required for structural business statistics, cf. De Jong (2002). Furthermore, the same work had to be done by fewer people of a higher educational level. The editing process is often a demanding and costly process. It was therefore decided to switch over to selective editing, cf. Granquist (1995), Granquist & Kovar (1997), Hidiroglou & Berthelot (1986). De Jong (2002) gives a detailed description of UniEdit 1, the new micro editing process for annual structural business statistics (ASBS) at Statistics Netherlands.

In this chapter, two steps in this new process are highlighted, namely the partition of records for automatic and manual editing, and automatic editing itself. The emphasis is on selective editing of ASBS. Business statistics differ from social statistics, because they mainly contain numerical data instead of categorical data. Furthermore, companies receive a questionnaire to fill in, while persons are often visited by an interviewer. Questionnaires that are distributed by mail often contain more errors than questionnaires that are dealt with by an interviewer, because in the latter case edit rules are checked directly.

In Section 2 the principles of selective editing and automatic editing are discussed and the new process for micro editing is highlighted. In Section 3 the purposes of plausibility indicators are stated. Partial plausibility indicators (PPI) need to be calibrated on the basis of raw and edited data of last year, before they can be used to make a selection of records that are implausible. In Section 4 the technique that is used to calibrate PPI's is explained. The computation of the overall plausibility indicator (OPI) is discussed in Section 5. Records with a low OPI are edited manually. In Section 6 the evaluation of plausibility indicators on the basis of raw and edited data is considered. The evaluation of SLICE 1 is treated in Section 7. Deviations as a result of selective automatic editing are treated in Section 8. Finally, some conclusions are drawn in Section 9.

2. SELECTIVE AND AUTOMATIC EDITING

A. Principles

First, some terminology is introduced based on Rivière (2002). The *right* value is the value that would be obtained with an ideal measurement process. A value is *correct* if a subject-matter specialist would agree to leave it unchanged in the database. We therefore assume that a record is correct when it has been edited manually. A value is *acceptable* if the data-editing program accepts it in the database without any requirement to check it manually or adjust it automatically. A record is acceptable when it has been edited. value is *raw* when it has not been checked at all.

Some types of errors are obvious, such as uniform 1000-errors (all financial variables are a factor 1000 too large), erroneous negative values, and empty (sub)totals. Ideally these types of errors should bother neither an editor nor an advanced program for automatic editing. These errors should be edited automatically in an early stage. Since they are obvious a simple program suffices to do the job.

In our view the goal of selective editing is to select those records for manual editing that have a large influence on the publication total and/or contain large errors. Records that do not satisfy either of these conditions can be edited automatically. When records are aggregated to publication totals small non-systematic errors will largely be cancelled out anyway. So, we use the principle of selective editing, cf. Granquist (1995), Granquist & Kovar (1997), Hidiroglou & Berthelot (1986). Plausibility indicators are used to decide whether a record can be edited automatically.

To obtain acceptable data it is sufficient to edit records automatically. When at least one edit rule is violated a record is *doubtful* and values of variables should be changed by means of imputation. At Statistics Netherlands automatic editing of ASBS is done with SLICE 1. It requires a description of the data, edit rules, confidence weights that give an indication of the reliability of each variable, and imputation rules. The generalised Fellegi-Holt paradigm for localisation of errors is used. This paradigm implies that values of variables within a record should be adjusted such that all edit rules are satisfied and the sum of the confidence weights for adjusted variables is minimal.

B. UniEdit

UniEdit 1 is the latest statistical process for selective micro-editing of ASBS of Statistics Netherlands. For many branches of industry it was first applied to the ASBS for the year 2000. UniEdit aims at a uniform editing process that is identical for all branches of industry so that the efficiency of production can be optimised.

After removing obvious mistakes, it is determined whether a record must be edited by hand or automatically. For this partition several plausibility indicators are used. The records are then changed by either editors or by SLICE 1 in such a way that all editing rules are satisfied.

UniEdit 2 is the latest statistical process for weighting and macro-editing of ASBS of Statistics Netherlands. It includes unit-imputation of large companies that did not respond, automatic outlier detection, weighting with auxiliary information, and validation of figures. Weights of records can be adjusted manually in the validation step when figures do not seem plausible.

3. PLAUSIBILITY INDICATORS

A. Selecting records for manual editing

For selective editing, we need reliable estimates of correct values of variables in a record. Records are therefore grouped into relatively homogeneous subgroups. Such a group is called an edit cell, which is an intersection of a publication cell and a company size class, see figure 2 in Appendix A. For each edit cell the plausibility of each record is assessed.

A plausibility indicator (PI) has to serve several purposes. The main purpose is to make a good selection of records that have to be edited manually. Records that contain errors that have a significant effect on the estimated population total should be selected for manual editing. Let's assume that *P%* of the records is to be selected and *(100-P)%* of the records is not edited. The selection should be such that a distance function, based on raw and correct values of variables for plausible records, is minimal. We first compute a sum of weighted differences between raw and correct values for variable y_j, relative to the (weighted) publication cell total for variable y_j

$$\Delta_j(y^c, y^r, S_{PI}) = \left| \frac{1}{Y_j} \sum_{i \notin S_{PI}} w_i (y^r_{ij} - y^c_{ij}) \right| , \tag{1}$$

where

y^c_{ij} y^r_{ij}

y^c, y^r	: matrices containing $\hat{y}^c_{ij}$ and $\hat{y}^r_{ij}$, respectively ;
S_{PI}	: selection of records for manual editing made by a plausibility indicator;
w_i	: weight of record *i* ;
Y_j	: estimated publication cell total of variable *j*, $Y_j = \sum_i w_i y^c_{ij}$.

The main problem is that y^c_{ij} is not known beforehand. It can be estimated using y^c_{ij} from last year, for instance multiplied by an estimate for the economic growth or inflation rate. The final weight for record *i* is also not known at the beginning of the editing process. It can be estimated by the inverse of the inclusion probability π_i.

We prefer to have an overall plausibility indicator that determines whether a record is either edited manually, or automatically. This OPI should for example minimise

$$\sum_{j=1}^{J} \alpha_j \Delta_j(y^c, y^r, S_{OPI}), \tag{2}$$

subject to the constraint that *P%* of the records are to be selected, where

α_j	: denotes the importance of variable y_j ;
J	: is the set of variables on a questionnaire.

In this chapter we will make use of (1), not of (2). Furthermore, we will only use (1) for evaluation purposes when the editing process is finished. The selection percentage *P* is then not a predetermined but an observed value.

B. Partial plausibility indicators

Another purpose of plausibility indicators is to assist an editor in the interactive editing of a record. Besides an overall plausibility indicator, seven partial plausibility indicators (PPI) are used to assess the plausibility of a specific part of the questionnaire. Each (partial) plausibility indicator can attain a discrete number between 0 (very implausible) and 10 (completely as expected).

For the construction of plausibility indicators we need to distinguish two important aspects: influence and risk. The influence component quantifies the relative influence of a record on an estimated publication total. The risk component quantifies either the extent in which a questionnaire is filled in properly or the extent in which it deviates from reference values. These reference values should be close to the correct value of a variable.

A questionnaire for an annual structural business statistic at Statistics Netherlands has four important parts, namely an employed persons block A, a business profit block B, a business costs block C, and a business results block D. For each block a partial plausibility formula (PPF) is constructed that has a range of $[0, \infty)$ and measures both influence and risk. The resulting PPF equals formula (9) in Appendix B. The reference values are the estimated population median and total for a subset of variables in a block. The risk is incorporated by the difference between observed values y_{ij} and the corresponding estimated population medians m_{cj}. The influence is mainly included through the inverse of the inclusion probability π_i and estimated population totals. These totals are estimated on the basis of edited records of last year for the same edit cell. Population medians are estimated on the basis of edited records of last year for the same median cell. A median cell is an intersection of a publication cell and company size, see Appendix A.

A record will obtain a high value for the partial plausibility formula for a block, when values of variables in a block differ much from the corresponding population medians. That is, a block PPF has a high value when values of variables in a record are either small or large compared to corresponding population medians. Raw values that are relatively small can then also cause a high block PPF. This is advisable, because it might be unjust that a raw value for one company is much smaller than raw values for other companies within a supposedly homogeneous group. Furthermore, a block PPF has a high value when a record contains many empty or zero entries for variables within this block for which this is considered to be unlikely.

Besides a PPF for each block (PPF **Block A, B, C**, and **D**), three other PPF's (**External**, **Indicators**, and **Quality**) are used that measure risk for variables across all four blocks. PPF **External** uses external information, like VAT-information and turnover from short-term statistics. Information from edited structural business records of last year is also used for four important variables. PPF **External** equals formula (10) in Appendix B. This PPF differs considerably from the other six, because reference values only relate to the specific company. It is assumed that the larger the ratio of raw values and reference values, the more likely that raw values are wrong.

Other important tools for editing records are ratios of two variables, for instance turnover divided by number of employees. PPF **Ratios** compares ratios within a raw record with medians for corresponding ratios based on edited records of last year. Seven ratios are used for this comparison. PPF **Ratios** equals formula (11) in Appendix B. If the values of ratios within a record differ much from corresponding medians then PPF **Ratios** will have a large value.

Finally, PPF **Quality** (formula (12) in Appendix B) is used to assess the quality of filling in questionnaires. This is the only PPF that considers all variables in the questionnaire. The number of empty entries and the number of violated edit rules are counted for a specific raw record before obvious mistakes are corrected. If these numbers are high then PPF **Quality** attains a large value.

4. CALIBRATING PARTIAL PLAUSIBILITY INDICATORS

A. Mark limits

Partial plausibility formulas have a range of [0, ∞) and they are transformed to corresponding partial plausibility indicators, which can attain discrete values between 0 and 10. In The Netherlands marks that are given in schools vary between 0 and 10, where 0 is very bad, 10 is excellent, and all marks below 6 are insufficient. Everyone therefore has developed a feeling for these marks. PPF's are transformed to marks by means of mark upper limits. These upper limits can vary across PPF's and edit cells. In table 1 an example is given of a set of mark upper limits. Note that if PPF **A** is lower than 6,29 then PPI **A** has a sufficient mark. When the upper limits are determined for each PPF and edit cell the resulting PPI's are PPI **Block A**, **B**, **C**, **D**, and PPI **External**, **Indicators**, and **Quality** respectively.

*Table 1. Upper mark limits for NACE 52110, number of employees 0-9 and PPI Block **A**.*

upper limit	Mark	upper limit	mark
1.35	10	8.61	5
1.82	9	9.87	4
2.38	8	13.15	3
3.47	7	14.20	2
6.29	**6**	16.10	1
		∞	0

Partial plausibility indicators are calibrated by the determination of mark limits. Mark limits for year *t* are computed using raw data of year *t-1* and edited data of both year *t-1* and year *t-2* for the same edit cell, as is shown below.

B. Sufficiency limit

The upper limit for mark six is important, because it determines whether a PPI obtains a sufficient mark. This limit is also referred to as the *sufficiency limit*. For determination of upper limits we make use of the empirical cumulative distribution function (*ECDF*) of a PPF for both edited and raw data of year *t-1*. Note that manually edited data is correct by definition and data that has been edited selectively is a mixture of correct and acceptable data.

For calibration of PPF **Block**, **External**, and **Indicators** we start with the *ECDF* of edited data for year *t-1*. The main part of this data should have a PPI of at least six. Ideally, values of variables in edited records are close to reference values and each PPF has a small value for those records. However, some outliers will often be present, because financial variables have skew distributions. Furthermore, we would like to select influential records in any case, although they might be correct. We define $P_{\geq 6}^{edited}\%$ as the percentage edited forms that have at least mark six for a specific PPI. For calibration of year 2000 we have chosen $P_{\geq 6}^{edited}\% = 90\%$ for PPI **Block**, **External**, and **Indicators**.

For calibration of PPF **Quality** we only use raw data of year *t-1*. PPF **Quality** will be very low for edited data, because violations of edit rules are not permitted for these data. The sufficiency limit is therefore based on $P_{\geq 6}^{raw}\% = D\%$, where $D\%$ is the average value of $P_{\geq 6}^{raw}\%$ for the other six PPF's within the same edit cell.

The procedure below is followed for each edit cell, provided that there are at least 50 edited records available. Otherwise, some publication cells are combined into an aggregated publication cell and mark limits are determined for the resulting aggregated edit cells. For every PPF, except PPF **Quality**:

1. Determine the quantile corresponding to $P_{\geq 6}^{edited}\%$ on the basis of edited data of year *t-1*, that is, $ECDF_{edited}^{-1}\left(P_{\geq 6}^{edited}\%\right)$, where $ECDF_{edited}^{-1}$ is the inverse empirical cumulative distribution function of a PPF for edited data. This quantile equals the sufficiency limit.
2. Determine $P_{\geq 6}^{raw}\%$ from $ECDF_{raw}^{-1}\left(P_{\geq 6}^{raw}\%\right)=ECDF_{edited}^{-1}\left(P_{\geq 6}^{edited}\%\right)$, where $ECDF_{raw}^{-1}$ is the inverse cumulative distribution function of the PPF for raw data of year *t-1*. Hopefully, edited data are more close to the reference values than raw data. In that case $P_{\geq 6}^{edited}\%$ will be larger than $P_{\geq 6}^{raw}\%$, because $ECDF_{raw}\left(PPF\right)$ will lie on the right of $ECDF_{edited}\left(PPF\right)$.

In Figure 1 an example is given; The upper curve is the *ECDF* of PPF Block A with edited *t-1*-data for NACE 52110. The quantile for which $P_{\geq 6}^{edited}\%$ is 90% equals 6.29. The lower curve is the *ECDF* of PPF Block A with raw *t-1*-data for NACE 52110. When we take 6.29 as the sufficiency limit then $P_{\geq 6}^{raw}\%$ is about 84%. That is, 84% of the raw data of year *t-1* for NACE 52110 has a PPI Block A of at least six. In practice $P_{\geq 6}^{raw}\%$ is often considerably smaller than 90%.

Suppose that the difference between edited data and raw data is large for many records in an edit cell, block A, and year *t-1*. Furthermore, let us assume that reference values are reliable. In that case the sufficiency limit will be such that a large percentage of raw records in year *t-1* has an insufficient mark for PPI **Block A**. Many records will then have an insufficient mark for PPI **Block A** in year *t* if the following two conditions hold

- raw data for year *t* are of the same quality as raw data for year *t-1*, that is, the differences between raw and edited data are about the same for both years
- differences between edited data for year *t* and year *t-1* are comparable with differences between edited data for year *t-1* and year *t-2*.

C. Remaining mark limits

For the construction of other limits than the sufficiency limit we solely make use of raw data of last year. For each PPF and edit cell, the sufficient and insufficient marks are distributed uniformly across the available raw forms. That is, the upper limits are determined such that the number of raw forms with marks 0, 1, 2, 3, 4, and 5 is about the same, and the number of raw forms with marks 6, 7, 8, 9, and 10 is about the same. Given the sufficiency limits, the remaining limits are determined using the percentiles:

$$P_{\geq c}^{raw}\% = P_{\geq 6}^{raw}\% + \frac{6-c}{c}\left(100\% - P_{\geq 6}^{raw}\%\right), \quad c=1,2,\ldots,5,$$

$$P_{\geq c}^{raw}\% = \frac{11-c}{5} P_{\geq 6}^{raw}\%, \quad c=7,8,9,10.$$

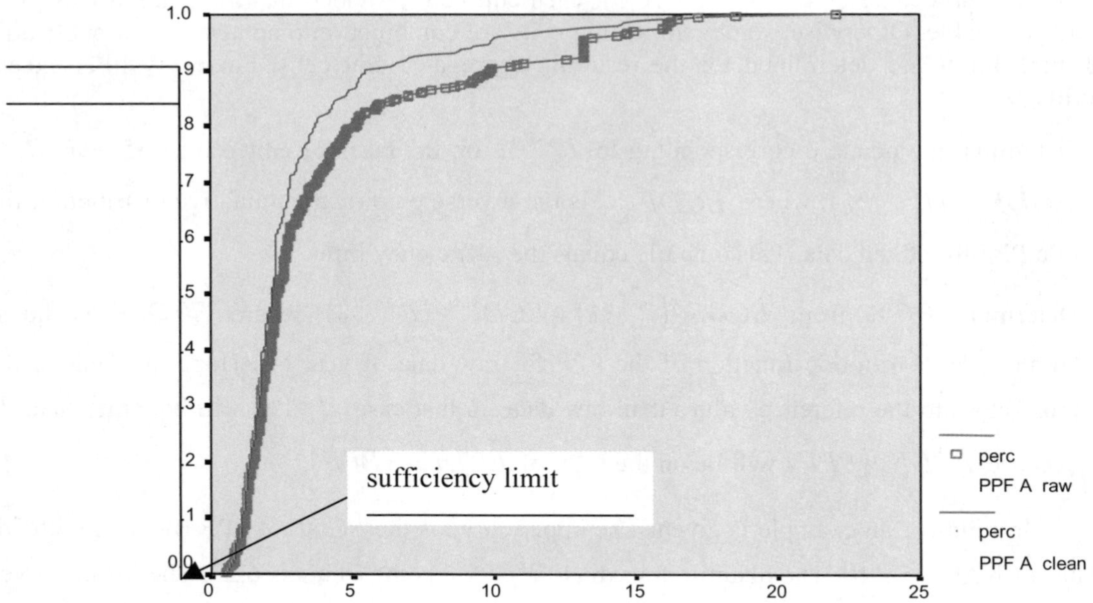

*Figure 1. Empirical cumulative distribution functions of PPF **Block A** for edited and raw data (without obvious mistakes) for NACE 52110.*

The upper limit for mark *c* now equals $ECDF_{raw}^{-1}\left(P_{\geq c}^{raw}\%\right)$. When all upper limits are determined the PPI's are calibrated for year *t*.

5. COMPUTATION OF OVERALL PLAUSIBILITY INDICATOR

The overall plausibility indicator serves to select records that have to be edited manually. In our view the mechanism that determines the overall plausibility indicator should satisfy four criteria:

1. It is rather simple;
2. The OPI cannot change dramatically due to small changes in a PPI;
3. An increasing PPI cannot cause the OPI to decrease;
4. A low mark for a PPI has a large influence on the OPI.

The overall plausibility indicator for a record is a truncated weighted mean of the values of the seven partial plausibility indicators for this record, where the weights are such that a lower mark has a larger weight. The resulting formula is

$$\text{OPI}=\left\lfloor \frac{\sum_{v=0}^{10} v n_v s_v}{\sum_{v=0}^{10} n_v s_v} \right\rfloor, \quad (3)$$

where n_v is the number of PPI's with value v for a specific record, s_v is the weight of value v, and $\lfloor \ldots \rfloor$ means that the expression between brackets is truncated. The weights s_v are given in Table 2.

Table 2. Weights s_v

v	s_v	v	s_v
10	1	4	9/3
9	9/8	3	9/2
8	9/7	2	9
7	9/6	1	18
6	9/5	0	36
5	9/4		

6. EVALUATION OF PLAUSIBILITY INDICATORS

A. Data requirements

If we have raw and correct values for all records then plausibility indicators can be evaluated. However, as soon as we make use of selective editing we do not have correct values for all records. Records that have been edited automatically are acceptable, but they are not always correct. Ideally, in the traditional editing process raw and correct values were kept. However, at Statistics Netherlands raw values were often not saved in the past. In the year before selective editing was introduced, editors were therefore instructed to save raw values.

The ASBS of year 2000 are produced with a new statistical process. An important problem is that variables are not always comparable between year 1999 and year 2000, because of new questionnaires for year 2000. Variables of 1999 have to be transformed to the 2000 format. However, a one-to-one transformation does not exist for some variables. Raw and correct data of 1999 can therefore be unavailable in the right format. Furthermore, raw data can be missing because some editors ignored instructions to save raw values. Because of data problems and time pressure an extensive evaluation of plausibility indicators by means of 1999 data has not been performed.

Plausibility indicators are therefore evaluated by means of 2000 data. The main problem is that records that are edited automatically cannot be considered as correct. Records that have been edited automatically are therefore also edited manually. This can only be done for a small selection of publication cells due to the availability of editors. The performance of SLICE, Statistics Netherlands` module for automatic editing, can then also be evaluated for these publication cells. Furthermore, when records that have been edited manually are also edited automatically, it can be investigated whether the percentage of records that is edited automatically should be adjusted.

B. Evaluation criteria

The performance of OPI as a selector of influential errors for variable y_j and a specific edit or publication cell can be assessed by computing (1) when correct values of variables are either available or estimated. Suppose that $P\%$ of the records has to be edited manually. When (1) is small for that edit or publication cell then OPI makes a good selection regarding variable y_j. To determine whether OPI makes a good selection for all variables in a record we can compute (2). However, in this chapter we only discuss the performance of OPI for each variable separately. Note that we only consider undetected errors and that we do not notice errors that OPI does detect.

The performance of a PPI as a selector of influential errors for variable y_j can also be assessed by computing (1). S is then defined as the selection of records that have an insufficient mark for this

PPI. Furthermore, we can compute (2) to assess the performance of a PPI as a selector of influential errors for a set of variables. J is then defined as the set of variables that is monitored by a specific PPI.

A disadvantage of (1) is that it does not take the number of records into account that are edited automatically. The less records are sent to SLICE, the better the value for (1). We therefore also use evaluation criteria that take the number of records with a sufficient PPI or OPI into account. We first define the error in variable j for record i as

$$e_{ij} = y_{ij}^{r} - y_{ij}^{c} \ .$$

For PPI **Block A, B, C, and D** we then use the following evaluation criterion for variable y_j

$$C_b^j = \frac{\sum_{i:PPI_b \geq 6} w_i \cdot |e_{ij}| / v_b}{\sum_i w_i \cdot y_{ij}^c / r} \ , \qquad (4)$$

where

- PPI_b is PPI **Block** b , b = **A, B, C, or D**;
- v_b is the number of records in an edit cell that has a sufficient PPI **Block** b ;
- r is the response in the edit cell.

For each variable y_j and edit cell we consider the records with a sufficient PPI **Block** and we compute the average of the weighted absolute error. This average is compared with the average contribution of a correct value in a record to the estimated total of an edit cell. The score on criterion (4) is considered as bad if larger than 0.1. In this case we speak of *large unseen errors*.

For PPI **External** we use a different criterion, because this PPI serves to detect large relative deviations of raw values with external data. For each variable y_j and edit cell we consider the records with a sufficient PPI **External** and we compute the average relative deviation between raw and correct values

$$C_E^j = \frac{1}{v_E^j} \cdot \sum_{i:PPI_E \geq 6} \left(\frac{y_{ij}^c}{y_{ij}^r} + \frac{y_{ij}^r}{y_{ij}^c} - 2\right) \ , \qquad (5)$$

where

- PPI_E is PPI **External**;
- v_E^j is the number of records with a sufficient PPI **External** where both y_{ij}^c and y_{ij}^r are unequal to zero and not empty.

For PPI **Ratios** we also use a different criterion, which considers the errors in ratios for records with a sufficient PPI **Ratios**. For each ratio r_j and edit cell we compute

$$C_R^j = \frac{1}{v_R^j} \cdot \sum_{i:PPI_R \geq 6} \left(\frac{r_{ij}^c}{r_{ij}^r} + \frac{r_{ij}^r}{r_{ij}^c} - 2\right) \ , \qquad (6)$$

where

- PPI_R is PPI **Ratios**;
- r_{ij}^c is the value for ratio j in record i for manually edited data;
- r_{ij}^r is the value for variabele j in record i for raw data without obvious mistakes;

– v_R^j is the number of records with a sufficient PPI **Ratios**, where both r_{ij}^c and r_{ij}^r can be calculated.

Criteria (5) and (6) take relative sizes of errors into account. Small companies therefore have the same impact as large ones. The score on criteria (5) and (6) is considered as bad if larger than 0.2. In this case we speak of *large unseen errors*. The value of 0.2 is for example attained on criterion (5) if 40% of the plausible records have a ratio that is a factor two too high.

Unlike the other partial plausibility indicators, PPI **Quality** is not calculated on the basis of raw values of variables, but on the basis of two characteristics of the questionnaire as a whole. It is therefore not useful to investigate unseen errors in separate variables and a criterion such as (4), (5) or (6) cannot be derived.

For OPI we use a comparable evaluation criterion as (4) for PPI **Block A, B, C, and D**. For each variable y_j and edit cell we compute

$$C_O^j = \frac{\sum_{i:OPI \geq 6} w_i \cdot \left|e_{ij}\right| / v_b}{\sum_i w_i \cdot y_{ij}^c / r} \quad . \qquad (7)$$

C. Selected publication cells

The returned questionnaires are divided into a number of publication cells depending on the SIC (Standard Industrial Classification; Dutch version of the NACE) of the respondent. These publication cells contain one or more SICs. During the editing process we no longer distinguish records with different SICs within a publication cell. This implies that the publication cells must be as homogenous as possible for the editing process to work well. In contrast with this is the demand that a publication cell must be big enough to allow the application of statistical methods.

The twelve publication cells used for evaluation are given in table 3. They contain 4651 records in total for ASBS 2000. Some 45% of these records have a sufficient PI. Because the PI was not ready in time for production, records were not edited automatically the first few months. Records that were edited automatically were later edited by hand in the course of this study. The records that were edited by hand during production were later edited automatically.

The enterprises in each publication cell are categorised by size class in three edit cells: size class 1 (less than 10 employees), 2 (from 10 to 100 employees), and 3 (at least 100 employees). Records in edit cells of size class three are completely edited by hand. These *crucial edit cells* contain major enterprises, which attribute so much to the published total, that it is very important that these enterprises have optimal quality data.The questionnaires consist of cover pages and inserted pages. Cover pages are less extensive for size class 1 than for size class 2-3, but they do not contain specific questions on publication cells. These are on the inserted pages. In the publication cells we studied there are five different inserted pages.

We encountered a problem when we re-edited the wholesale trade records in size class 1 by hand. We could not produce all necessary files for the interactive editing program. So for the corresponding edit cells we only have part of the records available that contain both raw and manually edited data. These edit cells were therefore eliminated from the study. After removing the records of wholesale trade size class 1 we had 4162 records left. All weighted totals were determined on the basis of these records.

Example

We give an example of the use of criterion (4) for PPI **Block B**. There are five important variables in this block of questions concerning operating profit. These variables have an importance weight α_j of 100, the remaining variables in Block B have an importance weight α_j of 0, see formula (9) in Appendix B.

In publication cell 163300 there are large (by PPI **Block B)** unseen errors for each important variable, see table 4. In some edit cells the average weighted unseen absolute error is even larger than the average contribution of a correct record to the estimated population total of the edit cell. That is, the nominator of criterion (4) is larger than the denominator of criterion (4). For publication cells Wholesale trade and Retail trade there are only large unseen errors for other operating profit.

	Wholesale trade
151200B	in flowers and plants
151300C	in food, beverages and tobacco excl. fruit, vegetables and potatoes
151600C	in tool, machinery for agriculture/textile production
	Retail trade
152110	in food, beverages and tobacco in shops; super markets
152121C	in furniture, household textile, lights, and household articles
152121E	in hardware, tools, paint and construction materials
	Transport
160220	Irregular transport of people by taxi
161100	Shipping at sea
161200	Inland shipping
163110	Loading, unloading, warehousing
163300	Travel organisation and mediation; information for tourism
163400	Shipping agents, cargo insurance and chartering brokers; weighing and measuring

*Table 4. Results for criterion (4) for PPI **Block B**, for each important variable and non-crucial edit cell.*

Publication cell	Size class	Net turnover	Net turnover for main activity	Net turnover for other activities	Other operating profit	Total operating profit
151200B	2	0.04	0.04	0.00	0.02	0.04
151300C	2	0.03	0.04	0.04	0.05	0.04
151600C	2	0.02	0.02	0.01	0.10	0.02
152110	1	0.01	0.01	0.00	0.00	0.01
	2	0.00	0.00	0.00	**0.11**	0.01
152121C	1	0.03	0.03	0.00	0.02	0.03
	2	0.00	0.00	0.00	**0.90**	0.01
152121E	1	0.02	0.02	0.00	0.00	0.02
	2	0.04	0.03	0.00	**0.24**	0.03
160220	1	0.00	0.00	0.05	0.05	0.00
	2	0.00	0.00	0.00	**0.10**	0.00
161100	1	0.01	0.01	0.00	0.02	0.01
	2	0.04	0.03	0.01	**0.30**	0.04
161200	1	0.01	0.03	0.02	0.00	0.00
	2	0.03	0.05	0.06	0.00	0.04
163110	1	0.00	0.01	**0.24**	0.00	0.01
	2	0.05	0.07	**0.16**	**0.24**	0.05
163300	1	**1.47**	**1.51**	0.00	0.00	**1.46**
	2	**0.38**	**0.38**	**0.51**	**0.33**	**0.38**
163400	1	0.01	0.01	0.00	0.02	0.01
	2	0.01	0.02	**0.12**	**1.52**	0.01

D. Evaluation results for plausibility indicators

The emphasis of our evaluation is on errors that are not detected by plausibility indicators PPI **Block**, PPI **External**, PPI **Ratios**, and OPI. We use evaluation criteria (1), (4), (5), (6) and (7) to assess their performance. We now summarize the performance of plausibility indicators according to the above mentioned criteria.

Table 4 shows that PPI **Block B** does not detect all large errors in variables for that block of questions. The same holds for other PPI **Block**. PPI **External** and PPI **Ratios** also miss some large errors for variables considered in these PPI's. PPI **External** mainly has a bad performance when external information is unavailable. However, most of the large unseen errors for one PPI are detected by some of the other six PPI's. The computation of OPI is such that a low mark for one PPI has a relatively large influence. A low mark for at least one PPI therefore often results in an insufficient OPI and the detected errors can then be solved by an editor.

The performance of a plausibility indicator varies across publication cells and variables. In general, it is better for important variables. These variables also have a larger weight in the computation of a plausibility indicator. Furthermore, important variables are often (sub)totals of entries in a questionnaire. These (sub)totals contain less substantial errors, because errors in underlying entries are often relatively small or cancelled out. In Table 7 in Appendix C results are given for OPI for three important variables: total number of employed persons, net turnover, and operating result. For total number of employed persons criteria (1) and (7) are acceptable. However, for publication cell 163300 criteria (1) and (7) have a large value for net turnover and operating result. This means that some large errors have not been detected by OPI. Furthermore, a large value for criteria (1) indicates that some of those errors are influential on the publication level and that they do not compensate each other.

In general, there are more unseen influential errors for publication cells Transport than for Trade. One of the reasons is that reference values are less accurate for Transport (Hoogland & Van der Pijll, 2003). Raw data for Transport also contain more errors than raw data for Trade. Transport companies seem to have more difficulties with understanding variable definitions on the uniform cover pages of questionnaires Trade & Transport. The main question becomes now whether SLICE 1 tackles unseen influential errors or not.

7. EVALUATION OF SLICE 1

A. SLICE 1

When a record is considered plausible on the basis of the calculated OPI, it is edited with the SLICE 1 program developed at Statistics Netherlands. SLICE 1 contains the module CherryPi, cf. de Waal (2000) and De Waal & Wings (1999). This module localises errors in a record on the basis of a number of edit rules that show the mathematical relationships between variables. It also contains an imputation module, which can apply mean, ratio, or regression imputation in the case of erroneous values. Finally, it contains a module that corrects imputed values when they violate edit rules.

The edit rules violated by a record have to be satisfied by CherryPi by changing the values of one or more variables. Usually there are several possibilities for editing a record. This requires a choice, which is made according to the *principle of Fellegi and Holt*, see Fellegi & Holt (1976). The principle states that it is more likely that there is one major error in one variable, than that there are smaller errors in more than one variable. The best solution for editing a record is to change as few variables as possible.

In practise some variables contain fewer errors than others, or are not allowed to be changed as frequently as other variables. That is why each variable in CherryPi is weighted for reliability. This implies that a change in one variable can weight a number of times heavier than a change in another variable. The best solution for the record is obtained by minimising the sum of the reliability weights of the variables changed, such that all edit rules are satisfied. The resulting constrained minimisation problem is solved with the Chernikova algorithm, cf. Chernikova (1965).

When several variables have the same weight, CherryPi often finds several equally good solutions. The output given by CherryPi contains all these solutions, from which one must be selected. In this case the first solution is always chosen. When many edit rules are violated, many variables must be changed. In such cases CherryPi cannot find a solution because there are too many possibilities to check and the record must be edited by hand anyway.

B. Available data

We have both manually and automatically edited data available for 4162 records, except for 247 records for which SLICE 1 could not find a solution. This is mainly due to the poor quality of these records, which means too many variables had to be adjusted. Although it may be possible to edit these records automatically anyway by improving SLICE 1, this is not the way we would go. The quality of these records is so low that they should be checked by an editor in any case. Table 5 shows that most of these records received an insufficient PI and would not end up with SLICE 1 during production. The percentage of records with a PI of four or more for which SLICE 1 could not find a solution was very small.

OPI	Total number of records	No solution	
		number	percentage
0	222	66	29.7%
1	560	76	13.6%
2	367	30	8.2%
3	303	20	6.6%
4	364	14	3.8%
5	373	11	2.9%
6	395	12	3.0%
7	593	14	2.4%
8	685	4	0.6%
9	292	0	0%
10	8	0	0%
Total	4162	247	5.9%

The crucial edit cells contain 216 enterprises. Together with the group that cannot be edited automatically, there are 449 records (11% of the total in the twelve publication cells) that have to be edited by hand in any case.[1] This means that the percentage of automatically edited records cannot exceed 90%.

C. Publication totals in evaluation versus actual publication totals

Part of the manually edited data in this evaluation come from the production of ASBS 2000 and part were edited especially for this evaluation. We assume that the editing quality of the records later edited by hand is as good as the editing of the records that were originally edited by hand. There are still differences between the ASBS 2000 production and our evaluation. This is mainly due to the following points:

1. The implementation of the plausibility indicators was not ready when manual editing was started for production. So at the start of the editing process, records with unknown OPI's went to the editors. Some of these may have had a sufficient OPI, and could have been edited automatically. In the analysis we assume that all records that would have had a sufficient OPI went to SLICE 1. So this means we could overestimate the inaccuracy of the published totals for ASBS 2000.

2. In the production of ASBS 2000 we used a new weighting method. However, during this analysis we used an old weighting method, because we were only interested in the trend breach as a consequence of the introduction of selective editing. In the old method direct weighting is done per SIC and company size on the basis of the population and survey sample sizes, excluding outliers. A number of records were already identified as outliers in the editing phase. These records were given a weighting factor of 1.

3. For the evaluation we used the production database as it was directly after micro-editing and before the UniEdit 2 process. So we did not have the outlier indications that were determined in that process.

[1] Because the two groups of records overlap somewhat, the total number is smaller than the sum of the sizes of the two individual groups.

The weighted totals we calculated are therefore not identical to the published totals. Furthermore, aggregated deviations between records that were edited manually and automatically, which are calculated in the next section, can differ from these deviations in practice.

Because more records were edited manually than was necessary on the basis of the OPI, and because the greatest deviations from the ASBS 1999 figures were smoothed out in the validation step, the bias in the published totals will be lower than the values we calculated. We are mainly interested in the effect of automatic editing as it will take place in the future. We therefore feel that it is more important to look at the ideal case, in which the PI is available from the very beginning, and no work has to be done during validation.

D. Evaluation criteria

The bias of a weighted total after selective automatic editing is the expected deviation from the real population total. Because this population total is unknown we cannot determine this bias. However, we are concerned with the difference between automatic and manual editing. So we can approximate the bias with the difference between the weighted total of 100% manually edited data and that of partly automatically edited data. We call this value the *pseudo-bias* due to selective automatic editing. It is expressed as a percentage of the manually edited weighted total.

The pseudo bias of SLICE 1 for variable y_j is assessed for a publication cell by computing

$$pb(y_j) = \frac{\sum_{\bar{S}} w_i (y_{ij}^a - y_{ij}^c)}{\sum_C w_i y_{ij}^c}, \qquad (8)$$

where

$\bar{S}$: is the set of records that were edited automatically in a publication cell;
C : is the set of all records in a publication cell;
y_{ij}^a : is an automatically edited raw value;
y_{ij}^c : is an interactively edited raw value that was edited automatically in production.

Note that (8) looks similar to the expression between absolute signs in (1). The only difference is that we now use automatic edited (acceptable) values instead of raw values. In section VIII we will present the nominator in (8) as a percentage of the denominator in (8).

The pseudo-bias of SLICE 1 depends on the selection of records that are edited automatically (and therefore on the OPI) and on the quality of automatic editing with SLICE 1. The aim is to keep the influence of automatic editing on the weighted totals to a minimum. So the pseudo-bias must be small.
However, it will differ across variables. The main reasons are:

- Some variables are given much more attention when the plausibility of a record is assessed. Therefore, SLICE 1 will mainly have to correct small errors for these variables.
- The number of times that SLICE 1 adjusts a raw value for variable y_j depends on the specified confidence weight, the number of empty/zero values for variable y_j and the number of times that variable y_j is involved in violated edit rules.

For variable y_j the percentage of records that are edited automatically might be increased when $|pb(y_j)| < \delta_j$, where δ_j is determined on the basis of quality requirements. For a set of variables the percentage of records that are edited automatically might be increased when

$$\sum_{j=1}^{J}\alpha_j\left|pb(y_j)\right| < \sum_{j=1}^{J}\alpha_j\delta_j \cdot$$

On the other hand, we might argue that none of the *important* variables are allowed to have an unacceptable pseudo bias. In this case the percentage of records that are edited automatically can only be increased for an edit cell when

$$\forall\, y_j, j = 1,2,\ldots,J, \quad \text{if } \alpha_j \geq \varepsilon_j \text{ then } |\, pb(y_j)\,| < \delta_j \quad ,$$

where ε_j denotes the minimal importance weight for a variable to be important.

8. DEVIATIONS AS A RESULT OF AUTOMATIC EDITING

A. Pseudo-bias as a result of selective editing

The pseudo-bias is calculated for all variables and twelve publication cells on the basis of the OPI as it could have been used in 2000. Due to problems, specified above, with the OPI calculation during production of ASBS 2000, the selection of automatically edited records in our study is not identical to the selection of automatically edited records during production.

There is a great deal of variation in pseudo-bias. For most variables the pseudo-bias is close to zero. This is because many variables are hardly changed by editors or SLICE 1. This is mainly true for less important variables. Variables that show major deviations, however, are also usually unimportant ones. For important variables the pseudo-bias is at most 15%. The pseudo-bias of 15% is caused by errors in the program that corrects obvious mistakes. These errors have been removed for ASBS 2001. Details of this research are given in Van der Pijll & Hoogland (2003).

Pseudo-biases in publication cells for transport are usually greater than those for trade. This is because questionnaires for transport are not filled in as well as those for wholesale and retail trade. One way to explain this is that cover pages of the questionnaires are the same for all publication cells trade and transport, while they are based on questionnaires for trade ASBS 1999. This may confuse respondents from transport, because definitions in variables may differ.

For some variables we found the cause of deviant editing by SLICE 1. These deviations were mainly found in the publication cells for transport. It will be possible to remove major deviations in these variables in the future by

- improving questionnaires (Bikker, 2003a; Bikker, 2003b; Van der Pijll & Hoogland, 2003);
- splitting heterogeneous publication cells (Van der Pijll & Hoogland, 2003);
- adapting the software that corrects obvious mistakes (Bikker, 2003a);
- improving plausibility indicators (Hoogland & Van der Pijll , 2003);
- adding a number of edit rules (Bikker, 2003a; Bikker, 2003b; Van der Pijll & Hoogland, 2003);
- adjusting reliability weights (Bikker, 2003a; Bikker, 2003b; Van der Pijll & Hoogland, 2003);
- improving the error localisation module within SLICE (De Waal & Quere, 2000; Quere, 2000);

– building an extra step in the statistical proces before SLICE, which removes systematic mistakes that do not follow the Fellegi-Holt principle (Bikker, 2003a; Bikker, 2003b).

B. The effect of more automatic editing

One key question is whether the percentage of records that is edited automatically can be increased or must be decreased. We can study this by varying the selection of records to be edited automatically. We can again calculate the pseudo-bias for each selection. This will generally be larger as the percentage of automatically edited records increases. In some cases the errors of the added automatically edited records can cancel out some of the existing deviation, so that the pseudo-bias is reduced. However, these are only incidental cases, and we should not count on them.

We varied the threshold for sufficient grades. This means we varied the number of records for which the OPI is considered sufficient. Table 6 shows the percentage of records that is automatically edited at the given threshold. When the threshold is six, as was the case for ASBS 2000, the percentage of automatically edited records is between 43 and 62 percent for most publication cells. It is impossible to determine the percentage in advance because the PPI are calibrated on the basis of raw and edited values of the previous year. Therefore the percentage of automatically edited records fluctuates for each publication cell. Apparently the PI was very severe for publication cell 152110, because only 28% of the records were deemed plausible enough for automatic editing. When the threshold is four the percentage of automatically edited records will exceed 60% in most publication cells, whereas a threshold of two will generally correspond to an automatic editing percentage from 72 to 90 percent.

In Appendix D we show how the pseudo-bias depends on the threshold for three key variables. Table 8 shows that it is very difficult to automatically edit the number of employed persons in publication cell 161200 (inland shipping) when the threshold is set at six. The deviation between automatic and manual editing is over 5% here. This is partly due to a systematic error made by the respondents, which is not always detected by the overall plausibility indicator. This systematic error cannot be corrected by SLICE 1. There are no significant problems in the other publication cells. When the percentage of automatically edited records exceeds 60%, the pseudo-bias in the total number of employed persons in publication cells 152121C and 163300 reaches more than 2%.

Publication cell	1	2	3	4	5	6	7
151200B	83%	72%	64%	60%	55%	48%	38%
151300C	83%	79%	73%	65%	58%	53%	44%
151600C	85%	74%	62%	52%	46%	43%	36%
152110	81%	65%	54%	46%	37%	28%	22%
152121C	88%	77%	68%	62%	53%	43%	41%
152121E	91%	82%	74%	65%	55%	48%	45%
160220	83%	73%	64%	59%	55%	44%	36%
161100	94%	90%	85%	80%	73%	62%	43%
161200	93%	86%	80%	77%	71%	62%	53%
163110	89%	81%	77%	77%	70%	61%	48%
163300	87%	72%	66%	59%	49%	38%	34%
163400	83%	72%	67%	62%	53%	44%	30%
All twelve cells	86%	76%	68%	61%	54%	45%	36%

The variable net turnover (table 9) is correctly edited automatically in almost all publication cells. Raising the percentage of automatically edited records to 80% causes virtually no problems for these variables. The only publication cell in which there is a major difference between manual and automatic editing is cell 163300 (travelling organisations and travel intermediation). This is because respondents often fill in some purchase value while the variable in this publication cell should almost always be zero. The editors usually remove the purchase value and balance it with net turnover, whereas SLICE 1 leaves the records unchanged. This leads to major pseudo-bias in these variables, because the overall plausibility indicator fails to detect some of those errors. The resulting bias cannot be avoided by applying extra edit rules. The problem will continue to show up in future, because the Fellegi-Holt principle does not hold. One long-term solution for this problem is an extra editing round focusing on specific errors such as these.

SLICE 1 does a fairly good edit of total operating result (table 10) for all publication cells. However, when SLICE 1 has to edit more records some difficulties show up in various publication cells. SLICE 1 cannot cope with all influential errors that are unseen by the overall plausibility indicator. For publication cell 163300 pseudo-bias occurs when the threshold is set at five or less. This corresponds to a percentage of records to be edited automatically of over 50%. In publication cell 163110 (loading, unloading, warehousing) the problems start around 75%.

The pseudo-bias for most variables and publication cells is small. It does not get much higher either when the number of records edited by SLICE 1 increases up to 70%. This is not true for variables with a large pseudo-bias in a publication cell. For these variables and publication cells we can see a rapid increase in pseudo-bias when the number of automatically edited records increases.

Tables 8-10 show several high percentages. This does not mean that these major deviations ended up in the published totals, though. The weighted totals of these variables may have been corrected by the automatic outlier detection, the new weighting method, or during validation, substantially reducing these deviations.

9. CONCLUSIONS

At Statistics Netherlands a uniform statistical process for annual structural business statistics has been developed. In this new process, some obvious mistakes in raw data are edited automatically in an early stage. A partition is then made between records for further automatic editing and records for manual editing. Records that are labelled as crucial are always edited manually. Non-crucial records with an insufficient overall plausibility indicator are also edited manually. The remaining records are edited automatically by means of SLICE.

Partial plausibility indicators are used to assess the plausibility of specific parts of a questionnaire. These indicators assist an editor in locating errors in a record. Every year the partial plausibility indicators have to be calibrated before the new annual structural business statistics are edited. For this calibration correct and raw data of annual structural business statistics of last year are needed. Calibration of PPI's is not straightforward due to possible lack of correct and raw data.

When records that have been edited automatically are also edited manually and vice versa, the performance of the overall and partial plausibility indicators, and SLICE can be assessed. Furthermore, it can be investigated whether the percentage of records that is edited automatically has to be adjusted. We examined differences between manually and automatically edited weighted totals of ASBS 2000 prior to validation. We assumed that the plausibility indicator was operative during the entire editing period. The evaluation was made for twelve publication cells in the wholesale and retail trade, and in transport.

The effect of selective editing differs per variable. Most variables are hardly changed during manual or automatic editing. This is true both for less important variables and for some key variables such as total operating costs, total labour costs and total operating profits. The weighted totals for these variables hardly change in most publication cells when selective editing is used. Even when the percentage of automatic editing increases to 80% the deviation in the weighted totals for these variables stays under 2%.

However, for some variables the deviations of selective editing are large. These are mainly variables from the results block of the questionnaire, such as the result before taxes and the financial result. The current 45% threshold for automatic editing already yields many deviations of more than 5% in the weighted totals of these variables. When the percentage of records for automatic editing increases, the quality of these variables will plummet.

We found the greatest deviations in publication cells in transport. The problems are such that these publication cells will have to be edited more by hand, rather than less. The deviations in wholesale and retail trade are smaller. It depends on the level of bias in the published figures that is considered acceptable whether we can gain in efficiency by more automatic editing. The biases mentioned in this chapter are based on how the PI and SLICE 1 worked during ASBS 2000. There may well be less bias in most variables in the future when the PI and SLICE 1 are improved.

We have found room for improvement on a number of points. By adding a few edit rules, by developing software that removes systematic errors, and by improving the questionnaires we can come up with considerable improvements for the variables. Some of these improvements can be applied to large numbers of publication cells, also well beyond the twelve cells we studied here. Other improvements are publication cell specific (for instance pertaining to inland shipping and travel organisations). When these improvements are implemented those publication cells where SLICE 1 currently produces major deviations may well be edited without major problems.

References

[1] Bikker, R.P., 2003a, *Evaluation of automatic versus manual editing of Annual Structural Business statistics 2000 Trade & Transport – additional explanations (In Dutch)*. Internal paper BPA-no 1900-03-TMO, Statistics Netherlands, Voorburg.

[2] Bikker, R.P., 2003b, *Automatic editing of Annual Structural Business statistics 2000 Building & Construction branche: four structural problems with solutions (In Dutch)*. Internal paper BPA-no 2263-03-TMO, Statistics Netherlands, Voorburg.

[3] Chernikova, N.V., 1965, Algorithm for finding a general formula for the non-negative solutions of a system of linear inequalities. *USSR Computational Mathematics and Mathematical Physics*, **5**, pp. 228-233.

[4] Granquist, L., 1995, Improving the Traditional Editing Process. In*: Business Survey Methods* (ed. Cox, Binder, Chinnappa, Christianson, and Kott), John Wiley & Sons, pp. 385-401.

[5] Granquist, L. and J. Kovar, 1997, Editing of Survey Data: How Much is Enough? In: *Survey Measurement and Process Quality* (ed. Lyberg, Biemer, Collins, De Leeuw, Dippo, Schwartz, and Trewin), John Wiley & Sons, pp. 415-435.

[6] Hidiroglou, M.A., and J.-M. Berthelot, 1986, Statistical Editing and Imputation for Periodic Business Surveys. *Survey Methodology*, **12**, pp. 73-83.

[7] Hoogland, J. J. en E.C. van der Pijll, 2003, *Evaluation of the plausibility indicator for production statistics 2000 Trade & Transport (In Dutch)*. Internal paper BPA-no 1971-03-TMO, Statistics Netherlands, Voorburg.

[8] Jong, A.G., 2002, *UniEdit: Standardised processing of structural business statistics in The Netherlands*. Invited paper for UNECE Work Session on Statistical Data Editing, 27-29 May 2002, Helsinki, Finland.

[9] Quere, R., 2000, *Automatic Editing of Numerical Data*. Report BPA-no 2284-00-RSM, Statistics Netherlands, Voorburg.

[10] Rivière, P., 2002, *General principles for data editing in business surveys and how to optimize it*. Contributed paper for UNECE Work Session on Statistical Data Editing, 27-29 May 2002, Helsinki, Finland.

[11] Van der Pijll, E.C. en J. J. Hoogland, 2003, *Evaluation of automatic versus manual editing of annual structural business statistics 2000 Trade & Transport (In Dutch)*. Internal paper BPA-no 286-03-TMO, Statistics Netherlands, Voorburg.

[12] Waal, T. de, 2000, SLICE: generalised software for statistical data editing and imputation. In: *Proceedings in computational statistics 2000* (ed. J.G. Bethlehem and P.G.M. van der Heijden), Physica-Verlag, Heidelberg, pp. 277-282.

[13] Waal, T. de, and Quere, R., 2000, *Error localisation in Mixed Data Sets*. Report BPA-no 2285-00-RSM, Statistics Netherlands, Voorburg.

[14] Waal, T. de, and Wings, 1999, *From CherryPi to SLICE*. Report BPA-no 461-99-RSM, Statistics Netherlands, Voorburg.

Appendix A: Different types of cells for selective editing of ASBS

company size class	company size	number of employees	NACE: publication cell (=NACE 52121+52122): 52121	NACE: publication cell (=NACE 52121+52122): 52122	NACE: publication cell (=NACE 5263): 5263
	0	0			median cell
Small	1	1			
	2	2-4	edit cell		sample cell
	3	5-9			
Medium	4	10-19			
	5	20-49	sample cell	sample cell	edit cell
	6	50-99			
Large	7	100-199	median cell		
	8	200-499			
	9	> 499			

Figure 2. Cells for selective editing of ASBS, which are combinations of NACE and company size.

Appendix B: Partial plausibility formulas

The partial plausibility formulas below are computed for each record in each edit cell. The quantities in the formulas can vary across edit cells.

PPF **Block** b , b = **A**, **B**, **C**, and **D** are computed as follows

$$\text{PPF}_i\ \textbf{Block} = \sqrt{\frac{\sum_{j=1}^{J_b} \alpha_j \cdot \left(\frac{y_{ij} - m_{cj}}{Y_j}\right)^2}{\pi_i^2 \cdot \sum_{j=1}^{J_b} \alpha_j \cdot \left(\frac{m_{cj}}{Y_j}\right)^2}}, \quad (9)$$

where

- $y_{ij}, j = 1,2,...,J_b$, are entries for business unit i and year t that are considered for a specific block;
- $m_{cj}, j = 1,2,...,J_b$, are the corresponding population medians for year t-1 and median cell c containing business unit i in year t;
- $Y_j, j = 1,2,...,J_b$, are the corresponding weighted edit cell totals for year t-1;
- $\alpha_j, j = 1,2,...,J_b$, denotes the importance of variable y_j, which can differ across edit cells;

- π_i is the inclusion probability of business unit i in year t.

If an entry y_{ij} is equal to 0 or empty then $y_{ij} = e_{cj} \cdot m_{cj}$ is used instead, where e_{cj} is the empty entry factor of variable y_j. If $m_{cj} = 0$ then m_{cj} is first given the value 1 and y_{ij} is then given the value e_{cj}. An empty entry factor is large when it is unlikely that the corresponding entry equals 0.

The PPF for external information is computed as follows

$$\text{PPF}_\text{i}\ \textbf{External} = \frac{\sum_{j=1}^{J_E} \alpha_{ij} \cdot \sqrt{\frac{1}{2}\cdot\left(\frac{y_{ij}}{x_{ij}}\right)^2 + \frac{1}{2}\cdot\left(\frac{x_{ij}}{y_{ij}}\right)^2}}{\sum_{j=1}^{J_E} \alpha_{ij}}, \qquad (10)$$

where

- y_{ij}, $j = 1,2,...,J_E$, are entries for business unit i and year t that are compared with external sources;
- x_{ij}, $j = 1,2,...,J_E$, are external sources for business unit i and year t;
- α_{ij}, $j = 1,2,...,J_E$, denotes the importance of y_{ij}.

If y_{ij} or x_{ij} is equal to 0 or empty then $\alpha_{ij} = 0$, otherwise $\alpha_{ij} = \alpha_j$. This is necessary because external information is often incomplete. If y_{ij} or x_{ij} is equal to 0 or empty for each $j = 1,2,...,J_E$ then PPF$_\text{i}$ **External** = (upper limit for mark 6 + upper limit for mark 7) / 2 . That is, if there is insufficient information to calculate PPF **External** then PPI **External** equals six.

The PPF for ratios is computed as follows

$$\text{PPF}_\text{i}\ \textbf{Ratios} = \frac{\sum_{j=1}^{J_R} \alpha_j \cdot \sqrt{\frac{1}{2}\left(\frac{r_{ij}}{k_{cj}}\right)^2 + \frac{1}{2}\left(\frac{k_{cj}}{r_{ij}}\right)^2}}{\sum_{j=1}^{J_R} \alpha_j}, \qquad (11)$$

where

- r_{ij}, $j = 1,2,...,J_R$, are ratios for business unit i and year t;
- k_{cj}, $j = 1,2,...,J_R$, are the corresponding population medians for year t-1 and median cell c containing business unit i in year t;
- α_j, $j = 1,2,...,J_R$, denotes the importance of ratio r_j, which can differ across edit cells.

The PPF for quality of filling-out is computed as follows

$$\text{PPF}_i\ \textbf{Quality} = \sqrt{\frac{w_{EMPTY}\cdot\left(\frac{\#EMPTY_i}{\#EMPTY_{MAX}}\right)^2 + w_{HARD}\cdot\left(\frac{\#VEDIT_i}{\#VEDIT_{MAX}}\right)^2}{w_{EMPTY} + w_{HARD}}}, \quad (12)$$

where

- w_{EMPTY} and w_{HARD} are weights for the two quality aspects;
- $\#EMPTY_i$ is the number of empty entries for business unit i in year t and $\#EMPTY_{MAX}$ is the total number of entries for an edit cell;
- $\#VEDIT_i$ is the number of violated edit rules for business unit i in year t and $\#VEDIT_{MAX}$ is an estimate of the maximum number of violated edit rules for an edit cell that will occur in practice.

Appendix C. Some evaluation criteria for the Overall Plausibility Indicator

Table 7. Evaluation criteria (1) and (7) for OPI, for total number of employed persons, net turnover, and operating result. Criterion (1) is printed in boldface if larger than 0.05 and criterion (7) is printed in boldface if larger than 0.1.

Publication cell	Size class	Number of employees		Net turnover		Operating result	
		Criterion (1)	Criterion (7)	Criterion (1)	Criterion (7)	Criterion (1)	Criterion (7)
151200B	2	0.01	0.06	0.00	0.00	0.00	0.00
151300C	2	0.01	0.04	0.00	0.00	0.01	0.00
151600C	2	0.00	0.00	0.00	0.00	0.01	0.00
152110	1	0.00	0.02	0.00	0.00	0.00	0.00
	2	0.00	0.01	0.00	0.00	0.00	0.00
152121C	1	0.01	0.10	0.00	0.00	0.03	0.00
	2	0.01	0.07	0.00	0.00	0.01	0.00
152121E	1	0.01	0.03	0.00	0.00	0.02	0.00
	2	0.00	0.00	0.00	0.00	0.00	0.00
160220	1	0.00	0.03	0.00	0.00	0.01	0.00
	2	0.02	0.08	0.00	0.00	0.00	0.00
161100	1	0.01	0.06	0.00	0.01	0.00	0.01
	2	0.00	0.01	0.00	0.00	0.00	0.00
161200	1	0.04	0.09	0.00	0.00	0.00	0.00
	2	0.00	0.03	0.00	0.05	0.00	0.04
163110	1	0.00	0.08	0.00	0.00	0.03	0.00
	2	0.01	0.05	0.00	0.01	**0.10**	0.00
163300	1	0.00	0.00	0.03	**0.70**	0.00	**0.69**
	2	0.00	0.01	**0.05**	**0.32**	**0.07**	**0.31**
163400	1	0.00	0.04	0.00	0.01	0.00	0.01
	2	0.01	0.05	0.00	0.00	0.05	0.00

Appendix D. Pseudo-bias in publication totals for several key variables

A column in table 8-10 shows the pseudo-bias resulting from automatic editing of records with a PI equal to the threshold or higher. When the pseudo-bias exceeds 5% it is printed in bold character. Pseudo-biases between 2% and 5% are underlined.

Publication cell	Threshold for plausibility indicator						
	1	2	3	4	5	6	7
151200B	1.1%	1.1%	0.5%	0.6%	0.6%	0.1%	0.3%
151300C	0.3%	0.1%	0.2%	0.3%	0.2%	0.2%	0.1%
151600C	0.8%	0.2%	0.1%	0.1%	0.1%	0.1%	0.1%
152110	0.8%	0.3%	0.1%	0.0%	0.0%	0.0%	0.0%
152121C	3.6%	2.4%	2.4%	2.5%	1.8%	1.5%	1.4%
152121E	0.1%	0.5%	0.4%	0.5%	0.8%	1.0%	1.1%
160220	2.5%	0.7%	1.2%	1.0%	1.0%	0.9%	0.8%
161100	1.5%	1.4%	1.4%	1.4%	1.4%	1.4%	1.3%
161200	**7.7%**	**5.4%**	**5.1%**	4.1%	5.0%	**5.4%**	4.2%
163110	1.2%	1.4%	1.4%	1.4%	1.4%	1.4%	1.1%
163300	2.3%	2.1%	2.1%	0.5%	0.2%	0.0%	0.0%
163400	0.1%	0.2%	0.3%	0.1%	0.2%	0.3%	0.0%

Publication cell	Threshold for plausibility indicator						
	1	2	3	4	5	6	7
151200B	0.2%	0.2%	0.0%	0.0%	0.0%	0.0%	0.0%
151300C	0.2%	0.1%	0.1%	0.1%	0.1%	0.1%	0.1%
151600C	0.2%	0.2%	0.0%	0.0%	0.0%	0.0%	0.0%
152110	0.1%	0.0%	0.0%	0.0%	0.0%	0.0%	0.0%
152121C	0.3%	0.1%	0.0%	0.0%	0.0%	0.0%	0.0%
152121E	0.6%	0.2%	0.2%	0.1%	0.0%	0.0%	0.0%
160220	0.0%	0.0%	0.0%	0.0%	0.0%	0.0%	0.0%
161100	**5.1%**	0.2%	0.0%	0.1%	0.1%	0.1%	0.1%
161200	0.8%	0.4%	0.4%	0.4%	0.4%	0.5%	0.0%
163110	0.6%	0.3%	0.3%	0.3%	0.2%	0.2%	0.2%
163300	**34.6%**	**21.6%**	**18.0%**	**16.8%**	**13.1%**	**8.7%**	**7.7%**
163400	0.4%	0.4%	0.4%	0.4%	0.2%	0.1%	0.1%

Publication cell	Threshold for plausibility indicator						
	1	2	3	4	5	6	7
151200B	0.8%	0.2%	1.3%	1.1%	0.7%	0.6%	0.2%
151300C	0.4%	0.5%	0.5%	0.9%	0.1%	0.1%	0.1%
151600C	0.6%	0.2%	0.5%	0.3%	0.3%	0.2%	0.2%
152110	1.5%	1.7%	1.4%	0.3%	0.2%	0.2%	0.0%
152121C	**10.1%**	1.0%	2.4%	1.9%	1.9%	1.7%	1.7%
152121E	**12.7%**	0.8%	0.8%	0.3%	0.3%	0.1%	0.1%
160220	1.4%	1.3%	1.3%	1.2%	1.2%	2.1%	2.0%
161100	**8.2%**	2.7%	0.0%	0.3%	0.2%	0.5%	0.5%
161200	0.5%	0.2%	1.0%	1.2%	1.2%	0.3%	0.5%
163110	4.9%	**5.3%**	**5.3%**	**5.3%**	1.0%	0.9%	0.6%
163300	**8.0%**	**7.8%**	**8.0%**	**8.2%**	**8.3%**	0.6%	0.6%
163400	**39.5%**	0.8%	1.1%	1.1%	0.2%	1.1%	0.2%

EVALUATING NEW METHODS FOR DATA EDITING AND IMPUTATION – RESULTS FROM THE EUREDIT PROJECT

by John Charlton, Office for National Statistics (ONS), United Kingdom

1. INTRODUCTION

Advances in statistical and computer science have created opportunities for the application of newer technologies such as neural networks and outlier-robust methods for edit and imputation. The EUREDIT project, now completed, set out to assist users to make informed choices regarding the methods they use for automatic edit and imputation, by evaluating alternatives systematically, using real data. This paper describes in overview the findings of the EUREDIT project, which was funded under EU Fifth Framework research programme - a large multi-national collaboration involving twelve partners from seven countries (see http://www.cs.york.ac.uk/euredit). The project was based on real data and real problems encountered in official statistical data, and had the following objectives:

- To establish a standard collection of data sets for evaluation purposes
- To develop a methodological evaluation framework and develop evaluation criteria
- To establish a baseline by evaluating currently used methods.
- To develop and evaluate a selected range of new techniques.
- To evaluate different methods and establish best methods for different data types.
- To disseminate the best methods via a software CD and publications.

The project involved 12 partners from 7 countries, and its methods has been described previously - see http://www.unece.org/stats/documents/2002/05/sde/35.e.pdf.

The first stage of the project involved developing a framework for statistical evaluation (Chambers, 2001) – see Tables 1,2. This framework was then used within the project to evaluate both existing methods and those developed within the life of the project. It is envisaged that NSIs could also use the framework outside the Euredit project to evaluate other edit and imputation methods, including new techniques developed in the future. Operational characteristics of the methods examined (Tables 3 – 5) were also recorded, such as general features, resource requirements, judgement/ experience required etc. In this paper an overview of the findings, with selected examples, will be presented. Here we use the term "edit" to describe the process of detecting values or records with errors, and "imputation" as the process of correcting these errors or filling in holes in the data. The edit and imputation methods examined and their characteristics are described in Tables 1 to 2 below. The web version of the Euredit publication will be available at http://www.cs.york.ac.uk/euredit/CDindex.html.

2. STATISTICAL PERFORMANCE MEASURES USED IN EUREDIT EVALUATIONS

Table 1

Measures for evaluating performance of edit methods	
Measures of editing efficiency – smaller values denote better performance	
Alpha	Proportion of false negatives resulting from edit process for variable j (errors that are accepted as valid by the edit process). Estimates the probability that the editing process does not detect an incorrect value.
Beta	Proportion of false positives resulting from edit process for variable j (correct values that the edit process identifies as errors). Estimates the probability that a correct value is incorrectly identified as suspicious.
Delta	Proportion of editing errors overall. Provides a global measure of the inaccuracy of the editing process.
A	Proportion of cases that contain at least one incorrect value and that pass all edits (false negatives)
B	Proportion of cases containing no errors that fail at least one edit (false positives)

C	Proportion of incorrect case-level error detections
G	Gini coefficient for measuring error localisation performance. N.B. only applicable to edit processes that assign probabilities of being in error to variables
Measures of influential error detection performance - based on size of errors in post-edited data. Smaller values denote better edit performance	
RAE	Relative average error (scalar variables only), the ratio of the mean of post-edit errors to the mean of the true values
RRASE	Relative root average squared error (scalar variables only), the ratio of the square root of the mean of the squares of the post-edit errors to the mean of the true values
RER	Relative error range (scalar variables only), the ratio of the range of post-edit errors to their inter-quartile range
Dcat	Categorical or nominal data measure of relative error – weighted proportion of cases where post-edit and true values disagree
t_j	t-test for how effective editing process has been for error reduction for variable j – values >2 indicate significant failure of edit process (continuous and categorical versions available)
Measures of outlier detection performance, smaller values denote better edit performance	
AREm1	Absolute relative error of the k-mean for 1st moment
AREm2	Absolute relative error of the k-mean for 2nd moment

Table 2

Measures for evaluating performance of imputation methods	
Performance measures for predictive accuracy of imputation	
Categorical data	
D	Proportion of imputed cases where true values differ from imputed values. The smaller the better - ideal is zero.
Eps	Test statistic for preservation of true values in imputation, based on D
Dgen	Generalised version of D that takes into account the distances between categories
Continuous data	
mse	Mean square error from regressing true values on imputed values (zero intercept) using weighted robust regression - the smaller the better
t-val	t-statistic for testing slope=1 in above (smaller is better)
slope	Slope of regression line - should be close to 1
R^2	R^2 for above regression - proportion of variance in Y* explained by $\hat{Y}$
DL1	Mean distance between true and imputed values (L1 norm)
DL2	Mean distance between squares of true and imputed values (L2 norm)
DLinf	Distance measure between true and imputed values (L infinity norm – maximum distance between imputed and true values)
Performance measures of distributional accuracy of imputation methods	
Categorical variables	
W	Wald statistic for testing preservation of marginal distributions of categorical variables - distribution is chi-square with degrees of freedom =c (number of categories) for large n for stochastic imputation methods. Compares marginal distributions of imputed and true values.
Continuous (scalar) variables	
K-S	Kalmogorov-Smirnov for testing preservation of distribution (compares distributions of imputed and true values)
K-S_1	Alternative Kalmogorov-Smirnov for testing preservation of distribution using L1 norm (compares distributions of imputed and true values)
K-S_2	Alternative Kalmogorov-Smirnov for testing preservation of distribution using L2 norm (compares distributions of imputed and true values)
Performance measures for estimation accuracy	
m_1	Absolute difference between 1st moments of true and imputed values
m_2	Absolute difference between 2nd moments of true and imputed values
MSE	Evaluation of outlier-robust imputation. Mean square error of imputed values compared with true values
R_k	For time-series data, a measure of the relative discrepancy between estimated lag k auto-correlates for true and imputed values

3. EDIT AND IMPUTATION METHODS INCLUDED IN EUREDIT EVALUATIONS

The methods have been described in http://www.unece.org/stats/documents/2002/05/sde/35.e.pdf and in more detail in the volume *'Towards effective statistical Editing and Imputation Strategies – Findings of the Euredit Project"* (Charlton (ed), 2003).

Table 3. Characteristics of Edit and combined edit/imputation methods evaluated in EUREDIT

METHOD	CANCEIS	SCIA	GEIS	MLP neural networks	SOM/ NDA	CMM	IMAI	Cherry Pie[22]
Is it:								
Based on Fellegi-Holt?	No	Yes	Yes	No	No	No	No	Yes
Does method cover:								
Logical edit rules?	Yes	Yes	Yes	No	See[11]	No	No	Yes
Logical imputation rules?	Yes	Yes	Yes	No	See[12]	No	No	No
Does method require:								
Pre-specified edits?	Yes	Yes	Yes	No	No	No	No	Yes
Pre-specified parameters?	No	No	Yes	Yes	No	No[18]	No	No
Which parameters?	N/A	N/A	See [5]	See [8]	See[13]	See[19]	N/A	N/A
Pre-specified imputation rules	Yes	Yes	Yes	No	No	No	No	N/A
Other pre-specified imputation parameters	Yes	Yes[3]	No	No	No	See[20]	No	N/A
Training sample with raw values	No	No	No	Yes	No	No	No	No
Training sample with target values	No	No	No	Yes	No	No	No	No
Pre-process scaling of data?	Yes[1]	Yes[4]	No	Yes	Yes	No	Yes	No
Other pre-process transformation of data?	Yes[2]	No	Yes[6]	Yes[10]	See [14]	See[21]	Yes	No
Post process rescaling of data?	No	No	Yes[7]	Yes	See [15]	No	No	No
Post process other transformation of results?	No	No	No	No	No	No	No	No
Methodological experts?	Yes	Yes	Yes	Yes	See [16]	No	Yes	No
IT experts?	No	No	Yes	No	See [17]	No	No	No
Does it operate:								
Sequentially for each variable?	No	No	No	Yes	No	Yes	Yes	No
Simultaneously for set of variables?	Yes	Yes	Yes	Yes[9]	Yes	Yes	No	Yes
Types of variables dealt with:								
Categorical, nominal variables?	Yes	Yes	No	Yes	Yes	Yes	Yes	Yes
Categorical ordinal variables?	Yes	Yes	No	Yes	Yes	Yes	Yes	Yes
Continuous variables?	Yes	No	Yes	Yes	Yes	Yes	Yes	Yes

Table 4. Characteristics of imputation methods evaluated in EUREDIT

METHOD	DIS	Multi-variate regression	Hot-deck ratio	Hot-deck donor	EC System	Censor-ing	EM	Time Series methods[1]	SVM
Does method cover:									
Logical imputation rules?	No	No	Yes	No	Yes	No	No	No	No
Does method require:									
Pre-specified edits?	No	No	No	No	Yes	No	No	No	No
Pre-specified parameters?	No	No	No	No	No	No	Yes	Yes	No
Which parameters?	N/A	N/A	N/A	N/A	N/A	N/A	See [8]	See [2]	N/A
Pre-specified imputation rules	No	No	No	No	No	No	No	No	No
Other pre-specified imputation parameters	No	No	No	No	No	No	No	Yes [-see 2]	No
Training sample with raw values	No	No	No	No	No	No	No	No	Yes
Training sample with target values	No	No	No	No	No	No	No	No	Yes
Pre-process scaling of data?	No	No	No	No	No	No	Yes	No	Yes
Other pre-process transformation of data?	No	No	No	No	No	No	No	Yes[3]	Yes[7]
Post process rescaling of data?	No	No	No	No	No	No	Yes	No	Yes
Post process other transformation of results?	No	No	No	No	No	No	No	Yes[4]	Yes
Methodological experts?	Yes	Yes	Yes	Yes	No	Yes	Yes	Yes[5]	No
IT experts?	No	No	No	No	No	No	No	No	No
Does it operate:									
Sequentially for each variable?	No	No	No	No	No	Yes	No	No	Yes
Simultaneously for set of variables?	Yes	Yes	Yes	Yes	Yes	No	Yes	Yes[6]	No
Types of variables dealt with:									
Categorical, nominal variables?	Yes	No	No	Yes	Yes	No	Yes	No	Yes
Categorical ordinal variables?	Yes	No	No	Yes	Yes	No	Yes	No	Yes
Continuous variables?	Yes	Yes	Yes	No	Yes	Yes	Yes	Yes	Yes

Table 5. Characteristics of outlier robust edit/imputation methods evaluated in EUREDIT

METHOD	TRC/ POEM	BEM/ POEM	EA/ POEM	Univa-riate WAID	Mutiva-riate WAID	Forward Search/ Regression Imputation
Is it:						
An edit method?	Yes	Yes	Yes	Yes	Yes	Yes
An imputation method?	Yes	Yes	Yes	Yes	Yes	Yes
Based on Fellegi-Holt?	No	No	No	No	No	No
Does method cover:						
Logical edit rules?[2]	No	No	No	No	No	No
Logical imputation rules?	No	No	No	No	No	No
Does method require:						
Pre-specified edits?	No	No	No	No	No	No
Pre-specified parameters?	Yes	Yes	Yes	Yes	Yes	Yes
Which parameters?	Tuning	Tuning	Tuning	Tuning	Tuning	Tuning
Pre-specified imputation rules	No	No	No	No	No	No
Other pre-specified imputation parameters	No	No	No	No	No	Yes[3]
Training sample with raw values	No	No	No	No	No	No
Training sample with target values	No	No	No	No[4]	No[5]	No
Pre-process scaling of data?[6]	Yes	Yes	Yes	Yes	Yes	Yes
Other pre-process transformation of data?	No	No	No	No	No	No
Post process rescaling of data?	No	No	No	No	No	No
Post process other transformation of results?	No	No	No	No	No	No
Methodological experts?	Yes	Yes	Yes	Yes	Yes	Yes
IT experts?	No	No	No	No	No	No
Does it operate:						
Sequentially for each variable?	No	No	No	Yes	No	Yes
Simultaneously for set of variables?	Yes	Yes	Yes	No	Yes	No
Types of variables dealt with:						
Categorical, nominal variables?	No	No	No	No	No	No
Categorical ordinal variables?	No	No	No	No	No	No
Continuous variables?	Yes	Yes	Yes	Yes	Yes	Yes

4. DATASETS USED FOR EUREDIT SIMULATION EXPERIMENTS

A range of *standard datasets* was selected (Table 6), representative of the different types of data encountered by National Statistics Offices and other potential users of edit and imputation methods. The datasets included in EUREDIT experiments needed to be suitable for the evaluation of a wide variety of edit and imputation techniques and cover a range of data sources, such as social surveys, business surveys, time series, censuses and registers. Within each dataset, a range of error types and missingness was required, allowing the data to exhibit inconsistencies, non-response (item and unit), outliers and missingness.

The specific reasons for including particular datasets were:

***The Danish Labour Force Survey*:**
A combination of information sampled from the register from a population register combined with a true non-response pattern for income from a social survey (Labour Force Survey). The Income variable (known from the register) needed to be imputed for non-respondents to the survey. This represents a real pattern of non-response, and known missing values.

U.K. Annual Business Inquiry
A business survey (self-completion questionnaire) containing commonly measured continuous variables such as Turnover and Wages. It is currently edited through re-contact of cases that fail logical edits checks. Information was available regarding the types of errors and pattern of missingness.

Sample of Anonymised Records from the 1991 U.K. Census
A random 1% sample of household records from a census. This was the largest dataset in EUREDIT, containing information on people within households – a hierarchical structure. From Census documentation, patterns of errors and missingness in the pre-edited data were recreated in the data distributed to participants.

Swiss Environment Protection Expenditures
A Business Survey containing some categorical variables plus mainly continuous data (expenditures), including a large number of true zero responses (i.e. where there was no expenditure), and outliers. The originators of the data themselves recreated the pattern of errors and missingness – missing in cases where data suppliers had to guess expenditure, and with errors as found in data as originally received.

German Socio-Economic Panel Survey
A social survey dataset, with a longitudinal aspect, consisting of information from a panel of people interviewed over a number of years. There is also an element of hierarchical data with information on people within households. Complete records were selected, and missing values for income were created according to the pattern of missingness in the full dataset.

Time Series Data for Financial Instruments
Financial time series, consisting of daily closing prices of over 100 stocks covering a time period of up to 5 years. This was the only dataset to contain time series information. The suppliers were also able to provide a simulated dataset for use in developing methods.

Table 6 Description of datasets used for EUREDIT evaluations

Dataset name	Type of dataset	Type of variables	Number of variables	Number of records
Danish Labour Force Survey (used for imputation only)	Administrative records with pattern of missingness from social survey.	Continuous variable for imputation (income), Ordinal, Nominal.	14	15,579
UK Annual Business Inquiry (ABI)	Business Inquiry Questionnaire	Mostly continuous (£000 sterling), 1 nominal (industry)	35	9,580
Sample of Anonymised Records from U.K.1991 Census (SARs)	Population Census	Categorical, Ordinal.	35	494,024
Swiss Environment Protection Expenditures (EPE)	Environmental Questionnaire	Continuous (SF 000), Binary, Categorical.	70	1,239
German Socio-Economic Panel Survey (GSOEP)	Panel Survey	Nominal, Ordinal, Continuous (income)	169	5,383
Times Series: Financial Instruments	Time Series	Continuous	124 time series	522 obs. per series

Treatment of datasets for evaluation purposes

Table 7 shows the notation used to describe the different versions of any single dataset. In the context of EUREDIT, a missing value is not an error, and is thus ignored in the evaluation of error detection - they are easily identified in the data and are the targets for imputation.

Table 7 – Notation to describe versions of datasets

Errors?	Missing?	
	Yes	No
Yes	Y_3	Y_1
No	Y_2	Y^*

The $\mathbf{Y}^*$ version of the dataset is assumed to be complete and without errors. For the purposes of the EUREDIT evaluations, 'true data' means data that the NSI provider considered to be satisfactorily cleaned by their edit and imputation procedures. One could also consider this as 'target data'. Version Y_2 (with missing values but no errors), and Y_3 (with missing values and errors) were distributed to partners for use in their experiments. No Y_1 (errors but no missing values) dataset was provided since it did not seem to represent a realistic situation.

The Danish Population Register/Labour Force Survey and GSOEP datasets each have two versions, Y^*, Y_2, as they are to be used solely for imputation. The other four datasets have three versions: Y^*, Y_2, Y_3, where Y_2 and Y_3 have different observation numbers for individual records to prevent potential disclosure of errors. For each dataset the Y^* data were retained by the co-ordinator (ONS), and the perturbed data, Y_2, Y_3, were distributed to partners for edit and imputation

Developmental datasets

Some methods, particularly neural networks, need to estimate parameters from clean data. In real life situations such networks would learn from data that had been meticulously manually edited – usually a previous survey of the same type or a sample of the actual data. In order to develop and test prototype systems, six development datasets based on a small subset of each original dataset were provided for use with these methods. Each of these were available in the three versions:

- True data (Y^*)

- Data with missing values but no errors (Y_2)
- Data with both errors and missing values (Y_3)

5. RESULTS

Altogether 191 experiments were run on the six datasets using the different methods, and each experiment involved a number of variables (see Table 6) and for each variable there might be around 30 evaluation formulae (Tables 1-2), for Y_2 and Y_3 versions of perturbed data. Thus there was a huge amount of information to synthesise in comparing methods. The full set of results will be published in the Project volume: *'Towards effective statistical Editing and Imputation Strategies – Findings of the Euredit Project"* (Charlton (ed), 2003). In this short paper it is necessary to be selective in presenting results, and we will present some results for just two of the six datasets.

Danish Labour Force Survey

The Danish Labour Force Survey (DLFS) contains one variable with missing values, which is income. All other variables contain full information. The missing values in the variable income are due to the fact that the respondent refused to participate in the survey or could not be reached at home. The income comes from Statistics Denmark's income register. All other variables are also found in registers. As income is known for all persons in the dataset it is possible to analyse the efficiency of the imputation concerning the bias of non-response. The following variables were available to assist imputation: Telephone/postal interview or neither; No. times interviewed in the panel; Telephone contact made; Postal follow up; Male/female; Age of respondent; Marital Status; Duration of education; Last employment; Employed/unemployed; Any children at home; Living with another adult; Area of residence. In all subgroups, except for persons aged 15-25, the persons who did not participate had lower incomes. This is attributable to characteristics associated with the non-response rate, e.g. persons with the lowest level of education and highest unemployed account for the highest non-response.

In order to describe the effectiveness of the imputation the linear regression model can, e.g. be estimated: $Y^* = \beta\hat{Y} + e$, here $\hat{Y}$ denotes the imputed value of Y and Y_i^* is the true value. It appears from Table 8 that for all 24 various imputations that have been tested on DLFS, a slope β, which is less than 1, are estimated. Thus, the imputation is not able to remove entirely the non-response bias.
The neural networks 'MLP quick 20' and SOM yielded the best estimation of the mean income ($|m(Y^*) - m(\hat{Y})|$), with total numerical errors of less than 1,000. But the CMM median, NN and SVM also yielded good results. However, the standard method linear regression (REG) is a comparatively good method, and is better than many of the other methods. Random errors are also imputed in cases where donor imputation is applied, reflecting the variation in the data material, which might suggest that the results achieved by e.g. RBNN and SOM with respect to the bias are not so good. This is especially true when looking at the slope and R^2. In the light of this, the results achieved by SOM are particularly good.
Another essential problem is the efficiency of the imputation used to describe the distribution and the variation in the material. The Kolmogorov-Smirnov distance (K-S) measures the largest difference between the two numerical distribution functions. The area between the two empirical distributions functions in first and second moment is also calculated. The area between the two distribution functions is lowest for SOM and NN, but also for "RBNN loglinear without noise" and "DIS without area". In general, SOM is superior with respect to the Kolmogorov-Smirnov distances. SOM is in general also among the best to minimize the mean error (m 1), but pays a price with respect to other measures of the quality of the imputation.

In summary, there is no clear winner, but "MLP quick 20", SOM and linear regression are the three best methods overall. In evaluating which imputation method is best suited, depends on the purpose of the imputation. It is therefore difficult to give a simple prescription, but it will be fair to say that SOM showed great strength. SOM was able to achieve total numerical errors of less than 1,000, which must be regarded as an impressive reduction of the bias in connection with non-response. Also, SOM was able to obtain good results with respect to imputing the variation in the data. In Table 9 the 5 best results on each measure have been underlined – some experiments have been omitted to save space.

Table 8 Results for various imputation methods on the DLFS data (some experiments omitted to save space)

EXPERI-MENT	METHOD	ESTIMATION/DONOR	SLOPE	T VAL	MSE	R*R	DL 1	DL 2	DLINF	K S	K-S 1	K-S 2	M 1	M 2	MSE
DL21120	MLP quick 20	E	0.939	-14.1	6241867909	0.457	46538	78639	868315	0.0711	0.0128	0.00035	604	5466857151	1020321
DL21130	MLP dynamic	E	0.892	-27.6	6400848668	0.445	47599	80042	829097	0.2072	0.0232	0.00165	9551	3162220193	7528796
DL21140	MLP multiple	E	0.913	-21.0	6235500054	0.458	47018	78701	848750	0.0922	0.0182	0.00072	5288	4197224414	2995240
DL21150	MLP prune	E	0.893	-28.1	6292790808	0.454	46804	79329	822795	0.1126	0.0221	0.00116	8771	3138454147	6509871
YL20001	CMM n. neighbour	D	0.832	-35.2	9569009086	0.262	62391	102680	850380	0.0599	0.0109	0.00036	7290	888155314	4904610
YL20003	CMM mean	E	0.886	-28.8	6648029533	0.424	48754	81714	834028	0.1492	0.0261	0.00190	11499	3050703655	10460707
YL20005	CMM median	D	0.946	-13.9	6679189	0.423	451	81157	834249	0.1349	0.0218	0.00111	1132	690499	10479

					338		32							7159	17
FL20001	N.neighbour	D	0.842	-28.1	10100000000	0.232	66379	103504	870720	0.0498	0.0082	0.00018	1322	1811656379	1197455
FL20005	RBNN log-linear w/o noise	D	0.835	-30.7	9882576471	0.250	64607	103779	880970	0.0517	0.0079	0.00018	4344	3745782	2446269
RL2002	SVM greedy bottom up	E	0.941	-14.7	6473310831	0.439	45113	79937	848858	0.0989	0.0180	0.00075	1400	6242058236	1109103
RL2003	SVM stratified	E	0.941	-14.1	6477665209	0.438	45695	79962	847997	0.0946	0.0185	0.00076	1446	6259512366	1117663
OL20001	DIS with all variables	E	0.807	-40.9	10200000000	0.224	64602	107385	870720	0.0822	0.0141	0.00067	11252	2286197959	10181466
OL20002	DIS without area vbl	E	0.834	-32.8	9658856881	0.243	63225	102042	869105	0.0580	0.0116	0.00037	6315	543320167	3927580
JL20003	SOM random donor	D	0.850	-27.3	10400000000	0.196	64992	104274	955189	0.0359	0.0080	0.00012	402	3611230060	1055018
JL20005	SOM n. neighbour	D	0.862	-28.6	9350027835	0.265	60267	98870	955189	0.0434	0.0076	0.00014	947	2533995253	1121543
Cl20001	REG Linear regression	E	0.922	-18.7	6352749474	0.449	46960	79278	836901	0.0771	0.0183	0.00063	3181	4974625603	1710695
DL21600	SOLAS Hot Deck	D	0.743	-44.7	13100000000	0.105	78753	124914	965724	0.0798	0.0137	0.00061	11553	3621201643	10704072

UK Census (SARS)

Editing

We present results for the census variables age, sex, relat (relationship to head of household), and mstatus (marital status). Tables 9 and 10 show the values for α and β respectively for each experiment where editing was carried out. For a good editing procedure both α and β should be small. Here we can see that the methods CANCEIS/SCIA and MLP achieved consistently low values for both α and β. The CANCEIS/SCIA, and MLP editing procedures show particularly good performance for the variable sex. Higher α values can be seen for the continuous variable age, but it should be noted that the perturbations for the SARS dataset included a large number of minor perturbations, for example, age may have been perturbed from 33 to 34, and most editing systems will ignore such minor perturbations as they are not considered important. Relationship to household head did not have a strong relationship with other variables so performance as measured by α was less good here. Overall the probability of identifying a correct value as suspicious (β) is small for the CANCEIS/SCIA method. Table 11 shows the statistic δ (the probability of an incorrect outcome from the editing process) for the variables age, sex, relat and mstatus. For all variables and all editing methods δ is small, with the CANCEIS/SCIA and MLP methods achieving smaller values than SOM.

Table 9 Alpha values (probability of accepting errors as valid) for four SARs variables where editing has been applied.

Experiment	Method	Age	Sex	Relat	Mstatus
IS30001b	CANCEIS/SCIA	0.593281	0.078518	0.435005	0.243563
IS30003	MLP	0.630947	0.105027	0.312877	0.302392
JS30001	SOM	0.800808	0.114187	0.198952	0.446133
JS30002	SOM	0.582831	0.113751	0.184758	0.446133

Table 10 Beta values (probability of identifying a valid value as an error)for four variables where editing has been applied

Experiment	Method	Age	Sex	Relat	Mstatus
IS30001b	CANCEIS/SCIA	**0.004183**	**0.000275**	**0.000821**	**0.000255**
IS30003	MLP	**0.00751**	**0.000373**	**0.011732**	**0.001585**
JS30001	SOM	0.008246	0.000862	0.047294	0.000746
JS30002	SOM	0.057456	0.002457	0.054983	0.000746

Table 11 Delta values for four variables where editing has been applied

Experiment	Method	Age	Sex	Relat	Mstatus
IS30001b (A)	CANCEIS/SCIA	0.045277	0.005354	0.028296	0.011676
IS30003 (A)	MLP	0.050999	0.007166	0.030788	0.015705
JS30001 (C)	SOM	0.063533	0.008218	0.056891	0.021653
JS30002 (C)	SOM	0.094104	0.009682	0.063195	NA

Imputation

We now assess the performance of the imputation processes. Imputation was carried out on both the Y2 and Y3 datasets. The Y2 dataset did not have errors in the data whereas Y3 was used to assess the ability to make imputations in the presence of errors. For categorical variables we can assess the *predictive accuracy* of an imputation procedure using the measure D. This measure gives, for each variable, the proportion of cases where the imputed value does not equal the true value. An imputation process with good predictive accuracy would achieve small values for D, ideally zero. The variable "Ltill" is whether or not the person has a limiting long-term illness.

Table 12 Measure of predictive accuracy, D, for four variables (Y3 data, with errors)

		D			
Experiment	Method	Sex	Relat	Mstatus	Ltill
IS30001a (B)	CANCEIS/SCIA	**0.24**	**0.11**	**0.18**	0.14
IS30002 (B)	MLP	**0.24**	0.17	**0.20**	**0.11**
RS3001 (B)	SVM	0.27	**0.09**	0.21	**0.12**
RS3005 (B)	SVM	0.27	0.11	0.21	**0.12**
RS3006 (B)	SVM	0.27	0.09	0.21	**0.12**
JS30001 (C)	SOM	0.45	0.68	0.48	**0.12**
JS30002 (C)	SOM	0.45	0.70	0.48	**0.12**
JS30004 (C)	SOM	0.45	0.70	0.48	**0.12**

For the Y3 data CANCEIS/SCIA, MLP, SVM do reasonably well in accurately predicting values but performance varies according to the variable imputed. SOM is less good, only slightly better than naive baseline methods (not shown here). As expected, for the Y2 data that are not contaminated with errors (Table 13) the performance is improved. CANCEIS/SCIA is overall best across the different variables. All methods do extremely well for the variable 'bath'. SVM also has good results for the variables sex, mstatus and relat. However, SOM and IMAI/SOM have not performed particularly well for these variables.

Table 13 Measure of predictive accuracy, D, for four variables (Y2 data, no-errors)

		D			
Experiment	Method	Sex	Relat	Mstatus	Bath
IS20001	CANCEIS/SCIA	0.23	0.05	0.16	0.0006
IS20002	MLP	0.23	0.15	0.17	0.0005
OS20001	DIS	0.33	0.35	0.32	0.008
RS2001	SVM	0.25	0.06	0.19	NA
RS2002	SVM	0.28	0.07	0.21	NA
RS2006	SVM	0.27	0.07	0.19	NA
YS20001	CMM	0.26	0.28	0.29	0.0005
JS20001	SOM	0.28	0.29	0.23	0.004
JS20002	SOM	0.34	0.24	0.36	0.014
JS20003	SOM	0.28	0.30	0.22	0.0009
FS20001	SOM/donor	0.30	0.25	0.34	0.0007
FS20002	IMAI/SOM	0.29	0.12	NA	NA

For the continuous variable Age we use the R^2, dL_2, m_1, m_2 and Kolmogorov-Smirnov statistics to assess imputation performance. Table 14 gives the results for R^2, dL_2, m_1 and m_2 for the Y3 data. The statistic R^2 should be close to one for a good imputation procedure. It can be seen that the methods CANCEIS/SCIA, MLP and SVM have values of $R^2 > 0.8$. For the method SOM however $R^2 < 0.5$. We assess preservation of true values using dL_2. This is a distance measure, so smaller values indicate a better imputation performance. We can see that the methods CANCEIS/SCIA, MLP and SVM achieve the smallest values, in fact SVM performs very well, especially in terms of preserving first and second moments m_1 and m_2. SOM has the highest dL_2 values. For all methods m_1 indicates that the mean of the empirical distribution for age has been reasonably well preserved by the imputation procedures, apart from SOM. We can see how well the variance of the empirical distribution is preserved by using the statistic m_2. The methods CANCEIS/SCIA, MLP and SVM perform better than SOM. For the methods CANCEIS/SCIA, SVM and SOM the Kolmogorov-Smirnov statistic has values ranging from 0.01 to 0.07 confirming that these imputation methods have preserved the distribution for the variable age, but results for MLP and SOM are not as good.

Table 14 Values for selected imputation criteria for variable age (Y3 data – with errors)

Experiment	Method	R^2	dL_2	m_1	m_2	KS
IS30001a (B)	CANCEIS/SCIA	**0.850**	**9.04**	**0.24**	**21.94**	**0.0075**
IS30002 (B)	MLP	**0.853**	8086	0.83	60.69	0.1092
RS30001 (B)	SVM	0.75	11.51	1.15	**2.65**	0.0692
RS30005 (B)	SVM	**0.92**	**6.67**	**0.40**	65.35	**0.0280**
RS30006 (B)	SVM	**0.92**	**6.62**	**0.43**	66.40	**0.0292**
JS30001 (C)	SOM	0.51	16.63	3.74	544.86	0.1764
JS30002 (C)	SOM	0.37	17.64	3.08	514.98	0.1591

We now assess the imputation performance on the Y2 data that was error-free. Table 15 gives results for R^2, dL_2, m_1 and m_2 for the continuous variable age. Again CANCEIS/SCIA, SVM MLP and CMM perform well. The methods IMAI/SOM and SOM with regression also perform very well. SVM and CANCEIS/SCIA achieved the smallest dL_2 values and values of R^2 > 0.9. CANCEIS/SCIA, SVM, CMM, and SOM with regression are best in preserving the mean (m1) while CANCEIS/SCIA, SOM/donor and IMAI/SOM achieved the best results for preserving the raw second moment of the empirical distribution. The Kolmogorov-Smirnov statistic is in the range 0.01 to 0.09 for the methods CANCEIS/SCIA, SVM, CMM and IMAI/SOM confirming that these methods have preserved the distribution for age. MLP, and DIS also have low values (<0.13). In summary the methods CANCEIS/SCIA, SVM, CMM, IMAI/SOM and SOM with regression show good performance for the imputation of the variable age, while the performance of the methods SOM and DIS was not as good.

Table 15 Values for selected imputation criteria for variable age (Y3 data – without errors)

Experiment	Method	R^2	dL_2	m_1	m_2	KS
IS20001	CANCEIS/SCIA	**0.926073**	**6.249487**	**0.171317**	**17.29991**	**0.00607**
IS20002	MLP	0.863691	8.482209	0.524163	148.7667	0.103244
OS20001	DIS	0.591329	17.45294	6.019617	593.8579	0.131801
RS2001	SVM	**0.946346**	**5.315706**	0.613262	79.23829	**0.036347**
RS2002	SVM	**0.937552**	**5.702528**	0.237599	58.01568	**0.024444**
RS2006	SVM	**0.942952**	**5.457148**	0.261328	36.08478	**0.022656**
YS20001	CMM	0.820548	9.721793	**0.025185**	46.32909	0.052261
JS20001	SOM	0.197077	24.05214	4.69175	335.1553	0.09484
JS20002	SOM	0.572164	14.92676	**0.181788**	234.4577	0.203346
JS20003	SOM	0.008383	29.13619	9.20166	574.4546	0.23152
FS20001	SOM/donor	0.865529	8.49288	**0.140562**	**6.962375**	**0.00613**
FS20002	IMAI/SOM	0.891531	7.638982	**0.152414**	**4.859234**	0.011724

In summary, for the imputation of the SARS dataset the donor method implemented in CANCEIS/SCIA performed better than the neural network methods. CANCEIS/SCIA was the best performer across all measures for the imputation of the continuous variable Age. SVM, CMM, IMAI/SOM and SOM with regression achieved good results on several of the measures. CANCEIS/SCIA and SVM may be better suited for imputation of datasets where most variables are continuous. The CANCEIS/SCIA and MLP editing procedures show promising results. It was apparent from the experiments that thorough exploratory analysis of the data is crucial to achieving a highly successful edited/imputed dataset and the extent to which this is done well will affect the results. The selection of appropriate matching variables and other tuning parameters may require many hours of analysis. In addition to this most systems require lengthy set up times and run times, but more time and expertise invested in preparation should result in higher quality imputed datasets.

6. CONCLUSIONS

In an ideal world the series of experiments conducted in the course of the project would enable the identification of general procedures for editing and imputation of statistical data that would be "best" across a wide variety of data types, including census data, business survey data, household survey data and time series data. Not unexpectedly, the conflicting requirements and data types implicit in these different data scenarios meant that it was impossible to find a "one size fits all" solution to the many different editing and imputation problems posed within them. In real life situations it is likely that a mixture of solutions will be needed, tailored to characteristics of the dataset being processed. Overall the Euredit project was very productive, achieved most of its objectives, and many important lessons were learnt in the process of carrying out the research, developing new methods, and in the evaluation stages. Due to lack of space it has only been possible to present results for two of the six datasets included in the experiments, but full details are available in the project's publications.

References

[1] Charlton JRH, 2002. First Results from the EUREDIT Project. UNECE Work Session on Statistical Data Editing: http://www.unece.org/stats/documents/2002/05/sde/35.e.pdf

[2] Chambers R, 2001. Evaluation criteria for statistical editing and imputation. NS Methodology Series No 28. See http://www.statistics.gov.uk/StatBase/Product.asp?vlnk=9227

[3] Charlton JRH (Ed), 2003 (forthcoming volume). *Towards effective statistical editing and imputation strategies – findings of the EUREDIT project.* (see http://www.cs.york.ac.uk/euredit)

Footnotes to Table 3.

1. Missing value cannot be represented by a blank;
2. Data must be split into strata and imputation groups; the household head variables must be located in first position;
3. Yes optionally: Key variables, auxiliary matching variable, degree of fixity of the variables, marginal variables, max no of times that each donor can be used, max size of donor record;
4. The system requires positive integer coded data;
5. Variable weights, max cardinality of solutions, data groups/edit groups, matching variable, max no of times that each donor can be used, max allowed time to find solutions, Hiroglou-Berthelot algorithm parameters;
6. Data translation in order to avoid negative values;
7. If data have been translated in order to avoid negative values, back transformation of data is required;
8. Network topologies (no of hidden layers, no of neurons per layer, error function, activation function, training rate, stopping criteria etc.;
9. Yes but it is time and resources consuming;
10. Possible preparation of error indicators for the training phase;
11. SOM does not need, but it can be used with edit rules;
12 SOM does not need but it can be used with imputation rules;
13. Always: number of neurons, selection of variables, Imputation: method and related parameters (if any), Editing: sigma1 and sigma2 (for robustness);
14., 15. Depends on the data set;
16. Some understanding is recommended;
17. Depends on the software implementation used;
18. Parameters determined automatically by system, but can be overridden by user.;

19. K (the number of neighbours for K-NN processing), also the number of quantisation bins. Parameters determined automatically by system. User can override these;
20. Five "modes" for imputation are available. Default mode selected by system generally gives good results. ;
21. Data is represented in a CMM binary neural network to allow fast identification of similar matching records.; 22. Cherry Pie is the only method described in this table that is not designed to perform imputations;
23. AGGIES was also part of the software investigated, but we could not get it to work properly and NAS and others were not able to solve the problems.

Footnotes to Table 4.
1. LVCF, R1, NP100,MARX1, AR5X, MLP, BSBASE, BSLVCF, BSEM, BSMLP;
2. Choice of covariates, choice of dependent variables, and choice of training set and number of intermediate nodes in the case of MLP and BSMLP;
3. Yes, log returns of each time series;
4. Yes, inverse log returns with consistency checking;
5. Yes, except for the LVCF method;
6. No, but all methods impute sequentially over time. The R1, NP100, MARX1 and BSEM impute simultaneously for a set of variables;
7. SVM requires normalisation of scalar independent variables and the target variable if it is scalar. Categorical independent variables may require 1 of n encoding (also known as design variables).
8. Max iterations, and sometimes interactions fitted

Footnotes for Table 5.
2. All edit and imputation methods using POEM have the capacity to also use user-specified edit rules. However, these are not required for the methods to work.
3. Reverse calibration imputation requires specification of outlier robust estimate for variable being imputed.
4. Optimal tuning for univariate WAID error detection requires access to training sample or historical data with target values.
5. Optimal tuning for multivariate WAID error detection requires access to training sample or historical data with target values.
6. All methods require initial transformation of data to linearity to achieve optimal performance. With the ABI and EPE data, this was achieved via log transformation. None of the methods work well where there are many zero or "special" values in the data.

A FUNCTIONAL EVALUATION OF EDIT AND IMPUTATION TOOLS

By Claude Poirier, Statistics Canada

1. INTRODUCTION

In the development of new surveys or the redesign of existing surveys, edit and imputation applications are regularly prepared. For these processes, survey managers have to decide whether they will develop custom-made systems or use existing software. Many statistical agencies, including Statistics Canada, develop and maintain generalized systems to offer managers basic tools for each survey step, but the choice of a system may sometimes be difficult. Internally developed generalized systems may offer only subsets of the required functionality, and so the managers perhaps have to look for potential systems outside of their agencies, be it for full implementation or simply to look for implementation ideas from other development teams around the world. The money and time anybody would invest to acquire, understand, adapt and/or extract good principles of external systems must be considered in any decision.

The goal of this paper is to evaluate the functionality of four editing and imputation systems. An empirical evaluation would also be interesting but the amount of common functionality across the systems is too limited to do so. Given the selected systems, the choice of any set of data would clearly favour one of those. The selected systems are the Generalized Edit and Imputation System from Statistics Canada, the New Imputation Methodology also from Statistics Canada, the Standard Economic Processing System from the U.S. Bureau of the Census, and Solas for missing data analysis from Statistical Solutions Inc. The evaluation identifies the strengths and weaknesses of these systems as well as the context in which they can better serve survey statisticians. The four targeted systems are clearly not an exhaustive set of editing and imputation packages. Other products exist and may be part of future evaluations. Examples are Plain Vanilla [(1)], AGGIES [(2)], MacroView [(3)], etc. Details on these systems are given in Graham (1997), Todaro (1998), and Van de Pol et al. (1997) respectively.

The four selected systems are described in Section 2. An evaluation and comparison exercise is documented in Section 3, elaborating on the systems' respective strengths and weaknesses, their expected future developments and the best use of each system. Concepts such as qualitative or quantitative data, deterministic imputation, hot-decking, nearest neighbour methods, weighted distance, minimum change, multiple imputation, imputation by estimators, and prorating are introduced and defined in this section.

2. THE SYSTEMS' FUNCTIONALITY

2.1. The Generalized Edit and Imputation System

The Generalized Edit and Imputation System (GEIS) was developed at Statistics Canada to meet the requirements of the Canadian economic surveys. The current version, GEIS v6.5, is not an editing system as such but targets more the imputation process. It is usually used after preliminary editing associated with the collection and capture phases and respondent follow-up have been completed. Linear programming techniques are used to conduct the localization of fields to be imputed and search algorithms are used to perform automatic imputations. The processing is entirely

---

(1) Plain Vanilla is a general-purpose edit and imputation system for economic censuses, U.S. Bureau of the Census

(2) AGGIES is an Agriculture Generalized Imputation and Edit System, U.S. Department of Agriculture

(3) MacroView is a graphical macro editing system, Statistics Netherlands

driven by edit/imputation linear rules defined by means of numeric variables. This section describes the main functionality of the system. More details are given in Statistics Canada (1998).

GEIS is usually applied in a step-wise fashion, and its structure facilitates this approach. The steps are edit specification, outlier detection, error localization, and automatic imputation.

The first step, the edit specification and analysis, serves to identify the relationships that characterize acceptable records. The relationships are expressed as a set of n linear edit rules in the form:

$$\begin{array}{c} a_{11}x_1 + a_{12}x_2 + \ldots + a_{1m}x_m \leq b_1 \\ \vdots \\ a_{n1}x_1 + a_{n2}x_2 + \ldots + a_{nm}x_m \leq b_n \end{array}$$

where the a_{ij}'s and b_i's are user-defined constants, and the x_j's represent the m survey variables. The rules are connected with logical *'and'*s, which means each rule must be satisfied for a record to pass the edits. The system checks for edit consistency, redundancy and hidden equalities. This step permits an iterative approach to the design of the best possible set of edits.

The second step aims at the detection of univariate outliers using the Hidiroglou and Berthelot method (1986). It performs comparisons of selected variables across records and identifies outlying observations based on the median M, and the first and third quartiles Q_1 and Q_3 of the population. An observed value x will be identified as an outlier if it is outside the acceptance interval $(M-kQ_1, M+kQ_3)$, where k is set by the user. This method can be used to identify variables to be imputed or to be excluded from subsequent calculations.

The third step is the error localization that uses a linear programming approach to minimize the number of fields requiring imputation. This is an application of the rule of minimum change as proposed by Fellegi and Holt (1976). The step identifies the fields that need to be imputed in order for the record to pass all the edit rules. The problem is expressed as a constrained linear program and solved using Chernikova's algorithm, as detailed by Schiopu-Kratina and Kovar (1989). The system also allows the use of weights for each variable when the user wishes to exert some influence on the identification of the fields to be imputed. Although the algorithm is costly to run, it constitutes one of the main features of GEIS.

The final step is the imputation function which offers three imputation methods: Deterministic, Donor, and Estimators. Based on the edit rules, the deterministic imputation identifies cases in which there is only one possible solution that would allow the record to satisfy the rules. For instance, in the case of two simple edit rules being $x \leq 2$ and $-x \leq -2$, GEIS would detect and impute the only possible value $x=2$. The donor imputation replaces the values to be imputed using data from the closest valid record, also referred to as the nearest neighbour. For a given record, a subset of the fields which do not need imputation are automatically used as matching fields, and the maximum standardized difference among these individual fields is used as the distance function. The donor pool includes the observations that satisfy all edit rules. The user can specify post-imputation edits to make sure the nearest neighbour is close enough to be used as a donor. The imputation by estimators provides a wide set of techniques using historical or current information. Built-in estimators are available in GEIS: Previous values, previous/current means, trends, and multiple regressions. If a non-standard estimator is required, a user-defined estimator can also be specified using any combination of the following operators: +, -, ×, ÷, *exp*. Error terms with specific variances can be introduced in these estimators.

GEIS allows the use of different imputation techniques across questionnaire sections and sub-populations. The use of a sequence of techniques is also possible where, at each step, the user can include/exclude previously imputed data in the process.

The system works in MVS and UNIX environments. It was developed in C language and currently interacts with Oracle databases. It includes an interface that helps the user in specifying the parameters and edit rules, but the interface is not the easiest one to work with. The functionality described above is quite adequate for economic surveys but the complex foundation software makes the system somewhat difficult to set up and maintain. Section 6 describes the newly initiated developments which target a more user-friendly system. The setup and maintenance of applications will be made easier from a user perspective.

2.2. The New Imputation Methodology

The New Imputation Methodology (NIM) is another system developed at Statistics Canada. As opposed to GEIS, NIM targets the social surveys because it deals mostly with qualitative variables. The system was initially developed and put in place for the 1996 Canadian Census. It uses donor imputation as a unique imputation method. As detailed in Bankier et al. (1995 and 1996), its goal is to minimize the number of changes while making sure the imputation actions are plausible. It always performs record imputation based on a single donor. Since the Census data are collected at the household level with information for each person within the household, the system is designed to identify donors for the entire household, not for individual persons.

NIM is an imputation system more than an edit system. It is used after the collection and capture editing has been completed. It uses edit rules to identify records that need imputation and records that can be used as donors. In practice, only conflict rules are implemented but in theory, validity rules can be used as well. A failed-edit record is identified if at least one of the conflict rules is true. The rules are defined through decision logic tables (DLT), using SPIDER, a Statistics Canada package (Ciok, 1992).

Table 1 provides a simple example of conflict rules for a two-person household. An observation that satisfies either of the two conflict rules will be flagged as a failed-edit record.

Table 1: An example of conflict rules

	Conflict Rules	
	1	2
Person1 is married	N	
Person2 is married		N
Person2 is the spouse of person 1	Y	Y

When failed edit and passed edit records are identified, the system tries to find, for each record to be imputed, a record that can be used as a donor. The search targets a donor coming from the set of passed records and being close to the failed edit record. In this process, the distance between a failed record *f* and a passed record *p* is defined as follows:

$$D(f,p) = \Sigma\, w_j\, D_j(f,p)$$

where w_j is a user-defined weight associated with the variable j, and $D_j(f,p)$ is a distance function associated with variable j (this distance function may be different for each variable). For instance, if variable j is qualitative in nature, the distance function $D_j(f,p)$ can be defined as 0 when the *j-value* in record f and record p are the same, and 1 when they are different. A more complex definition can be used for numeric variables. In making a choice amongst the records in the donor pool, the system takes into account all feasible actions for each potential donor. A feasible action is the transfer of donor data into a set of recipient's fields such that the newly imputed record, say a, passes the edit rules. NIM will randomly select a donor p and a final action a from the feasible actions which minimize the following composite distance, D_{fpa}, for the failed record f:

$$D_{fpa} = \alpha D(f,a) + (1-\alpha)D(a,p) \quad 0 \le \alpha \le 1$$

where α is a user-defined constant. In this equation, an α close to one would give more importance to the minimum number of changes than to the similarity of the imputed action and the passed record. Variations can be made by accepting not only the minimum D_{fpa} but also some near minimum changes as possible imputation actions. This is done by a random selection with unequal probabilities amongst the minimum and near minimum change scenarios.

Other modules also exist to specifically deal with the persons' sequence within the household in order to better identify couples and to optimize the process. In practice, the function described above becomes costly to minimize as the number of passed-edit records and potential actions grows. Highly efficient algorithms were introduced in order to alleviate the potential shortcoming.

The system was developed in the C language and runs in a mainframe environment. It works jointly with SPIDER, a PL-1 program that handles DLTs. Current limitations of SPIDER force the user to use a pre-processor to replicate DLTs for edits between persons. The system was used successfully for the Canadian Census of Population but a generalization would be required for other applications.

2.3. The Standard Economic Processing System

Sigman (1997) describes the basis behind the development of the Standard Economic Processing System (StEPS). While the Plain Vanilla system was designed to provide the Fellegi and Holt approach for the U.S. economic censuses, StEPS is to replace 15 existing systems used for U.S. economic surveys. Its development was initiated in 1996 by the U.S. Bureau of the Census to provide integrated tools for the processing of survey steps. As detailed in the system concepts and overview document (U.S. Bureau of the Census, 1996), StEPS is more than just an editing and imputation system. It includes a module to control the collection of information, a data review and on-line correction module, an estimation and variance calculation module, and a tabulation and disclosure module. It can provide general diagnostic tables, including response rates, imputation rates, etc. For the purpose of the present evaluation, the focus is constrained to the editing and imputation modules.

The data editing module of StEPS v1.0 allows simple verifications such as ascertaining the presence of data values for required items, range verifications, and verifications of valid categories. It also provides more complex tests such as balance tests which verify the additivity of items against selected totals, and survey rules to verify field relationships within observations. Skip pattern validations and field positivity verifications will eventually be implemented. The edit options offer the basic functionality and should a complex rule be required, the user can provide his or her own program statements. Such program coding is made easy by special windows integrated in the menus. The statements must be provided in SAS because SAS is the unique foundation software of StEPS. The system can validate the syntax of the statements before the user submits the program. All verifications can be performed on mixtures of current and historical values. In case of edit failures, concurrent users can individually modify reported data in an interactive manner. The system keeps track of all the modifications made by each user, and allows cancellations of user modifications done on any time period. The manual modification and the verification modules can be used iteratively until the data are ready for the automated imputation step.

StEPS has two modules for imputation, referred to as "simple imputation" and "general imputation". The simple-imputation module performs deterministic imputations and flags the resulting imputed values as if they had been reported. The imputation formulas used by the simple-imputation module are defined by the user through the use of SAS windows. Any group of SAS statements, regardless of their complexity, can be used to define the imputation formula. The following single-statement is just an example of such a formula.

$$y_i = max(k , x_i)$$

where k is a constant predefined by the user. These user-defined functions are built from data entries and constants, not from any macro information like population means or trends. The general-imputation module aims to replace with valid values, any invalid values identified in the above editing process. The strategy is user-defined, as opposed to the automated localization of minimum change offered by GEIS and NIM. The imputation techniques available in StEPS are mostly estimator type techniques. This includes the imputation by auxiliary data items, sum of data items, historical values, means, trends, ratios, and multiple regressions. All estimator functions can be evaluated from weighted or unweighted data. Similar to GEIS, the system can exclude several types of records from the calculation of estimators. Furthermore, for the ratio and mean estimators, StEPS allows the exclusion of records based on upper and lower bounds U and L. For instance, the value y_i of unit i can be imputed from a ratio estimator with the auxiliary value x_i as follows

$$y_i = x_i \, (\Sigma y_j / \Sigma x_j)$$

where the sums are taken over the subset of valid observations $\{ j \mid L \leq y_j/x_j \leq U \}$. Similarly, the calculation of the mean

$$y_i = \bar{y}$$

is carried out over the subset of valid observations $\{ j \mid L \leq y_j \leq U \}$.

The prorating transformation represents another imputation action offered in StEPS. The function consists of adjusting every component of a sum in order to obtain a known total. Currently, StEPS can prorate multiple one-dimensional sums that have a common total. Future versions of StEPS will be able to prorate nested one-dimensional sums ($A+B=C$ and $C+D=E$) and two-dimensional sums. The StEPS prorating functions are SAS versions of those developed for the Plain Vanilla system, as described by Sigman and Wagner (1997).

The system is developed entirely in SAS and works in a UNIX environment. A complete graphical user interface is available. The file and variable naming convention eases the processing of historical edit and imputation. Indeed, the field names include the numeric field codes, the field status (Reported, Adjusted, Edited or Weighted) and the survey period. The database architecture is based on a data point model. A record corresponds to a data item of a respondent unit. It includes three basic components: the unit identifier, the field name (code/status/period) and the value itself. These "skinny" records are different from the usual "fat" records which include all survey variables. In this architecture, the empty cells are simply dropped, as opposed to the usual architecture. For the user, this translates into a more efficient database where no record layout has to be maintained to port information across processes.

2.4. Solas for missing data analysis

Solas for missing data analysis is produced by Statistical Solutions Ltd., a statistical software company based in Ireland with offices in the United States. Websites for the company can be found at *www.statsol.ie* and *www.statsolUSA.com*. Solas v1.1 was designed for the imputation of missing data, primarily in biostatistical research. Although the documentation claims support for both numeric and ordered categorical variables, the imputation functions are more widely applicable to numeric variables. Solas also includes data analysis tools but these are used in the imputation process rather than being the main feature of the system.

The system does not include any edit function. It simply imputes fields having missing data. Its main feature is the multiple imputation option, a technique developed by Rubin (1978). It also includes the standard hot deck method, and two estimator type imputations, namely the current mean and the historical imputation.

The hot deck imputation attempts to find matching records that are similar to records to be imputed with respect to auxiliary matching variables and precedence rules defined by the user. Exact matches are targeted, and if no records are found, Solas will automatically drop the matching variables one by one given the precedence rules until it has found an exact match. The process is completed when an exact match is identified. Whenever several exact matches are found, one can be selected randomly to impute all the missing fields of the record to be imputed. If absolutely no matches are found, a random selection from the entire pool is possible. Due to the possible rareness of exact matches for continuous variables, these variables can be categorized within Solas prior to imputation.

The multiple imputation is a repetitive execution of an imputation strategy. It can be applied to both cross-sectional and longitudinal data and many imputation parameters can be controlled by the user. Solas will impute several, say *M*, values for each missing field. The results can be combined to produce overall estimates with variances for the variables of interest. The User reference manual (Statistical Solutions, 1997) describes the theory well. It states that:

> "*Solas applies an implicit model approach (using a logistic regression model) based on propensity scores and an approximate Bayesian bootstrap to generate the imputations. The multiple imputations are independent repetitions from a posterior predictive distribution for the missing data given the observed data.*"

The current mean is one of the two estimator functions. It consists of imputing the missing values with the basic mean of the other records in the imputation class. For ordered categorical variables, the mode is used. The historical imputation is the second estimator type imputation. It simply imputes the value from the previous data period, with no transformation. The value is copied as is.

Solas provides the capability to define a weighting variable, referred to as a "case frequency variable". As its name suggests, the weights are defined for each record, as opposed to the weighting concept introduced for GEIS and NIM to put more emphasis on some variables. Thus, a weighted observation will be processed by Solas as repetitions of an original observation.

The Solas system works on IBM compatible personal computers with 80-486 or higher processors. It can read and write data in different formats including ASCII, SAS, DBase, FoxPro Paradox, Excel, Lotus, BMDP, and others. The system can be installed by almost any user, with no support required. Its interface is user-friendly and the help function is quite complete.

3. COMPARISON OF THE SYSTEMS

3.1. Their strengths

The four systems we analyzed can process data by imputation classes or groups. Comparing GEIS with NIM, we note that the first one targets uniquely numeric variables while the second targets mainly qualitative variables. The strengths of GEIS are its capacity to find minimum changes for any set of rules being expressed as a series of linear equations, and its automated donor imputation function driven by the edit rules. This imputation function runs with almost no intervention from the user since it derives the matching fields by itself. It simply uses the response pattern, whatever it is, to look for a donor. The minimum change rule contributes to increase the chance of preserving a relatively good data integrity given the data in error. The flexible estimator module of GEIS, the several diagnostic reports and the on-line tutorial, coupled with a continuous user support constitute the desirable aspects of the system.

NIM, on the other hand, finds the donor before it identifies the minimum number of changes needed. Because the minimum changes do not necessarily guarantee a plausible imputation, NIM was developed to meet two objectives at once: to minimize changes and assure plausible imputations. Of the four systems we evaluated, NIM is the only one that includes a generic distance function for the donor imputation. This means the user can define the distance function for each matching field. Its first use for the 1996 Canadian Census was a success with the processing of 11 million households within a month (Bankier et al, 1997).

The StEPS project was initiated following a decision from upper management to build an integrated and standardized product, implemented in SAS, that is to be used by up to a hundred economic surveys. Not surprisingly, therefore, the major strength of StEPS is its integration of several survey processing modules: Information management, data review and on-line correction, editing, imputation, estimation, variance calculation, tabulation and disclosure. The system uses SAS files to input and output data so survey statisticians can take advantage of the analytical strengths of this product. For the edit and imputation modules, both the survey specifications and the implementations are integrated into the graphical interface. That means, a survey manager can provide his or her specifications directly through the system and the application developer just has to translate these into system rules. While doing so, both the specifications and the system rules are linked and displayed together in the graphical user interface. This feature is practical especially for managers who do not know SAS well enough to code their non-standard rules. The product standardization resulted in a good file and variable naming convention which simplifies all the processes. The completeness and effectiveness of its set of estimator imputations is comparable to the one offered in GEIS. Finally, we observed that the generalized imputation for two-dimensional balance edits seems to be unique to StEPS.

Solas presents a good multiple imputation function with many control options for that method. The nice graphical interface of the system represents another good aspect. Solas is easy to install and user-friendly. Its on-line help function is adequate for the functionality Solas provides. Once imputation is completed, a copy of the resulting data sheet appears on the screen. The imputed values are shown in blue, in contrast to the reported values which appear in black. Finally, the small size and the portability of the system makes it very practical. Some empirical evaluations (Kozak, 1998) have shown that the system is relatively quick. On a regular Pentium, the multiple imputation with cross sectional measurements could impute 600 missing observations from 15,000 records in about four minutes.

3.2. Their weaknesses

The foundation software of GEIS makes the system sometimes "too heavy" to run. Also, a user that built his or her own edit system will in most cases want a direct access to the imputation function. Unfortunately, the current imputation function cannot be run independently from its edit function. GEIS only deals with numeric variables. In the editing process, it assumes each variable takes non-negative values, which is not always true in practice, especially for financial surveys. Pre-processors have to be developed to overcome the problem.

NIM was developed essentially for the Canadian Census, which surveys persons within households. In its current form, it may be difficult to reuse NIM for a wide variety of surveys.

Although its generalization is being considered, its feasibility has not been demonstrated yet. NIM can process quantitative variables along with qualitative variables, but the performance of the system with more than a few quantitative variables has yet to be demonstrated. Some recent theoritical results, however, suggest this may be feasible.

StEPS does not provide a minimum change functionality nor any other automated error localization module. Thus, for every combination of errors, the user has to specify which fields need to be imputed. Also, StEPS does not offer a donor imputation function. This means the imputation strategy for a brand new survey, with no historical data nor administrative information, is limited to estimator imputations based on current values. Although the SAS windows in which users specify special rules are practical, a certain level of SAS knowledge is a prerequisite. In practice, this is not always available and thus some SAS training has to be provided in addition to the system-specific training.

As for Solas, the functionality aside from the multiple imputation is very basic. There is no control on the number of required records from which the information is extracted to perform the group mean or the donor imputation. The historical method includes no control on the imputation status of the historical information before its use in the process. The imputation techniques cannot be used in sequence. If missing values are still present after imputation is applied, the user must manually submit another run of Solas with a different method to complete the data set. Finally, no imputation summary report is produced after the imputation has been completed. Solas is mostly recommended for biostatisticians. It is less appropriate for complex surveys where we observe high numbers of variables linked together with complex relationships.

3.3. A subjective comparison

The four processing systems being evaluated can be compared in terms of their functionality. Such a comparison is difficult to do because the functions are implemented differently across systems, with different sub-functions, features, options and/or completeness. The goal here is to qualify rather than quantify the quality, flexibility, efficiency and reliability of each implementation. For this subjective comparison, a zero to three-stars rating, where three stars represent the best, is used in table 2 below to differentiate the implementations. A three-star (***) rating is given to a function when its implementation offers the sub-functions or options being required by a wide range of survey applications. This does not mean, however, that no improvement can be made to the function. A two-star (**) rating is given to an implementation having a less complete set of options. A one-star (*) rating means the implementation offers a partial functionality. That is, either its assumptions are too restrictive or its options are not generalized enough to make good use of the function. No stars are assigned when the functionality is not offered at all.

Table 2: A subjective comparison of systems

Characteristics	GEIS	NIM	StEPS	Solas
Type of variables:				
- Numeric	***	*	***	***
- Qualitative	*	***	**	*
Editing:				
- Data verification	*	*	***	
- On-line correction			***	
- Minimum changes	***	***		
- User-defined changes			***	
- Outlier detection	**		**	
Imputation:				
- Deterministic	***		*	

- Donor (random)	**	**		***
- Donor (closest)	***	***		
- Estimators	***		***	*
- Prorating			***	
- Multiple imputation		*		***
General:				
- User-friendliness	*	**	**	***
- On-line help			***	***
- On-line tutorial	***			**
- Diagnostic reports	***	***	***	
- Integration			***	
- Reusable code	***	**	**	***
- Portability	**	**	**	***
- User support [4]	***			*
Other information:				
- Size of code (Mb)	20	1	200 [5]	7
- Cost ('000 US$)	20	--	--	1

In the above evaluation table, the minimum change refers to the automated identification of the minimum set of variables that need to be imputed. On the other hand, user-defined change consists of the pre-identification of variables to be imputed in case of an edit failure. In the general category, the integration refers to the possibility of using the system within a suite of systems that provide other survey functions, like sampling, data collection and capture, estimation, etc. A reusable code is a program that can easily be adapted to any survey, regardless of its collection structure, its database structure and variable names. The portability depends on the platforms and foundation softwares being required to install, compile and run the system. Note that both the size and the cost figures are approximate and dated January 1999.

3.4. Future developments:

GEIS recently entered a major redesign phase. First, independent modules for the edit and the imputation functions are being created in order to ease the direct access to either of the two. Changes to the input and output statements will be made to make possible the interactions with SAS datasets, in addition to the Oracle databases. Finally, the development of new functionality including a prorating function and mass imputation function was recently initiated.

The NIM development team is currently defining the theory to allow a better and more complete processing of numeric variables mixed with qualitative variables. Its generalization is being investigated in order to make the code easily reusable for other surveys. Work was initiated to move the entire program into C language, to use generic DLTs and to make the system portable by using flat files as input information.

Future versions of StEPS will be able to prorate nested one-dimensional sums and two-dimensional sums. Improvements and some functionality will be added to the edit module. A long-range plan of the StEPS development team is to investigate the possibility of a minimum change function. This may be implemented using the Chernikova's algorithm that GEIS and AGGIES use.

---

(4) The user support refers to maintenance, services and help being offered to external clients.

(5) This size corresponds to the whole StEPS system, not only to the edit and the imputation modules

The additions to further versions of Solas are unknown to the author.

3.5. The best uses of the systems:

Given the characteristics listed in the above comparison table, we note that the systems do not duplicate their respective functionality as may be initially expected. An objective evaluation would only be possible if specific survey requirements were known. Thus, a comparison of the systems against each other is inappropriate here.

Nevertheless, it is possible to identify the context in which these systems can better serve survey statisticians. If a small and simple survey is being developed on micro computers, with a tight schedule and budget, Solas may present a good cost/benefit ratio. On the other hand, in the case of large-scale business surveys for which long questionnaires and complex field relationships are developed, GEIS or StEPS would be more appropriate. The required functionality is probably the main factor that would differentiate the two. Another factor to consider is the foundation software. Indeed, the existing in-house expertise with C/Oracle or SAS, the cost of these commercial products and the potential benefits of their acquisitions for the working units should be considered. Finally, a social survey that targets persons within households would clearly derive more benefits from NIM then from the other three systems. The possible generalization of NIM may eventually make the system more suitable for all kinds of social surveys and maybe some business surveys.

In summary, the performance of each system depends on the survey requirements: Numeric, or qualitative variables? Automated minimum changes, or user-defined changes? Donor, or estimator techniques? Good support/ high costs, or low support/low costs? . . .

4. CONCLUDING REMARK

In the evaluation of software, we can often say that the more complete the functionality, the less user-friendly the system is likely to be. In practice, we are tempted to forget this rule and to expect a full set of options and controls with a simple and user-friendly interface. When a system grows in complexity, the development of training tools is suggested in order to improve its uses. Also, for systems like StEPS, GEIS or NIM, there is an increasing need for auxiliary skills in SAS, ORACLE/SQL, or C. These auxiliary skills may encompass a better understanding of imputation so that users can better choose imputation options and keep induced errors to a minimum. This may also provide the users with some tricks to adjust input data so it better fits into the available methods or even generate variations of the existing functionality.

References

[1] Bankier, M., Luc, M., Nadeau, C., and Newcombe, P. (1995). "Additional Details on Imputing Numeric and Qualitative Variables Simultaneously". *Proceedings of the Section on Survey Research Methods*, American Statistical Association.

[2] Bankier, M., Luc, M., Nadeau, C., and Newcombe, P. (1996). "Imputing Numeric and Qualitative Variables Simultaneously". Statistics Canada Technical Report, 120 pages.

[3] Bankier, M., Houle, A.-M., Luc, M., C., and Newcombe, P. (1997). "1996 Canadian Census Demographic Variables Imputation". *Proceedings of the Section on Survey Research Methods*, American Statistical Association.

[4] Ciok, R. (1992). "SPIDER - Census Edit and Imputation System". Statistics Canada Technical Report.

[5] Fellegi, I.P. and Holt, D. (1976). "A Systematic Approach to Automatic Edit and Imputation". *Journal of the American Statistical Association*, 71, 17-35.

[6] Graham, R. (1997). "Functional Requirements of Plain Vanilla Modules and System Capabilities" Technical report from the U.S. Bureau of the Census.

[7] Hidiroglou, M.A. and Berthelot, J.-M. (1986). "Statistical Editing and Imputation for Periodic Business Survey". *Survey Methodology*, 12, 73-83.

[8] Kozak, R. (1998). "Solas for Missing Data Analysis: Software Evaluation". Statistics Canada Technical Report.

[9] Rubin, D.B. (1978). "Multiple imputations in Sample Surveys - A Phenomenological Bayesian Approach to Nonresponse". *Proceedings of the Section on Survey Research Methods*, American Statistical Association.

[10] Schiopu-Kratina, I. and Kovar, J.G. (1989). "Use of Chernikova's algorithm in the Generalized Edit and Imputation System". Methodology Branch Working Paper, No. BSMD-89-001E, Statistics Canada.

[11] Sigman, R. (1997). "How Should we Proceed to Develop Generalized Software for Survey Processing Operations such as Editing, Imputation, Estimation, etc.?". Technical report from the U.S. Bureau of the Census.

[12] Sigman, R. and Wagner, D. (1997). "Algorithms for Adjusting Survey Data that Fail Balance Edits". *Proceedings of the Section on Survey Research Methods*, American Statistical Association.

[13] Statistical Solutions, (1997). "Solas For Missing Data Analysis 1.0: User Reference". Cork, Ireland, Statistical Solutions Inc.

[14] Statistics Canada (1998). "Functional Description of the Generalized Edit and Imputation System". Statistics Canada Technical Report.

[15] Todaro, T.A. (1998). "Evaluation of the AGGIES Automated Edit and Imputation System". Technical report from the National Agricultural Statistics Service, U.S. Department of Agriculture.

[16] U.S. Bureau of the Census (1996). "StEPS: Concepts and Overview". Technical report from the U.S. Bureau of the Census.

[17] Van de Pol, F., Buijs, A., van der Horst, G., and de Waal, T. (1997). "Towards Integrated Business Survey Processing". *New Directions in Surveys and Censuses, Proceedings of the 1997 International Symposium*, Statistics Canada.

COMPUTATIONAL RESULTS FOR VARIOUS ERROR LOCALISATION ALGORITHMS

By Ton de Waal, Statistics Netherlands

Abstract: Over the last few years several algorithms for solving the so-called error localisation problem have been developed at Statistics Netherlands. For six data sets involving numerical data we present computational results for four of those algorithms in this paper. The algorithms are based on a standard mixed integer programming formulation, on the generation of the vertices of a certain polyhedron by means of an adapted version of Chernikova's algorithm, on a branch-and-bound algorithm using Fourier-Motzkin elimination, and on a cutting plane approach.

1. INTRODUCTION

In this paper we compare computational results for four different algorithms for automatic error localisation on six data sets involving numerical data. For the duration of this paper we define the error localisation problem as the problem of changing as few fields as possible so that all edit checks (or edits for short) become satisfied. That is, all algorithms we consider in this paper are based on the Fellegi-Holt paradigm of minimum change (see Fellegi and Holt, 1976). All four algorithms solve the error localisation problem to optimality.

The aim of our comparison study is not to perform a comprehensive evaluation study for all possible data sets, but rather to perform a succinct evaluation study that allows us to identify the most promising algorithm(s) for a number of realistic data sets. We restrict ourselves to data sets involving exclusively numerical data because automatic data editing of economic – and hence (mostly) numerical – data is a far more important subject for Statistics Netherlands than automatic data editing of social – and hence (mostly) categorical – data.

In literature some evaluation studies are already described, see Garfinkel et al. (1986 and 1988), Kovar and Winkler (1996), and Ragsdale and McKeown (1996). Garfinkel et al. (1986) concentrate on error localisation for purely categorical data. The other papers concentrate on error localisation for purely numerical data. It is difficult to compare our results to the described results for numerical data. First, because in most cases the actual computing speeds of the computer systems used in those studies are difficult to retrieve, and hence difficult to compare to the computing speed of present-day PC's. Second, because Garfinkel et al. (1988) and Ragsdale and McKeown (1996) use randomly generated data whereas we use realistic data. We feel that realistic data should be used for evaluation studies, because realistic data and randomly generated data have completely different properties. Kovar and Winkler (1996) use realistic data, but the data set used in their evaluation study is not generally available.

The algorithms we examine are:

- an algorithm based on a standard mixed integer programming (MIP) formulation that is solved by means of the commercial MIP-solver ILOG CPLEX;
- a vertex generation algorithm;
- a non-standard branch-and-bound algorithm;
- a cutting plane algorithm.

The remainder of this paper is organised as follows. In Section 2 we summarise the data sets that we have used for our evaluation study. In Section 3 we provide some information regarding the implementation of the above-mentioned algorithms. The computational results are summarised in Section 4. Section 5 concludes the paper with a brief discussion.

2. THE DATA SETS

In Table 1 below we give a summary of the characteristics of the six data sets. In this table the number of variables, the number of non-negativity constraints, the number of edits (excluding the non-negativity constraints), the total number of records, the number of inconsistent records (i.e. records failing edits or containing missing values), and the total number of missing values are listed. Besides, we present the number of records with more than six erroneous fields or missing values. For the purpose of our evaluation study we define these records to be 'highly erroneous' ones. In Section 4 we compare the computing time required for the records that are not highly erroneous to the computing time that is required for all records for two of the evaluated algorithms. Finally, we list the average number of errors per inconsistent record (excluding the missing values) and the average number of optimal solutions per inconsistent record.

Table 1. Characteristics of the data sets

	Data set A	Data set B	Data set C	Data set D	Data set E	Data set F
Number of variables	90	76	53	51	54	26
Number of non-negativity constraints	90	70	36	49	54	22
Number of edits[a]	8	20	36	15	21	18
Total number of records	4,347	274	1,480	4,217	1,039	1,425
Number of inconsistent records	4,347	157	1,404	2,152	378	1,141
Total number of missing values	259,838	0	0	0	2,230	195
Number of records with more than 6 errors or missing values	4,346	7	117	16	136	8
Average number of errors per inconsistent record[b]	0.2	2.5	2.6	1.6	5.8	3.0
Average number of optimal solutions per inconsistent record	6.1	12.0	6.9	23.3	1.2	11.6

[a] Excluding non-negativity constraints
[b] Excluding missing values

The numbers in the last two rows of Table 1 have been determined by carefully comparing the number of fields involved in the optimal solutions, respectively the number of optimal solutions, of the various algorithms to each other. The number of fields involved in the optimal solutions is assumed to be equal to the actual number of errors.

The number of variables, edits and records are in most of the six data sets quite realistic. Exceptions are data set A, where the number of edits other than non-negativity edits is very small, and data set B, where the number of records is very small. At Statistics Netherlands, a very large and complex data set to be edited automatically may involve slightly more than 100 variables, about 100 edits, and a few thousand records. These numbers are somewhat higher than for the data sets in Table 1, but for such large data sets the value of many variables equals zero. This simplifies the error localisation problem to some extent, for example, because this justifies replacing missing values by zeros in a pre-processing step.

The six data sets come from a wide range of business surveys, namely a survey on labour costs, a structural business survey on enterprises in the photographic sector, a structural business survey on enterprises in the building and construction industry, a structural business survey on the retail sector, and a survey on environmental expenditures. Besides these data sets we have also used the ABI data set; one of the evaluation data sets from the Euredit project. Due to confidentiality reasons the branch of industry to which the businesses in this data set belong has not been made public.

As far as we are able to tell, the six test data sets are not essentially different from other data sets arising in practice. In other words, to the best of our knowledge these data sets are representative for other data sets from business surveys. A good performance on the six data sets hence suggests that the performance on other data sets arising in practice will be acceptable. This is confirmed by practical experience at Statistics Netherlands, where nowadays almost all annual structural business surveys are treated by a combination of selective editing (for details on this implementation of selective editing see Hoogland, 2002) and automatic editing. For an overview of this approach for annual structural business surveys at Statistics Netherlands we refer to De Jong (2002). Automatic editing for annual structural business surveys is carried out by means of SLICE 1.0 (see, e.g., De Waal, 2001, for more information on SLICE), which is based on a vertex generation approach (see De Waal, 2003b). Because extensive use of time-consuming COM-components is made in the software architecture of SLICE, its computing times are of a higher order than those mentioned in Table 2 in Section 4 of this paper. Nevertheless, all involved structural business surveys can be treated by SLICE within a reasonable amount of time. Obviously, computing times vary over data sets of different surveys, but no data set with an exceedingly high computing time has been encountered so far. Our practical experience hence suggests that computational results for our test data sets can be carried over to other business data sets.

3. IMPLEMENTATION OF THE ALGORITHMS

The four algorithms we examine in this paper have been implemented in four prototype computer programs. We briefly discuss the implementation details of these programs in this section. The first algorithm, based on a standard MIP formulation (see e.g. Chapter 3 in De Waal, 2003a), we consider has been implemented by Van Riessen (Van Riessen, 2002), a student at the Hogeschool van Amsterdam (College of Amsterdam), while doing an internship at Statistics Netherlands. This algorithm has been implemented in Visual C++ 6.0, and calls routines of ILOG CPLEX (version 7.5), a well-known commercial MIP-solver, to actually solve the MIP problems involved (see *ILOG CPLEX 7.5 Reference Manual*, 2001). We refer to Van Riessen's program as ERR_CPLEX. It determines one optimal solution per erroneous record. ERR_CPLEX, or more precise the MIP-solver of ILOG CPLEX, suffers from some numerical problems. These problems arise because in (erroneous) records the largest values may be a factor 10^9 or more larger than the smallest values. Due to these numerical problems ERR_CPLEX occasionally generates suboptimal solutions containing too many variables. In some other cases it does not find a solution at all.

The second algorithm, based on vertex generation (see De Waal, 2003b, and Chapter 5 in De Waal, 2003a), has been implemented by the author. This program, CherryPi, has been developed in Delphi 3 (see De Waal, 1996). The implemented algorithm is an adapted version of Chernikova's algorithm. Improvements due to Rubin (1975 and 1977), Sande (1978), Schiopu-Kratina and Kovar (1989), and Fillion and Schiopu-Kratina (1993) on the original algorithm by Chernikova (1964 and 1965) have been implemented in CherryPi. The adapted version of Chernikova's algorithm uses a matrix to solve the error localisation problem. The number of rows of this matrix is implied by the number of edits and the number of variables. The number of columns is determined dynamically. Due to memory and speed restrictions a maximum for the allowed number of columns is set in CherryPi. If the actual number of columns exceeds the allowed maximum, certain columns are deleted. This influences the solutions that are found by CherryPi. Due to this pragmatic rule in some cases only non-optimal solutions may be found, and in some other cases no solutions at all may be found. Another effect of this pragmatic rule is that if columns have been deleted in order to arrive at solutions to an instance of the error localisation problem, the optimality of the found solutions is not guaranteed. The higher the allowed number of columns, the better the quality of the solutions found by CherryPi, but also the slower the speed of the program. Practical experience has taught us that in many instances setting the allowed number of columns to 4,000 gives an acceptable trade-off between the quality of the found solutions and the computing time of the program. In the version of CherryPi that was used for the comparison study the allowed number of columns was therefore set to 4,000. Besides the above-mentioned memory problems, CherryPi occasionally suffers from numerical problems, for the same reason as ERR_CPLEX. The program determines all optimal solutions for each erroneous record.

The third algorithm, based on a non-standard branch-and-bound approach (see, e.g., De Waal, 2000, and Chapter 8 of De Waal, 2003a), has been implemented in a prototype computer program called Leo. The program has been developed in Delphi 3. It requires that a maximum cardinality for the optimal solutions is specified beforehand. Leo determines all optimal solutions up to the specified maximum cardinality for each erroneous record. Records requiring more corrections are rejected for automatic editing by Leo. On two data sets, the data sets for which the computing times of Leo are comparatively bad, we have applied a special, alternative version of Leo in which equalities are treated more efficiently (see Chapter 8 in De Waal, 2003a). Leo sometimes suffers from memory problems, especially for records with many errors, because too many nodes with too many edits need to be stored. For records for which Leo suffers from memory problems, it cannot determine an optimal solution. Leo occasionally suffers from numerical problems, for the same reason as ERR_CPLEX and CherryPi.

The fourth algorithm is based on a cutting plane algorithm similar to the algorithms by Garfinkel et al. (1986, 1988) and Ragsdale and McKeown (1996) (see Chapter 10 in De Waal, 2003a). This algorithm has been implemented by Coutinho, while working temporarily at Statistics Netherlands. We refer to Coutinho's program as CUTTING. It has been developed in Delphi 3. The algorithm proposes potential solutions to the error localisation problem by solving a modified set-covering problem (see Ragsdale and McKeown (1996) and De Waal, 2003a). Subsequently, it checks the feasibility of each proposed solution, and generates additional constraints in case this proposed solution is infeasibility by eliminating the variables involved in the solution. A fundamental part of the program is a solver for modified set-covering problems. Using well-known ideas from literature, we have developed this solver, which is based on a recursive branch-and-bound algorithm, ourselves. We did not spend much time on optimising the performance of this solver. It may, therefore, be improved upon. CUTTING can determine all optimal solutions up to a user-specified maximum cardinality. Records requiring more changes than the user-specified maximum cardinality are rejected for automatic editing by CUTTING. The program can also work without such a maximum cardinality. Like Leo, CUTTING suffers from memory problems for some records containing many errors. For such records, it cannot determine an optimal solution. CUTTING occasionally suffers from numerical problems, for the same reason as the other three programs.

The computing times of ERR_CPLEX and CherryPi may possibly be improved upon if we include a restriction on the number of variables that may be changed, like we do for Leo and CUTTING. The stricter this restriction, the faster each program is likely to be. Including such a restriction in CherryPi will probably have less effect than for Leo and CUTTING, because the search process of CherryPi is based on manipulating edits rather than on treating variables directly. The effect of including a restriction on the number of variables that may be changed in ERR_CPLEX is not entirely clear. On the one hand, in order to include such a restriction an additional integer constraint would be required, which would slightly increase the computing time. On the other hand, the search process would be shortened, because certain possible solutions would not have to be examined. Considering the two opposite effects, we expect that including a restriction on the number of variables that may be changed in ERR_CPLEX leads to a reduced computing time, but this remains to be tested.

CherryPi, Leo and CUTTING determine all optimal solutions to each instance of the error localisation problem. This allows one to later use a more statistical criterion to select the "best" one. In contrast, ERR_CPLEX finds only one optimal solution to each instance of the error localisation problem. To find all optimal solutions we could – once an optimal solution to the current MIP problem has been determined – iteratively add an additional constraint, which basically states that the present optimal solution is excluded but other optimal solutions to the current MIP problem remain feasible, and solve the new MIP problem. This process of determining an optimal solution to the current MIP problem and adding an additional constraint to obtain a new MIP problem goes on until all optimal solutions to the error localisation problem have been found. We have not implemented this option, however. Resolving the problem from scratch for each optimal solution would be time-consuming. The alternative is to use a hot restart, where information generated to obtain an optimal solution to an MIP problem is utilised to obtain an optimal solution to a slightly modified MIP problem quickly. A problem with this possibility is that experiences at Statistics Netherlands with ILOG CPLEX so far, on linear programming (LP) problems arising in statistical disclosure control, show that ILOG CPLEX becomes numerical unstable if too many hot restarts in a row are applied.

The results of ERR_CPLEX are therefore only indicative. If the algorithms we have developed ourselves were clearly outperformed by ERR_CPLEX, this would suggest that standard MIP-solvers may be preferable to our algorithms. In that case, further studies with an extended version of ERR_CPLEX that aims to find all optimal solutions to the error localisation problem instead of only one would still be needed, however.

An important aspect in the evaluation of an algorithm is the time required to implement it in a computer program. The easiest algorithm/program to implement is ERR_CPLEX. The program only has to transform data and user-specified metadata, such as edits, into optimisation problems in a format that can be interpreted by ILOG CPLEX. To solve these optimisation problems routines from ILOG CPLEX are used. A bit more complicated is CUTTING. The two most important steps are the elimination of variables and solving modified set-covering problems. Both steps are actually quite simple to implement. Implementing CUTTING required about two months for a non-professional programmer. Slightly more complicated is Leo as this involves implementing a recursive algorithm, which is difficult to debug. The most complicated program to implement is CherryPi as several "tricks" (see De Waal, 2003b) need to be implemented in order to make this program sufficiently fast. To implement CherryPi about three to four months were required for a non-professional programmer.

4. COMPUTATIONAL RESULTS

For Leo and CUTTING we have performed two kinds of experiments per data set. In the first kind of experiments we have set the maximum cardinality N_{max} to six. For many realistic data sets setting N_{max} to six is a good option as for records containing more than six errors it is unlikely that automatic error localisation will lead to data of sufficiently high statistical quality. Possible exceptions are data sets that contain many missing values, such as data set A. In the second kind of experiments for Leo we have set N_{max} as high as possible without encountering memory problems for many, i.e. 20 or more, records. In the second kind of experiments for CUTTING we have removed a maximum cardinality all together. For ERR_CPLEX and CherryPi we have only performed experiments without a specified maximum cardinality.

The experiments have been performed on a 1500 MHz PC with 256 MB of RAM. This PC is connected to a local area network. Computing times may therefore be influenced by the amount of data that was transmitted through the network at the time of the experiments. To reduce and to estimate this influence we have performed five experiments per data set at various moments during the day. In Table 2 we have mentioned the average computing times of these experiments for the entire data sets, and between brackets the standard deviation of these computing times over the corresponding five experiments. Note that some programs, such as Leo, have a random aspect that also influences the computing time. This random aspect is reflected in a relatively high standard deviation.

Table 2. Average computing times of the error localisation algorithms in seconds (between brackets the standard deviation of these computing times)

	Data set A	Data set B	Data set C	Data set D	Data set E	Data set F
ERR_CPLEX[a]	233 (1)	10 (0)	86 (1)	93 (9)	13 (0)	35 (0)
CherryPi	570 (38)	96 (1)	540 (7)	498 (30)	622 (3)	79 (0)
CUTTING	601 (17)	513 (12)	1913 (7)	1101 (20)	90 (1)	94 (2)
CUTTING (N_{max} = 6)	156 (10)	395 (23)	695 (31)	1036 (137)	50 (2)	92 (5)
Leo[b]	18 (0)	308 (10)	531 (4)	21 (1)	59 (34)	7 (0)
Leo (N_{max} = 6)	7 (0)	51 (1)	94 (2)	19 (0)	4 (1)	8 (1)

[a] These tests were performed on a special server. On this PC the only fully licensed version of ILOG CPLEX at Statistics Netherlands has been installed. For comparison reasons we have also used CherryPi for data set A on this machine. The average computing time for data set A on this machine is 528 seconds (compared to 570 seconds on the usual PC) with a standard deviation of 0 seconds. To compare the computing times of ERR_CPLEX to those of the other programs, we have therefore multiplied the original computing times on the special server by a factor of 570/528 = 1.08.
[b] To find the results for Leo for $N_{max} > 6$, we have set N_{max} equal to 90 for data set A, to 8 for data sets B and C, and to 12 for data sets D, E and F.

Data set F contains only eight records for which six or more changes are required. The computing times of Leo and CUTTING are therefore almost equal to the computing times of Leo_6, respectively CUTTING_6 (i.e. Leo, respectively CUTTING with $N_{max} = 6$). In fact, due to the stochastic variability in the computing times Leo even outperformed Leo_6 in our experiments. Taking the standard deviation of the experiments into account, Leo and Leo_6 are about equally fast.

Due to numerical and memory problems, the programs could not always determine solutions. None of the programs can guarantee to find (all) optimal solutions for all records. For ERR_CPLEX, CherryPi, Leo, and CUTTING we have listed in Table 3 below for each data set the number of records for which these programs could not determine solutions to the error localisation problem. For all data sets, Leo_6 and CUTTING_6 found all optimal solutions for all records requiring six or less changes. Especially for data set A, this was very easy as there is only one record in data set A that has six or fewer errors or missing values (see Table 1).

Table 3. Number of records for which no solution could be found

	Data set A	Data set B	Data set C	Data set D	Data set E	Data set F
ERR_CPLEX	3	0	0	0	0	0
CherryPi	0	2	11	8	2	7
CUTTING	0	1	93	0	0	2
Leo[a]	0	1	58	0	53	0

[a] To find the results for Leo, we have set N_{max} equal to 90 for data set A, to 8 for data sets B and C, and to 12 for data sets D, E and F.

For 9 of the 58 records of data set C for which Leo_8 could not find a solution and for 13 of the 53 records of data set E for which Leo_12 could not find a solution, Leo suffered from memory problems. Those 9, respectively 13 records were excluded from the computational results for Leo in Table 2. As far as we have been able to determine, excluding these records from the computational results does not have a large effect and does not change the overall picture. Leo_8, respectively Leo_12, could not find solutions for the other records referred to in Table 3, because more than 8, respectively 12, changes were required.

Comparing the evaluation results of the various programs to each other is a complex task. If we rank the algorithms according to their computing times, and compare ERR_CPLEX, CherryPi, Leo (with $N_{max} > 6$) and CUTTING with each other we see that ERR_CPLEX performs best for three out of the six data sets and second best for the other three data sets. Leo (with $N_{max} > 6$) performs best for three out of six data sets and second best for two data sets. So, one might conclude that – purely looking at of the computing times – ERR_CPLEX is slightly better than Leo. Clearly worst is CUTTING.

Now, if we compare ERR_CPLEX, CherryPi, Leo_6, and CUTTING_6, and again rank the programs according to their computing times, we see that ERR_CPLEX performs best for two out of the six data sets and second best for three data sets. Leo_6 performs best for four out of six data sets and second best for the other two data sets. Here one might conclude that – purely looking at of the computing times – Leo_6 is better than ERR_CPLEX. The performances of CherryPi and CUTTING_6 are about equally good.

As we already mentioned in Section 3, for the two data sets for which ERR_CPLEX is faster than Leo_6, data sets B and C, we have applied a special version of Leo in which equalities are handled more efficiently. The results are given in Table 4. In this table we have mentioned the average computing times for the entire data sets, and between brackets the standard deviation of these computing times.

Table 4. Average computing times for Leo (in seconds) with more efficient handling of equalities (between brackets the standard deviation of these computing times)

	Data set B	Data set C
Leo[a]	308 (10)	531 (4)
Leo with efficient handling of equalities[a]	14 (2)	77 (1)
Leo ($N_{max} = 6$)	51 (1)	94 (2)
Leo with efficient handling of equalities ($N_{max} = 6$)	4 (1)	19 (1)

[a] To find the results for Leo for $N_{max} > 6$, we have set N_{max} equal to 8 for both data sets.

For data set B the version of Leo_8 with efficient handling of equalities could not find a solution for one record. For data set C the version of Leo_8 with efficient handling of equalities could not find optimal solutions for 58 records, just like the standard version of Leo. The version of Leo with efficient handling of equalities did not suffer from memory problems, however.

Examining the results of Tables 2 and 4, we can conclude that as far as computing speed is concerned ERR_CPLEX and Leo (either with $N_{max} = 6$ or with $N_{max} > 6$) are the best programs. We note at the same time, however, that this conclusion is not completely justified as ERR_CPLEX determines only one optimal solution whereas the other programs (aim to) determine all optimal solutions.

Comparing the results of Tables 2 and 4 we see that the special version of Leo that handles equalities more efficiently indeed has a reduced computing time, at least for the two data sets examined. With this rule, Leo_6 is clearly faster than ERR_CPLEX for all data sets.

Besides computing speed other aspects are, of course, important too. We note that all programs, even the commercially available ILOG CPLEX, suffer from numerical problems. In addition, Leo sometimes suffers from memory problems. Due to its matrix with a fixed maximum number of columns, CherryPi does not always determine optimal solutions. Instead, it sometimes determines a less good, suboptimal solution. Summarising, it is hard to give a verdict on the quality of the solutions found by the programs as the programs suffer from a diversity of problems.

5. DISCUSSION

McKeown (1981), in the context of Special Transportation Problems and Pure Fixed Charge Transportation Problems, remarks that 'It is unclear in any of these contexts as to what makes a problem "easy" or "difficult" to solve'. This remark has again been confirmed in the context of the error localisation problem. From the characteristics of the data sets it is hard to establish beforehand whether the corresponding instances of the error localisation problem will be "easy" or "hard". We can even extend the remark of McKeown to the following: it is unclear in our context as to what makes an algorithm a "good" or "bad" one. All algorithms we have examined have their good and bad aspects. In the end, the algorithm one favours is to some extent a subjective choice.

From our own developed algorithms, we consider the branch-and-bound algorithm (see Chapter 8 of De Waal, 2003a) the most promising one for solving the error localisation problem. The main reason for our choice is the excellent performance of Leo for records with up to six errors. For such records it determines all optimal solutions very fast. We admit that for records with more than six errors the results of Leo become less good, just like the other algorithms. The program begins to suffer from memory problems, and the computing time increases. To some extent these problems can be overcome by treating the equalities more efficiently as is done in the special version of Leo (see Table 4). Besides we feel that records with many errors should not be edited in an automatic manner, but in a manual manner. That is, we feel that records with more than, say, six errors should be rejected for automatic editing. Given this point of view, Leo seems to be an excellent choice.

In addition, it is not very complex to extend the branch-and-bound algorithm of Leo to a mix of categorical and continuous data. Statistics Netherlands has therefore decided to implement this algorithm in a module of version 1.5 (and future versions) of the SLICE system (see De Waal, 2001). This version reads an upper bound for the number of missing values per record as well as a separate upper bound for the number of errors (excluding missing values) per record. The former number is allowed to be quite high, say 50 or more, whereas the latter number is allowed to be moderate, say 10 or less. If the number of missing values or the number of errors (excluding missing values) in a record exceeds either of these upper bounds, this record is rejected for automatic editing. The new module is suitable for a mix of categorical and continuous data, and treats the equalities in an efficient manner. In addition, it contains a heuristic to handle integer data. The new module replaces the CherryPi-module, based on vertex generation, of SLICE 1.0.

One may argue that some users of SLICE will want to edit records with many erroneous fields, say 10 or more, automatically despite our arguments against editing such extremely contaminated records. Such users might then be disappointed, because the new module is not able to handle such records. To overcome this problem, we propose to opt for a simple heuristic treatment of these extremely erroneous records instead of applying the new module. We sketch three possible heuristics below.

The first heuristic is to split the set of edits into two subsets. First, we can apply the branch-and-bound algorithm on one of these subsets. One of the optimal solutions for this subset is chosen, and the corresponding fields are set to missing. Subsequently, we apply the branch-and-bound algorithm on the newly created record with possibly some additional missing values in comparison to the original record, using all edits. The solutions obtained in this way are, possibly suboptimal, solutions to the error localisation problem for the original record. This approach utilises the fact that the branch-and-bound algorithm works quite well for records with missing values.

A second approach, which utilises the same fact, to solve the error localisation problem for a record with many errors is to first determine a number of implausible values in a heuristic manner. These implausible values are set to missing. Subsequently, we apply the branch-and-bound algorithm on the newly created record with some additional missing values in comparison to the original record. The solutions obtained in this way are again, possibly suboptimal, solutions to the error localisation problem for the original record. Chung, a trainee at Statistics Netherlands, has studied this heuristic approach for solving extremely erroneous records (see Chung, 2003).

The final heuristic we mention consists of solving an LP approximation for the error localisation problem (see Section 13.2 in De Waal, 2003a).

All in all we are confident that records with many errors do not pose a threat for us if we apply the branch-and-bound algorithm in practice. We are willing to admit that our choice for the branch-and-bound algorithm is to some extent a subjective choice, but we feel that our choice is a justifiable one.

References

[1] Chernikova, N.V. (1964), Algorithm for Finding a General Formula for the Non-Negative Solutions of a System of Linear Equations. *USSR Computational Mathematics and Mathematical Physics* 4, pp. 151-158.

[2] Chernikova, N.V. (1965), Algorithm for Finding a General Formula for the Non-Negative Solutions of a System of Linear Inequalities. *USSR Computational Mathematics and Mathematical Physics* 5, pp. 228-233.

[3] Chung, W.H. (2003), *Effectief Automatisch Opsporen van Foute*n (*Effective Automatic Error Localisation*), Internal report (BPA number: 1057-03-TMO), Statistics Netherlands, Voorburg.

[4] De Jong, A. (2002), Uni-Edit: *Standardized Processing of Structural Business Statistics in the Netherlands*. UN/ECE Work Session on Statistical Data Editing, Helsinki.

[5] De Waal, T. (1996), *CherryPi: A Computer Program for Automatic Edit and Imputation*. UN/ECE Work Session on Statistical Data Editing, Voorburg.

[6] De Waal, T. (2000), *New Developments in Automatic Edit and Imputation at Statistics Netherlands*. UN/ECE Work Session on Statistical Data Editing, Cardiff.

[7] De Waal, T. (2001), SLICE: Generalised Software for Statistical Data Editing. *Proceedings in Computational Statistics* (eds. J.G. Bethlehem and P.G.M. Van der Heijden), Physica-Verlag, New York, pp. 277-282.

[8] De Waal, T. (2003a), *Processing Erroneous and Unsafe Data*. Ph. Thesis, Erasmus University Rotterdam.

[9] De Waal, T. (2003b), Solving the Error Localization Problem by Means of Vertex Generation. To be published in *Survey Methodology*.

[10] Fellegi, I.P. and D. Holt (1976), A Systematic Approach to Automatic Edit and Imputation. *Journal of the American Statistical Association* 71, pp. 17-35.

[11] Fillion, J.M. and I. Schiopu-Kratina (1993), *On the Use of Chernikova's Algorithm for Error Localisation*. Report, Statistics Canada.

[12] Garfinkel, R.S., A.S. Kunnathur and G.E. Liepins (1986), Optimal Imputation of Erroneous Data: Categorical Data, General Edits. *Operations Research* 34, pp. 744-751.

[13] Garfinkel, R.S., A.S. Kunnathur and G.E. Liepins (1988), Error Localization for Erroneous Data: Continuous Data, Linear Constraints. *SIAM Journal on Scientific and Statistical Computing* 9, pp. 922-931.

[14] Hoogland, J. (2002), *Selective Editing by Means of Plausibility Indicators*. UN/ECE Work Session on Statistical Data Editing, Helsinki.

[15] *ILOG CPLEX 7.5 Reference Manual* (2001), ILOG, France.

[16] Kovar, J. and W.E. Winkler (1996), *Editing Economic Data*. UN/ECE Work Session on Statistical Data Editing, Voorburg.

[17] McKeown, P.G. (1981), A Branch-and-Bound Algorithm for Solving Fixed Charge Problems. *Naval Research Logistics Quarterly* 28, pp. 607-617.

[18] Ragsdale, C.T. and P.G. McKeown (1996), On Solving the Continuous Data Editing Problem. *Computers & Operations Research* 23, pp. 263-273.

[19] Rubin, D.S. (1975), Vertex Generation and Cardinality Constrained Linear Programs. *Operations Research* 23, pp. 555-565.

[20] Rubin, D.S. (1977), Vertex Generation Methods for Problems with Logical Constraints. *Annals of Discrete Mathematics* 1, pp. 457-466.

[21] Sande, G. (1978), *An Algorithm for the Fields to Impute Problems of Numerical and Coded Data*. Technical report, Statistics Canada.

[22] Schiopu-Kratina, I. and J.G. Kovar (1989), *Use of Chernikova's Algorithm in the Generalized Edit and Imputation System*. Methodology Branch Working Paper BSMD 89-001E, Statistics Canada.

[23] Van Riessen, P. (2002), *Automatisch Gaafmaken met Behulp van CPLEX* (*Automatic Editing by Means of CPLEX*). Internal report (BPA number: 975-02-TMO), Statistics Netherlands, Voorburg.

Section 2.3

IMPACT ON PRECISION

Foreword – Pedro Revilla, Instituto Nacional de Estadistica, Spain

This section contains two papers covering the problem of variance estimation taking into account imputation and non-response. While one of the papers focuses more on the theoretical problems, the other one presents some empirical studies.

The paper by Rancourt presents an overview of the available theory and methods to measure and understand the impact of imputation and non-response on variance estimation. It presents specific software to carry out these tasks. It also proposes potential applications and research avenues.

The paper by Aparicio-Pérez and Lorca studies the performance of resampling variance estimation techniques under imputation, using data from the Structural Industrial Business Survey and the Retail Trade Index Survey. It applies the jackknife variance estimation based on adjusted imputed values and the bootstrap procedures. The performance of the two methods is measured through the Monte Carlo bias, the mean square error and the coverage rate of the 95 percent confident interval based on normal approximation.

ASSESSING AND DEALING WITH THE IMPACT OF IMPUTATION THROUGH VARIANCE ESTIMATION

By Eric Rancourt, Statistics Canada

Abstract: Imputation is a well-known approach to treat non-response in surveys. However, it can have a number of impacts on data and other processes, but more importantly, on estimates produced from these data. In recent years, imputation research has lead to the development of a number of methods and approaches as well as software to assess the quality of imputation by means of estimation of the variance under imputation. These methods are either based on a model, or on re-sampling techniques. In this field, we are now at a point where the main questions are about which method(s)/tool(s) should be used to perform variance estimation under imputation; about which quality measures should be developed based on these and about how to interpret results coming out of them. This paper attempts to respond to such questions by presenting the various aspects of the problems, by giving an overview of the existing methods and tools and by proposing potential applications and research avenues.

1. INTRODUCTION

Surveys are faced with the problem of missing and non-responding data. The missing information may be at the unit level (total non-response) or at the item level (partial non-response). Also, the information may be available but inconsistent or unusable. In this case, editing rules usually identify such records. In this paper, we shall consider all of these, but concentrate on non-response.

In the presence of non-response extra care must be taken to deal with this potential source of error. First, it must be detected from the data after collection. Then, it needs to be treated and finally, the resulting quality of estimates produced should be assessed.

In the context of surveys, non-response (especially partial non-response) is very often treated by imputation. To perform imputation, there are numerous methods that are all the resulting expression of a modelling exercise between the variable of interest and other variables present on the file. The degree of sophistication of the model will depend on the auxiliary information available, on the needs for simplicity and the analysts' needs.

Imputation is very attractive, because it leads to a complete data file that can be used by regular complete data software. However, this too often brings a false sense of security about the quality of data and estimates produced. Imputation has impacts that should and can be measured. These may be direct (on the process, on estimates) or indirect (on the next design, on secondary analysis). It is thus clear that quality measures are essential.

Statisticians have always been uncomfortable with inference from samples containing imputed data. In the last few decades, a significant amount of research has been carried out to provide a theoretical framework to imputation that would enable statisticians to measure the quality of imputed data and of estimates based on them. The first instance is in Rubin (1977) where the multiple imputation approach was introduced. Equipped with this tool, producers of micro data files can provide external users with properly imputed files from which correct inference can be made. In the 90's, then followed a number of approaches to estimating the variance under imputation. For instance, Lee, Rancourt and Särndal (2000; 2002) and Shao (2002) present a detailed account of such methods along with extensive comparisons, both qualitative and quantitative. Rao (1996) also presents a review of the topic.

There have been recent developments in the field of quality assessment of imputation, particularly with respect to tools, software and their application. Some methods can now be used to assess the quality of manual imputation (Rancourt, 1997) or the quality of editing (Rancourt, 2002). Further, a number of methods are now available in software such as SEVANI (Beaumont and Mitchell, 2002) or GENESIS (Haziza, 2003).

This paper is divided as follows: Section 2 briefly describes and discusses variance estimation methods under imputation. Then Sections 3 and 4 respectively present Statistics Canada's systems: GENESIS and SEVANI. Section 5 outlines potential applications of imputation variance estimation and Section 6 briefly describes some research avenues.

2. VARIANCE ESTIMATION METHODS

As described in Rancourt (2001), having at hand a method to evaluate the impact (variance) of imputation allows one to construct a better imputation strategy. Estimation of the total variance (including imputation) can be very useful. For example, it allows for:

- More precise estimation of the total variance, and as a result, a better knowledge of the data quality by the statistical agency;
- The possibility to make correct inferences;
- Better quality reporting to users, who can sometimes be misled by knowing only the sampling variance;
- Improved evaluation and choice of imputation methods by assessing the variations in precision (imputation variance) resulting from various approaches;
- Production of separate estimates of sampling and imputation variances to plan or adjust budgets between the sample size and the imputation/follow-up effort.

Variance estimation methods can be grouped into four categories: the two-phase approach; the reversed approach; re-sampling and multiple imputation.

Two-phase approach. The two-phase approach is based on the idea that the response mechanism is the second phase of a two-phase selection mechanism. It is similar to two-phase or double sampling but different in that the second phase process in NOT controlled by the survey statistician. In this approach, a model is necessary. One may use a model for the response mechanism, or a model for the data.

The response model approach was presented in Rao and Sitter (1995). The simplifying assumption that non-response is uniform is often made, but the approach is general enough to allow one to model non-response in any fashion. In the end, it is as if one tries to restore the second phase inclusion probabilities by estimating response probabilities. The resulting variance estimator conveniently splits into two terms, one that represents sampling and one that represents non-response (imputation)

$$\hat{V}_{\text{TOT}} = \hat{V}_{\text{SAM}} + \hat{V}_{\text{NRP}}.$$

The data model approach (Särndal, 1992) consists of using the relationships that exist between the variable of interest and other variables among the respondents to evaluate the expected model error caused by imputed nonrespondents. Under imputation, the total error of an estimator can be decomposed as the sampling error, the non-response (imputation) error and a mixed term. The estimator for the total variance is made of a sampling component which is the usual sampling variance estimator[1] under imputation and an imputation component. There is also a mix term, but in many situations it is exactly or approximately zero. The expression for the variance estimator is

$$\hat{V}_{\text{TOT}} = \hat{V}_{\text{SAM}} + \hat{V}_{\text{IMP}} + \hat{V}_{\text{MIX}}.$$

Reversed approach. In the reversed approach, being a respondent or a non-respondent is assumed to be a characteristic of every unit in the population. As a result, the *selection* of respondents can be viewed as taking place before selection of the sample. Therefore, we have a population of respondents selected from the population and a sample of respondents selected from the population of respondents. This approach was introduced by Fay (1991) and Shao and Steel (1999). The corresponding estimator still has two components, but their meaning is slightly different. In the case of negligible sampling fractions, the second component $(\hat{V}_2)$ becomes negligible and we obtain a simplified one-term variance estimator. In this case,

$$\hat{V}_{\text{TOT}} = \hat{V}_1 + \hat{V}_2.$$

Re-sampling techniques. The usual re-sampling techniques have now been adapted to the context of imputed data for estimation of V_1 above. The main ones are the Jackknife technique (Rao and Shao, 1992) and the Bootstrap technique (Shao and Sitter, 1996). They are reviewed in Shao (2002).

The jackknife technique (Rao and Shao, 1992) was developed to estimate the total variance. It is justified in the context of the reversed approach and actually measures its first term $(\hat{V}_1)$. The principle is that whenever a unit is deleted, a correction has to be made to all imputed values that were originally influenced by this value. Once the corrections are made, the usual jack-knife variance estimator can be used:

$$\hat{V}_{\text{JKNF}} = \sum \frac{n-1}{n} \sum \left(\hat{\theta}^j - \hat{\theta}\right)^2.$$

The Bootstrap technique is a natural extension of the idea of simulating non-response and imputation to measure their impact. In the bootstrap (Shao and Sitter, 1996), the principle is to repeat the non-response and imputation processes within each of the bootstrap samples, thereby allowing the ordinary formula to be appropriately used. However, it can be implemented without replicating non-response by using adjustments to imputed codes. For the bootstrap, the variance estimation formula is the usual one:

$$\hat{V}_{\text{BOOT}} = \frac{1}{L} \sum_{l=1}^{L} \left(\hat{\theta}^j - \bar{\hat{\theta}}\right)^2.$$

Multiple imputation. Multiple imputation was developed by (Rubin 1977, 1987), and Rubin (1996). It was develop to answer the needs for quality measure of estimates by external (or secondary) users of statistics. Multiple imputation is based on the approximate Bayesian bootstrap where more than one value is imputed for missing values so that a variance between sets of imputed values may be

[1] The usual sampling variance estimator can be used directly provided that errors are added to the imputed values for variance estimation purposes. For instance, see Gagnon, Lee, Rancourt and Särndal (1996). Otherwise, an adjustment component is required.

obtained. To get the final estimator, it is combined with the average variability within sets of imputed data. The estimator has the form:

$$\hat{V}_{\text{TOT}} = \hat{V}_{\text{BET}} + \left(\frac{M+1}{M}\right)\hat{V}_{\text{WITH}}.$$

There are also other approaches such as the balanced repeated replication method that was adapted for the case of imputed data, but they are not treated here.

In practice, the main issue with estimation of the variance in presence of imputation is not about how to proceed, but about which method to use. Each has its own merits and the choice should be made based on a number of considerations, including

- The approach implemented in production under full response;
- The need for separate components for sampling and imputation variance;
- Whether users are internal or external to the agency or group producing imputation;
- Simplicity;
- Complexity of the design and estimator.

Since the 1980s, Statistics Canada has invested in the development of generic software for various survey steps. Recently, two gaps have been identified with respect to imputation software: the ability to perform repeated simulation studies with missing data and imputation without having to write a new program each time and taking imputation into account while estimating the variance of statistics in surveys. The systems presented here (GENESIS and SEVANI) are major steps trying to fill the gaps.

3. THE GENERALIZED SIMULATION SYSTEM (GENESIS)

GENESIS v1.1 (Haziza, 2003) is a menu driven system based on SAS Release 8. It contains SAS macros linked to menus using SAS/AF. The system was developed to address the fact that several methodologists at Statistics Canada regularly conduct simulation studies in the presence of imputation. It therefore seemed appropriate to create a tool that would enable users to conduct such simulation studies without having to write a program each time. GENESIS is a simple to use and relatively efficient system in terms of execution time. The system assumes that a population data file is provided in SAS format. This population file is used as the starting point for simulations. The user then chooses a variable of interest and auxiliary variables. GENESIS contains three main modules:

(1) Full response module;
(2) Imputation module;
(3) Imputation/Reweighting classes module.

In the full response module, several sampling designs are available: simple random sampling, proportional-to-size sampling with and without replacement, stratified random sampling, Poisson sampling, one-stage and two-stage cluster sampling, two-phase sampling and the Rao-Hartley-Cochran method.

For several designs, GENESIS computes the Horvitz-Thompson, ratio and regression estimators. It displays several useful Monte Carlo results such as the relative bias of point and variance estimators, the mean squared error and coverage of the confidence interval. GENESIS also displays several useful graphics that facilitates the comparison between estimators.

In the imputation module, simulation studies can be carried out to test the performance of imputed estimators (and, in some cases, variance estimators) under different scenarios. From the population provided, GENESIS draws simple random samples without replacement of size *n* (specified by the user).

GENESIS then generates non-response to the variable of interest according to one of the following three response mechanisms:

- MCAR (Missing Completely At Random): the probability of response is constant;
- MAR (Missing At Random): the probability of response depends on one or more auxiliary variables;
- NMAR (Not Missing At Random): the probability of response depends on the variable of interest.

The user must specify the desired response rate. In the case of the MAR and NMAR mechanisms, the user can also choose to generate the non-response so that the probability of response increases or decreases with a function of the auxiliary variables or with the variable of interest.

In terms of imputation methods, the user may select one of the following:

- Previous value (or historical) imputation;
- Mean imputation;
- Ratio imputation;
- Regression imputation;
- Random hot deck imputation;
- Nearest neighbour imputation (for which the user may specify the choice of distance).

For some imputation methods, GENESIS estimates the variance of the estimators by the following methods:

- The two-phase approach under the MCAR mechanism (Rao and Sitter, 1995);
- The two-phase approach based on a model (Särndal, 1992);
- The reverse approach under the MCAR mechanism (Shao and Steel, 1999);
- The reverse approach based on a model (Shao and Steel, 1999).

Steps (1) to (4) are repeated *R* times where *R* is the number of iterations specified by the user. A number of Monte Carlo measures are proposed, such as the relative bias of the imputed estimators, their root mean squared error, the estimators of variance (when the estimation of variance option is selected), the relative bias of the variance estimators, etc.

GENESIS stores important results tables (SAS tables) in a database that gives the user more processing flexibility. For example, the user can easily calculate Monte Carlo measures other than those offered by GENESIS.

In the Imputation/Reweighting classes module, GENESIS allows the user to test the performance of methods for constructing imputation classes (method by cross-classification and score method).

GENESIS provides a means of examining the behaviour of two methods of forming imputation classes: the method by cross-classification and the score method. Within the classes, the user can choose to impute by mean or by random hot deck.

<u>Cross-classifying method</u>**:** This method involves forming imputation classes by cross-classifying auxiliary categorical variables specified by the user. He or she may also specify a number of constraints such as a minimum number of respondents per class or that the number of

respondents be greater than the number of non-respondents in the classes. If the constraints are not met, GENESIS will eliminate one of the auxiliary variables and the remaining variables will be cross-classified.

Scores method: The first step in this method is to predict the variable of interest or the probability of response using the respondent units, leading to two "scores": $\hat{y}$ et $\hat{p}$. The user must specify the desired number of classes *C*. After selecting one of the two scores (or both), the imputation classes are then formed using the equal quantiles method, which forms imputation classes of approximately equal size or using the classification method based on an algorithm that makes it possible to create homogeneous classes with respect to the selected score.

For both methods, GENESIS provides Monte Carlo measures, such as the relative bias of the imputed estimator or the relative root mean squared error (RMSE). For the scores method, GENESIS also provides graphics showing the behaviour of the relative bias and the RMSE when the imputation classes 1, 2,…, *C* are used.

4. THE SYSTEM FOR ESTIMATION OF THE VARIANCE DUE TO NON-RESPONSE AND IMPUTATION (SEVANI)

SEVANI v1.0 (Beaumont and Mitchell, 2002) is a SAS-based prototype system that can be used to estimate the non-response and imputation variance portions in a survey context when a domain total or mean is estimated. SEVANI is designed to function in a SAS v8 environment either directly using the macros or through the graphical user interface.

To be able to provide estimated variances, the system requires the sample data file, final survey weights and sampling variance estimates (before taking non-response/imputation into account). Then SEVANI will provide in a SAS file, the portion of the variance that is due to non-response, to imputation, their proportion to total variance as well as the total variance (total of sampling, non-response and/or imputation)

Variance estimation is based on the quasi-multi-phase framework (Beaumont and Mitchell, 2002), where non-response is viewed as additional phases of selection. Since the survey methodologist does not control the non-response mechanisms, a non-response model is required. When imputation is used to treat non-response, strength can be gained by using an imputation model. In SEVANI, it is possible to estimate the non-response variance associated to more than one non-response mechanism or, in other words, more than one cause of non-response. For example, most surveys suffer from unit and item non-response and these two types of non-response are likely to be explained by different non-response mechanisms. Moreover, they are often not treated in the same way. Unit non-response is usually treated by a non-response weighting adjustment technique while item non-response is usually treated by an imputation technique.

Non-response inevitably leads to an observed sample of smaller size than the sample originally selected. This sample size reduction is usually accompanied by an increase in the variance of the estimates, no matter which method is chosen to treat non-response. This increase in variance is called the non-response variance. The imputation variance is defined in SEVANI as a component of the non-response variance, which is due to the use of a random imputation method.

SEVANI can deal with situations where non-response has been treated either by a non-response weighting adjustment or by Imputation. If imputation is chosen, SEVANI requires that one of the following four imputation methods be used (within imputation classes or not):

- Deterministic Linear Regression (such as mean or ratio imputation);

- Random linear Regression (such as random hot-deck imputation);
- Auxiliary Value (such as carry-forward imputation) or
- Nearest Neighbour.

Note that auxiliary value imputation covers all methods for which the imputed value for a given unit k is obtained by using auxiliary data that come from this unit k only. Therefore, no information from the respondents is used to compute imputed values.

A good modeling effort is always required to minimize the non-response bias as much as possible and to find a non-response treatment method. If one model is better than all other models, then there is no need to estimate the non-response variance in order to choose a method. However, if there are competing models, estimating the non-response variance can be used as a criterion to make a decision on the non-response treatment method to be chosen.

5. POTENTIAL APPLICATIONS OF IMPUTATION VARIANCE ESTIMATION

Estimating the variance in the presence of imputation is only one dimension of measuring the overall quality of survey estimates. There is a large potential to extending the methods developed for estimation of the variance in presence of imputation. We outline the cases of manual imputation (or adjustments) and editing.

Manual imputation. This includes any type of manual intervention to modify data in the course of editing or analyzing the data. As in Rancourt (1997), manual imputation can be linked to previous value imputation. If the process can be replicated in a controlled setting (e.g. analysts making changes to values that are known to be correct), then the associated error can be evaluated using the data model method within the two-phase approach in paragraph 12.

Editing. It can be considered as part of the non-response mechanism. This is often the implicit assumption when dealing with the problem of missing data. However, the editing process is completely distinct from the actual response mechanism and should be studied accordingly. Since an editing model cannot be used, a *data* model (ratio) such as

$$\xi : y_k = \beta\, x_k + \varepsilon_k,\ \ \mathrm{E}_\xi(\varepsilon_k) = 0,\ \ \mathrm{E}_\xi(\varepsilon_k \varepsilon_{k'}) = 0,\ \ \mathrm{E}_\xi(\varepsilon_k^2) = \sigma^2 x_k$$

may be considered as in Rancourt (2003).

Under a data model, the editing process can be fixed, since the variables of interest are random. The total variance (sampling, non-response and editing) can be worked out to be

$$V_{\text{TOT}} = V_{\text{Editing}} + V_{\text{Nonresponse}} + V_{\text{Sampling}} + \text{ Small mix terms.}$$

Then with measures such as $\hat{V}_{\text{Editing}}$ and $\hat{V}_{\text{Nonresponse}}$, one can study various impacts of editing to monitor the editing process.

VI. RESEARCH AVENUES

The context of survey taking is in constant evolution and has increased in complexity from the original (theoretical) idea of univariate inference from a simply drawn sample to a population. Areas of research in the context on imputation could include

- The context of combining survey and administrative data through direct replacement of survey data whether they are adjusted or not;
- Rolling surveys and censuses, where data are missing by design for some areas or groups at any given point in time;
- Multivariate aspects of imputation and relationships between variables;
- Multi-level aspects of imputation when imputation classes are sequentially used in a hierarchical setting.

References

[1] Beaumont J.-F., Mitchell C. – The System for Estimation of Variance Due to Non-response and Imputation (SEVANI), *Proceedings of Statistics Canada Symposium 2002: Modeling Survey Data for Social and Economic Research*, 2002.

[2] Fay R.E. – A Design-Based Perspective on Missing Data Variance. Proceedings of the Annual Research Conference, US Bureau of the Census, 429-440, 1991.

[3] Gagnon F., Lee H., Rancourt E. and Särndal C.-E. – Estimation the Variance of the Generalized Regression Estimator in the Presence of Imputation for the Generalized Estimation System, *Proceedings of the Survey Methods Section,* 151-156, 1996.

[4] Haziza D. – The Generalized Simulation System (GENESIS), *Proceedings of the Section on Survey Research Methods*, American Statistical Association, 2003. To appear.

[5] Lee H., Rancourt E., Särndal C.-E. – Variance Estimation in the Presence of Imputed Data for the Generalized Estimation System, *Proceedings of the Section on Survey Research Methods*, American Statistical Association, 384-389, 1997.

[6] Lee., Rancourt E., Särndal C.-E. – Variance Estimation from Survey Data under Single Value Imputation, *Working Paper HSMD – 2000 – 006E*, Methodology Branch, Statistics Canada, 2000.

[7] Lee H., Rancourt E., Särndal C.-E. – Variance Estimation from Survey Data under Single Value Imputation, in *Survey Non-response*, Groves, R. et al eds., J. Wiley and Sons, New York, 315-328, 2002.

[8] Rancourt E. – Estimation de la Variance en Présence d'Imputation par Valeur Précédente. Colloque Francophone sur les Sondages, Rennes, 1997

[9] Rancourt E. – Edit and Imputation: From Suspicious to Scientific Techniques. *Proceedings*, International Association of Survey Statisticians, 604-633, 2001.

[10] Rancourt E. – Using Variance Components to Measure and Evaluate the Quality of Editing Practices, *Working paper No. 10*, Conference of European Statisticians, UN/ECE Work Session on Statistical Data Editing, Helsinki, 2002.

[11] Rancourt E. – Statistics Canada's New Software to Better Understand and Measure the Impact of Non-response and Imputation, *Working paper No. 10*, Conference of European Statisticians, UN/ECE Work Session on Statistical Data Editing, Madrid, 2003.

[12] Rao J.N.K., Shao J. – Jackknife Variance Estimation with Survey Data under Hot-deck Imputation, Biometrika, 79, 811-822, 1992.

[13] Rao J.N.K. – On Variance Estimation with Imputed Survey Data. *Journal of the American Statistical Association*, 91, 499-506, 1996.

[14] Rao J.N.K., Sitter R.R. – Variance Estimation under Two-Phase Sampling with Application to Imputation for Missing Data, *Biometrika*, 82, 453-460, 1995.

[15] Rubin D.B. – Formalizing Subjective Notions about the Effect of Nonrespondents in Sample Surveys. *Journal of the American Statistical Association*, 72, 538-543, 1977.

[16] Rubin D.B. – *Multiple Imputation for Non-response in Surveys*. New York, John Wiley, 1987.

[17] Rubin D.B. – Multiple Imputation after 18 + Years. Journal of the American Statistical Association, 91, 473-489, 1996.

[18] Särndal C.-E. – Method for Estimating the Precision of Survey Estimates when Imputation Has Been Used, *Survey Methodology*, 241-252, 1992.

[19] Shao J. – Replication Methods for Variance Estimation in Complex Surveys with Imputed Data, in *Survey Non-response*, Groves, R. et al eds., J. Wiley and Sons, New York, 303-314, 2002.

[20] Shao J., Sitter, R.R. – Bootstrap for Imputed Survey Data. Journal of the American Statistical Association, 91, 1278-1288, 1996.

[21] Shao J., Steel P. – Variance Estimation for Survey Data with Composite Imputation and Nonnegligible Sampling Fractions, *Journal of the American Statistical Association*, 94, 254-265, 1999.

PERFORMANCE OF RESAMPLING VARIANCE ESTIMATION TECHNIQUES WITH IMPUTED SURVEY DATA

by Felix Aparicio-Pérez and Dolores Lorca, Instituto Nacional de Estadistica (INE), Spain

1. INTRODUCTION

Survey data imputation is a widely used technique, employed to overcome some problems such as the presence of missing or non-valid information. In business surveys, several different imputation techniques are often applied, depending on the nature and quantity of the information that has to be imputed. Usually, data after imputation are handled as if they were true data, making inference inaccurate. (e.g. underestimating the real variance) The extent of this adverse effect depends mainly in the rate of imputed information. For a small rate of imputed data, the effects are negligible, but they can be substantial if the imputation rate is moderate or high.

Some methods have been proposed to overcome these difficulties with imputed data, but they still are far from being of routine use in many National Statistical Offices.

In this paper, we investigate the effect of some of these methods, namely two resampling techniques (the jackknife and the bootstrap) when used to provide a better variance estimation. Often, when these methods are described in research papers, a theoretical description is provided and the simulations are done with populations that are not real or, if they are, their size is very small. In this paper we conduct some extensive simulations using populations that are very similar to real populations, since they are taken from the frames of large sample data.

The remainder of this paper is organized as follows: in section 2 the jackknife techniques are studied using two different populations and several imputation methods. Section 3 deals with the bootstrap, using one of the populations of section 2 and finally Section 4 contains some conclusions.

2. JACKKNIFE

We consider the jackknife variance estimation based on adjusted imputed values proposed by Rao and Shao (1992). This takes into account the fact that some data are imputed values. If a respondent is deleted, a re-imputation is done using the response set reduced by one unit. The performance of the jackknife variance estimations is measured through its monte carlo relative biases and mean square errors and its coverage rates.

We work with artificial populations taken from large samples used in one structural business survey and in one short-term business survey. In the first case, we draw random samples from the business population. In the second case, we draw stratified random samples from the business population.

2.1. Background

2.1.A. Jackknife variance estimation

Let U={1...,k,...N} be the index set of the finite population and s a simple random sample without replacement of size n drawn from U. The set of respondents, r, is of size m and the set of non-respondents, o, is the size l=n-m. Let y be the variable of interest to be imputed using more than one imputation method and x the auxiliary variable.

We consider the jackknife variance estimation based on adjusted imputed values proposed by Rao and Shao (1992). This takes into account the fact that some data are imputed values. If a respondent is deleted, a re-imputation is done using the response set reduced by one unit.
Let $\hat{y}_k$ be the imputed value and $\hat{y}_k(j)$ the value obtained by computing the imputed values using the reduced response set after unit j has been deleted. The data after imputation are given by $\{y_{.k} : k \in s\}$ where

$$y_{.k} = \begin{cases} y_k & \text{If} \quad k \in r \\ \hat{y}_k(j) & \text{if} \quad k \in o \text{ and } j \in r \\ \hat{y}_k & \text{if} \quad k \in o \text{ and } j \in o \end{cases}$$

The jackknife variance estimator of $\bar{y}_{.s}$ is:

$$\hat{V}_J = (1-f)\frac{n-1}{n}\sum_{j \in s}\left(\bar{y}^r_{.s}(j) - \bar{y}_{.s}\right)^2$$

with $s(j) = s - \{j\}$

$$\bar{y}^r_{.s}(j) = \frac{1}{n-1}\sum_{s(j)} y^r_{.k}(j)$$

$$f = \frac{n}{N}$$

2.1.B. Imputation methods

Here we present the formulae used for ratio imputation with residuals and hot-deck imputation when they are both applied to the same data set. For ratio and mean imputation the formulae are provided by Rancourt, Lee and Särndal (1994).

The response set is divided into two parts: r_1 and r_2 of sizes m_1 and m_2 respectively and the non-response set is accordingly divided into two parts: o_1 and o_2 of sizes l_1 and l_2. We suppose that in r_1 and o_1 we have the values of the x variable available. Therefore we use ratio imputation in o_1. In o_2 we apply with replacement hot deck imputation. The imputed values are given by:

$$y_{.k} = \begin{cases} y_k & \text{if} \quad k \in r \\ \left(\bar{y}_{r_1}/\bar{x}_{r_1}\right)x_k + \varepsilon^*_k & \text{if} \quad k \in o_1 \\ \delta^*_k & \text{if} \quad k \in o_2 \end{cases}$$

where $\delta^*_k \in \{y_i : i \in r\}$, is a with replacement and equal probabilities realization from the observed values of y,

$\varepsilon_k^* \in \left(y_i - \frac{\overline{y}_{r_1}}{\overline{x}_{r_1}} x_i : i \in r_1 \right)$, is a with replacement and equal probabilities realization from the residuals of the complete observations.

The point estimator for $\overline{Y}$ after imputation is:

$$\overline{y}_{.s} = \frac{1}{n}\left(m\overline{y}_r + l_1\overline{x}_{o_1}\frac{\overline{y}_{r_1}}{\overline{x}_{r_1}} + \sum_{k\in o_1}\varepsilon_k^* + \sum_{k\in o_2}\delta_k^* \right)$$

The jackknife mean after deletion of unit is:

$$\overline{y}_{.s}^{r}(j) = \begin{cases} \frac{1}{n-1}\left(\left(m + \frac{l_2}{m-1}\right)\overline{y}_r - \left(1 + \frac{l_2}{m-1}\right)y_j + \frac{\overline{y}_{r_1}(j)}{\overline{x}_{r_1}(j)} l_1\overline{x}_{o_1} + \sum_{k\in o_1}\varepsilon_k^* + \sum_{k\in o_2}\delta_k^* \right) & \text{if } j \in r_1 \\ \frac{1}{n-1}\left(\left(m + \frac{l_2}{m-1}\right)\overline{y}_r - \left(1 + \frac{l_2}{m-1}\right)y_j + \frac{\overline{y}_{r_1}}{\overline{x}_{r_1}} l_1\overline{x}_{o_1} + \sum_{k\in o_1}\varepsilon_k^* + \sum_{k\in o_2}\delta_k^* \right) & \text{if } j \in r_2 \\ \frac{1}{n-1}\left(m\overline{y}_r + \frac{\overline{y}_{r_1}}{\overline{x}_{r_1}}\left(l_1\overline{x}_{o_1} - x_j\right) + \sum_{k\in o_1-\{j\}}\varepsilon_k^* + \sum_{k\in o_2}\delta_k^* \right) & \text{if } j \in o_1 \\ \frac{1}{n-1}\left(m\overline{y}_r + \frac{\overline{y}_{r_1}}{\overline{x}_{r_1}} l_1\overline{x}_{o_1} + \sum_{k\in o_1}\varepsilon_k^* + \sum_{k\in o_2-\{j\}}\delta_k^* \right) & \text{if } j \in o_2 \end{cases}$$

where

$$\sum_{k\in o_1}\varepsilon_k^* = l_1\overline{\varepsilon}_{o_1}^*$$

$$\sum_{k\in o_2}\delta_k^* = l_2\overline{\delta}_{o_2}^*$$

$$\sum_{k\in o_1-(j)}\varepsilon_k^* = l_1\overline{\varepsilon}_{o_1}^* - \varepsilon_j^*$$

$$\sum_{k\in o_2-(j)}\delta_k^* = l_2\overline{\delta}_{o_2}^* - \delta_j^* .$$

2.2. INDUSTRIAL BUSINESS SURVEY DATA

In Spain, the Industrial Business Survey completely enumerates businesses with 20 or more employees. We take these as our population. We simulate 200.000 samples from this population to test the performance of the jackknife variance estimation.

The variables considered in this section are turnover, payroll expense and total expense. Their distributions are strongly skewed and present very high correlation between them. We impute the turnover from each of the other two variables.

From our population of industrial businesses of size N=16438, simple random samples without replacement of sizes n=100, 500, 1000 and 5000 are drawn. Non-response in the y variable is randomly generated, assuming that the response mechanism is uniform. A loss of about 30 per cent is simulated. The number of replications is 200000 for each x variable, imputation method and sample size.

Within each replication, we compute the percentage relative bias, the relative mean square error and the coverage rate of the 95 percent confidence interval based on the normal approximation. Tables 1 to 4 show the simulation results for each sample size and imputation method.

Table 1. Imputed variable: turnover. Auxiliary variable: payroll expense
Imputation methods: ratio and mean imputation

Sample Size	Ratio: 100%			90%			70%			0%		
	Mean: 0%			10%			30%			100%		
	RB(%)	MSE	COVR(%)	RB(%)	MSE	COVR(%)	RB(%)	MSE	COVR(%)	RB(%)	MSE	COVR(%)
100	2.54	4.99	58.5	2.30	5.16	58.4	1.26	5.38	58.4	0.23	4.49	57.1
500	-0,30	2.05	68.0	-0.12	0.07	67.9	0.086	2.10	67.3	-1.22	1.95	65.8
1000	-0.89	1.40	74.3	-0.60	1.42	74.0	-0.78	1.42	73.7	-2.14	1.35	72.6
5000	-6.40	0.52	88.4	-7.0	0.53	88.1	-8.5	0.53	87.8	-11.4	0.51	87.3

Table 2. Imputed variable: turnorver. Auxiliary variable: total expense
Imputation methods: ratio and mean imputation

Sample size	Ratio: 100%			90%			70%			0%		
	Mean: 0%			10%			30%			100%		
	RB(%)	MSE	COVR(%)	RB(%)	MSE	COVR(%)	RB(%)	MSE	COVR(%)	RB(%)	MSE	COVR(%)
100	0.72	4.28	59.2	0.68	4.23	58.8	0.14	4.22	58.6	0.29	4.52	56.9
500	1.22	1.84	69.9	0.32	1.82	69.4	0.38	1.82	68.9	-0.90	1.96	65.8
1000	0.36	1.26	76.7	-0.07	1.25	76.5	-0.50	1.25	75.9	-2.12	1.35	72.6
5000	-2.22	0.47	90.3	-2.41	0.47	90.3	-4.25	0.47	89.8	-12.0	0.51	87.3

Table 3. Imputed variable: turnover. Auxiliary variable: payroll expense
Imputation methods: ratio with residuals and hot deck imputation

Sample size	Ratio: 100%			90%			70%			0%		
	Hot deck 0%			10%			30%			100%		
	RB(%)	MSE	COVR(%)	RB(%)	MSE	COVR(%)	RB(%)	MSE	COVR(%)	RB(%)	MSE	COVR(%)
100	2.47	4.88	59.5	3.17	5.13	59.2	1.79	4.96	59.3	1.44	4.69	58.7
500	-0.41	2.10	68.7	0.32	2.14	68.7	-0.36	2.13	68.3	-2.01	2.01	67.6
1000	-1.62	1.44	75.0	-1.35	1.46	74.8	-1.54	1.46	74.6	-2.45	1.39	73.8
5000	-9.70	0.54	88.1	-10.6	0.54	88.0	-11.7	0.54	87.6	-15.8	0.52	87.0

Table 4. Imputed variable: turnover. Auxiliary variable: total expense
Imputation methods: ratio with residuals and hot deck imputation

Sample size	Ratio: 100%			90%			70%			0%		
	Hot deck 0%			10%			30%			100%		
	RB(%)	MSE	COVR(%)	RB(%)	MSE	COVR(%)	RB(%)	MSE	COVR(%)	RB(%)	MSE	COVR(%)
100	0.61	4.26	59.4	0.52	4.25	59.1	0.64	4.26	59.2	-0.02	4.65	58.8
500	0.54	1.83	70.0	-0.05	1.81	69.8	0.64	1.84	69.6	-1.21	2.02	67.5
1000	0.34	1.25	76.9	-0.90	1.24	76.6	-0.94	1.26	76.3	-2.27	1.39	73.9
5000	-5.00	0.47	89.9	-4.35	0.46	90.1	-7.16	0.47	89.6	-15.5	0.52	87.1

As expected, the performance of the jackknife variance estimator is better for larger sample sizes, for ratio imputation and for total expense as auxiliary variable (this variable has a higher correlation with the y-variable, as shown in table 1). The relative bias is large for small sample sizes, then decreases and increases again when the sampling fraction becomes non-negligible. This effect has been reported by other authors (Lee, Rancourt, and Särndal, 1995, Full, S, 1999). The coverage rate is not close to the nominal one even for large samples. This is probably due to the skewed and heavy-tailed distributions of the variables.

2.3. SHORT-TERM BUSINESS SURVEYS

A sample of 9414 businesses from the Retail Trade Index Survey is taken as a sampling frame. Samples are drawn from this population mimicking the true survey design, missing data are generated following a distribution similar to the true missing value pattern observed in the survey. Two imputation methods are then applied: ratio and mean imputation. Three variables are the goals of these imputations.

The three variables under study are turnover, number of trading days in a month and number of establishments. The first and third variables are imputed using ratio and mean imputation, and only the latter method is applied to the second variable. Moreover turnover is imputed from two different variables: last month turnover and same month previous year turnover.

To prevent samples from becoming too small strata are defined as aggregations over regions of the real survey strata. Resulting strata are defined by industry and size. In each stratum missing data of the three variables are supposed to follow the same distribution as in the real survey. Missing data are also simulated for auxiliary variables used for ratio imputation, in order to study the effect of these covariates in the results. Accordingly, missing values in the auxiliary variables are simulated on a simple random sampling basis with 0, 10, 30 and 100 percent rates. The sizes of the samples drawn from our frame are 800, 1500, 2200 and 3000. For each variable, imputation method and sample size the number of replications is 200000.

Descriptive statistics are computed for the three variables. The skewness and kurtosys coefficients, even when computed within strata, are very high for turnover, high for the number of establishments and smaller (but significant) for the number of trading days. This explains the different performance of our statistics. Tables 5 to 8 show the simulation results for each sample size and imputation method

Table 5. Imputed variable: turnorver. Auxiliary variable: last month turnover

Sample size	Ratio	100%		90%			70%			0%		
	Mean	0%		10%			30%			100%		
	RB(%)	MSE	COVR(%)	RB(%)	MSE	COVR(%)	RB(%)	MSE	COVR(%)	RB(%)	MSE	COVR(%)
800	-19.7	1.15	61.7	-19.9	1.13	61.8	-20.1	1.12	61.7	-19.7	1.12	61.8
1500	-0.65	0.89	77.1	0.27	0.88	77.6	0.12	0.88	77.6	0.13	0.88	77.7
2200	-1.14	0.79	81.5	-0.69	0.79	81.7	0.006	0.79	82.0	-0.1	0.79	82.0
3000	-1.80	0.60	85.0	-0.68	0.61	86.0	0.18	0.61	85.5	0.36	0.61	85.5

Table 6. Imputed variable: turnorver. Auxiliary variable: same month year ago turnover

Sample size	Ratio	100%		90%			70%			0%		
	Mean	0%		10%			30%			100%		
	RB(%)	MSE	COVR(%)	RB(%)	MSE	COVR(%)	RB(%)	MSE	COVR(%)	RB(%)	MSE	COVR(%)
800	-19.8	1.15	61.7	-19.7	1.14	61.9	-19.9	1.13	61.9	-19.6	1.13	62.0
1500	-0.63	0.89	77.1	0.17	0.88	77.5	0.03	0.88	77.7	0.06	0.88	77.7
2200	-1.21	0.79	81.5	-0.58	0.79	81.8	-0.03	0.79	82.0	-0.15	0.79	81.9
3000	-1.92	0.60	85.0	-0.75	0.61	86-0	0.15	0.61	85.5	0.31	0.61	85.6

Table 7. Imputed variable: number of trading days

Sample size	Ratio	100%		90%			70%			0%		
	Mean	0%		10%			30%			100%		
	RB(%)	MSE	COVR(%)	RB(%)	MSE	COVR(%)	RB(%)	MSE	COVR(%)	RB(%)	MSE	COVR(%)
800										-1.0	0.25	94.6
1500										-3.18	0.17	94.5
2200										-4.28	0.14	94.3
3000										-7.6	0.13	94.0

Table 8. Imputed variable: number of establishments. Auxiliary variable: last month number of establishments

Sample size	Ratio 100%			90%			70%			0%		
	Mean 0%			10%			30%			100%		
	RB(%)	MSE	COVR(%)	RB(%)	MSE	COVR(%)	RB(%)	MSE	COVR(%)	RB(%)	MSE	COVR(%)
800	0.0	1.85	69.3	0.18	1.65	70.0	-0.05	1.60	70.3	0.47	1.57	70.6
1500	-3.7	1.26	75.3	-0.97	1.13	78.0	-0.014	1.10	78.6	0.57	1.10	78.8
2200	-6.31	0.97	81.1	-1.96	0.89	83.7	-0.59	0.87	84.3	-0.36	0.86	84.4
3000	-10.1	0.79	84.4	-4.04	0.69	86.8	-1.42	0.72	87.2	0.12	0.71	87.6

Regarding the results, we can see that the jackknife performs reasonably well for the third, and mainly the second variables. For turnover the performance is poor. This shows that strong skewness and kurtosys of the imputed variables can influence considerably the results. For example, for sample sizes of 3000 units true coverage rate is of about 85 per cent for turnover. It can be seen that imputation within survey design strata does not solve the problem. In our simulations increase of the sample size seems to be the only way to improve the jackknife performance. The effect of sample size on relative bias that other authors found and that we also mentioned in our previous section is confirmed in these simulations.

3. BOOTSTRAP

In this section we analyse the performance of the bootstrap, when estimating the variance and a confidence interval of a simple statistic in a survey with non-response and mean imputation. The relative bias and root mean square error of the variance estimator and also the coverage rate of the bootstrap confidence interval are calculated and compared with the ones obtained from the jackknife variance estimator in the previous section.

The data are taken from the Industrial Business Survey and are exactly the same as in section 2.2.

3.1. Background

Shao and Sitter (1996) proposed a bootstrap method for variance estimation with imputed survey data. This is the method that we are using. There are another modified bootstrap methods, like the ones proposed in Saigo, Shao and Sitter (2001). See also Lee, Rancourt and Särndal (2001) for a review of variance estimation methods under imputation.

Assuming a rather general sampling design, the method consists of the following steps:

a) Let $Y_I = Y_R \cup Y_O$ where $Y_R = \{y_k : k \in A_R(respondents)\}$ and $Y_O = \{z_k : k \in A_O(non-respondents)\}$. Y_O is obtained from Y_R using some imputation technique.

b) Let $Y^* = \{y_i^* : i=1,\ldots,n\}$ a simple random sample (bootstrap sample) drawn with replacement from Y_I, and $Y^*_I = Y^*_R \cup Y^*_O$ where $Y^*_R = \{y_k^* : k \in A_R^*(respondents)\}$/and $Y^*_O = \{y_k^* : k \in A_O^*(non-respondents)\}$ and Y^*_O is obtained from Y^*_R using the same imputation technique that was used in step a)

c) Obtain the bootstrap estimator $\hat{\theta}_I^* = \hat{\theta}(Y_I^*)$ of $\hat{\theta}_I = \hat{\theta}(Y_I)$, based on the imputed bootstrap data set Y_I^*.

d) Repeat steps b) and c) B times. The following bootstrap variance estimator for $\hat{\theta}_I$ is calculated:

$$v_B(\hat{\theta}_I) = \frac{1}{B}\sum_{b=1}^{B}(\hat{\theta}_I^{*b} - \bar{\theta}_I^{*})^2$$

where

$$\bar{\theta}_I^{*} = \frac{1}{B}\sum_{b=1}^{B}\hat{\theta}_I^{*b}$$

We are also calculating the percentile and the bootstrap-t confidence intervals of the statistic. The former is computed as the empirical confidence interval obtained after sorting the B bootstrap statistics. To build the bootstrap-t confidence intervals, we first compute the statistics

$t_b^{*} = (\hat{\theta}_I^{*b} - \bar{\theta}_I^{*}) \big/ \sigma_b^{*}$ where $\sigma_b^{*2} = v_B(\hat{\theta}_I^{*b})$, and then calculate $t_L^{*} = C\hat{D}F_t^{-1}(\alpha)$, $t_U^{*} = C\hat{D}F_t^{-1}(1-\alpha)$, where $C\hat{D}F_t^{-1}(x) = \#\left(t_b^{*};\ t_b^{*} \le x,\ b = 1....B\right)/B$. The bootstrap-t confidence interval is then given by $\left(\hat{\theta}_I - t_U^{*} v_B(\hat{\theta}_I), \hat{\theta}_I - t_L^{*} v_B(\hat{\theta}_I)\right)$

3.2. MONTECARLO STUDY AND RESULTS

From our population of industrial businesses we draw simple random samples without replacement of sizes n=100, 500, 1000 and 5000. We simulate a loss of about 30 per cent of our data with a uniform mechanism. The number of replications is 50000 for each sample size. The number of bootstrap samples is 999 for each replication.

An additional simulation with 23000 replications was conducted only for small sample sizes (n=100) calculating the bootstrap-t confidence interval. We used 999 bootstrap samples in the first level and 50 bootstrap samples in the second level (variance estimation of the first level bootstrap statistics).

The analysis variable is the turnover of the businesses. We use mean imputation. Within each replication, we compute the percentage relative bias, the relative root mean square error and the coverage of a nominal 95% bootstrap confidence interval. Table 9 shows the simulation results. It includes a part of Table 2 for comparison.

Table 9. Imputed variable: turnover.
Imputation method: mean imputation, 95% confidence intervals

Sample size	BOOTSTRAP T			BOOTSTRAP Percentile			JACKKNIFE		
	RB(%)	MSE	COVR(%)	RB(%)	MSE	COVR(%)	RB(%)	MSE	COVR(%)
100	0.07	4.51	56.9	-0.42	4.47	60.6	0.29	4.52	56.9
500				1.00	2.00	68.3	-0.90	1.96	65.8
1000				4.24	1.45	75.6	-2.12	1.35	72.6
5000				27.15	0.76	91.9	-12.0	0.51	87.3

4. CONCLUSIONS

From the point of view of jackknife performance ratio imputation should be used instead of mean and hot deck imputation whenever auxiliary information is available. The use of residuals and the hot deck imputation is not recommended over plain ratio and mean imputation from the point of view of the jackknife performance.

The definition of imputation classes should improve the quality of both the imputation and the jackknife performance, as also should the stratification of the sample. But in this empirical work, the strong skewness and kurtosys of the imputed variables seem to influence considerably the results and imputation within survey design strata does not improve noticeably the performance figures.

The results show that the percentile bootstrap performs better than the jackknife for coverage rate of the confidence intervals and the reverse is true for mean square errors and bias of the variance estimators.

There seems not to be any advantage in using the bootstrap-t confidence interval, in spite of its higher computational time, though only small sample simulations and small number of second level bootstrap samples are considered for this method.

References

[1] Aparicio-Pérez, F. and Lorca, D., (2002). Performance of Jackknife Variance Estimation using several imputation methods. UNECE work session on Statistical Data Editing. Helsinki.

[2] Aparicio-Pérez, F. and Lorca, D., (2003). Performance of Bootstrap Techniques with Imputed Survey Data. UNECE work session on Statistical Data Editing. Madrid.

[3] Full, S. (1999). Estimating variance due to imputation in ONS business surveys. International Conference on Survey Non-response. Portland, Oregon.

[4] Kovar, J.G and Whitridge, P.J (1995). Imputation of business survey data. Business survey methods. Eds B.G. Cox, D.A. Binder, B.N. Chinnappa, A. Christianson, M.J.Colledge, P.S. Kott), pp 403-423. New York. Wiley.

[5] Lee, H., Rancourt, E. and Särndal, C.E. (2001). Variance estimation from survey data under single imputation. In Survey Nonresponse. Eds. R.M. Groves, D.A. Dillman, J.L. Eltinge and R.J.A. Little, 315-328. Wiley. New York.

[6] Lee, H, Rancourt, E and Särndal, C. (1995). Variance estimation in the presence of imputed data for the Generalizad estimation System, Proceedings of the Section on Survey Research Methods, American Statistical Association, pp 384-389.

[7] Lorca, D and Aparicio-Pérez, F (2003). Variance Estimation under imputation in short-term business surveys. 54 th Session of the International Statistical Institute (ISI). Berlin

[8] Rancourt, E., Lee, H. and Särndal, C. (1994). Variance estimation under more than one imputation method. International Conference on establishment Surveys,pp 374-379.

[9] Rao, J.N.K and Shao, J (1992). Jackknife variance estimation with survey data under hot deck imputation. Biometrika, 79, pp 811-822.

[10] Saigo, Shao and Sitter (2001). A repeated half-sample bootstrap and balanced repeated replications for randomly imputed Data. Survey Methodology, vol 27,No. 2,pp.189-196

[11] Shao and Sitter (1996) Bootstrap for imputed survey data. Journal of American Statistical Association, 91,1278-1288.

Section 2.4

METADATA FOR STAKEHOLDERS

Foreword – Heather Wagstaff, Office for National Statistics, United Kingdom

There are three papers in this section that discuss what knowledge and metadata about the primary source data and the data editing process should be disseminated to the stakeholders.

The first, by Nordbotten, discusses the sharing of knowledge between producers and users of statistics. Nordbotten argues that statistics can become commercial commodities. Hence, he explores how the statistical market mechanism might work in the future to meet the information needs of the users. The discussion is mainly confined to metadata about the accuracy of statistics and statistical data editing processes. It acknowledges that, in reality, the users may place higher priority on other dimensions of quality. Emphasis is placed on the importance of understanding the needs of the end-users and how a statistical producer should provide these metadata. The paper concludes that further research should focus on: which data are needed by end-users; how the data should be collected; and the form in which the metadata about accuracy should be disseminated.

The second paper, by Luzi and Manzari, discusses the dissemination of knowledge within the National Statistical Institute. This is analysed from the perspective of information flows among the internal users of editing and imputation methods (the survey statisticians) and the centralized methodologists. The analysis is based on a functional model, the data editing method life cycle, as a conceptual framework. The paper concludes that there are significant gains to be made from having a good mechanism for information exchange. This in turn ensures that users understand the concepts and facilitates discussions on principles, techniques, methods and systems.

The last paper in this section, by Rouhuvirta, emphasizes the direct link between the content management of register data and the quality of the resulting statistical data. The paper considers ways to present the metadata about statistical data that have been compiled from register sources to ensure a good understanding and accurate interpretation by users of the data. A discussion follows of methods to ensure that adequate metadata about data from registers is available at the data editing phase and how to preserve metadata from the editing process for utilization in later stages of statistical production. A practical example - the problem of structuring of taxation metadata and its utilization - is presented.

METADATA ABOUT EDITING AND ACCURACY FOR END-USERS

by Svein Nordbotten, Statistics Sweden

1. INTRODUCTION

This paper focuses on the needs of the end-users of statistics for metadata about the statistics offered by the statistical producers. It is set within a framework proposed in an earlier paper [Nordbotten 2000a]. Since the discussion is in the context of data editing, the discussion is mainly limited to metadata about the accuracy of statistics and statistical data editing.

Several questions are addressed in this paper. The first is what are the end-users' needs for metadata and how will the users of statistics react on metadata. A second question addressed is how should a statistical producer react to the information needed by the users and provide metadata, which might serve the needs. At the end of the paper, a short discussion is included about required research and development for implementation of a metadata service.

2. INFORMATION NEEDS OF END-USERS OF STATISTICS

In the paper referred to above, it was proposed that statistics could be considered as ***products*** delivered from a statistical producer. We shall assume that each product is described by 4 production attributes: ***identification, accuracy, process data,*** and *size.* Identification determines which real world fact the product is assumed to reflect, accuracy indicates the quality of the measurement, process data explains how the product was generated, and size refers to the measured value of the product. The identification, accuracy and process data are ***metadata,*** which tell the user about the measurement while size is the statistical figure, which the end-users want to use to solve their respective problems.

Modern metadata systems are expected to include a number of data useful for the users and producers [Sundgren 1991, Nordbotten 1993]. Examples of metadata are conceptual and operational definitions of facts represented by identification attributes, description of procedures for and performances of the important processes such as the selection of units observed, the collection techniques, editing, estimation, presentation and dissemination of results, which are all components of the statistical production. This paper addresses metadata originating from the editing process because the main objective of this process is to contribute to the accuracy of statistical products.

The aim of editing is to detect and adjust errors in the collected microdata. From the process, important process data can be obtained useful for producers to improve the production design and useful for the end-users to evaluate the available statistics for their purposes [Nordbotten 2000b].

In early days, the main objective for producers of official national statistics was to provide statistics satisfying the needs of their national governments. The production was typically also funded by government grants and the producers were assumed to prepare the statistics as accurately as the granted funds permitted. In the 20th century, research and private industry became important users of official statistics. In the beginning of the present century, electronic technology, communication and globalisation trends dominate. In the future, we expect statistics, as any kind of information, to become of vital interest to new groups of users and to be valued as commercial commodities. This will require an exchange of information between producers of statistics and the growing variety of users.

It is therefore important to have a conceptual picture of which information producers and users need, and how the actors react to metadata about accuracy. We illustrate in ***Figure 1*** how the future statistical market mechanism may work. Each quadrant of the figure represents a special aspect of the market.

The ***Southwest quadrant*** explains the relation between production cost, ***C=C (A)*** and the accuracy, ***A***. It assumes that increasing the quality of a product requires resources and increases the cost of producing the product.

The ***Northwest quadrant*** reflects the number of uses of a product, ***N,*** as a function of its accuracy, ***A,*** assuming the product is free, ***N= G(A; P=0).*** The more accurate the product is, the more it will be used. This corresponds to the traditional situation when statistical products are available without cost for the users and they have to guess the accuracy of the products.

When a product is provided for a price set by the producer, the number of uses is assumed to be determined by ***3*** factors, the kind of product, its accuracy, and its price. For each accuracy level, there may be a different demand curve. As depicted in the ***Northeast quadrant,*** the demand curve, ***N= F(P; A=a),*** determines the number of uses of the product, ***N,*** as a function of its price, ***P***. A product with a higher accuracy is assumed to have a demand curve to the right of the curve for the same product with a lower accuracy. Note the relationship between the two functions in this and the previous quadrant.

Finally, the producers gross income, ***I,*** from a product with a given accuracy, ***a,*** *is* determined by the income curve ***I=F (P; A=a)*P*** in the ***Southeast quadrant.*** The gross income curve can be compared with the cost curve corresponding to the accuracy of the product, and the net income,
i-c, deducted.

In a statistical market in which the statistical products are free or charged only with the cost of printing and distribution, the number of uses is determined by the curve in the Northwest quadrant if data on the accuracy are available for the users. If the product is free and no accuracy data are available, the users will evaluate the product on basis of earlier experience, and decide if the product can be used or not for their specific. On the other hand, information on the product accuracy does not imply that the producer must request a price for his product.

For the statistical producer, several productions and marketing strategies are possible:

i) If the goal of the statistical producer is to maximize the number of uses of a product, he may choose to allocate as much as possible of resources to increase accuracy by editing, etc. Maximum of uses will then obviously be obtained when a product is offered free of charge, ***P=0***. The number of uses would in the example be ***N = n1***.

ii) An alternative strategy for the producer would be to recover production cost, ***C=c***, for a product with a given accuracy ***a***. The producer must then set the price, ***P=p2,*** such that, ***I=F (P=p2; A=a)* P=p2,*** equals the costs, ***C=C (A=a)***. The implementation of this strategy requires that the users have information about the product accuracy and that the producer knows the demand curve for this accuracy. The number of uses in this case would be ***n2***.

iii) A third producer's strategy would be to aim at a product price for a given accuracy, which would give a maximum income. This objective would be satisfied when the price is set to maximize the demand function ***I=F(P; A)*P,*** *i.e.* ***P=p3***. This also assumes that the producer has acquired knowledge about demand curves for the relevant accuracy level, and that the users are informed about the accuracy and the price set for the product. The number of uses would in this situation be $N=n_3$.

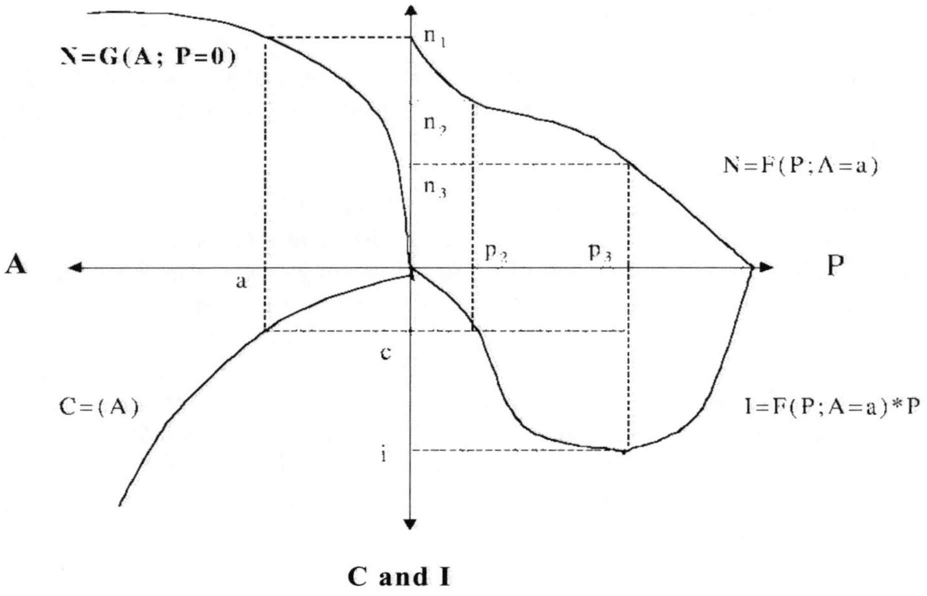

Figure 1: The statistical market

A more challenging problem would be to locate both the accuracy level and the price for the product, which simultaneously generates the maximum net income. All the above-indicated strategies are referred to a single product. In a real world system, there will be multiple products, and the producer must consider the optimum accuracy and price simultaneously for all products.

3. METADATA CONCERNING EDITING

In the previous section, we emphasized that providing the end-users with information on accuracy/editing must be a two-way communication to be effective. The end-users need to be informed about ***3*** meta-aspects of the statistical product as well as the price asked:

- identification of the social/economic fact measured,
- accuracy of the product,
- process data including how accuracy measurement was done ant its reliability
- price requested for the product.

This meta-information should be available in alternative forms depending on the wishes of the end-users.

On the other hand, statistical producers must also acquire knowledge of the users' reactions to the information about product accuracy and price setting in order to be able to adjust adequately to needs and accuracy.

A ***2-way*** exchange of information about the statistical products between the producer and the users as indicated in ***Figure 2*** is therefore needed. Without this mutual exchange of information, the users' behaviour will be arbitrary and dominated by uncertain knowledge and experience while the producer's choice of strategy for serving the market will be inefficient and dominated by traditions.

The conditions for the 2-way exchange to function effectively are:

i) procedures for providing the users with information about the existing products, and

ii) procedures for acquiring feedback responses from the users.

To fulfil the first condition, the statistical producers must decide on a marketing policy for providing meta-data about the accuracy of their products. Traditional marketing implied that a statistical product was provided with a name permitting the users to identify which real fact the product aimed at describing and a price, if not free. A modern marketing policy must also include a measure of the accuracy, information about how this accuracy was measured, and advice about how it should be interpreted and used.

A national statistical producer disseminates a large number of statistics each year, and it will probably never be possible to provide accuracy measures for each. The aim must be to give accuracy measurements for products which can be considered representative for others with respect to accuracy.

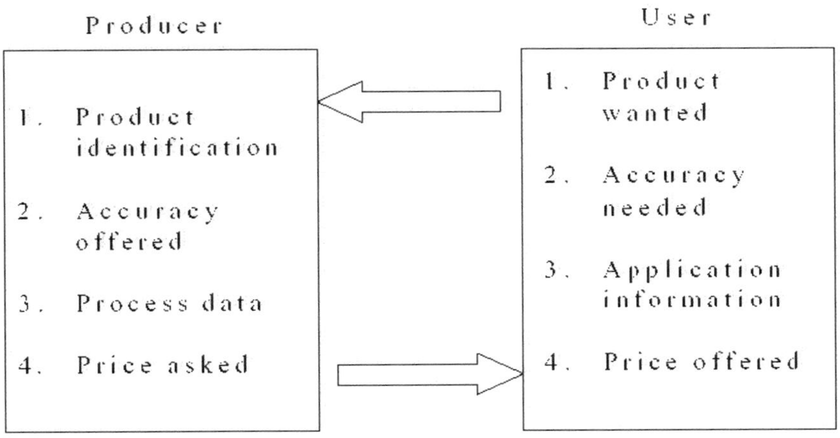

Figure 2: Exchange of metadata between producer and user of statistics

This policy has been an aim of national statistical offices for many years. Because of the implied costs, it has in most cases been postponed. With exploding needs for statistical information and a trend to consider statistical products as any other information products, it is now time for preparing a new marketing policy. As a starting point, a few products should be selected for introducing accuracy and editing process metadata. The best form of metadata presentation is not obvious and needs research in close cooperation with users.

Feedback from the users is equally important, but a much more difficult problem because it requires active participation of users. Because the statistical products traditionally have been supplied without any or for a small charge, the statistical producer has not had any strong incitement for acquiring data and knowledge about the users needs and their evaluations of products disseminated. However, up to ***40%*** of the typical statistical survey costs, is spent on editing for improving accuracy [Granquist 1996 and 1997]. It should be justified to systematically ask users about their accuracy needs and evaluation of products disseminated. Users should be recruited for representative panels to provide the wanted information.

4. METADATA ON ACCURACY

So far, we have referred to metadata on editing in general terms. We need, however, to decide how accuracy from editing should be measured and provided to the end-users. We shall refer to the accuracy measurements as ***accuracy indicators.*** The general question of measuring product quality was discussed in detail previously [Nordbotten 2000a]. In the present paper, we shall concentrate the discussion on alternative accuracy indicators.

Manzari and Della Rocca distinguished between ***output-oriented approaches*** and ***input oriented approaches*** for evaluation of editing procedures [Manzari and Della Rocca 1999]. Both approaches can provide metadata reflecting the accuracy of the product. An output-oriented approach focuses on evaluating the impact of editing on the final output comparing edited and true values (in real surveys this can only be possible for small samples), while in an input-oriented approach the evaluation is based on the changes of input data during the editing process. We shall follow a similar distinction for different indicators of accuracy.

4.1 Output-based indicators

The most obvious form for an output-based accuracy indicator is the ***error indicator*** expressing the size order of the error in the product size. Since the error of a statistical measurement can only be determined exactly in controlled experiments (if we in a real survey knew the exact errors, we would of course adjust the estimates to their correct values), we have to be satisfied with an error indicator of accuracy subject to uncertainty. An example of an indicator of this type is an ***upper bound D*** for maximum error specified with a certain degree of confidence. This means that the actual error may be less then the indicator, but that there is also the specified risk that it may be larger.

Formally, the indicator ***D*** and a confidence probability p can be presented as:

$$Pr\ (|Y'-Y|<=D)=p$$

where ***Y'*** is the size of the statistics prepared and ***Y*** is the unknown, true value of the fact estimated.

It is not a trivial task to present a probability statement of this type to the end user in such a way that it is understood correctly. It may be formulated as a quality declaration in different ways. In ***Figure 3***, the probability statement is presented in four different examples, two by text, and two by means of graphical tools. Do we know which type will be understood and correctly interpreted by a majority of users? The formulation of the declaration requires careful consideration to be useful for the end-users. The four examples in the figure also illustrate the difficulty in conveying the content of probability statements in a simple way.

In any case, there should always be an option for the users to obtain more specific meta-information about the indicators and how they were computed.

The product Y' is a measurement of a fact defined as ...... There is a risk of 100*(1-p) that the error in the product Exceeds +/- D.

Example 1 [More process data]

The data on which the statistical product Y' was based, have been carefully edited. The product may, however, deviate from the fact it is describing. The National Bureau of Statistics has made an accuracy evaluation of Y' by means of a careful examination of a random sample. If repeated samples were examined, 100* p% of the samples would show a deviation +/- D from the fact Y which the estimate Y' aims at.

Example 2 [More process data]

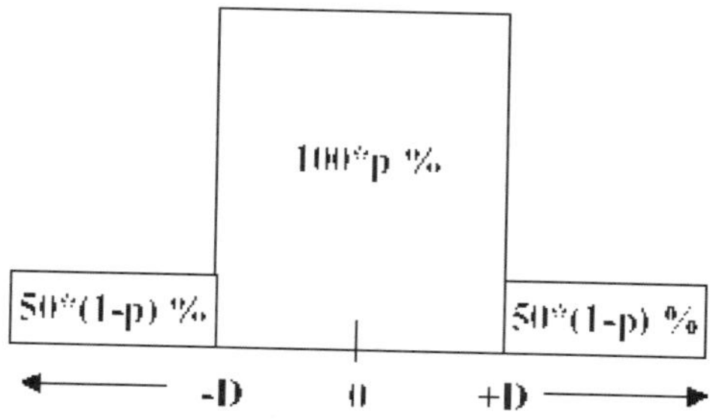

The risk for the size of error in the statistics Y'.

Example 3 [More process data]

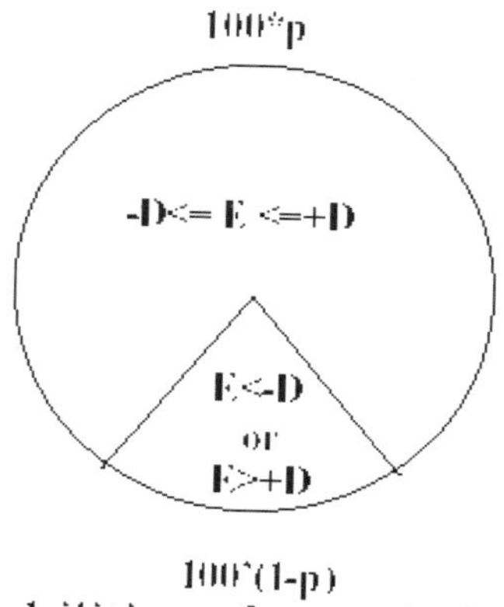

Probabilities of error in Y'.

Example 4 [More process data]

Figure 3: Four simple examples of accuracy indicators for a statistical product

A serious drawback of output-based accuracy indicators is that they require a second, time-consuming and expensive editing of a sample of already edited data.

4.2 Input-based indicators

In the input-based approach, focus is on raw, input data and edited data. Three types of accuracy indicators, ***frequency, ratio,*** and ***relative*** indicators, can be developed from process data. A typical ***frequency indicator*** based on process date from the editing process is:

Reject frequency** = **No. of rejected observations/ Total no. of observations.

This indicator tells the users that a certain number of collected values were identified as suspicious, and submitted for further inspection. What does a large frequency indicate? It may indicate that many records have been reinspected and many errors are probably eliminated, i.e. the product has a high quality. Alternatively, it may indicate that the original raw input data had a low quality in general. It will always be difficult to interpret the differences expressed by such an indicator from one survey to another. In most cases, more process information will be useful, for example about possible changes in the collection process.

A number of editing process performance measures can easily be developed as a by-product of the editing process without significant expenses. Assume that a total of imputed values obtained during editing and a corresponding total of the original raw values are computed. We can then define the ***ratio indicator:***

Imputation ratio = Total of imputed values/ Total of raw values

> The accuracy of the statistics has been monitored and evaluated during the processing, and it is considered to have improved by x % compared with the accuracy of the statistics for the previous period.
>
> More information on the accuracy can be obtained from the National Statistical Office.
>
> *Example 1* [More process data]

> The data used for preparation of these statistics have been screened. X% of the collected data were rejected as suspicious and re-inspected. As a result Y% of the estimate values is based on data which have been changed.
>
> More information on the accuracy can be obtained from the National Statistical Office.
>
> *Example 2* [More process data]

Figure 4: Two examples of relative accuracy indicators

A large imputation ratio can indicate high accuracy because the editing process changed many dubious raw values. This conclusion is correct if the adjustment of rejected values always will improve the data. Unfortunately, this cannot always be assumed for example when an automatic imputation has been used. A large imputation ratio may in this case indicate a high degree of uncertainty with respect to the accuracy of the product.

Usually, correct interpretation of process data indicators requires an extensive knowledge of the production process. The metadata reflecting this knowledge should therefore be available to end-users. The statistical producer should select the process data indicators, which he believes to be the most reliable indicators of accuracy and present these for the end-users in the form of ***relative indicators*** with reference to a base year or the previous period.

4.3 Comparative remarks

Two alternative approaches to inform the end-users about the accuracy of statistical products have been outlined. Each has its comparative advantages and drawbacks. Comparing the approaches, we can sum up the results:

(a) The output-based indicators permit the end-users to evaluate the probably maximum errors he shall have to deal with. He can also compare the errors of different statistics. The main drawback with this kind of error indicators is the extra resources and time needed for computing the indicators.

(b) The input-based indicators can be considered as inexpensive by-products from the editing process and are frequently required for improving the process. In many situations, experienced statisticians can deduce accuracy information from these indicators and present it for the end-users. Because the preparation of input-based indicators do not include a comparison with any true values, they can not inform about accuracy levels, but about the direction of change in these levels. The user-friendliest form may be to make them available as relative indicators.

(c) Metadata about the editing process should always be available as an option for end-users wanting more information about the reliability of the accuracy indicators.

5. REQUIRED RESEARCH AND DEVELOPMENT

To provide metadata to users about editing and accuracy about statistical products is a challenging objective. Several research and development tasks have been mentioned:

Which data do the end-users need and how to collect the data?
The answer requires a 'market analysis'. A first step may be to extend the producer's established contact with established user groups to discuss the needs for metadata about editing and product accuracy. As a more permanent solution, representative user panels may be needed. These panels should be exposed to experimental market scenarios and express their reactions. Recruiting members for such panels may require that those serving be offered some kind of payment.

In which form should the accuracy meta-data be disseminated?
Accuracy data can be presented in several alternative forms, which may not exclude each other. Most metadata could be presented as plain text. The challenge will be to find a balance between a shorter presentation, which is read, but frequently misinterpreted, and a longer version needed for correct interpretation, but read only by few. Alternatives can be tabular and graphical presentations.

How to disseminate the accuracy meta-data?
Should metadata be printed and made easily available as promotional material with product prices, and if so how should this be made known to the general user community? Should links metadata, etc. be made available at the producer's web site?

References

[1] Granquist, L. (1996): An Overview of Methods of Evaluating Data Editing Procedures. Statistical data editing. Vol. 2, Methods and Techniques. Statistical Standards and studies No. 48. UN/ECE Work Session on Statistical Data editing, Voorburg.

[2] Granquist, L. (1997): The New View on Editing. UN/ECE Work Session on Statistical Data editing, Voorburg. Also published in the International Statistical Review, Vol. 65, No. 3, pp.381-387.

[3] Manzari, A. and Della Rocca, G. (1999): A Generalized System Based on Simulation Approach to Test the Quality of editing and Imputation Procedures. UN/ECE Work session on Statistical data editing. Rome.

[4] Nordbotten, S. (1993): "Statistical Meta-Knowledge and –Data," Presented at the Workshop on Statistical Meta Data Systems, EEC Eurostat, Luxembourg, and published in the Journal of Statististics, UN-ECE, Vol. 10, No.2, Geneva, pp. 101-112.

[5] Nordbotten, S. (2000a): Evaluating Efficiency of Statistical Data Editing: General framework. UN/ECE Conference of European Statisticians. Geneva.

[6] NORDBOTTEN, S. (2000b): Statistics Sweden's Editing Process Data Project. Presented at the ICES II Conference. Buffalo.

[7] Sundgren, B. (1991): "What Metainformation should Accompany Statistical Macrodata?" R&D Report, Statistics Sweden, Stockholm.

DATA EDITING METHODS AND TECHNIQUES: KNOWLEDGE TO AND FROM USERS

By Orietta Luzi and Antonia Manzari, ISTAT, Italy

1. A FUNCTIONAL MODEL FOR DISSEMINATING KNOWLEDGE IN THE DATA EDITING FIELD

The number and the variety of statistical production processes characterizing any National Statistical Institute (NSI in the following) generally determines an intensive and diversified demand of specialized statistical and technological knowledge coming from the Production Units (i.e. the staff responsible for surveys). In this context, an important objective is to ensure the dissemination inside the NSI of all the available knowledge on data editing methods and techniques. In particular, all the available information about the best solutions (from the point of view of costs and quality) for particular classes of problems have to be disseminated to the statisticians responsible for surveys. This requires the management and optimization of information flows to and from users (i.e. the statisticians responsible for the surveys).

A functional model based on a given *data editing method life cycle* is designed to ensure that knowledge and expertise are as widely shared as possible within the NSI. In that model, a fundamental assumption is that a centralized unit in charge of the search and the definition of the best methods does exist.

We define *a data editing method life cycle* as the following sequence:

(i) *analysis of demand:* for any class of homogeneous statistical information production processes:

- identification of actual and potential needs (requirements);
- analysis of problems and limits due to the current existing procedures, if any;

(ii) *search for best solutions* already available: in the market, in the academic environment, in other NSIs;

(iii) if best solutions are not available, *research and development of new methods and techniques;*

(iv) *software acquisition* (if already available) or *development* (otherwise);

(v) *testing of the selected method,* by applying it to selected situations, representative of the entire class;

(vi) *evaluation,* and, if positive,

(vii) *generalized dissemination* of the method to the entire class of production processes.

The need for information exchange arises in steps i) and vii). In step i) the flow is mainly from internal users to methodologists in the central unit. On the contrary, there is an opposite flow in step vii).

In the following paragraphs we will analyse more in depth some of the above-mentioned phases: in Section 2 some aspects of the first phase of the functional model are discussed; Section 3 deals with the search of the best solution for a particular class of surveys; in Sections 4 and 5 some aspects related to the development and the evaluation of the selected solutions are analysed, respectively. Section 6 describes some approaches that seems to be appropriate for disseminating the acquired knowledge about the evaluated methods to the entire class of surveys. Section 7 contains some concluding remarks.

2. ANALYSIS OF DEMAND

In any NSI there are several kinds of statistical information production processes, characterized by different features and objectives. Different classes of survey processes can be defined depending on: - target population,

- characteristic of investigated phenomena,
- survey organization,
- available resources and time,
- statistical objectives and kind of produced figures,
- data processing features.

Generally speaking, the common problem of any of these situations is the *optimization of the overall survey process and, more specifically, of the data processing phase, in terms of quality, cost, time, respondent burden.* In many NSIs there exists a central unit in charge of collecting and organizing the demand of methodological and/or technical solutions coming from users (i.e. the statisticians responsible of the surveys), whose main goal is studying, evaluating and providing the "best solutions" for each class of problems. In other words, all the actual (and potential) requirements have to be gathered and all the possible solutions have to be evaluated in order to find (classes of) best solutions for that requirement.

In particular, the identification of operational, technical or methodological solutions to the problem of designing best data E&I strategies, can be simplified if surveys are grouped in subsets (or 'clusters') that are homogeneous with respect to some classification criteria. For example, clusters could consists of statistical survey processes similar in terms of target population (business or household surveys), type of surveyed variables (quantitative or qualitative), survey typology (censuses, periodic sample surveys, panel surveys, administrative surveys, etc.), survey organizational features (mode of data collection, mode of data-entry, available budget, technological and human resources, timeliness requirements, and so on). This makes it possible to build a sort of *classification tree* in which pre-defined criteria are used as branching rules and each node contains survey processes similar with respect to all the criteria considered in the higher levels. An example of a survey process classification tree is shown in figure 1, where the *Business Survey* root node generates several more specific nodes at lower levels corresponding to particular sets of surveys identified on the basis of some simple criteria.

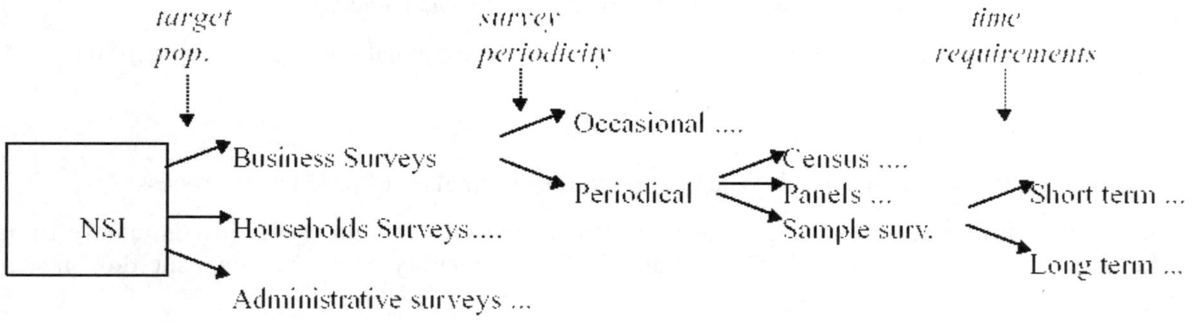

Figure 1 - An example of structured tree of survey processes

Even if the improvement or the re-design of the E&I strategy of a specific survey implies in any case the development of *ad hoc* data processing flows, the task of identifying possible solutions can be simplified if the above-mentioned survey and methods classification structure has been defined.

3. SEARCH FOR BEST SOLUTIONS

The general scheme described in the previous section also makes it possible to classify the already available or known E&I methodologies and techniques on the basis of an evaluation of their usefulness and applicability to the specific context of each node. This classification facilitates the search for the best solutions for each class of survey process, in the sense that the set of possible solutions is restricted to a particular subset of alternatives. It should be noted that, in the above tree structure, some of the possible methodological or technical solutions could be 'inherited' from a higher level node to one or more of its lower level nodes: for example, the use of generalized automatic systems[1] for numeric variables can be considered appropriate in any subsequent node of the general *Business surveys* class (see figure 1). On the other hand, editing and/or imputation techniques requiring the use of historical information on the same respondent unit are peculiar to the *Panel business surveys* node; similarly the use of macro or selective editing criteria, that implies follow-up activities, are more appropriate in *Short-term business surveys,* where timeliness and costs are the most important production constraints.

It should be emphasized that a 'best solution' for a given survey or class of surveys generally consists of a *set of combined single 'best solutions',* referred each to a particular step or to a specific problem constituting the whole E&I process. In this sense, in order to identify an overall best solution for a given node, it is required to analyse each step of its peculiar processing flow in order to define the corresponding (set of) best method(s). Therefore, in the following, we will denote with 'best solution' a given set of best methods or software.

In any case, it is also possible that, in the choice of the best solution for a given survey belonging to a certain class, the constraints represented by costs, time, human and available technological resources may be really strong. In extreme situations, these limits could determine even the impossibility to adopt the best solution identified for a given class to a survey belonging to that class.

Once the best solution has been found, further problems arise relating to its actual availability. In particular, it is necessary:

- to verify if either the best solution has been already developed as consolidated methodology, or an original theoretical development is needed;
- to verify if either the identified solution is already included in some generalized or *ad hoc* software, or its implementation has to be planned (inside or outside the NSI);
- to verify if either the eventually available software including the solution is already available in the NSI, or it has to be acquired from outside,
- to assess if either the solution has been already tested, or an experimental activity has to be designed,
- to evaluate if either the solution is easy to transfer to users, or its dissemination requires that training activities, documentation production and other activities have to be planned and performed.

As for the first two points, if the identified solution has not been already developed and/or implemented in any software, an evaluation of the costs and resources required for these activities has to be done. In particular, if a useful software exists but has to be acquired from outside, the above-mentioned evaluation represents a benchmark for the costs and resources needed to obtain or buy it. In the Italian National Statistical Institute (ISTAT in the following) there have been very different experiences in this context. For example, to satisfy the general demand in the *Household surveys* area for an automatic system in order to improve quality, timeliness and costs of final results, the use of automatic generalized systems implementing the Fellegi-Holt probabilistic methodology (Fellegi et Holt, 1976) was identified as best solution. In that situation, the development and implementation of that

---

[1] Several generalized software handling economic variables have been implemented by various NSIs: GEIS (Kovar et al. 1988) by Statistics Canada, CHERRYPI (Ton De Waal, 1996) by Statistics Netherlands, AGGIES (Todaro,1999) by the U.S. NASS, SPEER (Winkler, 1997) by the U.S. Bureau of the Census.

software (called *SCIA, Automatic System for data Check and Imputation)* (Riccini et al. 1995) has been carried out with existing ISTAT resources (already available budget and human resources). The same process characterized the life cycle of two other ISTAT automatic systems: the software RIDA for missing data integration based on the lowest distance donor imputation method (Abbate, 1997), and the software ESSE *(Editing Systems Standard Evaluation) (Luzi* and Della Rocca 1998; Manzari and Della Rocca, 2000) for evaluating the quality of E&I procedures. A different life cycle characterized the acquisition of the software GEIS *(Generalized Editing and Imputation System)* developed by Statistics Canada and dealing with numerical, continuous and non-negative variables. Recently, the demand for methodological and technical solutions coming from the *Business Surveys* field, and regarding the problem of dealing with large amounts of stochastic non-influential errors, has rapidly increased. Also, in this case, the best solution has been considered an automatic generalized system implementing the Fellegi-Holt methodology. But in this case, for organizational, costs and resources reasons, it was preferred to acquire such a software instead of developing it with internal resources.

4. DEVELOPMENT OF THE SOLUTION

When an identified solution has not already been implemented in any existing software, either developed inside or available outside the NSI, the only chance is to develop it. Statistical software development requires performing the following steps:

- Algorithm identification,
- Resource allocation and cost evaluation,
- Implementation,
- Training to users,
- Maintenance.

When dealing with computational problems, the knowledge of mathematical methodology, then of the algorithm, is a fundamental prerequisite. The algorithm has to be fully defined, as well as input and output data. Once the algorithm has been identified, its optimization from a computational point of view, is also a crucial aspect to consider: software must be not only reliable, but also highly performing in terms of time and resource allocation. This phase requires strong and productive relationships between methodologists/statisticians and software developers.

Software development requires a careful planning and evaluation of resources (in terms of people, environment and time needed to develop the software).

Software implementation consists of three main phases: *design, code implementation* and *performance test.* The design of the application requires the definition of technical specifications: target platforms (Unix, Windows, etc.), type of users interface (graphically, by command line, etc.), format and structure of both input/output data and diagnostic reports tracing specific E&I actions. The code implementation requires the availability of expert programmers and development environments (machine, programming languages and compilers, debugging tools, etc.). The development phase implies also that developers write user manuals (user guide, installation guide, readme files, etc.). Once the code has been developed and debugged by the programmers, a suitable test phase needs to be performed by users. This test is aimed to evaluate: programme quality (detect residual bugs), requirements satisfaction, performance (computational time, system resource used) and ease of use. Based on the feedback from testing, an iterative reworking of the code is generally performed.

In order for users to start using the new application effectively, training is necessary, including theoretic and practical (hands-on) sessions.

Finally, future maintenance of the programmes also has to be guaranteed. The need for maintenance comes from: residual bugs in the code, interaction conflict with additional applications installed later, operating system upgrade. Maintenance is also related to the implementation of small programme enhancements solicited by users. Maintenance also requires a careful "skill transfer" stage to people in charge of it, in case they are different from developers. To facilitate maintenance of an application code, all the tasks of the development process as well as all the technical characteriztics of the code itself are to be properly documented.

5. EVALUATION OF THE SOLUTION

When a solution has been developed and/or implemented in a software, testing of its performance and evaluation of its impact on the survey process is demanding for every search of "best solution" process. The evaluation process is, in fact, an essential support for choosing or discarding an E&I method or strategy for its application in a specific class of surveys.

Comparison of different solutions requires a metrics definition, in other words, standard evaluation criteria have to be defined and proper indicators have to be computed for each solution. A universal definition of quality of E&I methods is a difficult task because of the numerous aspects of quality. Generally speaking, a main distinction is made between accuracy and efficiency characteristics. Quantifying the *accuracy* of the E&I procedure means to provide a measurement of the closeness between the actual (true) values and the output determined by the investigated procedure. The output of an editing method is the classification of each observed value as correct or erroneous, while the output of an imputation method is the new assigned value. Whatever the output (classification result, individual data items, frequency distribution or parameter estimates), the computation of quality indicators of E&I methods requires comparisons among *actual* data set (true values), *raw* data set (collected values) and *clean* data set (edited and imputed values). Generally speaking, the availability of *actual* values corresponding to *raw* values is quite rare because of the high cost for carrying out careful re-interviews of respondents (professional interviewers, computer assisted interviewing, reconciliation of current answers with previous ones, etc.). In case of non-availability of true data, it is possible to arrange *actual* and/or *raw* data by a simulation approach. Instead of simulating both artificial true data and corresponding raw data, ISTAT strategy is based on the use of production data as true data, and therefore only the simulation of a *raw* data set is needed. In experimental applications, *actual* data are obtained as a result of processing a set of observed data according to an E&I procedure (straightforward and less expensive solution), while corresponding *raw* data are obtained by inserting artificial errors in *actual* data. To perform the simulation step the generalized ESSE software has been developed (Luzi and Della Rocca, 1998). ESSE performs controlled generations of artificial *erroneous values,* according to predefined error generation models (the ones most commonly occurring in the phase of the compilation of the questionnaire and in the data entry phase), and provides reports containing accuracy indices to assess the capability of the E&I process in localising errors and restoring the true values without introducing new errors in data. Accuracy indices are computed on the basis of the number of detected, undetected and introduced errors. An example of such indicators is given in Manzari and Della Rocca, 2000.

For the sake of clarity we point out that the only comparison between *a raw* data set and *clean* data set does not provide indicators about quality of the E&I method in terms of its accuracy. It just allows to measure the effect of E&I method on *raw* data and gives insights into the quality of the data collection procedure and, therefore, of the collected data set. An example of indicators to evaluate the quality of the collected data set is given by the quantitative information provided by the Italian Information System for Survey Documentation (SIDI) (Fortini et al., 2000).

Quantifying the *efficiency* of the E&I procedures means to provide a measurement of costs reduction in terms of *time* of data processing, *technical* (hardware and environment) and *human* resources required in applying the given E&I method.

Further information useful for the evaluation of the impact of an E&I method on survey process are its *reproducibility,* its *flexibility* to changes (in number of variables, codes, and edit rules), and the automatic *availability of standard documentation* of the E&I actions (diagnostic reports).

Finally, in relation to the evaluation issue, it is recalled that, when in a periodic survey a new E&I procedure replaces a traditional one (because of changing in organizational aspects or in resources availability, or because a new methodology suggests a solution better than the current one), the comparative evaluation of the quality of the new procedure against the traditional one should be followed with an evaluation of the impact of the new procedure on the time series of events. The impact measurement requires processing a set of raw data according to both the previous and the new procedure, and it is generally performed in terms of distances between estimates computed from the two sets of clean data.

6. STATISTICAL E&I KNOWLEDGE DISSEMINATION

This phase is one of the most critical of the entire life cycle, because at this stage all the collected information about the identified best solutions, their effectiveness, their usefulness, their requirements and implications have to be transferred to users. In particular, the main objective here is not only to transfer the acquired knowledge, but also to allow the users be able to evaluate all the consequences produced by the possible use of that particular E&I technique in its survey (in terms of quality of data and organizational impact).

There are different ways to fulfill the above-mentioned information requirements. The most effective ones can be considered the following:

(a) developing *a knowledge base* containing all the available information on the particular methods, techniques and software representing the best solutions; in particular it has to be stressed to what type of data and processes they can be applied, and what requirements must be considered (for example in terms of environment and resources);
(b) preparing and providing documentation of experiments and past experiences in the application of a given method: quality indicators and estimates of cost should be available in an information system for the documentation of surveys (SIDI for example);
(c) in order to allow the user to apply the method, user manuals should be available, and training courses should be organized on a regular basis *(indirect assistance);* in any case, *direct assistance* given by the methodologists in implementing first applications is the best way to disseminate knowledge (under certain conditions), as a form of *training on the job.*

Among the possible ways of implementing *a knowledge base* on existing available E&I methodologies, the following seems to be the most effective ones:

- producing internal documentation like methodological and/or technical manuals describing the selected E&I approach, method or software, its field of application, its technical characteristics, possible advantages and disadvantages in its usage and so on. In general, this documentation can consist of methodological monographic volumes dealing with specific subjects in the case of an E&I method or technique, or it can be represented by *user manuals* and/ or *application guidelines* in the case of software or generalized systems. All these materials have to be organized in such a way that users could easily access to it, in order to guarantee the higher level of its diffusion and sharing;
- producing *statistical guidelines* dealing with the process underlying the design, implementation, test and application to statistical survey data of E&I methods and techniques. These manuals have to point out the theoretical and operational steps to be performed, the essential factors and the

major distinctive elements to be taken into account in building an E&I strategy;

- developing an Intranet site, dedicated to the specific area of data E&I, structured in such a way that all information (internal and external references, related topics, meetings, etc.) related to new solutions is available and easy to find. In this context, the creation of a *discussion group* could facilitate the sharing not only of knowledge but also of problems and related solutions regarding the use of the various best methods.

The work of sharing all the acquired information on new E&I methodologies and approaches for a given class of surveys can be greatly facilitated by documenting and disseminating experiments and past working experiences performed using these methodologies on surveys belonging to that class. In this way, it is possible to highlight not only the peculiar characteriztics and properties of any selected technique, but also to provide users with important additional information, allowing a more precise evaluation of the advantages and disadvantages of using it in terms of quality of results, costs, timeliness, impact on data and survey organization. For each experience, documentation should be available in a standard format in order to allow the evaluation of the E&I method by analysing its performance on surveys the method was applied to. The availability of quality indicators and cost estimates could be useful, particularly if stored in an information system for the documentation of surveys. This is the case of the already mentioned SIDI system developed by ISTAT, providing users with standard quality indicators on the E&I phase related to a number of surveys.

A useful way for disseminating knowledge about new E&I solutions (editing methodologies, imputation techniques, generalized software, outlier detection approaches and so on) consists in supplying *training courses* on these specific topics. In general, these courses are planned to be held more than once, in order to allow as many people as possible to attend them. Generally speaking, as these courses have very specific objectives in terms of discussed subjects, they have a particular target, for example people with some specific background and experience, or subject matter involved in particular survey areas (e.g., business, households or administrative surveys). Training courses in the area of E&I have to be not only *information processing courses,* where only theoretical and/or technical knowledge about the discussed methodologies, techniques or software is provided to the participants, but also *experience processing courses,* where the users have to play a key role. In other words, the course should be the result of the continuous interaction between participants and teacher (generally a methodologist), in the sense that the users expert contribution can have an impact on the degree of accuracy assigned to the discussion and the development of each topic dealt with during the course.

An important feature of training courses is their capability of generating *a feed-back* process from the users to the teacher, in order to both verify the course quality in terms of its contents and structure, and evaluate its impact on final users and survey processes. In particular, information could be collected from participants in order to evaluate the course usefulness in terms of: - comprehension degree of discussed topics by the participants,

- degree of users autonomy in experimenting the acquired methods,
- potential impact of integrating the discussed techniques in survey processes,
- potential demand from production processes by monitoring the number of users interested in adopting the new methodologies or tools in their surveys.

Another important characteristic of training courses on E&I solutions is the portion of time reserved to practical applications and experimentation of the considered method and/or software, allowing the user to better understand and acquire knowledge on it. By adopting this pragmatic strategy, it is also possible to anticipate in this phase an important amount of knowledge transferring work that otherwise will have to be performed as *a training on the job activity* (also called *direct assistance),* i.e. in the context of working co-operation activities devoted to the improvement or the re-design of the survey E&I processes. In this case, a given amount of time and costs has to be spent by subject matter people in acquiring the new E&I solution, in order to be able to eventually introduce it in the survey process. In any case, the direct assistance provided by the methodologist to the survey statisticians in the form of training on the job can be in some situations the best or the only way of transferring knowledge in this area. This is the case, for example, of initial design or re-design of E&I strategies for complex or strategic surveys (like population or business census and other important exhaustive or sampling surveys). In these cases, an important initial investment in terms of planning, implementing, testing and evaluating the overall E&I strategy is needed. In this context, the methodological contribution is not only possible, but necessary in all the phases of the E&I strategy building process, and the user training on the newly introduced techniques and/or tools become an essential activity incorporated and distributed in the overall co-operation process.

Two examples of different approaches in disseminating knowledge, deriving from ISTAT experience, are represented by the processes of knowledge sharing, in the case of two generalized software: SCIA and GEIS. In the case of SCIA, with its first applications performed on very important and strategic surveys (1991 Census of Population, Labour Forces survey, Multipurpose survey, Household Expenditures survey), the training of users on that software has been performed very often by direct assistance provided by methodologists of the Methodological Studies Office in designing and developing the overall data E&I strategies. A different approach has been followed in the case of GEIS: in order to disseminate as much basic knowledge about that system as possible, specific training courses, addressed only to subject matter working in the *Business surveys* area, have been planned. In order to stress not only the advantages (for example, in terms of quality of final results, completeness, possibility of monitoring each data processing step, and so on), but also the limits of the software, a large amount of practical applications on experimental data were performed during the course. As feed-back, after the course, the participants were asked to perform an evaluation of the system in terms of:

i) its potential usefulness in their operational and statistical context,
ii) its potential overall impact on their survey processes,

in order to make a first evaluation of the future potential demand of direct assistance coming from that area.

7. CONCLUSIONS

The proposed *functional model* for disseminating the best data editing methods and techniques inside National Statistical Institutes is characterized by a strong interaction between the users (i.e. the statisticians responsible of the surveys) and the methodologists working in the centralized unit that are in charge for identifying and analysing those methods. This holds particularly in the *analysis of demand* and *knowledge dissemination* phases, where the information flows to and from users has to be optimized. In the other phases of the data *editing method life cycle,* critical activities are represented by the *evaluation* steps of the identified best solution in terms of:

- the quality of produced results and costs related to its implementation or acquisition from outside,
- the overall impact of its introduction in the statistical production processes.

Another critical point relates to the identification of the best way of transferring the acquired knowledge on the best solution to users, i.e. to allow the users to know:

- if the method is suitable to their particular survey,
- the advantages in terms of costs and/or quality in using the new method in their survey,
- how to apply the method.

Different solutions have been presented and discussed, that can be simultaneously adopted in order to improve the knowledge dissemination process. Among others, the production of a *knowledge base* on the selected methodologies or software and the *training* of users by specific courses or by direct assistance can be considered the more appropriate in terms of effectiveness and dissemination extent.

References

[1] Abbate C. (1997) "La completezza delle informazioni e l'imputazione da donatore con distanza mista minima", ISTAT, *Quaderni di Ricerca,* n.4/1997.

[2] De Waal, T. (1996) "CherryPi: a computer program for automatic edit and imputation", Report presented at the *Work Session on Statistical Data Editing of the United Nations Statistical Commission and Economic Commission for Europe,* Voorburg, 4-7- November 1996.

[3] Fellegi I.P., Holt D. (1976), "A systematic approach to edit and imputation", Journal of the American Statistical Association, Vol. 71, pp.17-35.

[4] Fortini M., Scanu M., Signore M. (2000) "Measuring and analysing the data editing activity in ISTAT Information System for Survey Documentation", in ISTAT *Essays* n. 6/2000, 17-29.

[5] Kovar J.G., MacMillian J.H., Whitridge, P. (1991), "Overview and strategy for the generalized edit and imputation system", Statistics Canada, Methodology Branch.

[6] Luzi O., Della Rocca G. (1998) "A Generalized Error Simulation System to Test the Performance of Editing Procedures", *Proceedings of the SEUGI* 16, Prague 9-12 June 1998.

[7] Manzari A., Della Rocca G. (2000) "A generalized system based on a simulation approach to test the quality of editing and imputation procedures", *in ISTAT Essays* n. 6/2000, 83-103.

[8] Riccini E., Silvestri F., Barcaroli G., Ceccarelli C, Luzi O., Manzari A. (1995) "The editing and imputation methodology for qualitative variables implemented in SCIA", ISTAT Internal Report.

[9] Todaro T. (1999) "Overview and evaluation of the AGGIES automated edit and imputation system", Report presented at the *Work Session on Statistical Data Editing of the United Nations Statistical Commission and Economic Commission for Europe,* Rome, 2-4 June 1999.

[10] Winkler W. E. and Draper L. R. (1997) "The SPEER Edit System", in *Statistical Data Editing, Volume* 2, U. N. Statistical Commission and Economic Commission for Europe, Geneva, Switzerland, 5155.

CONCEPTUAL MODELLING OF ADMINISTRATIVE REGISTER INFORMATION AND XML - TAXATION METADATA AS AN EXAMPLE

by Heikki Rouhuvirta, Statistical Methodology R&D, Statistics Finland

1. INTRODUCTION

As register-based statistics production is becoming more general, one of the main factors influencing the use of register data is the content of register data. Content management of the existing register data used in statistics production has a direct effect on the end result of the use of administrative data, which in this case means statistical information, its quality and extent. Similarly, content management of register data essentially influences the key stage of statistics production, i.e. editing and its end result.

The first issue we address is the question of how to form a conception of the information content of the administrative register. At present the means for this are fairly limited and quite conventional in their use. The usual way is to look up a description of administrative data from fairly short administrative register descriptions produced by authorities themselves and from printed handbooks or their electronic copies. For statistics production these descriptions and administrative handbooks are external and separate information sources that are difficult to handle in information technology and are managed manually.

In addition to being about an adequate informative basis for editing, it is also a question of whether contentual information created in editing can be saved as descriptions of the results of editing work to be used further in later stages of statistics production. It is not only a question of that producers of statistics have full contentual command of the register data but also how the content of the statistical information collected from register sources is described and transmitted to users of statistics so that they can form a correct perception of the content of statistical information and have a possibility to interpret and use the thus formed statistical information as accurately as possible.

It is a process where a conception of the register data must be passed on to statistics producers and they must be able to transfer that information to users of statistics in a form understandable to them. The only way to transmit the meaning and purpose of the data is to ensure easy availability of adequate content information in all stages of data processing. The challenge is how the present process, where the description of administrative data can mostly be read from the authorities' administrative handbooks (see Figure 1.), can be transformed into such that it meets the requirements for the usability and presence of the contentual description of data both in the production process to statistics producers and in the distribution of statistical information to users of statistics.

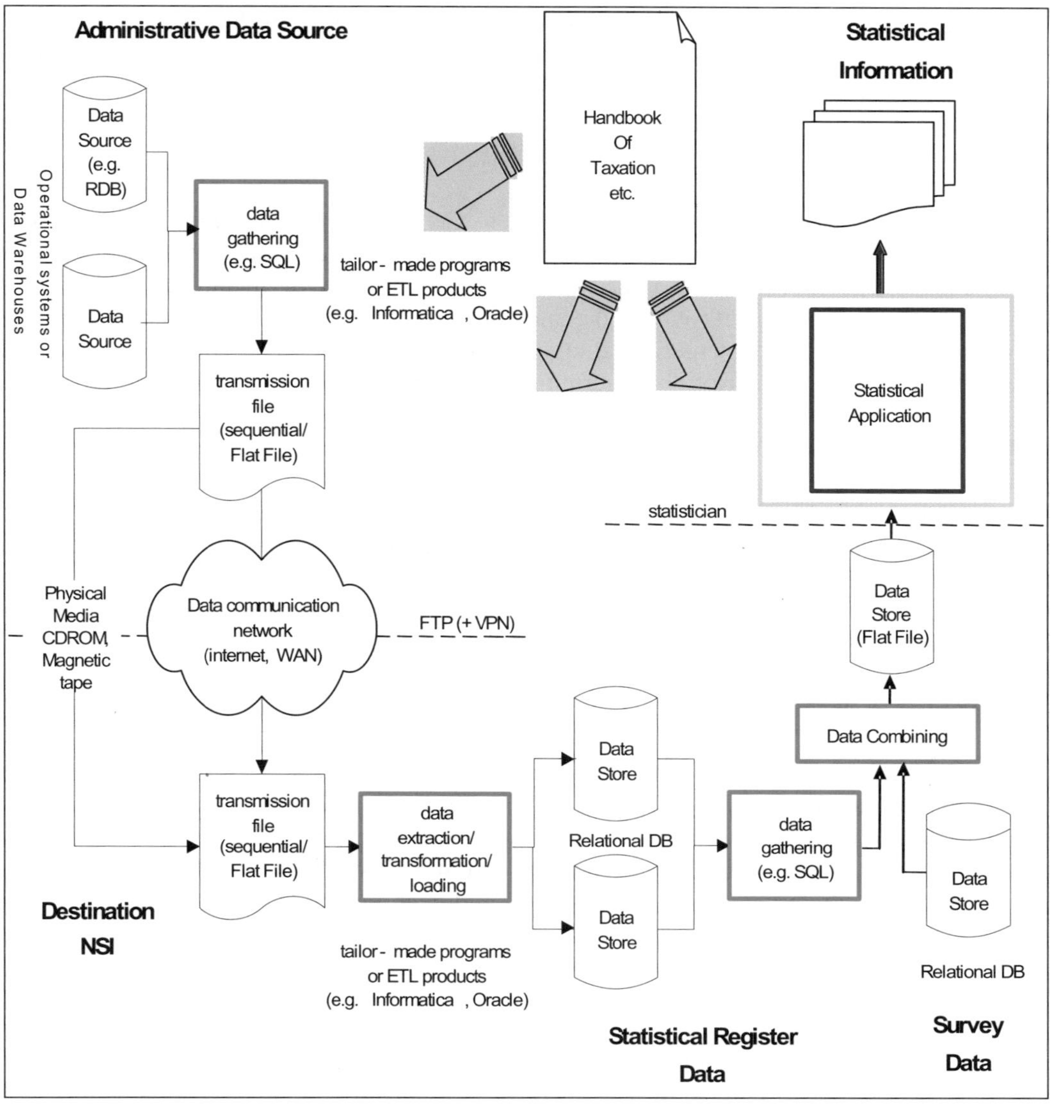

Figure 1. *Present state of compilation of administrative data*

In case these external information sources for content and the new contentual information produced in editing can be flexibly integrated as part of technological information systems of statistics production, such integration could at the same time intensify statistics production as well as improve its quality.

2. DATA SEMANTICS OF ADMINISTRATIVE REGISTER

In order to better integrate the contentual information into statistics production in its different stages, we need to extend the conventionally used data models so that they will also include a semantic description of the data. Similarly, the data model of the register information used in data processing should contain a semantic description of administrative data as fully as possible. Secondly, data models should be revised so that they would allow optimally unambiguous and contentually permanent transferability for the semantic definition. Thirdly, the revised data models should enable presentation of statistical information and register data semantics in a uniform reference frame and in as standard manner as possible.

The methods and technologies conventionally used in statistics production did not as such point at any clear solution model for the intended extension and editing of the data model for administrative register information. The situation was also the same for the technologies used by producers of administrative data in their activity. They could not offer any ready-made solutions that could be applied as semantic data models for administrative register information.

In absence of ready-made applicable models it was quite natural to look for solutions from the starting points applied at Statistics Finland for conceptualisation of statistical metadata[1][1]. This is quite reasonable also because in semantic data it is partly a question of metadata, or to put it more accurately, of metadata in respects where the metadata is semantically significant. In addition, this application model offers a fundamental advantage as the concrete solution of statistical metadata is the one into which the semantic description of administrative information should be integrated.

3. CoSSI AS THE REFERENCE FRAME OF METADATA

In modelling of statistical information[2] the starting point of the definition of metadata is that in the conceptualisation of the contentual description of statistical information use is made as far as possible of the concepts characteristic of statistical information, the concepts and concept structures it contains and the logic that allows sufficiently multifaceted and complex concept structures for an exhaustive description of the information content. As the used description method allows implementation of complicated structure descriptions, the procedure does not have essentially any factors that would per se somehow force to contract or limit the contentual description.

Correspondingly, attention was paid in the conceptualisation of information content of administrative material to the simplification of the characteristic concepts of the administrative information in question and to the definition of the logical structure of the concepts and the concept model. By analysing the information related to administrative data and the existing contentual information about it to the extent that it is produced and accumulated by administration, the aim was to produce a fully defined and logical information structure characteristic of the current administrative information, within the frame of which the semantic description of administrative data can be produced.

The first approach was applied to the personal taxation material and to the administrative information describing it, from which the results presented here are taken[3].

4. TAXATION AS AN INFORMATION SYSTEM

Taxation is generally seen as a process of tax collection, which results in paid taxes. Taxation as a process includes several different types of information recorded in taxation, such as that describing reporting of income, determination of taxes, complaints about them, etc. This standpoint is not very useful in this connection because the process view of taxation obscures taxation as a conceptual information system.

As we are not interested in the collected taxes as such, i.e. taxes paid, but in what kind of information taxation as a process is based on, we can get closer to the content of tax information by viewing taxation from the determination bases of taxes, forgetting now the information related to the implementation of taxation and the information saved on that. The latter would naturally be interesting

---

[1] See Rouhuvirta, H., An alternative approach to metadata-CoSSI and modelling of metadata, CODACMOS European seminar Bratislava 7th October 2004, Project IST-2001-38636.

[2] See for further details Rouhuvirta, H. and Lehtinen, H., Common Structure of Statistical Information (CoSSI) - Definition Descriptions, 2nd December 2003, Version 0.9, Statistics Finland 2003.

[3] Rouhuvirta, H., Lehtinen, H., Karevaara, S., Laavola, A., Harlas, S., Demonstration Report on Taxation Metadata in Secondary Data Collection - How to connect the metadata of taxation to numeric taxation data and use them at the same time. Codacmos 2004. Project IST-2001-38636.

only in case we intended to describe, explore or study the case-specific taxation practice and its problematics. But our purpose lies elsewhere: to produce a description of the data contained in the taxation material that will universally explain what is the actual meaning of the data collected to the register on payment of taxation.

In addition to the determination basis of taxes, i.e. the income concept, the logical basic components of taxation include deduction and the tax itself as the end result of calculation. When tax is not examined, we end up with the concept space of income, or rather that formed of income sources and deductions presented in Figures 2 and 3.

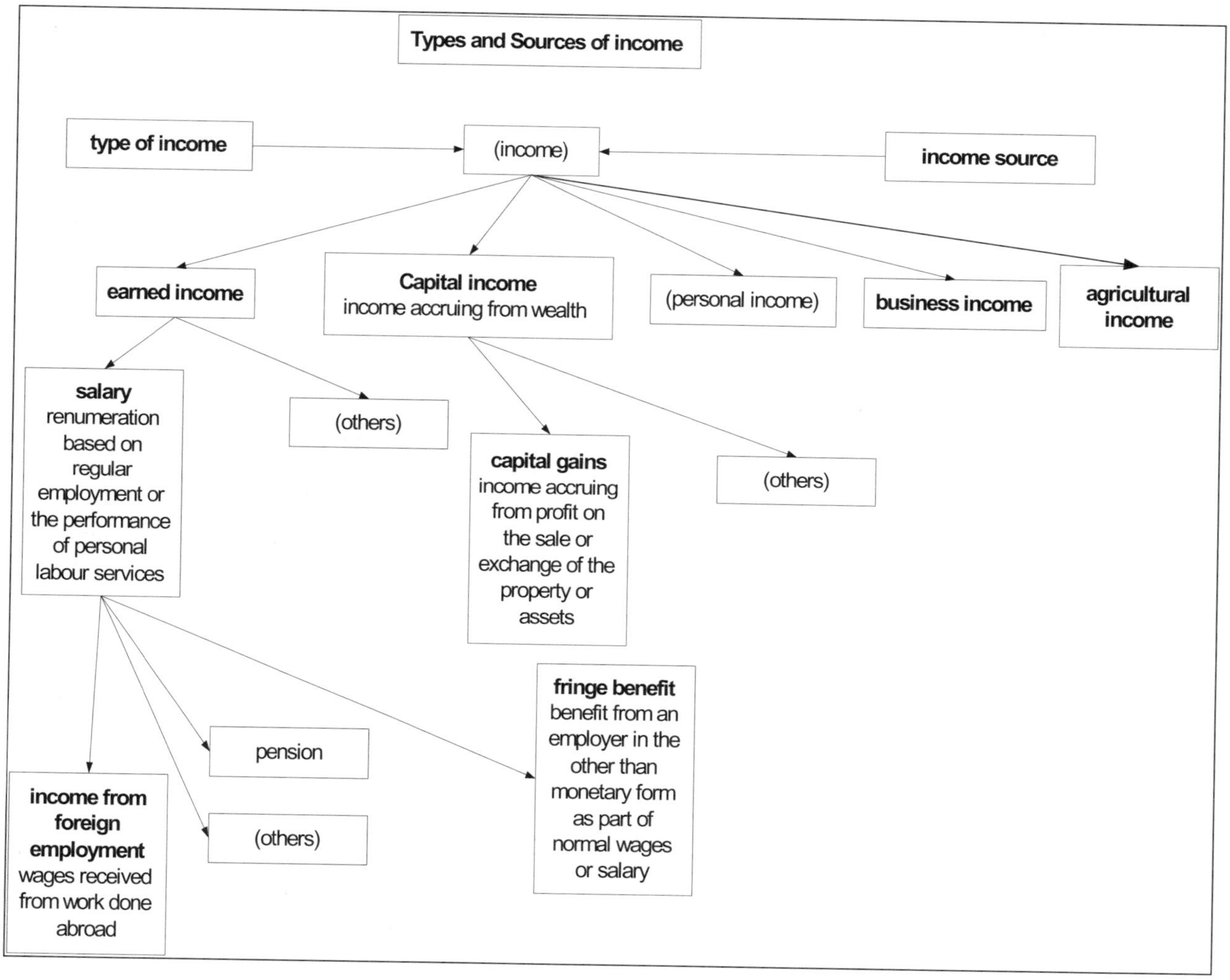

Figure 2. Types and sources of income

The types of income are earned income and capital income. Income source indicates the activity in which the income of a taxpayer originates. A taxpayer may have three sources of income: business (business income), agriculture (agricultural income) or other activities (personal income). The source of income determines which law is applied in calculating a taxpayer's taxable income.

Deductions can be made either from income or taxes. Deductions made from income include such as deduction for pension insurance premiums, discretionary allowance for circumstantial incapacity to pay taxes, pension income allowance, earned income allowance and low-income allowance. The deductions made from the taxable income are, for example: child maintenance credit, domestic help credit and credit for capital income deficit.

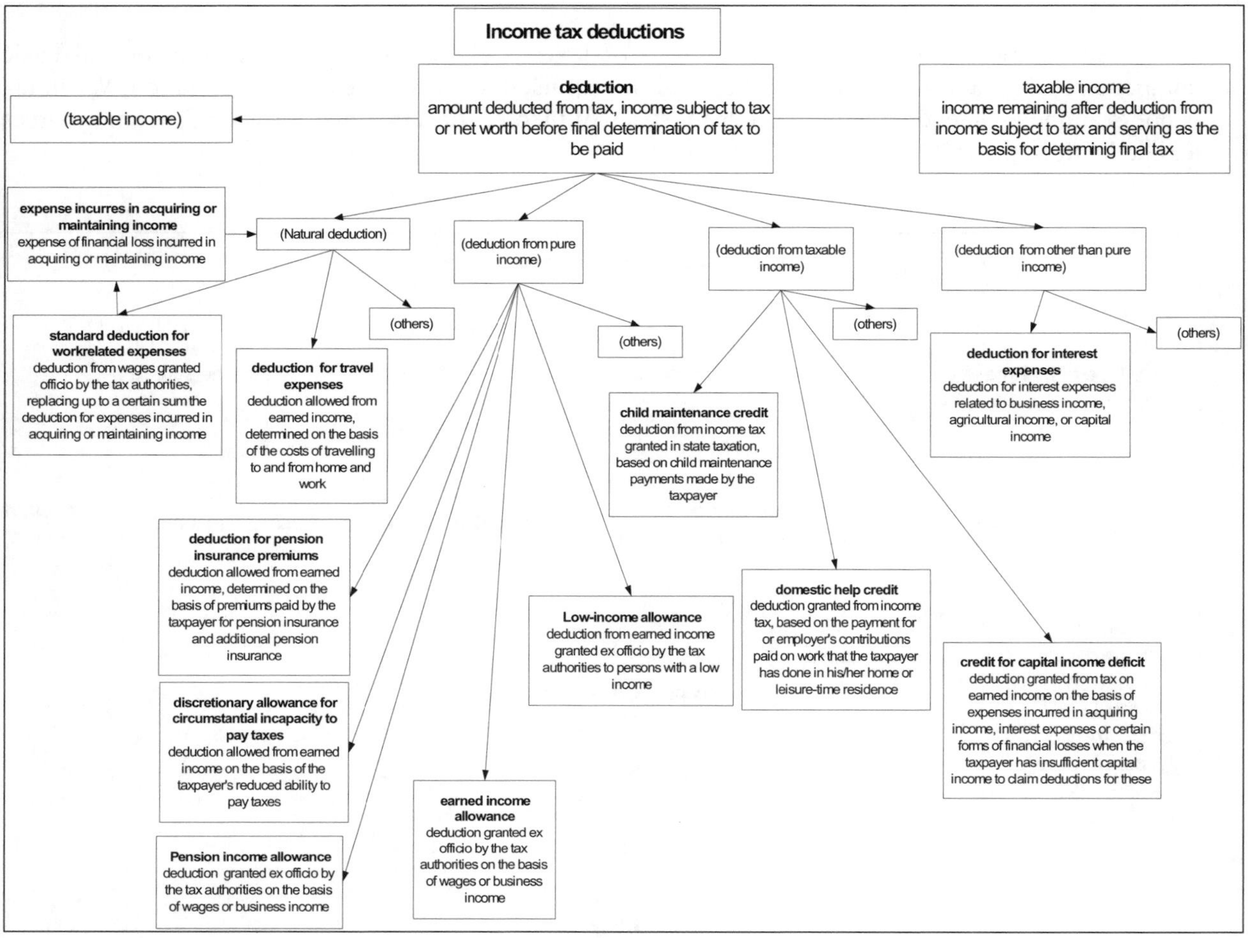

Figure 3. Income tax deductions

5. SOURCES OF CONTENT INFORMATION FOR TAXATION

Although all the data handled in taxation is collected with various tax forms, the information defining the data collected on the forms is contentually fairly concise. The main contentual information concerning taxation is stored in the Tax Administration's various instructions and handbooks. The Tax Administration also has technical descriptions of its information systems. The joint reference frame for all these information sources is formed by the taxation legislation. In Finland legislative texts are stored in a public electronic database on acts and decrees accessible to all through the Internet.

The contentually largest source for the information describing personal taxation is the Tax Administration's handbook on personal taxation. The handbook is a printed publication and it is used at Statistics Finland, for instance. The size of the handbook is about 800 pages. It describes in detail the entire personal taxation practice and the related legal cases. The handbook also has references to the legislation concerning personal taxation. An updated version of the handbook is produced separately for each starting tax year.

There is an electronic original of the handbook mainly for printing, which is also used for storing the information to be updated. For production of the electronic original there is a document definition, which mainly describes the external structure of the handbook. A printed publication can thus be produced automatically from the original. The scarce contentual structure in the document definition (e.g. legal cases and search words) does not however follow the contentual logic of taxation information.

6. FROM SEMANTIC DATA TO STRUCTURED METADATA

In addition to the theoretical bases certain practical matters also have an effect on editing of the concept model for semantic taxation information. The concept structure to be created for taxation information is formed into such that in its scope it is easy and widely possible to utilise the existing electronic data defining the information content and to transfer this information to the user of taxation data without losing the information. In addition, the idea was to employ the structure definition so that it is in a technologically suitable form for information processing.

From the presented starting points a logical concept model for taxation information was defined, which as a tree structure[4] is shown in the figures below (see Figures 4a. and 4b.).

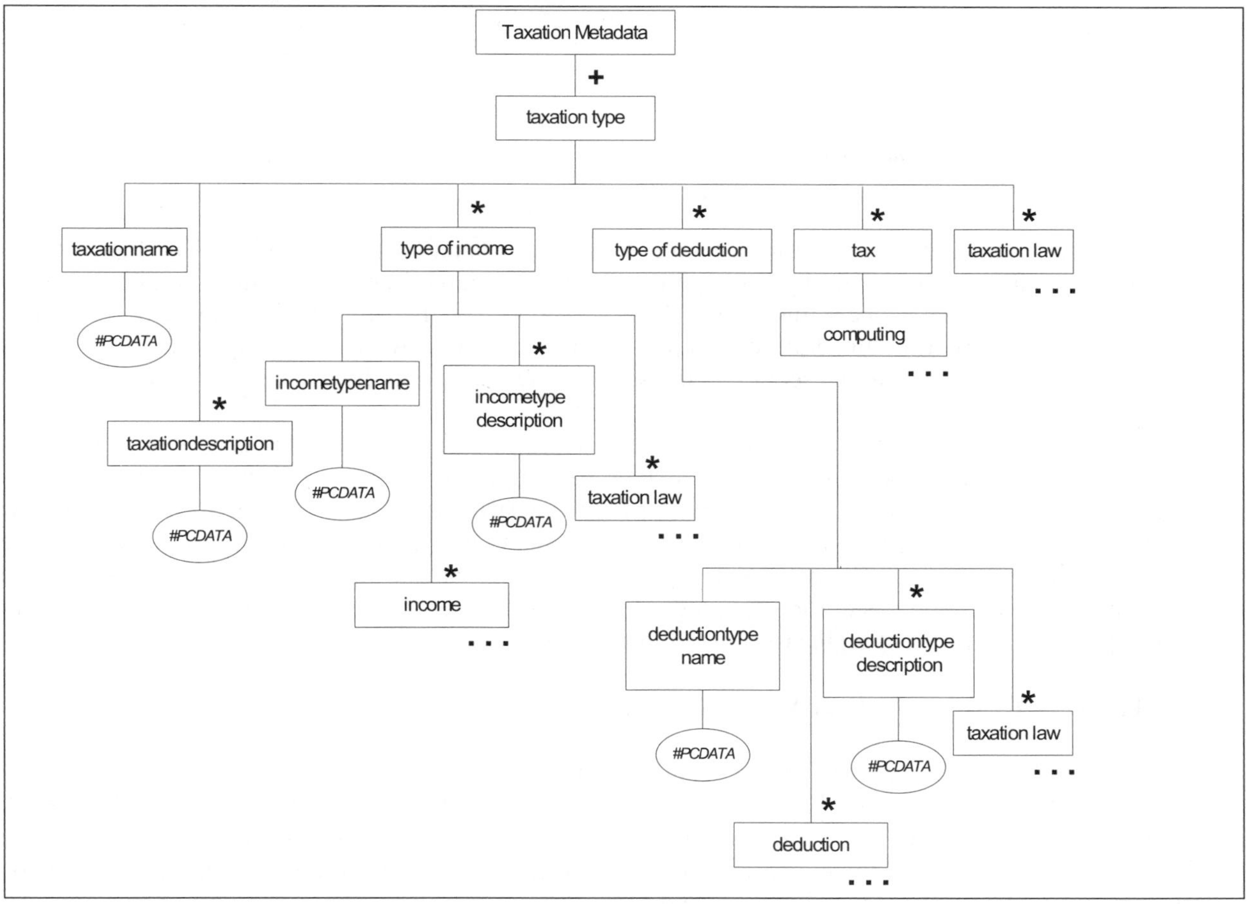

Figure 4a. Logical concept model for taxation

[4] Method of tree structure description, see Maler, E. & El Andaloussi, J. 1996. Developing SGML DTDs. From text to model to markup. Upper Saddle River (NJ), USA: Prentice Hall.

Within the framework of the structure it is possible to describe the key concepts of taxation except for the process description of taxation, which was excluded from the analysis as a factor defining the semantic content of information secondarily and thus omitted from the concept model. The detailed structure definition was implemented as XML DTD[5]. The XML definition was also used as the basis for application development. In its present form, the implemented detailed structure definition does not comprise tax calculation algorithms, but they can be included in the structure definition as the concept model for determination of taxes to be paid.

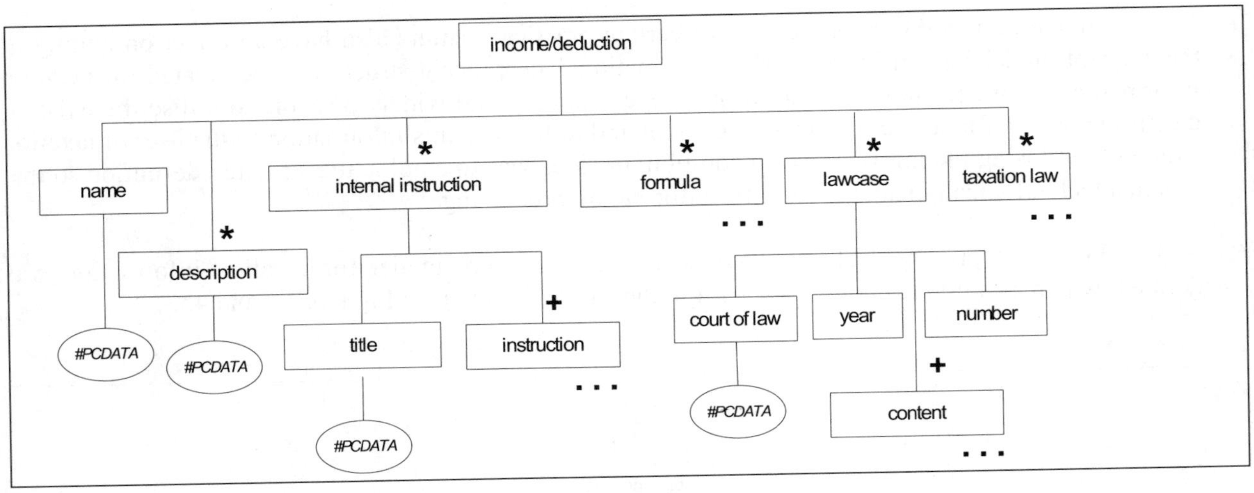

Figure 4b. *Logical concept model for taxation – income and deduction*

In the implementation the information structure of taxation is hierarchical. The hierarchy of taxation metadata is determined by tax type that contains income items and deduction items and the contentual information concerning them. The structure of the information consists of name, description and instruction. In addition, it is possible to attach to different hierarchy levels descriptions of the legal cases concerning the section in question and references to the legislation regulating it.

Within the scope of the structure definition it is possible to present the information contained in the taxation handbook following the contentual logic of taxation and taxation information. Information contents may change in the scope of the structure. For example, formation of new taxation items as the legislation changes yearly or production of new taxation information when the tax authorities review their instructions do not yet compel to make any changes to the structure of the information model. The need for changing the structure arises only when a completely different philosophy and the relevant logic are adopted in taxation.

7. STRUCTURED METADATA - REGISTERS

The electronic version of the personal taxation handbook was used in testing the information model for register information. The electronic information content was arranged on a one-off basis according to the structured information model. The use of the information was tested in the development environment[6], where structured register metadata was linked to the information selected from the relational database (see Figure 5. and 6.).

[5] Rouhuvirta, H. and Lehtinen, H., Taxmeta DTD. Codacmos 2004. Project IST-2001-38636.
[6] The software solution of the development environment was made by Laavola and Harlas from Tietokarhu Oy. About the development environment, see the demo report p. 15 (Rouhuvirta et al., Demonstration Report on Taxation Metadata in Secondary Data Collection - How to connect the metadata of taxation to numeric taxation data and use them at the same time. Codacmos 2004. Project IST-2001-38636).

The first of these user interface images (see Figure 5.) shows the information of one person's tax register record in the relational database: first is given the code used in the register, second the value in euro and the third field has a plain-language register code, which can be either a column code of the relational table or an individualising code for the calculated information content. The information identified by a code in the relational database is such as pay, proceeds from sale of timber, membership fees paid, etc. Metadata can be searched for each tax record field by using these codes.

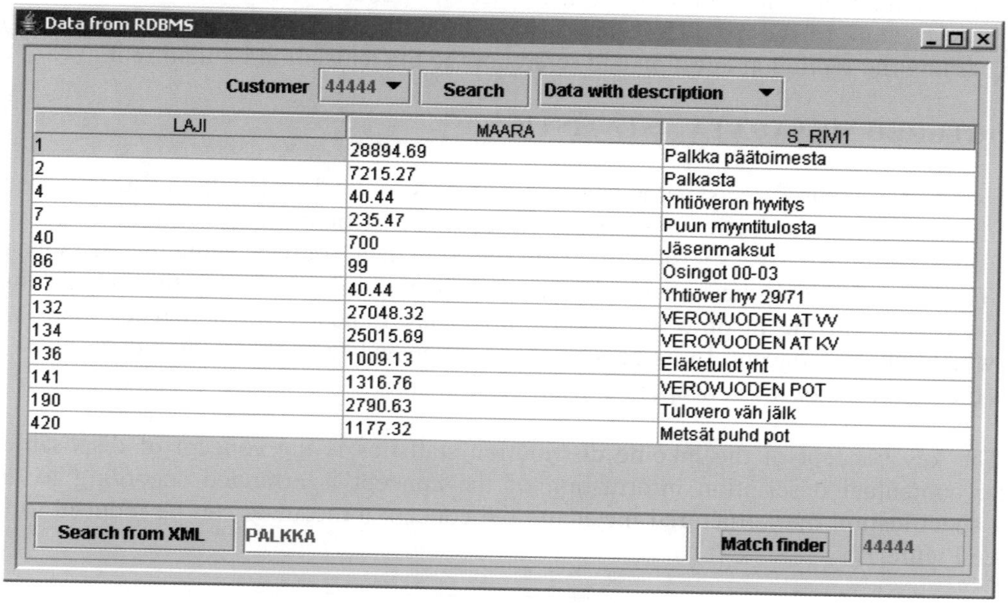

Data from RDBMS
Customer 44444
Search
Data with description
LAJI
MAARA
S_RIVI1
1 28894.69 Palkka päätoimesta
2 7215.27 Palkasta
4 40.44 Yhtiöveron hyvitys
7 235.47 Puun myyntitulosta
40 700 Jäsenmaksut
86 99 Osingot 00-03
87 40.44 Yhtiöver hyv 29/71
132 27048.32 VEROVUODEN AT VV
134 25015.69 VEROVUODEN AT KV
136 1009.13 Eläketulot yht
141 1316.76 VEROVUODEN POT
190 2790.63 Tulovero väh jälk
420 1177.32 Metsät puhd pot
Search from XML
PALKKA
Match finder
44444

Figure 5. Taxpayer's tax record selected from the relational database (user interface screen)

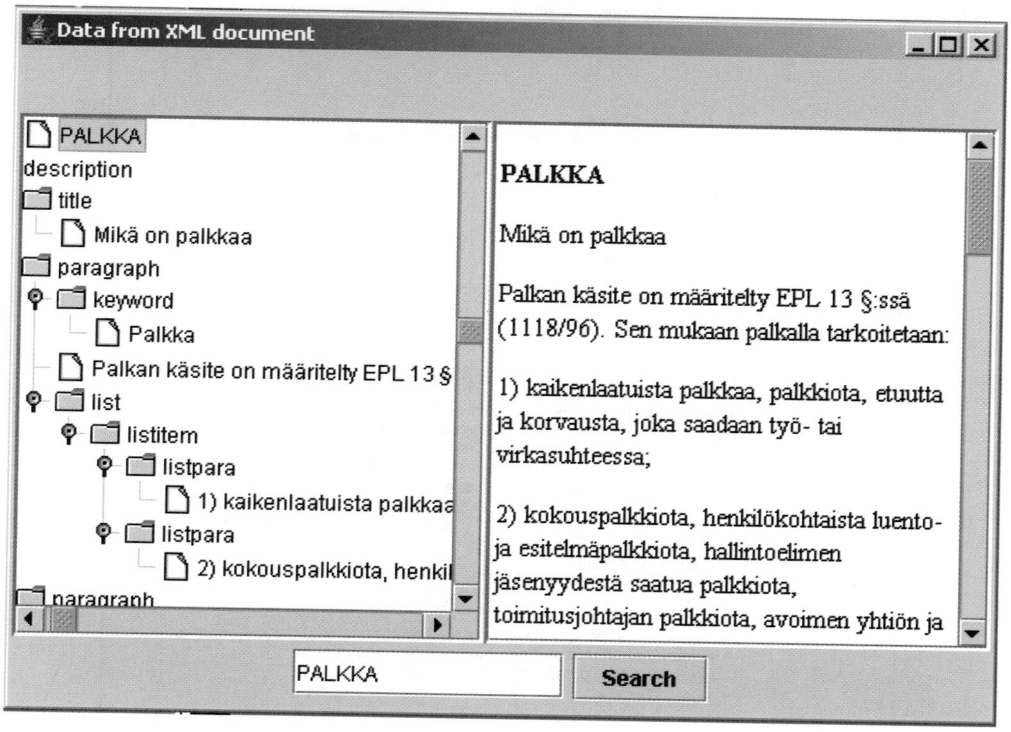

Figure 6. Metadata of register data (user interface screen)

Metadata is presented (see Figure 6.) as a structure and an XML document. The structure follows the concept hierarchy and it can be browsed along the hierarchy in both directions. By browsing the structure it is possible to go deeper from a more general concept to the concepts it contains and their metadata. Thus it is possible to move by browsing from a more general concept, such as earned income, to pay and its metadata and from wages to the concept of shunting and its metadata.

The hierarchy is made similarly both for taxable items and deductions made from them. In addition, the structure of the metadata enables in different hierarchy levels descriptions of the legal cases concerning the section in question and references to the legislation regulating it.

8. STRUCTURED METADATA – STATISTICS

Using of structured register metadata as part of statistical metadata is illustrated here by an example from income distribution statistics. The data for income distribution statistics are mostly collected from administrative registers, one of the key data sources being the personal taxation register. The way in which the register data is used in the compilation of the income distribution statistics is defined in the income formation rules. They indicate which register item is used for forming which income concept. In its present scope the metadata of the income distribution statistics describes the definition of the concept and its possible source.

The key concept of the income distribution statistics is the concept of disposable income. When the contentual description information of the concept is arranged according to the CoSSI metadata specification into structured metadata, the concept's metadata can be reduced to the figure below (see Figure 7.).

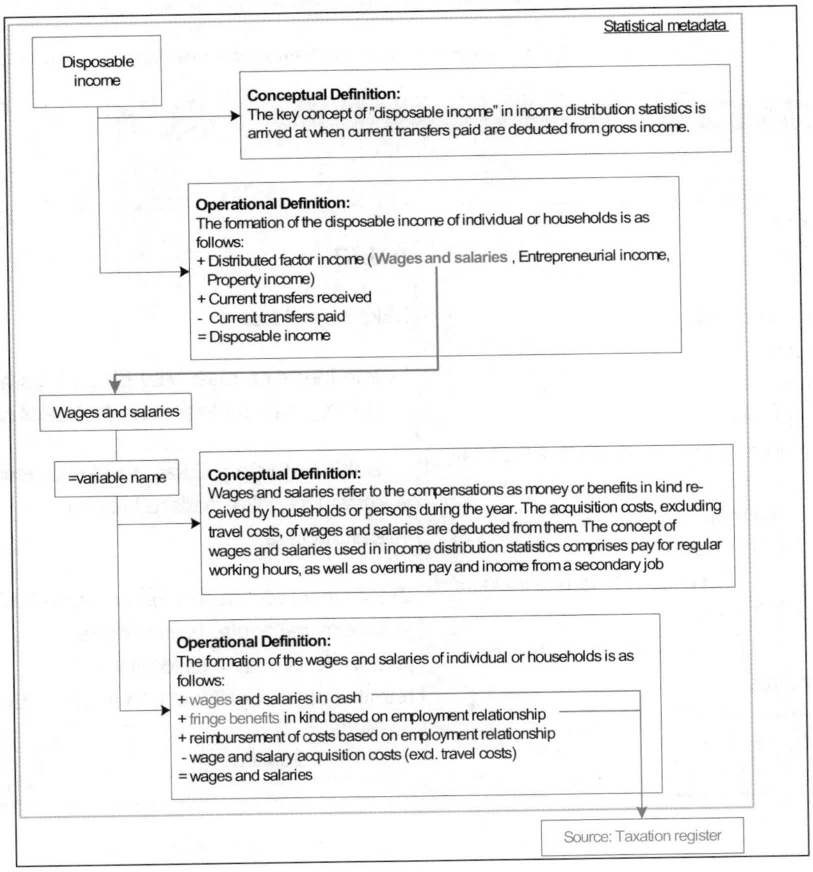

Figure 7. Statistical metadata of the income concept

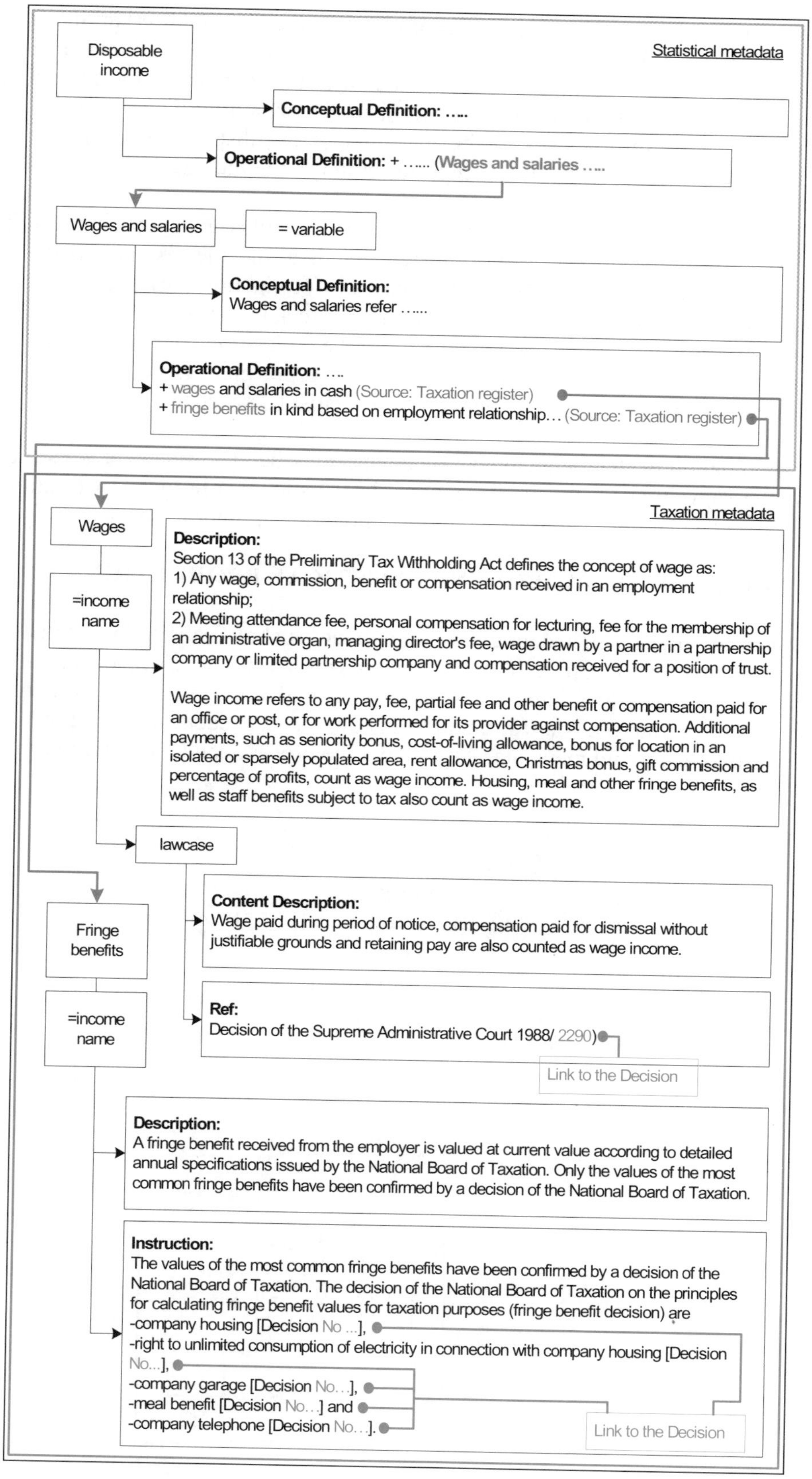

Figure 8. Extended statistical metadata of the income concept

The main factor collecting and transmitting the information in the structured statistical metadata is variable. When for register data there is available structured metadata as that produced in the development environment, the register metadata can be connected by quite simple procedures as part of statistical metadata when using register data. The resulting metadata is illustrated in Figure 8, which shows in a simplified manner the metadata of the disposable income concept extended by combining and corresponding to the concept formation of the income distribution statistics.

Thus arranged, metadata makes the processing rules and procedures followed in taxation available to statistics producers editing the register data and the tax authorities' direct information influencing the interpretation can be used in statistics production during editing as well. The created metadata structure also enables linking of original sources to the metadata, whereby this material can also be used by statistics producers. These links to the legislation database or guidelines, for example, directed to both taxpayers and taxation officials for reporting and revising tax information can be opened directly and their content can be viewed by statistics producers.

Combination of the metadata can be done only when the metadata are structured as presented above. At the same time it will become possible for statistics production to automate the handling process of metadata and to exploit structured technologies in other ways as well.

9. TOWARDS METADATA-DRIVEN STATISTICAL PRODUCTION

When the register metadata can be integrated as shown above into statistical metadata in the production process of statistics, it opens the possibility to develop a genuinely metadata-driven production process. In a genuinely metadata-driven production process rich metadata is present and available in all production stages, including editing, and metadata accumulates as the process advances without losing old metadata. As a model the process can be described as in Figure 9.

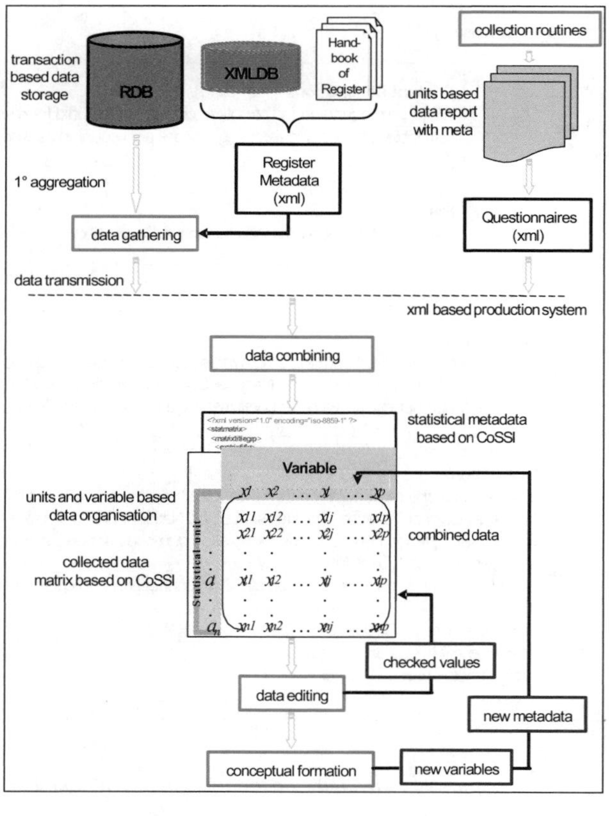

Figure 9. Compilation, combination and editing of collected information in the CoSSI reference frame

In the model the selection of register data and collection of primary data both produce structured metadata. Metadata is transferred to the editing stage of statistical production where the data are checked and edited in many ways. During editing new conceptual variables and metadata describing them are formed to the data. Thus we end up with final statistical data, which also contain statistical metadata. When tables and other outputs are produced from the data by tabulation, the metadata necessary for the interpretation of statistical figures can be included fully in statistical tables, similarly as in other outputs.

References

[1] Maler, E. & El Andaloussi, J. 1996. Developing SGML DTDs. From text to model to markup. Upper Saddle River (NJ), USA: Prentice Hall.

[2] Rouhuvirta H., An alternative approach to metadata – CoSSI and modelling of metadata, CODACMOS European seminar Bratislava 7th October 2004, Project IST-2001-38636. Available on the web at: http://www.stat.fi/org/tut/dthemes/papers/alternative_approach_to_metadata_codacmos_2004.pdf

[3] Rouhuvirta, H. and Lehtinen, H., Common Structure of Statistical Information (CoSSI) - Definition Descriptions, 2nd December 2003, Version 0.9, Statistics Finland 2003. Available on the web at: http://www.stat.fi/org/tut/dthemes/drafts/cossi_definition_descriptions_v_09_2003.pdf

[4] Rouhuvirta, H. and Lehtinen, H., Taxmeta DTD. Codacmos 2004. Project IST-2001-38636. Available on the web at: http://www.stat.fi/org/tut/dthemes/drafts/taxmeta_dtd_v_01.txt

[5] Rouhuvirta, H., Lehtinen, H., Karevaara, S., Laavola, A., Harlas, S., Demonstration Report on Taxation Metadata in Secondary Data Collection - How to connect the metadata of taxation to numeric taxation data and use them at the same time. Codacmos 2004. Project IST-2001-38636. Available on the web at: http://www.stat.fi/org/tut/dthemes/papers/demoreport_on_taxation_metadata_codacmos_2004.pdf

Chapter 3

IMPROVING QUALITY

Foreword – Leopold Granquist, Statistics Sweden

This chapter contains three sections on how data editing could improve data quality in surveys.

The first section comprises three papers containing an underlying principle: editing should primarily focus on identifying and eliminating error sources before cleaning up the data. The Process Data System (PDS) that is outlined in the first paper, or metadata systems as described in the second paper, play a key role. Learning from editing is the main element of the system. An application of the concept in the third paper concludes the section by showing that costs for both the producers and data providers can be greatly reduced, ease the respondent burden and at the same time significantly improve the data quality.

The second section has five contributions that focus on web surveys or computerized self-administered questionnaires (CSAQs). Such data collections offer ideal opportunities to obtain valuable information on how respondents interpret questions and understand the survey concepts. For CSAQs and other modes of data collection, respondents should be interviewed. Moving editing to the reporting phase of data collection facilitates the task for the respondents and improves incoming data quality. By giving them valuable feed-back, respondents would be convinced that using this mode of reporting is advantageous when other alternatives are provided.

Section three presents five papers on topics using alternate sources in data collection and on improving quality in both business and social statistics areas. These include:

- Defining concepts for incorporating administrative data into an editing and imputation framework for multi-source data collection.
- Evaluating administrative records for their accuracy and completeness
- Linking multiple data sources at the unit level to decrease the amount of editing necessary.
- Analysing all available information, especially metadata that contain information about the coverage of the survey frame, non-respondents, field investigation and other data processing stages to improve quality.
- Using administrative data throughout the entire data processing phase of a survey. An interesting feature of the survey is the need to develop a complete census for all units in the population using mass imputation procedures based on sample and administrative sources.

Section 3.1

CONTINUOUS IMPROVEMENT

Foreword – Carsten Kuchler, Statistisches Bundesamt, Germany

The best errors are those that do not occur. This describes the direction of data editing efforts since the mid 1990s. By interrelating data editing to previous and subsequent stages of the survey process, past knowledge acquired from correcting errors is valuable in identifying and suppressing potential error sources within the entire survey process. In addition, enhancements in other sub-processes have been based on indicators and statistical measures derived during data editing, and vice versa. Finally, data editing methods have been improved in such a way that they preserve the methodological requirements of other statistical processes. However, these cross-connected improvements remain ad hoc until they are embedded and reflected in feedback loops that relate sub-processes of subsequent surveys.

The papers in this section address the question how to proceed from single improvements concerning methods and applications towards a continuous improvement of the entire survey process. They suggest that dealing with continuous improvement requires conceptual orientation as provided by data quality objectives, adaptable application flows, and – as the contributions unanimously agree – metadata for monitoring, evaluating and relating sub-processes. The focus moves from basic methodological considerations towards their concrete implementation in national statistical agencies.

The first paper by Engström and Granquist shows one of the first and most influential attempts at consolidating different data editing approaches ensuring data quality in an integrated and interrelated application flow. Several of the ideas proposed by Engström and Granquist reemerge in the remaining papers of this section. They discuss concrete approaches like establishing current best practice through identifying data error sources and standardizing editing processes. These approaches imply that single improvements rely on metadata to become the subject of continuous improvement. Based on the general standards of how to monitor application flows, the authors describe the Process Data Subsystems (PDS) that are intended to store quality characteristics, information about the methods applied and their performance.

In the second contribution, Tate describes the way the data editing process is embedded into the Statistical Value Chain, underlying the ambitious modernization programme of the Office for National Statistics (ONS). The message expressed is that metadata are the lubricant of a complex and highly interdependent process flow. In describing the relation between the chain links of the survey process as considered by the ONS, the paper specifies types of metadata and their application in processing a precise data set or managing and evaluating the entire survey process. To provide each survey sub-process with the required metadata, the ONS has established a Central ONS Repository for Metadata (CORM) that can be considered a descendant of the Process Data Subsystems introduced by Engström and Granquist.

The CORM (meta-) database demonstrates the crucial role of software for the requirements of planning, performing, monitoring and evaluating editing processes. Implementing tailor-made software for specific survey processes offers the chance to link these processes by metadata streams that are provided by well-defined and general interfaces. The paper by Kuchler and Teichmann presents the implementation of such a metadata stream in the Federal Statistical Office in Germany. A point of reference is the embedding of an IT tool for data editing in an office-wide software standard. The PL-Editor is considered a gateway for metadata utilized in previous and subsequent sub-processes. The paper deals mainly with the question of how methodological enhancements can be easily integrated into an existing application flow. Thus, a flexible software standard is required to allow for continuous improvement of survey processes.

This section reviews the implementation of actions ensuring continuous improvement. Then it addresses the question of how this may be applied in a specific survey. Thus, the last paper by Jean-Sébastien Provençal describes a concrete process of continuous improvement - the Unified Enterprise Survey (UES) - conducted by Statistics Canada since 2002. The author refers to both the collection and the post-collection processes. He introduces the effects of setting up quality control processes in the collection phase and shows how the use of external data sources (such as fiscal data) improve post-collection processes. Comparisons with the past situation show a remarkable improvement. The author finally states that this is considered just another stepping-stone for ongoing further improvements.

IMPROVING QUALITY BY MODERN EDITING

By Per Engström and Leopold Granquist, Statistics Sweden

Abstract: The paper treats two principal aspects of improving data quality by means of editing: continuous improvement of the whole survey, and the design of edits. The Continuous Improvement Approach is a direct consequence of the new editing paradigm that emphasises identifying and eliminating error sources ahead of cleaning up data. Related issues discussed are collection of data on error causes, the need for and the requirements of a high qualitative Process Data Subsystem (see section 2.2), and standardisation of editing process by developing and implementing Current Best Methods (see section 2.3). Design of the query edits is considered a crucial issue in quality improvement. Of particular interest for improving data quality by editing is inlier edits. A useful technique for developing inlier and outlier edits is using Exploratory Data Analysis methods in a graphical environment.

1. INTRODUCTION

Traditionally, editing is considered the procedure for detecting, by means of edit rules, and for adjusting, manually or automatically, individual errors in data records resulting from data collection or data capture. It is considered a necessary survey operation because errors in survey data may distort estimates, complicate further processing, and decrease user confidence. It should be noted that here editing is considered a tool also for improving quality beyond cleaning up data.

Here we discuss the most common setting of editing: The computer identifies erroneous or suspicious data by means of a large number of edits provided by subject-matter specialists; the flagged records are manually reviewed, very often by follow-ups with respondents, (see Granquist and Kovar 1997 for details).

Practically all published studies of traditional editing processes indicate that many originally reported values are being changed by insignificant amounts and that few errors are responsible for the majority of the total change. The studies present data like: 10 to 15 percent of the changes contribute to more than 90 percent of the total change; 5 to 10 percent of the changes bring the estimate within 1 percent of the final estimate. The hit-rate (the proportion of flags that result in changes) lies between 20-30 percent in the few studies where hit-rates are estimated. These facts suggest two things: 1) the entire set of edits should be designed to identify errors more efficiently; 2) many errors could be left unattended or subject to automatic treatments. Many statistical agencies are aware of these problems and devote considerable efforts to raise the productivity of editing systems.

1.1. Increasing Productivity

During the last 15 years a number of selective editing methods have been developed, that can decrease the number of unnecessary flags and order the errors (or the suspect data) with respect to their (potential) impact on estimates either prior to or during survey processing, without having examined all the cases. Selective editing includes any approach, which focuses the editor's attention on only a subset of the potentially erroneous micro-data items that would be identified by traditional editing methods. Those methods are known as macroediting, aggregate editing, top down editing, graphical editing, Hidiroglou-Berthelot bounds, score function editing (identifying data records that need to be followed up), and others (see e.g. ECE 1994 and ECE 1997, Hidiroglou and Berthelot 1986, van de Pol and Bethlehem 1997). We have now a continuous ongoing research on refining this kind of edits and on new types of edits and editing procedures. Furthermore, interactive editing procedures at the data entry stage or when collecting data have proven to be good ways of rationalising the editing of survey data.

It is empirically shown that selective editing methods put together in a system, where rework and recontacts to respondents are minimised can increase productivity by 50 percent and more (Granquist and Kovar 1997). But for improving quality we have to go further!

1.2. Quality issues

One quality benefit of selective editing is that over-editing is prevented or essentially limited as the editors' work is directed to influential records and items in priority order. Further quality improvements will depend on how the gains in productivity are invested. If the editors are not given more time and higher capacity for solving questionable data further quality improvements should not be expected.

Many authors claim that suggested selective editing methods improve quality, but do not provide data to show it. Note that the suggested selective editing methods are evaluated only against the current editing. Thus concerning quality, it can only be stated that the new method is practically as good as the current one, and in data where the new method was evaluated. Certainly, the new method will detect erroneous data that the current method misses, but we do not know whether quality is significantly improved or even improved.

Suppose for example that reported data contain both negative and positive errors. Then the edits have to address both types of errors equally. Otherwise, a bias will be introduced by the edits, irrespective of the skill of the reviewers in finding accurate data to replace the flagged data. Thus, edits still play a crucial and determining role for improving quality. Note that generally selective editing primarily means that priority is built into the edits to make them focus on influential items or records. Therefore, programmed edits have to be continuously evaluated and improved to get them to identify all erroneous data that have impact on quality. Special attention has to be paid to parameter based programmed edits. They depend heavily on how well the parameters are estimated and whether underlying assumptions really hold in the data to be edited. Generally, the populations we are surveying are subject to dynamic changes, why we cannot rely on edits and edit bounds used in passed periods. We will return to this issue in the next Chapter.

2. CONTINUOUS IMPROVEMENT - A PROCESS PERSPECTIVE

A wider definition on editing has been suggested. It is focused on identifying and collecting data on errors, problem areas, and error causes to provide a basis for a continuous improvement of the whole survey.

The key objective of the paradigm is that quality should be built into the processes to prevent errors rather than identify errors once they have occurred and replace them with more accurate data. This is advocated in editing literature, for example in Granquist (1995), Jong (1996), Granquist and Kovar (1997), Weir (1997), and Nordbotten (1998). A successful way of doing it is to apply the concept of continuous quality improvement to the whole survey process, where editing is but one process, Linacre (1991). Note that editing under this paradigm is a key process, in that it will furnish data on errors as a basis for measures to eliminate root causes of errors from the survey. This role of editing will probably improve the quality much more than the editing of data per se. The less error prone the survey process is the higher the resulting quality. It will also reduce the cost of editing substantially provided the editing process is effective in finding and removing the errors that still occur. Thus continuous improvement also applies to the editing process.

The process perspective in surveys is described in for instance Linacre (1991), Morgenstein and Marker (1997) and Lyberg et al. (1998). It is based on Deming's Total Quality Management (TQM) principles, in particular Deming's Plan-Do-Check- Act (PDCA) procedure. It implies a shift from mass inspection to controlling the survey processes, because product quality is achieved through process improvement. Lyberg et al. (1998) give an example from experiences at the Research Triangle

Institute (RTI), where the coding error rate was reduced by about 75 percent in an application to industry and occupation coding. Costs were reduced and at the same time quality improved.

2.1. Collecting Data on Error Causes

The paradigm imposes a new and probably rather heavy and difficult task to the editors. They have not only to verify flagged data and find acceptable values, but also they have to identify and register quality indications of the new data, error causes, respondent problems, and possible problem areas of the survey. It will require deep subject matter knowledge of and insight into the survey design. Furthermore editors have to understand that this task is substantially more important in recontacting respondents than verifying suspicious data. This contrasts with the common comprehension that flagged data should be changed to pass the edits (creative editing). To build quality into the survey also means that recontacting respondents includes educating the respondents in answering the questions in continuing surveys.

Engström (1997) presents a study from the 1995 Swedish European Structure of Earnings Survey (SESES), where data collection on error causes was integrated in the survey process. The editors had to identify and code error causes like misunderstanding, questionnaire problems, typing problems etc. Furthermore, they had to indicate whether respondents were contacted to solve flagged items. Engström found that the edits were rather efficient. The error cause data for the most erroneous item (4000 cases out of 16000) showed that 90 percent of the errors were due to respondent misunderstanding. It was judged that most of these errors could be avoided by changing the wording of the question and improving the instructions to the respondent. However, the coding was burdensome and the editors had problems in refering the error cause to the erroneous item. Engström (1997) concludes that error cause data are extremely useful and that the system has to be carefully designed to facilitate the work of the reviewers.

Linacre and Trewin (1989) indicates that rates for item non-response and form/system design errors are both about 30 percent of the errors in business surveys and concludes that improving questionnaire design would improve the quality of incoming data. The example given by Engström (1997) emphasises that a significant number of errors can be prevented by improving the questionnaires and that a tight co-operation between questionnaire designers and survey managers would be extremely beneficial for the organisation. Of course, questionnaires should always be carefully tested. Australian Bureau of Statistics established a forms design unit, when facing the results of a number of evaluations of editing processes as pointed out in Linacre (1991). The cited paper states that the quality of statistical estimates is largely influenced by the respondent's ability to understand questions unambiguously and to have relevant data available. If respondents do not have data for a particular item in their accounting systems, the strategy of collecting data of that variable has to be revised. Note that respondents are likely to deliver the data they have irrespective of any difference in definitions.

2.2. Statistics on the Survey Process

In addition to final product quality indicators, the continuous quality improvement approach requires data on the applied editing system architecture as background data and on the performance of the process including interactions with respondents and others to evaluate the process. The editing architecture data are results of the design of the system, while performance data have to be collected and stored during the editing. The product quality, the editing system architecture and the performance data have to be collected and stored in a well-designed system, here called the process data subsystem (PDS). Cost and timeliness constraints particularly for short period surveys exclude post evaluations for this purpose. The data have to be analysed and measures have to be taken to improve the current editing.

A PDS has many purposes. Performance measures are needed during the editing process for monitoring and regulating the process while maintaining quality goals, and for improving future system designs as to quality and performance objectives (Weir 1997).

The effectiveness of the query edits has to be continuously evaluated, because query edits have expiration dates, although unknown, due to rapid changes in the surveyed populations. For example Hogan (1995) reports that the edit bounds of a used edit did not cover the median. Furthermore, note that (at least initially) bounds are often set on purely subjective grounds. Weir (1997) and Engström (1996) discuss and suggest performance measures and how they can be displayed in user-friendly graphics that can be easily understood by the editors and the survey manager.

A PDS should give data on quality for both the user and the survey manager. The users want data about quality to evaluate whether the supplied statistics are suitable for their needs, while the survey manager need data on quality to analyse alternative production strategies (Nordbotten 1998).

Editing processes have to be described in a uniform way, making it possible for a statistical agency to compare the effectiveness of the editing between surveys. The top-level managers need data in order to allocate their methodological resources, select surveys for revisions, and see the effect of research and development efforts.

Key issues associated with a process perspective are definition of key process variables (Morgenstein and Marker 1997), how the measurements should be made to assure that data are collected with high quality, and how statistics should be presented to the different users.

Research on designing a PDS beyond as a means for improving individual surveys as well as developmentsa of prototypes or systems are going on in some statistical agencies, e.g. ISTAT (Italy), Statistics Canada, DESTATIS (Germany), INE (Spain), ONS (United Kingdom). The PDS must be an integrated part of a general meta data system permitting research in the origins of errors, improved survey design in general and of improved editing systems in particular. Nordbotten (1998) presents a Process Data Project outline for systematic collection and storing of data on editing architecture, quality and performance for individual surveys which combined with other meta data provide a basis for survey design improvements. Papers on this subject have been presented in Work Sessions on Statistical Data Editing in 2000, 2002, 2003 (see http://amrads.jrc.cec.eu.int/k-base/), and an important implicit subject in the forthcoming Work Session in Ottawa May 2005.

2.3. Standardizing Editing Processes

Lyberg et al. (1998) state that probably the most effective way to improve quality is to develop Current Best Methods (CBM) for its major recurring processes, to have them implemented and continuously updated as new knowledge is generated. The role of CBMs in the improvement of survey quality is discussed in detail in Morgenstein and Marker (1997). Granquist (1997) presents the development of a CBM o n editing, Edit Efficiently, that is used at Statistics Sweden since April 1997. In 2002 that CBM was replaced by “Guide to Editing” (Arvidson, Elffors, Granquist, Norberg 2002)

Agency manuals on editing, papers on editing strategies, and generalised software may have similar effects as CBMs in getting sound, recommended practises communicated and used within the agency. The advantage of CBMs is that they are supported by the top level management and developed by the agency’s experts together with a number of carefully selected users (here statisticians responsible for editing processes) to assure that each CBM will reflect the organisation’s apprehension of what are best practises.

A first important step in continuous improvement is to understand the process. Morgenstein and Marker (1997) stress that the staff actually working with the processes under study should use flowcharts to visualise all processes related (in this case) to the editing of the survey. Editing activities are usually carried out in several phases of the survey implying a high risk of lots of rework, see for example Linacre and Trewin (1989). Generally, avoiding rework is one of the most efficient ways of rationalising processes. Thus identifying rework should be important in revising editing processes. At Statistics Sweden process changes are organised as Total Quality Management projects. The CBM on editing (Granquist 1997) has been appreciated by project teams working on improving the editing process. In general, the data editing should be carried out in the early stages of processing, preferably when the respondent is still available (Granquist 1995, Lepp and Linacre 1993). There should always be an output editing subprocess to identify serious errors that were missed in earlier subprocesses. When incoming data have few errors one may rely fully on output editing, in particular when graphical editing is applied (e.g., Granquist 1995, van de Pol et al. 1997).

3. DESIGN OF EDITS

We have established that the edits play a crucial role in improving data quality, and that they have to be continuously evaluated in repetitive surveys to control that their good qualities are maintained. As pointed out in the introducion (Chapter 1), edits should not only be considered as constraints on data but powerful means for detecting serious errors. Analysts or methodologists should be involved in the design of edits. The situation has changed the last 15 years and suggestions of improved methods appear on conferences and in the editing literature rather frequently. Most of these methods may be characterized as outlier progammed edits, that is data points outside acceptance regions are flagged as suspicious. Here we will only discuss graphical editing.

3.1. Graphical editing

Graphical editing is established as a powerful and efficient method for accurately identifying outliers. It is a parameter free method that allows for efficient examination of large amounts of data at once. The data points are visualised in graphs that are linked to each other, which means that marking data points with the mouse will highlight the data points in all the graphs. The editor clicks on the potentially most interesting cases, reviews the up-popping reported values of the selected record, changes the faulty values, and notes the effect on graphs, distributions and so on.

Graphical editing systems put in practice are intended for output editing. They use top-down approaches in a macro-editing setting to search for probable contributors to suspect estimates (e.g., Esposito et al. 1994, Houston and Bruce 1992, Weir 1997, Engström and Ängsved, 1997). This means that the search is driven by programmed edits. Hence the quality improvement depends on the edits like other selective outlier editing methods.

Explorative Data Analysis (EDA) methods can now be succesfully used to edit data on-line, thanks to the advent of powerful PCs and EDA software. EDA can be described as "a set of tools for finding what we might have otherwise missed" in a set of data (see Tukey 1977). Hogan (1995) characterises EDA techniques by the "4 R's," resistance, re-expression, residuals and graphical revelation. Biennias et al. (1997) illustrate with practical examples how they used these "4 R's" to improve the outlier detection in two establishment surveys. The paper can be considered an introduction to using EDA methods in editing. It points out the following advantages. The methods of fitting data to be relatively resistant to the presence of outliers in the data are useful. Removing linearity in the scatter plots to examine the residuals from the linear fit is valuable. Various methods exist to transform data (re-expressing) so that patterns can be more easily discerned. Establishment survey data are often skewed. Therefore, it is essential to have methods for transforming data to be rather symmetric which make it easier to find data points that are particularly unusual.

DesJardins (1997) is an excellent introduction to graphical EDA techniques using SAS/INSIGHT or JMP and the implementation strategy used at the U.S. Bureau of the Census. He describes a number of EDA-techniques and presents a number of new EDA graph techniques developed by him to fulfil needs at the Census Bureau. Furthermore the paper stresses the power and the usefulness of the point and click SAS/INSIGHT software making it possible to produce a number of linked EDA graphs of millions of data in a few seconds. Novices in SAS can do it. However, the editors have to be trained in EDA to be able to understand what graphs are telling. It means that analysts should do the editing.

3.2. Inlier edits

Outlier checks cannot identify for example data that are affected by small but systematic errors reported consistently by a number of respondents in repeated surveys. Such errors are termed inliers and are defined as faulty data which lie within any reasonable bounds of ordinary used edits. Inlier methods are probably of greater importance for the quality than outlier methods, irrespective how efficient they are in detecting erroneous outliers. Inliers occur whenever there are discrepancies between the survey definitions and the definitions used in the firms' accounting systems. Werking et al. (1988) present an illustrative example. In an ongoing Response Analysis Survey (RAS) designed to focus on differences in definitions and how to get firms to apply the survey's definitions, they found that the estimate of the main item "production worker earnings" for the RAS units became 10.7 (standard error 3.2) in contrast with 1.6 for the control group. A method to cope with that type of inliers is to add some questions into the questionnaire, asking the respondent whether he or she included/excluded certain item components in the answer. In web surveys this method is strongly recommended.

Mazur (1990) reports from the Livestock Slaughter Data Survey at the U.S. Department of Agriculture, where many respondents reported the same values every week. Therefore they created an inlier edit by using historical data and Tukey's biweight (see also Hoaglin et al. 1983).

Research on inlier methods is fairly new. Winkler (1997) presents a description of the problem and suggests a number of methods of converting inliers to outliers using additional information that may be available in the files being edited.

However, Exploratory Data Analysis (EDA) methods using SAS/INSIGHT or JMP is an excellent method for identifying the presence of inlier problems as they are focused on discerning patterns in data.

References

[1] Arvidson G., Elffors, C., Granquist, L. and Norberg, A. (2002): Guide to Editing (Guide to granskning). CBM 2002:1 (in Swedish).

[2] DesJardins, D. (1997): Experiences With Introducing New Graphical Techniques for the Analysis of Census Data, Work Session on Statistical Data Editing, Prague, Working Paper No. 19.

[3] Economic Commission for Europe, (1994): Statistical Data Editing: Methods and Techniques, Volume No. 1, Statistical Standards and Studies - No. 44, United Nations New York and Geneva, 1994.

[4] Economic Commission for Europe, (1997): Statistical Data Editing: Methods and Techniques, Volume No.2, Statistical Standards and Studies - No. 48, United Nations New York and Geneva, 1997.

[5] Esposito, R., Fox, J. K., Lin, D. Y., and Tidemann, K. (1994), "ARIES -- A Visual Patch in the Investigation of Statistical Data," *Journal of Computational and Graphical Statistics*, **3**, pp. 113-125.

[6] Engström, P. (1995): A study on using selective editing in the Swedish survey on wages and employment in industry, ECE, Work Session on Statistical Data Editing, Athens, Room Paper No. 11.

[7] Engström, P. (1996): Monitoring the Editing Process, Work Session on Statistical Data Editing, Working Paper No. 9, Voorburg 1996.

[8] Engström, P. (1997): A Small Study on Using Editing Process Data for Evaluation of the European Structure of Earnings Survey, ECE, Work Session on Statistical Data Editing, Prague, Working Paper No. 19.

[9] Engström, P and Ängsved, C. (1997): A Description of a Graphical Macro-Editing Application, in ECE, Statistical Standards and Studies, No. 48, Geneva pp. 92-95.

[10] Granquist, L. and Kovar, J.G. (1997): Editing of Survey Data: How much is enough? in *Survey Measurement and Process Quality*, New York: Wiley, pp. 415-435.

[11] Granquist, L. (1997): On the CBM-document: Edit Efficiently, ECE, Work Session on Statistical Data Editing, Prague, Working Paper No. 30.

[12] Hidiroglou, M. A., and Berthelot J.-M. (1986): Statistical Editing and Imputation for Periodic Business Surveys, *Survey Methodology*, **12**, pp. 73-84.

[13] Hoaglin, D. C., Mosteller, F., and Tukey, J. F. (1983), *Understanding Robust and Exploratory Data Analysis,* New York: Wiley.

[14] Hogan, H. (1995): How Exploratory Data Analysis is improving the way we collect business statistics, Proceedings of the American Statistical Association, August 1995 pp. 102 – 107.

[15] Houston, G. and Bruce, A. G. (1993): gred: Interactive Graphical Editing for Business Surveys, *Journal of Official Statistics,* Vol. 9, No. 1, 1993, pp. 81-90.

[16] de Jong, W. (1996): Designing a Complete Edit Strategy, Combining Techniques, Statistics Netherlands, Research paper No. 9639.

[17] Lepp, H., and S. Linacre (1993), "Improving the Efficiency and Effectiveness of Editing in a Statistical Agency," *Bulletin of the International Statistical Institute: Proceedings of the 49th Session*, Florence, Italy, Contributed Papers Book 2, pp. 111-112.

[18] Linacre, S. J. (1991), "Approaches to Quality Assurance in the Australian Bureau of Statistics Business Surveys," *Bulletin of the International Statistical Institute: Proceedings of the 48th Session*, Cairo, Egypt, Book 2, pp. 297-321.

[19] Linacre, S. J., and Trewin, D. J. (1989), "Evaluation of Errors and Appropriate Resource Allocation in Economic Collections," *Proceedings of the Annual Research Conference*, Washington, DC: U.S. Bureau of the Census, pp. 197-209.

[20] Lyberg, L., Biemer, P., and Japec, L. (1998): Quality Improvement in Surveys – A Process Perspective, Proceedings of American Statistical Association, Dallas August 8-13, 1998.

[21] Mazur, C. (1990): Statistical Edit System for Livestock Slaughter Data, Staff Research Report No. SRB-90-01, Washington, DC: U.S. Department of Agriculture.

[22] Morganstein, D. and Marker, D. A. (1997): Continuous Quality Improvement in Statistical Agencies in *Survey Measurement and Process Quality*, New York: Wiley, pp. 475-500.

[23] Nordbotten, S. (1998): Improving Editing Strategies, Proceedings of the third International Conference on Methodological Issues in Official Statistics in Stockholm, October 1998 pp 107-117.

[24] van de Pol, F. and Bethlehem, J. (1997): Data editing perspectives, Statistical Journal of the United Nations ECE 14 (1997) pp. 153-171.

[25] van de Pol, F., Buijs, A., van der Horst, G., and de Wal, T. (1997): Integrating Automatic Editing, Computer-Assisted Editing and Graphical Macro-Editing, Statistics Netherlands, Research paper No. 9739.

[26] Tukey, J.L., (1977) *Exploratory Data Analysis,* Addison-Wesley Publishing Company, 1977.

[27] Weir, P. (1997): Data Editing Performance Measures, ECE, Work Session on Statistical Data Editing, Prague, Working Paper No. 38.

[28] Weir, P., Emery, R., and Walker, J. (1997): The Graphical Editing Analysis Query System in ECE, Statistical Standards and Studies, No. 48, Geneva pp. 96-104.

[29] Werking, G., Tupek, A. and Clayton, R. (1988): CATI and Touchtone Self-Response Applications for Establishment Surveys, *Journal of Official Statistics,* **4**, pp. 349-362.

[30] Winkler, W. (1997): Problems With Inliers, ECE, Work Session on Statistical Data Editing, Prague, Working Paper No. 22.

THE ROLE OF METADATA IN THE EVALUATION OF THE DATA EDITING PROCESS

By Pam Tate, Office for National Statistics, United Kingdom

1. INTRODUCTION

The Office for National Statistics (ONS) has embarked on an ambitious modernization programme out of which it aims to deliver a standard technical infrastructure, methodologies and statistical tools.

The aim of this programme is to apply common recognized standards and practices in a highly efficient way. It will enable the ONS to:

- be expert in using a smaller range of standard software;
- use simpler, more automated processes that provide greater efficiency;
- use an integrated information management system, that will expand the opportunities to assemble information from a wider range of sources;
- use the web as the main medium for our day to day business.

One of the key elements of this programme is a series of statistical infrastructure projects to provide corporate statistical tools and methods for use across the ONS. These projects are based on the statistical value chain, (SVC), shown in Figure 1, which describes statistical components from survey design to data dissemination.

The project for the editing and imputation component of the SVC has the objective of developing and implementing cost-effective, standard editing and imputation tools for all ONS data sources, incorporating methodological best practice, and operating within the new Information Management environment.

This paper discusses the place of the data editing process within the new statistical infrastructure, and its relationships and interfaces with the other statistical processes. It considers particularly the role of metadata in these interfaces, and its contribution to the management and evaluation of the processes themselves, and to the measurement of the quality of the statistical outputs.

Figure 1: Statistical Value Chain

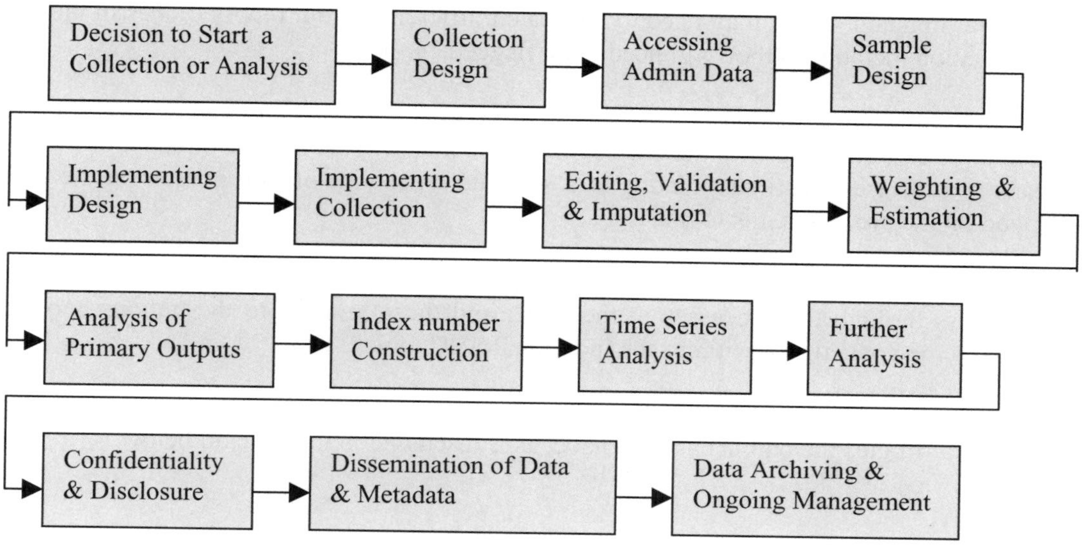

2. MANAGING THE EDITING AND IMPUTATION PROCESS WITHIN THE STATISTICAL VALUE CHAIN

As one would expect, data editing and imputation is, in the SVC, most closely linked with data collection on the one hand, and with weighting and estimation on the other. In most circumstances, the editing and imputation processes and tools would be applied after data collection, and before weighting and estimation.

The traditional model of statistical data processing is to apply the various individual processes in sequence to a dataset deriving from a specific data source. However, increasingly we may expect to see multiple modes of data collection deployed within a single data source, some modes being able to apply editing at the point of collection, and collection instruments tailored to subgroups or even individual respondents.

Thus, although some processes will by their nature continue to be applied to whole datasets, some may be applied to different subgroups or individual cases at different times, or in different ways, or not at all. To avoid too much complication of the language, the discussion that follows refers generally to datasets in the traditional way, but the reader is asked to bear in mind that more complex sequences of operations may often be applied in practice, and that these may demand more complex structures of data and metadata.

In the new statistical infrastructure, the methods employed should incorporate best practice, and should be applied in a standard fashion. One implication of this is that there should be no need for any human intervention in deciding which process should be applied to a dataset when, or in what order. This therefore needs to be determined by metadata accompanying the dataset, and interpretable by the data management systems and the statistical tools.

In order for the transition from data collection to editing and imputation to operate correctly, the editing and imputation tool must be able to: recognise a dataset which is due to be subjected to editing and/or imputation; recognise which editing methods should be applied to it, and with what parameters.

Furthermore, in order for the transition to weighting and estimation to function correctly, the editing and imputation tool must be able to indicate that the dataset is next due to be subjected to weighting and estimation, and with which methods and parameters.

Some of this information will derive from the results of the editing and imputation process. For example, imputed values may need to be treated differently from reported ones in the application of the estimation method, so they will need to be flagged.

Some of the information however will derive from processes applied at an earlier stage, and will have to be carried along with the dataset in some manner. This may be directly, or more probably by means of a dataset identifier pointing at a separate repository of information on the dataset as a whole, and on the processes it is to undergo.

We therefore need two kinds of process management metadata for each dataset: those relating to its progress through the processes in the SVC; and those relating to the options and parameters which need to be applied to it within each individual SVC tool.

These metadata depend primarily on what outputs are to be produced from the dataset, and what quality attributes the outputs need to have, as is discussed in more detail below.

3. EVALUATION OF THE QUALITY OF THE EDITING AND IMPUTATION PROCESS, OTHER ELEMENTS OF THE SURVEY PROCESS, AND THE SURVEY OUTPUTS

There is a close relationship between the editing process and the quality of the outputs, in several different ways. Editing changes to the data affect the accuracy of the outputs, as does the extent to which imputation is used. The time taken for editing affects the timeliness of the outputs. The nature of the edit checks affects the comparability and coherence of the outputs, as does the imputation methodology used. Some of these processing measures therefore contribute, either directly or as proxies, to the quality indicators for the outputs.

We also need measures of the quality of the editing and imputation process itself. Some of these measures can suggest possible ways of improving the performance of the process. For example, information on the number of cases failing each edit check, and on the number of these for which changes in the data resulted, indicates whether the checks are working efficiently in detecting errors.

Yet other editing process measures may be able to suggest ways of improving other elements in the survey process. For example, information that a particular variable is frequently changed as a result of failing edit checks may indicate that the question on which it is based should be assessed for quality of concept and wording.

Finally, management information on the operation of the editing process can contribute to the management of the survey process as a whole. In particular, up to date information on the progress of data through the editing process, and other individual processes, can enable resources to be switched between the different processes and datasets in the most productive and efficient way, thus improving the quality of the overall survey process.

4. THE ROLE OF METADATA IN THE EVALUATION OF QUALITY

These measures of the quality of the editing and other processes, and of the survey outputs, are dependent on the creation and use of various kinds of metadata. Working through the SVC from the beginning, the evaluation of the Collection Design stage needs information on how effectively the data collection process has functioned in the past. Some of this comes from the past results of the editing process in identifying errors in the data. Metadata are thus needed on what edit checks were applied, what proportion of records failed each check, and what changes were made to the data in response to edit failure.

In Implementing Collection, metadata need to be gathered on the mode of collection, and whether computer-assisted methods were used, since these factors may affect the processes applied later. Where computer-assisted methods are used, information should be gathered on the performance of the editing element of the process, to be used for evaluating its efficiency and effectiveness and identifying improvements for the future.

The metadata needed for evaluation and future improvement of the Editing, Validation and Imputation process itself include what edit checks were applied, what proportion of records failed each check, and for what proportion of these failures the data were subsequently changed.

For Weighting and Estimation, metadata are needed to identify records that may need special treatment in this process. This includes whether data have been imputed; and also whether data have been identified as implausible by statistical edit checks and then confirmed – these may be outliers.

Also, there may be circumstances in which data are considered to be unsuitable for use in imputation, for example if they have been left unedited through a selective editing procedure. This needs to be indicated through metadata.

In Analysis of Primary Outputs, metadata are needed to support assessment and evaluation of the quality of the outputs. Where data have been identified as implausible by statistical edit checks and then confirmed, the metadata should include the reasons for the implausibility of the data.

For each key output, the quality indicators need to include the proportions of records that had data changed during editing, the proportion that had imputed data, the difference made to the output by editing, and the proportion of the value of the output that derived from imputed data.

5. IMPLICATIONS FOR DATA AND METADATA STRUCTURES

There is thus a wide range of metadata needed for evaluation of quality, relating to data at different levels of aggregation, from an individual variable in an individual record to a complete dataset. Before discussing the implications of this for data and metadata structures, we need to consider the ways in which data and metadata are to be stored and managed in the new ONS infrastructure.

The Central ONS Repository for Data, or CORD, was mentioned earlier as an element of the modernization programme. It is proposed that it will hold all forms of ONS data, cross-sectional and longitudinal, from surveys and administrative sources of all kinds, at all levels of aggregation.

It is also proposed that within CORD there be a Central ONS Repository for Metadata, or CORM. It is envisaged that this will contain metadata about entities, such as method, survey, dataset, data item, classification, question. These metadata will be updated at defined trigger points of the SVC.

The CORM will then be a convenient vehicle for ensuring that metadata are automatically made available to users of data aggregates and other outputs, which are disseminated through the web tools. Additionally, in parallel, the microdata and associated unit level metadata will still be available internally for analysis.

When considering the structure of the metadata needed for the interfaces of the editing process, we therefore need to distinguish between unit or record level metadata, sometimes called micrometadata, and summarised or aggregated metadata.

Unit level metadata includes for example the failure of a record to pass an editing check, a change in the value of a data item, the reason for the change, and so on. Summarised metadata includes the number of records that have failed a particular edit check, the number that have been changed, the proportion of an estimate that derives from data changed through editing, and so on.

Micrometadata are created as each individual record passes through the survey process. They describe the characteristics of the data in that record as identified by the survey process, and the interaction of the data with the survey process.

The summary level metadata are derived from the micrometadata, but describe for example the characteristics of the dataset as a whole, or of an estimate derived from that dataset, or an edit check applied to that dataset. They relate to a variety of higher-level entities, in contrast with the micrometadata which relate to an individual data item.

The unit level metadata need to accompany or be linked to the unit level data in the data repository. They are needed for monitoring the operation of the process itself, (providing *inter alia* management information), and for monitoring the performance and quality of the process.

The summary level metadata are more appropriately held in the metadata repository, together with other information about the dataset as a whole. This implies that the design of the data repository needs to take account of the needs for unit level metadata; that the design of the metadata repository needs to take account of the needs for summary level metadata derived from the unit level metadata; and that there need to be (automatic) processes for deriving the summary level metadata from the unit level metadata.

In addition, there are some items of unit level metadata that need to be accessible across various data sources, for example information gathered from a particular respondent about the reasons for an implausible but confirmed piece of data - this may well explain other implausible data gathered from that respondent in another survey, and may also be of use to compilers and users of more aggregated data.

This category of metadata, which relates more to the unit in general than to the specific data item, sometimes has implications for the survey frame, and sometimes just for other operations on that unit. In either case, the most convenient location for it is likely to be in or linked to the frame or register in which the general data about the unit are held.

6. MANAGING THE PROCESS INTERFACES THROUGH METADATA

The interfaces between the editing process, and the adjacent processes of data collection and weighting and estimation, are managed by two types of metadata. One consists of the micrometadata that accompany the data, and include information about the history of the data, at unit level, as it passes through the various processes in the SVC. An example of the contents of this, at the points of entering and leaving the editing process, is sketched in Figure 2.

The second type of metadata needed for managing the interfaces between processes is information relating to the whole dataset on the processes that are to be applied to it, and the options and parameter settings within those processes that are applicable to this dataset. These need to be held in a repository of process control settings, as part of the operational management of the survey process.

For the editing and imputation process, the options and parameters need to define such things as the edit checks to be applied, the actions to be taken in case of failure to pass an edit, the automatic correction procedures to be applied, the imputation methods to be used, and in what circumstances, and so on.

The choice of these options needs to be based on a thorough understanding of the subject of the survey, analysis of past and related data, and up to date knowledge of best practice in editing and imputation methodology. It also needs to be determined in co-ordination with the other elements of the survey process, and informed by assessment of the interactions between them.

Figure 2: Example of micrometadata input to and output from the editing process INPUT

Unit level

Unit identifier

Collection mode

Response category

Capture date/time

Explanatory commentary on implausible data obtained from computer-assisted collection

Process history (which tools applied at what date/time)

Variable level

Variable identifier

Whether data obtained, data missing or variable not applicable to unit (may be separate metadata variable or special data values)

OUTPUT (in addition to input metadata)

Unit level

Updated process history

Explanatory commentary on implausible data from scrutiny or respondent follow-up

Whether each edit check failed

Selective editing category

Whether any data changed during editing

Whether any data imputed

Whether unit excluded from providing imputed values

Variable level

Whether data failed each relevant edit check

Selective/priority editing score

Whether data confirmed

Whether data changed

By what/whom data changed or confirmed (e.g. automatic correction, editor scrutiny, respondent follow-up)

New data (in addition to original data)

Date/time of data change

Whether new data imputed

Imputation method

7. CONCLUSIONS

Data editing is linked to other elements of the survey process in many and various ways. Some relate to the management of the editing process itself within the Statistical Value Chain; and some to the ways in which information about the editing process and its effects contributes to the operation of that and other processes, and of the survey process as a whole.

These relationships can contribute greatly to evaluating and hence improving the quality of the survey outputs, and the efficiency and quality of the survey process. But the achievement of these improvements depends very much on creating the right metadata, and being able to use them effectively in conjunction with the survey data to evaluate the outputs and processes.

This involves three elements. Firstly, the necessary metadata must be specified, at both unit and aggregate levels, to support the evaluation of quality. Beyond that, it is essential to specify data and metadata structures that can facilitate the use of the metadata in managing and evaluating the survey process. And lastly, these structures must also support the analysis of the metadata together with the survey data, in order to determine how to improve the quality of both processes and outputs in future.

LINKING DATA EDITING PROCESSES BY IT-TOOLS

By Carsten Kuchler and Corina Teichmann, Federal Statistical Office, Germany

1. INTRODUCTION

In 2002 the Federal Statistical Office of Germany (Destatis) started to re-structure its data editing process. The focus of its ambitious new data editing concept is on enhancing both the planning and the execution of the underlying work steps. In a prior evaluation of the previous practice, a variety of sub-processes was identified. By re-arranging these sub-processes, the crucial role of tailor-made software in linking related sub-processes became apparent, and the provision of software tools was considered the tie between realising methodological improvements on the one hand and optimising work flows on the other (Wein 2004, 2005, Kuchler 2003).

The integration of data editing processes by means of appropriate software is primarily based on the provision and accessibility of metadata in the entire survey process. Advanced survey methods generally depend on metadata from previous steps of processing and at the same time produce metadata on their part. Since most of these methods are implemented in specific software tools, it is obvious to establish the required metadata streams by providing well-defined interfaces and routines for activating them. Engstrom and Granquist (1999) were the first to propose so called Process Data Subsystems that are intended to allocate information about methods applied to a survey at hand and their particular performance. Since then several approaches and implementations extended this starting point towards the provision of general metadata information systems which are available in any step of the survey process (for recent examples see the description of the SIDI system at ISTAT by Brancato et. al. 2004 or the CORD and CORM system of the ONS briefly introduced by Tate 2003).

The focus of this paper is rather on the integration of survey process on the level of application software than on the description of general depository systems. Point of reference is the so-called PL-Editor that is a key element of the software strategy flanking the new data editing concept at Destatis. It is intended to support almost any specification task to be accomplished in preparing the data editing process of a particular survey. By this means the PL-Editor is one of the central gates through which metadata enter the survey process. In order to make the PL-Editor satisfy existing and future information claims raised by related processes of data production, much attention was paid on the specification of its interfaces with respect to an office-wide software standard. This paper treats the PL-Editor with respect to problems of linking processes on both the data editing level and the general data production level, as introduced by examples in section three and four. In preparing this, the following section provides an outline of basic concepts of the PL-Editor. Finally the fifth section reports some experiences made in launching the PL-Editor in different surveys, and gives an outline of its future prospects.

2. BASIC CONCEPTS OF THE PL-EDITOR

The PL-Editor is intended to support almost any specification task concerning the physical and logical description of data structures and processes related to data editing like particularly the compilation of data set descriptions, data checks and sequences of data checks. Specifications are stored in an office wide depository system and are made available by direct data base access, specific XML-based interfaces common to any software tool recently developed by Destatis or automatically generated source code to be processed by other software tools. By this means specifications of an ongoing survey are utilised throughout the entire survey process, and specifications of completed surveys can easily be included in current application flows. Thus the PL-Editor as part of the integrated office-wide software standard supports the reuse and harmonisation of specifications and increases the efficiency of the executing department.

The PL-Editor mainly consists of four interrelated components, as shown in figure 1, each of them conceptually independent from the others: (a) the actual editing interface as illustrated in detail by a screenshot in figure 2 provides input fields for the specification tasks, (b) the data base interface transfers metadata entered by the PL-Editor to an office wide depository system, (c) a collection of source code generators allows for generating metadata driven source modules and finally (d) an interface layer organises the complete data exchange between these components. This section mainly provides an outline of the basic concepts of the PL-Editor. Embedding and transferring metadata and the functionality of the source code generators is discussed in the subsequent sections in their context of application.

Due to the strictly object-oriented office-wide software standard (like any recent Destatis software, the PL-Editor is implemented in Java), modelling a survey by means of the PL-Editor is an object-oriented task. Metadata entering the system via the editing interface are thus considered instances of objects. Figure 3 reveals the aggregation of the involved objects and the cardinality of their (non total!) part-whole-relationships.

The atomic object is a variable. The essential attributes of a variable are its type (integer, real, date, string, etc.), storage information like field length, its domain (set of legal values and missing codes), variable and value labels, etc. Data checks and associated correction instructions that solely refer to the modelled variable (like domain and coding checks) are considered methods of the variable object.

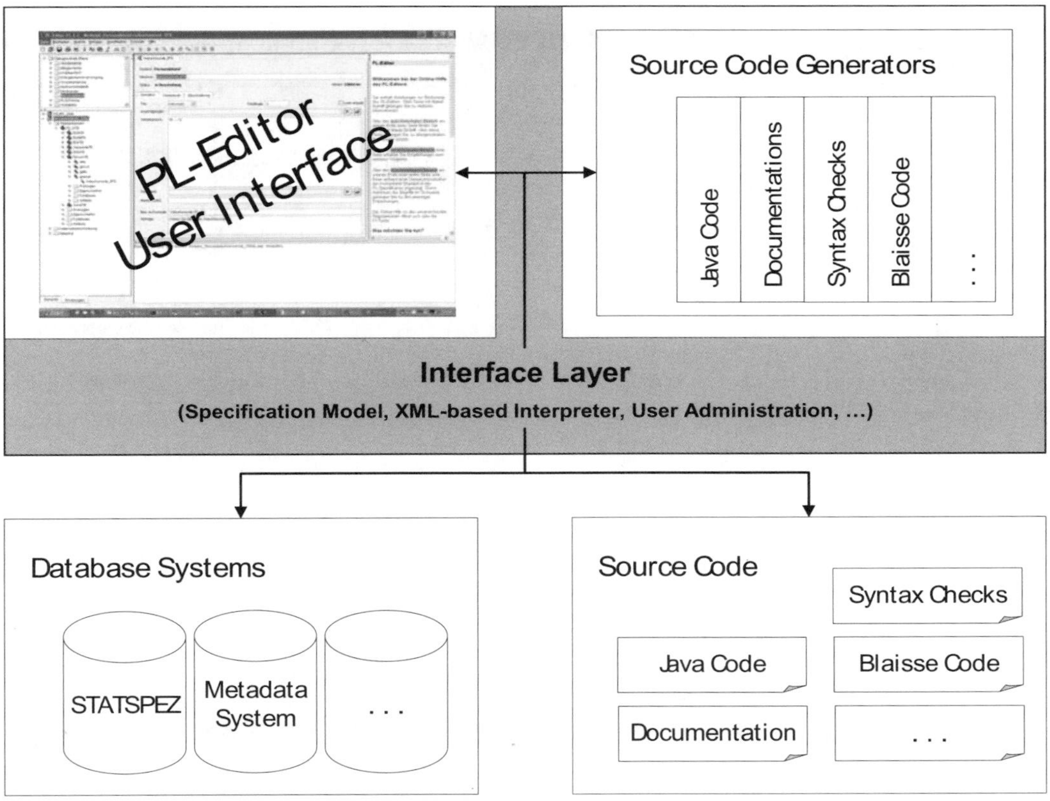

Figure 1: Components of the PL-Editor

On the next higher level of aggregation, so-called topics combine variables and topics of lower aggregation. Topics are basically disjoint sets of variables sharing a context of content (like item blocks or sections in a questionnaire). Figure 4 shows an example of the aggregation of two topics by a superior topic. The resulting contexts induce relational data checks referring to at least two of the subsumed variables. Relational data checks and the associated correction instructions are considered methods of a topic. Combining topics thus allows for structured modelling of data checks of increasing complexity. Finally a major topic, i.e. the one that is not covered by another topic, refers to the entire survey.

The selection and order of data checks applied to a particular data set may vary due to the intended product, i.e. releasing micro data requires another sequence of data checks than the computation of aggregates published in first release, etc. A natural way of dealing with this problem in terms of object orientation is to provide sequences of data checks as an additional method of topics.

Each specified instance refers to a one-to-one identifier according to an office wide catalogue of surveys within the program of official statistics. Following the aggregation arrows in figure 3 in reverse direction or de-referencing the corresponding inclusions, this key attribute allows for the access to the instances of the subsequent objects. Thus the PL-Editor may be considered a user interface for the convenient enter of editing rules and data set descriptions as well as a front end of the underlying data bases and metadata streams. By this means specifications from already completed data editing processes can easily be included in current application flows and thus support the reuse and harmonisation of specifications. Additionally the specifications can be made available throughout the entire process of data production and for the respective software applications.

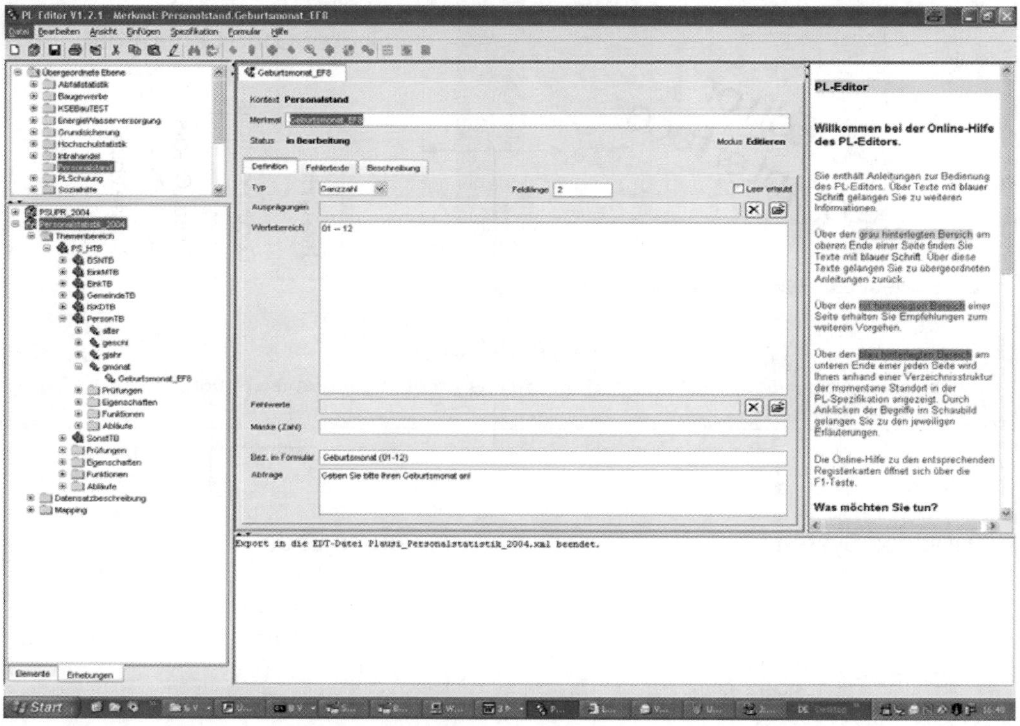

Figure 2 Screenshot of the PL-Editor, showing a register card of a variable that provides facilities for specifying the data type, the field width, the domain and the missing declarations of the variable. The two boxes on the left allow for the navigation between surveys (upper box) and within the selected survey. The box on the right shows the online help for the current work step (specifying a variable). The footer contains a box with log information about the execution of functions.

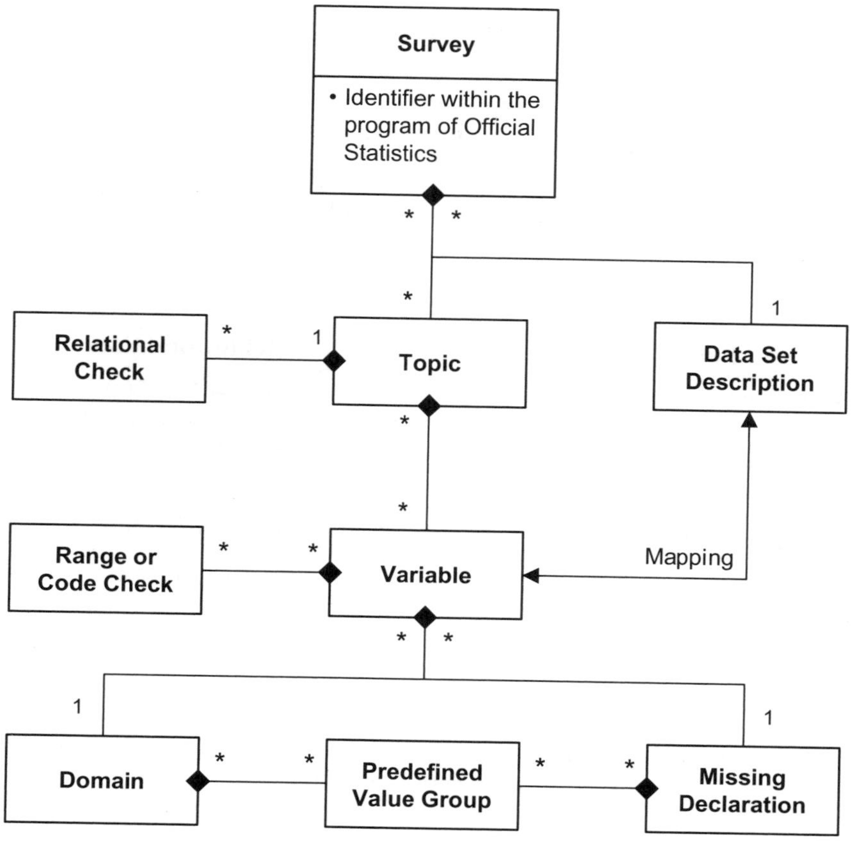

Figure 3 Aggregation of the objects provided by the PL-Editor (incl. cardinalities of the non total part-whole relationships, where "" denotes an arbitrary natural or null).*

Data checks are specified in a script language specific to the PL-Editor that provides advanced syntax constructs like for- and while-loops, the definition of functions and data structures and particularly facilities for de-referencing external data sources. The deposition of the specified instances takes place in an interface layer that connects the PL-Editor with the office wide depository system and the source code generators (see figure 1). Since the interface layer conceptually separates the specification syntax from the data structures the specified instances are processed in, the actual specification of instances remains unaffected by any change of the application flow. The price to be paid for this encapsulation is a rather advanced definition of the interface layer and the associated interfaces of counterpart software. This is done due to an office wide standard for data base structures and XML-based interfaces that is subject to the next sections.

3. LINKAGE OF DATA EDITING PROCESSES BY THE PL-EDITOR

The logical and relational structures of any instance specified with the PL-Editor are described in a specific XML-based format called DatML/EDT, that is assigned to the interface layer and thus separating specifications from the data structures they are subsequently processed in. The term DatML (Data Markup Language) denotes a family of XML-based formats and document-types for respectively describing any type of data and metadata occurring in the entire survey process (from surveying to archiving data). The provision of DatML formats based on a common XML core allows for a consistent and integrated (meta-)data flow. Beside DatML/EDT that was specifically developed

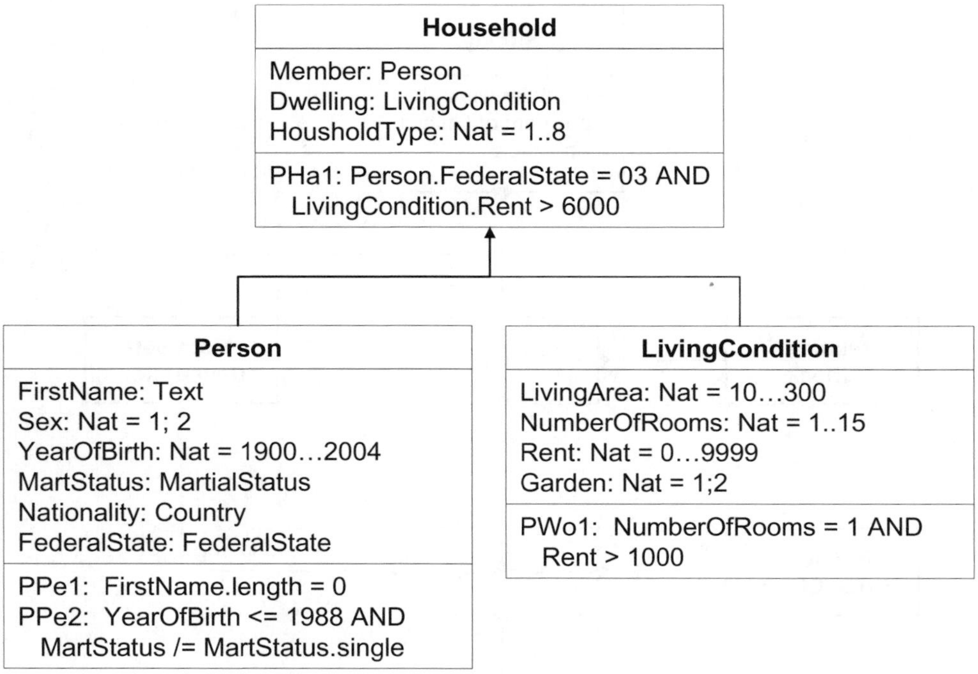

Figure 4 Imaginary example for the aggregation of topics ("Person" and "LivingCondition") with the associated fields and data checks by a superior topic ("Household"). Note the de-referencing of fields by the data checks of the "Household" topic.

for the interface layer of the PL-Editor, for instance DatML/RAW was implemented for handling and exchanging raw data or DatML/SDF is used for the description of survey properties with respect to automated processes.

As illustrated in figure 1 the interface layer passes the DatML/EDT descriptions to office wide depository systems or to source code generators. Based on the DatML/EDT descriptions of the instances and some meta-information which is also available in XML format, the source code generators produce source files executable by target applications. A typical use case is the generation of Java classes that are simply included by other programs written in Java as well. But the generality of the XML-based interface layer in principle allows for arbitrary target programming languages and formats.

A basic example for the application of source code generators is the provision of documentation facilities for the PL-Editor. For this purpose a documentation-generator is available that transfers the descriptions of the instances from the DatML/EDT format into the csv-format common to Microsoft Office products. Another application within the PL-Editor is the generation of consistency and syntax checks applied to the specified data checks that are also implemented by an automatic code generator and then returned to internal check functions.

A rather advanced example for the use of source code generators is the generation of executable source code that implements the data checks related to a survey at hand. This functionality is particularly useful when specifications of data checks or their sequence of application are changed in the data editing process. Typical target applications are interactive correction programs and software for the automatic identification of erroneous values. Due to the object-oriented software standard of Destatis, the recent interactive correction applications are written in Java. So it is natural to make available the data checks and their sequence of application by appropriate Java classes that are embedded into the target application. For this purpose the PL-Editor disposes of a Java code generator that receives the descriptions of the data checks and their sequence of application from the interface layer in DatML/EDT format as input and produces the according Java classes. The Java code generator already proved its reliability in several surveys (see the fifth section for an overview of use).

Due to the new data editing concept introduced at Destatis, a software tool for the identification of erroneous values in an observation is currently implemented. According to an approach proposed by de Waal and Quere (2003) a minimal missing pattern is computed for any observation that violates at least one relational data check. Since the underlying algorithms are of high complexity, they need to be implemented in a programming language that allows for faster processing than Java. For this purpose the prototype implementation was written in C. Applying this programme in a data editing process, where data checks and their sequence of application are usually reviewed for several times, requires the provision of a C code generator that produces the according C modules at the push of a button.

4. LINKAGE OF SURVEY PROCESSES BY THE PL-EDITOR

The focus of the previous section was on examples of integrating applications within the data editing sub process. This section widens the focus and deals with the linkage of the data editing with other survey processes by metadata streams provided by the PL-Editor. The exchange of metadata via the interface layer of the PL-Editor is in principle open for any counterpart software disposing of the required XML-based interfaces or having direct access to the underlying database. Since the recent applications at Destatis were programmed due to the office-wide software standard, various survey sub-processes are already supported by metadata entering the application flow via the PL-Editor. In this section we give two examples concerning exchange of metadata in XML format via the interface layer and a third example for direct data base access.

A typical field for re-using variable and data check specifications outside of data editing processes is the design of electronic questionnaires. Once the variables and data checks are entered, the basic structure of an electronic questionnaire can be considered fix. Even though the PL-Editor is intended to support data editing that does not mean that the respective specifications need to happen right before or within this process. In the majority of cases these specifications can be done prior to the process of questionnaire design. The IDEV software by Destatis supports the design of electronic questionnaires by processing metadata entered by the PL-Editor. Of particular interest is the PL-Editor facility to treat sequences of data checks as methods of topics. Due to methodological considerations one may select a subset of data checks specific to the purposes of the electronic questionnaire, which is then related to the associated fields of the electronic questionnaire. In subsequent stages of data editing one may apply other sequences of data checks. The metadata are released by the PL-Editor via the interface layer in the DatML/EDT format, and are entering the IDEV system via an XML interface also based on DatML/EDT. The resulting questionnaires are described in an XML-based format belonging to the DatML family as well, which is called DatML/ASK.

This year the Federal Statistical Office and the Statistical Offices of the Länder released the so-called .CORE software package that provides a variety of tools and transfer formats for surveying enterprise data straight from the accounting software used by a particular enterprise. The exchange of the questionnaire (which is a rather outmoded term in this context) and the data is carried out by save internet connections. The obvious effect of this approach is a significant increase of data quality both in terms of accuracy of the surveyed data and the efficiency and timeliness of subsequent steps of data production. In addition the respondents´ burden is reduced to a minimum. In close collaboration with well-known suppliers of accounting software and representatives of involved enterprises, multiple XML-based exchange formats were agreed, each of them fitting specific purposes (one of them is the DatML/RAW format mentioned above). These formats became part of the DatML family and are supplemented by specific software tools realising the data exchange from the first request to a final acknowledgement of receipt. Any specification of variables and data checks necessary for the particular enterprise survey is done with the PL-Editor. Since each of the subsequent processes relies on members of the DatML family, which are all based on the common XML-interface standard, these metadata are directly available via the interface layer of the PL-Editor. So changes of specifications only result in a re-integration of the associated metadata in subsequent applications. The .Core project is the 2005 winner of the 5th eGovernment competition in the field of "Economy and Labour", which is arranged by the international consulting firms BearingPoint and Cisco systems.

Finally the example of the so-called STATSPEZ software illustrates the reuse of specifications by direct data base access. STATSPEZ is a client/server application for specifying, generating and presenting results of statistical analysis in a unique manner and due to the standards of the publication program at Destatis. These tasks require specifications of the variables to be analysed like data set descriptions, storage information, domains, etc., which are all provided by the PL-Editor. As shown in figure 1, the interface layer of the PL-Editor directly feeds a database underlying the STATSPEZ application. The data formats and structures required by the database are due to a predefined standard and can thus be generated by the interface layer of the PL-Editor.

5. INTRODUCING THE PL-EDITOR AT DESTATIS

The PL-Editor was released for use at Destatis in July 2004. About three month earlier a preparatory training program started that still continues. Since the PL-Editor is a rather complex application, only staff members are trained that are concerned with surveys that are to be restructured with respect to the application of new software tools and editing methods. At the moment the PL-Editor is applied in about twenty surveys, with twelve of them generating an electronic questionnaire. Since the reorganisation of surveys is going step-by-step, the gain of efficiency achieved by sharing and re-using specifications in multiple surveys related by a similar context of content is not yet the major improvement realised by the PL-Editor. At the current stage of launching, departments chiefly benefit from the facilities for entering and administrating specifications with the PL-Editor and their high-grade availability in other survey processes. In particular the departments appreciate that changes in the specifications of data checks do not any longer require a re-programming of highly nested if-else constructions but only re-generating and re-embedding of source files into a target applications of subsequent processes which is regularly done within minutes.

However, with an annual survey, there may be periods of several months where staff does not work with the PL-Editor. In order to meet this "once-in-a-blue-moon" problem, the PL-Editor provides multiple help and documentation facilities. Of particular importance is the context sensitive online help in the right third of figure 2. It provides suggestions for workflows that can be seized by hyperlinks calling the demanded views and functions. In addition the F1-key is associated with a context sensitive help function providing information about currently activated input boxes and links to the intranet pages describing the method or work step in question.

Further developments of the PL-Editor are primarily related to the improvement of internal functionalities and the ergonomics of the application. Due to the strict separation of specifications and data structures realised by the PL-Editor, changes and enhancements in the linkage of processes and their associated software tools do not affect the actual PL-Editor, but only the interface layer and the underlying DatML formats. The primary enhancement to be released in next update versions of the PL-Editor is the provision of a modular testing environment for performing extended syntax and semantic checks on specifications in general and on data checks and their sequences of application in particular.

References

[1] Brancato, Giovanna, Concetta Pellegrini, Marina Signore and Giorgia Simeoni (2004): Standardising Evaluating and Documenting Quality: The Implementation of Istat Information System for Survey Documentation – SIDI. Proceedings of the European Conference on Quality and Methodology in Official Statistics (Q2004), Mainz.

[2] De Waal, Ton and Ronan Quere (2003): A Fast and Simple Algorithm for Automatic Editing of Mixed Data. In: *Journal of Official Statistics*, Vol. 19 (4), 2003, 383-402.

[3] Engström, Per and Leopold Granquist (1999): Improving Quality by modern Editing. UNECE, Work Session on Statistical Data Editing 1999, Rome, WP.23.

[4] Kuchler, Carsten (2003): IT Tools for an integrated Data Editing Concept. UNECE, Work Session on Statistical Data Editing 2003, Madrid, WP.19.

[5] Tate, Pam (2003): The Data Editing Process within the new Statistical Infrastructure of the Office for National Statistics. UNECE, Work Session on Statistical Data Editing 2003, Madrid, WP. 9.

[6] Wein, Elmar (2004): Improvement of Data Editing Processes. Proceedings of the European Conference on Quality and Methodology in Official Statistics (Q2004), Mainz.

[7] Wein, Elmar (2005): Concepts, Materials, and IT Modules for Data Editing of German Statistics. UNECE, Work Session on Statistical Data Editing 2005, Ottawa, WP.37.

AN UPDATE OF ANALYSIS OF DATA SLICES AND METADATA TO IMPROVE SURVEY PROCESSING

By Jean-Sébastien Provençal, Statistics Canada

Abstract: In May 2002, in Helsinki, Finland, a paper submitted by Statistics Canada on the Unified Enterprise Survey (UES) was presented at the UN/ECE Work session on Statistical Data Editing. The title of the paper was "Analysis of Data Slices and Metadata to Improve Survey Processing". The paper provided an overview of the UES Collection and Post Collection processes. It also presented the findings of a study evaluating those two processes. Conclusions and actions to be taken were discussed in the paper. Three years later, we provide an updated version of the paper. This paper gives an overview of the collection and post collection processes. It puts the emphasis on the major changes that have taken place in the last few years. It explains how those changes have modified and improved the UES.

Acknowledgements to Hélène Bérard, Sylvie DeBlois, Anthony Dupuis, Judy Lee and Claude Poirier of Statistics Canada for their contribution.

1. INTRODUCTION

The Unified Enterprise Survey (UES), initiated at Statistics Canada (STC) in 1997 with seven industries, now integrates close to 50 annual business surveys into one centralised survey system. In this paper, we will use the term industry to refer to a specific economic sector. Businesses of all sizes are in scope for the UES. Larger firms are always selected in the sample while the smaller businesses are randomly selected each year.

Many things have changed since the beginning of the UES in 1997. In the first few years of the UES, most industries employed two questionnaires – a long version and a short version. In subsequent years this process was changed to simplify the processing and to lower response burden for those that were filling a long form. Now, only one version of the questionnaire is used. This new version is much shorter than the initial long version.

Also, a graphical tool was developed to evaluate and monitor the impact of all the changes performed during a complete survey cycle. More details about this tool are given by Hazelton (2003).

The most important change that affected the collection and post collection processes is the increased use of fiscal data, also referred to as tax data. In the recent years, this source of data improved drastically in terms of accessibility, accuracy and timeliness facilitating its use in the post collection process. For example, for reference year 2003, tax data accounted for close to 50% of the final estimate for some variables in certain industries.

In this paper, we provide a review of the collection and post collection processes. We summarize the collection process prior to 2002 that was documented by Martin and Poirier (2002). We review the findings related to collection that were pointed out in a study conducted in 2002. We summarize the updates that have been made to the collection process since 2002, and finally we discuss how various issues were addressed by the recent changes that were implemented. We go through the same steps to describe the post collection process.

2. REVIEW OF THE COLLECTION AND POST COLLECTION PROCESSES

A. Background of the collection process and review of the findings resulting from the 2002 study

A. 1. Overview of the collection process prior to 2002

Survey data for the UES were collected via mail-back questionnaire or by telephone. All initial contacts were made via regular mail questionnaire. Follow-up activities in the presence of total non-response and for certain edit failures were conducted by telephone.

Mail-back questionnaires were captured using a Quick Data Entry (QDE) system with virtually no editing. Captured data were then batch edited and categorized according to the severity of their edit failures.

Two slightly different follow-up strategies were applied to mail-back units that failed capture edits. For the non-manufacturing sector, questionnaires categorized as having severe edit failures were flagged for follow-up. For the manufacturing sector, only "critical" units categorized as having severe edit failures were flagged for follow-up. Critical units were identified through a score function. Mail-back questionnaires having only non-severe edit failures and manufacturing "non-critical" units were not flagged for follow-up.

All total non-responses, i.e. units that do not mail back their questionnaire, were flagged for follow-up. A major concern was the cost associated with the follow-up strategy. In 2002, it was estimated that a telephone follow-up takes on average 15 minutes. This estimated time did not account for the unsuccessful follow-up attempts that often precede a final contact.

A. 2. Review of the findings on collection resulting from the 2002 study

In this sub-section, we provide a summary of the findings and highlights that were pointed out by the study carried out using results from reference year 1997 to reference year 2000. The study made the following recommendations.

Edit failure and Follow-up Rates

- *The need to find a way to encourage respondents to use the mail-back questionnaire in order to minimize the cost associated with telephone data collection;*
- *The need to re-visit the edits, paying stricter attention to what should constitute an edit follow-up, so that those units responding by mail would not be contacted by telephone simply to have their reported data confirmed;*
- *The need to find a way to prioritise individual units for follow-up in an even stricter fashion than was currently employed for the manufacturing sector.*

Impact of Follow-up

- *The need to direct the attention to the problem of edit failure caused by improper capture.*

To conclude, the use of a shorter questionnaire, starting in 2002 for reference year 2001, was expected to improve the response rate and reduce the edit failure rate.

B. Updates made to the collection process since 2002 and their impact

B.1. Updates made to the collection process since 2002

Through the last few years, several new methodologies and processes were put in place in order to improve the collection process. One of these was the implementation of a Quality Control (QC) process for QDE starting in 2003 (collection for reference year 2002). Overall, QC results showed that QDE was efficient. It was estimated that less than 1% of the records were found initially in error and less than 0.5% were still in error at the end of the process. Similar results were observed for reference year 2003.

Another major change made to the collection process is related to the follow-up strategy. Starting in 2003 (collection for reference year 2002), a score function was implemented for the non-manufacturing sector. The score function provides a day-to-day operational plan for collection. It identifies the units that are the largest potential contributors to the final estimates in each domain (e.g. industry by geography) and follow up is performed only for these most important units. The score function is a tool that helps to better manage the collection effort and reduce the collection cost. It also serves to meet the collection goal of obtaining a high weighted response rate. More details about the score function are given by Poirier, Phillips and Pursey (2003).

The follow-up strategies used for manufacturing and non-manufacturing sectors are now more similar. Both sectors are now using a score function to identify critical (followed-up) and non-critical (not followed-up) units. However, each sector uses a different methodology to derive their score function.

Finally, more pre-contact activities took place. This was done to account for the increasing contribution of fiscal data to the final estimates. The main purpose of the pre-contact is to validate the geographical and industrial classification of units for which it was intended to use fiscal data instead of survey data.

B.2. Impact of the updates on the collection process

The QC done on QDE confirmed that data obtained from the capture process were of good quality. Analysis done on reference years 2002 and 2003 showed similar results.

The implementation of a score function was certainly a major change to the collection process. The score function allows for the prioritizing of units selected for follow-up activities in order to reach a maximum coverage for a given domain.

On the other hand, the introduction of a score function raises a few issues. The use of the score function led to a minimal collection effort for a large portion of the sample. Units with a low priority are not followed-up and consequently we observe a very low response rate for these units. One could wonder why having an optimal sampling design for a given sample size if we cannot afford a process with a follow–up strategy for each surveyed unit? Should we consider reducing the sample size in order to be able to put a greater collection effort for each sampled unit? There are also some concerns regarding the respondent perception if no effort is done to contact them if they do not respond.

These issues are currently being studied. We might want to come up with a strategy where a minimal follow-up effort is carried on for each unit. For example, the score function could be used to control the effort's intensity.

Also, since reference year 2002, we reduced resources allocated for collection, and increased the use of tax data. The use of the score function may also be revisited given the increased use of tax data. Since non-financial data can only be obtained from respondents, there is more pressure to obtain even higher response rate from respondents.

C. Background to the post collection process and review of the findings resulting from the 2002 study

C.1. Overview of the post-collection process prior to 2002

There were three main steps in the post-collection process: 1) post collection review and correction by survey data analysts, 2) automated imputation, and 3) post-imputation review and correction. This section focuses mainly on automated imputation.

The automated imputation included three distinct parts. First, we imputed missing key variables, (e.g. three or four variables, generally totals), identified for each industry, for all partially filled questionnaires or empty questionnaires with historical data available. Second, we imputed missing details (e.g. totals breakdowns or characteristics like number of employees), for all partially filled questionnaires or empty questionnaires with historical data available. Finally, we imputed all empty questionnaires.

C.1.1 Imputation of missing key variables

For missing key variables, the automated system imputed a value by using different methods. The choice of the method depends on the data available for the record. The methods are applied in the following order:

- Derivation of rules involving other reported data for the individual record
- Previous year's ratios amongst key variables for the individual record
- Current year ratios amongst key variables within a group of similar records
- Year over year trend for each key variable within a group of similar records

These processes ensured that we have key variables for all units that reported at least one key variable, and for all units that were in the survey in the previous period.

C. 1.2 Imputation of details

For units that have a value for their key variables, (either reported or imputed) the distribution of details for the short questionnaires was taken from each unit's tax data report. The distribution of missing details, for the long questionnaires, was obtained through donor imputation. The imputation is done independently for each section of the questionnaire. Key variables are used to find the nearest neighbour for each section.

C.1.3 Imputation for total non-response

Empty records underwent mass imputation using the data of a single donor for all sections of the questionnaire and for all variables, both key variables and details. During the 1997 to 1999 period, tax data were used to find the nearest neighbour. Ratios observed between the donor and the recipient tax data were applied to the donor's reported data to get a more tailored result for the recipient (rather than simply copying the donor's data).

C.2. Review of the findings on post-collection resulting from the 2002 study

In this sub-section, we provide a summary of the findings and highlights that were pointed out by the study carried out using results from reference year 1997 to 2000.

Manual Imputation Rates

Findings strongly indicated that we should be concerned with mass imputation and changes to reported data.

- The need to find a substitute for tax data or improve the processes leading to a version of tax data so that there would be a consistent correlation between auxiliary data and survey data;
- The need to address the issue of badly captured data, so that analysts could feel confident that "reported" data were truly reported;
- The need to revisit the content/wording of the questionnaires, so that respondents would not misunderstand.

Impact of Manual Imputation

- The need to find a way to identify fewer, large impact units that would yield the greatest improvement in the estimates.

D. Updates made to the post-collection process since 2002 and their impact

D.1. Updates made to the post-collection process since 2002

One major update to the post collection process is the increasing use of tax data as a proxy for some pre-designated variables upfront in the process. Another very important update, that had an impact on the post collection process, is the replacement of the long and short form questionnaires by one redesigned single-form questionnaire.

Since reference year 2001, we have been using tax data as a proxy value for specific variables in case of total non-response. Since reference year 2002, we extended this approach in using tax data in lieu of survey data for a portion of the sample where no questionnaire was sent. For reference year 2002, we implemented this process for a limited number of records across a few industries. For reference year 2003, we extended it. For example, for the non-manufacturing sectors, we used this process for less than 6,000 sampling units for reference year 2002 and for over 13,000 sampling units (out of 44,000) across 7 industries for reference year 2003.

This process allows us to reduce response burden and the collection cost. However, the use of tax data has its limitation: tax data are easily usable only for simple business structures and not all the traditionally surveyed variables can be obtained through tax data. Variables for which tax data can be used vary from one industry to another. For reference year 2003, the number of financial variables used ranged from 7 to 25 depending on the industry.

Records for which we use tax data are treated like records with a partially filled questionnaire and are dealt with in the first two parts of the automated imputation process. At these stages, we process survey data and tax data together. Ratios and trends used to impute key variables are calculated using survey and tax information. Generally, we used survey filled questionnaires as donors to impute the missing details from questionnaires that were partially filled using tax information. Several studies had shown enough similarities between these two sources to justify this approach.

We are now using only one form of questionnaire for all sampled units rather than the two forms (a short and a long) that were previously used. The new form is shorter than the old long form. The processing is now simpler. As well, partially completed questionnaires are now more likely to be imputed by one donor.

Finally, with a simplified process, we were able to expand the set of techniques used to impute missing details on each partially filled questionnaire. The techniques described below represent the result of the improved imputation strategy.

- Derivation of rules involving other reported data for the individual record
- Carry forward of last year information for the individual record
- Previous year's ratios amongst variables for the individual record
- Current year ratios amongst variables within a group of similar records
- Donor imputation using the nearest neighbour method within a group of similar records

Since different imputation situations may call for different techniques, the expansion of the number of techniques helped to better tailor the imputation strategy for each industry.

D.2. Impact of the updates on the post collection process

The main factor that had the most impact on the UES Post Collection Process is linked to the increased use of tax data. Tax data have continued to improve over the years in terms of availability, timeliness and consistency that gave us the opportunity to increase their use.

The use of tax data significantly reduces the number of questionnaires with total non-response. Hence, it reduces the use of massive imputation that often leads to major sources of manual revisions by the data analysts. For reference year 1998, 67% of the manual revisions were for units that had been imputed through mass imputation. For example, for the retail trade store industry, the percentage of cases for which we used mass imputation decreased significantly. It went from 25% for reference year 2000 to 7% for reference year 2003 which represent a decrease of few thousand records that needed imputation.

Recently, the UES questionnaires have been redesigned to better represent accounting principles that are more easily understood by respondents and that are also used in the tax forms. This initiative should also help reduce partial non-response as the concepts measured should be more readily understood by the respondents. Some surveys have already gone through this process, and others will undertake this task very soon. This project will be finalised in the upcoming years. This initiative will increase the number of variables for which we can use tax data. Hence, it will reduce the imputation rate for these variables.

Finally, despite these many improvements, there is still a need to develop a method in order to better identify units that should be reviewed by the data analysts. An improvement in this area would certainly optimize the use of resources, and would contribute to improve quality of the final product, especially its timeliness.

3. CONCLUSION

The main purpose of this paper was to give an update of the recent progress regarding UES Collection and Post Collection processes issues that have been reported by Martin and Poirier (2002). Both processes have considerably evolved.

On the data collection side, we made changes in order to use the available resources more efficiently and optimize the follow-up strategy. Work is still on going on this issue as the UES context is changing with the increasing use of tax data. We will have to develop new surveys focussing on characteristics for some industries. Optimal use of the resources is necessary in order to achieve the targeted objectives of timeliness, data accuracy and cost reduction. The collection process will need to adapt in order to face all these challenges.

On the post collection side, major improvements have been made. Fiscal data is a reliable source of data that helped to improve the process. This source was used to reduce significantly the major cause of manual reviews e.g. records that were imputed through mass imputation. On the other hand, we still need to develop a method to target more efficiently which records should be reviewed manually.

Our goals remain to reduce respondent burden, reduce collection cost and make better use of tax data. Our efforts to harmonise our questionnaires with the concepts used by accountants (our respondents) and the tax forms may lead us in different directions. For example, how can we best integrate survey data and tax data?

The integrated use of survey data and tax data will require the development of new quality indicators in order to inform the users about the data quality and accuracy of the final products.

References

[1] Hazelton, F. (2003), Impact of Data Processing on Unified Enterprise Survey Micro Data, Proceedings of the UN/ECE Work Session on Statistical Data Editing, Spain (Madrid). (http://www.unece.org/stats/documents/2003.10.sde.htm)

[2] Martin, C. and Poirier, C. (2002), Analysis of Data Slices and Metadata to Improve Survey Processing, Proceedings of the UN/ECE Work Session on Statistical Data Editing, Finland (Helsinki). (http://www.unece.org/stats/documents/2003.10.sde.htm)

[3] Poirier, C., Phillips, R. and Pursey, S. (2003), The Use of a Score Function in a Data Collection Context, Proceedings of the UN/ECE Work Session on Statistical Data Editing, Spain (Madrid). (http://www.unece.org/stats/documents/2003.10.sde.htm)

Section 3.2

THE EFFECT OF DATA COLLECTING AND DATA QUALITY

Foreword – Pedro Revilla, Instituto Nacional de Estadistica, Spain

This section includes five papers about the effect of data collection methods on data quality. The main focus of the papers is the impact of electronic data reporting on the design of the editing strategy.

The paper by Nichols et al. presents the United States Census Bureau's experience with data editing strategies used in business surveys. It describes the interactive editing approach currently incorporated into Computerized Self-Administered Questionnaires (CSAQs), which are delivered to the respondent by downloadable files or transmitted electronically over the Internet.

The paper by Paula Weir presents changes in electronic data reporting options and usage for the U.S. Energy Information Administration. She examines in detail one fully Web-based survey that recently implemented an editing module to better understand the respondents' views and use of the edit feature. Respondents were asked how they used the edit function and how clear and useful they found the information provided for edit failures. The responses regarding the edit function for this survey are then compared to a study of the edit log that records information each time the edit function is invoked.

The paper by Gonzalez et al. explores the possibilities of Web questionnaires to improve editing. It discusses the possibilities and challenges that Web questionnaires offer to the editing tasks, in particular the combination of built-in edits and selective editing approach. Some practical experiences in the Spanish Monthly Turnover and New Orders Survey are presented.

The paper by Laroche focuses on the evaluation of the Internet option offered to the respondents in the 2004 Census test. A satisfaction survey of the respondents using the Internet and a follow-up survey of those not using the Internet are described. For the 2006 Census, all households will be offered Internet access. Comparisons between these two data collection methods are presented.

The last paper by Ceccarelli and Rosati, (if you have one comma after 'paper', then you need another after the authors. Or you can omit any comma) describes the data editing method used for the Italian Labour Force Survey. It presents the data edit and imputation strategy implemented for the whole survey process. A discussion on the main outcomes of the effect of using a combination of the Computer Assisted Personal Interviewing (CAPI) and Computer Assisted Telephone Interviewing (CATI) for data collection is also presented.

DESIGNING INTERACTIVE EDITS FOR U.S. ELECTRONIC ECONOMIC SURVEYS AND CENSUSES: ISSUES AND GUIDELINES

By Elizabeth M. Nichols, Elizabeth D. Murphy, Amy E. Anderson, Diane K. Willimack and Richard S. Sigman, U.S. Census Bureau, United States

Key Words: Electronic reporting, establishment surveys, usability testing, computerized self-administered questionnaires (CSAQs), data editing, electronic data collection.

1. INTRODUCTION

The purpose of this paper is to document the U.S. Census Bureau's experience with interactive data editing strategies used in collecting data from business survey respondents. Such surveys are subject to many classes of unintentional human error, such as programming mistakes, omissions, miscalculations, typing errors, and interviewer misclassifications. The contribution of each class of inadvertent error to total survey error, however, may be controlled or at least somewhat mitigated by good survey design practice, forethought and planning, and by the advances of computer technology. In the survey context, all such efforts to detect and correct respondent errors fall under the purview of *data editing*.

In mail surveys of establishments, data editing has typically been performed during post-data-collection processing. Computer-assisted establishment surveys, however, may perform data editing interactively, during data collection. For example, in surveys that use computer-assisted telephone interviewing (CATI) or computer-assisted personal interviewing (CAPI), data editing rules, referred to as *edit checks*, can be incorporated into the CATI/CAPI instrument so that the interviewer is notified of an entry that fails one or more edit checks. The interviewer can then probe the respondent for an alternative response or for verification that the flagged response is correct.

Edit checks are also incorporated into computerized self-administered questionnaires (CSAQs), which are delivered to the respondent by mailing disks or CD-ROMs (downloadable) or transmitted electronically over the Internet's World Wide Web. Browser-based CSAQs are also called *online Web-survey* or *Internet* questionnaires. When collecting data using CSAQs, respondents – not interviewers – are notified when a response fails one or more edit checks. The remainder of this paper focuses on interactive edit checks in downloadable and Internet questionnaires.

For comparison purposes, Section 2 describes the interactive editing approach currently incorporated into CSAQs collecting economic data from businesses. In Section 3, we offer preliminary guidelines for incorporating edit checks into CSAQs, based on several usability studies of electronic surveys of businesses or organizations. In Section 4, we discuss our findings and propose themes that emerge from the Census Bureau's approaches to interactive data editing; and we raise some issues for future research in Section 5.

2. EXPERIENCES WITH EDIT CHECKS AND IMPLEMENTATION STRATEGIES FOR U.S. ELECTRONIC ECONOMIC SURVEYS AND CENSUSES

CSAQ edit checks prompt respondents to clarify or resolve ambiguous or discrepant responses. Fields containing information that respondents can edit, including name, address and contact information, may be subject to interactive edit checks. Thus, the kinds of edit checks incorporated into the Census Bureau's economic CSAQs cover a broader range of potential discrepancies than do those conducted during post-collection.

Economic CSAQs borrowed the following kinds of edit checks from post-collection edit routines:

- Balance edit: Verifies that the sum of detail data equals the appropriate total.
- Survey-rule test/Ratio edit: Verifies that the ratio of two data values lies in the range defined by specified minimum and maximum values.
- Survey-rule test/Logical edit: Verifies that data reported for related items are logically valid.
- Required item or Missing value/Incomplete edit: Verifies that data have been reported.

The following kinds of edit checks tend to be administered only within CSAQs:

- Preventive edit: Blocks respondents from completing an action, occurring upon the first invalid keystroke.
- Alphanumeric edit: Verifies that the data meet the proper alphanumeric rules established for that field.
- Format edit: Verifies that the data have been entered in the expected form (e.g., date entered with dashes instead of slashes).
- Rounding Test: Checks to see if rounding has occurred in the data. (Some post-collection balance edit checks may use rounding tests.)

CSAQ designers have control over when and how the results of various edit checks are displayed to respondents. *Immediate edit checks* present edit messages instantly upon detection of discrepant data, and the system prompts the respondent for a correction or explanation. The result of an immediate edit check can be presented as either a pop-up window or an icon located near the questionable item. The results of *deferred edit checks* are presented to the respondent after the data have been entered and reviewed, usually in a list format. *Server-side edit checks* employ a type of deferred approach, since data have to be submitted to the server in order to generate the edit message.

Two questions are frequently asked in survey development: 1) How many edit checks are too many? 2) Should we allow submission of data with edit failures remaining? It is difficult to devise empirical rules to answer these two questions since each data collection situation is different. Instead we can speak to what we have done, what seems to work, and a general philosophy we have adopted.

Table 1 summarizes the editing features of six Census Bureau economic programs offering either downloadable or browser-based CSAQs – the Survey of Industrial Research and Development (R&D), the Manufacturer's, Shipments, Inventories, and Orders Survey (M3), the 2002 Economic Census, the Company Organization Survey (COS), the Annual Survey of Manufactures (ASM), and the Quarterly Financial Reports (QFR).

Table 1 shows that economic programs at the Census Bureau have embedded numerous edit checks into each electronic survey and, in two cases, that the number of edit checks exceeds the number of items collected. Although the number of edits could be related to respondent burden, our experience indicates that respondents are generally receptive to edit checks. In situations with numerous edit checks, respondents could be bombarded with edit failures if they happen to trigger each edit rule. Fortunately this does not typically happen.

The question survey designers must address is the likelihood of a respondent triggering an edit check. If a respondent is highly likely to trigger a large number of edit checks, then perhaps the number of edits embedded into the CSAQ should be reduced or they should be tuned to produce fewer "hits." If it is likely that a large number of edit checks will be triggered, perhaps the edit rules are too strict or there is a problem in the question phrasing or response field placement causing respondents' answers to trigger multiple edit checks. From the respondent's perspective, the purpose of edit checks is to help the establishment submit accurate, internally consistent data. Edit checks that do not clearly foster this result may be annoying to respondents.

Table 1 also shows that the Census Bureau's economic programs typically do not require respondents to resolve all edit failures before submission. For the situations where certain fields are required to pass the edit test before the survey can be submitted (also known as "hard" edits), failing to satisfy the edit test results in unit non-response. These items are considered so critical to survey response that missing or inaccurate responses make the submitted form unusable.

The philosophy of accepting data with unresolved edit failures stems from two principles: 1) Let the user be in control to the extent possible (a usability principle); and 2) Obtaining some data, even edit-failing data, is better than obtaining no data at all. Since the first principle is respondent-centered and the second is from the survey management perspective, CSAQ editing strategies become a balancing act. Generally, however, respondents want to provide accurate data; thus, if they have not changed data in a way to satisfy the edit failure, we should assume their response is correct in their business context. We also suspect that the more difficult it is to submit data electronically (by difficult we mean that we do not allow submission until all data edit failures are resolved), the more likely is unit non-response.

3. PRELIMINARY GUIDELINES FROM USABILITY RESEARCH ON ORGANIZATIONAL SURVEYS

A. Census Bureau Usability Research Methodology for Organizational Surveys

To learn about respondent interaction with various approaches to edit-failure notification, the Census Bureau tests candidate editing approaches with respondents. We observe test respondents interacting with edit messages during usability testing. Do respondents recognize edit-failure notifications? Do respondents read the edit messages? If they read the messages, do they understand them? What kind of action do they take regarding the message? A response might consist of ignoring the edit check, modifying data values, or writing a remark to explain why data are accurate even though they failed the edit check. The latter task is particularly characteristic of business surveys since it is not uncommon for valid data to lie outside an expected range. Finally, how easy is it for respondents to interact with the CSAQ to respond to the edit check? For example, respondents may have to navigate to items referred to in the edit message.

Because it is virtually impossible to recruit business respondents to travel to the Census Bureau's usability lab, researchers travel with a video camera and laptop to the business locations to conduct usability testing. With the respondent's consent, video tape recording allows one or more researchers to analyze the session afterwards; the laptop is a necessary backup in case the CSAQ does not work properly on the respondent's workstation. Using a think-aloud protocol, a method often used in cognitive testing, we watch and listen as respondents interact with the CSAQ in their offices. Often we use internal staff members as supplemental subjects, since the usability literature typically recommends between five to 12 subjects (e.g., Dumas and Redish, 1999). As few as five subjects is considered sufficient to identify 80 percent of the usability issues (Virzi, 1992). Even with a small number of participants, usability methods are effective in uncovering issues in comprehension and navigation of the CSAQ.

Usability testing has its limits, however. Since usability testing uses a small number of subjects, generally from convenience samples, results cannot be tested for statistical significance. Statistical hypothesis testing is not appropriate in a usability-testing context because usability testing is not controlled experimentation. Usability testing is intended to identify problems that actual respondents might have with the CSAQ, not to find significant differences between groups.

Further, interview time devoted solely to edit checks is limited since usability testing focuses on the entire instrument. Edit behavior is often not fully functional when usability testing is conducted; such was the case during testing of the 2002 Economic Census prototype. Given these disclaimers, the best practices we recommend for designing edit behavior arise from limited usability testing and should be subjected to additional research.

B. Preliminary Guidelines

The following design guidelines summarize our interpretations of respondent reactions to interactive edits encountered during usability tests. After we state the guideline, we include evidence from our usability tests to support the guideline. In addition to the usability tests performed on surveys listed in Table 1, we also drew from usability reports for two institutional surveys: the Library Media Center Survey (LMC) and the Private School Survey (PSS). At the time of those tests, the LMC and PSS surveys were browser-based.

1) **Minimize edit failures through good design.** Good questionnaire design includes communicating to respondents which data fields require answers and which are optional. For example, instructions should inform participants to click on "none" if the answer is zero or to enter a number when an entry is required (Bzostek and Mingay, 2001). For dates or amounts, format can be built into fields automatically. Additionally, question text can include instructions on the correct format (Bzostek and Mingay, 2001; Nichols et al., 2001).

2) **Perform edit checks immediately unless checking for missing data or performing an inter-item edit. Defer activating those edit checks. Run them either immediately before the respondent finishes the form or after all the items in the inter-item edit have been entered**. Study participants preferred immediate notification of edit failures, rather than receiving a list of edit messages at the end (Bzostek and Mingay, 2001; Rao and Hoffman, 1999). Participants can learn to avoid similar mistakes if they are notified immediately. However, we caution against triggering edit rules too early. This happened during usability testing of the Quarterly Financial Report (QFR). A QFR edit checking the consistency between two items triggered the edit as soon as data were entered for the first of the two items. Participants thought the edit check was ill-placed. This edit check should have been invoked on the second of the two items. We recommend activating the edit check when all the relevant fields have been manipulated, no matter the order of manipulation (Nichols et al., 2000).

3) **Research edit checks before implementing an edit that might be too strict**. Not all individual records will conform to broad-based edit rules, but they may still be correct. Some participants during the Annual Survey of Manufacturers (ASM) usability testing did not think the edit took in all the relevant factors when calculating ranges for a ratio edit (Saner et al., 2000). In usability testing of the Library Media Centers Survey (LMC), some participants correctly entered a number, which exceeded a range edit check. These participants changed the value to reflect the upper bound of the range. Based on the number of participants who triggered this edit check during usability testing, we determined this range edit was too strict (Nichols et al., 1998). Some LMC respondents began ignoring edit messages when they received numerous edit failures with which they disagreed (Hoffman et al., 1999).

4) **Avoid violating user expectations for single-purpose functions.** For example, do not mix editing and submitting. Problems arose in the Public School Survey (PSS) because the server-side editing process was invoked when the respondent pressed the "Finished" button, thinking that the form would be submitted. When they saw that an edit check was run and edit messages appeared, they changed their understanding of the "Finished" button. They then believed that clicking on "Finished" again would iteratively check for edits until their forms were correct. This was not the case. Edit checks were only run the first time the "Finished" button was pressed. Although this design was most likely created to ensure respondents invoked the edit checks, the design violated respondents' understanding twice. Initially it violated their understanding of the word "Finished." It then violated their expectation of the ability to iteratively check for edits (Bzostek and Mingay, 2001). During usability testing of the Company Organization Survey (COS), respondents were also surprised that the edit report was rerun when they tried to submit (Nichols, 1998). Some Census Bureau

CSAQs continue to be designed with editing and submitting as a final verification check. Research is needed to find a less confusing mechanism to run final editing.

5) **Allow edit failure reports to be run iteratively, as expected by respondents.** In some CSAQs, edit failures for the entire CSAQ can be run as a batch (usually at the end of the questionnaire) and presented together as a list of failures. The batch process of presenting edit messages is not a problem in itself. The problem arises if the CSAQ does not allow this batch processing to be rerun and updated. For example, the PSS was designed for all the edit messages to appear together, at the top of the scrollable form, once the form was submitted. Most likely designers thought respondents would make their way through the list, correcting each one in turn. During usability testing, however, some participants wanted to recheck their form after correcting only one edit, hoping that the list would reappear without the edit they had just corrected. They could not do this with the original design of the PSS CSAQ (Bzostek and Mingay, 2001). In the ASM, we also observed respondents wanting to return to the review screen after correcting a failure. In this case, each time the review screen was invoked, the edit checks were rerun, generating an updated list (Saner et al., 2000). This design met respondent expectations.

6) **Allow for easy navigation between an edit failure list and the associated items.** In both the COS and ASM, respondents easily navigated from the list of edit failures on the review screen to an item by clicking on the hyperlinked edit-failure text. Once at an item, however, returning to the review screen was confusing (Saner et al., 2000). PSS users wanted to be able to navigate easily back to the list of edit failures, once they were at an item. When they discovered the list was at the top of the form, they complained about having to scroll up to see the list (Bzostek and Mingay, 2001). In the 2000 Orders Survey (M3) CSAQ design, server-side edit checks were run, and the edit messages appeared on a separate page. Users had to exit that page to return to the form and correct their responses. They could not easily navigate between the two pages. Usability experts working on the M3 recommended placing the messages directly on the form, eliminating the need to navigate between two windows (Rao and Hoffman, 1999). The 2002 Economic Census attempted to alleviate this problem by using a separate pane for edit messages. Hyperlinks between the edit pane and the item pane provided the navigation. In theory this design solution satisfies this guideline, but for confirmation purposes we recommend future usability testing of this approach.

7) **Clearly identify which edit failure goes with which item.** In the PSS, clicking on the edit-failure message at the top of the scrollable form reset the page to display the data-entry field that had failed the edit check. The page was reset so that the line containing the data-entry field was at the top, but the question text for this field was above the fold. To see the question text, respondents had to scroll up; thus they had to perform two tasks to find the item associated with the edit failure (Bzostek and Mingay, 2001). In the LMC, the pop-up edit messages were invoked when the respondent's cursor gained focus in (i.e., went to) another data field. If respondents scrolled down this browser-based scrollable form, the item with the failed edit could be off the screen when the pop-up message appeared (Nichols et al., 1998).

8) **Include a location, a description of the problem, and an action to take in the edit message.** Respondents were always trying to decipher where the edit was located and what they needed to do to fix it. Every participant for the 2002 Economic Census prototype testing commented that many of the edit messages would have been easier to work with had the item number been available. Participants also wanted to know what action they needed to take to resolve an edit failure. The easiest messages to understand were those that said, "Please complete item x" (Nichols et al., 2001).

9) **Avoid jargon, be polite, use good grammar, be brief, use active voice, and use words that match the terminology used in the question.** Problems arose when words used in the edit

message did not match the terminology used in the item. Respondents were not sure they were on the right question (Nichols et al., 2001). Unclear edit messages were also a problem during usability testing for the LMC field test (Tedesco et al., 1999).

10) **Prior to implementation, cognitively test any edit messages offering a solution.** Offering one of many possible solutions seems to "lock" the respondent into that solution, which may not be the appropriate one. Problems also arose when solutions such as, "Check for a typing mistake" were in an edit message. Sometimes these solutions led respondents astray (Nichols et al., 2001). We noticed participants changing their answer to fit the upper bound of a range edit check in the LMC when the range edit provided the bounds (Nichols et al., 1998).

11) **Do not automatically erase data that fail an edit check.** In the LMC testing, we tested messages containing an "OK" and a "Cancel" button to close the pop-up edit message window. The edit messages warned participants that their data would be erased by clicking on the "OK" button, but clicking "Cancel" would retain their entries. At least four participants did not understand the difference between the two buttons. We found that when participants' entries were erased by clicking the "OK" button, some were reluctant to re-enter data (Tedesco et al.,1999).

12) **Inform respondents about the policy for submitting data with unresolved edit failures.** Respondents in both the ASM and QFR testing were not sure whether they could send data with edit failures remaining, although this was permissible (Saner et al., 2000; Nichols et al., 2000).

13) **Give the respondent as much control as possible.** One design for communicating edit failure messages is to include them in a pop-up window. In this design, when a respondent finishes entering data, if the data fails the edit, a pop-up window containing the edit failure message automatically appears. Unsolicited pop-up windows containing edit messages caused problems for respondents in usability testing for the LMC Field Test. Several respondents did not read the message but automatically clicked a button in the window to make it disappear. When probed at the end of a testing session, one respondent didn't even remember a pop-up window. Others thought it was a computer bug (Nichols et al., 1998; Tedesco et al., 1999). The QFR also used pop-up windows to display the edit message, but the participant needed to click on an icon next to the field to invoke the pop-up. Participants used this icon successfully, and could choose when to open and read the edit message (Nichols et al., 2000). In the 2002 Economic Census, the respondent could run edits at any time, which is an example of giving the respondent control. We recommend further usability research on this concept of respondent-initiated editing.

14) **Use newly created icons with caution since they do not have universal meanings. Use standard icons only for expected purposes.** Both the QFR and the ASM use icons to immediately notify the respondent of an edit failure. A red circle with a white "X" icon was used successfully by the QFR respondents. When the respondent clicked on the icon, an edit message was displayed. The yellow "!" warning messages were rarely clicked on in the QFR testing, and a few ASM respondents were unaware of their clickable property. The white bubble "i" icon was only used in the QFR. When probed, respondents thought the "i" bubble icon meant additional information and were surprised to find the message reminded them to make a remark (Nichols et al., 2000). The standard use for an "i" bubble is to convey information, not to suggest a user action. Users will be confused by standard icons used to mean something different and by ambiguous icons. A flag icon was used in the 2002 Economic Census to indicate an edit failure. There is no current standard icon for edit failures. We recommend usability testing of icons until a standard develops. Standard usability guidelines say to use a text label for any icon. Another option is to use text instead of icons to denote editing functionality or edit failures. The LMC contained a button labeled

"Check your work." If selected, this button would list all the edit failures. Respondents, however, assumed the button simply allowed them to review their work. They did not expect to receive a list of edit failures when they selected the button (Hoffman et al., 1999).

4. DISCUSSION AND EMERGING THEMES

We summarize by discussing several themes that emerge from Census Bureau survey practices and research on incorporating interactive editing into CSAQs and Web instruments:

The use of edit checks has increased for several reasons over the years. Historically, early CSAQs incorporated only a few basic edit checks because of a grave concern for additional respondent burden, which might result in unit non-response. In addition, early software could support only a few simple edit checks. Over time, more edit checks have been added to existing CSAQs and to newly created CSAQs. Indeed, the ratios of the number of edit checks to the number of questionnaire items presented in Table 1 seem high: A recent Web instrument developed by the Census Bureau, the M3, averages more than two edit checks per item on the questionnaire. This growth has occurred, in part, because of enhancements to the software, enabling the creation of edit checks that were not previously possible. Moreover, the number of edit checks has increased as survey-staffs' experience and confidence have grown over multiple survey iterations.

A reasonable number of embedded CSAQ edits will not necessarily increase respondent burden or lead to unit non-response. Even though the number of edit checks has increased, it appears that embedded CSAQ edits do not necessarily lead to unit non-response. This is corroborated by usability research suggesting that respondents seem to appreciate edit checks, wanting to be informed of discrepancies in their data so they can make corrections. Thus, respondents do not necessarily consider edit checks to be "bad", and they do not appear to abandon the response task just because they received edit messages. In our experience, computer-literate respondents actually expect some automated checking of their data entries along with a capability to make interactive changes to their responses, and they are surprised if these features are not built into an electronic survey.

Only some post-collection edit checks can be embedded in CSAQs. The source of edit checks added to CSAQs is the set of edits typically applied during post-collection processing. For various reasons, however, not all post-collection edit checks can be moved into the interactive CSAQ environment. Programming or technical issues may constrain development of embedded edit checks. For example, not all the edit checks typically performed at headquarters were incorporated into the 2002 Economic Census because the system's design inhibited implementation of some edit checks. The utility of some edit checks is also limited by "one-size-fits-all" approaches to the design of electronic instruments. Because the correctness of many establishment survey data items depends on the industry, editing parameters vary by industry. CSAQs are not currently tailored by industry or size of business, limiting the value of certain kinds of edit checks. Other edit checks may be too complex to communicate to respondents and too cognitively challenging for respondents to interpret during the course of completing an electronic survey. Moreover, macro-level edits that look at summary results across all respondents can only be done post-collection, and thus cannot be moved into the CSAQ.

Mission criticality, typical levels of data quality, and certain respondent characteristics guide the inclusion of edit checks in CSAQs. Because of various constraints, survey managers at the Census Bureau must prioritize edit checks incorporated into electronic surveys. Priorities are placed on items deemed mission-critical. Subject area knowledge of respondents' abilities to report particular data items and typical levels of response accuracy also guide the definition and selection of edit checks for CSAQs.

Respondent acceptance of edit checks depends on several factors, including perceived usefulness. Respondent reaction remains a valid concern. Research shows that, to a great degree, instrument control needs to remain with respondents. Usability research suggests a number of guidelines for user-centered design and implementation of CSAQ edit checks to improve the usability of electronic surveys. Operational experience suggests that respondents easily accept edit checks ensuring that the data they enter meet required formats, and these kinds of edits are effective. In addition, different levels of edits– information, warning, and edit failure – provide respondents with information about severity and let respondents choose how to deal with edit messages.

Acceptance of electronic forms containing edit-failing data reflects a greater willingness to deal with measurement error rather than to absorb non-response error. Usability research suggests that the issue of respondent control over resolving edit failures is perhaps most critical at the data-submission stage. Many current Census Bureau CSAQs allow respondents to submit completed electronic survey forms with data that have failed the embedded edits. The main reason for this strategy is to avoid encouraging survey non-response due to unresolved edit failures. All survey programs prefer edit- failing data to no data (unit non-response), and they continue to rely on post-collection editing and imputation to cleanse reported data. Thus, it appears that survey managers are more willing to accept measurement error, than they are to accept non-response error, in the collected data.

5. FUTURE DIRECTIONS AND RESEARCH ISSUES

In general, the Census Bureau's incorporation of interactive edit checks into electronic data collection for economic surveys embodies a conservative philosophy. At a minimum, the Census Bureau receives data from cooperative respondents. Those data may or may not pass basic edit checks. Research is needed to support a more ambitious philosophy, allowing the inclusion of additional post-collection edit checks in electronic instruments in order to reduce costs and increase data quality, while maintaining respondent cooperation.

Survey practitioners would very much like to have "generally accepted practices" or "rules of thumb" for resolving electronic survey-design issues, including the open issues in data editing. However, we expect this to be virtually impossible given the variety of surveys, administrations, and trade-offs related to data quality and response. Instead we think it would be more appropriate to develop a set of research-based guidelines to aid decisions related to editing. Derived from goals and principles, and supported by research, these guidelines should be revisited periodically to ensure their relevance as technology changes. Research is needed to determine whether a core set of best practices and heuristics could always be implemented.

Issues concerning data quality and resource allocation can arise when large mail surveys offer automated data collection. Large mail surveys have high variable costs (with respect to the number of respondents and the number of survey cycles) associated with data editing because clerks and subject matter experts review edit failures produced by post-data-collection edit checks. On the other hand, editing at the time of data collection, by respondents reviewing edit messages generated by automated edit checks, can have high fixed costs for programming and questionnaire testing; but the corresponding variable costs associated with interactive data editing should be much lower than those for traditional post-data-collection editing. Such a paradigm shift would require modifications to survey organizational cultures, structures, and resource allocation.

Survey managers' preferences for receiving edit-failing data from respondents – as opposed to no data – raise the question of whether "submission with unresolved edit failures" is a satisfactory, cost-effective, "optimum" strategy in terms of data quality, which is affected by both non-response error and measurement error. Investigations into data quality suggest that the potential benefits of CSAQ edit checks are realized, resulting in fewer data items failing post-collection edits (Sweet and Ramos, 1995) and fewer items being changed during analyst review (Evans, 2003). Further research is needed to corroborate this encouraging conclusion, and to evaluate the trade-offs between measurement error and non-response error related to interactive edit checks in electronic data collection.

6. ACKNOWLEDGEMENTS

This report is released by the U.S. Census Bureau to inform interested parties of research and to encourage discussion of work in progress. The views expressed on methodological issues are those of the authors and not necessarily those of the Census Bureau. The authors wish to thank the following Census Bureau staff for helping us gather information for this paper: Patrick Kent, Joyce Kiessling, Yvette Moore, John Nogle, Yolando St. George, and Rita Williamson. Material in this paper was previously presented to the Federal Economic Statistics Advisory Committee, March 2003, and to the Annual Conference of the American Association for Public Opinion Research (AAPOR), May 2004.

References

[1] Anderson, A., Cohen, S., Murphy, E., Nichols, E., Sigman, R., and Willimack, D. 2003. *Changes to Editing Strategies when Establishment Survey Data Collection Moves to the Web*, Presented to the Federal Economic Statistics Advisory Committee, Washington, D.C., U.S. Bureau of Labor Statistics.

[2] Bzostek, J. and Mingay, D. 2001. *Report on First Round of Usability Testing of the Private School Survey on the Web*, U.S. Census Bureau, Statistical Research Division, Usability Lab, Human-Computer Interaction Memorandum Series #42.

[3] Dumas, J. and Redish, J. 1999. *A Practical Guide to Usability Testing*. Portland, OR: Intellect.

[4] Economic Electronic Style Guide Team. 2001. "Style Guide for the 2002 Economic Census Electronic Forms," U.S. Census Bureau, Economic Planning and Coordination Division.

[5] Evans, I. 2003. "QFR CSAQ Evaluation." Internal Memorandum. U.S. Census Bureau, Company Statistics Division.

[6] Hoffman, R., Moore, L., Perez, M. 1999. *Customer Report for LMCQ Usability Testing,* U.S. Census Bureau, Statistical Research Division, Usability Lab, Human-Computer Interaction Memorandum Series #23.

[7] Nichols, E. 1998. *Results from Usability Testing of the 1998 Report of Organization CSAQ,* U.S. Census Bureau, Statistical Research Division, Usability Lab, Human-Computer Interaction Memorandum Series #19.

[8] Nichols, E., Murphy, E., and Anderson, A. 2001a. *Report from Cognitive and Usability Testing of Edit Messages for the 2002 Economic Census (First Round),* U.S. Census Bureau, Statistical Research Division, Usability Lab, Human-Computer Interaction Memorandum Series #39.

[9] Nichols, E., Murphy, E., and Anderson, A. 2001b. *Usability Testing Results of the 2002 Economic Census Prototype RT-44401,* U.S. Census Bureau, Statistical Research Division, Usability Lab, Human-Computer Interaction Memorandum Series #49.

[10] Nichols, E., Saner, L., and Anderson, A. 2000. *Usability Testing of the May 23, 2000 QFR-CSAQ (Quarterly Financial Report Computerized Self-Administered Questionnaire),* U.S. Census Bureau, Statistical Research Division, Usability Lab, Human-Computer Interaction Memorandum Series #33.

[11] Nichols, E., Tedesco, H., King, R., Zukerberg, A., and Cooper, C. 1998. *Results from Usability Testing of Possible Electronic Questionnaires for the 1998 Library Media Center Public School Questionnaire Field Test,* U.S. Census Bureau, Statistical Research Division, Usability Lab, Human-Computer Interaction Memorandum Series #20.

[12] Rao, G. and Hoffman, R. 1999. *Report on Usability Testing of Census Bureaus M3 Web-Based Survey*, U.S. Census Bureau, Statistical Research Division, Usability Lab, Human-Computer Interaction Memorandum Series #26.

[13] Saner, L., Marquis, K., and Murphy B. 2000. *Annual Survey of Manufacturers Usability Testing of Computerized Self-Administered Questionnaire Findings and Recommendations Final Report*, U.S. Census Bureau, Statistical Research Division, Usability Lab, Human-Computer Interaction Memorandum Series #30.

[14] Sweet, E. and Ramos, M. 1995. "Evaluation Results from a Pilot Test of a Computerized Self-Administered Questionnaire (CSAQ) for the 1994 Industrial Research and Development (R&D) Survey," Internal Memorandum. U.S. Census Bureau, Economic Statistical Methods and Programming Division, #ESM-9503.

[15] Tedesco, H., Zukerberg, A., and Nichols, E. 1999. "Designing Surveys for the Next Millennium: Web-based Questionnaire Design Issues," *Proceedings of the Third ASC International Conference*. The University of Edinburgh, Scotland, UK, September 1999, pp. 103-112.

[16] Virzi, R. 1992. "Refining the Test Phase of Usability Evaluation: How Many Subjects Is Enough?," *Human Factors*, 34:457-468.

Table 1. Summary of Interactive Editing Features in U.S. Census Bureau Computerized Self-Administered Questionnaires (CSAQs)

Survey Program [1]	**Type of CSAQ**	**Ratio of edit checks to data-entry fields**	**Kinds of edit checks** [2]	**Timing of the edit-check messages**	**Display of edit-check messages**	**Resolution required to submit?**
R&D	Downloadable	67/205 = 0.33	P, R, M	Immediate, Deferred	Review panel	N
M3	Browser-based	103/58 = 2.43	P, B, R, A, M	Deferred	Highlighted text	N
2002 Economic Census	Downloadable	66/95 = 0.69	B, P, L, M, F	Immediate, Deferred	Icon next to item, review panel	Y (for failure on one edit check)
COS	Downloadable	36/23 = 1.57	P, R, L, M, F, RT	Immediate, Deferred	Pop-up messages, review panel	Y (for a few key edit-check failures)
ASM	Downloadable	Unavailable/88	Unavailable	Immediate, Deferred	Pop-up messages, review panel	N
QFR	Downloadable	29/94 = 0.31	B, P, L, M	Immediate	Icon next to item	N

[1] R&D = Survey of Industrial Research and Development; M3 = Manufacturer's Shipments, Inventories, and Orders Survey; COS = Company Organization Survey; ASM = Annual Survey of Manufactures; QFR = Quarterly Financial Report.

[2] B=Balance, P=Preventive, R=Ratio, L=Logical, A=Alphanumeric, M=Missing value/Incomplete, F=Format, RT=Rounding Test

EDR AND THE IMPACT ON EDITING — A SUMMARY AND A CASE STUDY

By Paula Weir, Energy Information Administration, Department of Energy, United States

1. INTRODUCTION

It has been well documented that data editing is one of the most resource intensive aspects of the survey process, if not *the* most. Much of survey literature and research is dedicated to methodologies, approaches and algorithms focused on defining edit rules and building editing systems with the goal of identify and correcting actual/potential response error. Unfortunately, much less has been written documenting the actual survey performance of the varied editing approaches, and the net effect on data quality. Concerns have frequently been raised that surveys often suffer from over-editing which results in increased respondent burden and frustration from edit failure resolution, introduction of error and bias as edits are resolved, and increased survey processing time and cost. While recognition has been given to the prevention of errors through better survey forms design, respondent instructions, interviewer training, etc., these efforts have been limited in their effect. Data editing as a traditional post-collection process has been challenged to some extent by CATI and CAPI surveys, but now, electronic reporting and internet data collection/web surveys have expanded that challenge through self-administered surveys by providing the potential for editing at data capture by the respondent. The presence and the extent of edits in electronic data reporting through computer self-administered questionnaires (CSAQ) via web surveys, downloadable software, and e-mail attachments that are implemented at the initial data entry and capture, versus those implemented in the traditional data editing stage depend on: the amount of development resources dedicated; the sophistication of the electronic option selected; the security of the transmission that is required; the quality of the data that is required; the amount of respondent burden that is acceptable, and the related concern for increased non-response.

This paper examines the change in electronic data reporting options and usage from 2003 to 2004 for one statistical agency. One fully web-based survey that recently implemented an editing module is then examined in more detail to better understand the respondents' views and use of the edit feature. In particular, for this survey, respondents were asked how they used the edit function, as well as, about the clarity and usefulness of the information provided for edit failures. The responses regarding the edit function for this survey is further compared to a study of the edit log which records information each time the edit function is invoked.

2. RECENT PROGRESS IN ELECTRONIC DATA COLLECTION

A review of surveys conducted by the U.S. Energy Information Administration (EIA) revealed that electronic reporting on 65 surveys had dramatically increased from 2003 to 2004. The U.S. Government Paperwork Elimination Act of 1998 was an encouragement for Federal statistical surveys to move into more electronic modes, but little progress had actually been made in the first years following the Act. However, the discovery of anthrax, which shut down the main post office for government mail, provided the impetus for change for historically mail surveys. The short-run solution of posting surveys in PDF format on EIA's web site, along with facsimile return, kept mail surveys operating, but this crisis-based approach did not represent the most efficient electronic collection method. As a result of the perceived threat to respondents, respondents were ready also to accept more electronic modes of data collection, especially methods for which they had already developed a certain comfort level. After the immediate surge in survey responses via unformatted emails and facsimiles, an alternative method was implemented fairly quickly making use of formatted Word files, or Excel files in the survey form image. To encourage secured reporting, a link was placed directly on the electronic survey form that directed the respondent to secured transmission.

The implementation of the formatted files on EIA's website was successful because respondents felt comfortable with this option. From the respondents' viewpoint, this method was convenient, simple and safe. From EIA's viewpoint, data were received more quickly and forms were more readable. Total or net values were calculated as the respondent entered data on the spreadsheet, so some potential errors were avoided, but very little editing at collection was attempted beyond integrity checks to insure loading of the data to a database. These mostly included automatic totals, checks on field lengths, numeric vs. character, or valid codes (state, month, etc). Despite these limitations, the ease of implementing this option resulted in the number of surveys offering this option increasing 17% from 2003 to 2004. Surprisingly though, of the surveys offering both secured and unsecured transfer options, 86% of the surveys had more respondents choosing unsecured transfer in 2003. But, the number of respondents choosing secured has grown as the number of surveys offering secured transfer has increased approximately 52% in 2004 (from 27 to 41 surveys), as shown in Table 1. Yet, for those surveys that had previously offered secured transfer, only a few of the surveys experienced a large increase in usage of secured transfers, ranging from 18 to 54%, while roughly half of the surveys had more modest increases, and two surveys experienced decreases (ranging from 10 to 20%) in secured transmission usage. This finding is interesting in view of the frequent reference that security concerns are respondents' primary concern about reporting via the Web.

While this electronic option of formatted files on the web has been appealing to the respondents, the benefits have also been limited because of the complexity of data capture. Although some of the surveys utilize a Visual Basic conversion and SQLLLOADER to an Oracle database, many surveys continued to print the electronic responses, and re-key the data into the respective survey processing systems/databases, potentially introducing new errors. This along with limited editing capability has restricted the benefits to the agency of these electronic forms.

Internet data collection (IDC), using a browser-based approach, has become the alternative, requiring more resources to develop, test, and implement. The usage of this reporting option for surveys that offered the option of IDC has been steadily growing as more surveys have provided this option. Most of this growth has occurred in the last year with 20 surveys offering IDC in 2004, compared to 12 in 2003. More importantly, the percent of IDC respondents choosing the IDC option for those surveys has significantly increased. One survey offering this option for the first time realized a 51% usage by respondents, while the other surveys with the IDC option showed an average increase in usage of approximately 40%. One particular series of surveys made a concerted effort to increase electronic reporting, resulting in the achievement of usage rates greater than 50% across their IDC option surveys. The IDC surveys have successfully incorporated editing by respondents using server-side information, such as, respondent's previous period's data. Fatal edits are clearly the most commonly implemented, driven by database requirements. Edit rules that depend on fixed values or within form reported values are the next most commonly implemented. Edit rules that depend on external values, such as, previous period's report require that data be accessible to the respondent at data capture, or quickly returned to the respondent in an interactive mode. Therefore, these edits are more resource intensive to implement and require that security concerns be addressed for confidential data. The surveys with an IDC option vary in approach to the respondent's requirement for edit failure resolution. Some require data correction or edit override with comment (hard edits), while others require no response or action from the respondent (soft edits).

Table 1. Electronic Usage 2003 and 2004

Electronic Method	Number of surveys using method and range of % respondents using method (2003)	Number of surveys using method and range of % respondents using method (2004)	Change in surveys using method from 2003 to 2004	Data Capture?	Editing within electronic collection?
Unformatted e-mail	5	11	120.00%	no	no
	10-90%	.35-100%			
Unsecured transfer Word or Excel file	39	36	-7.69%	no	Only totals
	1-100%	.17-80.8%			
Secured transfer Word or Excel file	27	41	51.85%	some	simple
	1-70%	.16-55%			
Diskette/CD software (e-mail, fax or mail back)	4	9	125.00%	only if diskette is mailed back	yes
	3-57%	1-100%			
PEDRO (mail CD, install and electronic submission) and download software	23	23	0.00%	yes	simple
	1-27%	2.5-51.4%			
Internet	12	20	66.67%	yes	yes
	2-99%	.1-100%			

Despite the increased usage of editing at the data reporting phase, editing is still being performed in the traditional data processing stage for not only non-IDC respondents, but also across respondents from all reporting modes for edits requiring integration of responses, as well as for IDC respondents by-passing the (soft) edit failures. It is important in the survey process that the edits performed are consistent across collection modes, and, that data from all collection modes are integrated and higher level edits performed across respondents, or across surveys as appropriate. This is necessary to optimize the editing process, in an attempt to not only prevent error in the most effective manner by exploiting the respondents' knowledge at data capture, but also continue to draw on the more comprehensive information available for validation at post-collection. Some balance of the two phases of editing is viewed as optimal for improving efficiency and data accuracy without negative side effects on response rates, particularly for mixed mode data surveys.

3. CASE STUDY

Editing in Internet surveys has brought about a new set of issues and concerns. In addition to the traditional problem of determining the most effective and efficient edit rules, the internet survey edit process has to address how and when to invoke the edits to maximize data quality and minimize respondent break-off. Should the edits be performed after each data item is entered or after all items have been entered? Should hard edits be used requiring the respondent to take action, or soft edits to alert the respondent but require no action? How should the edit failures be presented—in a separate window or directly on the data entry/survey instrument screen? Should the edit failures be presented one at a time or all together? Edit messages take on a different role than in traditional editing, communicating directly with the respondent and taking on the role or "social presence" of the interviewer in resolving an edit failure. These messages need to be written in simple, non-confrontational language, and convey meaning to which the respondent can relate and take the appropriate action. How much information should be conveyed with the edit failures?

One fully web-based survey that recently had implemented an editing module was examined in terms of the how the respondents used the edit feature in reporting. In this survey, State officials are the respondents who reported prices charged by the sampled businesses operating in their State. The overall reaction to the new edit, which identified businesses whose price change since the previous report was out of range, was very positive. The edit module was intended to be invoked by the respondent after all the data for that period had been entered. The system required the edit to be run prior to submission, but did not require the respondent to make any changes to the flagged data prior to submitting the data. Respondents were encouraged to provide comments on the edit failures but were not required to do so. The system, however, actually allowed the respondents to "Review Prices Before Submit", thereby running the edit, at any point in their data entry. This was an area of concern because the edit rule was based on the mean change of all the prices that were entered, and different expectations for editing would result if run on partial data. After respondents had used the edit feature in the IDC for four reporting periods, they were sent a questionnaire asking five basic questions regarding the new function exploring: 1) when they invoke the price review/edit; 2) the process they use once the review screen is displayed (ignore, recall companies, etc); 3) their understanding of the information provided on the review screen; 4) the navigation between the review screen and the main survey screen for error correction; 5) other comments or suggestions regarding the edit function and the review screen.

Figure 1. Main Screen

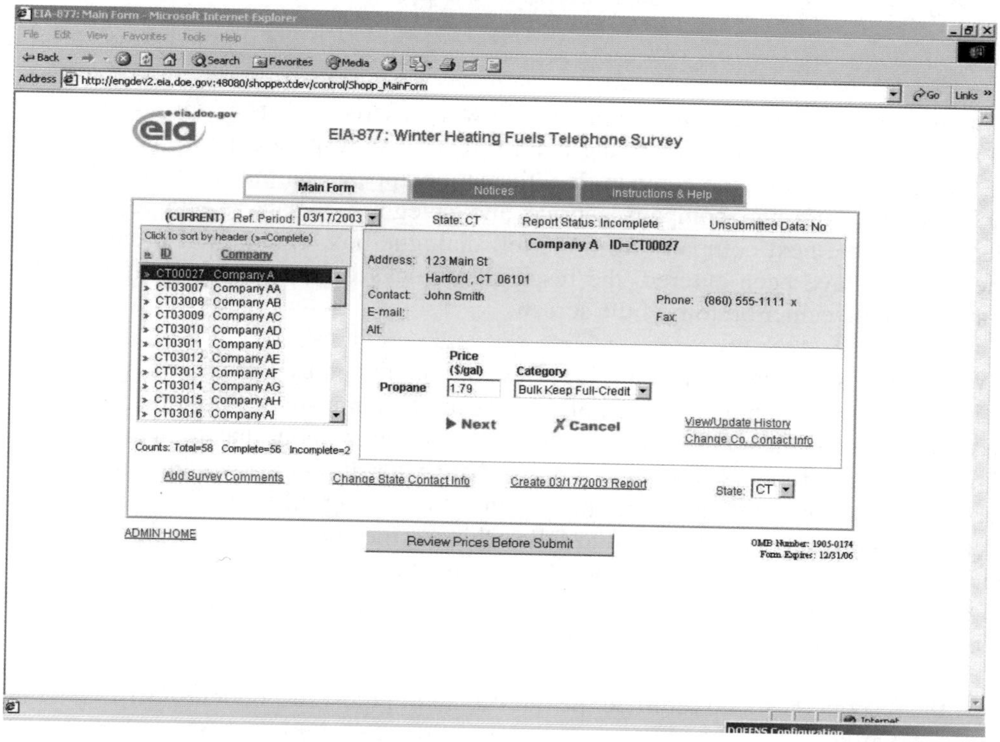

Figure 2. Review Screen

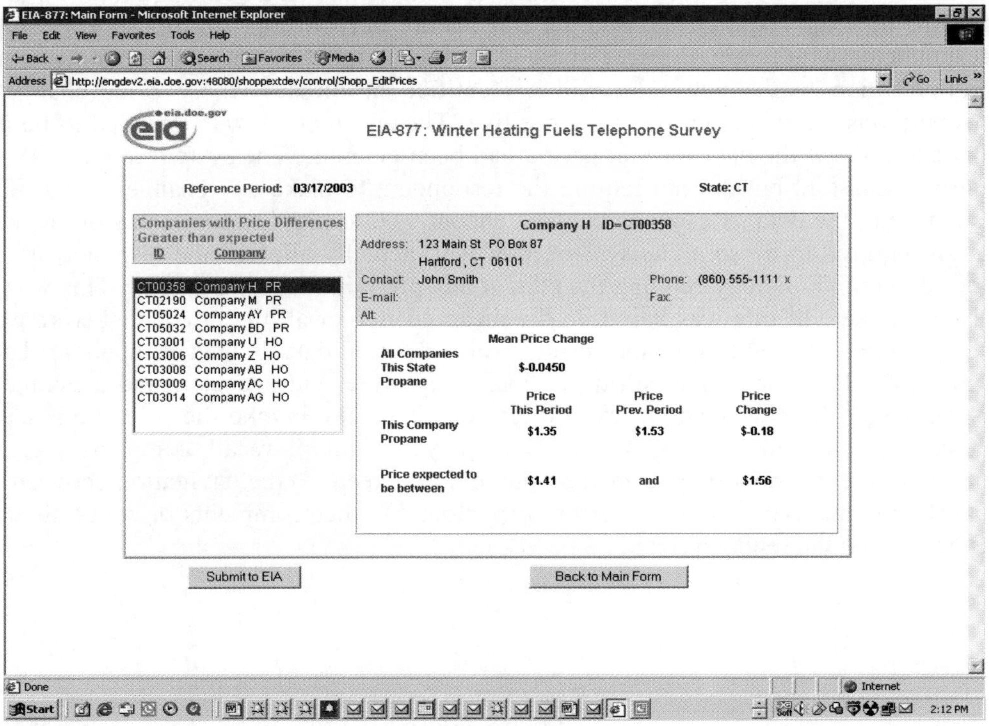

In order to better understand the process flow, two screen prints are provided. The first screen (figure 1) shows the data entry screen, the main screen. The respondent selects a company from the dialogue box on the left, and the company's information appears on the right side of the screen along with the boxes to enter the company's price and category of sale. After entering a price, the respondent selects the next company from the left dialogue box, enters their price, etc. Once all the companies' prices have been entered, the respondent clicks on the "Review Prices Before Submit" button located on the center bottom of the screen.

When the respondent clicks on this review button, the edit failures are displayed in the second screen (figure 2) shown. On the left side of the screen, the companies whose prices failed the edit are displayed. As the respondent clicks on a company, information about that company is displayed to the right. This information includes the mean price change for all companies in that State, the previous and current period's price, and the price change since the last period for the company selected, and the price interval the company was expected to fall within for the current period. To make a change to the data, the respondent clicks on the "Back to Main Form" button shown in the figure at the bottom right to return to the data entry screen. If no data changes are needed, the respondent clicks on the "Submit to EIA" button at the bottom left to send the data to EIA.

Of the respondents who returned the questionnaire, most respondents (86.7%) indicated that they ran the edit after all prices had been entered, just prior to submission of the data, as shown in Table 2. However, a few respondents (12.5%) indicated that they invoked the edit when an individual company's data seemed anomalous. Similarly, a few respondents indicated they used their own method outside the system to review the data, frequently making use of a longer historical series than just the previous period, or compared price changes to a fixed amount they had set. The respondents also varied as to their process for reviewing the prices flagged by the IDC edit.

Table 2. Edit Function Questionnaire Results

Q1. When invoked (can check more than one):	
After each entry	0%
After some but not all entries	12.5%
After all entries	86.7%
Other	20.0%
Q2. Process for review flagged entries (can check more than one):	
Ignore	25.0%
Review one-by-one, calling and correcting	25.0%
Review by noting outside system, call all, correct all, review again, then submit	25.0%
Review by noting outside system, call all, correct all, then submit (no final review)	6.7%
Other	25.0%
Q3. Understand:	
Why failed	80.0%
Mean change	80.0%
Mean includes only entered data	73.3%
Flagged company information	86.7%
Expect company value	86.7%
Q4. Is navigation to/from review screen a problem?	
No	100%

Finding One: Approximately 25% of the respondents reported that they ignored the information provided regarding the failed prices. Another (25%) reviewed the information for each failed company one at a time, verifying the information and correcting as necessary by returning to the main screen, before proceeding to the next flagged company. On the other hand, 31% of the respondents make note (outside of the system) of the edit failure information provided and then follow-up. Of particular concern is the finding that 25% of the respondents ignore the edit, and 7% perform no second review of edit failures after corrections are made in the main file, prior to submitting the data, despite the fact that that the re-edit information is presented to them on the submit (review) screen.

Finding Two: Also of interest is the finding that 87% of the respondents understand the information regarding the particular company's price that failed, and, in particular, the information regarding the company's reported price this and last period, and also understand the expected interval for the company's price for this period. Yet, only 80% understand why the price failed the edit, and understand the information on mean price change of all companies they report for. Furthermore, only 80% understand that the mean price change represents only the prices that were entered at the point at which the review button was hit. These last two findings can be used to further interpret the 87% --- 87% understand that the price is expected to fall within the specified interval, but a few of those respondents do not understand *why* the price should be within the interval, and therefore, do not understand *why* the price failed.

Finding Three: All the respondents reported that the navigation between the review screen and the main form (in order to correct a price) was not a problem for them. This finding was curious in view of the first finding that 20% of the respondents indicated that they flip back and forth between the main screen and the review screen for each company (after having entered all or most of the data), and that 33% of the respondents record information from the review screen to another location outside the system to further evaluate the data.

Each time the respondent selects the "Review Prices Before Submit" button, the edit failures that are displayed are also written to an error log. This log records for each edit failure the individual company's data, the reference period, the time the edit was invoked, and whether the price failed as too high or too low. This log was analyzed for the first twelve reference periods. A summary of the edit failures written to the log is shown in Table 3.

As mentioned previously, each time the respondent clicks the "Review Prices Before Submit" button, each of the edit failures is written to the error log, regardless of whether the edit failure had been written before, as long as the price still failed the edit rule. Therefore, the number of failed records shown in Table 3 reflects the number of times the button was hit times the number of failures at that time. Even though this created a large number of virtually duplicate records written, that characteristic of the log made it useful for tracking and measuring the respondents' process flow. The number of first time failures shown in Table 3 was derived from the log to measure the set of unique edit failures. If the same set of failures occur each time the review button is clicked, then the ratio of the number of failed records to unique records indicates the number of times respondents went to the main screen from the review screen, and returned to the review screen. Across both products, respondents clicked on the review button an average of 5.7 times per reference period, but the rate by respondent and product varied from a low of 1.5 times to a high of 11.8 times review clicks, averaged across reference periods. These respondent rates for changing screens were further compared to the respondent average rate for edit failures to shed light on the respondent's process for invoking the edit and resolving the edit.

Table 3. Summary of Edit Failure Log

PRODUCT	PRICE HI or LO	Data	Total	Avg/ wk.	Avg # Failures	Avg. # Screen Changes	Screen Changes/ Failure
Heating Oil	H	# Failed records	3478	289.8	13.2		
		# Changed and fail again	1		0.0		
		# First time failures	584	48.7	2.2	6.0	2.7
	L	# Failed records	4410	367.5	16.7		
		# Changed and fail again	5		0.0		
		# First time failures	728	60.7	2.8	6.1	2.2
Heating Oil # Failed records			7888	657.3	29.9		
Heating Oil # Changed and fail again			6	0.5	0.0		
Heating Oil # First time failures			1312	109.3	5.0	6.0	1.2
Propane	H	# Failed records	3841	320.1	13.3		
		# Changed and fail again	19	1.6	0.1		
		# First time failures	705	58.8	2.4	5.4	2.2
	L	# Failed records	2722	226.8	9.5		
		# Changed and fail again	13	1.1	0.0		
		# First time failures	504	42.0	1.8	5.4	3.1
Propane # Failed records			6563	546.9	22.8		
Propane # Changed and fail again			32	2.7	0.1		
Propane # First time failures			1209	100.8	4.2	5.4	1.3
Total # Failed records			14451	1204.3	50.2		
Total # Changed and fail again			38	3.2	0.1		
Total # First time failures			2521	210.1	4.4	5.7	1.3

The average respondent failure rate across both products was 4.4, compared to the 5.7 screen change rate, but again, the failure rate varied by product and respondent from a low of 1.4 failures to a high of 10 failures averaged across reference periods. The average number of screen changes per edit failure is displayed in the last column of Table 3. This shows a rate of 1.3 screen changes per failure overall, indicating that on average, the respondents return to the main screen one or more times per failure. This finding at first would lead one to think the respondents are viewing the edit failures one at a time and returning to the main screen to apply a correction. However, in general, this is not the case, because when the respondent returns to the review screen, the same edit failures with no data changes appear for the most part. What the log of failures can not show, however, is the possibility that respondents return to the main screen and enter new data that do not fail nor impact the previously failed data sufficiently to change their edit failure status.

The screen change rates per edit failure were also compared to the findings from the questionnaire. Comparing the screen change to failure rates to the responses to question 2, we find for the respondents who answered that they ignored the information provided on the review screen, their screen changes to failure rates, lower than most, as determined from the log ranged from .2 to 1.3 failures per response period, across the products. Clearly, these respondents do not go back and forth from review to main for each edit failure, but they are using the review button more than would be expected, given that they said they ignored the information.

Similarly, we can compare information for the other extreme of respondents who reported on the questionnaire that they reviewed the information for each failed company one at a time, verifying the information and correcting as necessary by returning to the main screen, before proceeding to the next flagged company. This would imply screen changes to failure rates of 1.0 or greater. These respondents would be expected to have the largest screen changes to failure rates. The log showed that one of these respondents had a rate less than expected of only .6, but the remaining respondents ranged from 1.2 to 3.0 screen changes per edit failure across the two products.

Those respondents that reported making a note (outside of the system) and then following-up on the edit failures had, in general, the highest rates, ranging from 1.1 to 5.1 screen changes per failure across the products.

The concern regarding the finding that only 80% of the respondents to the questionnaire understood that the mean price change represents only the prices that were entered at the point at which the review button was hit was investigated. Review of the individual respondent logs for the 20% that did not understand showed that most of these respondents (75%) had very high screen changes per edit failure and showed evidence of editing data based on partial information, thereby effecting the edit rule and resulting failures. The logs for these respondents did not show the same set of edit failures each time the review screen was clicked. As expected, this was particularly true of the subset of respondents who had also answered on the questionnaire that they invoked the edit after each/some entries were made, but not all entries.

Further study of the edit failure log by reference period by create date revealed that a substantial number of the records were created after preliminary estimation by the survey, and some even after final estimation (one week after the preliminary estimate). The separation of failures by preliminary and final estimates' dates is now highlighted as an area of future study. Future research will also include an examination of the logs to determine the efficacy of the edit rule, and examination by company to highlight repeat failure companies to discover whether the data are repeatedly reported erroneously, or the edit rule is not appropriate for them.

4. CONCLUSIONS

While substantial progress has been made in EDR, both in the number of surveys providing the option and the increased usage of the option by respondents, significant work remains in developing and EDR editing strategy. The strategy must recognize the balance of possibly conflicting quality goals of maximizing the use of the EDR option by respondents, and minimizing the errors on the submitted data. The EDR strategy must take into account when/if to use hard or soft edits, when to invoke the edit in the data entry process, how to present messages regarding the edit failures, and how to navigate efficiently to correct errors and/or submit the data. The use of cognitive testing and respondent interviews/questionnaires are useful in designing an EDR editing strategy or improving an EDR editing approach already in use.

EDR expands the "self-administered" role of the respondents to include their interaction with the edit process. As a result, new indicators on the performance of the edit process must be constructed and analyzed. As demonstrated in this case study, logs generated by the respondent actions are useful not only in measuring the performance of the edit rules, or to validate information obtained by cognitive testing or questionnaires, but just as importantly, as hard evidence on how the respondents actually use the edit process. This case study demonstrated that understanding the respondent process of how and when the edit is invoked, and how and when the failures are resolved may impact the resulting edit failures, which in turn effect the quality of the data.

References

[1] Best, Sam (2004): "Implications of Interactive Editing", FCSM-GSS Workshop on Web Based Data Collection, Washington, D.C.

[2] Nicholls, W.L. II, Baker, R.P., & Martin, J. (1997): "The Effect of New Data Collection Technologies on Survey Data Quality" in L. Lyberg, P. Biemer, M. Collins, C. Dippo, N. Schwarz, & D. Trewin (editors) *Survey Measurement and Process Quality.* New York: Wiley.

[3] Weir, Paula (2003): *Electronic Data Reporting—Moving Editing Closer to the Respondent,* UN/ECE Work Session on Statistical Data Editing, Madrid.

[4] http://www.eia.doe.gov/oil_gas/petroleum/survey_forms/pet_survey_forms.html

[5] http://www.eia.doe.gov/cneaf/electricity/page/forms.html

[6] http://www.eia.doe.gov/cneaf/electricity/edc/contents.html

EDR IMPACTS ON EDITING

By Ignacio Arbues, Manuel Gonzalez, Margarita Gonzalez, José Quesada and Pedro Revilla, National Statistics Institute, Spain

1. INTRODUCTION

Electronic Data Reporting (EDR) and, in particular, Web surveys offer the opportunity for new editing strategies. Moving editing closer to the respondent can significantly contribute to improving editing effectiveness. We can go a step further by integrating the respondents into the editing processes. Electronic questionnaires offer new possibilities of moving editing closer to the respondent. The possibility of using built-in edits allows respondents to avoid errors as they are made. The elimination of data keying at the statistical agency directly gets rid of a common source of error. Hence, some of the traditional editing tasks could be reduced.

Many statistical institutes are offering electronic questionnaires as a voluntary option in order to improve the efficiency of statistical processes and to reduce respondent burden. Hence, a mixed mode of data collection (partly paper, partly electronic) is used. Global strategies should be designed, because data editing strategies may differ when using paper than when using an electronic questionnaire. Some crucial questions arise: What kind of edits should be implemented on the electronic forms? How many? Only fatal edits or fatal edits and query edits? What kind of edits should be mandatory?

Like many other statistical institutes, the National Statistical Institute of Spain (INE) has a significant interest in Web-based data reporting. An example of this was the possibility offered to all citizens to fill in the Population Census 2001 using the Internet. The INE is working on a general project of giving reporting enterprises the option of submitting their responses to statistical surveys using the Internet. A major target of this project is to offer the reporting enterprises another option to fill in the questionnaires, in the hope of reducing respondent burden, or, at least, improving our relationship with them.

While there are a lot of expectations about the role of Web questionnaires in the years to come, the use of Web questionnaires is often lower than expected. More research is needed to look for the reasons why the rate of using electronic questionnaires is quite low, while technical conditions are available for many of the respondents. Probably, the electronic forms do not have as many advantages for the respondents as for the statistical offices. For this reason, encouraging the use of Web questionnaires by respondents is a key issue. Several methods can be used. For example, explaining the benefits to the respondents or considering statistical Web questionnaires in a wider context of all administrative duties and all EDR (e-commerce, e-administration, etc.). Given incentives (temporary access to information, free deliveries of tailored data) is another method to increase the take-up of Web questionnaires.

This paper explores the possibilities of Web questionnaires in order to reduce editing tasks. The combination of built-in edits and selective editing approach appears very promising. Our target for the future is that, after implementing correct Web edits, no traditional microediting will be needed. Some practical experiences in the Spanish Monthly Turnover and New Orders Survey are presented. For this survey, we offer tailored data from the Web. When an enterprise sends a valid form, it immediately receives tailored data from the server. Taking this advantage into account, we expect more enterprises to use the Web survey.

In the following section, the challenges and opportunities of electronic questionnaires are discussed. In section 3, some practical experiences are presented. The paper concludes with some final remarks.

2. CHALLENGES AND OPPORTUNITIES OF ELECTRONIC QUESTIONNAIRES

Web surveys offer new opportunities on moving editing closer to respondents. Whereas Computer Assisted Interviewing (CAI) integrates into one step previously distinct phases such as interviewing, data capture and editing, Web surveys go a step further by shifting such activities to the respondent. Hence, Web surveys offer the opportunity for re-engineering editing processes, in a way reporting enterprises may play a more active role in data editing.

Many statistical offices are experimenting with the use of different EDR options in data collection. Web surveys offer some advantages over other more complex EDR methods. The Web is a mature technology for EDR because of widespread public acceptance in enterprises and institutions (and increasingly, also in households). The prerequisites are only a PC, access to the Internet, and a browser. There is no need, in principle, to incorporate other software on the reporting enterprises. The Web makes it simple to put electronic forms at the disposal of almost every enterprise, whatever its size.

Several advantages could be expected from using Web surveys. These include improving accuracy and timeliness, and reducing survey cost and enterprise burden. Improving accuracy results from built-in edits, which allow the reporting enterprises to avoid errors as they are made. The elimination of data keying at the statistical agency directly gets rid of a common source of error. Moreover, this elimination of data keying reduces the processing time of the survey. There are other factors that can also contribute to improve timeliness. Data transfer on the Web can be done much faster than using the postal system. Some electronic devises (automatic data fills and calculations, automatic skipping of no applicable questions, etc.) could help the respondent to fill in the questionnaire faster. The cost for statistical offices to carry out a survey using the Web could decrease. Savings could be achieved from reducing storage, packing, postal charges and eliminating data keying and keying verification. Some of the editing task could be reduced from built-in edits.

Nevertheless, to get the target of reducing enterprise burden using Web surveys is not so straightforward. The reduction in the enterprise burden is not always obvious. The respondents' benefits depend largely on the way metadata support the respondent in filling in the questionnaire (help texts, auto-fill rules, pre-filled data, etc). In any case, the respondents' benefits need to be clearly explained to convince them to use the Web questionnaire. An important element to improve the acceptance of Web surveys among reporting enterprises is to consider Web questionnaires in a wider context of all their administrative duties and of all electronic data reporting. It is unlikely that reporting enterprises are willing to adapt their systems only for statistical purposes. Hence, statistical offices should be aware of the habits of respondents and try to adapt electronic questionnaires to these trends (for example, e-commerce, e-administration, etc.).

There are a lot of expectations about the role of Web surveys in the years to come. Nevertheless, the implementation of Web surveys and other EDR methods in enterprise surveys (and, even more, in household surveys) has often been lower than expected. The take-up of electronic data reporting for statistical data by business providers is generally less than 10%, and often less than 5% (Branson 2002). Other studies also find low rates of response via Internet. For example, Grandjean (2002) finds a rate of 18% for a survey used to construct the Index of Industrial Production in France. Different rates are found in this study by enterprise size (higher for large enterprises than for small and medium ones) and by sectors (for example, electronic and electric industries more than the average, furniture industries less than the average). In another study, Mayda (2002) finds a rate between 5% and 25% in two quarterly surveys on business and agriculture in Canada. Even though the usage of the electronic option by respondents has increased lately (for example, Paula Weir, 2005) it still leaves room for improvement.

More research is needed to look for the reasons why, up to now, the rate of using EDR is quite low, while technical requirements are available for many of the respondents. Probably, electronic forms have not the same advantages for the reporting enterprises than for the statistical offices. For many of the questionnaires, the most time consuming tasks are to look for the required data and computing the answers. There is no time difference between keying data on a screen and to fill in a questionnaire on paper. The advantages for the reporting enterprises would probably be bigger if the information could be extracted straight from their files. But this procedure may be expensive for both reporting enterprises and statistical agencies, because an initial investment is needed.

In any case, for most of the surveys, it is clear that, at the moment, EDR cannot be the only way of data collection. Paper data collection and associated procedures (like scanning) are probably going to stay with us for some years. Hence, a mixed mode of data collection (partly paper, partly electronic) should be used. Global strategies should be designed, because data editing strategies differ when using paper to an electronic questionnaire.

There are two contradictory targets – on the one hand, to implement a single point of entry for all agency surveys, with a uniform security model and a common look across the entire site and, on the other hand, to allow decentralized applications to cope surveys singularities. One aspect where the difference among surveys has to be taken into account is data editing. Combining the two targets (i.e. integrating a centralized platform with decentralized applications) is a non-trivial task.

Some crucial questions arise: What kind of edits should be implemented on the Web? How many? Only fatal edits or fatal edits and query edits? What kind of edits should be mandatory? When should the edits be performed? After each data item or after the whole form has been sent to the server?

On one hand, we need to include some edits. If we do not, then the information collected by a Web survey should be treated to the editing procedures in exactly the same way as collected by paper. In that case, we would lose an essential advantage of Web surveys: no need to editing again the information with a suitable set of edits implemented in the Web application. On the other hand, we need to be extremely careful with the set of edits to be implemented in the Web survey, because if we implement a big set, then respondents will give up and prefer the freedom they have in paper. Too many edits could even irritate the reporting enterprises and increase the burden. In that case we will lose all the advantages of Web surveys, as users will prefer the easy way (paper).

How to cope with the too few/too many edits dilemma? If we are trying to implement a Web questionnaire in an existing survey, a way is to analyse the current set of edits in order to determine the efficient set of edits to be used in the Web implementation. Hence, the implementation of new procedures obliges to the revision and redesign of the current procedures of the survey. But we should make that revision from the user's point of view. Otherwise, it would be impossible to find out if the users are going to get fed up with the task of filling in a Web form or not. It must be stressed that making that sort of analysis is strictly necessary in order to implement a suitable set of edits that will not discourage users and that will make possible not to edit the Web information in the traditional paper way.

In order to achieve this target an analysis similar to that of Martin and Poirier (2002) should be carried out. It is important to have procedures allowing access to versions of data and additional processing metadata that describe how the data were transformed from collection to dissemination.

3. SPANISH EXPERIENCES ON WEB SURVEYS: THE TURNOVER AND NEW ORDERS SURVEY

Like many others statistical agencies, the INE has a significant interest in Web-based data reporting. An example of this was the possibility offered to all citizens to fill in the Population Census 2001 using the Internet. The INE is working in a general project of giving respondents the option of submitting their responses to statistical surveys using the Internet. A major target of this project is to offer the respondents another option to fill in the questionnaires, in the hope of reducing respondent burden, or, at least, improving our relationship with them.

Moreover, an ad hoc prototype Web system to collect establishment data for the Turnover and New Orders Survey is also being implemented. This monthly survey uses a very simple form. Many problems using the Internet might be due to the various configurations and products installed on the respondents' machine. Each respondent's computer can have different components, different versions of operating systems and browsers, and different modem speeds. For this reason, and from using a very simple form, all the programs are going to be run through the server, without the need to install any software on the respondents' computer.

The Web form is being offered to the sample of reporting enterprises as a voluntary option to respond to the Survey. We think that, probably, many enterprises will not change to the Web form. For this reason, we offer tailored data to them. When an enterprise sends a valid form (i.e. passing the mandatory edits), it immediately receives tailored data from the server. These tailored data consist of tables and graphs showing the enterprise trend and its position in relation with its sector. Offering this data through the Web has some advantages (speed, possibility to edit the file) over sending this same data on paper by mail. Taking these advantages into account, we expect more enterprises to use the Web survey.

A. Editing in the New Orders/Turnover Industrial Survey

A monthly survey provides data to publish the Short Term Indicators of Industrial New Orders and Turnover. The sample size is of about 13,200 local units, for which 14 variables are requested:

- Orders: Total new orders, domestic market, eurozone non-domestic, European Union non-eurozone, non-EU, stock at the beginning of the month, cancelled orders, orders invoiced and stock at the end of the month.

- Turnover: Total turnover, domestic market, eurozone non-domestic, European Union non-eurozone, non-EU.

Hereafter, the variables Total Turnover and total New Orders will be referred as 'main variables'. Since these variables are used for the computation of the indices, they receive a different, more exacting, editing process. When in the future, new indices are calculated, e.g. for the different markets, more variables will have the same consideration.

The data is collected in three different ways: a little more than 90% of the sample is collected by the local offices of the INE, about 8% is obtained directly by the national headquarters and from January 2005 a web reporting system (WRS) is working experimentally.

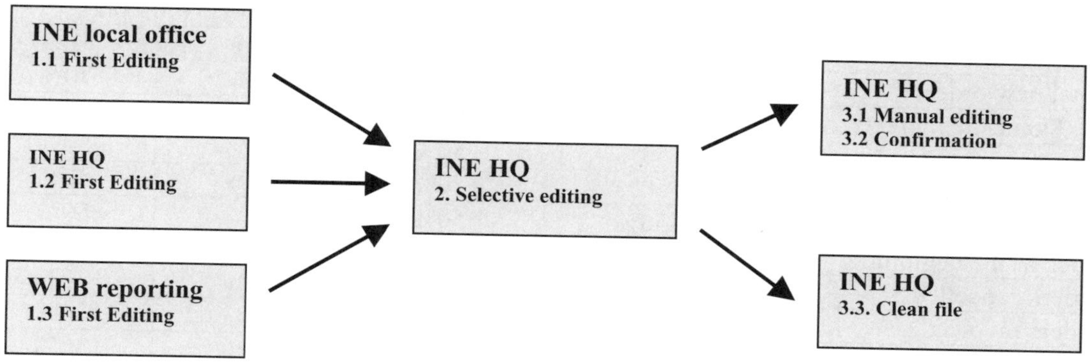

Figure 1 Microediting scheme

B. First editing of paper questionnaires

The processes 1.1 and 1.2 are very similar, since the edits implemented are the same. The main differences are due to the closeness of the 1.2 editing team to the people in charge of the calculation of the indices and the fact that the same team performs also phase 3. Thus, the result of 1.2 is intended to be more reliable, since the team receives a more direct feedback from the computations and analysis done with the edited microdata. Moreover, the team in 1.2 is more specialized (working only in this survey) and more qualified (university degree).

The interest of having this data collecting channel in the INE headquarters is to guarantee the quality of the data from some enterprises of great importance for the computation of the indices.

Two kinds of edits are distinguished in **phases 1.1 and 1.2**: type I and type II.
I edits are mandatory, checking that:

- There are no non-numeric characters and the values are within the range [0,9999999999]. The upper value is due to the format of the files used for transmitting the data. Negative values are not allowed.
- All the variables are reported.
- The market desegregation sums up to the main variables.
- The stock at the end of the month equals the stock at the beginning plus new orders received, minus orders cancelled, minus orders invoiced.

II edits are not mandatory. The only effect is that the person in charge of recording the questionnaire is forced to type a remark. These edits check that:

- The stock of orders at the end of the month equals the stock at the beginning of the next month. This edit was decided to be non-mandatory because some enterprises argued that due to price changes, the value of the stock is recalculated when passing from one month to another.
- The change rate of any variable is within a defined range. The rates are computed comparing the current value with those of the previous month and the same month of previous year. The intervals are described in Table 1. It should be noted that they are very narrow, so there is an important risk that the frequency of errors, most of them unnecessary, makes the staff keying the questionnaires to type standard remarks which are of no use to the subsequent process.

Variable	Previous month		Previous year	
	Min	Max	Min	Max
Total new orders	-30%	+30%	-30%	+30%
Domestic market	-50%	+50%	-50%	+50%
Eurozone non-domestic	-50%	+50%	-50%	+50%
EU non-eurozone	-50%	+50%	-50%	+50%
Non-EU	-50%	+50%	-50%	+50%
Stock at the beginning	-30%	+30%	-30%	+30%
Orders cancelled	-30%	+30%	-30%	+30%
Orders invoiced	-30%	+30%	-30%	+30%
Stock at the end	-30%	+30%	-30%	+30%
Total Turnover	-30%	+30%	-30%	+30%
Domestic market	-50%	+500%	-50%	+500%
Eurozone non-domestic	-50%	+500%	-50%	+500%
EU non-eurozone	-50%	+500%	-50%	+500%
Non-EU	-50%	+500%	-50%	+500%

Table 1

C. First editing in the web reporting system

The process in the **web reporting system 1.3** is somewhat different. The mandatory edits are the same but for the fact that some variables in the market desegregation are allowed to remain blank. In this case, the system assumes that their real values are zero (which implies that the remaining variables sum up to the total value reported).

There is a strongly reduced list of informative errors, since the change rates are checked only for the main variables. The ranges also differ between the annual and monthly rates and are much broader. The larger width of the monthly intervals is due to the seasonality of some series. A further difference is that in this case, the remarks are optional. The ranges are described in Table 2.

Variable	Previous month		Previous year	
	Min	Max	Min	Max
Total New Order	-99%	+9800%	-90%	+4000%
Total Turnover	-99%	+9800%	-90%	+4000%

Table 2

D. Selective editing

The questionnaires from the 1.1, 1.2 and 1.3 proceed to phase 2. Some questionnaires are selected for manual editing according to the following criteria:

- Strong **variation** from the previous values.
- **Influence** on the value of the branch indices, i.e., the value of the index is very different depending on whether the microdata is used in the calculation or not.

E. Variation

At this stage, the microdata files are augmented with two flags indicating whether the variation rates of the main variables exceed some limits. There is one flag for each main variable which activates if any of the ranges is exceeded. The limits are the ones in Table 2. In fact, these ranges were applied to the web reporting system after being used for selective editing. One aim of the experiment is to know if the fact that the reporter is warned of the values exceeding the limits allows a relaxed later editing.

When the flag is activated, the microdata is not used in the computation of the index unless it is validated in the phase 3 of the editing scheme. Otherwise, the data is considered as validated, so it is used in for the computations, unless its validity is revoked in phase3.

F. Influence

The influence is computed in a different way depending on whether the variation flag is activated or not.

- In the first case, the aim of computing influence is to **know the effect of validating the microdata**. Thus, we compare the monthly rate of the branch with and without the microdata. By compaing the variation rate instead of the index, we remove the effect of the index level, which can be very different between activities.

- In the second case, the influence has a further function, that is **to detect anomalous values**. Thus, due to the seasonality of many series, it proved more useful to compare the annual rate on the branch with the one obtained **removing the value** under analysis from the **current total** (month t) and removing the value of previous year to the corresponding total (month t-12).

The first influence is easy to calculate. We compute the variation rates:

$$V^M = \frac{\sum_j \widehat{x}^t_{i,j}}{\sum_j \breve{x}^{t-1}_{i,j}} \qquad V^M_k = \frac{x^t_{i,k} + \sum_j \widehat{x}^t_{i,j}}{x^{t-1}_{i,k} + \sum_j \breve{x}^{t-1}_{i,j}}$$

EQ1

- V^M is the monthly rate of variation with all data and V^M_k is the rate obtained adding the value under analysis.
- $\widehat{x}^t_{i,j}$ is the value of unit *j* in activity *i* at time *t*, among the validated units common to time *t-1*.
- $\breve{x}^t_{i,j}$ is the value of unit *j* in activity *i* at time *t*, among the validated units common to time *t+1*.
- $x^t_{i,k}$ is the value of the (non-validated) unit under analysis *k* in activity *i* at time *t*.

The influence thus, is computed as:

$$I^M_k = 100 \times \left(V^M_k - V^M\right)$$

EQ2

The influence measure used for the validated microdata involves more complex calculations. The following formulae are used:

$$V^A = \prod_{s=1}^{12} \frac{\sum_j \widehat{x}_{i,j}^{t-s+1}}{\sum_j \breve{x}_{i,j}^{t-s}} \qquad V_k^A = \frac{\sum_{j\neq k} \widehat{x}_{i,j}^{t}}{\sum_j \breve{x}_{i,j}^{t-1}} \left(\prod_{s=2}^{11} \frac{\sum_j \widehat{x}_{i,j}^{t-s+1}}{\sum_j \breve{x}_{i,j}^{t-s}} \right) \frac{\sum_j \widehat{x}_{i,j}^{t-11}}{\sum_{j\neq k} \breve{x}_{i,j}^{t-12}}$$

EQ3

Where:

- V^A is the yearly rate of variation with all data and V_k^A is the rate obtained removing values as explained above.
- $\widehat{x}_{i,j}^t$ is the value of unit *j* in activity *i* at time *t*, among the validated units common to time *t-1*.
- $\breve{x}_{i,j}^t$ is the value of unit *j* in activity *i* at time *t*, among the validated units common to time *t+1*.

Thus, the influence can be computed as:

$$I_k = 100 \times \left(V^A - V_k^A\right)$$

EQ4

G. Interpretation of the influence

We can express the monthly influence in a different form:

$$I_k^M = 100 \times \left(\frac{x_{i,k}^t + \sum_j \widehat{x}_{i,j}^t}{x_{i,k}^{t-1} + \sum_j \breve{x}_{i,j}^{t-1}} - \frac{\sum_j \widehat{x}_{i,j}^t}{\sum_j \breve{x}_{i,j}^{t-1}} \right) = 100 \times \frac{\left(x_{i,k}^t + \sum_j \widehat{x}_{i,j}^t\right)\sum_j \breve{x}_{i,j}^{t-1} - \left(x_{i,k}^{t-1} + \sum_j \breve{x}_{i,j}^{t-1}\right)\sum_j \widehat{x}_{i,j}^t}{\left(x_{i,k}^{t-1} + \sum_j \breve{x}_{i,j}^{t-1}\right)\left(\sum_j \breve{x}_{i,j}^{t-1}\right)}$$

If the value of $x_{i,k}^{t-1}$ is small compared with the total $\sum_j \breve{x}_{i,j}^{t-1}$, we can make the approximation:

$$I_k^M \cong 100 \times \frac{\left(x_{i,k}^t + \sum_j \widehat{x}_{i,j}^t\right)\sum_j \breve{x}_{i,j}^{t-1} - \left(x_{i,k}^{t-1} + \sum_j \breve{x}_{i,j}^{t-1}\right)\sum_j \widehat{x}_{i,j}^t}{\left(\sum_j \breve{x}_{i,j}^{t-1}\right)^2} = 100 \times \frac{x_{i,k}^t \sum_j \breve{x}_{i,j}^{t-1} - x_{i,k}^{t-1} \sum_j \widehat{x}_{i,j}^t}{\left(\sum_j \breve{x}_{i,j}^{t-1}\right)^2} =$$

$$= 100 \times \frac{x_{i,k}^{t-1}}{\sum_j \breve{x}_{i,j}^{t-1}} \left(\frac{x_{i,k}^t}{x_{i,k}^{t-1}} - \frac{\sum_j \widehat{x}_{i,j}^t}{\sum_j \breve{x}_{i,j}^{t-1}} \right)$$

EQ5

Thus, the influence is approximately equal to the **weight of the unit** *j* in *t-1*, multiplied by the **difference between the rates of variation** of the unit and of the whole branch.

In a similar way, for the annual influence we can compute:

$$I_k^A \cong 100 \times A \frac{x_{i,k}^{t-12}}{\sum_j \breve{x}_{i,j}^{t-12}} \left(\frac{x_{i,k}^{t}}{x_{i,k}^{t-12}} - \frac{\sum_j \widehat{x}_{i,j}^{t}}{\sum_j \breve{x}_{i,j}^{t-12}} \right)$$

Where:

$$A = \left(\sum_j \breve{x}_{i,j}^{t-1} \right)^{-1} \left(\prod_{s=2}^{11} \frac{\sum_j \widehat{x}_{i,j}^{t-s+1}}{\sum_j \breve{x}_{i,j}^{t-s}} \right) \sum_j \widehat{x}_{i,j}^{t-11}$$

The factor A is common for all units k, so it has no effect for comparison between the units of a branch.

H. Selection

The questionnaires are then distributed according to Table 3.

CASE	EDITING
Validated	The microdata with greater influence are selected for manual editing. The threshold is decided by the editing team depending on several criteria, such as the weight of the branch and results from the macro editing.
Non-Validated and Monthly influence in [-1%,1%]	The microdata are edited manually one by one.
Non-Validated and Monthly influence out of [-1%,1%]	Confirmation with the reporting enterprise is requested.

4. FINAL REMARKS

A prerequisite of any editing strategy is obtaining high quality incoming data. The problem of how to get high quality incoming data can be faced from the perspective of the Total Quality Management (TQM). Using a TQM approach, it is considered that the suppliers (i.e. the reporting enterprises) are part of the production system. Hence, the statistical process begins with the production and transmission of microdata by the reporting enterprises. Data collection has to be adapted to the respondent conditions and possibilities. Also, statistical agencies should implement strategies to encourage the respondent to fill in questionnaires with confidence and care. A key success factor in achieving high quality incoming data is improving our relationship with reporting enterprises. One of the ways this is being achieved is by offering the enterprises free of charge data tailored to their needs. According with our experience, this new practice (Gonzalez and Revilla, 2002) has seen an increase of interest on the part of the enterprises, which are consequently filling in questionnaires more carefully. Moreover, an "auditing system" carried by reporting enterprises comes from that practice (Revilla, 2005).

The combination of the TQM approach, the built-in edits using in EDR and the selective editing strategy appears very promising. Our target for the future is that, after implementing correct Web edits, no traditional microediting will be needed. A selected editing approach based on statistical modelling will be used in a way that the most influential suspicious values could be detected. Hence, all fatal errors and the most important query errors could be corrected before the survey is disseminated.

References

[1] Branson, M. (2002), "*Using XBRL for data reporting*". Australian Bureau of Statistics. Unece/Eurostat Work Session on Electronic Data Reporting, Working Paper No 20. February 2002.

[2] Gonzalez, M. and Revilla, P. (2002). "*Encouraging respondents in Spain*". The Statistic Newsletter. OECD. Issue No. 12.

[3] Gradjean, J.P. (2002), "*Electronic data collection in Official Statistics in France*". French National Institute of Statistics INSEE. UN/ECE/Eurostat. Work Session on Electronic Data Reporting. Working Paper No 7. February 2002.

[4] Martin, C. and Poirier, C. (2002), "*Analysis of data slices and metadata to improve survey processing*". Statistics Canada.. UN/ECE Work Session on Statistical Data Editing. Working Paper No 2. Helsinki. May 2002 .

[5] Mayda, J. (2002), "*Experiences with implementation of EDR into existing survey programs 2002*".Statistics Canada. UN/ECE/Eurostat. Work Session on Electronic Data Reporting. Working Paper 23. February 2002.

[6] Revilla, P. (2005), *"Auditing by reporting enterprises"*. 55th Session of the International Statistical Institute. Sydney. April, 2005.

[7] Weir, P. (2005), *"The Movement to Electronic Reporting and the Impact on Editing"*. 55th Session of the International Statistical Institute. Sydney. April, 2005.

EVALUATION REPORT ON INTERNET OPTION OF 2004 CENSUS TEST CHARACTERISTICS OF ELECTRONIC QUESTIONNAIRES, NON-RESPONSE RATES, FOLLOW-UP RATES AND QUALITATIVE STUDIES

By Danielle Laroche, Statistics Canada

1. INTRODUCTION

By law, Statistics Canada (STC) is required to conduct a census every five years, and all households are required to complete a census questionnaire. The last census took place in 2001, while the next is scheduled for May 16, 2006. The *de jure* method is followed, meaning that people are counted at their usual residence in Canada regardless of their location on Census Day. In 2001, Canada had nearly 12 million households and a population of more than 30 million. Approximately 98% of households were counted using the self-enumeration method and the remaining 2% counted via interview.

Major changes are being implemented for the 2006 Census in relation to data collection and processing methods. These changes are primarily as follows: questionnaires will be mailed out to two-thirds of dwellings, with enumerators delivering questionnaires to remaining dwellings as in the past; completed questionnaires will be returned to a single processing centre rather than to enumerators; questionnaires returned via the mail will be scanned and their data captured automatically; telephone follow-up for incomplete questionnaires will be conducted from the Census Help Line sites using a Computer Assisted Telephone Interview (CATI) application; and, last but not least, all households in private dwellings will have the option to complete and submit their questionnaire via the Internet.

Use of the Internet in data collection is not new to Statistics Canada; several business surveys have been conducted using this collection method. However, the Internet option for household surveys is relatively recent. That is, it has only been utilized in the Census, first with a major test during the 2001 Census, then as part of the Census Test in May of 2004 when Statistics Canada carried out the testing of almost all systems and operations to be used during the 2006 Census.

As for the Census, two types of questionnaires were used to collect the majority of the Census Test data. The short-form questionnaire, or form 2A, was distributed to four households out of every five. The long-form questionnaire, referred to as form 2B, was distributed to one of every five households. This questionnaire contains all of the questions appearing on form 2A plus questions on a range of various topics. The 2004 Census Test was conducted within a limited number of test regions in Nova Scotia, Quebec, Manitoba and Saskatchewan. These sectors were selected based on their socioeconomic characteristics, proportion of francophone and anglophone households and availability of farms with a view to establishing a sample of both mail-out and list/leave areas.

This report describes the characteristics of the electronic questionnaires, presents the main results of the qualitative tests and summarizes the analyses of partial non-response and failed-edit follow-up rates for the 2004 Census test questionnaires. Assessment of the preliminary quality of the data collected consisted of analysis of partial non-response rates and the percentage of questionnaires sent to failed-edit follow-up. These two indicators are key factors in determining the initial data quality that can reveal problems related to specific questions.

2. CHARACTERISTICS OF ELECTRONIC QUESTIONNAIRES

In general, the electronic questionnaire is identical to the paper questionnaire in terms of question wording, instructions and response options. In terms of functionality, respondents have the option to save an Internet 2B questionnaire and complete it over multiple sessions from different computers. Respondents can also switch the questionnaire language, i.e., French or English. Additionally, the Internet application was made to be as consistent as possible with standards and guidelines for presentation of federal government Web sites. All Web pages of the Government of Canada strive to have similar characteristics, and the electronic questionnaires follow the same straightforward, efficient format. The Government of Canada places great emphasis on the uniform presentation of its Web sites, which provides the benefit of ensuring users a consistent experience visit after visit. The use of strict standards also enhances the satisfaction level of respondents using government sites.

The first screen is a **welcome page** giving users the opportunity to verify their computer requirements and settings. If respondents have an adequately recent and properly configured browser, then the next screen is displayed. If not, then respondents can click links to view troubleshooting information to help them modify their browser settings or download a more recent version of the required browser or Java Virtual Machine (JVM).

The second screen is the **access code page**. Access codes are printed on the front page of the paper questionnaires. They are unique, randomly generated, 15 digit numbers segmented into five groups of three digits to make them more user-friendly. After entering their unique access code, respondents click the *Start* button at the bottom of the page to validate their code. If the code is valid, then the application automatically selects the appropriate questionnaire type in the appropriate language and displays the first page of the questionnaire.

In the first part of the census questionnaire, respondents are asked to provide their telephone number and household **address**. If the household received its questionnaire via the mail, then the access code is associated with the address in the Master Control System (i.e. master list of dwellings which includes addresses used for mail-out), and the address is displayed for the respondent to confirm. The paper and electronic questionnaires are identical in this regard. If the dwelling is in a list/leave area where the questionnaires are delivered by enumerators, the respondent is required to provide the household address. The Province field has a drop-down list containing the possible response options. Respondents simply click this field to view a list of provinces and territories.

In the electronic questionnaire, all fields for province selection use this **drop-down list** format. The month and day of the date of birth question follow the same format.

A bar representing respondents' **completion status** or progress in the questionnaire appears in the left-hand column on all screens. This feature provides respondents an indication of how much of the survey they have completed and how much remains.

A **help function** appears in the form of a link in the left-hand column on the screen under the completion status bar. Respondents can click the help link for assistance with the current question. The help function contains instructions and examples to help respondents ensure that their responses are as accurate as possible to all questions. In addition to the help link, the left-hand column is configured with explanations for respondents as to **why they are being asked each question** and how the information they provide will be used. This information has been found to enrich the user experience when completing the online census.

Questions and response options appear in a box at the centre of the screen to make them stand out. Each question is displayed on a background colour corresponding to the colours used in the paper questionnaire.

Internet **standards** are followed, including **check boxes** to indicate that multiple responses are possible and circles, or **radio buttons**, to indicate that only one response is possible. When a radio button associated with a write-in response is selected, the cursor moves automatically to the field in which respondents are expected to type their answers. If respondents simply start typing a response in a write-in field, then the corresponding radio button is selected automatically.

Respondents navigate within the questionnaire using **control buttons** located at the bottom of each screen. When respondents click the ***Next*** button, the data are encrypted and sent to Statistics Canada's secure server, where they are then decrypted and verified. If no problem is detected with the answers, the server sends to the respondent's browser the next appropriate screen. If there is a problem with the respondent's answers, the server encrypts the current screen's data, sends it back to the respondent's browser where it is decrypted and displayed with a validation message. This process is called two-way encryption. That is, data entered by respondents are encrypted by their browser and sent to the server where they are decrypted. Data coming from the server are encrypted and sent to the respondent's browser where they are decrypted. Respondents may also return to the previous screen by clicking the ***Go Back*** button. The ***Stop and Finish Later*** button gives respondents the option to save a partially completed questionnaire and fill in the remainder later. After clicking this button, respondents are prompted to choose a password or to let the application assign one. When they return to finish their questionnaire, they are prompted to enter their original access code and then given five attempts to enter their password correctly. For security purposes, if respondents are unsuccessful or if they do not log back in within the prescribed period, then their partially completed questionnaire is submitted on their behalf. Finally, respondents can click the ***Cancel*** button to simply exit a session. No data are saved if they exit in this manner.

Four types of **validation messages** are possible. **Non-response** messages appear when respondents have not answered a question. **Partial response** messages appear when respondents provide only a partial response to a question, for example, if they omit the city name from their address. **Invalid response** messages appear for numerical responses when respondents enter a number outside of the range established for a question. Finally, **soft edit** messages appear only for questions relating to money amounts whenever the amount in a response appears unusual. This type of message asks respondents to verify that they have entered the correct amount, for example, "*Please verify the amount you entered for part (f), if correct leave as is*". All of these messages follow the same approach. When respondents click the *Next* button, the information on the current page is validated, and, if necessary, the application displays the same screen again noting any problems at the top of the page in red text, for example, "*Please answer question 5 about John Doe.*" The question and field requiring attention appear in red, and a red arrow highlights the missing response to assist the respondent, who can then either fill in the missing information or continue to the next screen. If the respondent chooses to move on without making any changes, then the next screen is presented. If the respondent adds or changes any information, then the responses are validated again. This approach is consistent with the Common Look and Feel guidelines prescribed for Canadian government Web sites in that pop-up windows should not be used within pages to convey information to respondents.

The electronic questionnaire follows primarily the **matrix format** but also, in places, the sequential format. With the matrix format, each question appears only once, and response options are repeated under the name of each person in the household. Usability tests have demonstrated that this format reduces the response burden, since respondents have to read each question only once and can then respond for all members of the household. Another advantage of the matrix approach is that it reduces the number of screens and, as a result, requirements with regard to system infrastructure. With the **sequential format**, questions are asked about one person at a time. As a result, questions are repeated as many times as there are persons in the household. The sequential format supports increased customization of questionnaires. For one, it allows a respondent's name to be directly incorporated into each question. The sequential format is used in two places on the electronic version of form 2B: questions 40 to 46 concerning labour market activities and question 52 on income. Usability tests have indicated that it is easier for respondents to focus on one person at a time in responding to these particular questions.

The electronic version of form 2B has two types of automated **skip patterns.** The first relates to all members of the household. With this skip type, any questions deemed non-applicable are not displayed. However, since the questions are numbered, a message appears at the top of the screen for the next applicable question to indicate to the respondent that one or more non-applicable questions were skipped. In this situation, a skip message like this would be presented: "*Based on your response to Question 11, Question 12 is not applicable. Therefore, proceed with Question 13*". The second type of automated skip relates to questions applicable to one or more persons but not to all persons in the household. With this skip type, the question must be displayed since it applies to some members of the household. In this event, a message appears under the names of persons as appropriate to indicate that the question does not apply to them. By skipping any questions deemed non-applicable, we hope to reduce the response burden, thereby making the user experience more pleasant and less frustrating in comparison to the paper questionnaire. For example, with paper questionnaires respondents sometimes do not follow skip instructions which results in a considerable increase in response burden.

The electronic questionnaire has two **mandatory questions**, one on the number of persons staying at the address on Census Day (Step B1), the other on the names of the members of the household (Step B2). The second screen depends on the first; for example, if a respondent indicates "3" for the number of persons in the household, then the application generates three lines to type the names of these persons. The respondent must provide a first or a last name for each person. These names are subsequently used to customize responses and selected questions. These two questions are the only mandatory questions in the Internet questionnaire.

One of the main **differences** between paper questionnaires and their electronic versions relates to the population coverage Steps questions. In the electronic questionnaire, respondents are required to enter the names of all persons staying at their address on Census Day and three additional questions are then used to eliminate any temporary residents (persons whose usual residence is at another address in Canada) or foreign residents (visitors or government representatives from another country). On the paper questionnaire, respondents list only the names of usual residents at their address. The three questions of the electronic questionnaire are presented in the form of instructions on the paper questionnaire. In either response mode, if all residents at an address are temporary or foreign, then respondents (i.e. the persons filling out the questionnaire) list their name and usual telephone number, and there is no need to respond to any further questions. The application can accommodate up to 36 persons, although it is possible to indicate more persons in the corresponding question.

Age is particularly important in the long-form questionnaire (2B), as persons less than 15 years of age are subject to different validation for the questions on marital or common-law status and are not required to respond to a portion of the questionnaire, including questions on mobility status, education, activities in the labour market and income. **Age confirmation** provides respondents the opportunity to verify the ages calculated based on the responses given to the question on date of birth. This confirmation occurs only for the electronic questionnaire. If a date of birth is not indicated, then the message "*Date of birth not indicated*" appears next to the appropriate person's name; if it is invalid, then the message "*Impossible to calculate age*" appears. Respondents can go back to the previous screen to modify their response to the date of birth question or go on to the next screen. If they opt to move on or not to provide a date of birth, then the person in question is presumed to be more than15 years of age, and all applicable questions on the form 2B are asked.

On the last page of the electronic questionnaire, the completion status bar indicates that the questionnaire is complete. Respondents then have the option to document any suggestions or **comments** in the designated space. The ***Submit*** button is located at the bottom of the page. When respondents click this button, the application submits the questionnaire and displays an acknowledgment page containing a **confirmation number**. Respondents can click a button at the bottom of this page to print the number to retain as evidence that they have submitted their questionnaire in case an enumerator telephones or knocks at their door.

3. RESULTS OF QUALITATIVE STUDIES (INTERNET RESPONDENTS)

Qualitative studies of the electronic version of form 2B were carried out in respondents' homes in May and June of 2004, in parallel with the 2004 Census test. Approximately 50 interviews were conducted in both official languages.

Most respondents stated that they enjoyed using the application and that they found their experience to be positive and pleasant. They found the electronic questionnaire easy to complete, efficient and user-friendly. Some respondents stated that they appreciated not having to fill out the form manually, while others said it was easier to correct mistakes on the electronic copy. The majority of respondents liked the interactive nature of the application and its "smart" features (personalized questions and answers with the respondents' names, age confirmation, automated skips, etc.). Moreover, the collection method saved respondents the trouble of going to the post office or finding a mailbox.

One of the problems found was not related to the questionnaire itself but rather to the process for gaining access to it. This is because respondents who had to modify their computer settings were generally unable to do so without assistance from an interviewer. The majority of respondents did not know what type or version of browser they had or how to find this information. This could mean lower response rates at census time as a result of unsuccessful attempts to gain access to the electronic questionnaire.

During qualitative tests, it seemed to us that the 2B Internet questionnaire did not offer respondents significant time savings compared to paper, and may in fact have taken longer in some cases. However, data collected by the Internet application, that is, from the time each respondent logged-in to the time the respondent submitted their form, did not confirm this. In fact, the electronic questionnaires take less time to complete than the paper version, except in cases where Internet respondents do not use a high-speed connection. In addition, most Internet respondents, even those with "dial up" connections, reported that they thought the electronic version was faster to use and much more efficient than the paper version. This perception was likely due in part to the interactive aspects of the application and to the fact that after respondents complete the electronic questionnaire, they can submit it instantly as opposed to the paper version, which must be mailed.

Validation messages, particularly those for non-response or partial response, were effective in that they helped to ensure that respondents provided responses for questions they had inadvertently skipped. In spite of this, respondents found the messages to have a negative connotation in that they only appeared when respondents did something "wrong." In addition, generally held conceptions of Internet respondents with regard to how forms on the Internet should be completed can lead them to believe that they must provide a response to every single question, without exception, before moving on. For the Census, this false impression could result in undesirable behaviours that might impact data quality. For example, some respondents might invent responses or pick them at random in order to move on. An issue of this nature may be difficult to detect.

4. COMPARISON OF PARTIAL NON-RESPONSE RATES FOR INTERNET AND PAPER QUESTIONNAIRES (UNWEIGHTED)

The rate of partial non-response to questions can provide an indication of the difficulties encountered by respondents. It is useful in assessing the overall level of understanding of questions and provides a preliminary indication of data quality. A question is generally deemed to be missing a response when a response is required but none has been provided. However, the situation may not always be as obvious. For example, if question 11 (landed immigrant) has no response, it is impossible to know whether a respondent was or was not supposed to respond to question 12 (year of immigration). In this event, it is presumed that the respondent was not supposed to respond to the question. As such, the rate of partial non-response studied in this section corresponds to actual rates in that only responses for which we were certain there should have been a response were taken into consideration. For some questions, the rates also include incomplete and invalid responses. These rates are unweighted and were calculated based on all non-blank questionnaires returned.

Wherever possible, the Internet questionnaire mirrored the paper form in terms of question wording, instructions provided and response options. However, in comparing non-response rates, certain characteristics of the electronic questionnaires need to be taken into account. Firstly, the use of radio buttons in the response options for certain questions makes it impossible to select more than one response for these questions. Secondly, when respondents click "Continue" at the bottom of each page, any appropriate non-response, partial response, invalid response (for numerical responses) messages or soft-edit messages (for amounts) are displayed automatically. Respondents can then choose to enter or correct a response or to simply move on. In addition, all skips are automated.

Form 2A is divided into two parts, coverage steps and persons data. **Form 2B** has three parts: coverage steps, person data and household data. In terms of coverage steps, we did not evaluate non-response but rather only situations requiring confirmation from a household. These results appear in the section on rejection rates.

The following chart illustrates the non-response rates calculated for both collection methods by questionnaire type (i.e. 2A or 2B) and data type (i.e. person data or household data).

Chart 1: Partial Non-Response Rates by Questionnaire Type and Data Type

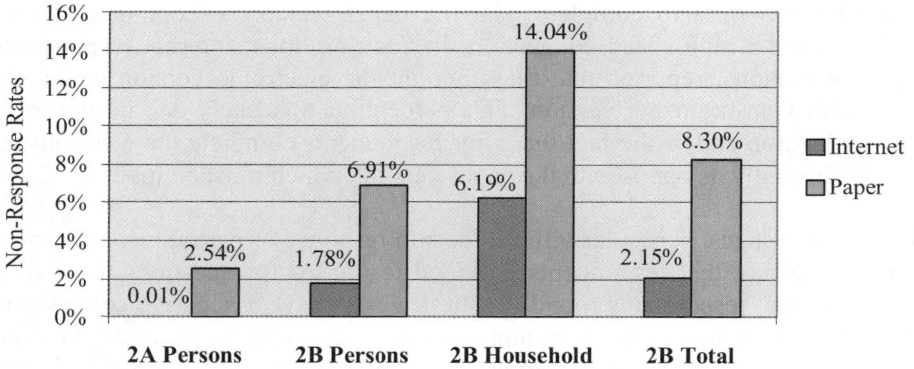

As the chart indicates, the non-response rate was almost nil for the Internet version of form 2A (0.01%), while the same rate was 2.54% for the paper questionnaire. For form 2B, the non-response rate for person data was four times as high for the paper questionnaire (6.91%) as for the Internet version (1.78%). With regard to household data, the non-response rate for the paper version of form 2B was twice as high (14.04%) as for the Internet version (6.19%). When all questions are considered together, the rate of partial non-response of 2B was nearly four times as high for the paper questionnaire (8.30%) as for the Internet version (2.15%).

It appears, therefore, that the validation messages used for the Internet version are effective in reducing non-response. Qualitative studies appear to confirm this hypothesis. However, these studies have also revealed that many Internet respondents believe that they must provide a response to every single question before moving on. For some respondents, non-response messages are interpreted as a confirmation of this. Nevertheless, it would appear that the non-response messages assist inattentive respondents in correcting the majority of unintentional errors or omissions.

Analysis of rates of partial non-response for each question indicates that some question types are more likely to have non-response than others for either collection method. These are generally questions that respondents deem non-applicable (for example, question 5 on common-law status for married respondents or young children, question 8B on activity limitations at work or at school for respondents not working or attending school, question 30 on major field of study for respondents without certificate or for those who only have a secondary certificate, question 33 on the number of hours spent caring for children for respondents without children or question 39 on the last date worked for respondents who are not working or have never worked). Other questions, meanwhile, are more difficult to respond to as a proxy respondent, i.e., on behalf of another person (for example, question 17 on ethnic origin, question 43 on the main activities performed at a person's work or question 46 on place of work). Finally, still other questions are simply more difficult to respond to in that they depend on memory recall (for example, question 24 on mobility status over the previous five years or question H5 on period of construction of dwelling) or require retrieval of documentation (for example, question 52 on income or the questions in section H6 on amounts paid for electricity, oil, gas, wood, water or other municipal services) or in that respondents do not know or refuse to provide the answer (for example, question 52 on income or on income tax paid). In most cases, the types of questions listed above tend to have higher non-response rates for both collection methods. However, these rates are consistently twice as high for paper as for electronic questionnaires.

According to this analysis, non-response rates also increase as we progress on the questionnaire regardless of collection method. Internet questionnaires include both questionnaires submitted by respondents and those submitted automatically by the system (that is when a respondent saves a questionnaire and then does not return within the prescribed time, the system submits the questionnaire on the respondent's behalf). In addition, respondents who did not respond to the question on date of birth were required to respond to all questions on form 2B (although this proportion was negligible at 15 cases out of 7,526, or 0.02%). This explains in part why non-response rates tend to increase as we progress in an Internet questionnaire. Additional factors to explain this increase might include increasing question difficulty, increasing effort required or respondent fatigue.

5. COMPARISON OF FOLLOW-UP RATES FOR INTERNET AND PAPER QUESTIONNAIRES (UNWEIGHTED)

After data entry, questionnaires are transmitted to data processing where automated edits are performed. These edits identify any questions requiring follow-up and compiles a score for each household. Follow-up requirements are calculated based on these scores and weights assigned to each question. The data for households with a score exceeding a predefined value are forwarded to follow-up. These households are grouped to classify follow-ups by priority; those with the highest scores are given higher priority in terms of number of contact attempts. In other words, the higher a household's score, the higher its priority for follow-up.

In terms of coverage steps, we do not evaluate non-response but rather the situations requiring verification with households. The first situation in this regard concerns households identifying themselves as temporary or foreign resident households (Step B). It is necessary to confirm that these households actually do include only temporary or foreign residents. The second situation relates to doubts concerning the exclusion of a person from the questionnaire (Step C). In the event of doubt concerning whether to exclude a person from a questionnaire, respondents are supposed to indicate the person's name, the reason for exclusion and the person's relationship with Person 1. It might be necessary to contact the household to confirm that the person is, in fact, not a usual resident at the address. Should one of these situations arise that cannot be resolved through analysis of the questionnaire, then verification must take place with the household.

The following chart illustrates the follow-up rates by reason for forms 2A.

Chart 2: Follow-Up Rates by Reason – Forms 2A

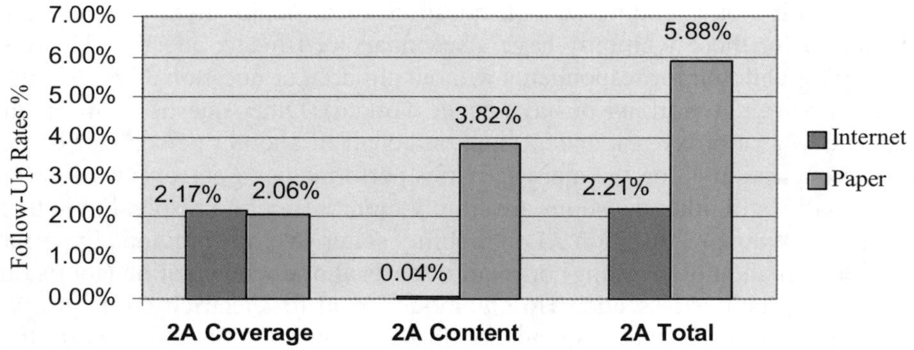

In terms of coverage steps, the Internet and paper versions of form 2A rank more or less equivalent (2.17% and 2.06%). For either collection method, nearly three-quarters of all coverage issues relate to Step C. In terms of content, on the other hand, follow-up rates are negligible for the electronic version of form 2A (0.04%) in comparison to the paper version (3.82%). Overall, the paper versions of form 2A require follow-up three times as often as the Internet versions (5.88% versus 2.21% respectively).

The following chart illustrates the follow-up rates by reason for forms 2B.

Chart 3: Follow-Up Rates by Reason – Forms 2B

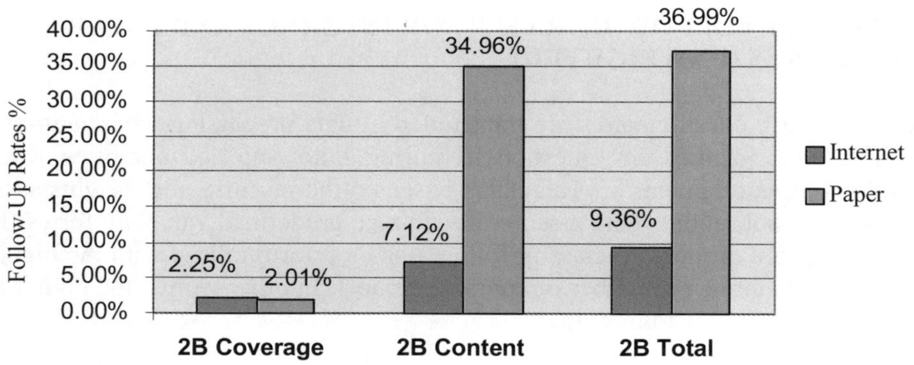

With regard to coverage steps, follow-up rates for form 2B are similar for either collection method (2.25% for electronic versions, 2.01% for paper). These rates are also similar to those for form 2A, with the majority of coverage issues relating to Step C for either collection method. With regard to content, the follow-up rate was nearly five times as high for the paper questionnaire (34.96%) as for the Internet version (7.12%). Overall, the follow-up rate was nearly four times as high for the paper questionnaire (36.99%) as for the electronic version (9.36%).

The following chart illustrates the follow-up rates by reason for all questionnaires combined.

Chart 4: Follow-Up Rates by Reason – Forms 2A and 2B Combined

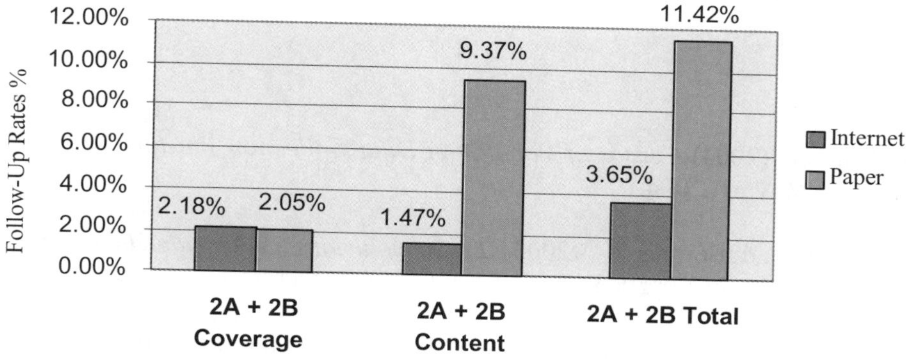

In terms of overall coverage steps, follow-up rates were similar for the electronic and paper versions (2.18% and 2.05% respectively). Follow-up rates relating to content were six times higher for paper questionnaires than for their electronic versions, at 9.37% and 1.47% respectively. Overall, the follow-up rate was three times as high for the paper questionnaire (11.42%) as for the electronic version (3.65%).

The analysis of non-response and follow-up rates leads to the conclusion that the electronic questionnaires are more complete than the paper questionnaires and consequently less expensive in terms of follow-up than the paper questionnaires.

6. CONCLUSION

Data collection via the Internet offers a range of both new possibilities and new challenges. As demonstrated in this report, partial non-response rates and follow-up rates (i.e. failed edit questionnaires) are much lower for electronic versions of questionnaires than for their paper versions. With regard to the validation messages, it is possible to conclude that in general, they are effective in obtaining answers to questions respondents might otherwise have overlooked and in having them correct errors they inadvertently committed. Along with the automated skips of non-applicable questions, these messages result in a general perception among respondents that the electronic questionnaire is "smart". This responds in part to the high expectations the general public have with regard to Internet questionnaires.

The results provided in this report are thus highly encouraging. They demonstrate that data collected via the Internet are more complete and consequently less expensive from a failed edit and follow-up perspective than data collected via paper questionnaires. Moreover, electronic questionnaires are ready for processing upon submission since they are already in electronic form. A number of countries have invested significant financial and other resources into this new collection method, as the new technology offers hope in terms of reducing the cost of future censuses if we obtain a high take-up rate using this methodology. The infrastructure for collecting data via paper will always be required, at least for a Census. With an on-line option, organizations must invest additional funds for a second infrastructure. The saving can only be realized if the Internet take-up rate is high enough to reduce the paper processing infrastructure and eliminate operations costs related to processing paper questionnaires.

However, it is also appropriate to explore more fully the reasons for the differences in non-response and follow-up rates between these two data collection methods. Do the differences in format between electronic and paper questionnaires influence the quality of the responses collected? Are data collected from households via the Internet and via paper questionnaires strictly comparable? Is the quality of responses equivalent from one collection method to the next and do we need to implement additional processing steps to control for the differences? More detailed studies are necessary and are currently underway with a view to finding the answers to these questions.

References

[1] Laroche, Danielle (2004) *Census of Population Data Collection Via Internet.* Statistics Canada, SSC Montréal, May 31, 2004.

[2] Boudreau, J.-R. and Bornais K. (2003) *Les conclusions de l'étude du contrôle et du suivi.* Statistics Canada, 20 février 2003.

[3] Statistics Canada, 2006 Census Processing *Response Integration and Verification Task – Coverage and Collective Edit Systems Requirements.* Version 9 – February, 2005.

[4] Statistic Canada, Bornais, K. (2004) *Rates by response Channel.* Internet questionnaires derived from Booklet Id. E-mail October 21, 2004.

DATA EDITING FOR THE ITALIAN LABOUR FORCE SURVEY

By Claudio Ceccarelli and Simona Rosati, National Institute of Statistics, Italy

1. INTRODUCTION

The European Council has approved a new Regulation (n.577/98) that aims to produce comparable information about labour market in the European Member States. The Council Regulation requires that Labour Force Surveys have to be carried out complying with both the contents and the methodologies that are set at Community level. In order to accept this Regulation the Italian Labour Force Survey (LFS) has been completely revised. The rotating panel design, the frequency of the survey and the complexity of the questionnaire are the main reasons which led to adopt a different data collection strategy, which is a combination of different *Computer Assisted Interviewing* (CAI) techniques. More exactly, CAPI (*Computer Assisted Personal Interviewing*) technique is used for the first interview, while CATI (*Computer Assisted Telephone Interviewing*) technique is used for the interviews following the first. To conduct the interviews with CAI technique, professional interviewer network has been realised.

As known, one of the major advantage of using CAI is the improving of data quality, especially in case of complex questionnaires. This is mainly due to the fact that the use of CAI allows to reduce large amounts of potential errors due to interviewer or to respondent. For example, routing errors are eliminated because the script automatically routes to the next questions. In addition, CAI makes it possible to check range and data consistency during the interview. As a consequence, the problem of imputing missing or inconsistent data at the post-data capturing stage is significantly reduced, even if not completely solved. A certain amount of records indeed may present a few internal inconsistencies, since some edit rules may be left unsolved during the interview. Moreover, the choice to introduce a limited number of edits, in order to do not compromise the regular flow of the interview, increases the number of records with unsolved logical inconsistencies.

Nevertheless, most of errors do not have an influential effect on publication figures or aggregate data, which are published by Statistical offices. On the other hand, if data have been obtained by means of a sample from the population, an error in the results due to the incorrect data is acceptable as long as this error is small in comparison to the sampling error. The question we pose is: "It is necessary to correct all data in every detail when CAI is used as data collection method?". From a first point of view, data which are collected by means of computer-assisted methods would not need to be further corrected. On the other hand, if some edits are not solved during the interview, some records will remain internally inconsistent and may lead to problems when publication figures are calculated. Data editing helps to reduce the errors and make sure that records become internally consistent, but a caution against the overuse of query edits must be heeded.

It is well recognized that the ideal edit strategy is a combination of selective editing and automatic editing, although macro-editing can not be omitted in the final step of editing process. For our purpose automatic editing is especially suited for identifying all incorrect records, since performing this activity is low cost and not time-consuming. After that phase, the records are split into two stream: critical records (they may have an influential effect on aggregate data) and noncritical records (they do not affect significantly aggregate data). The critical records which are incorrect for systematic errors are imputed by a deterministic algorithm, while those which are incorrect for probabilistic errors are automatically imputed according to the Fellegi and Holt methodology (1976). The remaining noncritical records, which may be incorrect for different types of errors, could be either not edited or could be imputed automatically. If the latter solution is adopted, it is expected that software systems implementing the Fellegi and Holt method will not be able to function properly. This is also the case of the LFS. In this paper we do not give a solution to such a problem, but we are confident that useful results will be provided in the future. Suggestions, which we intend to verify, are presented in the last section.

The work is organised as follows: the characteristics of the LFS sample are presented in Section 2; Section 3 analyses the survey process as a whole; the edit strategy for the LFS is described in Section 4; some results about the imputation are also reported. The paper concludes with a brief discussion about the main outcomes and the issue concerning data editing in CAI surveys. For brevity all the results presented in the paper refers to 2004 fourth quarter data.

2. SAMPLE DESIGN

The most relevant aspect about new LFS is the time continuity of reference weeks spread uniformly throughout the whole year. For this reason, all solutions adopted to realise the survey are conditioned by this characteristic. Sample design is realised taking into account Council Regulation 577/98 constraints about frequency of the survey and the representativeness of the sample.

The sample has two-stage of selection. The primary units are the Municipalities stratified into 1,246 group at the Province level. The stratification strategy is based on the demographic size of the Municipality. The sample scheme provides for one primary unit for each strata. The secondary units are the households and they are selected from the Municipality population Register. For each quarter 76,918 households are interviewed (i.e. sampling rate equal to 0.4%). The LFS sample is designed to guarantee annual estimates of principal indicators of labour market at Province level (NUTS III), quarterly estimates at the Regional level (NUTS II) and monthly estimates at the national level.

Council Regulation 577/98 indicates the quarter as the reference period about the estimates of principal indicators of labour market, so the sample of households to be interviewed is split into 13 sub groups homogeneous regarding to the size. In similar way to the old version of LFS, the sampling households follow the rotation scheme 2-2-2. For example, if we consider a sampling household that is interviewed in the third week of the first quarter of 2005, it will be interviewed again in the third week of the second quarter of 2005, then it will go out to the sample in third and fourth quarters of 2005 and, finally, it will be interviewed again in the third week of first and second quarter of 2006.

The weighting factors are calculated taking into account the probability of selection and the auxiliary information relating to the distribution of the population being surveyed, by sex, age (five-year are groups) and region (NUTS II level), where such external data are referred to the Register statistics.

The weighting strategy adopted by LFS is developed in the following there steps. In the first one, the initial weights equal to inverse of probability of selection are calculated. In the second step, non-response factors, by household size and referent person characteristic are calculated to correct initial weight from non-response effects. Finally, final weight relating to the distribution of the population being surveyed, by sex, age (five-year are groups) and region are calculated using calibration estimators methodology.

3. SURVEY PROCESS

Quality in statistics refers to an undefined concept. Each survey process is based on a multiple elementary operations, which have an influence over the final outcome, consequently quality has progressively become a central issue in official survey designing. Starting from these considerations, the new LFS is planned to analyse the process, in terms of elementary activities. In this way, it's possible to associate each activities to a specific type of error and to define a complex quality monitoring system for all steps of the survey.

In order to control all elementary actions about the LFS process, the quality monitoring system is introduced and can be divided into three main phases: "preventive checks phase", regards some of preventive actions implemented before data collection, to prevent the errors; "checks during the survey phase", regards some actions for detecting the errors that can be made during the process; "*a posteriori* checks", to evaluate non sampling error using quantitative indicators linked to each elementary operation. Double strategy of interview (the first one with CAPI and the other three with CATI) call for a high level of automation on the interviews management, transmission and execution, which have to be strictly observed. Monitoring system give the possibility to put the new LFS process under control and to adjust it in "real time" in case of error (Giuliani et al, 2004).

Mixed mode techniques has been due to the need of interviewing the households belonging to the sample for four waves: the first interview is generally carried out by CAPI technique, the three successive interviews are carried out by a CATI technique. In particular cases, for example when the household do not have a fixed telephone, the previous scheme can be changed.

To carry out CAPI interviews, ISTAT decided to realise a network of 311 interviewers, one for each specific sub-regional area, directly trained and managed by ISTAT experts. Each ISTAT Regional Offices manage weekly interviewer job. Through a web connection the interviewers receive the electronic questionnaire and related changes and the information about the weekly sampling households.

ISTAT provided to realise a complex automatic system that has to be able to manage all information regarding the core of new LFS. In particular, the system manages the flows of data between sampling Municipalities and ISTAT, allocates the interview according to techniques, governs the flows of information in data treatment phase and so on. The information system guarantees that all activities, achieved by reliable hardware and software tools, respects all the requirements of a secure information system (data privacy, data availability and data integrity) and simultaneously, provides for monitoring system based on a series of indicators defined to plan and control all the elementary activities. (Bergamasco et al, 2004).

The sample Municipalities select a list of households that are the theoretical sample to be interviewed. This sample is composed by "base household" and its three "replacing households". This information are collected and managed by a software system called SIGIF (*SIstema Gestione Indagini Famiglie* – system for the management of households surveys). SIGIF distributes the sampling households according to data collection techniques (CAPI or CATI).

Using SIGIF, ISTAT Regional Offices allocate to the CAPI interviewer the weekly sample of households. In order to solve eventual not planned events, ISTAT Regional Offices re-assign the job between interviewer. Each interviewer try to interview the "base household" and, if it is not possible, he can replace the household with a "replacing" one chosen automatically by the CAPI system. The interviewers have about 4 weeks to carry out the interview: the first week is dedicated to fix the appointments, the second week to the interview, the following two weeks to complete pending interviews. As soon as possible, the interviewers send, using web connection to a toll-free number, the results of the weekly job to the SIGIF divided into interview and field-work data (Bergamasco et al, 2004).

Using SIGIF, the list of the households is sent to the private service company that has the responsibility of carrying out the telephone interview. Weekly, the service company sends to ISTAT the results of the interview and daily a set of field-work indicators. In Table 1 are reported the sample size of the LFS and the response rate by survey technique.

Table 1. Sample size and response rate by survey technique

Households			Respondent households			Response rate		
Universe	Sample	Sampling rate (%)	CAPI	CATI	Total	CAPI	CATI	Total
21,810,676	76,872	0.4	26,985	42,567	69,552	90.2	92.1	90.5

The European Council Regulations n. 1575/00 and n. 1897/2000 introduce other innovations, as typology of questions, type of variables (continuous or categorical), acceptance range of variables, and explore in details the concept of "unemployed person" and gives further methodological indications on data collection.

In order to observe these European Council Regulations and simplify the interview, electronic questionnaire has developed. Characteristics like: automatic branching, online help, interactive codification of open items using a search engine for certain key variables (such as economic activity and profession), root and coherence rules, confirmation items for waves following the first, improve significantly data quality.

The questionnaire is composed by a section regarding general personal information on household members. Individual questionnaire is divided into 9 sections that should be submitted to each member in working age (over 15 years); the themes treated are: labour status during the reference week, main job, second job, previous work experiences (only for the not employed persons), search of employment, registration to public and private employment office, education and training, main labour status and residence. To close the interview there are 2 section called: other information on the household, general trend of interview. The last section regards pending codification used if the interviewer do not codify some particular variables, like economic activity and profession, during the interview.

Rotation scheme 2-2-2 of the sampling households allows to make a panel of information. Traditionally, ISTAT produce "three months transition matrix" and "one year transition matrix" referred to longitudinal information carried out for all sampling persons. To give the possibility to reconstruct the working history of the respondent for more than one year, the longitudinal information required about the labour status has been improved.

European Council Regulation n. 1897/00 gives the possibility to conduct the interviews following the first asking to the sampling person to confirm the information given in the previous interview. In this way, when the labour status and/or other characteristics of the respondent does not have substantially changed we are able to reduce the time of interview. CAI technique help to realise a "confirmation questionnaire", in which the "confirmation questions" are the fundamental nodes of interview flow. In case of the status of respondent is not changed, all information regarding a sub-flow of the questionnaire depending on certain "confirmation question" are automatically registered.

The LFS process and the new interviewers network represent the core of a crucial transformation of ISTAT's surveys, and has allowed, for the first time in ISTAT history, the implementation of an innovative survey management process. The attention given to data quality moved from the final product to the methodologies and the tools used to keep the whole production process under control. With this new system, the evaluation of the quality of the LFS, in terms of correctness and transparency, are set.

4. DATA EDITING

4.1 Error detection

After data captured contradictory information and item non-response are detected principally by using an automatic system based on Fellegi and Holt model of editing. It is worth noting that this operation can also be performed every week in order to notify in time possible errors due to the electronic questionnaire.

In editing process some edits (rules) are specified by experts with a knowledge of the subject matter of the survey. An edit expresses the judgment of some experts that certain combinations of values, corresponding to the different questions on the questionnaire, are unacceptable. The set of such edit rules is referred to as *explicit edits*. A record which fails any of the edits does need to be corrected. Conversely, a record which passes all the stated edits does not need to be corrected. The explicit edits relating to categorical variables (i.e. variables which are not subject to a meaningful metric) are implemented in SCIA (System for editing and automatic imputation), developed by ISTAT according to the Fellegi and Holt methodology (Barcaroli and Venturi, 1997). More exactly, the version of SCIA included in CONCORD (CONtrol and Data CORrection), a system designed for Windows environment, is used (Riccini Margarucci and Floris, 2000).

The remaining edits related to continuous variables are translated into a SAS program including if-then-else rules (SAS Institute Inc., 1999). Two different systems are used, given that a software which handle mixed data, i.e., a mix of categorical and continuous data is currently unavailable. Developing such a system is generally considered too hard, although in 1979 Sande showed how to this. He first showed how to convert discrete data to continuous data in a way that would allow solution of the error-localization problem. He then showed how to put a combination of discrete and continuous data into a form to which Chernikova's algorithm could be applied (1964, 1965). To our knowledge only recently two researcher of Statistics Netherlands proposed an algorithm based on Fellegi and Holt methods for automatic editing of mixed data (de Waal and Quere, 2003).

For a single variable we also distinguish two types of errors: "random error" and "systematic error". Although it is not a clear cut on their definition, we say that random errors can be assimilated to normal measurement errors, they have equal probability to occur in different variables and, for a generic variable, they are not correlated to errors in other variables. Systematic errors may be defined as non-probabilistic errors; they are generally due to some defects in surveying structure (e.g. a question wrongly specified).

Table 2 shows the number of explicit edits for the LFS. With regard to the SCIA system, the large number of edit rules and the complicated skip patterns of the questionnaire poses several computational problems that the entire set of edits need to be partitioned into two subsets. The problems arise since the Fellegi and Holt system runs to check the logical consistency of the entire edit system. We suppose that such a problem could be solved changing something into the software system by using more powerful processor. As result of the stage of error detection in Table 3 are reported the proportion of incorrect records per type of error.

Table 2. Number of explicit edits

Edit	Number of edits
SCIA system	2,358
- Set 1	961
- Set 2	1,397
SAS system	142

Table 3. Erroneous records per type of error

Error	Percentage of records
Systematic	2.5
Probabilistic	2.8

4.2 Imputation

The imputation of item non-responses depends on the nature of errors which generated them, although practical considerations and other issues should be considered in implementation of imputation procedures. When missing data are imputed it has been shown that deterministic imputation methods distort the distributions and attenuate variances, whereas probabilistic methods yield approximately unbiased estimates of distributions and element variances (Kalton and Kasprzyk, 1982). Nevertheless, we can reasonably assume that deterministic imputation is more suitable for correcting systematic errors, while probabilistic methods are more specific for errors generated from random error models.

Deterministic imputation assigns only one value, *a priori* determined, on the base of other values considered "true" by experts. On the contrary, probabilistic imputation assigns a value according to a stochastic model (e.g. a regression model) or using a donor unit which is similar to record to be imputed. A *distance function* is generally used to define similarity.

The Fellegi and Holt methodology can be counted among the probabilistic methods. It is concerned primarily with the stages of data editing and of imputation. Data editing process localizes errors in the record identifying a *minimal set* of variables (the smallest set), whose values can be changed in such a fashion that the resulting record would pass all the edits. Finally imputation will provide suitable values for those variables.

One of the major objectives of the Fellegi and Holt methodology is to retain the structure of the data. This means that univariate and multivariate distributions of survey data reflect as nearly as possible the distributions in the population. This goal is achieved by the use of *hot-deck* imputation. Hot-deck imputation consists of imputing for a variable of the current record the value recorded in the same field of some other record, which passed all the edits and which is similar in all respects to the current record. This can be done one variable at time (*sequential imputation*) or all variables at once (*joint imputation*). The former aims to preserve the univariate distributions of the variables, whereas the latter preserves the multivariate distributions.

To solve the error-localization problem, Fellegi and Holt showed that both explicit and implicit edits are needed. *Implicit* edits are those that can be logically derived (or generated) from a set of explicit edits. If the implicit edit fails, then necessarily at least one of the explicit edits fail. For the LFS the current algorithm in the SCIA system can not generate the full set of implicit edits because the amount of computation needed for generation grows at very high exponential rate in the number of edits. The same limitations were found when the Fellegi and Holt system ran to check the logical consistency of the explicit edits.

On the other hand, it seems to be not convenient to divide further the two subsets of explicit edits: we would obtain more than three subsets, which would be not independent each from other, with additional restrictions for the imputation method. Moreover, if some records are incorrect for systematic errors, it would be better correct them by using deterministic imputation. For these reasons we adopt a procedure which is a combination of selective editing and automatic editing. After errors detection, the incorrect records are split into two stream: critical records (they are influential on aggregate data) and noncritical records (they do not affect significantly aggregate data).

The critical records which are incorrect for systematic errors are imputed by choosing one value *a priori* determined, while those which are incorrect for probabilistic errors are automatically imputed according to the Fellegi and Holt methodology. Currently, only probabilistic logical inconsistencies which do not depend on rules of questionnaire are automatically imputed. In order to achieve this aim 137 explicit edits are used to detect probabilistic errors and 213 edits form a complete set of edits to solve the error-localization problem, i.e., which variables change in an erroneous record to ensure that the record passes all of the edits.

The remaining noncritical records, which may be incorrect for different types of errors, could be left unsolved without reducing data quality. Otherwise they could be automatically imputed too. In fact, the small number of errors and the variety of failing edits make the use of probabilistic imputation acceptable. At present, the remaining incorrect records are not automatically imputed since the amount of computation needed for generating the full set of implicit edits is prohibitive. These records are imputed by a deterministic algorithm whose implementation is not only time-consuming, but need to be modified for each quarter. In order to verify that the deterministic actions are correct, all the records are checked through the edit system a second time. If they pass, then nothing else is done. If they still fail edits, then it means that either some if-then-else rules need to be adjusted or that other rules must be considered in the algorithm.

As result of the impact of imputation in Table 4 are reported some findings related to the records which have been corrected by sequential or joint imputation. Table 5 shows the percentage of records per number of imputations at the end of the editing process. Note that the percentage of records that are corrected for four or more variables is equal to zero. Really this percentage is equal to 0.05, which means that there are at least four variables that have been imputed in 100 records. The maximum number of imputations is equal to 16.

Table 4. Erroneous records per type of imputation

Imputation	Percentage of records
Joint	41.1
Sequential	58.9

Table 5. Records per number of imputations

Number of imputations	Percentage of records
0	95.5
1	3.5
2	0.7
3	0.3
4 or more	0.0

5. CONCLUDING REMARKS

The advantage and also the aim of imputation is to complete a data set with "full" information for all observed individuals, which reduces bias in survey estimates and – from a point of a data user – also simplifies the analysis. Nevertheless, when CAI is used the increase of data quality due to editing process is usually negligible. In addition, for large complex data set implementing an automatic system for imputing contradictory information may be too costly in terms of timeliness and resources.

Therefore it seems to be unnecessary to correct data in every detail when CAI is used, while the information on error detection can play an important role in the improvement of the electronic questionnaire and the data collection. The LFS data could be checked frequently, since they are captured continuously week by week. Thus fatal errors can be identified just in time so that the errors can be eliminated. This process allows to get immediate feedback and monitoring on how interviewer are filling in the electronic questionnaire.

Although the impact of editing is considerably reduced by new technologies, we found that some errors may continue to be in the data and may have an influential effect on aggregate data. A combination of selective and automatic editing may be used to correct errors. Nevertheless, we also argued how it was hard implementing a system based on Fellegi and Holt methods when numerous edits are specified.

For the future we suggest applying the Fellegi and Holt method step by step. Initially the method is applied only for edits which fail. They are drawn from the set of the explicit edits. Then the records, which have been imputed, are checked through the edit system a second time. If they pass, then nothing else is done: all the records are correct. If the records still fail edits, the failing edits are added to the subset of edits previously selected in order to impute the incorrect records. The algorithm is reiterated until the records pass all the edits.

References

[1] AMENDOLA A. CAROLEO F.E., COPPOLA G. (1997) Differenziali territoriali nel mercato del lavoro e sviluppo in Italia, Celpe, Università di Salerno Discussion Paper n. 36.

[2] APPEL M. V., NICHOLLS II, W. L., NICHOLLS, W. (1993) New CASIC Technology at the U.S. Census Bureau, ASA, U.S. Census Bureau, vol. 2, pp. 1079-1084.

[3] BAFFIGI A. (1999) I differenziali territoriali nella struttura dell'occupazione e della disoccupazione: un'analisi con dati a livello provinciale (1981-1995). In: Struttura della contrattazione: differenziali salariali e occupazione in ambiti regionali, a cura di M. Biagioli, F.E. Caroleo e S. Destefanis.

[4] BAKER R.P., BRADBURN N.M., JOHNSON R.A. (1995) Computer-assisted personal interviewing: an experimental evaluation of data quality and cost, *Journal of Official Statistics*, vol.11 n.4, pp. 413-431.

[5] BARCAROLI G. (1993) Un approccio logico formale al problema del controllo e della correzione dei dati statistici, Quaderni di Ricerca, n.9, ISTAT.

[6] BARCAROLI G., LUZI O., MANZARI A. (1996) Metodi e software per il controllo e la correzione dei dati, ISTAT, Documento interno.

[7] BARCAROLI G., VENTURI, M. (1997) DAISY (Design, Analysis and Imputation System): Structure, Methodology, and First Applications. In: J. Kovar and L. Granquist, (eds.) Statistical Data Editing, Volume II, U.N. Economic Commission for Europe, 40-51.

[8] BERGAMASCO S., GAZZELLONI S., QUATTROCIOCCHI L., RANALDI R:, TOMA A., TRIOLO V., (2004) New strategies to improve quality of ISTAT new CAPI/CATI Labour Force Survey, European Conference on Quality and Methodology in Official Statistics, Mainz, Germany, 24-26 May.

[9] CHERNIKOVA, N.V. (1964) Algorithm for Finding a General Formula for the Non-negative Solutions of a System of Linear Equations, *USSR Computational Mathematics and Mathematical Physics*, 4, 151-158.

[10] CHERNIKOVA, N.V. (1965) Algorithm for Finding a General Formula for the Non-negative Solutions of a System of Linear Inequalities, *USSR Computational Mathematics and Mathematical Physics*, 5.

[11] COUPER M.P. (1996) Changes in Interview Setting Under CAPI, *Journal of Official Statistics*, Statistics Sweden, vol.12, n.3 pp.301-316.

[12] DE WAAL T., QUERE R. (2003) A Fast and Simple Algorithm for Automatic Editing of Mixed Data, *Journal of Official Statistics*, Statistics Sweden, Vol. 19, No. 4, 383-402.

[13] DECRESSING, J. E FATÀS, A. (1995) Regional Labor Market Dynamics in Europe, *European Economic Review*, n. 3, 1627-1655

[14] FABBRIS L. (1991) Abbinamenti tra fonti d'errore nella formazione dei dati e misure dell'effetto degli errori sulle stime, Bollettino SIS, n. 22.

[15] FABBRIS L., BASSI F. (1997) On-line likelihood controls in Computer-Assisted Interviewing, Book 1, 51° session ISI, Istanbul.

[16] FELLEGI I.P., HOLT D. (1976) A Systematic Approach to Automatic Edit and Imputation, *Journal of the American Statistical Association*, 71, 17-35.

[17] FILIPPUCCI C. (1998) La rilevazione dei dati assistita da computer: acquisizioni e tendenze della metodologia statistica e informatica, Sorrento, XXXIX Riunione Scientifica della S.I.S.

[18] FUTTERMAN M. (1988) CATI Instrument logical structures: an analysis with applications, *Journal of Official Statistics*, Statistics Sweden, vol.4, n.4 pp.333-348.

[19] FUTTERMAN, M. (1988) CATI Instrument logical structures: an analysis with applications, *Journal of Official Statistics*, Statistics Sweden, vol. 4, no. 4, pp. 333-348.

[20] GIULIANI G., GRASSIA, M. G., QUATTROCIOCCHI L., RANALDI R. (2004) New methods for measuring quality indicators of ISTAT's new CAPI/CATI Labour Force Survey, European Conference on Quality and Methodology in Official Statistics, Mainz, Germany, 24-26 May.

[21] GRASSIA, M. G., PINTALDI F., QUATTROCIOCCHI L., (2004) The electronic questionnaire in ISTAT's new CAPI/CATI Labour Force Survey, European Conference on Quality and Methodology in Official Statistics, Mainz, Germany, 24-26 May.

[22] GROVES, R. M. et al. (1988) Telephone Survey Methodology, New York, John Wiley.

[23] KALTON G., KASPRZYK D. (1982) Imputing for Missing Survey Responses, Proceedings of the Section on Survey Research Methods, American Statistical Association, 22-31.

[24] KELLER W.J. (1995) Changes in Statistical Techonology, *Journal of Official Statistics*, Statistics Sweden, vol.11.

[25] MASSELLI M. (1989) Manuale di tecniche di indagine: il sistema di controllo della qualità dei dati, Note e Relazioni n. 1, ISTAT.

[26] NICHOLLS, W. L., BAKER, R. P., MARTIN, J. (1997) The effects of new data collection technologies on survey data quality. In: Lyberg, L. et al. (eds), Survey Measurement and Process Quality, J. Wiley & Sons, New York.

[27] RICCINI MARGARUCCI E., FLORIS P. (2000) Controllo e correzione dati - Manuale utente, Istat, Roma.

[28] SANDE, G. (1979) Numerical Edit and Imputation, Proceedings of the 42nd Session of the International Statistical Institute, Manila, Philippines.

[29] SARIS W.E. (1991) Computer-Assisted Interviewing, Newbury Park.

[30] SAS INSTITUTE INC. (1999) SAS OnlineDoc®, Version 8, Cary, NC: SAS Institute Inc.

Section 3.3

MAKING USE OF ALTERNATE DATA SOURCES

Foreword - Natalie Shlomo, Central Bureau of Statistics, Israel and Southampton Social Statistics Research Institute, University of Southampton, UK

The focus in this section is twofold: effective edit and imputation procedures when combining multiple data sources for producing statistical data which ensure consistent, logical and high quality records; and the enhancement and augmentation of survey data by incorporating administrative data into the edit and imputation phase of data processing. The section contains five papers on these topics in both business and social subject-matter areas.

The Blum paper defines and elaborates the concepts of incorporating administrative data into the framework of edit and imputation, in particular for a multi-source data collection. It outlines the benefits from using multiple sources of data as well as the impact on quality dimensions. To obtain high quality output from the integration of several data sources, the administrative records need first to be evaluated for their accuracy and completeness. Administrative records are used for enriching information to obtain better imputation models, for creating a reference file for error localization and for continuous quality assurance during data processing. The paper also describes other statistical processes relating to edit and imputation that are supported by administrative data.

The Gåsemyr paper also emphasizes the need for prior knowledge on the quality of each administrative data source to ensure overall high quality for the final records of the statistical data. Methods for editing a single administrative source are similar to survey data. However, when linking multiple data sources at the unit level, more errors and inconsistencies may occur, especially when data sources have common variables with conflicting values. The paper demonstrates methods for editing and imputation to obtain a complete Employment File based on linking multiple sources of administrative data.

The Shlomo paper is more technical than the previous papers. It develops a probabilistic method for linking multiple data sources at the unit level, which ensures consistent and accurate records and less need for editing and imputation. The method determines the best values of variables which a priori pass edit constraints, taking into account the quality of each data source. The method can also be used to enhance and improve the edit and imputation phase of survey data by linking it to administrative data at the unit level and enabling secondary sources for obtaining basic demographic and geographic variables. More sophisticated modeling can then be carried out on survey target variables and indicators.

The Laaksonen paper discusses the need for high-level auxiliary data to improve the quality of survey data by exploiting all available information, especially important metadata that contain information about the coverage of the frame, non-respondents, field investigation results and other data processing stages. The three main tasks in editing and imputation according to the author are the following: model building for a pre-imputation phase to obtain preliminary values which assist in the editing process; error localization; and imputation to obtain predicted values for missing and erroneous variables.

The Mathews and Yung paper describes the use of administrative data in business surveys. Administrative data can replace some of the statistical data that are collected through surveys for some parts of the population. An example is shown in Statistics Canada's Annual Survey of Manufactures where administrative data is used throughout the entire processing of the survey data. An interesting feature of this survey is the need to develop a complete census for all units in the population using mass imputation techniques based on the sample and administrative sources. The paper also presents an analysis on the impact of combining administrative and survey data and the quality of the estimates and their variances.

EVALUATION OF EDITING AND IMPUTATION SUPPORTED BY ADMINISTRATIVE RECORDS

By Olivia Blum, Central Bureau of Statistics, Israel

1. INTRODUCTION

Administrative files support editing and imputation (E&I) processes directly and indirectly: On the one hand, they enable error detection and cold-deck imputation that enhance the end product, and on the other hand, administrative files improve model based imputation and lead to a better prediction of missing values (Ardal & Ennis, 2001; Ruotsalainen, 2002). In their direct use, they are used as an independent reference against which the edited data are compared. Once more than one administrative data-source is used, the comparison criteria are less direct and rely on integrated estimates. Furthermore, administrative data are used to simulate an alternative editing process after which the edited files are compared (Barcaroli & D'Aurizio, 1997; Di Zio et al, 2002).

In many cases, administrative files are considered to contain true values; on a micro level, individual records are linked and values are borrowed, and on a macro-level, shapes of frequencies are adopted and variance and variability are kept. However, administrative files carry their own errors and since they are initially intended to serve other agencies and reasons, the definition of their population, variables and categories do not always correspond to those of the edited file. Hence, the administrative data should support the formation of a reference-file, accepted as a good proxy for the true values, rather than serving as such. The reference-file can be used as a ruler by which other data-files are measured and edited, but it can also be the target data-file itself. When it is the target file, the selection of data sources usually use registers as pivot-files, since they cover whole populations and carry their basic identifying attributes (Blum, 1999; Roos et al, 2001; Shlomo, 2003). Other characteristics are selected from different administrative records, while controlling coherence within the created file.

The logic behind the building of a reference file serves the process of multi-source data collection. The selection of the best data source for populations and variables, while controlling quality within the created file, includes embedded editing and uses editing logic and tools. This reduction of future editing by applying its rules in the collection stage rather than postponing it to the post-collection stage, expands the meaning of editing to include processes of editing-prevention actions.

This extensive use of administrative data necessitates quality evaluation and control, throughout the statistical production process. The evaluation encompasses products, like the data sources, the raw file and the end-file, and elected processes among which are E&I. The evaluation apparatus depends on the available resources; it relies on internal indices, calculated within the treated file, on external attributes like frequent use or interests involved that lead to accurate and updated registration, and on external sources, usually administrative ones. The available resources stipulate different combinations of quality dimensions, which are relevant to the imputation-type involved, and answer the needs of the end users.

The structure of this paper is as follows: Section 2 refers to the merits of using administrative data for editing and imputation and other supporting and supported processes. Section 3 refers to the quality dimensions relevant to the different imputation procedures, stipulated by available data sources. Section 4 expands editing to a multi-source data collection and section 5 closes the arguments with contemplation about future developments.

2. USING EXTERNAL DATA-FILES FOR E&I: CONCEPT AND MERITS

External information supports both parts of data editing: editing, in its narrow meaning, and imputation. Detecting possible or certain errors in a data-file requires the implementation of logical rules within or between data sets, or the existence of a ruler or a reference-file against which the values are compared. Correcting errors in a data-file entails a well-defined model to predict the value of a variable, the availability of records, variables and values to enable the implementation of the model, or an external true value, or its proxy, to be imputed. While detecting errors is better off with the support of additional data sets, the correction will more often rely on them, if they are available and surpass a quality threshold.

An illustrating analogy would be the editing of a proverb. One can locate the suspected or certain wrong word in the proverb from the sentence itself, once it doesn't make sense. However, the introduction of external information, that includes proverbs, enables the comparison, the indication that there is a difference between the sentence to be edited and the external proverbs, or the identification of the wrong word itself. The value added to the error location process by the external information is two folded: the tagging of the sentence as erroneous even if it makes sense (avoiding false-positive errors), and the specification of the word that causes the sentence to be illogical (the cause of the failed edit-check). Correcting a word in a sentence, when no additional information is brought about, results in a logical sentence whether it forms the right proverb or not. However, it is just rational to turn to accessible proverbs-book (true file) or quality texts with proverbs, rather than to choose a word from a collection of possible ones, since they form an already agreed upon, accepted proverb.

A. Mechanisms and Merits

Administrative records support E&I via three main mechanisms: the enrichment of the relevant information needed (Roos and Roos, 2001), the expansion of the ability to create a ruler or a relatively accurate reference-file, and the continuous quality assurance performed throughout the statistical production process.

The additional data files allow for a better specification of an imputation model, either by adding variables not included in the treated data file, or by adding records that improve the representation of small groups in the edited file. In a hot-deck imputation, which can be considered as a special case of a model-based imputation, the administrative records improve and refine the selection of sort-variables and enrich the pool of possible donors. Moreover, the augmented information is used directly, on the individual level, in a cold-deck imputation. In the previously phase of editing, administrative records enable error locating by identifying unexplained differences in values of variables involved in failed edit-checks.

In their role as an external ruler, the administrative records support the editing process in locating errors and corroborating values in variables involved in failed edit check; they improve the ability to identify the erroneous variable. Moreover, they help to avoid false-positive errors, through a comparison between the edited file and the reference-file. As for the imputation process, if specific variables in a single administrative data source are found to be qualitative enough to serve as true values, cold-deck imputation is called for. This is usually the case in registers, like the population register, where variables like place and date of birth are accurate for people who were born in the state that the register refers to, after the establishment of the register. Moreover, registers supply the population or the sampling frame, and as such, they facilitate the identification of missing records in the edited data-file and enable cold-deck imputation of missing units.

However, if no single register or administrative source is found to carry accurate values, every additional file with variables common to both, improves the ability to create a reference-file with relatively accurate values. This process involves the selection of the best value using different processes: *the majority rule*, which implies the selection of the value that most files carry independently; *the qualitative-file rule*, that tests the file rather than the variable and implies the selection of values from the data source with the highest quality indices; *the corroborated-variable rule*, implies the selection of values of variables that were corroborated by empirical tests.

The third mechanism, in which E&I is supported by administrative records, is the continuous quality assurance. It is more of a preventive measure. Edit-checks and values comparisons between the processed data and the administrative data are carried out in order to identify missing values, errors in the collected data and errors added during data processing. Since it is done online, the error source itself can correct the error or indicate that the edit-check is incorrect, almost immediately. Future E&I can be significantly reduced, especially the micro-level errors.

Recapitulation-Table 1: Merits of using administrative records in E&I, by mechanism.

	Mechanism	Supporting Editing	Supporting Imputation
1	Enrichment of information	· Corroborating values. · Locating possible erroneous variables in failed edit-checks.	· Enabling cold-deck imputation. · Improving the specification of the imputation model, including small area estimates and sort-variables in hot-deck.
2	Creating a Ruler or an accepted Reference-File	· Corroborating values. · Locating the erroneous variables in failed edit-checks. · Avoiding false-positive errors	· Enabling qualitative cold-deck imputation. · Improving model-based imputation, including frame related errors.
3	Continuous Quality Assurance	· Reducing micro-level editing: · Online editing, which enables error detection during data collection. · Avoiding errors accumulated throughout the production process.	· Reducing the need for imputation.

B. Other Aspects of E&I Supported by Administrative Records

Extending farther the meaning of E&I, incorporates other aspects of data processing to those who benefit from the support of administrative records, through the enriched information mechanism. Three of the most routine aspects are record linkage, coding and imputation of new variables.

Record linkage is a tool to facilitate and enable heterogeneous statistical processes. One of which is the definition and identification of the entity behind the record. Once the records of the same individual are linked, critical variables can be corrected using cold-deck imputation. For example, when the individual's unique ID number in a survey is not identical to the one in the register, but a linkage, based on other variables, is possible, the ID number in the survey data-file can be corrected. It enables further linkages with less variable-rich data-sources. Statistical record linkage on an aggregate level, using a group profile, supports macro editing and hot-deck imputation and it also improves model-based imputation through the enrichment of relevant data.

E&I are embedded in the process of coding; especially in the more complicated variables, like industry and occupation. Actually, each coding process, which is not based on exact match, engages editing. It is implemented directly in the text, or indirectly, by the interpretation of the text within a context, drawn by other variables. The administrative data support the interpretation by creating or enhancing the context.

As for imputing new variables, there are two main aspects to be considered; the direct cold-deck imputation of variables not included in the basic data-file or of new indices calculated with the support of external data, and the replacement of the data source by an administrative one. New variables and indices are possible due to the unique information in designated data files, built for administrative purposes. For example, an index of well-being, on the locality level, can be calculated based on census data or it can be better specified by including data from other sources, like the subsidies per capita from the social security institute and the air pollution level from the environmental ministry. The inclusion of data from other sources in the editing process is going a long way, from the substitution of erroneous values to the substitution of data source. In this context, it is a preventive measure, carried out when an extensive E&I is foreseen, either for correction or for supplementing the data. Further implications are elaborated in section 6.

Recapitulation-Table 2: Extension of E&I supported by admin records, by process

	Process	Process Feature	Enabled E&I Processes
1	Record linkage	Individual level	Cold-deck imputation
		Aggregate level	Macro editing
2	Coding	Text	Text editing
		Context	Context interpretation
3	Imputation of new variables	Calculated indices and variables	Direct and indirect cold-deck
		Substitution of data source	Ex-ante E&I

3. USING EXTERNAL DATA-FILES FOR E&I: QUALITY DIMENSIONS

Evaluation of quality of an edited data set depends on whether there are other data sets that have been used in the E&I process or can be used for evaluation. Moreover, the supporting data influence the scope of the possible evaluation of the E&I results. The number of administrative files available, the inter-dependency between them and their coverage and content have an effect on what quality dimensions are applicable.

Quality dimensions that are directly related to E&I processes are coherence within, consistency between, comparability, completeness and accuracy. Other dimensions are relevant to the output product and are not directly related to E&I. Among them are core dimensions like relevance, accessibility, timeliness and punctuality, and non-core dimensions like response burden, confidentiality and data integrity. The following theoretical analysis refers to those directly related to E&I.

The concepts of coherence and consistency are used at times as synonyms with regard to quality dimensions, however, it is functional to separate them, as implied in Holt and Jones (1998); Coherence is measured within a file and refers to the relative number of failed edit-checks (Elvers and Nordberg, 2001). Consistency is measured between data sources and refers to differences of definitions, data collection processes, etc. These two dimensions are independent in so much as the data set can be coherent within but not consistent with other data-sets, or it can be consistent with others but not coherent within. Another closely related quality dimension is comparability. Comparability is a necessary but not sufficient condition for consistency. Data sets can be comparable in spite of the differences between them, since they share data elements like population and variables. The results of the comparison may point at the attributes that cause the inconsistency and require harmonization. E&I improve quality measured in terms of all three: coherence, consistency and comparability.

Another multifaceted quality-dimension is completeness. It refers to missing values and missing records before E&I, and those remained missing after editing. Incompleteness can be a result of a choice (not to impute values in specific variable, for example), impossibility (when no model can be specified or too many values are missing, etc.) or as a result of unawareness (like missing records due to partial frame). Improvement of quality as a product of E&I measures relative completeness rather than the absolute one.

The most common and basic quality dimension in E&I processes is accuracy (Holt and Jones, 1998). Accuracy is a relative term, measured against accepted or agreed upon values, hence the importance of the availability of external information. As most quality dimensions, accuracy measured by bias and variance, support decision-making during editing and serve a process of continuous quality assurance, which feeds back the E&I.

The above quality aspects are not always applicable. They depend on the data sources available and on the editing processes that have taken place, which in turn, depend on the data sources used. The increasing abilities to implement E&I processes and to evaluate the derived statistical quality is unfolded as data sources from different types are added, either by record linkage or with longitudinal data (Roos et al, 2001);

If the edited file is the only data source to be used, one may detect errors by activating edit-checks that are implied by logical rules, concerning the relations between variables within the dataset. One of the main problems is how to determine what value involved in a failed edit-check is the wrong one. The idea of erasing minimum values that satisfy maximum rules is one of the solutions suggested and is applicable in many datasets. The limited abilities to manipulate data in order to correct it are also manifested in the imputation process. Cold-deck imputation is not possible, while hot-deck and model-based imputation depend on the richness of the attributes within the dataset and the correlations between them. More variables enable a better specification of an imputation model if they are correlated and characterize homogeneous groups. In this realm of a single data-file, editing is done on a micro level. Macro-level problems are not easy to detect and once they are identified, correction is quite impossible since no external information is available. For example, a macro-level failure can be a too high proportion between children and women in the fertility age. How and where to correct is a question to be answered with more information than the edited file alone. As for the quality dimensions, quality can be evaluated by internal cohesiveness and by completeness related to the attributes within the file, whether they are item nonresponse or erased errors, and completeness related to unit nonresponse within the sample. Problems of a frame are not presented.

If the edited file is a part of a survey conducted in several waves, or part of an ongoing survey, the E&I possibilities are expanded. Potential errors are detected by comparing waves, cold-deck imputation can be used by borrowing background variables or by borrowing slow-pace changing attributes, and model-based imputation is enhanced, by including changes over time. A limited macro level editing is also introduced, if an accepted dataset has been formed. Evaluation of quality is also broadened by consistency and comparability between datasets of the same survey and by a limited accuracy dimension, measured against the best 'true file' the same survey in different time points could supply.

The existence of other surveys or administrative files widens the information scope that comes from independent sources. Macro editing has the supporting information needed for detecting errors and correcting them, and cold deck imputation is expanded to more variables and has more candidate values to be imputed. Furthermore, the introduction of additional data, coming from independent sources enables a better-specified imputation model. The quality evaluation is more reliable, especially the accuracy dimension, since this wealthy information facilitates the development of an accepted reference-file.

The uniqueness of registers, with regard to other administrative sources, is the completeness of the frame and the continuous updated information. Registers are reference-files and as such, they influence directly and indirectly processes and results. Hot-deck imputation is an example of an indirectly influenced process. After exhausting the cold-deck imputation with the support of the register, hot-deck imputation is engaged for missing values of variables not included in the registers. The register information improves the stratification of the population in the edited file, needed for hot-deck imputation to be performed within homogeneous strata. Other sources of information may do it as well, but registers have the advantage of having the whole population, as censuses do in infrequent points of time. This attribute contributes to the completeness dimension when evaluating coverage of a relevant population.

Recapitulation Table 3: Quality dimensions by imputation type and by data source

	Sources of data	**Imputation type**	**Level**	**Quality dimension** (Relevant to E&I)
1	File to be edited	Model-based Hot-deck	Micro	· Coherence within · Completeness (sample related)
2	File to be edited Neighboring waves (same survey) Previous rounds (same survey)	Extended model-based Hot-deck Cold-deck	Micro & Macro (Partial)	· Coherence within · Consistency between sources · Comparability over-time-same survey · Completeness (sample related) · Accuracy (limited)
3	File to be edited Other surveys Administrative files	Extended model-based Hot-deck Extended cold-deck	Micro & Macro	· Coherence within · Consistency between sources · Comparability between sources · Completeness (sample related) · Accuracy
4	File to be edited Registers (Census)	Extended model-based Extended hot-deck Extended cold-deck	Micro & Macro	· Coherence within · Consistency between sources · Comparability between sources · Completeness (sample and frame related) · Accuracy

4. EVALUATION OF E&I IN A MULTI-SOURCE DATA COLLECTION

The use of several data sources in the data collection phase presents questions with regard to the meaning of editing and the statistical production-process that it encompasses. There are many reasons for the use of administrative sources to substitute direct data collection. However, in the editing context, a rational decision making, which leads to indirect data collection and integration of several data sources, have to see the merits in terms of a lesser need for E&I, easier implementation and a high quality end-product.

Editing has always been a part of data collection. Field supervisors have checked the paper questionnaires and returned them to the interviewers in order to correct errors or to complete missing values. The introduction of computer assisted data collection, has allowed for avoiding errors by implementing online edit-checks, where the interviewers can correct either the answers given or the data capture, while still interviewing (Bethlehem and Hofman, 1995; Wein, 2004; Kozjek, 2004). The use of administrative records as an alternative data source deepens editing avoidance by bringing its implementation to an earlier stage of the statistical data production, the selection of data source.

Since the issue of data quality is not the only reason for multi-source data collection, editing is not shunned completely and new types of errors are introduced. Consequently, evaluation of the data to be used is a pre-requisite. Accuracy and completeness are the critical quality dimensions that support decision-making concerning sources of information to be used, in order to form the population frame and fill-in its relevant attributes. For example, a good population register has to be used as a pivot, since it covers the designated population (Roos et al, 2001; Shlomo, 2003) and its geo-demographic attributes. So is the case with a business register. However, if registers are not available, the population frame is a result of an extensive record linkage between data sources, which have been evaluated and identified as relevant, regarding completeness of units and their unique identification. The incorporation of the population attributes is also stipulated by previous evaluation that refers to the data source and the relevant variables in it. For example, files of authorities that provide subsidies have a relative accurate geographic address since the people have an interest to be located. They may also provide information about wages and income although downward biased.

Quality of a data source at this stage is a result of frequent use and interests. Frequent use acts as an ongoing quality check. For example, files of authorities that sell services, like telephone and electric companies, are used and updated on an ongoing basis. Therefore, they are expected to include all service buyers with the attributes relevant to the transaction. As for interests, they involve subsidies and other benefits, given by the file holder. They serve as an incentive to be registered in the administrative file with true attributes, as is the case with children allowances given by the social security institute. Yet, the very same interests may instigate over coverage and biased information, in order to be eligible for the benefits. Therefore, corroborating information is needed; either from another administrative source or from a field survey. Editing, in its error avoidance meaning, is inherent to this evaluation and selection process. Moreover, editing is also embedded in the integration of data sources, implemented in harmonization and ongoing quality assurance processes, in order to ensure coherence, consistency and comparability.

Despite the careful building of the raw data file, additional editing is required since attributes like data availability and costs interfere with the quality considerations. Imputation is needed since sources of data are either carrying missing values or having values that lead to failed edit-checks, and therefore are erased. Macro editing is required since it is more difficult to perform online, while building a file. The problem is that the external accepted reference-files have already been incorporated into the data collection stage. It means that all these files can be used partially, if at all, by using directly and indirectly variables and values that have not been used. The availability of other administrative files, not used in the data collection stage, may improve the E&I processes. Editing, at this stage, plays its traditional role of correcting the errors accumulated in previous stages; errors made in the selection process and errors originated in the data sources themselves.

Evaluation of the end result is the third time the data are evaluated; the first is the evaluation of the separate data sources, the second is the evaluation of the raw data file, and the third is an out-going quality evaluation that refers to the end file. It is a result of the expansion of the editing life cycle, in Luzi and Manzari (2000) terms. Evaluation of the end result includes quality dimensions measured in relative terms and refer to the quality change contributed by E&I. The main challenge at this stage is finding or building an independent reference-file to serve as the truth, since the process of building the file and editing it has already used evaluation and selection of the best data source.

There are two main approaches for evaluation in this situation: The first is to point at the distances of key attributes from the truth, which is represented by a new accepted reference file, and the second is to evaluate key processes that lead to the end file (Nordbotten, 2000).

Qualitative administrative files that have not been used or a combination with files that have been used can serve the first approach. It is possible to use an already used file since the result of the different combination may vary significantly from the one created and used before (although it questions the stability of the selection results). An alternative data source can also be a designated field survey, used as another source of information and not THE true file since it carries its own unique errors (Poulsen, 1997). Comparing the differences between the raw and the reference file, and between the end and the reference file brings about the effect of E&I (Granquist, 1997; Luzi and Manzari, 2000). The implementation of this approach is costly and concentrates mainly on the accuracy and completeness dimensions of quality.

The second approach is the evaluation of the processes rather than the products. Its implementation means checking decision rules, repeating processes and checking the effect of different processes within the realm of the statistical operation. For example, there is a leading principle to define edit rules; it can be a number of checks, like the maximum checks possible in a given computer resources, or the minimum checks needed to trace errors between key variables only. An alternative principle can be a context related one, like edit-checks that keep maximum coherence within the file. The activation of different principles, possibly on samples, enables the evaluation of the principle chosen and the edit-rules implied.

The process of evaluating processes may end up with many segmented results or it can add up to a single evaluation picture. In order to have the later, the evaluated processes have to be complementary. For example, the evaluation of imputation should include the evaluation of the main processes and methods used, in order to assess the quality of the imputation product, rather than the evaluation of the effect of cold deck imputation solely. Evaluation of processes may also call for a field operation and may end up being quite costly. Its advantages reside in cases where administrative files are not available and where critical selected processes have to be evaluated. The quality dimensions attached to the evaluation would be those that were aimed for, in the different processes.

Recapitulation Table 4: Quality considerations in a multi-source data collection

	Stage	Editing Type	Quality Considerations
1	Building the raw data-file: Selection and integration of data-sources	Preventive, ongoing	· Completeness and accuracy refer to single sources in addition to the integration of the selected sources. · Coherence, consistency and comparability should stipulate the integration
2	E&I of the raw data-file	Traditional: correction of accumulated errors	· The result of the integration carries source and selection errors. · Evaluation is against alternative sources or alternative selection.
3	Evaluation of the end-file	--	Two approaches: · Creating a new true-reference-file with a combination of old sources or with new ones, administrative or field products. · Evaluating processes rather than products.

5. FURTHER CONTEMPLATION AND CONCLUDING REMARKS

In a realm where multiple data sources are available and accessible, the boundaries of editing and imputation become fairly blurry. Administrative files support errors detecting and correction, yet they are evaluated as a potential data source with the very same logic and rules used for editing. Both uses aim to the same goal; a data-file of the quality traits that the end users ask for or need.

As a result of the moving boundaries and because of the extensive use of administrative data, the line between editing and evaluation is constantly moving. It happens in spite of the different goals of the two, since evaluation tools and dimensions are also used for the definition of edit-rules. Moreover, the process and results of the selection of data that have passed a quality threshold, when developing a reference true-file, is actually narrowing down the options opened for imputation. It dictates the imputation processes and essentially lays down part of the imputed values.

In this sphere, there is a real danger of creating a tautology by using administrative data that have supported editing, for evaluation purposes. Since the unlimited wealth of administrative information is still utopia, and since more and more statistical offices strive to exhaust the use of administrative data as an alternative data-source for a fieldwork operation, it seems that independent evaluation operation will be THE process to be carried out in a field survey.

The challenges of evaluating a complex product, that relies on administrative information, in a fieldwork operation, is in getting the big picture from which future work will benefit. The samples are required to be efficient since they are meant to enable the quality evaluation of the administrative files, the different processes that led to the final statistical product and the evaluation of the end product itself. If the result is a large sample and elevated costs, direct data collection will be again part of the possible data sources used for a survey or the only source for it. One way or another, statisticians will have to equip themselves with editing knowledge and tools that will enable a qualitative editing of any source of information or the product of their integration.

References

[1] Ardal, Sten and Sherri Ennis (2001). "Data Detectives: Uncovering Systematic Errors in Administrative Databases". Proceeding of Statistics Canada Symposium 2001: Achieving Data Quality in a Statistical Agency: A Methodological Perspective.

[2] Barcaroli, Giulio and L. D'Aurizio (1997). "Evaluating Editing Procedures: The Simulation Approach". UNECE Work Session on Statistical Data Editing. Prague, Czech Republic.

[3] Bethlehem, Jelke and Lon Hofman (1995). "Macro-Editing with Blaise III". IBUC International Blaise Users Conference. Helsinki, Finland.

[4] Blum, Olivia (1999). "Combining Register-based and Traditional Census Processes as a pre-defined Strategy in Census Planning". FCSM Research Conference. Washington DC, USA.

[5] Di Zio, Marco, Orietta Luzi and Antonia Manzari (2002). "Evaluating Editing and Imputation Processes: The Italian Experience". UNECE Work Session on Statistical Data Editing. Helsinki, Finland.

[6] Elvers, Eva and Lennart Nordberg (2001). "A Systematic Approach to Quality Measurement and Presentation". Q2001, European Conference on Quality and Methodology in Official Statistics. Stockholm, Sweden.

[7] Holt, Tim and Tim Jones (1998). "Quality Work and Conflicting Quality Dimensions". 84th DGINS Conference. Stockholm, Sweden.

[8] Granquist, Leopold (1997). "An Overview of Methods of Evaluating Data Editing Procedures". Statistical Data Editing: Methods and Techniques, Vol.2. UNECE Statistical Standards and Studies No. 48.

[9] Kozjek, Pavle (2004). "Error Reporting and User Interface for Post-Collection Data Editing". IBUC International Blaise Users Conference. Ottawa, Canada.

[10] Luzi, Orietta and Antonia Manzari (2000). "Data Editing Methods and Techniques: Knowledge To and From Users". UNECE Work Session on Statistical Data Editing. Cardiff, UK.

[11] Nordbotten, Svein (2000). "Evaluating Efficiency of Statistical Data Editing: General Framework". UNECE. Geneva.

[12] Poulsen, Marius Ejby (1997). "Evaluating Data Editing Process Using Survey Data and Register Data". Statistical Data Editing: Methods and Techniques, Vol.2. UNECE Statistical Standards and Studies No. 48.

[13] Roos, Leslie L and Noralou P. Roos (2001). "Of Space and Time, of Health-Care and Health". Journal of Health Services Research and Policy, Vol.6 (2).

[14] Roos, Leslie L., Ruth-Ann Soodeen and Laurel Jebamani (2001). "An Information Rich Environment: Linked-Record Systems and Data Quality in Canada". Proceeding of Statistics Canada Symposium 2001: Achieving Data Quality in a Statistical Agency: A Methodological Perspective.

[15] Ruotsalainen, Kaija (2002). "Use of Administrative Data in Population Censuses – Definition of Main Type of Activity as an Example". UNECE Work Session on Statistical Data Editing. Helsinki, Finland.

[16] Shlomo, Natalie (2003). "The Use of Administrative Data in the Edit and Imputation process". UNECE Work Session on Statistical Data Editing. Madrid, Spain.

[17] Wein, Elmar (2004). "Improvement of Data Editing Processes". Q2004, European Conference on Quality and Methodology in Official Statistics. Mainz, Germany.

EDITING AND IMPUTATION FOR THE CREATION OF A LINKED MICRO FILE FROM BASE REGISTERS AND OTHER ADMINISTRATIVE DATA

By Svein Gåsemyr, Statistics Norway

1. INTRODUCTION

When using administrative data for statistical purposes editing (checks and corrections) has to be based on computerized procedures. The volume of data (records x variables), of administrative sources is simply too large to base the editing on manual methods alone. Usually the micro file of a statistical survey is linked to base registers and other administrative sources. The advantage of integrating surveys and administrative sources is to utilize the strength of each source. This paper concentrates on editing and imputation of linked files from base registers and other administrative sources.

The procedures of editing and imputation are integrated parts of data collection and processing. Section 2 of the paper describes the infrastructure that is developed to promote electronic collection and processing of data and reduced response burden for enterprises and households. Section 3 presents problems and methods in editing and imputation for creating a system of linked files by describing problems and methods in creating the job file. The job file is an integration of the following administrative and statistical units: employee jobs, self-employed jobs, spells of unemployment, and periods in a labour market measure. The integrated job file has a key role in developing integrated and coherent social statistics and in integration of economic and social statistics. The job file was developed for the Norwegian register-based Population Census 2001. The job file might be the most difficult component to develop within a system of register-based statistics. Other topics discussed in this paper are; extended job file in section 4, measuring quality of linked files in section 5, and linked files for administrative purposes in section 6.

2. INFRASTRUCTURE TO PROMOTE ELECTRONIC COLLECTION AND PROCESSING OF DATA

Since the start of the 1960s in the Nordic countries, the development and use of computerized administrative data systems in private sector and government agencies has been based on the same infrastructure and strategy of data collection:

- Operation of computerized central administrative base registers of the total population for the most important units, (i) person, (ii) business and (iii) land property/dwelling;

- Assignment of an official and unique ID number for the main units, PIN (Person Identification Number) BIN (Business) and DIN (Dwelling) and use of the unique and official ID numbers in administrative data systems of government agencies and the private sector and in statistical surveys;

- Infrastructure under development for a few years is operation of a common portal for EDI reporting (Electronic Data Interchange), methods for designing electronic questionnaires and common meta information systems.

The task of the base registers is to identify target populations. The tasks of the ID numbers are to ensure reliable identification of a unit and efficient linkage across sources at unit level and to follow a unit over time.

A. Uses of a common portal and electronic questionnaire and how these measures affect methods for editing and processing

Since 1996 Statistics Norway has put considerable efforts into the area of electronic data collection. Three systems have been implemented, Kostra for the municipalities, Idun for web questionnaires in business surveys and Altinn as a common portal for data reporting to the government sector. Household surveys conducted by Statistics Norway are based on CATI.

Electronic data collection implies that respondents are doing a large part of editing. Furthermore, the respondents have become users of a NSI system, where you introduce the need for traditional service support, and finally, when the respondents press the send button, they expect an immediate response indicating whether everything has been accepted or not. Therefore, electronic data collection will have a great impact on the internal workflow and responsibilities concerning the data collection process. These impacts will occur immediately when you provide electronic data reporting as an alternative for most of your paper surveys.

Mixed mode data collection will emphasize the need for a central reception of all incoming responses. The editing defined and carried out in the electronic questionnaire could be reused both on file extracts and on the paper versions of the same questionnaire during scanning and verify operations. While the respondents can decide how to react on a warning made by a programmed rule, the scanning and verify operator will not always be able to take the same decision. This introduces the need for 1) training of staff and 2) automated edits and tracking flags. The objective however, should be to hand over to the subject matter division a micro-file with as few differences as possible caused by different data collection methods. This would allow the subject matter divisions to concentrate more on data analysis and editing from a macro perspective.

When reporting electronically, respondents need immediate feedback when they deliver their information. This introduces the need for common procedures to verify that they have completed their reporting duty. In most cases, central staff and procedures will be sufficient. Data reported by different methods should be handled equally.

B. Main data sources for official Norwegian statistics

Statistics Norway (SSB) uses administrative data as a source for statistics whenever it is possible. The policy of the Norwegian government is that an enterprise should report a variable to government agencies only once. Of 200 official statistics in SSB about 100 are based on administrative data. The volume of the data (records * variables) is much bigger for administrative sources than for statistical surveys.

<u>Administrative base registers:</u> Central population Register (CPR). Legal Unit Register (LUR). Property and Dwelling Register (GAB).

<u>Administrative data for both social and economic statistics:</u> Income and wealth, labour market data.

<u>Sources based on a combination of administrative data and surveys</u>: data for wage statistics, Kostra (system for EDI collection from municipalities), and database for completed educational programs.

<u>Administrative data systems to be used in social statistics:</u> Social security, social care, health, culture and crime.

<u>Important administrative data systems used for economic statistics</u>: foreign trade, VAT, enterprise accounts (all enterprises are covered from 2005).

Household surveys: Labour Force Survey, Household Budget Survey, Coordinated surveys on living conditions, Survey on culture and media, Time use survey (every 10 years).

Business surveys for short-term statistics: Production and turnover of key industries, Retail trade, CPI, Investment of key industries, Orders of key industries, Use of Internet by households and enterprises.

Business structural statistics surveys: Annual structural survey of most industries.

3. METHODS FOR EDITING AND IMPUTATION OF A LINKED JOB FILE

Usually some editing is executed by the agency that is responsible for an administrative data system and there are some controls and editing when an administrative source is received by Statistics Norway. Methods for editing a single administrative source are more or less the same as for surveys, i.e. linkage to a base register and control of consistency between variables for each unit. This paper concentrates on editing of linked files i.e. linking of files that are edited as single sources. The main challenge in developing integrated systems from a large number of sources is that *cases of inconsistency* are identified when two sources are linked at unit level.

The more sources to be linked the more errors are found and corrected for. The correction of an error is part of the editing. The starting point is a through knowledge of the quality of each source that contributes to the linked file. When contradictory information between two sources is identified, it is important to know which of the two sources should be the most reliable. Even the order in which the files are linked affects the final result. In principle, the quality of a linked file should improve when an additional source is integrated. Three challenges in the process of editing and imputation of a linked job file are discussed:

- to identify the same unit of job from different sources;
- to ensure consistency between periods jobs are active when a person changes jobs;
- to develop methods for imputing and calculating variables on the job file.

A. Definition of the unit of job and list of variables in the job file

The unit of job is defined within the SNA (System of National Accounts): A job is defined as an explicit or implicit contract between a person and an institution to perform work in return for compensation for a defined period or until further notice. Variables that identify a job:

[1] PIN, BIN, T1 - T2

The PIN of the employed person, the BIN of the work place and the period, T1-T2, a job is active identify the unit of job. The concept of job is based on integration of three statistical units, *person*, *work place* and *job*. Examples of variables in the job file listed by the statistical unit are:

person: sex, age, residence, family, educational attainment
establishment: locality, industry, institutional sector, size group
job: occupation, hours paid for, hours actually worked, wage sum of the calendar year

The unit of job represents a link between the CPR and the LUR. This link makes it possible to make statistics for the staff of an establishment from variables such as age, sex and educational attainment. Variables related to the establishment such as industry and size group can be specified on statistical files for persons.

B. Data sources for the job file

The job file is based on linkage of base registers and a large number of other administrative sources. The process of editing and imputation might affect the operational definition of a variable, for example the classification of a person as employed, unemployed or not in the labour force.

<u>The main administrative data sources for the job file:</u>

Unit of employee jobs:	**A.** Social Security data system on employee jobs
	B. Data system of Tax Agency, where the employer reports the annual wage sum for each employee job
Self-employed jobs:	**C.** Data system of Tax Agency on annual mixed income of self-employed jobs
Spells of unemployment and periods in labour market measures:	**D.** Data systems of Employment Service

In source A the BIN of the unit of *establishment* identifies the work place. In source B and C the BIN of the *enterprise* identifies the work place. Most enterprises comprise only one establishment. For the minority of enterprises that are profiled into more than one establishment, Statistics Norway has to control that the enterprise reports to source A are in accordance with the agreement on identifying the unit of job by profiled establishments. The controls on the employer reporting are mostly based on computerized procedures. The follow up of errors in the employer reporting are based on contact with the enterprise. The unit of establishment is a statistical concept and this is an example that Statistics Norway has succeeded to have a unit for mainly statistical purposes implemented in administrative data systems such as the LUR (base Legal Units Register) and source A.

During the year 2001 source A identifies *2,903,000* employee jobs. An employer reports employee jobs with a working week of 4 hours or more and jobs with a continuous duration of 6 days or more. The employer reports annual wage sum for *4,331,000* employee jobs to source B. A large number of these are very small jobs that are not reported to source A. The number of annual tax returns for self-employed jobs of source C are *330,000*. The number of spells of unemployment and periods in labour market measure reported to Employment Service during 2001 are *763,000*. Some of the jobs reported to A and B refer to persons not resident in Norway.

The task is to integrate these 8,427,000 units into *one* integrated and consistent statistical micro file. The number of persons involved are 2,500,000, i.e. in average there are 3.4 units registered for each person. Most persons are registered with one unit in A and one in B

C. To identify the unit of employee job across sources

<u>First step</u>, Linkage of A and B

The result for the year 2001: about 90 % of the jobs in A are linked to a unit in B, i.e. a Social Security job is registered with compensation or labour income in the Tax register. One reason for not finding a job in source B is that the same job is identified with different BIN in the two sources.

<u>Second step</u>, identifying more linked jobs of A and B

About 7% of the jobs of A without linkage to B are reported to source B with a BIN for another enterprise than that reported to A. A procedure to identify these jobs and find the enterprise unit used in source A has been developed. The design of the procedure is based on empirical studies of jobs registered in B without a match to a job in A. Usually the difference in the unit of enterprise used in reporting to A and B refers to the whole staff of an employer. There are other sources from labour income than B and the final result of the identification procedure is that 97 % of the jobs in source A have information on the wage sum for the year 2001.

The remaining 3% of employee jobs of source A are registered without compensation (labour income) in year 2001 and classified as not in active employment in 2001, i.e. the date of termination of these jobs are corrected to 31 December 2000 or earlier.

Third step, identification of employee jobs registered in B only

When the identification procedure is fulfilled there is an annual wage sum registered in source B without match to a job in source A for *1 428 000* employee jobs. Some of these wage sums refer to employment performed in the year 2001. A large number of the employee jobs without match to a job in source A refer to a very small wage sum. To classify a person as employed during the year in Census 2001 there is a limit of 100 hours paid for. This equal an annual wage sum of about 15 000 NOK (2 600 USD). About 250 000 persons are classified as employed on the basis of the 1 428 000 employee jobs without match to a job in source A.

For employee in enterprises with two or more establishments the establishment of the job is selected by a statistical model based on variables of residence and information on staff of the same enterprise that live in the same municipality.

D. Methods for ensuring consistency in the dates of start and termination of a job

There are some delays in employer's reporting of start and termination of a job to source A, and more delays for termination than for start. The result of this practice is that according to source A, a person might be registered with two active full-time jobs for the same day.

Fourth step, correcting the period an employee job is active

For each person there is an edit procedure to ensure that all full-time jobs registered in source A are without overlap to other jobs for the period a job is active. One problem for employee jobs that are reported only to source B is that the majority of the jobs are reported to be active for the period 1 January - 31 December of the reference year.

Fifth step, linking employee jobs and spells of unemployment and measures

To improve the dates of start and termination of the employee jobs the units of source D, spells of unemployment and periods in a labour market measure are linked to the file of employee jobs at the level of person. The result of this linkage is that for some persons, inconsistency between the period of an employee job and the period of unemployment or in a labour market measure becomes visible. The result of this confrontation is correcting of dates that improve the quality both for jobs and spells of unemployment. The editing is based on rules that decide the most reliable source. These rules are complicated and the decision depends on information of delays in reporting.

The integration of employee jobs and spells of unemployment means that the LFS concept of labour force based on administrative sources is implemented.

E. Linking employee jobs and self-employed jobs

Some employed perform a secondary job in parallel to the main job. Some employed perform both employee jobs and self-employed jobs in parallel or move from one type of job to the other during the calendar year.

Sixth step, classification of main jobs

For each employed person all employee jobs are classified as a main job or as a secondary job. The same classification is implemented for self-employed jobs.

Seventh step, Linking employee jobs and self-employed jobs

For employed that perform both employee and self-employed jobs during a year there is a second round of adjustment of dating of jobs and then there is a classification of which of the main jobs should be the most important - the employed person is classified as self-employed or as an employee.

F. Editing and imputation of hours paid for

The process of editing and imputation covers other variables than the variables that identify the unit of job, examples are calculation and imputation of hours paid for each job and imputation of item non-response of occupation of jobs classified as a main job.

Hours paid for during the calendar year are calculated for each job. The calculation of hours paid for is based on relation [2]

[2[Wage sum = Hours paid for * wage rate

Wage sum is registered in source B. Mixed income of self-employed jobs is registered in source C. Wage rates are based on imputation for groups of jobs.

Imputation of wage rates for homogenous groups of jobs

The method for imputing wage rates is based on a set of groups of jobs that are expected to be homogenous with regard to wage rate. So far average wage rate for a group of jobs are used in the calculation of hours paid for. The source for calculation of wage rates is the linked file of A and B. Information on occupation is not utilized in the groupings. In future imputation of wage rates should be based on statistical models and calculation of wage rates should include sources such as micro files for wage statistics and the variable of occupation.

Persons with an employee job that is registered as a full-time job in source A are sorted in 160 groups by sex, 4 age groups, 1 digit economic activity and 3 groups of educational attainment. Number of working days of a job is based on date of start and eventually date of termination of the job. Average full-time working week is based on the LFS - 38.5 hours for male and 36.6 for female. The total of employee jobs are allocated to one of the 160 groups and hours paid for are calculated by using the average wage rate for the full-time jobs.

The source of hours worked for self-employed jobs is the LFS. Groups based on the LFS, sex, primary industry, other industry, 3 groups of hours paid for, 1-9, 20-29 and 30-. According to the LFS, most self-employed work is full-time.

It would be useful to split mixed income of a self-employed job in a labour component and a capital component. A staring point could be to study how the Tax Agency splits mixed income into labour and capital components. The next step would be the development of some kind of statistical model to impute labour income for each self-employed job.

G. Editing and imputation of occupation

Occupation of a job is specified in source A (Social Security data system on employee jobs), but not in source B (annual wage sum) or C (self-employed). Information on occupation is missing for 3 groups of the job file: (i) employee jobs registered both in A and B, 1 905,000, for 6.4% of these jobs information of occupation is missing, (ii) for employee jobs based on source B only, 210,000, there is no information on occupation from administrative sources, (iii) for self-employed jobs source C, 152,000, there is no information on occupation. For these 3 groups statistics on occupation is based on imputation at the level of job. The figures refer to occupation for main job of employed per 1st November 2001.

The imputation of item non-response of source A is based on information on occupation registered in source A. Imputation of occupation for jobs based on source B and C is based on information in the LFS.

The grouping for imputation of occupation of main jobs, response homogeneity group (RGH) model, is common for the 3 sources A, B and C. The grouping is designed to create groups that are homogenous with respect to occupation.

Educational attainment: 6, 4 and 2 digits groups of ISCED

When the code for educational attainment of a person indicates study field, 4-6 digits the education is often directed towards a specific occupation or a limited group of occupations. This information is utilized in the RHG grouping. In Norway (and other Nordic countries) there is a database of complete registration of fulfilled educational programmes. The system is based on administrative sources and statistical surveys. The current reporting started in 1970 and is linked to information on educational attainment in the Population Census 1970.

Economic activity: 5 and 2 digits groups of NACE (European version of ISIC)

The source for economic activity is the statistical Business Register

Age: 4 groups for source A and 2 for the LFS

Sex. Grouping by sex is not used for small groups.

42. For each group the distribution function of occupation is specified. 352 occupational groups are specified. The distribution function for the actual group is allocated to main jobs of this group.

The method for imputation of occupation should be improved. More sources, such as micro files for wage statistics, and variables such as institutional sector, labour income and or wage rate and country background, should contribute to the grouping. Statistical stochastic models should be developed for the different groups of non-response. The statistics on occupation is based on the distribution function for groups. This method should be replaced by imputation of occupational code for each main job with.

4. EDITING AND IMPUTATION IN DEVELOPMENT OF THE EXTENDED JOB FILE

In 2004 Statistics Norway launched two projects that will be of importance for the development of demographic and social statistics. The first project is related to development of the infrastructure of base registers. A second project is a program to develop a coherent and integrated statistical system on person, family and household. Both projects are a further development of the Population and Housing Census 2001. The extended job file developed for the Census 2001 is to be improved and operated as an annual file. The extended job file includes other time use units such as unemployment and education and income sources such as pensions. The job file and extended job file are sources in statistics on labour, living conditions and population census and sources for research projects on labour market and living conditions.

The extended job file includes units of *time use activities* in addition to paid work such as: spell of unemployment, period in a labour market measure, period in current education and in household work and units of *sources of livelihood* in addition to labour income such as: sickness and unemployment benefit, disabled and old age pension, education grant, student loan and contributions from parents.

Integration of these units into a linked file needs editing and imputation. In Norway and the other Nordic countries, information on persons in current education from administrative sources are of good quality and have good coverage. Information of hours used in education is limited to some indicators and has to be based on imputation in a system outlined here. For household work there is some administrative sources that indicate that the person is in full-time household work. Most adults living in a private household perform household work and an integrated system would be based on imputation of hours used in household work. In a satellite to the National Accounts the value of household work are calculated. According to the Time Use Surveys the total hours used in household work are about the same level as hours actually worked in the labour market and should be covered in statistics on living conditions. One important aspect of the integrated statistic is that an activity has to be classified as main or secondary activity and an income source as main or secondary source.

5. METHODS FOR MEASURING THE QUALITY OF A LINKED FILE

Methods for measuring the quality should cover base registers, use of ID numbers, the sources received by Statistics Norway and systems of linked files. Work on methods is based on studies of linked files of administrative sources and on linkage of administrative sources and household surveys. For both methods it is not enough to describe gross deviations between two sources. To decide which of the two sources should be the most reliable one has to know the reason why the value of a variable is different in the two sources. A much more systematic development of methods is needed. TQM (Total Quality Management) would be the frame for this work. Some projects are in the pipeline.

When a statistical variable is derived from a linked file of base registers and a number of other administrative data systems it would be useful to have information on the quality of the variable. Measurement of the quality of a linked file should be based on information of each source and by linking the integrated file of administrative sources and statistical surveys at the level of person. Information on the quality of the integrated file affects the methods for editing and imputation and it should be of interest to improve the methods to measure quality, and as a result of this information improve the methods for editing and imputation.

6. EXAMPLES OF RECORD LINKAGE IN ADMINISTRATIVE PROCEDURES

Record linkage of administrative data in administrative cases and procedures is under development in government agencies. For administrative use procedures for editing and imputation need to be based on some kind of documentation to confirm changes. Additional information could be collected when inconsistent information within a source or between sources is identified and the client could confirm what should be the correct information.

The Norwegian Tax Agency has succeeded in preprinting the annual tax return for the majority of households and person. By use of record linkage of administrative data on income and wealth from employers, banks etc. detailed information on income posts are registered. The proposal from the Tax Agency for the tax return for a person is sent by mail and the person has to confirm the proposed tax return or to make corrections. This system has improved the administrative sources on income and wealth, more detailed information is available.

The Government plans to unite the local offices and central agencies of Social Security, Employment Service and municipal Social Service. This reform is aiming to reduce sick leave by measures to reduce the sickness period, to find measures to reduce the increasing number of persons that receive disabled pension and early retirement pension. Administrative cases of the new unit would have to be based on a linked file close to the extended job file described above. The information would have to be organized as longitudinal data. Improved procedures for editing and imputation compared to similar procedures for official statistics would be necessary at the united office.

References

[1] Svein Nordbotten (1966): A statistical file system, Statistisk Tidskrift No 2.

[2] O. Aukrust and S. Nordbotten (1970): Files of individual data and their potential for social research, Review of Income and Wealth.

[3] Svein Nordbotten (1965): The Effiency of Automatic Detection and Correction of Errors in Individual Observations ….., ISI Proceedings.

[4] Denmark Statistics and Eurostat, (1995): Statistics on Persons in Denmark - A register-based statistical System, Eurostat.

[5] Statistics Sweden (2004): Registerstatistik - administrative data for statistiska syften.

[6] Frank Linder (2003): The Dutch Virtual Census 2001. (Paper for WS on Data Integration and Record matching, Vienna 2003).

[7] Svein Gåsemyr (2005): Record linking of base registers and other administrative sources - problems and methods. Paper to Siena Group meeting Helsinki, February, *2005.*

THE USE OF ADMINISTRATIVE DATA IN THE EDIT AND IMPUTATION PROCESS

By Natalie Shlomo, Central Bureau of Statistics, Israel

Abstract: In recent years, Statistical Agencies are putting more effort into incorporating administrative data into their data processing either as separate statistical databases (registers, censuses) or for enhancing and augmenting survey data. The motivation is to reduce both the response burden on statistical units (persons, businesses) and the financial burden on the Agency by collecting available statistical data at much less expense. A methodology is needed for the edit and imputation procedures of statistical data based on administrative data which will ensure consistent, accurate and high quality records. This paper will demonstrate the methodology on the Integrated Census that is being developed at the Israel Central Bureau of Statistics. The Integrated Census combines administrative based Census data with large scale Coverage Surveys for adjusting population estimates. The edit and imputation processes when constructing the Integrated Administrative File (IAF) of the Census and for correcting survey data obtained from the Coverage Surveys will be demonstrated.

1. INTRODUCTION

Many Statistical Agencies have access to high quality administrative data which can be used to supplement, augment and even replace survey data. Administrative data can be used as both a primary and direct source for statistical data or as a secondary source to enhance and improve the quality of survey data. The main uses of administrative data in the statistical processes are:

- Building registers, sampling frames and censuses,
- Defining parameters for designing samples and size variables for drawing the samples,
- Auxiliary data for calculating sample weights based on ratio or regression estimators,
- Covariates for modeling synthetic estimates that can be used in small area estimation,
- Improving the edit and imputation phase of survey data by enabling more complete and consistent data for error localization and cold-deck imputation,
- Identifying non-respondents and developing better data capture techniques and improved imputation models for both unit and item non-response.

Before incorporating administrative data into the statistical processes, it must be carefully analyzed and assessed so that bias will not be introduced into the statistical data. In particular, the coverage, timeliness and reliability of the administrative data need to be evaluated and quantified so that appropriate adjustments can be made if necessary. The cost effectiveness and the impact on the quality of capturing, editing and preparing administrative data for use as statistical data needs to be weighed against the cost for collecting the statistical data directly through surveys or censuses.

This paper will focus on edit and imputation procedures for obtaining high quality statistical data using administrative data. The first section of the paper demonstrates how edit and imputation procedures can be incorporated directly into the process of combining multiple sources of data (survey data, administrative data). Inconsistencies between data sources may occur because of the different quality and accuracy of the sources, raising the possibility of obtaining conflicting values for common variables. A method is demonstrated which chooses the optimum values for the variables which will ensure high quality, consistent, and logical final records. The second section of the paper demonstrates how administrative data can be used in the edit and imputation procedures for enhancing and improving survey data. This is possible when administrative data can be directly linked back to the respondents and non-respondents of a survey at the unit level through a record linkage procedure. By filling in accurate demographic data from administrative sources, better methods for modeling and imputing both item and unit non-response can be developed and applied.

To illustrate the use of administrative data for constructing statistical databases and for improving edit and imputation procedures on survey data, we will use as an example the Integrated Census under development at the Israel Central Bureau of Statistics (CBS). This census is based on an Integrated Administrative File (IAF), which is constructed by linking multiple sources of administrative files. The IAF serves as the core administrative census file from which large scale Coverage Surveys are drawn. As in post-enumeration surveys, the Coverage Surveys are used to estimate under-coverage (those that belong to the census target population in the specified area but are not listed in the IAF) using a standard dual system estimation procedure. The main challenge, however, when conducting an administrative based census is the over-coverage due to out-dated address information (those that are listed in the IAF but not found in the specified area because they have moved or emigrated out of the country). Therefore, a second stage of the Coverage Surveys is used to estimate the amount of over-coverage, which is then incorporated into the dual system estimation model. Based on the two stages of the Coverage Surveys, each person in the final IAF receives a coverage weight representing the net coverage for a particular area. The error localization of the survey data obtained from the Coverage Surveys is determined by the linked administrative data at the unit level. Direct replacement and cold deck imputation is carried out for the basic demographic variables: age, sex, marital status, religion, country of birth, etc. For other survey target variables, more sophisticated modeling can be carried out based on the complete demographic and geographic variables.

2. COMBINING MULTIPLE SOURCES OF ADMINISTRATIVE DATA

The Integrated Census IAF file is based on multiple administrative files that ensure the best coverage of the population and the most updated information, in particular address information. In Israel, there exists a National Population Register (NPR) and every person by law has to have a unique identity number upon birth or upon immigration. This is the most accurate source of administrative data for demographic data, although the register suffers from coverage problems because of emigrants that have left the country, non-citizens living permanently in the country, and persons not living in the addresses where they are registered. Other administrative sources for the construction of the IAF are Property Tax Files, Postal Address Changes, School Enrollment Registers, and Border Control Files for incoming tourists staying for long periods and outgoing citizens away for long periods.

Each administrative file chosen for the construction of the IAF undergoes soft-editing, harmonization and standardized coding, and parsing of names and addresses. Soft-editing includes checking the validity of the identity numbers based on the number of digits, the ordering and the check digit. Duplicates and out-of-scope populations are removed, including those who have emigrated or died. In the NPR, the identity numbers of parents and spouses are given for most of the records in the file, so administrative family units can be generated. For those without identity numbers of family members, the algorithm for constructing households includes joining individuals with the same last name living at the same address. Also, married couples with different address information are joined and placed in one of the addresses most likely to be the true address. To obtain the relationships in the administrative household, a full matrix is calculated so that every member of the household has a vector containing the definitions of the relationships to other members of the household. This greatly aids in the edit checks at the household level.

The linkage of the administrative files is based on exact matching by identity numbers, sex and date of birth. Subsequent passes on the residuals from the exact matching process are based on probabilistic matching using first and last names, sex and date of birth. The matching passes are carried out under different blocking criteria. The matching weights for names are calculated by string comparator measures, taking into account variations in spelling, similar letters, and the distance between similar letters (Winkler, 1990 and Yitzkov and Azaria, 2003). The matching weight for date of birth is based on a scaled exponential function of the difference between the years of birth from the two files being linked. In some cases, depending on the file being linked, there may be other matching variables involved. Population groups that appear in one file and are not represented in other files are added to the matched files in order to obtain maximum coverage of the population.

The linked administrative file containing all of the data from the multiple administrative sources needs to undergo logic checks and edits as would any other file containing statistical data. In this case, however, there could be several possible choices of values for each of the variables to be included in the IAF and we need to choose the values that satisfy the logic checks and edits of the Integrated Census, both on an individual level and on the household level. Basically, this means that we are implementing a large scale deterministic or cold-deck imputation module, where the choice of the best value for each of the variables is based on a priori passing edit constraints and on obtaining the value of highest quality. To explain the following algorithm for this module, we will consider the example of records as shown in Table 1. The table contains records of individuals in the same administrative household from two different administrative files.

Table 1: Example of Individuals in an Administrative Household from Two Files

File	Relation	Sex	Date of Birth	Marital Status	Date of Marriage	Date of Immigration	Country of Birth
A	head	male	19601115	married	19820416	19920820	USA
	spouse	female	19821014	married	19820416	19920820	USA
	son	male	19870214	single	-	19820110	Israel
B	head	male	19601115	married	19620416	19920000	USA
	spouse	female	19621014	married	19820000	19920820	USA
	son	male	Blank	single	-	19920820	USA
	mother	female	19421211	widow	-	19820110	Poland

There are seven variables in common between the two administrative files. The head of the household has discrepancies in both "Date of Marriage" and "Date of Immigration" between the two files and therefore has four (2^2) possible combinations of records. The spouse also has four possible record combinations with both “Date of Birth” and “Date of Marriage” in discrepancy. The son has eight possible record combinations and the mother one record combination. All of these individuals make up 128 possible combinations of households.

Starting with the record combinations of the individuals, each possible combination will be defined a **total field score** that will quantify the probability that the record is correct. The total field score is calculated as the sum of **single field scores**. The single field score is calculated separately for each variable in the record combination and is based on the number of administrative files that agree with the value of the variable as well as the quality of each file. The single field scores are calculated as follows:

Let $i = 1,..,I$ be the number of administrative files for a variable j ($j = 1,..,J$). In the example in Table 1, the number of files I is 2 and the number of variables J is 7. Based on empirical and subjective considerations, we define a weight w_{ij} for each variable j in file i. The weights must be adjusted to meet the constraint that the sum of the weights across the different files for a given variable equals the total number of files contributing to the variable:

$\sum_i w_{ij} = I$. The weight w_{ij} represents the accuracy and validity of variable j on file i. Files that are more accurate and of higher quality will receive higher weights. For example, files with full address information will receive a higher weight for the address field than files with only partial address information. The proportion of blanks and invalid values in a variable can be used to calibrate a weight for each file. Files with high levels of erroneous or missing values result in lower weights. Files with similar characteristics with respect to quality and validity for a given variable j will have equal weights, $w_{ij} = 1$ for all files i. This occurs when some of the administrative files are "fed" off another administrative file for a particular variable. For example, the NPR often provides data to other administrative files and therefore there is equal quality between them.

In the example in Table 1, "Date of Birth" has missing values in file B but in general the values are of high quality. Assuming that the proportion of missing and invalid values in file B is 15%, the adjusted weight is 0.9 for file B and 1.1 for file A. Both of the variables "Date of Immigration" and "Date of Marriage" have missing values and partial missing values in file B and are of lesser quality, so the weights are adjusted downwards. After subjective and empirical considerations, the weights chosen for "Date of Immigration" are 1.2 and 0.8 for files A and B, respectively. The weights for "Date of Marriage" are 1.4 and 0.6 for files A and B, respectively. The other variables in the two data sources were evaluated to have the same quality, so both files A and B each receive a weight of 1.0 for each remaining variable: relation to head, sex, marital status, and country of birth.

Let $C_j = (C_{1j},...,C_{Ij})$ be the profile of the values of variable j from the I linked files having weights $(w_{1j},...,w_{Ij})$. Let f_{j_c} be the weighted frequency of value c in profile C_j: $f_{j_c} = \sum_{i:C_{ij}=c} w_{ij}$. If all of the weights are equal to one, f_{j_c} will be the number of files that have value c in variable j. If the weights are not equal between the data sources, f_{j_c} will be the sum of the weights for those files that have value c in variable j. The probability of value c being the correct value for variable j given the profile C_j is $\frac{f_{j_c}}{I}$. If there is total agreement in the categories for variable j in all of the files, and therefore the particular variable does not cause different combinations of records, then $f_{j_c} = 1$ and the probability will be one. This probability defines the **single field score**. If the value of the variable is missing or blank, we define the single field score as zero.

In the example in Table 1 and recalling the weights that were given for each variable in each file (see paragraph 8.1), there are disagreements in the variables "Date of Marriage" and "Date of Immigration" for the head of the household. The single field score for "Date of Marriage" is $\frac{1.4}{2} = 0.7$ for file A and $\frac{0.6}{2} = 0.3$ for file B and the single field score for "Date of Immigration" is $\frac{1.2}{2} = 0.6$ for file A and $\frac{0.8}{2} = 0.4$ for file B. The other single field scores are all equal to one since the categories in the fields are in agreement between the two files.

The initial total field score is the sum of the single field scores. In this example, for each of the record combinations of the head of the household, we obtain the results in Table 2 before the logic checks and edits of the records.

Table 2: Initial Total Field Scores for Record Combinations of the Head of Household

Relation	Sex	Date of Birth	Marital Status	Date of Marriage	Date of Immigration	Country of Birth	Initial Total Field Score
head	male	19601115	married	19820416	19920820	USA	5+.7+.6=6.3
head	male	19601115	married	19820416	19920000	USA	5+.7+.4=6.1
head	male	19601115	married	19620416	19920820	USA	5+.3+.6=5.9
head	male	19601115	married	19620416	19920000	USA	5+.3+.4=5.7

The methodology is the same for three or more files. For example, consider three administrative files with a discrepancy in one of the variables. Let two of the files agree on a category and the third file have a different category. This results in two possible record combinations, so the single field scores for equally weighted files will be $\frac{2}{3}$ for the category in agreement and $\frac{1}{3}$ for the category in disagreement. If the files have different weights, for example 0.5 , 0.7, 1.8, respectively, the single field scores will now be $\frac{1.2}{3} = 0.4$ for the category in agreement and $\frac{1.8}{3} = 0.6$ for the category in disagreement.

Each of the different record combinations of the individuals and the households undergo the logic checks and edits of the Integrated Census. Section 3, paragraphs 12-13 describe the exact method for carrying out the logic checks and edits according to the algorithm in Fellegi and Holt (1976). In the example in Table 1 for the head of the household shown in Table 2, the third and fourth record combination fail the edit constraint {"Year of Marriage"-"Year of Birth"<15}=F. The record combinations that do not pass the edit constraints automatically receive a zero for the final total field score.

Table 3 presents the eight possible record combinations for the son where the single field score for "Date of Birth" is $\frac{1.1}{2} = 0.55$ for file A and 0 for file B because of the missing value.

Table 3: Final Total Field Scores for Record Combinations of the Son

Relation	Sex	Date of Birth	Marital Status	Date of Mariage	Date of Immigration	Country of Birth	Initial Total Field Score	Final Total Field Score
son	male	19870214	single	-	19820110	Israel	1+1+.55+1+1+.6+.5=5.65	0
son	male	19870214	single	-	19820110	USA	1+1+.55+1+1+.6+.5=5.65	0
son	male	19870214	single	-	19920820	Israel	1+1+.55+1+1+.4+.5=5.45	0
son	male	19870214	single	-	19920820	USA	1+1+.55+1+1+.4+.5=5.45	5.45
son	male	blank	single	-	19820110	Israel	1+1+0+1+1+.6+.5=5.1	0
son	male	blank	single	-	19820110	USA	1+1+0+1+1+.6+.5=5.1	5.1
son	male	blank	single	-	19920820	Israel	1+1+0+1+1+.4+.5=4.9	0
son	male	blank	single	-	19920820	USA	1+1+0+1+1+.4+.5=4.9	4.9

The first two record combinations fail the edit constraint: {"Year of Birth">"Year of Immigration"}=F, so the final total field score is zero. The first, third, fifth and seventh combinations fail the edit constraint: {"Date of Immigration" ^= null and "Country of Birth"="Israel"}=F. Thus, only three record combinations pass the edit constraints and receive a positive final total field score. If no combinations pass the edit constraints, the combination with the highest total field score prior to the edit checks is flagged and will go through the imputation process for each individual.

The record combination for each individual with the highest final total field score enters the household edit checks. If this household passes the edit checks, the process is complete and those records enter the final IAF. The household edit constraints include checks for examining the relationships in the household, the ages of the family members, and other demographic variables. By taking advantage of the full matrix defining all of the relationships in the household separately for each individual, checking the consistency of the ages and other demographic details in the household is straightforward. Thus, the edit constraint defined as {"Year of Birth of Mother"-"Year of Birth of Child"<14}=F can be compared to all of the mothers and their children in the household regardless of their position in the household and their age. In our continuing example, the record combinations of the individuals with the highest positive final total field scores make up the following household as shown in Table 4:

Table 4: Household of the Individuals with the Highest Final Total Field Score

Relation	Sex	Date of Birth	Marital Status	Date of Marriage	Date of Immigration	Country of Birth	Final Total Field Score
head	male	19601115	married	19820416	19920820	USA	6.3
spouse	female	19621015	married	19820416	19920820	USA	6.25
son	male	19870214	single	-	19920820	USA	5.45
mother	female	19421211	widow	-	19820110	Poland	7

This household passes all of the edit constraints on the household level and thus these records will enter the final IAF.

Households that do not pass all of the edit constraints on the basis of the record combinations of the individuals with the highest final total field scores are further examined. From among the possible record combinations, the record combination of the individual with the next highest final total field score enters the household and replaces its record combination that was checked at an earlier stage. This results in a new combination of the household, which is then checked against the household edit constraints. By sequentially replacing record combinations of individuals with the next highest positive final total field score, all of the household combinations are checked until one is found that passes the edit constraints.

If no combinations of individuals or households exist that ensures the logic checks and edits, the following cases are flagged for follow-up and imputation:

- All of the individual record combinations have at least one combination with positive final total field scores, but together no household combination exists that passes the household edit constraints.
- At least one of the individual record combinations has missing values or did not pass the edit constraints on the individual level, but a household was found that passed the edit constraints.
- No household combination was found that passed the edit constraints and at least one of the individual record combinations has missing values or did not pass the edit constraints on the individual level.

Inconsistent records and records with missing items need to undergo an imputation procedure. Since there are overall few individual and household records that will fail edit constraints because of the large-scale cold deck imputation integrated into the method for constructing the IAF, we can use standard procedures. One approach particularly useful in the Census framework where there are many potential donors, is the NIM methodology (CANCEIS) successfully carried out on Canadian Censuses (Bankier, 1999). In this method, households and individuals failing edit constraints undergo a hot-deck imputation procedure. Potential donor households that have passed all edits are chosen for a failed household having the same characteristics with respect to matching variables such as broad age and sex distribution of the household and other geographic and demographic variables. For each of the potential donors, fields are identified that differ from the failed household. A donor is chosen randomly for the imputation from among the possible donors that ensure the minimum change principle of the Fellegi-Holt paradigm.

3. IMPROVING THE EDIT AND IMPUTATION PHASE OF SURVEY DATA

As mentioned, one of the most complete administrative sources available for use at the Israel CBS is the NPR. Extensive use of the NPR has been carried out for analyzing characteristics of non-respondents for specific surveys, such as the Family Expenditure Survey, in order to improve current estimation practices (Yitzkov and Kirshai-Bibi (2003)). In the remainder of this section, we present an algorithm for improving the edit and imputation phase of survey data using as an example the Coverage Surveys of the Integrated Census. We use the NPR for error localization, checking inconsistencies and filling in illogical or missing values of demographic data. The purpose is to reduce the amount of stochastic imputations necessary on the basic demographic data. Based on the more complete demographic variables and the geographic variables obtained from the survey data, more sophisticated modeling can be carried out for full non-response and item non-response on survey target variables.

The procedure that was described in Section 2 will again be implemented for choosing the best value for each variable in the record which ensures a priori that records pass all edit constraints. In addition to the survey data, we can link to the administrative based NPR data, which has high quality basic demographic variables. The adjusted weight for the survey data in the algorithm may be higher (or lower) than that of the administrative file to reflect higher (or lower) credibility. The highest scoring records that pass both the individual and household edit constraints enter the final file of the survey. Only households and individuals that do not pass the edit constraints at the different stages of the process will undergo imputation, thus the number of records that need to undergo stochastic imputation is minimized.

The Coverage Surveys for the Integrated Census will cover about 10% - 20% of the IAF. The example used in this paper to describe the method is based on the pilot of the Coverage Surveys, which was carried out in one town in Israel with about 50,000 inhabitants. In this example, the town was mapped into enumeration areas with about 50 dwellings in each area. A 20% area sample was selected which included 52 enumeration areas. In each enumeration area, computer-assisted personal interviews were carried out for all persons in the dwellings. The survey included 9,913 persons, thereof 9,422 persons were linked to the NPR by exact matching based on the identity numbers, sex and date of birth, as well as probability matching on the residuals from the exact matching based on first and last names. The remainder was not linked to the NPR because they live permanently in the country without citizenship and do not have identity numbers. Some initial editing was carried out based on logic checks incorporated into the computerized questionnaire and crude mistakes were corrected in the database, such as deleting duplicates. On this survey data, we will demonstrate how the edit and imputation phase for the demographic data was carried out based on the NPR.

Before beginning the edit and imputation process, a list of explicit edit rules were drawn up by the subject matter specialists. For the purpose of demonstrating the algorithm, we will use the following 16 explicit edit rules for the demographic data:

E_1 ={"Sex" notin (male, female)}=Failure
E_2 ={"Year of Birth"< 1890 or "Year of Birth"> 2002}=Failure
E_3 ={"Year of Marriage" - "Year of Birth" <15}=Failure
E_4 ={abs("Year of Birth" - "Year of Birth of Spouse") >25}=Failure
E_5={"Year of Birth " – "Year of Birth of Mother" <14}=Failure
E_6={"Year of Marriage " ^= "Year of Marriage of Spouse" }=Failure
E_7={"Sex " = "Sex of Spouse"}=Failure
E_8={"Year of Birth " > "Year of Immigration"}=Failure
E_9={"Year of Birth " – "Year of Birth of Father" <14}=Failure
E_{10}={"Marital Status" notin (married, single, divorced, widow)}=Failure
E_{11} ={"Marital Status" in (married, divorced, widow) and "Year of Birth" >1987}=Failure
E_{12} ={"Marital Status" =single and "Year of Marriage" ^=null}=Failure
E_{13} ={"Marital Status" ^= "Marital Status of Spouse"}=Failure
E_{14} ={"Marital Status" = married and "Year of Marriage" =null}=Failure
E_{15}={"Date of Immigration" = null and "Country of Birth" ^=Israel}=Failure
E_{16} ={"Date of Immigration" ^= null and "Country of Birth" = Israel}=Failure

Each one of the above edit rules are defined by logic propositions. The logic propositions are in standard SAS programming language using the exact names of the fields as defined in the data dictionary. For example, the edit E_5={"Year of Birth " – "Year of Birth of Mother" <14}=Failure involves three logic propositions:

- yearofbirth>1890 and yearofbirth<2002
- yearofbirthofmother>1890 and yearofbirthofmother<2002
- yearofbirth-yearofbirthofmother<14

In order for the edit to fail on a particular record, all of the logic propositions for that edit have to be true on the record. All of the above edits were broken down into logic propositions. Out of the 16 edit rules, 34 logic propositions were constructed. The consistency and logic of the edit rules were extensively tested by using test data, although more sophisticated techniques for checking the edit rules will be further developed in the future.

The edit rules are defined in an edit matrix and for this purpose we used a standard Excel spreadsheet. The first column of the matrix includes all of the logic propositions for all of the edit rules. Each column following the first column of logic propositions represents one edit rule, where a one is placed in the cell if the logic proposition is included in the edit rule, and zero if the logic proposition is not included in the edit rule. The number of columns in the matrix (besides the first column of logic propositions) is equal to the number of edit rules, or 16 in this case. The number of rows in the edit matrix is equal to the total number of propositions that make up the edit rules, or 34 in this case. The edit matrix is then imported into a SAS file.

Before incorporating the NPR data, the survey data was checked against a subset of the above edit rules. The survey data did not include year of marriage so edits: E_3, E_6, E_{12} and E_{14} were dropped. In order to check the edit rules automatically we developed the following algorithm according to the framework of Fellegi and Holt (1976):

- A SAS program transforms the logic propositions into Boolean logic statements (if-then-else) and defines a new SAS program which is then applied to the records in the dataset.

- As a result of running the new SAS program containing the Boolean logic statements on the dataset, new fields are added to each record which contain the results of the logic propositions. If a particular logic proposition is true on the record, the value of one is placed in the field, and if the logic proposition is false on the record, the value of zero is placed in the field.

- The output of this SAS program is therefore a new matrix where each row is a record of the dataset and each column represents a logic proposition containing either a one if the proposition is true or a zero if the proposition is false on the record. In this case, we have a matrix of 9,422 rows representing the records in the data and 34 columns of logic propositions.

- The records matrix (9,422 records $\times$ 34 propositions) is multiplied by the edit rules matrix (34 propositions $\times$ 16 edit rules) resulting in a new matrix consisting of 9,422 records and 16 edit rules and each cell of the matrix contains the scalar product of the vectors from the two original matrices. If the scalar product is equal to the total number of logic propositions for a particular edit, then the record fails that edit.

This algorithm was applied on the Coverage Survey data before incorporating the NPR administrative data and the results are presented in Table 5.

Table 5: Failed Edit Rules for the Coverage Survey Dataset

Edit Rules	Number of Records with Failed Edits	
	Total	Percentage
Total Records Checked	9,422	-
Records Failing: E_1	171	1.81%
E_2	203	2.15%
E_4	5	0.05%
E_5	3	0.03%
E_7	2	0.02%
E_8	0	-
E_9	5	0.05%
E_{10}	0	-
E_{11}	0	-
E_{13}	7	0.07%
E_{15}	4	0.04%
E_{16}	26	0.28%

In addition, not including the edit checks pertaining to year of marriage, 250 records had had least one edit failure, thereof: 76 records had one edit failure, 172 records had two edit failures, and 2 records had three edit failures.

By incorporating the NPR data we can correct a priori failed edit rules by choosing the best values of the variables that ensure that edit rules will not be violated. In this small survey, there were nine common variables between the survey data and the NPR data: sex; marital status; country of birth; year, month, and day of birth; year, month and day of immigration. Each one of the variables was checked to see if there is a discrepancy between the value in the survey data and the value in the NPR data. For each record in the survey data, all possible combinations of records were built from among the different values of the variables. In general, the number of record combinations depends on the number of variables in discrepancy and the number of data sources available. For this simple example where there are only two data sources (survey data and administrative data), a discrepancy in one variable on the record will cause two records to be constructed, each one having a different possible value for the variable and no changes in the other variables. With two variables in discrepancy between the two data sources, four possible records are constructed, and so on. Out of the 9,422 records in the survey, 2,922 had at least one discrepancy in one of the variables that did not involve a missing value. These resulted in 11,050 different record combinations not including combinations with missing values according to the distribution in Table 6.

Table 6: Number of Records and Record Combinations for Fields with Discrepancies

Number of Fields with Discrepancies	Number of Records	Number of Record Combinations
Total	2,922	11,050
1	1,785	3,570
2	694	2,776
3	348	2,784
4	74	1,184
5	19	608
6	2	128

The total number of record combinations to undergo edit checks is 17,550 records (6,500 single records with no discrepancies and 11,050 multiple records with discrepancies). For each one of the record combinations, a total field score is calculated as described in paragraph 8, which represents the validity and the reliability of the record combination. The total field score is the sum of single field scores that are calculated for each one of the nine variables that differ on the record combination. In general, the single field scores depend on weights that are defined by the user as described in paragraph 8.1 according to the variable and the source of the data in the record combination. In this small example, it was decided that more weight would be given to the demographic variables on the NPR as compared to the survey data. In addition, all variables on each of the data sets have the same weight. Thus, all values of variables coming from the NPR received a weight of 0.6 and all values of variables coming from the survey data received a weight of 0.4. The single field score for each of the fields where there are only two sources of data and all fields in each source have the same weight is trivial and is equal to the weight itself. Fields with no discrepancies in the values between the NPR and the survey data have a single field score of 1.

The record combinations underwent the full edit checks. After selecting the records with the lowest number of edit failures and the highest total field score the results in Table 7 were obtained.

Table 7: Failed Edit Rules for Record Combinations and Records with Highest Total Field Score

Edit Rules		Number of Record Combinations with Failed Edits		Number of Records with Highest Total Variable Field Score and Lowest Number of Failed Edits	
		Total	Percentage	Total	Percentage
Records Checked		17,550	-	9,422	-
Records failing:	E_1	0	-	0	-
	E_2	4	0.02%	0	-
	E_3	4	0.02%	1	0.01%
	E_4	22	0.13%	4	0.04%
	E_5	5	0.03%	0	-
	E_6	159	0.91%	52	0.55%
	E_7	0	-	0	-
	E_8	3	0.02%	0	-
	E_9	13	0.07%	2	0.02%
	E_{10}	0	-	0	-
	E_{11}	0	-	0	-
	E_{12}	43	0.25%	0	-
	E_{13}	67	0.38%	14	0.15%
	E_{14}	3,205	18.26%	1,162	12.33%
	E_{15}	49	0.28%	14	0.15%
	E_{16}	615	3.50%	10	0.11%

For the records that had the highest total field score and the lowest number of failed edits, we compared the results of the subset of the edit checks that were carried out in paragraph 18. Recall that edits E_3, E_6, E_{12} and E_{14} were dropped in paragraph 18. Based on the edits in common, only 44 records had at least one edit failure after incorporating the administrative data using the above method compared to 250 records with at least one edit failure based on the survey data alone. This is an improvement in the number of records that have to be corrected using stochastic imputation. As for the total set of edit checks (including edits E_3, E_6, E_{12} and E_{14}), 8,165 records had no edit failures, 1,255 records had one edit failure and 2 records had two edit failures. Table 8 presents the source of the data that was selected for building the final records of the Coverage Survey. Note that for each one of the variables the NPR data had a larger weight than the survey data and therefore the NPR variables were mostly selected for producing for the final record.

Table 8: Source of Data Chosen for Final Records of the Survey

Field	No Discrepancy	Discrepancy between Survey and NPR File		
		Total	NPR Data Chosen	Survey Data Chosen
Sex	9,232	190	190	0
Date of Birth	8,905	517	516	1
Date of Immigration	2,467	6,955	6,924	31
Country of Birth	7,713	1,709	1,615	94
Marital Status	9,019	403	308	95

Most of the edit failures that still remained after applying the NPR data were a result of missing data. A considerable amount of records were corrected using a deterministic approach based on plausible imputation from other family members, in particular for religion, marital status, year of marriage, date of immigration and country of birth. Additional administrative sources may also be available that could assist in the correction and imputation stage. The remainder of the records with missing values was imputed using hot-deck imputation by finding nearest neighbors on common matching demographic and geographic variables. In this example, the few records that had inconsistent data were corrected manually. For the large scale Coverage Surveys, an approach such as the NIM methodology (CANCEIS) mentioned in paragraph 12 would be useful.

6. CONCLUDING REMARKS

Because of the large cold-deck module that ensures that individuals and households in linked administrative data and survey data pass a priori edit constraints, the scope of actual hot-deck imputations needed at the final stages of processing is limited. This is the main advantage when incorporating administrative data into the edit and imputation processes as compared to conventional methods on survey or census data. We have shown in this paper a methodology for using administrative data in the edit and imputation process, both when the administrative data is used as a direct statistical source of data and when it is used to enhance survey data processing. Incorporating high quality sources of administrative data into the survey processing improves the error localization problem, the imputation models that can be used and the overall quality of the statistical outputs of the Agency.

References

[1] Bankier, M. (1999), "Experience with the New Imputation Methodology Used in the 1996 Canadian Census with Extensions for Future Censuses", U.N. Economic Commission for Europe Work Session on Statistical Data Editing, Rome, Italy, June1999, www.unece.org/stats/documents/1999/06/sde/24.e.pdf .

[2] Fellegi, I.P. and Holt, D. (1976), "A Systematic Approach to Automatic Edit and Imputation", *Journal of the American Statistical Association*, 71, 17-35.

[3] Shlomo, N. (2002), "Smart Editing of Administrative Categorical Data", UN/ECE Work Session on Statistical Data Editing, Helsinki, Finland, May 2002,

[4] www.unece.org/stats/documents/2002/05/sde/21.e.pdf .

[5] Shlomo, N. (2003), "The Use of Administrative Data in the Edit and Imputation Process", UN/ECE Work Session on Statistical Data Editing, Madrid, Spain, October 2003,

[6] www.unece.org/stats/documents/2003/10/sde/wp.30.e.pdf

[7] Winkler, W. (1990), "String Comparator Metrics and Enhanced Decision Rules in the Fellegi-Sunter Model of Record Linkage", *Proceedings of the Survey Research Methods Section, ASA* ,354-359.

[8] Yitzkov, T. and Azaria, H. (2003), "Record Linkage in an Integrated Census", FCSM 2003 Research Conference, Washington DC, November 2003,

[9] http://www.fcsm.gov/03papers/Yitzkov_AzariaFinal.pdf.

[10] Yitzkov, T. and Kirshai-Bibi, N. (2003), "Demographic Characteristics of Non-respondents to the Family Expenditure Survey", Internal Report Israel Central Bureau of Statistics, May 2003.

NEED FOR HIGH QUALITY AUXILIARY DATA SERVICE FOR IMPROVING THE QUALITY OF EDITING AND IMPUTATION

By Seppo Laaksonen, Statistics Finland and University of Helsinki, Finland

Abstract: The paper is focused on discussing the need of good auxiliary data when dealing with editing and imputation. A typology of 10 different types of auxiliary variables is given. These variables may be derived both from external sources, such as registers and other surveys, and from internal sources, that is, from the survey concerned. Auxiliary data can be aggregated or micro-level. When dealing with editing and imputation, micro-level auxiliary data are of the highest interest. Some auxiliary data should be available at the beginning of the editing process, for example, when deciding how to exploit selective editing. At the same time, the so-called pre-imputations may be done to facilitate editing. Later, at the estimation phase, final imputations and weightings will be done. It is important to note that the available auxiliary data are usually poorer at the beginning of the process than at the end of it. Each time, best possible data should have been exploited. This does not seem to be the common style in most survey institutes, quite often the same (initial) auxiliary data are used in each step of the process. However, many other alternative variables may be available, and the initial data could be updated for the reference period of the survey. This may lead to serious biases in estimates, especially in business surveys, where even the basic statistical units (businesses) may change radically after the sampling selection. In order to exhaustively exploit such data, the paper proposes a specific auxiliary data service system for survey institutes. How to organise and implement such a service should be discussed next. The author has no exact proposals for this but the success in this activity requires some centralisation, for example.

The examples of the paper are mainly from business surveys but the problems and issues are fairly similar in other surveys, too.

1. INTRODUCTION

There are various ways of classifying the tasks involved in the provision of survey data to users. I present here the following list that focuses on the requirements in editing and imputation:

(i) Users' needs,
(ii) Survey designing,
(iii) Sampling designing,
(iv) Data collection,
(v) Editing and imputation (pre-imputation, automatic and manual editing, final imputation),
(vi) Initial weighting (design weights, basic weights),
(vii) Re-weighting (post-stratification, response propensity modelling, g-weighting, outlier weighting, calibration),
(viii) Output data (aggregated macro data and micro data for special users),
(ix) Data integration, e.g. linking and matching files together (post-editing, post-imputation),
(x) Dissemination. (confidentiality included, special methods often required).

We do not look here in detail at all these steps of a survey, but the rest of this paper is focused on *step (v)*, that is, standard editing and imputation. It is important, however, to note that the impact of the editing and imputation work needs to take into account in all the subsequent steps. For example, the output data should have been *flagged* with all special operations done to them, both at the aggregate and individual level. Moreover, I wish to draw attention to the fact that when continuing to exploit several files including the initial survey file, new post-editing and imputation steps may be necessary because otherwise the data may be too 'dirty' to use.

The rest of this paper is organised so that in Section 2 I give a typology for the so-called auxiliary variables used in the various steps of a survey. Some examples of business data are given in this typology table. The typology gives systematisation for the next Sections that discuss motivations for an auxiliary service. We do not give an exact solution for the administration of such a service, because it is dependent of the institute concerned. Section 4 gives some examples on how to operate such a system in the case of business survey data. The final section 5, concludes few crucial points.

2. A TYPOLOGY OF AUXILIARY VARIABLES

The author of this paper has been dealing with various surveys, both concerning human and business entities, over a number of years. When trying to improve the quality of survey data, it is sensible to exploit all available information exhaustively. Usually, we denote the target variables of a survey with Y, whereas the so-called auxiliary variables or covariates are symbolised by X. These latter variables may also be used as survey variables Y, in which case these certain Y variables have been exploited for improving the quality of some other survey variables. Over the years, I have tried to systematise these auxiliary or X variables. Before this paper, I have only published any systematisation once (Laaksonen 1999). In this earlier paper, I had a typology of 8 types of auxiliary variables, but I now consider it important to extend this number to 10 (see Table 1).

The examples of Table 1 are from business surveys, but the corresponding variables may be given for household surveys or others, too. However, when speaking about editing and imputation, as in this paper, some types of these variables receive less focus in social surveys. For example, changes in the statistical units themselves are not as dramatic in standard social surveys than in business surveys. Nevertheless, the composition of a household may change essentially over a long period, and a large unit problem may arise in some surveys, such as income and wealth surveys (extremely rich person/household, very poor). Correct handling of outliers is important for continuous variables in all surveys, but especially in business and other economic surveys.

Table 1. A Typology of Auxiliary Variables in Surveys with Business Survey Examples
(t = survey period, t-1 = earlier available period: some months, one year or maybe many years earlier)

Type of Auxiliary Data	Examples (period)	Use
1. Actually used sampling design variables from population level	Size band (t-1), Industry class (t-1), Region (t-1).	Designing, Design weights for sampled units
2. All variables from the sampling frame, population level	Same as in type 1 plus some others e.g. forming post-strata	Initial or post-stratified weights for respondents, excl. over-coverage, based on sample information
3. Updated sampling frame variables from population level	Same as in types 1 and/or 2 but updated for period t as well as possible	Better weights than in the previous, sample and population over-coverage, under-coverage, deaths, births, mergers, splits, re-constructions
4. Other population level data from registers, other administrative sources and recent surveys (estimated)	Aggregated register turnover, employment (t-1, t); aggregated turnover from parallel short-term survey (around t)	*Macro editing, Macro imputation* G-weights based on ratio estimation or advanced (modelling) methods (calibration)
5. Micro data at sample level (respondents, over-coverage, non-respondents) from administrative sources, independent surveys and other *external sources*	Categorical: size band and industry (t, t-1); Continuous: register turnover (t, t-1), register employment (t, t-1), parallel survey turnover (around t) The above are available quickly (designing time), but others maybe later	*Micro editing*: error localisation, selective editing, … *Imputation*: modelling and task for key variables with missingness Re-weighting: GREG, response propensity modelling
6. Micro data at respondent level from *internal sources* (same survey)	In addition to type 5: any survey variables from t , e.g. survey turnover, survey employment, survey value added, total output, imputed *y* value	*Editing* incl. selective editing using 'best guess' (preliminary imputed value = *pre-imputation*); *Imputation*: modelling using auxiliary vbles either independently for each imputation task or sequentially (imputing first missing values of one vble, then the next)
7. Micro data as a sub-sample of non-respondents or respondents	In addition to standard vbles: key variables of the survey concerned	Quality checking Re-weighting, *Imputation*
8. Micro data from previous waves of the same repeated survey (panel)	Any categorical and continuous variables for the same unit (if unit changed, this should be taken into account) from t-1, t-2,… Note: also changes in weights	*Micro editing* *Imputation* Re-weighting if needed for longitudinal analysis (longitudinal weighting)
9.'Super-auxiliary' variables for specific small groups at micro level if possible	Large and other unique businesses are often so special that observations for modelling or donors cannot be found reasonably from the same survey. Hence multi-national data or other super data could be feasible.	*Micro editing*: plausibility checking *Imputation* Outlier weights
10. Hypotheses on the behaviour of variables, based on previous experiences from the same survey, international harmonisation purpose, etc.	Distributions (normal, log-normal, binomial, Poisson), link functions, conditions (CMAR, MAR, NMAR), sensitivity, bounds, relevant time series	Models for editing, *imputation*, weighting, outlier (out-error) and inlier (in-error) detection

3. NEED FOR AUXILIARY DATA SERVICE

One may think that exhaustive use of auxiliary variables is natural for survey statisticians, or that their own surveys at least have exploited them completely. They may also say that we have not many auxiliary variables available, because we have no register data, for example. These are good starting points for discourse, but in my experience some new variables or their specifications may be found almost always after detailed consideration. I give 10 examples, anonymously.

(1) An international social survey: the sampling frame of administrative sources (registers, election list, etc.) was available – not up-to-date, but not poor, either. The interviewers collected useful information about over-coverage and non-respondents, but nothing of this information was saved into any electronic file in order to try to exploit such data in quality checking or adjustments. The reason: it was the house style and they thought that no advantage could be taken of these auxiliary data.

(2) A household survey: the interviewers contacted most households but no information was saved from refusals, although many of these were willing to give their household composition, at least. This information would have been very useful for analysing non-respondents. Likewise, partially completed questionnaires were not exploited, not even saved in the file.

(3) A household panel survey: a quite good population register was available in a country. A certain number of over-coverage and non-responding units were found and saved for the year *t* file, but in the next year, no follow-up for the year *t* non-respondents was done in year *t+1*. This task could have been done at low cost at the same time as the normal update of the survey when linking register and survey data together. Moreover, the unit non-response rate for year *t+1*was calculated as the average of the non-response of the initial non-response rate of *t* and the additional non-response of the second year. This method, naturally, gives too low non-response rates. Respectively, the panel effect cannot be exploited in editing, imputation and weighting.

(4) A survey for elderly people: this kind of a survey is sensitive to changes in population, because older people may move to sheltered homes or hospitals and mortality rate among them is fairly high. Hence, it is useful to collect as much auxiliary variables both via the interviewing system, and from registers, if available. In our example case, many useful variables were not requested from the register authority although these were available without additional cost. The reason was that these variables were not asked earlier and it was thought that they were not needed for this survey, either. Second, refusals and non-contacts were not checked against an up-to-date register although this could have been done easily.

(5) Non-response analysis has become increasingly common in household surveys, in particular. Useful auxiliary information has been collected, and good methods (such as response propensity techniques) are also exploited. Made analyses have given interesting results, as well as appropriate information for future surveys, including ideas for improving fieldwork practices. Yet, these are not necessarily exploited. For example, the impact on the next sampling design has not been recognised. Maybe more importantly, the results are not used for improving the estimates of the particular surveys concerned, thus they have only been included quality reports, not for adjusting estimates.

(6) An annual business survey without rotating panel: register turnover and register employment were available for sample designing. The information was more or less old (some months' old for all but much older for most small businesses). This cross-sectional information would be excellent for editing, imputation and weighting, if was up-to-date for the survey period. Such an update could be done using the newest register data at the estimation phase, but is not done for unknown reasons. The reason may be an administrative one because the updating requires contacting another department within the NSI. Some additional costs may also arise if the updating is not done at the same time as other downloading of data. It should be noted that all information is not as important. It is most useful

to check changes in businesses, such as real births vs. artificial births, real deaths vs. artificial deaths, mergers and splits, and to concentrate on large or maybe medium-sized businesses.

(7) An annual business survey with rotating panel: longitudinal information has been overlooked, although this would facilitate both editing and imputation considerably. This also requires checking of changes in businesses, thus these changes should be considered as key auxiliary variables.

(8) A two-stage business survey of wage and salary earners. This kind of a survey uses businesses of certain sectors as the sampling frame, but the smallest businesses are not included in the frame. In principle, all workers of each sample unit are to be surveyed from a certain period. There are several error sources in such a survey: first-stage unit non-response, second-stage unit non-response, and item non-response, over-coverage and under-coverage. Completely coding of all these cases into the data file may be an impossible task. This leads to difficulties in using auxiliary data exhaustively from the same source, that is, from the business register and the data collection system. In some countries, following types of other sources may also be exploited:

(i) register information from the businesses in annual or short-term surveys, and
(ii) register variables from workers derived from a taxation or other register.

The two sources may not be fully consistent with each other due to different reference periods, or the concepts of the variables may not be exactly identical. Nevertheless, it is possible to find the relationships between these differences and then to exploit the auxiliary data in adjustments.

(9) A monthly (short-term) business survey with few questions on e.g. sales and employment. Quite a long time series of the harmonised variables was available, in principle. Some auxiliary information was also used, mainly from one or two earlier months, or maybe from the corresponding month of the previous year, too. However, no systematic evaluation of a longer series was not. Second, and more problematically, problems emerged with unit changes, including births and deaths. This kind of information was only available from the same survey, that is, from the responding businesses. Although it was available, it was difficult to construct a consistent time series. In an optimal situation, information about business demographics should be obtainable from a central business register, for example, and consequently this auxiliary information should be used in all business surveys.

(10) Any individual social or business survey that has been handled independently of other surveys and censuses. Thus the surveyors have not linked or matched possibly useful information from registers, censuses or other surveys with this survey. There are several reasons for this situation: (i) administrative problems, (ii) the linking is not easy, for example, because different identity codes are used in the linked databases, (iii) after data linking, new editing checks are often needed, and (iv) there is neither time nor resources for these extra operations.

I cannot say how typical the above-mentioned examples are in various countries, but I have come across them continually even in Finland where the possibilities for exploiting auxiliary variables from various sources are relatively good. Yet this is not done systematically, and doing it seems to depend on the competence and willingness of the staff responsible for a survey.

Hence, in my opinion, it is beneficial to establish some type of an auxiliary service system within a survey institute like an NSI. In practice, because business surveys and social surveys are so different two sub-systems may be a better solution. This service system may not need any special unit, but certainly some responsible persons. The development of such a system requires evaluation of the needs of each survey from this perspective, i.e. what improvements could be achieved in survey designing, editing, imputation, weighting and data analysis with more complete and qualified data files.

There is, I guess, also a need to harmonise identity codes, variable labels, classifications and other metadata. The question of how to harmonise such operators as non-applicable value, missing value, fatal error, another error, warning, and initial, edited and imputed value, is a special problem. Success in these tasks, on the other hand, is supported by IT solutions with as automated mechanisms as possible.

Finally, I want to discuss the standards of data files in a good system of auxiliary data service. In my experience, a typical micro file available to users consists of the respondents only, with only variables Y and sampling weights included. Maybe this is enough for some users, but not for sophisticated ones, such as (i) a methodologist who tries to check and improve data quality, and (ii) an advanced analyst who wants to exploit the available data exhaustively. Thus, the maximum number of variables X, also for unit non-respondents and over-coverage units, should be linked (or linkable) with the proper survey file.

The easiest solution for a user may be one where aggregate data are contained in the same file or system (e.g. regional totals of X would be put in each region). Naturally, full information of the sampling design should be included, not only the sampling weights. Attention should also be paid to the flagging of special values, such as the imputed and other ones mentioned above. The optimal file may become very large, especially if it contains several levels, such as household plus household members or business unit plus employees. This could be bypassed correctly with various technical tools, but I exclude this discussion from this paper. In practice, a user does not analyse the full dataset in any separate operation but instead chooses just the optimal, reduced set for each handling. This is easier if good indicators for this purpose are included in the file.

4. USE OF AUXILIARY DATA FOR EDITING AND IMPUTATION: Illustrative Model-based Examples for Structural Business Survey

The examples of this Section do not show real empirical results, although the author has done a considerable amount of analogous work. The purpose of this general presentation is to illustrate how the opportunities for the exploitation of auxiliary data vary during the survey process, in this case an annual business survey.

Section 1 mentions that the editing and imputation process contains three main steps: (i) pre-imputation, (ii) editing and (iii) final imputation. Of course, the number of steps may be much higher if the desire is to give more details, but we regard these main steps to be sufficient especially when speaking about an auxiliary data service. The following three major tasks are needed within each of these steps:
A. Model building,
B. Error localisation (and other editing) and
C. Imputation.
We will next discuss these tasks.

A. Model Building

The common feature in each step is *model building* and this is thus the first step after data collection. So, we have to build a model for pre-imputation, editing and final imputation. Each model takes advantage of the best possible auxiliary variables available at that time of the process. The model type depends, of course, on various factors, but any linear or non-linear model may be considered.

Examples of models: good guess, known function, edit rules (gates), linear regression model with constant term, linear regression with noise term, linear regression with constant and noise term, linear regression with slope (and noise), linear regression with constant , slopes and noise, logit (logistic) regression, probit regression, multinomial logit regression, Poisson regression, multi-level modelling, non-parametric regression models, regression tree, classification tree, neural nets such as SOM (self-organising maps), MLP (multi-layer-perceptron), CMM (correlation matrix memory), SVM (support vector machine). (see e.g. the Euredit Project website: (http://www.cs.york.ac.uk/euredit/)

In the editing step, errors have been localised as well as possible, and then corrected manually or automatically. If an error is minor with high probability, it may be allowed.

How to specify such a model? When considering the missingness or erroneousness of a single variable *y* it simply means either
(a) That the dependent variable is just this *y* or its good transformation (e.g. logarithm) and all possible auxiliary variables *x* have been tried as explanatory variables. Variable y thus may be categorical or continuous. The model has been fitted for the dataset without missing and erroneous values, thus making it into a so-called clean data set. Note, however, that variables *x* should be available for the full dataset, although not used in the modelling. If there is a missing *x* value, this may be imputed first, or the respective unit must not be included in the model building.
or
(b) That the dependent variable is categorical so that
= 1 if the value is missing or erroneous and
= 0 if the value is correct
(more categories may be used, too, but I have not done such exercises up to now).
This thus leads to a model of a missingness/erroneous indicator. The model is fitted for the clean dataset in the other sense, that is, variables *x*, as well as the categories of variable *y* should be correct. Note that in case (b) the dataset for fitting is larger.

Examples for business survey data
Case (a)
variable *y* = survey turnover or log(turnover+1) from period *t*,
variables x (all these may be re-scaled):
= register turnover from period *t-1,* from later period *t* if available,
= register turnover from period *t-2* if the business existed already at time *t-2*,
= survey turnover from period *t-2* if the panel used,
= turnover from a parallel monthly survey, period, e.g., some months from *t*,
= industry class from period *t-1*, maybe from t,
= region from period *t*,
= register employment from *t-1*, *t-2* and maybe from *t*, respectively,
= taxes and possible other information from registers,
= wages paid from register,
= purchases from the same and previous survey, maybe not available for all responded units,
= business demographics indicators such as = new business in *t*, dormant in *t-1* (*t-2*), not in *t*,
split after *t-1*, merged after *t-1*, other re-construction
Case (b)
variable *y* = 1 if survey turnover differs from initially coded value of turnover in the training data set, that is, it is erroneous; else = 0;
this is for the error localisation model,
for the missingness model, respectively.
variables *x*: there are similar opportunities as in case (a) but the specification and scaling may be different.

B. Error Localisation

Case (a): A simple way to continue from the estimated model that has been fitted for the cleaned dataset is to estimate also the confidence intervals for that model and then to predict this model with confidence intervals within the same clean dataset, say *y*low* and y**high*. We may consider the values outside this confidence interval as erroneous.

On the other hand, we find from the same dataset those initial values of variable *y* which are really edited, say $y,^e$ and the corresponding units. If those modelled edits and the real edits are equal, our error localisation has been successful in that clean dataset. Consequently, we may find three other cases: no error based on the model and in reality (success case), no error based on the model but error in reality (no success) and error based on the model and no error in reality (no success). Because we may use a training dataset, we may benchmark the confidence intervals so that the optimal result may be achieved.

Next, we go to look at really dirty data and make the same predictions with the benchmarked confidence intervals to this dataset, and will get the predictions for errors. The success in this operation depends, in particular, on how similar the dirty dataset and the training data are. It is assumed that variables *x* are correct; if this not the case, these should first be corrected. It is possible to increase the number of possible errors and error checkings by extending the confidence interval.

Case (b): The model gives now the predicted values for error probability. Typically, logistic regression (probit and log-log link can sometimes be better) is used in this estimation. This probability may be compared as in case (a) against the real data, and the decision about error checking done subsequently. The higher the error probability, the more values will need checking.

Examples for business survey data

In principle, variables similar to those given in the examples of model building may be tried, but in practice, fewer variables with real *x* values are available. This is because these *x* values should be available both for the training dataset and for the initial survey dataset. I suppose that register turnover from *t-1* and *t-2* (maybe from *t*) could be available, at least, and the respective values for register employment and register taxes. Some categorical variables should, in addition, be applicable.

C. Imputation

The estimated model gives some predicted types of values for using in the imputation task. These values may be very simple or complex. Basically, there are only three types of values: (i) imputation cells or classes or groups (these may also be formed automatically by parametric models or non-parametric ones, such as regression or classification trees, see Chambers et al. 2001), (ii) pure predicted values, (iii) predicted values with (random) noise terms. An imputation cell may be very simple like the whole population or based on a complex multi-dimensional non-parametric model, like in SOM technology.

When exploiting the estimated imputation model, the following two alternatives (or mixture of both) can be tried for the imputation task, see e.g. Laaksonen (1999) and (2003):

1. In case of *model-donor imputation* the imputed values are *directly* derived from a (behavioural) model.

2. In case of *real-donor imputation* the imputed values are *directly* derived from a set of observed values, from a real donor respondent, but are still *indirectly* derived from a more or less exactly defined model.

Alternative 1: an imputed value is a predicted value of the model, adding a noise term if necessary.
Alternative 2: how to choose a donor is the big question:

- Generalising: it is always a value from the neighbourhood.
- Many terms for this method are used, such as random hot decking (random raw with or without replacement), sequential hot decking, nearest neighbour, near neighbour.

All these methods thus have either a *deterministic* or *stochastic* feature, or both. A stochastic feature may be included both in the model and in the imputation task itself. Multiple imputation always requires some stochasticity but, naturally, single imputation may be performed stochastically, too.

When using the nearest or another near neighbour method, the nearness metrics may be constructed in various ways, including exploitation of edit rules, as in NIM software, for example (e.g. Poirier 2000). When using an explicit model, like regression model, it is logical to continue to use this information. Thus: exploit these predicted values with or without a noise term for determining the nearness metrics as well (Regression-Based Nearest Neighbour = RBNN). The advantage of this method is its objectivity, the weights for the explanatory variables of the model are estimated from the clean data, they are not taken from a black box or from the brain of the imputeur. This, like all nearness methods may be problematic if a reasonable number of (real) donors is not available in the neighbourhood of the units with missing values. This, for example, is often the case when trying to impute values for large firms. This just leads to the need for 'super-auxiliary' variables (Table 1) although I do not know any examples about this. Such information is obviously becoming to use when developing more global business statistics so that, for instance, the entities of multi-national companies will be observed in a global dataset, and not like now so that they are spread in national datasets and cannot be analysed.

The *model-based nearest neighbour technique* (real-donor method) may be used both for continuous and categorical variables. The former gives the 'continuous' predicted values of variable *y* for all the units, with or without missing values. The latter case also provides the continuous values, but for the probability (propensity) of missingness. From these values, the nearest real donor for the missing one can also be found without problems, and the values taken to replace the missing one, consequently.

Examples for business survey data

Now, imputation may be tried both at an early stage which is here called here *pre-imputation*, and at the very end of the validation process which we here call *final imputation*. Pre-imputation gives some preliminary values to facilitate the editing process. I think that, in principle, all the values of the key variables of the sampled units can be pre-imputed in order to get a preliminary understanding on the final results at aggregate and at individual level. Up to now, I have not come across any NSI where this type of system would be introduced into use.

I believe that especially in some regular business surveys this kind of a large-scale pre-imputation system could be useful if too much effort is devoted to it. The system should, therefore, be fairly simple and automatic, but perhaps not as simple as in some *selective editing* (or *significance editing*) exercises where the preliminary value is a mean imputed value at the industry level. If the survey is panel-based, a previous available value for the same unit is somewhat better (this method is called *cold decking* or *last-value-carried forward)* unless the business unit has been changed essentially.

Lawrence and McKenzie (2000, 245-246) use the term 'expected amended value' that may be taken using the editing model I have demonstrated in this paper. In any case, it is best to try with a simple robust model-donor imputation method in this pre-imputation step. When using the respective explanatory variables for turnover for error localisation as described above, it is possible to get rough imputed values for the significance editing process. I think that this needs more research.

For the final imputation, more effort is needed, including:

- Better model specification
- Attempts to apply various transformations (log, logit, ratios, ...)
- Updated auxiliary variables
- New auxiliary variables from other surveys as well
- Careful imputation

What does careful imputation mean in the context of regression model?

- Large businesses are useful to impute but it is not necessary to use these values in the final dataset (except for non-key variables). It is best to contact them again in order to get the real values or at least rough real values.
- Predicted values as in pre-imputation are perhaps not reasonable as imputed values, some noise (but with care) should be added.
- However: predicted values (with or without noise term) may be used as metrics for nearest neighbours, not as often in cases of large businesses where good real donors are not available as for small and medium-sized businesses.
- Final imputation is often useful to perform within homogenous imputation cells.
- Sampling weights should be taken into account in final imputation.
- Sequential imputation is becoming more and more common in business surveys, for example, so that key variables are imputed first and their imputed values are used as explanatory variables when imputing non-key variables.
- Make results consistent with each other using edit rules.
- Check completed results against available benchmarking data (aggregate level).

V. CONCLUSION

All available and 'useful' internal or external data related to each survey may and should be used as auxiliary information. It is not always clear how these data could best be exploited because they are often not in the same database. A solution is to establish a so-called *Auxiliary Data Service (ADS)* within an NSI or another survey institute. Currently, such a system exists in all NSIs, implicitly at least, but I would like to see it exist more explicitly. In practice, it may be best to organise this service separately for business surveys and household surveys, since the needs and the variables of these surveys are quite different. Naturally, surveys that are in-between, such as those on wages take advantage of both business and individual variables.

References

[1] Chambers, R.L., Hoogland, J., Laaksonen, S., Mesa, D.M., Pannekoek, J., Piela, P., Tsai, P. and de Waal, T. (2001). *The AUTIMP-project: Evaluation of Imputation Software*. Research Paper 0122. Statistics Netherlands.

[2] Laaksonen, S. (1999). Weighting and Auxiliary Variables in Sample Surveys. In: G. Brossier and A-M. Dussaix (eds.). "Enquêtes et Sondages. Méthodes, modèles, applications, nouvelles approches". Dunod. Paris. pp. 168-180.

[3] Laaksonen, S. (2000). Regression-Based Nearest Neighbour Hot Decking. *Computational Statistics* 15, 1, 65-71.

[4] Laaksonen, S. (2003). Alternative Imputation Techniques For Complex Metric Variables. *The Journal of Applied Statistics,* 1006-1021.

[5] Lawrence, D. and McKenzie, R. (2000). The General Application of Significance Editing. *Journal of Official Statistics* 16, 243-253

[6] Poirier, C. (2000). A Functional Evaluation of Edit and Imputation Tools. The Cardiff UNECE meeting

[7] Euredit Project Website: http://www.cs.york.ac.uk/euredit/

[8] Dacseis Project Website: http://www.dacseis.de/deliverables/ .

USE OF ADMINISTRATIVE DATA IN STATISTICS CANADA'S ANNUAL SURVEY OF MANUFACTURES

by Steve Matthews, Canada Post and Wesley Yung, Statistics Canada

1. INTRODUCTION

In an ongoing effort to reduce respondent burden, to reduce the cost of survey programs and to improve data quality, Statistics Canada has been working to increase the use of administrative data in its survey programs. One survey that makes extensive use of administrative data is the Annual Survey of Manufactures (ASM). The ASM is an annual survey covering all manufacturing establishments as defined by the North American Industrial Classification System (NAICS). Information collected by the ASM includes financial variables (revenues, expenses and salaries for example) and commodity variables (manufacturing inputs and outputs for example). Due to certain agreements with principal data users, the ASM is required to produce micro-data for a large portion of its target population. This pseudo-census is achieved by extensive use of tax data. This paper describes the use of the tax data in the ASM, with particular attention to the Edit and Imputation stage. Section 2 provides a quick overview of the tax data used by ASM. The ASM is described in section 3 and the use of tax data in the ASM is presented in section 4. Section 5 provides a summary of the work done to evaluate the impact of the use of tax data on the quality of the survey estimates. Conclusions and future work are given in section 6.

2. TAX DATA

Statistic Canada has long recognized the advantages of an increased use of administrative data for Statistics Canada's Business Survey Program in terms of reducing respondent burden and potential cost savings. In response, extensive programs have been put in place to provide administrative data to Statistics Canada surveys. Two of these programs, covering incorporated and non-incorporated businesses, are administered by the Tax Data Division of Statistics Canada. The tax data is collected by the Canadian Revenue Agency (CRA) and Statistics Canada has access to the tax files for statistical purposes through a data sharing agreement with the CRA. In this section, the two programs responsible for producing the required data are described.

A. T1 (Non-incorporated) Tax Data

While detailed data for incorporated businesses are available through the T2 tax program, for the non-incorporated businesses only estimates of totals for specific variables at the industry by province level are available through tax data. These estimates are produced based on a simple random sample of non-incorporated businesses, for which several variables are obtained by transcribing data from paper tax forms or from electronically filed tax forms. The set of variables available for the non-incorporated businesses is not nearly as extensive as the set for incorporated businesses and the data are available only for the sampled units. The data for non-incorporated businesses are subjected to an edit and imputation process, and the estimates are produced using a calibration estimator that benchmarks the estimates to the total revenues for the T1 population. For more information on Statistics Canada's T1 tax program, see Hutchinson, Jocelyn and Cooray (2004).

B. T2 (Incorporated) Tax Data

Incorporated businesses in Canada are now required by law to provide the information contained in their financial statements (T2 tax form) in the Generalized Index of Financial Information (GIFI) format. The GIFI format is an extensive list of financial statement items where each item has a unique code. CRA captures the tax files from all incorporated businesses in Canada and makes this data available to Statistics Canada. This data source provides a very detailed breakdown of the expenses, revenues and inventories for each business (approximately 700 variables divided into 7 sections) but only eight fields are mandatory (the 7 section totals and Net Income/Loss). CRA collects the data throughout the year and provides the data to Statistics Canada on a monthly basis where several verification processes are performed. These processes include editing the data to ensure that the data are clean and that the data balance; a generic to detail allocation where totals are allocated to the detailed level necessary; and transforming the data to a standard format to facilitate tax data use by business surveys. Once a year, annual processes, such as imputation, are executed. For more details on the processing of GIFI data at Statistics Canada, see Hamel and Belcher (2002).

3. THE ANNUAL SURVEY OF MANUFACTURES

The Annual Survey of Manufactures is administered as part of Statistics Canada's Unified Enterprise Survey Program (UES). The UES has united separate business surveys into a single master survey program with the goals of collecting more industry and commodity detail at a provincial level, of having survey questionnaires with a consistent look, structure and content, of reducing respondent burden by avoiding overlap in survey questionnaires and of employing similar survey methodologies. Although the ASM uses the same sampling frame as the UES, it does differ in some aspects, such as the survey methodology, due to the nature of the details collected and the importance of its estimates. The estimates from the ASM are used fairly widely since the Manufacturing industry represents a significant portion of the business activity in Canada; roughly 17% of the Gross Domestic Product. In this section, some details of the ASM methodology will be presented.

A. Target Population

The target population for the ASM consists of all incorporated and non-incorporated businesses in Canada who are involved in the manufacturing industry. A survey frame is produced on an annual basis using Statistics Canada's Business Register (BR), which contains all businesses in Canada. All businesses on the BR have a statistical structure consisting of four levels in the following order: the enterprise, the company, the establishment and the location. An enterprise can consist of one or many companies and a company can consist of one or many establishments and so on. For the majority of businesses in Canada, the four levels coincide and the business is known as a simple business. If a business is not simple, then it is considered a complex business. In addition to the statistical structure, a number of administrative variables are available on the BR including the industry classification based on NAICS, geographic classification and an estimate of annual revenues.

The target population of the ASM is highly skewed with relatively few businesses representing a large share of the total revenue and expenses. In order to reduce survey costs and respondent burden on the smaller businesses in the target population, a large number of units are assigned to a 'take-none' portion where no data collection is performed. Based on frame information, units in the take-none portion represent less than 10% of the overall economic activity. Estimation of the contribution from the take-none portion is done using tax data and is discussed in section 3.5. Once the take-none units are identified, the remaining units make up the survey portion.

B. Sample Design

The sample design within the survey portion is a stratified simple random sample with take-all strata and take-some strata. All complex units, i.e. units that are not defined as simple, are placed in the take-all strata and are sampled with probability 1. The remaining units, i.e. the simple units, are then stratified according to industrial classification (at the 3-digit NAICS level), geographic classification (provinces and territories) and a size measure based on annual revenues from the BR. Stratum boundaries and sample allocation are determined by applying the Lavallée-Hidiroglou (1988) method within each industry by province cell for pre-specified target CVs. Note that the Lavallée-Hidiroglou algorithm identifies additional take-all units.

C. Data Collection

The ASM questionnaire consists of two parts; a financial portion and a commodity portion. The financial portion is quite detailed and asks for a detailed breakdown of revenues, expenses and inventories. These data items are referred to as financial variables and are similar to information available from tax data. The commodity portion of the questionnaire asks for details such as the amount of each type of goods manufactured and those used as a manufacturing input. These items are referred to as commodity variables and will not be discussed further in this paper.

The ASM is a mail-out/mail-back survey with telephone follow-up. The mail-out occurs between November of the reference year and March of the year following the reference year depending on the fiscal year end of the selected business. Follow-up is managed by a score function to ensure efficient follow-up procedures. For more on the ASM score function, see Philips (2003).

D. Edit and Imputation

As with most large business surveys, edits are applied to the data at various stages of the processing system to ensure accuracy and coherence. In terms of imputation, the ASM is different than most business surveys due to the need for complete financial data for all units in the survey population. As the collection budget for the ASM is limited, imputation methods using T2 tax data extensively are used to produce this pseudo-census. In addition to the use of T2 data in the survey portion, it is used in conjunction with T1 data to estimate the contribution of the take-none portion. Take-none estimation is described in the following section and the use of T2 data in the survey portion is described in section 4.

E. Estimation

Once imputation is complete, micro-data is available for all units in the survey portion and estimation for the survey portion consists simply of aggregating the micro-data to obtain estimates. For the take-none portion, only Total Revenues is estimated and this estimate is based on T1 and T2 tax data as both incorporated and non-incorporated businesses make up the take-none portion. The contribution from the incorporated businesses will be obtained from the T2 tax data and non-incorporated portion will come from the T1 tax program. For the incorporated businesses, revenue values will come from their GIFI forms and will simply be added up. For the non-incorporated businesses, a sample of their T1 tax records will be selected, processed and a weighted estimate, benchmarked to Total Revenues from the T1 population, will be produced.

4. USE OF TAX DATA IN E&I FOR THE SURVEY PORTION

As with most types of administrative data, there are certain limitations to the T2 data as pertains to the ASM. Some of the challenges faced by the ASM were the differences in the collection units between tax and ASM and the availability of tax data corresponding to ASM variables. One important difference between the T2 data and the data collected by the ASM is the collection unit. The CRA receives data at the legal entity level (a unit defined according to legal concepts), while the survey data is generally collected at the statistical entity level as defined by the statistical structure on the BR. For simple businesses, the legal entity and the statistical entity correspond and the use of tax data for these units is straightforward. However, for complex businesses the use of tax data is much more difficult as an additional process is required to allocate the tax data from the legal entity to the statistical entity (which do not correspond in complex businesses). Due to this difficulty, the ASM uses tax data for simple businesses only and the complex businesses, treated as take-all units, will continue to be surveyed.

Of the 81 financial variables collected by the ASM, T2 data is able to provide 46 variables that are equivalent in concept to the ASM variable. A number of approaches were proposed for the use of tax data for these variables, including direct tax replacement, and use as auxiliary variables for model-based imputation methods. The first priority was to identify the variables that could be directly tax replaced. Before accepting the data from the tax files at face value, an evaluation study was done to compare the values obtained from the tax data with the data collected via the reference year 2001 ASM survey. Comparisons were done at the micro level according to several criteria to evaluate each variable individually. The analysis included a number of aspects, based on the set of businesses for which we have both reported tax data and reported survey data (approximately 6,000) including:

(a) Correlation Analysis: The correlation between the reported tax and survey data was calculated at several levels to determine if a linear relationship exists between the survey and the tax value. The analysis showed that for some variables, such as Total Expenses, the correlation was very high (approximately 90%) but for others, such as Maintenance and Repair Expenses, it was essentially zero.

(b) Consistency of Details: Since not all businesses incur expenses of a certain type, it is valid to receive zero values for many of the detailed revenues, expenses and inventories. This analysis verified whether or not the same units tended to report zero values for the same details according to the tax data and the survey data. The analysis showed similar results as the correlation analysis. That is, some variables matched very well (98% for Total Expenses) and some not so well (50% for Maintenance and Repair Expenses)

(c) Distribution of Ratios: The ratio of the survey to the tax value was calculated for each unit and for each variable, and histograms of the ratio values were produced to identify potential biases or increased variances that would result from substituting tax data for missing survey values. The results of this analysis showed that the ratios of survey to tax data are not that stable. The percentage of ratios that were in the range of (0.9, 1.1) varied from 60% for Total Expenses to 17% for Maintenance and Repair Expenses.

(d) Population Estimates of Totals: Weighted estimates were produced based on the set of units for which both sources of data were available, using the survey data and the tax data to measure the variable of interest. The relative difference between the tax-based estimate and the survey-based estimate was calculated. The relative differences obtained varied from a low of 0.7% for Total Manufacturing Output to a high of 20% for Amortization and Depreciation Expenses.

The results of this analysis can be generalized to conclude that for variables that relate to very general concepts (for example Total Revenues, Total Expenses), direct tax replacement will not have an important impact on the data quality (both in terms of microdata and aggregated estimates). However, for many variables that relate to detailed concepts (Expenses for Advertising, Expenses for Depreciation/Amortization) direct tax replacement may affect the data quality. This could be in terms of a bias or an increased variance. For this reason, based on these analyses a group of 7 variables was identified for which survey data will be replaced with tax data for some businesses. For a more detailed description of the study and recommendations, please refer to Batten and Matthews (2003).

Assuming that these 7 variables will be completed by direct substitution of tax values, the challenge remains to produce micro-data for all of the other financial variables. Since these 7 variables correspond to the totals of each financial section, this task consists of estimating the distribution of detailed revenues, expenses and inventories that should be imposed on the record requiring imputation. This is done in the general imputation system using the following methods:

(a) Historical Imputation – In this method, if the business reported their survey data in the previous reference year, the reported distribution from each section is copied to the current year and pro-rated to the totals coming from the tax data. Note that for the majority of records that are non-sampled, historical data will not be available.

(b) Ratio Imputation – This method is used if the business did not report their survey data in the previous reference year (this would be the case for most of the non-sampled records). Using the set of respondents from the current reference year, the ratio between the total and each detail is estimated within imputation groups, and these ratios are applied to the total coming from the tax data. Each section is then pro-rated to ensure that the totals are respected.

(c) Nearest Neighbor Donor Imputation – This method is used if the auxiliary data that is required for Historical or Ratio Imputation is not available. In Nearest Neighbor Donor Imputation, the data from the responding record that is most similar to the record requiring imputation is used to complete the entire record. All of the donor-imputed values are adjusted to reflect the difference in annual revenues of the donor and recipient.

These methods are applied within imputation classes, which are constructed according to geographic, and industry classifications. In general, we attempt to construct these classes at a detailed level to reduce biases, but in some cases the groups need to be aggregated to produce a suitable number of respondents in each group.

5. IMPACT OF TAX DATA

In order to evaluate the impact of using tax data on the quality of the estimates produced, estimates of population totals and corresponding variances were calculated under three different scenarios. The first scenario was under the assumption that tax data is not available and the population total is estimated using weights based on the sample design. The second scenario assumed that tax data is not available, but a pseudo-census is produced using revenue from the BR as an auxiliary variable for imputation purposes. The final scenario assumed that tax data is available for use for replacing non-responding and non-sampled units as described in section 4. For variance estimators, we use the Shao-Steel approach (1999) to take into account the imputation performed. The imputation variance could be considerable under the scenarios where imputation or tax data replacement is used for non-responding and non-sampled units.

In the Shao-Steel approach, the traditional view of non-response and sampling is reversed. Traditionally, it is assumed that a sample is drawn from the population, and some of the sampled units do not respond. For the Shao-Steel approach, it is assumed that the units in the population are divided into respondents and non-respondents and then a sample is drawn from this population. This allows one to derive the variance estimators using reversed conditional arguments. For example, under the traditional approach, the expectation with respect to the non-response mechanism is conditional on the realized sample, whereas under the Shao-Steel approach, the expectation and variance with respect to the non-response mechanism is not conditional, but the variance and expectation with respect to the sample is conditional on the non-response mechanism. The two approaches yield similar results with small sampling fractions, however the variance estimators from the Shao-Steel approach can be simpler to derive, can be extended to complex imputation strategies, and are valid regardless of the sampling fractions.

We now compare three estimators that could be used to produce population level estimates from the ASM data. The first two would be possible in the absence of tax data, and the third relies on the availability of tax data in the population. Note that under all three scenarios, we assume that the imputation classes are mutually exclusive and exhaustive subgroups, which consist of aggregates of sampling strata. We assume that within each imputation class there is a uniform response mechanism when deriving the Shao-Steel variance estimates. That is, within each imputation class the probability of a unit responding is the same for all units and is independent of other units. Since the imputation classes are independent of each other in terms of both sampling and imputation, the variance estimates calculated at this level can be aggregated to produce variance estimates for estimates of totals at more aggregated levels.

A. Tax data unavailable, macro estimates only

If the tax data were not available, the massive imputation approach would not be feasible, and we would be relegated to a Horvitz-Thompson estimator. Ratio imputation (using an annual revenue estimate from the survey frame as the auxiliary variable x) could be used to complete the non-responding records among the sample, but would not produce micro-data for non-sampled records as is currently required. In this case, the estimator of the total is given by

$$\hat{Y}^{(1)} = \sum_h \sum_{i \in s_h} w_{hi} y'_{hi}$$

where (hi) represents the i-th unit in the h-th stratum, s_h is the set of sampled units in the h-th stratum, w_{hi} are the survey weights defined by the sample design, $y'_{hi} = a_{hi} y_{hi} + (1 - a_{hi}) \hat{R}_x x_{hi}$, a_{hi} is the response indicator variable defined as $a_{hi} = 1$ for responding units and $a_{hi} = 0$ otherwise and

$$\hat{R}_x = \frac{\sum_h \sum_{i \in s_h} a_{hi} w_{hi} y_{hi}}{\sum_h \sum_{i \in s_h} a_{hi} w_{hi} x_{hi}}.$$

The estimated variance for this estimator derived under the Shao-Steel approach is given by $v^{(1)} = v_1^{(1)} + v_2^{(1)}$, where

$$v_1^{(1)} = \sum_h \left(1 - \frac{n_h}{N_h}\right) \frac{N_h^2}{n_h} \frac{\sum_{i \in s_h} (\xi_{hi} - \xi_{h\bullet})^2}{(n_h - 1)}$$

with $\xi_{hi} = y'_{hi} + a_{hi} \hat{c}_{hi} \hat{\varepsilon}_{hi}$, $\hat{c}_{hi} = \dfrac{\sum_h \sum_{i \in s_h} w_{hi} (1 - a_{hi}) x_{hi}}{\sum_h \sum_{i \in s_h} w_{hi} a_{hi} x_{hi}}$ $\xi_{h\bullet} = \dfrac{\sum_{i \in s_h} \xi_{hi}}{n_h}$, $\hat{\varepsilon}_{hi} = y_{hi} - \hat{R}_x x_{hi}$ and

$v_2^{(1)} = N\hat{p}(1 - \hat{p}) \tilde{s}_d^2$ with

$$\hat{p} = \frac{\sum_h \sum_{i \in s_h} w_{hi} a_{hi}}{\sum_h N_h}$$

and

$$\tilde{s}_d^2 = \frac{\sum_h \sum_{i \in s_h} w_{hi} a_{hi} \hat{\varepsilon}_{hi}^2 (\hat{c}_{hi} + 1)^2}{\sum_h \sum_{i \in s_h} w_{hi} a_{hi}}.$$

B. Tax data unavailable, pseudo-census

In order to satisfy the requirement for a pseudo-census, in the absence of tax data, an estimator could be used where the non-sample and non-responding units could be imputed using ratio imputation (with the annual estimated revenues, x_{hi}, as the auxiliary variable). In this case, we would produce a full population dataset so no weighting would be required and the estimator of the total would be

$$\hat{Y}^{(2)} = \sum_h \sum_{i \in s_h} \delta_{hi} y'_{hi} + \sum_h \sum_{i \in U_h \setminus s_h} (1 - \delta_{hi}) y^*_{hi} ,$$

with y'_{hi} as defined above, $y^*_{hi} = \hat{R}_x x_{hi}$, δ_{hi} is the survey portion indicator variable defined as $\delta_{hi}=1$ for units in the survey portion and 0 otherwise, U_h is the set of population units in the h-th stratum and $U_h \setminus s_h$ is the set of non-sampled units in the h-th stratum. Since we proceed with the assumption of a census with non-response, the variance estimator includes only one term, representing the non-response variance. The estimated variance for this estimator derived under the Shao-Steel approach is given by $v^{(2)} = N\hat{p}(1-\hat{p})\tilde{s}_d^2$, with

$$\hat{p} = \frac{\sum_h \sum_{i \in U_h} a_{hi}}{\sum_h N_h} , \quad \tilde{s}_d^2 = \frac{\sum_h \sum_{i \in U_h} a_{hi} \hat{\varepsilon}_{hi}^2 (\hat{c}_{hi} + 1)^2}{\sum_h \sum_{i \in U_h} a_{hi}} , \quad \hat{\varepsilon}_{hi} = y_{hi} - \hat{R}_x x_{hi}$$

and

$$\hat{c}_{hi} = \frac{\sum_h \sum_{i \in U_h} w_{hi} (1 - a_{hi}) x_{hi}}{\sum_h \sum_{i \in U_h} w_{hi} a_{hi} x_{hi}} .$$

C. Tax data available, pseudo-census

The methodology that will be used in production would directly replace the tax data for non-respondents and out-of-sample units. Clearly this would not be possible without the availability of the tax data for all population units, and this satisfies the requirement to produce data for a pseudo-census. For the variables that are directly tax replaced, the estimate of the total is given by

$$\hat{Y}^{(3TR)} = \sum_h \sum_{i \in s_h} \delta_{hi} y'_{hi} + \sum_h \sum_{i \in U_h \setminus s_h} (1 - \delta_{hi}) z_{hi}$$

with $y'_{hi} = a_{hi} y_{hi} + (1 - a_{hi}) z_{hi}$, a_{hi} and δ_{hi} as defined above and z_{hi} is the corresponding tax data value for the (hi)-th unit.

25. The estimated variance for this estimator derived under the Shao-Steel approach is given by $v^{(3TR)} = N\hat{p}(1-\hat{p})\tilde{s}_d^2$ with $\hat{p} = \frac{\sum_h \sum_{i \in U_h} a_{hi}}{\sum_h N_h}$, $\tilde{s}_d^2 = \frac{\sum_h \sum_{i \in U_h} a_{hi} \hat{\varepsilon}_{hi}^2}{\sum_h \sum_{i \in U_h} a_{hi}}$, and $\hat{\varepsilon}_{hi} = y_{hi} - \hat{R}_z z_{hi}$.

For variables that are imputed via ratio imputation based on a variable directly replaced by tax, the estimator of the total is given by

$$\hat{Y}^{(3RI)} = \sum_h \sum_i \delta_{hi} y'_{hi} + \sum_h \sum_i (1 - \delta_{hi}) y^*_{hi} ,$$

with y'_{hi} and δ_{hi} as defined above, $y^*_{hi} = \hat{R}_z z_{hi}$ and

$$\hat{R}_z = \frac{\sum_h \sum_{i \in s_h} a_{hi} w_{hi} y_{hi}}{\sum_h \sum_{i \in s_h} a_{hi} w_{hi} z_{hi}}.$$

The estimated variance for this estimator derived under the Shao-Steel approach is given by

$$v^{(3RI)} = N\hat{p}(1-\hat{p})\tilde{s}_d^2 \text{ with } \hat{p} = \frac{\sum_h \sum_{i \in U_h} a_{hi}}{\sum_h N_h},\ \tilde{s}_d^2 = \frac{\sum_h \sum_{i \in U_h} a_{hi} \hat{\varepsilon}_{hi}^2 (\hat{c}_{hi}+1)^2}{\sum_h \sum_{i \in U_h} a_{hi}},\ \hat{\varepsilon}_{hi} = y_{hi} - \hat{R}_z z_{hi} \text{ and}$$

$$\hat{c}_{hi} = \frac{\sum_h \sum_{i \in U_h} w_{hi}(1-a_{hi}) z_{hi}}{\sum_h \sum_{i \in U_h} w_{hi} a_{hi} z_{hi}}.$$

Using this approach, the estimates of totals and their corresponding variances were calculated for all possible domains at the All Manufacturing, Province, 3-digit NAICS, and 3-digit NAICS by Province level. The population used for the study was from reference year 2002, the latest data available. This population was reduced by excluding the imputation classes with fewer than 5 responding units from the total manufacturing population. This was done to avoid dealing with variance estimates that were based on very few observations and extremely sensitive to outliers. As well, we assume that all complex units responded so that we can measure the variance associated with the treatment of non-responding and non-sampled simple structured units only. Two variables were selected to provide examples of the quality achieved for tax-replaced variables and ratio imputed variables. For the tax replace variable, Total Expenses is used, and for the ratio-imputed variables, Total Energy Expenses is used. Table 1 provides a summary of the relative differences between the estimates of totals produced under each methodology, relative to the estimates produced by the Horvitz-Thompson estimator. The values given in the table are the median values of the absolute relative differences for the estimates at each level.

Table 1 - Median Value of Relative Differences between Estimates of Total Revenue at each level

	Tax data unavailable, pseudo-census		Tax data available, pseudo-census	
Level	**Total Expenses**	**Total Energy Expenses**	**Total Expenses**	**Total Energy Expenses**
All Manufacturing	1.81%	1.18%	0.53%	0.80%
PROVINCE	0.73%	0.47%	0.77%	0.64%
NAICS3	1.42%	0.92%	1.05%	1.50 %
NAICS3 x PROVINCE	0.03%	0.02%	1.32%	1.20%

It is clear from these results that the estimates from the different estimators are very similar. We know that the Horvitz-Thompson and Ratio Imputed estimators are unbiased, and the estimates for Total Expenses are in line with these, so it appears that the direct use of tax data has not introduced an appreciable bias to the estimates of the Total Expenses variable. This is not unexpected since the variables to be tax-replaced were selected based on a similar criterion. In fact, the relative difference Total Expenses at the "All manufacturing" level is smaller for the Tax Data Available/Pseudo-Census scenario (difference of 0.5%) than the Tax Data Unavailable/Pseudo-Census scenario (difference of 1.8%).

Table 2 – Comparison of CV's at each level

Level	Median CV of Horvitz Thompson		Relative Efficiency of Tax data unavailable, pseudo-census		Relative Efficiency of Tax data available, pseudo-census	
	Total Expenses	**Total Energy Expenses**	**Total Expenses**	**Total Energy Expenses**	**Total Expenses**	**Total Energy Expenses**
All Manufacturing	0.28%	0.31%	0.96	1.23	0.46	1.41
PROVINCE	0.64%	0.66%	0.97	1.02	0.41	0.97
NAICS3	1.09%	1.48%	1.13	1.11	0.41	1.15
NAICS3 x PROVINCE	1.46%	1.80%	1.00	1.00	0.46	1.01

Table 2 gives the median of the estimated co-efficients of variation (CV) at each domain level from the Horvitz-Thompson weighted estimator, and the median of the relative efficiency of the alternative estimators for the estimates at each level. The relative efficiency is calculated as the CV of the estimator divided by the CV of the Horvitz-Thompson estimator. A median relative efficiency less than one is an indicator that the variance of the estimator is generally lower than that of the Horvitz-Thompson estimator for the estimates at that level.

We first note that the estimated CV's are relatively low for the Horvitz-Thompson estimator at each level. This is to be expected as the sample is composed so heavily of large take-all units, which don't contribute to the variance. For the Tax Data Unavailable/Pseudo-Census scenario we note that the estimated efficiencies are approximately one for Total Expenses and are slightly higher than one for Total Energy Expenses. This can be interpreted to mean that the relationship between Total Expenses and the auxiliary variable is strong enough that the extensive imputation yields variability that is similar to the sampling variability in the Horvitz-Thompson estimator. On the other hand, we notice a slight loss in efficiency for the estimates for Total Energy Expenses (the linear relationship with the auxiliary variable is not as strong). For the Tax Data Available/Pseudo-Census scenario we notice an important efficiency gain for Total Expenses. The CVs of this estimator are notably decreased from those of the Horvitz-Thompson estimator. The results for Total Energy Expenses show a loss of efficiency compared to the Horvitz-Thompson estimator, particularly at the "All manufacturing" level.

6. CONCLUSIONS

This paper has given some background on the T1 and T2 tax programs at Statistics Canada and the use of tax data by the Annual Survey of Manufactures. It has also outlined and presented a comparison of three methodologies that could be used to produce population level estimates from the ASM. These methodologies vary in terms of the amount of imputation that is involved and the extent to which they make use of auxiliary data that is available. According to our results, the three estimators yield similar point estimates. We have demonstrated that the use of the Horvitz-Thompson estimator could produce estimates with a smaller CV, but there would be many challenges associated with producing a pseudo-census dataset that yields the same population level estimates. This pseudo-census dataset is required in order to provide the analytic capabilities that data users need. Thus, in order to make efficient use of the data (i.e. select a methodology that yields a small CV), the imputation approach that makes use of tax data is the preferred option. The availability of the tax data allows us to produce estimates with a CV that is lower than we could otherwise achieve through imputation based on auxiliary information such as annual revenues. In particular, to produce estimates with the same level of quality, we would need a larger sample size if we did not have the tax data available.

A. Future Work

Future work on this project will be concentrated in three main areas. First of all, it may be possible to expand the direct use of the tax data to more variables by applying some editing to the tax data to improve its quality. This may be possible through fully automated edits, or through editing systems that require subject-matter input, but it is suspected for some variables that by removing outlying observations, the data may be more suitable for use in the survey programs.

Another area that may be explored is the use of tax data in less direct ways. For example, the direct use of the tax data (as described in this paper for the ASM) relies on a relatively solid linear relationship between the tax data and the survey data, with no intercept term. While this is reasonable to expect, what we have observed in our analysis is that this is not always the case for a variety of reasons. It may also be possible to reap the benefits of the available tax data through modeling of the other variables. For example, models with an intercept, or multiple regression models may be fitted to try to find models that would lead to efficiency gains for the variables that are not currently tax replaced.

Finally, quality indicators that reflect the variance associated with imputation need to be developed. Given the large fraction of records that are completed via imputation, it is important to select a suitable quality indicator; one which conveys the increased variance and the potential for bias. This challenge is not specific to the Annual Survey of Manufactures and will be explored in the near future.

References

[1] Batten, D. and Matthews, S. (2003). Direct Use of Tax Data for the Annual Survey of Manufactures, Variable Selection Study, Internal Statistics Canada Document.

[2] Hamel, N. and Belcher, R. (2002). Edit and Imputation of the General Index of Financial Information, Contributed Paper to the Work Session on Statistical Data Editing, Helsinki, May, 2002.

[3] Hutchinson, P., Jocelyn, W. and Cooray, L. (2004). Design of the T1 TEP/UES Tax Sample TY 2003, Internal Statistics Canada Document.

[4] Lavallée, P. and Hidiroglou, M. (1988). On the Stratification of Skewed Populations. *Survey Methodology*, **14**, 33-43.

[5] Philips, R. (2003). The Theory and Applications of the Score Function for Determining the Priority of Followup in the Annual Survey of Manufactures, *Proceedings of the Survey Methods Section*, Statistical Society of Canada.

[6] Shao, J. and Steel, P. (1999), Variance Estimation for Survey Data with Composite Imputation and Non-Negligible Sampling Fractions, *Journal of the American Statistical Association*, **94**, 254-265.

Chapter 4

IMPROVING SURVEYS – WHERE DOES EDITING FIT IN? Some thoughts

By Leopold Granquist, John Kovar and Svein Nordbotten

Abstract

This paper considers a broad view of improving surveys as it relates to four groups of stakeholders: users, respondents, government and producers. From the user perspective, data quality is the main issue – fitness for use, including data quality in all its dimensions, but in particular, relevance, timeliness, accuracy, coherence, and interpretability. From the respondents' point of view, response burden is likely the greatest issue while from the government's point of view, provision of required statistics, confidentiality and efficiency are of greatest importance. From the statistical producers' point of view, professional knowledge, efficient planning and production, and employee job satisfaction are the main concerns.

It can be argued that editing impacts on all of the above aspects. Traditionally we concentrated narrowly on non-response as well as on response to obviously misunderstood questions, while hopefully correcting response and some processing errors and reducing non-response bias. In this chapter we review what has been done, and what was planned, but not done, in evaluating quality aspects of editing in the last decade or so, and we argue that editing should be considered in a wider perspective, specifically as it should provide valuable information to other survey processes and other surveys in a systematic way.

1. INTRODUCTION

We take a broad view of quality as it relates to our four groups of stakeholders: users, respondents, government (ultimately, the tax payers) and producers.

From the users' perspective, data quality is the main issue. That is, its fitness for use, including data quality in all its dimensions, but in particular relevance, timeliness, accuracy, coherence and interpretability. Clearly editing plays a crucial role related to timeliness. Numerous studies and reports speak to the fact that excessive, traditional editing leads to delays in publication, while automation of the process should have the opposite effect. Streamlining the process is clearly of great importance. Accuracy is affected both positively as well as negatively. On the positive side, it is hoped that editing will correct for at least some of the response errors, processing errors and non-response bias. On the negative side, editing may introduce new systematic errors and uncertainty. More specifically, the imputation process will introduce a variance component that needs to be accounted for as discussed in Section 2.3 of this Volume. In Section 3 we will see that many studies have been conducted that address the impact of editing as it relates specifically to accuracy. Thirdly, appropriate editing strategies can go a long way in improving coherence within as well as between surveys. Automation of the process lends itself particularly well to making the process reproducible and consistent. Use of administrative data in the edit and imputation phase can help to greatly improve coherence, as well as bias and precision. Finally, interpretability, especially as it relates to appropriate provision of metadata should be enhanced by the use of automated, well documented, methods that are tractable and which can be evaluated.

From the respondents' point of view, response burden is likely the greatest issue. Editing in real time, while with the respondent, be it in person or on-line, can have a great impact on not only the data quality but also on respondents' co-operation. An appropriate balance needs to be struck to realize all the potential benefits, as too much editing may add unnecessary response burden in terms of both time as well as annoyance factor. If used properly, editing can go a long way in improving the survey process in general and the survey vehicles in particular, resulting in reduced response burden.

From the government's point of view, comparable and timely statistics easily available for the public, government and international organizations, as well as efficiency, are the issues. Editing using reusable, automated systems that are well documented and thoroughly evaluated will help achieve these objectives.

From the statistical producers' point of view, professional knowledge, sound technical infrastructure, efficient planning and production, employee job satisfaction, or from the negative side, misallocation of resources, are all issues of concern. Learning from past experiences, as gleaned from the edit process metadata is paramount, and will lead to a continuous improvement of not only the edit process but the entire survey process as well.

Traditionally we concentrated narrowly on issues of reducing non-response bias and the effect of response errors resulting from obviously misunderstood questions, while hopefully correcting some response and processing errors. A number of the papers in this Volume go beyond that, by considering data quality more broadly. In this short note we argue that editing should be considered in even a wider perspective, specifically as it should provide valuable information to other survey processes and other surveys in a systematic way.

In Section 2 we briefly describe the aims of editing as they were, as they are, and as they should be. Section 3 discusses the impact of editing on data quality by reviewing the contributions presented in this Volume as well as the preceding Volume 2[1]. Section 4 elaborates on the strategies that have been put in place in order to improve the edit process, while Section 5 suggests some directions that could be pursued in the future. We conclude the note with some observations in Section 6.

2. THE AIMS OF EDITING

Traditionally, the role of editing was to identify and "correct" important errors. Emphasis was often on formal errors and those due to negligence. More realistically, editing was used to find better or plausible values. More recently (the last 10 years or so), this role took a second place in importance, though perhaps not universally. The role of editing was enlarged to include identification of error sources in the first place and, only secondly, identification and "correction" of important errors. This thinking has not yet fully found its way into practice. The focus is often still on only the second aim.

However, we propose that even a wider view should be considered, and suggest that the role of editing should be considered to comprise of the following:

- Identifying problems in data collection and processing with a focus on getting accurate responses, or getting "true" values, from all of the respondents.
- Providing intelligence related to both survey design as well as data dissemination.
- Identifying means of improving data quality.

The best way to help reduce errors is for editing to identify problems faced by the respondents, that is, problems in data collection. This can be done by having the editors systematically record information gathered from the respondents in follow-ups and by encouraging analysts to study

[1] In this paper, when referring to the contributions printed in Volume 2 as well as this Volume, we use the cryptic notation of V.x.x.x, where, for example, V3.1.1:Nordbotten refers to Svein Nordbotten's paper in Volume 3, section 1, paper 1; or V3.2.2.3: Charlton refers to John Charlton's paper in Volume 3, Section 2.2, paper 3, etc.

the process data, especially of problem areas, using a top-down approach. Careful analyses of the process data (particularly important in this context, edit failure rates and other editing information), extra questions to gather information about the respondent, and behaviour testing for possible misunderstanding are just some of the possible approaches. Usability testing, that is, performing cognitive studies on focus groups preferably with real respondents, can also prove to be useful.

Beyond the immediate problems associated with data collection and processing, such analyses can go a long way in influencing future occasions of the same surveys as well as new occasions of related surveys, by demonstrating what is and what is not possible. In that way, the survey design can evolve in the appropriate direction. With respect to dissemination, appropriate analyses will help subject matter specialists produce informative metadata that must accompany the data products. Editing processes can and must provide knowledge of problems in survey design and in presentation of results.

In this way, editing can provide the needed data to form a basis for where and maybe how to take measures to improve overall quality by improving the content relevance of the survey, the survey design, the collection vehicle, the edits themselves, the imputation procedures, as well as other steps of the process. Here survey planners, questionnaire designers, editing specialists, processing staff and subject matter specialists have to co-operate. To get the extended role of editing into practice, this role must be efficiently communicated to all staff that is involved in the editing exercise. This is likely the greatest challenge facing us, because appropriate communication tools and best practices are yet to be established. To this end, it must be understood by all concerned that this role of editing is the most important role if we are to reap all of the possible benefits of editing. If we want editing to become an instrument of improving the quality of a survey, it must be set up as a goal of the exercise.

3. IMPACT OF EDITING ON DATA QUALITY

Volume 2 and this Volume 3 contain more than 30 selected papers on evaluations of different kinds. The papers can be divided into two main groups: (1) Framework papers, including theoretical and method development papers, and (2) Empirical evaluations and reports on experiences. Most of these papers are summarized in the Appendix with the focus on the aims and methods of the empirical evaluations. The distribution between the two groups is roughly 1:2 and indicates that more work has been invested in applying and evaluating available methods than in considering the theoretical basis and developing new methods. In our opinion, this has been a wise approach.

In almost all types of method evaluations there is a need for reference data (that here and in the evaluations, are called "true values") to which the results are compared. These "true values" are defined differently or collected in different ways in each of the evaluations. The examples given in the papers include "true values" based on:

- re-interview studies (V2.4.3: Granquist),
- manual inspection by methodologists or subject matter experts on samples of edited questionnaires (V2.4.3: Granquist), or error lists/error messages (V2.4.2: Stefanowicz), (where the actions taken by the system and the editors were visible),
- edited data (V2.4.3: Granquist; V3.2.2.2: Hoogland),
- manual editing of automatically imputed data and data that were not edited due to the selective editing used when the survey was processed (V.3.2.2.2: Hoogland), and,
- register data (V2.4.4: Poulsen).

The impacts of editing on raw data are studied by producing tables and graphs of the editing changes sorted by the absolute magnitude of the changes (e.g., V2.4.3: Granquist). This method can be refined by plotting the estimates of the mean for decreasing values of a score variable and having the confidence interval on the other axes (V2.4.3: Granquist). This method has shown in many applications that many changes are insignificant in impacting the quality of published estimates and thus need not be identified. This should influence the design of the edits.

New or alternative methods are tested by applying the method to raw data and measuring the impact of the changes made in the current process based on a data set from a benchmark method to those which are identified and to those which are not identified. The editing changes made in the current process are considered "true" errors and the editing with the tested procedure is simulated by giving flagged items the tabulated value (e.g., V2.4.3: Granquist). The same technique is used when conducting studies on score functions for limiting the manual review of flagged records to the most important ones. This technique has been used to show that the new procedures do not compromise the quality (the estimates are the same) but leads to a considerable reduction of error flags.

The above methods are all based on currently available sources. It could be argued that re-interview studies provide a superior alternative to collecting "true" data and hence also for evaluating the editing exercise. Re-interview studies reported here are used to measure: accuracy of published totals of selected items; type of errors for possible improvements of questionnaire design; response quality improvement in repeated establishment surveys; and quality measures of Fellegi-Holt imputations in a test survey (V2.4.3: Granquist). However, these studies are generally very costly and there is no guarantee for obtaining the true values. Therefore simulations with defined true data sets provide an attractive alternative, but it is difficult to produce realistic simulations because errors must also be simulated. The framework paper by Italy (V.3.2.1.1: Di Zio, et al.) indicates this quite clearly.

Other studies aimed at improving incoming data quality, eliminating systematic errors, and alleviating problems in data collection are: manual inspection by methodologists or subject matter experts on samples of edited questionnaires (V2.4.3: Granquist); comparing survey data with the corresponding register data (V2.4.4: Poulsen); and simulations according to the framework paper (V.3.2.1.1: Di Zio, et al.)).

Data collection in co-operation with the respondent offers an excellent opportunity to evaluate and improve the edit process, because the respondent can be asked whether the provided data are obtained directly from the accounting books, whether the respondent has difficulty providing the answer, whether the survey concepts correspond to those of the respondent, and other similar questions. The types of questions noted in the paper on Response Analysis Surveys (RAS) (V2.4.3: Granquist) are simple enough to include in surveys conducted directly with the respondent. The RAS asked the respondents whether they included or excluded certain components of a survey variable and if they did not follow the survey definitions whether they could change their response behaviour in the future. Web surveys should permit to obtain intelligence on how respondents interpret the questions and what their data represent.

4. STRATEGIES FOR IMPROVING EDITS AND EDIT SYSTEMS

As seen in Section 3, a lot of work has been done on evaluating the impact of the edit process on data quality. In parallel, much has been accomplished with respect to improving the process itself. A number of methods have been proposed to rationalize editing, including selective editing, macro editing, and use of external (administrative) sources among others. Work also continues on strategies for removing errors by sharpening the questions and concepts as a result of feedback from the edit process. Finally, inroads are being made with respect to "web-editing", that is, editing of electronic questionnaires. Below, we offer a few thoughts on these topics.

Selective editing (including macro editing) refers to methods that select items or records to be edited manually because their impact on estimates of specified totals may be significant. When such units are erroneous, leaving them unchanged would jeopardize the realization of stated quality goals. As a result, data that exceed a certain limit (e.g., a plausibility indicator) will be treated manually, usually by follow-ups with the respondents while other data or records are left unattended or left to an automatic editing procedure. A key issue in this process is to estimate the limit or the parameters in the limit function. Several ideas are suggested in some of the papers of this Volume. A pragmatic way used in practice is to let the available resources for manual follow-ups influence the limits, for example, when data are sorted by size of the potential errors measured as deviations from the expected value of the edit.

External sources (administrative data) are used or suggested to be used in applications to widen the possibilities to check for errors (consistency errors), for imputation of missing data, and for evaluations. They should also be used for identifying error sources.

Methods focusing on special problems connected with respondent misunderstanding have not yet been a concern for editing methodologists and are yet to become an issue in editing exercises. However, the Response Analysis Surveys (V2.4.3: Granquist) could be considered as a method to deal with respondent misunderstanding.

An important issue in obtaining accurate response, or getting "true" values from respondents, can be summarized as follows: Do the respondents fully understand the questions and the underlying concepts? High edit failure rates may be an indication of conceptual problems. Can they report the required data within reasonable effort? Partially filled reports may indicate otherwise. Do business survey respondents have the requested data in their accounting systems? If not, and approximations are being reported, this fact should be noted. If too many approximations are being provided, the concepts, definitions and requested variables may need to be revisited. Systematic collection and transfer of information collected during editing to other parts of the production process is essential. In other words, what is needed is an integrated metadata system that feeds questionnaire design, concepts definitions, survey scope, etc. It is only when such integrated metadata systems exist that we will be able to make the quantum leap from having edit systems serve concerns of accuracy and timeliness to those of relevance, coherence and interpretability. At the same time, we must understand that the edit systems cannot remain static and they too must evolve with our increased knowledge of the response process.

Web editing is becoming more and more important because of the growing number of respondents getting access to Internet and the requirements for increased timeliness and accuracy as well as reduced editing costs. There are many issues connected with web editing. Which types of edits can or should be embedded in the collection process to take advantage of the cooperation of the respondents? Should there be any post collection editing? How should error (or warning) messages be communicated to respondents? How can information on specification errors be obtained? Can embedded experiments be conducted and how? What should trigger the edits and should pop up edits be used? Most studies of these topics are relatively new. A few are reported within this Volume, but more needs to be done. The technology offers an easy means of tracking much of the needed meta-information, but ways to efficiently analyze this information are yet to be developed.

5. POSSIBLE FUTURE WORK

Where should we be going in the longer term? How can the stated aims of editing be accomplished? Ultimately what needs to be done so that editing would improve the survey process and data quality?

Basic concepts

To date, evaluations of editing methods have without exception assumed the existence of a set of "true", usually unknown, values for sets of variables on which statistics are produced. In the finite population context, this creates two distinct problems: How to measure the values of variables to be used for production of statistics, and how to measure the true values of variables to be used for evaluation?

It may seem that solving the second problem may also provide the best solution for the first. But what is the true value of a variable? Unfortunately, ideal observation and processing methods are in general associated with prohibitive execution costs and time. Traditionally, it was assumed that the editing performed by human experts was approximately ideal and gave approximately a true value set. Research in the last ten to fifteen years indicates that this may not be a valid assumption. Still, a number of new editing methods have been evaluated and ranked based on benchmarks from manual editing.

One experimental solution used to avoid this problem, is to create an artificial set of true values, distort these by errors and apply the editing methods to be evaluated on the resulting values. However, the problem now emerges as to how to define and measure error distributions. Can we be certain that assuming the existence of only a single set of true values for each survey, is a useful approach? The interpretations of the questions asked and the statistics disseminated may vary among groups of producers, respondents and users. Instead of a single set of true values for each survey, several sets or distributions of plausible values might provide a better approach.

Automation

Currently-used automatic editing and imputation systems are often based on the Fellegi-Holt methodology. Their contribution to improving quality is limited to timeliness improvements for large surveys or censuses. When used in a selective editing setting they can contribute to accuracy by focusing the editing to potential influential errors. However, the assumptions underlying the Fellegi-Holt methodology are seldom met in practice. In particular the notion that errors are independent and that they occur at random, which leads to the minimum change principle, is often questionable. More research is needed to establish conditions under which the systems can contribute to quality improvements and how they should be developed to facilitate learning. In the Euredit project, a number of automatic imputation methods have been proposed and evaluated, but much more research has to take place before they can be used in practice, including research on how such methods could improve the quality of surveys.

Technological application trends

During the last decade, the application of information and communication technology has changed the way we communicate. This trend, including how statistical organizations communicate with respondents and users, will probably continue.

In a few years, data collection by ordinary mail will be too slow, face-to-face interviewing will require too much travel, and even telephone interviewing will require too many resources. More and more data will be collected on the web by dynamic questionnaires supported by voice, videos, etc. In order to reduce response burden and to reduce processing time and costs, editing must be expected to be embedded in dynamic and interactive electronic questionnaires supported by cross-sectional data for the individual respondent, so that the respondent can be actively included in the editing process during data collection.

The development of interactive editing of electronic questionnaires has merely started. Further development integrating the respondent side with the producer side in such a way that the three aims of editing are being satisfied, contains new and interesting challenges.

Globalization

It is frequently said that the world is becoming 'flat' due to globalization and advances in communication technology. This is also true for statistics. With a few exceptions, for example, foreign trade and migration statistics, statistical organizations do not yet take full advantage of available data from outside their own domains in their editing processes. Some work on macro editing has been done in this field, but obviously statistical data from other countries can be used extensively in editing/verifying domestic, raw data (political considerations notwithstanding).

User orientation

Traditionally, official statistics have been focused on the needs of governing bodies and on needs considered as necessary to describe the state and development of a country. Today, more needs, such as the needs of the business sector and other lobby groups are also taken into account. In the future, more systematic observations of all types of needs for statistical information should be performed in order to be able to calibrate the different quality dimensions of the statistical products and plan the editing of the collected data.

We offer these speculations in order to indicate that conceptual work is still needed and that it should be part of the future work tasks on data editing and on statistical quality in general. Further, the technological development continuously opens avenues for implementing both new and old ideas based on solutions that previously were prohibitive for practical use.

6. CONCLUDING REMARKS

Statistical quality has developed from considering the bias and precision in a complex context. Moreover, the statisticians have earlier indicated how bias and precision should be combined into one quality measure. However, today, we still do not know how to integrate timeliness with bias and precision, let alone with coherence, interpretability and other quality dimensions. Similarly, ideas on how to allocate resources appropriately to strike a balance between efficiency, respondent burden and quality are also in short supply.

In Section 2 we recommended an extension of the aims of editing, and ranked the importance of the three objectives. Are there any good arguments for our ranking? If we imagine two alternative editing processes contributing differently to the three objectives, how should we decide which process is more efficient?

In section 3, we surveyed recent reports on the development and evaluation of alternative editing methods, and concluded that useful studies have been carried out in experimenting with new ideas and empirical evaluations of available methods.

We discussed the need for strategies for continued future work in the general field of statistical editing, and offered a few ideas about specific tasks in the next two sections. We emphasised particularly the importance of discussing the concept of "true data sets", and the possibilities of web editing.

Finally, we would be remiss not to stress the need for reducing our reliance on editing as a correction tool. We must strive to make editing part of the continuous improvement process, rather than a mere correction tool.

Appendix: Methods of evaluating (systematic input errors in) the editing processes

This summary is based on selected papers from Volumes 2 and 3. They are identified in the first column using the cryptic notation described in Footnote 1 of the Introduction.

Paper	Aim	Method	Remark
United Kingdom: (V2.4.1: Thomas)	Planning: " Data Quality Monitoring System for 2001 census of population"	Developing a system to produce standard and ad hoc reports to facilitate comparisons of distributions before and after editing. A team of experts to analyse and interpret the results.	Planning paper
Poland: (V2.4.2: Stefanowicz)	Suggesting indicators on measuring different aspects of quality	Theoretical discussion with example. Using error lists to get, for example, true data, sources of errors.	Theoretical. Indicators used in many papers.
Australia: 1985-86 ABS Retail census (as described in V2.4.3: Granquist)	Manual analysis of the frequency and effect of the manual data review to identify areas of potential rationalizing	Inspection of samples of questionnaires. Effect on values of 5 key data items to get informed of respondent errors.	Hit-rate good indicator. Clerical intervention should be reduced. Fixing totals to equal the sum of components to avoid flags from computer edits.
Australia: 1983/1984 Agricultural census (as described in V2.4.3: Granquist)	Investigate possible resource savings through reduced editing and/or increased use of automatic imputation, and to assess the effect of data editing to improve the efficiency	Create a SAS-database of original, pre-edited and computer values on a number of selected items from a systematic sample of 1000 units, and compute different measures for analyses. It was used also for simulation studies.	Analysis of editing changes: Frequency and type of edit flags by item, by domain of study Magnitude of change by item, by domain of study. Indicators of distortion effects.
USA: Re-interview studies (as described in V2.4.3: Granquist)			
a) 1977 U.S. Economic Censuses	Measuring the accuracy of the published totals of selected items.	Personal visit re-interview	Estimates and variances of different ratios
b) Content Evaluation of the 1982 US Economic Censuses: Petroleum Distribution	Examined types of errors for possible improvements of questionnaire design.	Personal visit re-interview	The largest types of errors: using estimates instead of book values
USA: Response analysis survey (as described in V2.4.3: Granquist)	Improve the response quality in repetitive establishment surveys	Surveying respondents to review the survey item definitions against the firm's book-keeping definitions.	Results: over half of the enterprises studied did not entirely apply the survey definitions!

Paper	Aim	Method	Remark
Spain: Studies on Fellegi-Holt systems. (as described in V2.4.3: Granquist)	Evaluate Spanish system DIA by using real LFS-data by simulation of planted errors	Compare estimates of using DIA for E&I for erroneous data with 1) accepted data, and 2) randomly error planted data	Measure: the distance between the relative distribution of the values of each item of each method to the relative distribution of the target data file
UK: Development of automatic editing of missing values for a census (as described in V2.4.3: Granquist)	Study the quality of F-H imputations of missing values	Compare automatic imputed values with re-interview data	Imputation by F-H a better method for the Census than proportional distribution of missing values
USA, Canada: Measuring the impact of editing on original (raw) data (as described in V2.4.3: Granquist)	Study the impact of editing changes on totals by size of changes.	Analyse tables or graphs of changes of raw values to tabulated or edited values sorted by size of absolute change.	Indications whether the edits might be improved to focus only on big errors
World Fertility Survey: Performing analysis on raw data (as described in V2.4.3: Granquist)	Study the impact of machine editing on quality relative to the intended use of the survey.	Perform analysis on raw data (after field editing) and tabulated data	No differences were found.
Canada, Netherlands: (as described in V2.4.3: Granquist) Evaluating new methods	Evaluate a new method against the editing outcome of the current method.	Measure the impact of those changes made in the current editing process to those errors which are identified and those which are not identified.	The editing changes made in the ordinary data processing are considered as “true” errors and the editing is simulated by giving flagged items the tabulated value.
Calculating pseudo-bias	Evaluate a new method or the impact of different reviewing rates.	Plotting the estimates of the mean for decreasing values of the score variable.	Selective editing: A score variable is developed to prioritise edits.
Using graphs and confidence intervals.	Compare edited to unedited data	Compare the change to the confidence interval	
Denmark: Evaluating data editing processes using survey data and register data (V2.4.4: Poulsen)	Find potential error sources or where editing processes might be improved.	Compare and analyse individual data from two data sources.	

Paper	Aim	Method	Remark
UN/ECE: The Frame Work Paper (V3.1.1: Nordbotten)	General framework for evaluating the efficiency of statistical data editing in improving the quality of statistical products.	Suggesting some research topics: Development of a conceptual framework for description of editing processes. Collecting empirical data sets suitable for experimentation.	Comparison and evaluation of relative merits of available editing tools. Research on causal model description of the editing process. Exchange of information on research.
Italy: Evaluating the quality of editing and imputation: The simulation approach (V3.2.1.1: Di Zio, et al.)	Frame Work Paper Present some aspects relating to the use of simulation for evaluating.	Using the software ESSE for evaluating E&I procedures. Evaluate different methods for specific error typologies: to model the distribution of the raw data conditional on the true ones.	Data models suitable for reproducing statistical in the different survey contents. Error models suitable for reproducing the most typical errors and error patterns in the different survey contexts. Approaches and measures for assessing the quality of E&I taking into account the impact (at different data levels) of the stochastic elements possibly induced by E&I itself.
Canada: Using variance components to measure and evaluate the quality of editing practices. (V3.2.1.2: Rancourt)	Use the imputation variance estimation theory to apply it to editing. Disregard implausible values and let them cause holes in the data matrix and impute new values	Add the editing variance to the estimated variance. It allows for analysts to make more precise inference and for data users to be better informed of data quality.	Estimates are assumed to be unbiased.

Paper	Aim	Method	Remark
Italy: Evaluation framework (using simulation): Evaluating the Quality of Editing and Imputation: The Simulation Approach (V.3.2.1.1: Di Zio, et al.)	Get a system of statistical measures to support the survey managers in monitoring and documenting the quality of their surveys. To compare the quality of different surveys. To provide the Istat management with periodic reports concerning the quality of Istat surveys.	Create an Information System for Survey Documentation (SIDI). Compare and calculate measures of edited and raw data. Implement all in a system (IDEA Indices for Data Editing Assessment)	When true data are available the quality of the E&I process can be measured by comparing final and true data. IDEA is a big success among the 65 quality facilitators. IDEA has stimulated them to further analyses, e.g., when they have found big changes, they try to understand in which phase of the process the errors corrected by E&I where mostly originated, and, if possible take actions in order to avoid them in successive survey occasions.
UK and USA: Using principal components analysis (V3.2.1.4: Smith & Weir)	Concentrates on a small number of indicators which provide most of the information about the data quality	Uses principal components analysis to find measures which best capture the underlying variation in quality measures	They give two examples: from a UK survey and a U.S. survey.
Canada: The Impact of Editing on Data Quality (V3.2.2.1: Whitridge & Bernier)	The Unified Enterprise Survey (an integration of surveys into a single master survey program) is designed to incorporate quality improvements in a number of areas. Presents the results of a study that was conducted to examine the impact of data editing on the quality of the final survey estimates.	Descriptive information is given about the sample and what happened to it as the data moved through the different processes. The results section presents and compares several sets of estimates that can be produced under different scenarios.	Some general conclusions are drawn. (The impact on quality seems to consist of assessments by the analysts.) Some respondent problems in providing and understanding questions are mentioned.
Netherlands: Selective editing using plausibility indicators and SLICE (V3.2.2.2: Hoogland)	Study differences between raw, manually edited, and automatically edited data and the influences of selective editing on the publication totals.	Edit manually those data that were edited automatically for twelve publication cells. Calculate the Pseudo-bias. Manually edited data are considered true data.	Room for improvements: e.g., add a few rules, develop software that removes systematic errors, and improve questionnaires.
UK: Evaluating new methods for data editing and imputation – results from the EUREDIT project	Evaluate new methods for automatic edit and imputation by using real data. Develop a comprehensive list of performance measures on	Introduce errors by random error mechanisms.	The error mechanisms were not reflecting the detected errors in the experimental data files. It was found that it was impossible to find " a

Paper	Aim	Method	Remark
(V3.2.2.3: Charlton)	the assumption that the original edited data are true.		one size fits all”
Canada: A functional evaluation of edit and imputation tools (V3.2.2.4: Poirier)	Evaluate the functionality of the systems: GEIS, NIM, STEPS, and SOLAS	Define and use a set of criteria to compare the functionality of systems.	Outline strengths of systems.
Netherlands: Computational results for various error localisation algorithms (V3.2.2.5: de Waal)	Evaluate the results for automatic error localisation	Perform error localization on six data sets of real data under Minimum change principle.	Four methods are evaluated.